Historic

Georgia

Families

Historic
Georgia Families

Compiled by

L. W. RIGSBY

CLEARFIELD

Originally Published
Cairo, Georgia, 1925-1928

Reprinted
Genealogical Publishing Company
Baltimore, 1969

Reprinted for
Clearfield Company, Inc. by
Genealogical Publishing Co., Inc.
Baltimore, Maryland
1992, 1998

Library of Congress Catalogue Card Number 69-17128
International Standard Book Number: 0-8063-0298-4

Publisher's Preface

The present offering is a reprint of L. W. Rigsby's "Historic Georgia Families" as originally published in a series of
brochures between 1925 and 1928, with a cumulative title,
preface, contents page, and index to the whole of the work
which appeared with the concluding, 1928, brochure. As such,
it is without doubt one of the most valuable collections of genealogies of the early families of Georgia, with lists of early
settlers, biographical and historical data, documents, and so
forth. As part of our continuing program of making available
those basic genealogical reference works, including compen-
diums, the reprinting of this work should be welcomed by
genealogical researchers, historians, librarians, as well as the
general public.

The reader's attention is called to the existence of two
pages numbered 84 which appeared in the original and, consequently, in our reprint. In an apparent attempt to correct this,
the verso of 164 was left unnumbered and blank in the original
and, consequently, in our reprint, and beginning with page 165
the recto pages are again odd numbers as they should be. Users
of the Index should consult both page 84's when referred to
that number, since both pages are indexed as such. Finally, the
individual brochures which were published between 1925 and
1928 were paginated separately at the bottom of the pages. To
avoid confusion we have removed these page numbers in our
reprint. Otherwise, our reprint is an exact facsimile of the
original edition.

GENEALOGICAL PUBLISHING COMPANY
1969

PREFACE

Before the death of my mother, which occurred in 1916, she requested me to make a record of the facts relating to her family. I neglected to do this during her life. I fully intended to do so but kept delaying and procrastinating. In 1921, I had a sudden attack of appendicitis which necessitated an operation. This brought me face to face with the danger of delay. I made a vow then, that as soon as I recovered, I would comply with my mother's request. During the days of my convalescence I planned the general scope of the work and outlined in my mind what it should contain, viz., genealogies, ancestral chart, family register with forms for recording those facts essential to such records, biography, and portraits. I conceived that this should be in departments, loose-leaf, so that the typewriter could be used, and have a convenient system of reference and index.

Upon my recovery, I made drawings and diagrams and outlines and began the work for such families as I was interested in because of their relationship to my children. Once a year I published a brochure containing genealogies of those families of whom I had sufficient information justifying a release. At first I had no thought of incorporating them into a book but finding that there was some general demand for these brochures I thought it best to hold them off the market until a sufficient number had accumulated to make up into a volumn. The small quantity of the first numbers published, however, made the number of volumns rather limited and the number was further reduced by the extravagant price sometimes paid for one of the brochures.

In the last brochure I have given some conclusions reached as the result of the study and investigation made, necessary to the work. I have added an index to the compilation to make the work of more value as a work of reference.

Page 19 contains an outline designed as a guide in writing biographical sketches for use in family records. Two sketches have been included from my records, more as a matter for suggestions than anything else; one of these is on page 17 and one on page 89.

The forms first designed and used in making this compilation of information have been revised and are published and for sale under the title "Memories of Home and Family."

Whether or not this work will be of benefit to humanity time alone will show. It has been profitable to me in that I have gained a more accurate knowledge of history, a clearer understanding of religion and a keener insight into the motives of mankind.

Cairo, Georgia, September, 1928.

L. W. RIGSBY.

CONTENTS

Service Section Number One

The Pioneer Family Record Reference Chart

Prepared for Descendants of Thomas Coram, Richard Hill McRae Swann, Daniel Brunson, Frederick Watson, Allen Rigsby and Johnson Blair.

JULY 4, 1925

CORAMS OF BENEVOLENCE, GEORGIA.

Thomas Coram, the English philosopher, was the first of this name connected with Georgia. He was born in Dorcestershire, England in 1668. He was named by King George as one of the Trustees of Georgia, together with James Edward Oglethorpe. Afterward, he established a Foundling Hospital in London in 1741. He was also interested in the settlement of Nova Scotia. There is no record of his ever having come to Georgia, but he resided in Massachussetts for a short time.

The next Thomas Coram claiming our attention came to South Carolina from England, and was a celebrated painter. The picture of Christ blessing little children, now hanging in the Orphan Home in South Carolina, is one of his most celebrated works. An interesting story is related of the painting of this picture. At the time there was residing in Charleston a little girl who was related by blood to the Duke of Argyle. The suspicion developed that Thomas Coram was a British spy trying to steal this little girl. This was during the War of the Revolution, and the people became very indignant. An investigation was made, when it was found that Thomas Coram was painting this picture and using this little girl as one of the models for the group of children. He also engraved and cut the money for paying the Revolutionary soldiers of South Carolina. He was deeply interested in charity, and bequeathed his property to the orphan house at Charleston. Revolutionary documents in South Carolina bear the following entry "April 5, 1785, paid to Thomas Coram 6 pounds, 4 shillings and 5 pence for engraving and cutting paper money in the year 1778." It is shown further that on March 30, 1776, a list of names of reputable Charleston people was presented to the General Assembly of South Carolina, as being suitable men for filling the position of Justice of the Peace. There were some two or three dozen names, and the name of John Coram is one of them. (From letter from W. D. Harris, Greenville, South Carolina, 321 Laurens Street.)

Thomas Coram, the third was probaby born in South Carolina on March 17, 1776. He married Deborah Hayes in Warren County, Georgia. Very little is known of the Hayes family, we being ignorant of the name of her father and mother. She had brothers: Ambrose, William and Ezekiel, and a sister, Charlie, who married Vincent Smith.

There is a powder horn in the Coram family, now in possession of W. D. Harris, of Greenville, South Carolina, known as Washington's priming piece, and which tradition says was the property of the father of this Thomas Coram and used by him in the war of the Revolution.

Thomas Coram moved from Warren county to Randolph county very early, and was named in one of the old books as being one of the earliest settlers of this county. The little town of Benevolence now marks the place of this settlement, and he gave the land for the church, school and cemetery. He always took a leading part in the community activities, and was a deacon in the church, one of the first Tax Collectors in the county, and was loved and respected by all who knew him.

His death occurred in 1864 and his body lies buried in the old cemetery in Benevolence. He was truly a worthy progenitor of this noble family. We have no positive proof as to his ancestry.

We would have been glad to have recorded the names of every one of his dscendants, but this has been found impossible for the reason that some of the members of the family have been entirely lost and others have failed co supply us with information. His children were:

First—William Madison.
Second—Sarah.
Third—Mary Ann.
Fourth—Nancy.
Fifth—Susan.
Sixth—John Jasper.
Seventh—Thomas Jefferson.
Eighth—George Washington.
Ninth—Deborah S.
Tenth—Indiana.

First Line.

William Madison Coram, born September 4, 1810, died April 19, 1855. Married Elizabeth Cook. Children:

1. Thomas M. Coram, born September 25, 1837, at Benevolence, Ga., died at Sylvester, Ga., August 16, 1917, where he was buried; his grave being marked by a marble slab. He was married February 8, 1866, to Mollie E. Edwards at Springdale, Randolph County, Ga. Children:

A. Parkel Algienon Coram, born January 4, 1867, P. O. Sylvester, Ga., married Ella Roper Sikes at Sylvester, Ga., January 17, 1897. Children: (a) Kathreen, married Luther Thomas Outler, P. O. Moultrie, Ga., no issue. (b) Albert Coram, unmarried, P. O. 1310 S. W. 13th Street, Miami, Fla. (c) P. A. Coram, Jr., P. O. Sylvester, Ga.

B. Minnie Ola Coram, born January 4, 1861, died July 22, 1902. Married J. H. Westbury, September 7, 1887. Children: (a) Lovelace, married a Godwin, and lives at Fort Lauderdale, Fla. (b) Gladys, married a Price, and lives at Tifton, Ga. (c) Miss Merry. (d) Miss Ida (e) J. H. Westbury, Jr., Sylvester, Ga.

C. Ida Bird Coram, born May 12, 1875, died July 21, 1896.

2. Jason Hayes Coram married Mrs. Elizabeth McConnell, who before her marriage the first time was Miss Elizabeth G. Clayton. She died November 25, 1919. Children:

A. Alma B. Coram. B. Mary Coram died in infancy.

C. Jason Richard Coram, died February, 1920.

D. John Mercer Coram, born January 14, 1895, P. O. 2905 Highland Avenue, Tampa, Fla. Married Hazel Ardell Marble, April 19, 1915. Mr. Coram is mail carrier at Tampa and is secretary of the Florida Association of Letter Carriers. Children: Charlie Hayes Coram, born July 10, 1916, died January 18, 1922.

3. Dr. J. J. Coram, P. O. Lake City, Florida, married Miss Magnolia Niblock; a son, name unknown, is at Florence, S. C., and a daughter married Dr. E. O. Roberts, of Lake City. They probably reside now at Plant City, Florida. (This branch fails to answer letters.)

4. Edward Oscar Coram, born October 7, 1855, P. O. Punta Gorda, Florida. Married (1) Alma J. Young, of Lake City, Florida; (2) Julia Phillips of Forsyth, Ga., February 2, 1896; (3) Alice Buchanan of Charlotte Harbor. Chlidren by first marriage:

A. Eddie Young Coram, born February 1, 1881, married W. V. Husted at Charlotte Harbor. They have three children: (a) Ellsworth Ostram, P. O. Sarasota, Fla. (b) Willington Victor, Jr., now attending the University of Florida, at Gainesville. (c)Alma, who is with her parents.

B. Ruth, died at 11 months of age. Children by second marriage:

C. Elizabeth Juliett, born November 10, 1901. Married J. T. Lamb, June 27, 1921. P. O. Avon Park, Fla. Children: (a) John Edward Lamb, born March 3, 1922.

5. Sallie Deborah Coram, born May 22, 1842, at Benevolence, Ga., married Madison W. Bell, who was second cousin of Judge R. C. Bell of the Court of Appeals of Georgia. Children:

A. Cora Lee Bell, born May 18, 1867, died July 2, 1906. Married J. N. Price on January 26, 1890. Children: (a) James Eunice Price, born October 18, 1890, married B. Strickland, June 24, 1917. P. O. Edison, Ga. No children.

B. Minnie Thomas Bell, born September 3, 1869, died October 16, 1870. Buried at Benevolence, Ga.

Second Line.

Sarah Coram, born December 12, 1811, died May 15, 1891. Married William B. Mitchiner, September 10, 1838. He was married twice, (1) to Charlotte Oliver and (2) to Sarah Coram. Children by his first wife were: John, Lizzie, Amanda, Charlotte, Tom, Raymond, and Jim. Children by second marriage:

1. William, 2. Louisa, 3. Mattie, 4. Daniel, 5. Josephine, 6. Sue. 7. George.

8. Fannie Mitchiner, born January 30,1849, married May 17, 1882, W. T. Breedlove. P. O. Sale City, Ga. Children:

A. Lula, born December 12, 1884. B. Sallie, born August 28, 1886. C. Donie, born August 8, 1890. D. Albyrta, born July 30, 1892.

9. Robert.

10. David R. Mitchiner, born July 7, 1852 at Benevolence, Ga. Married (1) Mary Elizabeth Keese, (2) Annie Lou Hartsfield, November 14, 1899. Children all by first marriage:

A. Dessica Radford, born July 21, 1876, P O. 1575 Venton Ave., Memphis, Tenn. B. William Keese, born August 1, 1880, P. O. Dawson, Ga. C. Maxwelton, born July 29, 1882. D. Robert Clinton, born September 22, 1886, P. O. Gordon, Ga. E. Mary Eunice, born December 7, 1890, died February 25, 1922.

Third Line.

Mary Ann Coram, born July 15, 1813, married Harmon Butler. Died without issue.

Fourth Line.

Nancy J. Coram, born October 5, 1814, in Warren county, Ga., died April 12, 1870, in Quitman county, Ga. She married James A. Nobles March 1, 1838. James A. Nobles was born May 15, 1816. Family probably came first to Orangeburg, S. C., where the named was spelled Knobles. He died April 16, 1903. Served in Indian War in 1836 and in Confederate War from July, 1864, until close of war. Children:

1. Jeremiah T. Nobles, born August 25, 1839, married Rebecca Floyd. Joined Confederate service March 12, 1862, and died at Richmond, Virginia, August 6, 1862. One child.

A. James T. Nobles, who lives it Georgetown, never having married.

2. William J. Nobles, born August 30, 1843, and died November 13, 1862.

3. Mattie E. Nobles, born July 22, 1846, in Quitman county, Ga., married Hardy Floyd on July 20, 1865. He was born July 16, 1844, died September 3, 1922. Served in 29th Alabama Regiment from July, 1861 until close of war. Children:

A. Jeremiah J. Floyd, born March 27, 1866, P. O. Georgetown, Ga. Judge Floyd moved from Quitman county, Ga., to Pike county, Alabama, in 1890. Served as Postmaster at Deleon, Ala., from 1892 to 1903. Elected Justice of the Peace in Pike county, Ala., in 1900 and served until 1903. Moved to Quitman county Ga., in 1904, where he was elected Justice of the Peace, serving until 1917, when he was appointed Judge of County Court in 1917 and reappointed in July, 1921. On February 22, 1894, he married Mary M. Finlayson in Pike county, Ala. Children: (a) Addie R.. born February 26, 1895, married James Warren Griffin, August 17, 1913, P. O. Georgetown, Ga. Children (1) Mary Lois, born June 22, 1914. (2) Hazel Christine born May 6, 1916. (3) James Warren, Jr., born July 24, 1917. (4) Janie Lou, born July 2, 1919. (5) Alton Clifton, born September 16, 1922. (6) Jasper Norman, born August 29, 1924.) (b) Mattie V., born November 2, 1897, married Henry T. Rice on October 20, 1918. (c) Jimmie Ethel, born June 18, 1900, died January 16, 1901. (d) Alva Gertrude, born August 10, 1902, died February 28, 1925. (e) Florence Lucille, born January 8, 1905. (f) Julia Mae, born May 2, 1909. (g) Mary Clare, born March 17, 1912. (h) Dixie, born July 8, 1914.

B. Ella M. Floyd, born February 18, 1868, married Morgan L. Graddy on November 14, 1886, P. O. Georgetown, Ga. Children: (a) Henry K. Graddy, born August 23, 1887, married (1) Lucile Rice, April, 1909. (2) Lola Graddy, December, 1911, P. O. Cuthbert, Ga. (b) James R. Graddy, born March 14, 1889, died March 2, 1907. (c) Mattie L. Graddy, born July 27, 1891, married Walter Reeves on January 4, 1910, P. O. Saco, Ala. (d) Fannie Pearl Graddy, born December 28, 1892, married Reuben Finlayson, April, 1914, P. O. Perots,

4

Ala. (e) William W. Graddy, born December 4, 1894, married Lula Dunn December, 1919, P. O. Clayton, Ala. (f) Durwood E. Graddy, born January 28, 1897, married Ila Mae Bates, December 12, 1915, P. O. Georgetown, Ga.

Fifth Line.

Susan Coram, born June 19, 1816, married Fernando Sanders. Died without issue.

Sixth Line.

John Jasper Coram, born November 19, 1818, died May 12, 1890. Married Elizabeth Cook. Children:
1. Sophronia, married Judge O. A. Harris. She is dead but Judge Harris lives at Cuthbert, Ga. Children:
A. W. D. Harris, of Greenville, S. C. Mr. Harris has been of considerable assistance in supplying information for this sketch.
B. J. C. Harris, of Cuthbert, dead.
C. Aurora, married a McCormick and lives at Chipley, Fla.
D. Miss Willye Harris, of Cuthbert, Ga.
2. Annah, who married John Gauldin and moved to Texas. The family lost connection with this branch after the death of Mrs. Gauldin.
3. Sallie, married Thomas Franklin Meadows. She died and Mr. Meadows married (2) Lula Lee Coram, who was a daughter of Thomas Jefferson Coram. (For children of second marriage, see 6 in seventh line.) Children of first marriage:
A, J. C., B, T. C., C, Bessie. All dead.
4. Willie, died at 14 years of age.

Seventh Line.

Thomas Jefferson Coram, born July 10, 1820, married Martha J. Wamble, September 22, 1858. Mr. Coram was distinguished by his simple life and childlike faith and by the lives of probity which his children have lived. Mr. Coram, the elder, lived to be eighty-four years of age and never used profanity or was under the influence of strong drink or used tobacco in any form. Neither have any of his six sons indulged in any of these excesses. What further eulogy could we give him that would strengthen? Died Nov. 22, 1904. Children:
1. Thomas Allen Coram, born August 9, 1859, P. O. 212 May Street,

Montgomery, Ala. He married Mollie R. Hart, Dec. 21, 1886. She was a daughter of Henry Hart and was born Nov. 7, 1867. Children:
A. Minnie Fredonia, born January 10, 1888, married Edward C. Tinsley, April 22, 1906, in Mitchell county, Ga. P. O. Pelham, Ga., Route No. 1, Box 41. Children (a) Theodore L. born September 29, 1907; (b) Essie Mae, born March 25, 1909. (c) J. Milton, born May 14, 1911. (d) Audrey L. born July 23, 1913. (e) Henry Bernard, born Feb. 5, 1916. (f) John Allen, born July 23, 1924.
B. Nannie Mae Coram, born April 8, 1890, married Robert E. Brunson (born Jan. 19, 1883), Dec. 2, 1906. P. O. Cairo, Ga. Children: (a) Vera Elberta, born Sept. 2, 1907, (b) Thomas Lee, born Nov. 25, 1908, died Nov. 25, 1908. (c) Berma Nadine, born Nov. 26, 1910. (d) Robert Fallen, born Sept. 14, 1912. (e) Emma Jewell, born Feb. 3, 1915. (f) Mona Vermel, born Nov. 11, 1916. (g) Trener Hazel, born Jan. 9, 1919. (h) Lillian L. born May 2, 1922. (i) Bobbie May born July 27, 1924. (See Brunson Notes Swann-Watson Family.)
C. Rosa Elberta Coram, born August 7, 1892, married William S. Little, July 28, 1912. P. O. 212 May St., Montgomery, Ala. Children (a) Docia Christine, born May 4, 1913. (b) William Steiner, born June 5, 1916. (c) James Thomas, born November 5, 1918. (d) Jesse Edward, born Sept. 22, 1922.
D. Willie Lois, born Feb. 26, 1895, married Lewis H. Hopson, Feb. 14, 1913: Children (a) Rosa Oza Mae Julia, born April 8, 1916.
E. Henry Hart Coram, born October 20, 1899, P. O. 212 May Street, Montgomery, Ala.
2. William Watson Coram, born April 15, 1861 in Randolph county, Ga. P. O. 803 Lake Ave., Tampa, Fla. married Emma Elizabeth Murdock Oct. 10, 1883. Children:
A. Jefferson Cleveland Coram, born Sept. 25th, 1884, died Sept. 13, 1887.
B. William Alva Coram, born Jan. 1, 1890, married Feb. 28, 1924, Dorris Eugene Collins. P. O. 803 Lake Street, Tampa, Fla.
C. Ralph Eugene Coram, born August 29, 1892, married Hattie Belle Bishop, December 28, 1913. P. O. 811

Baker Street, Tampa, Fla. Children: (a) Walton Marion, born October 13, 1915. (b) Eunice Belle, born July 29, 1917. (c) Curtis Eugene, born February 25, 1920.

D. John Edwin Coram, born January 19, 1896, married Annie Belle White, December 16, 1916. P. O. Route No. 6, Orient Avenue, Tampa, Fla. Children: (a) Edwin Marvin, born September 26, 1917. (b) Emily Lorene, born May 12, 1921. (c) James Lynward, born July 31, 1924.

E. Henry Truman Coram, born October 9, 1899, P. O. 810 Curtis St., Tampa, Fla. Married Winnie Mae Southerland, August 10, 1919. One child (a) Henry Jean Clemons, born June 12, 1922.

F. Ruby Catholee Coram, born May 10, 1902, P. O. 803 Lake Street, Tampa, Fla. Married, June 15, 1920, Oscar Douglas Bryan.

3. J. Madison Coram, born November 13, 1865, P. O. Benevolence, Ga. On December 24, 1891 married Minnie O. Knighton, daughter of S. E. Knighton. Children:

A. Sammie J. Coram, born October 28, 1892, died February 28, 1919.

B. Clarence, born September 24, 1894.

C. Roy, born March 13, 1896. Married August 17, 1919. Name of wife not given.

D. Myrtie Mae, born June 28, 1897. (She was married September 1, 1918 her husband's name being Sorrell.)

E. Nina T., born August 15, 1911.

F. Clera, born April 18, 1916, died at Benevolence, Ga., Feb. 25, 1918.

4. Eulalah Indianah, died in 1864.

5. John E., born December, 1866, lives at Cuthbert, Ga. He is connected with the Cuthbert Liberal Enterprise.

6. Lula Lee, (same as Martha Telula) born July 15, 1869, married Thomas Franklin Meadows. (See also Sixth Line No. 3.) on January 2, 1890. Children:

A. Albert J., born December 10, 1890, died September 14, 1891.

B. Birdie M., born April 3, 1893, died April 5, 1893.

C. Hugh, born October 21, 1895, died December 26, 1895.

D. Thomas O., born August 11, 1897, died September 5, 1897.

E. Clyde, born Oct. 22, 1898.

F. Kattye

G. Lottie. Kattye and Lottie are twins. Born September 17, 1901. Lottie married a Wise in Americus, Ga., and Kattye is living at Benevolence, Ga.

H. Robert E., born Feb. 9, 1907, died July 27, 1907.

7. Maggie Coram, born August 27, 1871, married Charlie H. Pittman, December 6, 1903. P. O. Benevolence, Ga. Children:

A. Mary H., born September 13, 1904.

B. Charlie Max, born January 14 1906.

C. Lizzie Pauline, born November 17, 1910.

D. Cora Lee, born April 1, 1915.

8. George Jefferson Coram, born August 26, 1873, P. O. Benevolence, Ga. Married Lillie Pauline Jenkins, December 11, 1895. Mr. Coram is a rural carrier on route No. 1 from Benevolence, having begun this service in 1909. His father carried the mail during the Civil War once each week without charge, and his brother, Allen, was Star Route Carrier from Benevolence from 1892 to 1894. He left school in the tenth grade to assist his father with the farm, helping to earn a living for the large family. He has always been true to his family ties, loyal to his country, obedient to God and helpful to humanity. Sober, industrious, truthful, not given to disputations, and free from profanity and vulgarity, it is no wonder that he is liked by the patrons of his route and esteemed by the community in which he lives. His assistance in the preparation of this sketch in furnishing information has been of incalculable benefit. He is a faithful member of the Baptist church. Taking pattern from his father before him, he does not use tobacco. Children:

A. Broadus L., born February 5, 1899, now living at Orlando, Fla.

B. Raymond W., born September 26, 1901, now living at Orlando, Fla.

C. Marvin, born October 19, 1906, living at Orlando, Fla.

D. Sadie, born October 21, 1908, living at Benevolence.

9. James L., born October 20, 1876, died in 1905.

Eighth Line.

George Washington Coram, born February 10, 1825, married Susanah Manor. (See biographical section for sketches of both of these parties.) Children:

1. Willard N. Coram, born January 8, 1848, died ....
.... Married (1) Emma Morrison. Children by first marriage:

A. Henry, died about 18 years of age, without issue.

B. Elmore

C. Ollie

D. Homer

E. Minnie. Minnie Coram, born May 21, 1886, married Joseph Stephen Bush, January 16, 1904. Children: (a) Homer Elmo, born June 20, 1905. (b) Ila Montey, born January 22, 1907. (c) Infant son, born July 22, 1908, died October 28, 1908. (d) Thomas Jefferson, born June 30, 1910. (e) Infant son, born September 18, 1911, died November 30, 1911. (f) Infant daughter, born November 12, 1912.

F. Susan Emma

Married (2) Nannie Bartlett. Children by second marriage:

G. Maud

H. Edna

I. Annie Laurie

J. Rebecca

2. Eugenia Coram, born May 6, 1849, died April 15, 1890. Married Luther Hester, P. O. Sparks, Ga., R. R. No. 2. Children:

A. Ludie, died July 22, 1898, left a daughter who married Ural Stokes and lives in Terrell county, Ga.

B. Minnie Lee, born Feb. 10, 1875, P. O. Pavo, Ga., R. F. D. No. 2. Married W. P. Kirby: Children (a) Lillie Mae, born August 12, 1895, married Jimmie Parker, Feb 10, 1911, at Sparks, Ga, P. O. Adel, Ga. (b) Hughie Micheal, born March 14, 1898, married Mary Hester, died at Mulberry, Fla., on Dec. 23, 1914. (c) Hilda Marie, born Oct. 17, 1905, married Frank Holland, April 16, 1923, address 496 Capitol Ave., Atlanta, Ga.

C. Thomas Hester.

D. George Hester, born Oct. 26, 1878, married Mary Missouri Holland, Feb. 2, 1902. Children (a) Ethel Vivian, born Nov. 3, 1902. (b) Eugene Thomas born March 24, 1905.

E. Carl G. Hester, born Aug. 31, 1880, married Carrie Lee Forte, Aug. 21, 1909, P. O. Sparks, Ga., R. F. D. No. 2. Children: (a) Etna Lucile, born July 21, 1910. (b) Jewell Gynn Hester, born December 13, 1912.

F. Annie Hester married Joseph C. Bryan, P. O. Tifton, Ga. Children: (a) Bessie Irene, born Nov. 29, 1904. (b) Howard and (c) Carson, twins, born Aug. 1, 1907. (d) Helen Grace, born Sept. 2, 1910, (e) Ruby Eugenia, born March 25, 1913. (f) Luther, born Nov. 21, 1914. (g) Raymond, born Oct. 9, 1918. (h) Laura Lee, born July 28, 1921.

G. Bessie Hester, born September 10, 1884, married Eugene Adams, Feb. 11, 1906, P. O. Sparks, Ga. Children: (a) Inez, born Dec. 9, 1907, died Feb. 10, 1910. (b) Hazel, born July 7, 1909. (c) Hoke Smith, born November 7, 1910. (d) Eugene Guy, born Oct. 25, 1912. (e) Triplet daughters died Oct. 8, 1914. (f) Odus Noel, born Aug. 30, 1915.

H. Eugenia.

3. George Washington Coram, born February 6, 1851, P. O. Fort Gaines, Ga. Married Lou Eldo Rish, Jan. 8, 1890. Mr. Coram has been engaged as a teacher and farmer during the greater part of his life. He acquired through his own efforts a classical education and soon became a leader in his community. He now wns a large tract of land in Clay county, Ga. near Ft. Gaines. Children:

A. Leila Beatrice Coram, born November 18, 1890, married Frank Gunn Hartley on August 28, 1921.

B. Byron Wesley Coram, born July 14, 1892, Unmarried, resides with father.

C. Jennings Bryan Coram, born December 19, 1895, now located at Fairbanks, Alaska.

D. Ila Grace Coram, born October 18, 1900, married J. F. Ing:am, P. O. Blackshear, Ga. One child (a) Naomi, born April 10, 1920.

4. Susannah Sofronia Coram, boin January 20, 1853.

5. Thomas Jasper Coram, born June 4, 1854, P. O. West Bay, Fla. Married Mollie E. Savelle on June 7, 1883. She was born at Georgetown, Quitman county, Ga., on March 14, 1862, and died at West Bay, Fla., on June 29, 1924. Children:

A. Ida, born January 7, 1889, married B. F. Powell. Have several children, but fail to answer letters.

B. Samuel Wayne Coram, born September 30, 1891, married Alma Fleming on November 9, 1913.

C. Charles Harrison Coram, born September 30, 1894, died at West Bay, Fla., on June 28, 1924, just one day before his mother. He served in the World War from August 26, 1918, until he was honorably discharged. He was the support of his father's and mother's declining years, a friend of everybody and his death a great shock, especially being followed so soon by that of his mother.

6. Martha Elizabeth Coram, born July 8, 1856, married William D. Fort. May 18, 1882. Children:

A. William Henry, born Sept. 12, 1883 married Ida Paul. Died Aug. 29, 1907.

B. Emma Pearl, born March 30, 1885, died Dec. 23, 1885.

C. Annie May, born Dec. 24, 1886, married Clarence Ammons. P. O. Lumpkin, Ga.

D. Carrie Lee, born Aug 11, 1888. married Carl Hester, (See 2-E this line.)

E. Lillian Nanna, born April 18, 1890, married Colon Britt, April 14, 1907.

7. Mary Caledonia Coram, born May 7, 1858, married J. R. LeGear, Jan. 17, 1885. Children:

A. Mattie Eleanor, born October 28, 1885, married J. H. Shaw, October 17, 1909. Children: (a) Annie Claire, born April 1, 1911. (b) Eldridge Aldine, born October 8, 1912. (c) Geraldine, born December 12, 1919, died December 17, 1919. (d) James Henry, born November 16, 1920, died February 18, 1924; both of dead children are buried at the Bush cemetery at Cuba, Early county, Ga.

B. Allie Beatrice, born January 6, 1890, died April 20, 1890.

C. and D. Callie and Tallie, born July 11, 1892, died July 12, 1892.

E. Susie Annie Irene, born October 9, 1894.

F. Ella Lota, born June 27, 1898, died October, 1898.

8. Sarah Amanda Coram, born August 28, 1859, married William Savelle and moved to Alabama. We failed to locate any member of family.

9. Ella Tallula Coram, born December 25, 1861, P. O. Milford, Ga. Married Walter T. Ozmore, June 3, 1885. Children:

A. Raymond Leon, born March 19, 1888. Married Laura Lake Brinson in Grady county, Ga., June 2, 1908. Names of children not furnished to us.

B. Etna Irene Ozmore, born September 29, 1891, P. O. Tallahassee, Fla. Married Albert L. Burton on April 8, 1909. Children (a) Edith Lucile, born January 13, 1910. (b) Margaret Olivia, born September 28, 1915. (c) Lawrence Leland, born March 6, 1920.

C. Flora Inez Ozmore, P. O. Tallahassee, Fla., was born October 13, 1895. Married Henry Lee Fountain (Leesburg, Ga.), May 26, 1921. Children: (a) Charlie Ozmore, born Mar. 27, 1922. (b) Nezzie Lee, born July 27, 1923.

10. Laura Leander Coram, born December 2, 1863, married J. P. Swann. (For the continuation of her line see Swann-Watson Sketch. First Line.)

11. Emma Lenora Coram, born June 18, 1867, P. O. Columbia Ala. Married William Charles Harris, December 20, 1908. Charles Harris had been married before. No children by last marriage.

Ninth Line.

Deborah S. Coram, born April 22, 1824, died November 25, 1852. Married Martin H. Brown. Children:

1. Susan.

2. Julia.

N. B. Family moved to California. The last heard of them Julia had married a man by the name of Yenewine and was living at San Diego, California.

Tenth Line.

Indiana Coram, born September 11, 1825, and d.ed August 20, 1846. Married Frank Ware. Left no issue.

Watson-Swann Family.

Watson.

Origin of name. The name Watson and the name Watts mean the the same thing, that is, "the son of Walter." Walter signifies a woodmaster, or keeper of the woods, hence the name Watson "a son of the keeper of the wood."

Swann.

To understand the name Swann and its origin, it is necessary for us to go back to that period of time in which inns, shops and business houses were designated by pictures placed over the shops for the purpose of identifying the place of business. This was before family names became common and before the art of reading had been acquired by the majority of people. This whole matter is treated on pages 39 and 40 of an an essay on the Origin and Import of Family Names, as written by William Arthur, with the assistance of his son, Chester A. Arthur, who later became president of the United States.

"Many names were taken from the signs over the doors of inns, or the shops of various tradesmen, where goods were manufactured and sold."

Camden informs us, "that he was told by them who said they spake of knowledge, that many names that seem unfitting for men, as of brutish beasts, etc., come from the very signs of the houses where they inhabited. That some, in late time, dwelling at the sign of the Dolphin, Bull, Whitehorse, Racket, Peacocke, etc., were commonly called Thomas at the Dolphin, Will at the Bull, George at the Whitehorse, Robin at the Racket, which names, as many other of the like sort, with omitting at, became afterward hereditary to their children."

In olden times, in London, might be seen the sign of the Boar's Head, the Crosskeyes, the Gun, the Castle, the Crane, the Cardinal's Hat, the Angell, the Bell, the SWAN, the Bowles, the Barrel, the Crosier, the Griffin, the Coney, the Jugg, the Kettle, the Potts, the Pitcher, Sword, Shears, Scales, Tabor, Tub, etc."

Preliminary Notes.

Frederick.

The Frederick family united with the Watson family by the marriage of Martha Frederick to Frederick Watson. It is possible that the families were related before this, but we have no proof. Tradition is that this marriage occurred in Houston, Twiggs or Washington county, Georgia, and that the family lived in each of these three counties. (Information furnished by Mrs. Eliza Swann.)

In the History of Savannah and South Georgia, we find on page 1053, in the Sketch of Daniel Frederick Davenport, that Colonel Davenport married Mary Frederick, a native of Orangeburg, South Carolina. Her father, Daniel Frederick, was born, reared and married in South Carolina. Subsequently, he came with his family to Georgia and purchased a plantation in Houston county. His wife before her marriage was Caroline Rumph.

The Roster of Georgia Revolutionary Soldiers mentions Thomas Frederick, who drew land in Washington county, Georgia.

From the History of Orangeburg county, South Carolina, we find the following mention of the Frederick family:

Andrew Frederick appointed Road Commissioner, page 11.

Presbyterian meeting house erected on Cattle Creek, 1778, was called the Frederican Church after Andrew Frederick, who was its principal founder.

Andrew Frederick mentioned as being present at the baptism of John Frederick, son of Christopher and Angelia Miller, September 4 ,1754.

Hans Peter Frederick, son of Andrew and Margaret Frederick, born June 20, 1758, according to his baptismal record.

Jacob Frederick, son of Andrew and Margaret Frederick, was born June 20, 1758, as shown by baptismal record.

Church records also mention that Maria, wife of Andrew Frederick, was at baptism of Catherine Margaret Sondel.

Watson.

The records of the War Department show that one Frederick Watson served in the War of 1812, as a private in Capt. John Cox's Company, 2nd Regt. (Tisdale's) N. Carolina Militia. His service commenced September 28, 1814, and ended March 22, 1815.

The records of Archives and History State of Georgia show that Frederick Watson was Tax Collector, Houston county, 1828, 1830, 1831, 1832 1833, 1835, 1836, 1837 and 1838. These records do not show who was tax collector for the year 1834, but it is likely that this was Frederick Watson.

D. A. R. Lineage Book, Vol. XLV, No. 44205, shows Michael Watson to have married Martha Watson. His son, Elijah, married Chloe Wimberly. The following extracts are taken from mention of Michael Watson in the History of Orangeburg County, South Carolina. "Some of Watson's Company, who had also taken to flight on seeing their Captain fall, took possession of a farm house near by, occupied by only a mother and her child. There was little or nothing to eat on the premises, and they now feared pursuit more than ever, believing that the woman would report them to their enemies. One of them was chosen by lot and sent off to Orangeburg for help. Colonel Rumph came out to them as soon as possible, but before the arrival of his company, the poor woman and child, with their unwelcome guests, were all nearly starved to death." Page 484.

"Near the close of these troubles in South Carolina, in May 1782, Captain Watson (Foot Note says Michael Watson) heard of a body of tories in Deans Swamp, near Orangeburg, and, in conjunction with Captain William Butler, his .friend and neighbor, it was determiend to attack them. Watson's men were mounted Militia, armed with rifles and muskets; Butler's men were cavalry, armed with pistols and cutlasses. *******When they approached the edge of the swamp, two men were observed, as if endeavoring to hide themselves. Butler, Watson and Vardel—a very brave man—road rapidly forward to cap-

ture them. Watson first discovered that these men were only a decoy. * They arose on being discovered and poured on their assailants a well directed fire which brought down Watson, Vardel, and several others of the foremost Whigs."

"Watson survived until the Americans reached Orangeburg. In that village he was buried with the honors of war, and his grave was watered with the manly tears of his fellow soldiers."

Brunson.

This family is of German origin, the name was originally written Brunzon. There appears to have been several who came over with the colony of Germans and Swiss who settled in Orangeburg, South Carolina, from 1735 to 1737. Others of this colony whose names are familiar in Georgia, being probably born by descendants, are: Ott, Frederick, Huber, Rumph, Rickenbacker, Zeigler, Tilly, etc. They appear to have been Lutherians ih religion, and the church was called the Frederican Church after its founder, Andrew Frederick. In these church records appear the entries relating to the Brunson family:

On Tuesday, May 26th, 1750, married by J. Giessendanner, Robert Lammon, to Barbara, widow of Jacob Brunzon, deceased.

On Sunday, October 28th, Isaac (Baptized), son of Jacob and Barbara Brunson, born ....

Above information obtained from the History of Orangeburg, South Carolina.

Revolutionary Soldiers in Georgia bearing name of Brunson—

David Brunson drew land in Washington county, Ga. David Brunson is mentioned twice in the list compiled from the papers in the office of the Secretary of State, it should be probably in one place, Daniel. Also William, John and Samuel and the heirs of Ebenezer.

Jacob Brunson died in Orangeburg county, N. C., leaving widow Barbara, who married Robert Lammon.

Isaac Brunson was a son of Jacob and Barbara Brunson and the father of David Brunson, who served in South Carolina, was wounded in the foot at the battle of the Cowpens, died in

Decatur county, Ga. Left numerous descendants. His wife before her marriage was Zilphy Lee.

A son, Thomas W., married Cornela Cassels. Their son, Thomas Jefferson Brunson married Mary Ann Lydia America Wilder, a daughter of Isaac and Lydia Wilder. Thomas J. Brunson, father of Robert E. Brunson, who married Nannie Mae Coram.

Daniel Brunson married Francis Stanton, and drew land in St. Andrews Parrish 1774, and also in St. John's Parrish in 1774.

Stanton.

John Stanton drew land in Newton county, Georgia.

Swann.

Tradition is that this family in Georgia was founded by an Irish Immigrant that cames to America with two other brothers, one of the brothers locating in North Carolina, one in Virginia and the other in Georgia. Mentioned in the old records in connection with the Revolution, we find the names of James Swann, John Swann, William Swann (Drew Pension from Harris county) William B. Swann, Elijah Swann and the widow, Mary Swann, who was the widow of a revolutionary soldier. The others drew lands in Washington and Newton counties ,Mary in Monroe county. The land drawn by Mary was soon cut off into Pike.

From the above facts and traditions, when taken together with the following sketches, I have reached the conclusion that the Watson line, together with those with whom they have intermarried, come of original Orangeburg county, South Carolina, stock with the exception of the Stanton branch. In passing, I will say that the Harlow ancestry will be barren of results for further investigation. The family came to North Carolina early in the 17th century and mention will be found of the family in the Colonial records of North Carolina, but investigation will be fruitless, in my opinion. I would have been delighted to have followed up my investigation of these lines further, if the interest of the members of the family had justified the expenditure of the time and money.

John Green Berry Watson, who was a son of Frederick Watson, mentioned above, and his wife, Martha (Frederick) Watson, was born March 31, 1812, was a Democrat in politics, a member of the Baptist Church, and was Tax Collector of Randolph county, Georgia, 1887-8-9 and 1890. He married Mary Brunson in 1835. She was a daughter of Daniel Brunson and Francis (Stanton) Brunson. Children:

First—Daniel Frederick, married Emily Swann January 3, 1836. Their children are: (1) James Watson. (2) John Watson, (3) Tobe Watson, (4) Robert Watson, (5) Ada Watson, (6) Emma Watson, (7) Richard Watson, (8) George Watson. (George and Tobe are dead, the others take no interest.)

Second—Martha Eliza, born April 7, 1837, in Stewart county, Ga., P. O. Carnegie, Ga. Married Ross Swann, who was a soldier in the Confederate war, being killed in battle. Their children (1) Mary Jane Swann, born October 11, 1856, married James W. Bass and left several children. (2) John Walter Swann, born January 3, 1859, married Betsie Bass and left several children, who reside in and around Carnegie. (3) Green Ross Swann, born September 3, 1862, married Mattie Martin, a daughter of Rev. John Martin on January 2,1884. Mr. Swann lives at Carnegie and is a farmer and merchant at that place, priding himself more in his farm than in the store however. Their children are: (A) Lily, born January 24, 1885, (B) Ruby, born September 13, 1891, (C) Nellie, (D) Cleo, (E) Bart, (F) Mattie.

Third—Sarah Elizabeth, born 1838, married Richard Price. Children: To the best information obtainable. (1) Malrey, (2) Corene, (3) John, lives at Hartsfield, but refuses to answer letters. (4) Ida, (5) Richard, Jr., (6) Arrey.

Fourth—Francis Dewilder, married Joseph H. Swann, which line see.

Fifth—Mary Delilah, born February 5, 1842, married Thomas Stevens. Their children: To the best information obtainable. (1) Lena, married Nat. McKimmie, and lives at Cuthbert, Ga., but refuses to answer letters. (2) Laura Mae. No further information.

Sixth—William Stanton, born February 15, 1844, married James R. Patterson on December 23, 1869. He died April 2, 1916. (Inscription on Tombstone 'Asleep in Jesus, Blessed Sleep, from which none ever wake to weep. Gone but not forgotten.') Mrs. Patterson lives at Norman Park, Ga. Children: (1) John Allen Patterson, born August 18, 1871, married (1) Rushabel McMath, on September 9, 1914. (2) Alice Patton, on January 9, 1916. (2) Mary Edna Patterson, born April 13, 1873, married J. M. Reynolds on July 10, 1889. (3) Ada James Patterson, born February 9, 1878, died June, 1903.

Seventh—Emma Laura, died at 11 years of age.

Eighth—Elbert David Watson, born April 14, 1849, married about 1875 Sallie Martin, daughter of Rev. John Martin, and sister of the wife of G. R. Swann and first cousin of the wife of J. B. Watson. Mr. E. D. Watson fails to respond to letters, but records in the Department of Archives and History of State of Georgia show "E. D. Watson, Tax Collector, Randolph county, 1912-14, 1914-16,1916-20, 1920-24." Children: (1) Mattie Mae, married Dr. Weathers (brother of J. S. Weathers, of Cairo, Georgia). (2) Huddie, (3) Robert, (4) Flossie. These may not be correct.

Ninth—John Brunson Watson, born June 7, 1851, married Catherine A. Martin, February 10, 1874, in Calhoun county, Georgia. She is a daughter of Rev. Charles C. Martin and wife, Rachel A. Martin. Mr. Watson lives at Carnegie. Children: (1) Charlie Green Watson, born August 29, 1875, married Lenora Hicks, and lives at Moultrie, Ga. (2) Willie May Watson, born March 20, 1877, married Will Grubs 1897. She had children: (a) Katie, (b) Joe M., (c) J. Watson, Willie May is dead. (3) Mamie A., born January 10, 1879, P. O. Carnegie, Ga. (4) Alice B., born January 27, 1881, married E. Hatsten. She has four children: (a) Catherine, (b) Charlie M., (c) L. Watson, and (d) M. Nell.

Tenth—Green R. Watson, born April, 1854, died September 6, 1911. Married Mollie Bass, sister of Betsie, ..., March, 1877. Children: (1) I. F. (2) J. H. (3) W. B. (4) G. B. (5) T. C. (6) E. D. (7) J. A.

Joseph Hambleton Swann.

Joseph Hambelton Swann was a son of Richard Hill McRae Swann and Sarah Lewis (Harlow) Swann, who was born Mar. 4, 1797, died Jan. 6, 1877. Richard Hill McRae Swann was born April 7, 1798, died July 26, 1857. Was living in Monroe county, Georgia, the first known of him, moved from there to Stewart county, Georgia. Had children: William, James, Ross, Joseph Hambleton, Jane and Emily. W illiam and James went back into middle Georgia, and the other members of the family lost sight of them. Ross is included in the Watson Sketch Second Line, Emily in Watson Sketch first line, Jane married James Pritchard, from whom are descended the Fullers of Thomasville, Georgia, and the Owens of Moultrie, Georgia.

Joseph Hambleton Swann, born February 2, 1836, died February 2, about 1910, in Stewart county, Ga. He was a prosperous, thorough going farmer who provided well for his family, and by industry, thrift, judgment and economy accumulated considerable property. He was a Democrat in politics, and of the Baptist persuasion in religion. He joined the church but never took an active part, either in politics or religion, giving his energies and talents to his farming operation. He was married three times—(1) Francis Dewilder Watson. (2) Mrs. Mollie Wamble. (3) Annie Howell.

Francis Dewilder Watson, born May 7, 1840, died July 24, 1882. She was a consecrated Christian and took particular pains with the training of her children, but unfortunately she was not spared to finish her work. However, the second wife of Mr. Swann proved herself an excellent stepmother and as nearly as possible fulfilled a mother's place until her death.

Children of Joseph H. Swann and Francis Dewilder (Watson) Swann were: (1) Joseph Pinckney Swann. (2) Mary Lou, (3) Willie Jane, (4) Annie, (5) Nettie Laura, (6) Green M., (7) John Osborn.

First Line.

Joseph Pinckney Swann, born October 1, 1862, married Laura Leander Coram, who was born December 7, 1860, and died April 24, 1921, on December 21, 1881. (See biographical section for detailed sketches of their lives.) Children:

1. Bertha May (See Sketch of Rigsby Family No. 4 for continuation of this line.)

2. Roy, born June 15, 1888, was snake bitten and died ....

3. Nymie, born August 23, 1891, married Mark Howze Jan 26, 1908, who is a son of Matthew Howze and .... (Singletary) Howze. He was born in Thomas county, his parents and grandparents also lived in Thomas county. P. O. Phelham, Ga. Children:

A. Chester, born April 2, 1912.

B. Ione, born March 12, 1916.

C. Maston, born February 12, 1919.

D. Earnest, born August 27, 1923.

4. Lella, born February 12, 1893, married Marshall Hester Dec. 31, 1911. Marshall Hester and his wife live at Pelham, Ga., where he and Mark Howze, who married Nymie Swann, are engaged in the Market Business. Children:

A. Joseph Edgar, born December 7, 1920.

B. Laura Emily, born August 12, 1924.

5. Wilma, born August 5, 1898, married Arthur M. Prince on September 24, 1916. He is a son of George E. Prince and his wife, Jane (Bartlett) Prince. Wilma (Swann) Prince died June 23, 1920, at the birth of her first child:

A. Wilma Janice Prince, born June 22, 1920.

6. Joseph Paul Swann, P. O. Miami, Fla., Box 1864. c|o Orange State Oil Company, was born May 7, 1901. He married Flora Mae Shiver, daughter of Byron M. Shiver and Lilla (Spence) Shiver, who was a daughter of Asbury Spence. Byron M. Shiver is a son of M. Shiver and "Dollie" (Joiner) Shiver, who was a daughter of Asa Joiner of Mitchell county and a sister of Alfred Joiner, who married Josephine, the widow of Samuel D. Rigsby.

Children of Paul Swann and May (Shiver) Swann are:

A. Douglas Ledon, born April 25, 1922.

B. Richard McRae, born August 16, 1923.

7. Grace born June 27, 1904, died young with measles.

Second Line.

Mary Lou Swann, Norman Park, Ga., was born September 11, 1866, at Weston, Ga. On December 22, 1885 she married Thomas W. A. Wamble, a son of Lawrence L. Wamble, who is a brother of Martha J.Wamble, who married Thomas Jefferson Coram. Thomas W. A. Wamble lived and reared his family in Colquitt county, Ga., near Hartsfield, where he was a prosperous farmer. After his children were all nearly grown, he was appointed Attendance Officer for the schools of Colquitt county and moved to Moultrie. Before his appointment, he had been a member of the Board of Education for Colquitt county. He lived in Moultrie only a short time discharging the duties of his office to the satisfaction of all, when he had a slight stroke of paralysis. He partially recovered from this stroke, but it was not long before he suffered an attack of appendicitis, for which he underwent an operation but never recovered. He was a member of the Baptist church and an earnest worker in the Sunday Schools, and it may be truly said of him that he enjoyed the love and respect of all who knew him. Children:

A. Emmett, born December 24, 1886, died March 24, 1896.

B. Wiley, born August 24, 1888, died March 7, 1905.

C. Clyde, born July 31, 1892, died January 6, 1894.

D. Lonnie, born November 15, 1894, died December 6, 1894.

E. Willie Jewell, born March 5, 1897, married T. A. Stokes on Thanksgiving Day, 1914. P. O. Irvine Kentucky. Children: (a) Francis Helene, born June 18, 1916. (b) Thomas Alexander, born August 11, 1919.

F. Irene, born April 20, 1890, married G. F. Stokes on June 14, 1914. P. O. Sale City, Georgia. Children: (a) Thomas Fulton, born April 15, 1917.

G. Bernard, born March 5, 1901, married Nadine McDonald on January 4, 1920. P. O. Moultrie, Ga. Children: (a) Ivan Allen, born June 1, 1921.

H. Royal, born August 11, 1903.

I. Irma, born January 24, 1907, attending school at Norman Institute.

Third Line.

Willie Jane, born ....
1868, married L. L. Blanchard, in 1886.
She died ....;
her body lies buried in Liberty Hill
Cemetery, Colquitt county, Ga. No issue.

Fourth Line.

Annie E. Swann, born May 13, 1869,
in Stewart county, Ga., married Wil-
liam A. Wamble, brother of Thomas
W. A. Wamble, on December 2, 1888.
P. O. Esto, Florida, Holmes county.
Children:

A. Owen A. Wamble, born November 7, 1889, married Lucindy E.,Gay
on December 22, 1907. P. O. Esto,
Florida. Children: (a) Bessie Reba,
born August 21, 1912. (b) Leroy Aus-
telle, born April 16, 1916, died July
15, 1917. (c) Charlie, born September
26, 1917. (d) Hilda Francis, born August 31, 1920.

B. Willie G. Wamble, born March
13, 1893, married George W. Sellers
on July 20, 1917. P. O. Bay, Georgia. (Colquitt county) Children: (a)
Infant, born April 19, 1918, died
same day. (b) Leon Woodrow Sellers,
born July 7, 1919, died May 21, 1923.
(c) Clydie Mae, born January 31,
1921. (d) Grace Linelle, born March
12, 1922. (e) George W. Sellers, Jr.,
born June 28, 1923. (f) James Edward, born January 22, 1925.

C. Joseph L. Wamble, born January 21, 1896, married Lula Balcom on
February 15, 1920. P. O. Esto, Fla.
Children: (a) Sarah Eloise, born January 15, 1922.

D. Annie Mae Wamble, born May
26, 1900, married Charles S. Moody.
P. O. Graceville, Fla. Children: (a)
Edna Lurlene, born August 24, 1921.
(b) Syble Daphen, born May 10, 1923.
(c) Charles Ishmael, born December
29, 1924.

E. Ernest O. Wamble, born August 4, 1902, married Katrina Lloyd
on November 11, 1923. P. O. Day-
tonal, Fla., 510 Orange Avenue. Chil-

dren: (a) Ernestine Wamble.

F. Ruby Wamble, born January
15, 1905, died May 11, 1905.

G. Silas O. Wamble, born January
4, 1908.

H. Nymmie P. Wamble, born January 21, 1910.

I. Maggie P. Wamble, born March
9, 1911, died June 9, 1911.

Fifth Line.

Nettie Laura Swann, born April 10,
1871, married John Enoch Wamble,
another brother of Thomas W. A.
Wamble, P. O. Noma, Fla. Children:

A. Ethel Dewilda, born May 20,
1899, married Martin H. Register, on
November 21, 1920. P. O. Noma, Fla.
Children: (a) Ambrose Milton, born
October 2, 1921. (b) Broward, born
October 28, 1923, died June 5, 1924.

B. Bernice Stanton, born January
31, 1902, P. O. Albany, Ga.

C. Elnor Faye, born February 11,
1904.

D. Oris Binion, born May 10, 1906,
San Antonio, Texas.

E. Vita May, born January 12,
1908, died January 20, 1908.

F. Clyde McRee, born October 26,
1910.

G. Edna Avis, born Harch 13,
1912.

H. Blonnie E.air, born July 19,
1914.

Sixth Line.

Green McRae Swann, born Sept. 18,
1876, married Minnie Lee Jones Dec.
27, 1899 at Richland, Ga., ceremony
performed by Rev. W. W. Mabry:
Children:

A. Green M. Jr., born Sept. 20,
1905.

B. Clyde C., born Oct. 30, 1907.

C. Mary Frances, born Sept. 10,
1911.

D. Irma Myrtice, born Dec. 30,
1900 and died Dec. 24, 1902.

Seventh Line.

John Osborn, killed by negro on
father's farm in Stewart county, Ga.

Rigsbys of Georgia

The present form of this name evidently came from Rigby which itself came from Rigbi. It is probable, however, that its origin came from the words "Riggs" and "By". Riggs is a Danish word meaning wealthy or denoting a steep elevation, a range of hills or the upper part of such a range. "By" means a dwelling, a village, or town when used as a termination and is of Danish origin. The name Riggsby then would denote a dweller among or by or on hills or mountains. This family came into England with William the Conqueror and it is probable that the name Riggsby was conferred upon those of of his soldiers who came from among the hills and that all of the people bearing this name do not come of one common ancestor.

1

Allen Rigsby was born in North Carolina about 1770. Nothing positive is known about his parentage. He married Margarett Johnson who was a daughter of Irish parentage. Her mother's given name was Margarett and she lived to be one hundred eighteen years old, so tradition says.

Allen Rigsby served in the war of 1812 as did his sons John and Sam. Allen Rigsby was sergeant in Captain Abraham Massias Company and was discharged at Camp Point Peter, near Wilmington, North Carolina. He was a farmer, school teacher and cooper. In religion he was of the Baptist belief and both he and his wife were earnest consistent Christians, well versed in the Bible and he was a Deacon of the Church. Both he and his wife lived to be near the century mark, he dying about 1862 and she a short time before, both being buried at old Rocky Mount Church cemetery in Randolph county, Ga. Children:

A. John, who raised a family at Marietta, Ga.

B. Sam, who raised a family at Cuthbert, Ga.

C. Lewis, married in Georgia but moved to Texas.

D. Thomas, died in Alabama.

E. Jefferson.

F. Andrew.

G. Eliza, married Ause Langley.

H. Polly, married Ab Hopson.

I. Charity, married Sam Day and moved to Texas, a son, John, was for a time Captain of Co. G. 55th Ga. Regiment in Civil War but died in service.

2. J. Wiley Taylor Rigsby.

2

Wiley Taylor Rigsby was born in North Carolina, Jan. 7, 1809. His father moved to Georgia before his recollection where he grew to young manhood and married Jane R. Blair about 1831. She was a daughter of Johnson Blair (who may have been the same person mentioned in Roster of Revolutionary soldiers in Georgia) who tradition says immigrated from Ireland to America with his wife. If this tradition is true, then it is probable that he was married twice and that Jane R. Blair was the daughter of his second marriage. Johnson Blair died soon after the birth of Jane R. Blair and her mother married a man by the name of Vatin and had one son named Robert, who moved to Texas and married but left no issue. Tradition says that Jane R. Blair had a brother named John and another named William, but I have been unable to positively identify descendants of Johnson Blair so far. (For further information the reader is referred to a sketch of Wiley Taylor Rigsby and Jane R. (Blair) Rigsby, their Ancestry and Posterity and also to a Biographical sketch of the life of Wiley Taylor Rigsby now in preparation) Children:

A. Mary Ann Margaret.

3 B. Lewis Johnson.

C. James Roberson, born May 2, 1835, died Nov. 23, 1861 in the Confederate service, Richmond, Va.

D. Andrew Jackson born July 15, 1837; died Feb. 23, 1862.

E. Eliza Jane.

F. Amos Vatin, born April 7, 1841, died 1851.

G. Samuel David.

H. Thomas Wiley.

I. John Allen.

J. William Jefferson, born Nov. 29, 1851; married first Josephine Rigsby, Granddaughter of Sam Rigsby (1B) and second Mollie Faircloth, died 1916 without issue.

2 A

Mary Ann Margarett Rigsby, born June 11, 1832 married James Little. Children: (a) Mary Catherine born Nov. 18, 1853 married Elisha Barfield and died without issue, (b) Martha Elizabeth, born Oct. 24, 1856. Married Elijah D. Barfield, have children, (c) Eliza Rebecca born Feb. 1, 1860, married Jasper Brock and died without issue, (d) Margarett Nancy, born February 1862, married John F. Harrell, March 29, 1888, moved to Florida and left several children: (e) Alice Elmira, born Feb. 20, 1866, married Charles Edenfield Nov. 24, 1886 and have two children, (f) William Harrison, born August 6, 1868, died Oct. 16, 1872, (g) Lutisha Laura, born October 18, 1871, married William Edenfield October 3, 1890 and left issue.

James Little was a private in Company A, 22nd Georgia Regt., during the Civil War. The remainder of the Little geneaologies are given in sketch of Wiley Taylor Rigsby, etc.

2 E

Eliza Jane Rigsby, born March 29, 1839 married William B. Dunlap Nov. 10, 1858, children, (a) John B. born Sept. 27, 1860 and died young, (b) William Jefferson born April 17, 1862 married Ella Beasley and left issue, after her death he married a second time but left no issue by this marriage, (c) Mary Elander born Dec. 20, 1863, died Sept. 8, 1869, (d) Jennie Luella born Nov. 20, 1865 married John T. Oder May 6, 1883, moved to Florida where both died leaving issue, (e) Anice Elizabeth born Feb. 3, 1868 and died in childhood. (f) Telula Gertrude born Sept. 2, 1869 and married William Martin Prince Nov. 11, 1891, and have several children, (g) Thomas Wiley born March 20, 1872 married Florence Mathis, May 12, 1895 and died leaving children, (h) Annie Eliza born July 28, 1876 married C. C. Miller July 21st 1899 and have three living children, (i) Mollie Missouri born June 27, 1881 and married Rufus Harper, Nov. 29, 1903 and have several children (j) James Robert born Oct. 5, 1883 married first Annie Sarette, who died leaving children; married second Ocie Palmer and has several children by her.

William B. Dunlap served as a private in Company F., 50th Georgia Regt., in Civil War and lost a leg from a gunshot wound in the first battle of Manasses.

2 G

Samuel David Rigsby born Nov. 1, 1843 married Emily Josephine Draffin April 24, 1870, one child, (a) Sammie May married John T. Dollar and died near Cairo, Ga., leaving several children.

Samuel D. Rigsby served as a private in the Civil War in Company A 22nd Georgia Regt.

2 H

Thomas Wiley Rigsby born Aug. 15, 1845 married Vienna Brown Aug. 30, 1871. She was a daughter of James B. Brown and Zilpha (Hornsby) Brown. Children: (a) James Taylor born Dec. 8, 1873 married Alice Burnett and have children. (b) Elizabeth born March 13, 1875 married Milton Cooper Sept. 1, 1892 and have children. (c) Mamie born Dec. 8, 1879 married Edwin H. Shingler June 9, 1901 and have children. (d) Rebecca born Jan. 7, 1880 married Hardie B. Barwick Jan. 23, 1897 and have numerous children. (e) Wiley born March 16, 1884 married Mattie Marshall April 1, 1906 and have several children. (f) Myrtle born Feb. 28, 1887 married John P. Thomas Sept. 8, 1912 and have children. (g) Katie Born Feb. 22, 1887 married John Franklin Gay Dec. 11, 1910 and have several children. (h) Docie born Feb. 6, 1892 married James Johnson and have children. (i) John J. born Jan. 6, 1895 married Rhoda Mae Shiver and have children.

Thomas Wiley Rigsby was a private during the Civil War in Company A, 22nd Georgia Regt.

His oldest son James T. Rigsby is a Baptist preacher.

Edwin H. Shingler who married Mamie Rigsby was born and reared in London England, was ordained as a Baptist preacher by the Rev. Chas. Spurgeon, went as a Missionary to China where he served five years, coming from China to America he married Mamie Rigsby and continued his ministerial duties until his death.

John J. Rigsby above was a soldier in the world war serving in Company K., 30th Infantry, 3rd Division, receiving a slight wound.

2 I

John Allen Rigsby born Aug. 20, 1847 married Lds Cooper Dec. 10, 1874. She was a daughter of David Cooper and Nancy Whigham Cooper. Children: (a) Eula Genoa born Nov. 20, 1875 married John James and have several children. (b) Norma Estella born Oct. 5, 1877 married Charles Warren Nazworth March 15, 1899, (N. B. See sketch at close of this paragraph). (c) Lawson McElvey born Aug. 9, 1879. (d) Sherwood John born July 6, 1881, died Oct. 10, 1909. (e) Shirley Myrtilla born Jan. 19, 1888 married Robert E. Cox, Dec. 9, 1906, died leaving two boys. (f) Essie born Oct. 30, 1890 married J. L. Harrell June 2, 1918.

John Allen Righby served during the Civil war at a private in Company A, 22nd Ga. Regt.

The children of Norma (Rigsby) Nazworth and Charles Warren Nazworth are:

A, Herschel Thompson born Jan. 18, 1900. He served in the Army of Occupation in Germany, Co. L., 5th Inf., 2nd Brigade, A. F. B. in G. He made many friends and went safely through the war but was murderel soon after his discharge from the army without any cause or justification.

B. Virgil Scovil born Jan. 18, 1902.

C. Ray Rigsby born Sept. 1, 1903.

E. Maston Oneal born Dec. 15, 1905.

F. Lds born July 15, 1908.

G. Devola born and died 1910.

H. Charlie Hill born Oct. 30, 1912.

I. Donald Lewis born Aug. 20, 1914.

Having considered the Collateral branches of the family we will now take up the regular line:

4

Lewis Johnson Rigsby, born Jan. 9, 1834 married Behethland Luvinia Clay Dec. 11, 1866. Children:

A. Istalina Atwood born Nov. 1, 1867 and died Nov. 12, 1876.

5 B. Lewis Wiley.

Lewis Johnson Rigsby served in tne Civil War as First Sergeant Company G, 55th Georgia Regt. He was a Deacon in the Baptist Church, a Master Mason, the president of the Farmers Alliance and a Democrat in politics.

N. B. See Bigraphical section for extended biography of Lewis Johnson Rigsby and also of Behethland Luvinia (Clay) Rigsby.

5

Lewis Wiley Rigsby, born May 1, 1874, married Bertha May Swann Oct. 3, 1900. Children:

6 A. Hettie Lee.

B. Attie May.

C. Lewis Wilton.

D. Ila Paunee.

E. Lamar Joseph

F. Frank Park.

G. Lucia Elaine.

H. Roy Edward.

I. Ruth Claire.

J. Opal Elizabeth born Dec. 4, 1922. died Dec. 16, 1923.

Lewis Wiley Rigsby began his life's work as a teacher, and has been surveyor, was admitted to bar 1912, probation officer and is now (1925) Judge of the City Court of Cairo and the City Court of Whigham and Judge of Juvenile Court of Grady county and the author of these sketches and also of "Home and Family."

N. B. See Biographical section for a more extended biography of L. W. Rigsby and also of Bertha May (Swann) Rigsby.

6

Hettie Lee Rigsby born July 7th 1902 married James Othan Golden August 3, 1921 in Mitchell county, Georgia. Children:

A. William Valentine, born Feb. 22, 1923.

James Othan Golden is a son of Ella (Godwin) Golden and H. F. Golden, who is a son of William E. Golden and Laura (Taylor) Golden. William E. Golden was a son of Thomas Golden and Uriah (Alday) Golden. Laura (Taylor) Golden was a daughter of the Rev. John Taylor, a Baptist preacher who was born April 8, 1811 and died Oct. 29th, 1894 and is buried at Pleasant Grove cemetery, Grady county, Ga. His wife, Sallie (Parker) Taylor, died March 1, 1916, aged 111 years and is buried by the side of her husband.

Ella (Godwin) Golden is a daughter of John K. Godwin and his first wife Rebecca (Ray) Godwin. John K. Godwin took an active part in the creation of Grady county, Ga., being present at the signing of the bill, creating the county, by Governor Ter-

rell. He was a son of Valentine Godwin and his wife ....
(Kelley) Godwin. Valentine Godwin was a son of Alex Godwin who married a Yawn and came to South Georgia from North Carolina about 1823.
.... (Kelley) Godwin was a daughter of John Kelley (a son of William Kelley) and his wife Sarah (McElvey) Kelley who was a daughter of William McElvey, who was born and educated in Dublin, Ireland ,married Barbara Reeves and immigrated to America. He was a Baptist minister and was one of the presbytery that constituted Tired Creek (Baptist) Church 1826.

From Wm. McElvey's old family Bible we copy the following records:

William McElvey and Barbara his wife were married April 23, in the year of our Lord seventeen hundred and ninety-nine.

Second marriage of William McElvey to Elizabeth, his wife, February the 19th 1839 A. D.

John McElvey was married to Margaret L. Patterson Nov. 7th, 1824.

L. G. McElvey was married to Julia M. Booth Nov. 7th, 1843. A. D. 1843, A. L. 5843.

George R. McElvey was married to Catherine Rutherford December, 22, 1830 A. D.

Sarah G. McElvey was to John Kelley married 20th day of September, 1832. A. D. 1832.

Rachell Ann Blount and Harmon H. McElvey were married on the 29th day of December 1842, A. L. 5843, was married 55 years and 76 days at his death Feb. 14th, 1897.

Mary McElvey, daughter of William McElvey and Barbara, his wife. was born Aug. 18, A. D. 1799.

John McElvey was born March 7, A. D. 1801.

George McElvey was born April 29, A. D. 1802.

Noah McElvey was born Feb. 6, A. D. 1805.

William McElvey was born Dec. 10, A. D. 1807.

Martin McElvey was born Feb. 5, A. D. 1809.

Francis McElvey was born Feb. 2, A. D. 1811.

Frank McElvey was born April 25, A. D. 1812.

Elizabeth McElvey was born April 30, A. D. 1814.

Sarah McElvey was born May 2, A. D. 1816.

Harmon McElvey was born Aug. 25th in the year of our Lord 1819.

Lawson Gamble McElvey was born Sept. 10, in the year 1822.

Rachael A. Blount was born Sept. 9, 1826.

Thomas W. McElvey was born Dec. 9, 1856.

The preceding sketches have been prepared for binding with Home and Family in Section 1 as a part of the service rendered in connection with sales of that publication. Others will be prepared from time to time as the demand justifies and the interest of parties suggest and later a brochure of biographical sketches will be published of those so desired. We now have in preparation a sketch of the Clay-Jones family which connects up a great many of the Georgia branch of the Virginia Clays and will show the beginning of this branch in America and will give some history of the collateral branches in Kentucky and Alabama. In connection with this we expect to publish some notes on the following families:

Harrison, Singletary, Taliaferro, Hardin and Harden, Bass, Martin, etc.

These sketches will be furnished only with Home and Family at $10.00 each bound in imitation leather looseleaf or for $12.50 with genuine leather binding and name of purchaser stamped on cover in gold. Cash must accompany order. Orders should be given before publication as only enough are printed to satisfy the present demand.

Below we are suggesting an outline for biographical sketch and also giving a specimen sketch as prepared to this outline.

Laura L. (Coram) Swann.
B2S-2

Laura Lee Coram was born Dec. 7, 1863 in Randolph county, Georgia at Benevolence. Her father was George W. Coram and her mother, Susana (Mainor) Coram.

She was surrounded with a moral influence and Christian environment during her childhood which was spent at the place of her birth. She attended the public schools, the Sabbath schools and the church at Benevolence, winning the prize for the best record in school, which prize was offered by

Professor Orr who was then teaching the school at Benevolence. She was one of a large family and was denied the privilege of a college training.

Romance entered her life early and she was united in marriage to J. P. Swann, of Richland, Ga., Stewart county, Dec. 21, 1881. Her uncle T. J. Coram performed the ceremony consummating the marriage, some of the attendants being T. W. Wamble and Miss Mary Lou Swann who later married.

Her husband became a teacher and minister of the Gospel which occupation he followed until her death. During all of this period she was his constant helper and advisor and in his absence she managed the home with rare dilligence and judgment, taking most of the cares and worries from his mind. She was his constant helper in his church work filling that most difficult position of "minister's wife" so as to merit and receive the commendation of all who knew her.

Her life was domestic—a devoted wife and indulgent mother—she gave herself to her family.

She was fair with blue eyes and dark brown hair, five feet and four inches in height and weighed one hundred and twenty-eight pounds. She had unusually good health until worn by the trials of life.

Her perceptive faculties were much above the average and she had the artistic ability to reproduce what she saw leaving several drawings illustrating passages of scripture. She was a good composer and original writer and thinker, had an excellent memory reasoned well, had good judgment and was a good listener.

She was emotional and her affections deeply seated; she was sincere without guile. Without a moral blemish, with strong religious convictions and a bright hope of immortality her life was an example that her children may well emulate.

She was true to her God, her home and her fellow man.

She had talent for music and enjoyed good singing.

She was courageous and in her darkest hours never faltered, or became unbalanced or unreasonable.

She had a keen sense of humor and enjoyed innocent pleasures.

It was her delight to render service to those to whom service was due, to her God, her home, her country and her neighbors or the poor and needy.

She united with the Baptist Church at Mt. Pisgah, at Weston, Ga.. in 1883 and was baptised by the Rev. J. G. Corley. She remained a consistent Christian until her death, her membership then being with the Pleasant Grove Baptist Church, Grady county, Ga. She was active in Sunday School work and also in Missionary endeavors. She also joined the Masonic Lodge (Master's Daughter's Degree) in 1904.

She died at her home in Grady county, Georgia on the 24th day of April 1921, pneumonia being the immediate cause and she was buried at Pleasant Grove Cemetery on the 26th day of April, 1921, the funeral service being conducted by the Rev. Martin Taylor, of Cotton, Ga., and Rev. P. C. Barkley, of Cairo, Ga. Her grave is marked by a monument.

(Written by Mrs. Lella (Swann) Hester, a daughter.)

The above illustrates what a biographical sketch should show and is given as a specimen of sketches which we are collecting for publication for insertion in section seven of Home and Family, hoping that we may be able to collect a sufficient number of these sketches together with family histories to be incorporated into one large volume for reference for future generations.

The Pioneer Institute, Cairo, Ga.

OUTLINE FOR AN ANALYTICAL BIOGRAPHICAL SKETCH.

(1) Birth
    (2) Date
        Place
        Lineage
(1) Childhood and Youth
    (2) Enviroment
        Brothers and Sisters
        Educational Advantages
(1) Marriage
    (2) Place and Date
        Name of Wife or Husband and Other Facts
        Record of Marriage Together with Name of Minister or
            Officer Performing the Ceremony.
(1) Occupation or Profession
    (2) Qualifications
        Measure of Success
(1) Characteristics
    (2) Physical
        (3) Complexion
            Features
            Height and Weight
            Health and Constitutional Disease.
    (2) Mental
        (3) Perception
            Attention
            Memory
            Thought
            Reason
            Judgment
    (2) Emotional
        (3) Moral
            Religious
            Musical
            Courageous
            Temperamental, Sense of Humor
(1) Service
    (2) Of God
        (3) Details of Religious Life
            Membership in Church
            Official Position in Church
    (2) Of Humanity
        (3) Individual Efforts
            Fraternal Life
    (2) Of Country
        (3) Civil
            Military
    (2) Of Family
        (3) Parents
            Children
            Companion
            Collateral Kindred
(1) Death
    (2) Cause
        Place
        Date
        Burial Service
        Location of Grave
(1) Children
    (2) Marriage
        Location with Post Office Address, or Death.

The Georgia Branch of the Virginia Clays And Their Celebrated Cousins

With Harden and Jones Genealogies and Notes of Related Families.

Written and Published by L. W. Rigsby

For Service Section No. 1 "Home and Family."

July 4, 1926.

Literature and Early History of the Family.

The first effort made to preserve the history of this family appears to have been made by General Green Clay. I have been unable to obtain a copy of his manuscript, but Cassius M. Clay made a statement in his "Memoirs," and quoted a letter from Porter Clay, who was a brother of Henry Clay, the well known orator, who was known as the "Mill Boy of the Slashes." Both of these statements are incorporated in "The Clay Family" which was written by Hon. Zachary Smith and Mrs. Mary Rogers Clay and the statement is made that they had access to the MSS of General Green Clay while compiling their history. Their book has been indispensable in my work. For convenience it is cited merely "Clay Family."

The "Clay Family" gives considerable of the early history of the family, but deals principally with the Kentucky descendants. The authors appear to have lost trace of the branch which came to Georgia, and say very little of the Alabama Branch of the family. The history of the Alabama Branch, however is contained in the "Early Settlers of Alabama," by Col. James E. Saunders, which I have used and found of considerable assistance. It is cited merely "Saunders." Saunders, however, appears to also have been in ignorance of the Georgia Branch of the family.

Fortunately, there was published in 1906, by David E. Johnston, "A History of the Middle New River Settlements and Contiguous Territory," which supplied the key needed to con-

nect many of the Georgia Clays with their kindred throughout the other Southern States.

Notes left by Beheathland (Clay) Rigsby at her death connect the Georgia Clays with the Clays mentioned in the above History, which will be cited as "Johnston" and from the information supplied in these notes and in this history, I have connected the various lines and joined them to a common ancestry, so far as possible.

The notes referred to as left by Beheathland (Clay) Rigsby above differ, in the names and number of brothers who came from England to America, from the statement made by Porter Clay and Cassius M. Clay. They each, that is Cassius and Porter, say that three brothers came. My mother, Mrs. Beheathland (Clay) Rigsby, gives the number as two. Cassius and Porter gave their names as Charles, Thomas and Henry. My mother was not sure, but gave the names to the best of her recollection, as John and Lewis. She was correct as to the number who came and as to one of the names, that is, John. The other was named William. Now John and William had another brother named Richard, who was older than either John or William, and he had two sons who came to America, that is, Francis and Edward. It was evidently the sons, John, William and Richard, who Porter and Cassius had in mind, but they incorrectly named them; my mother evidently had in mind John and William.

In addition to the above manuscript

I have had the Manuscript of Miss Frances Powell Otken, of McComb, Miss., as well as a Manuscript furnished me by Mrs. Mary Clay, of Americus, Ga.

Other information has been obtained from County Records, numerous books, by personal interviews and by correspondence and questionnaires supplying information from more than a hundred members of the family in Georgia and other states. The Manuscript of Miss Otken is cited simply "Otken," of Mrs. Mary Clay, Americus, Ga., simply "Clay", the other citations give the title of the book or other authority. Where no citation is given information has been obtained by means of questionnaires or is within the knowledge of the author.

The "Georgia Branch of the Virginia Clays" begin their descent from the traditional Sir John Clay of England. His son, John "Claye" came to Virginia on the ship Treasuror, Feb. 1613, servant William Nicholls in the Dutie, May, 1619, wife Anne, in the Ann in August, 1623. He received grants of land as follows: 100 acres as an old planter before the government of Sir Thomas Dale and 1100 acres for the transportation of 23 persons on the "West" July 13, 1635. Land in Charles River County, (Clay Family).

William Clays (1638) brought over to Charles River County, Richard Bucher, Snalter Jochett, Adrian Marner, Thomas Stoakes and Tho. Seawell. (Early Immigrants, Geo. C. Greer.)

Richard Clay had a son, Francis Clay who came to America, 1649 (New England Historic Genealogical Register, Vol. 37, page 202). He brought over to Northumberland County, Virginia, 1653, the following parties: Wm. Bethell, Tho. Cleaves, Wm. Jones and Edwd. Simpson. Evidently Richard was the elder son and inherited his father's title and it is evident that Richard died between 1653 and 1655, because we find in 1655 that Francis Clay, Gent. brought over to Northumberland County, Virginia, the following parties: Wm. Bethell, John Cess, Tho. Cleaves, Mary Edwards, Henry Evans, Wm. Jones, Elizabeth Norman and Edward Simpson. (Early Virginia Immigrants, Greer.)

Daniel Clay was administrator on the estate of Francis Clay and bond was made before William Clay, steward of the Manor of Mansfield, who sealed with his arms. This William Clay was probably the eldest son of Francis Clay, inheriting the title from his father, who inherited it from his father, Richard, who inherited it from his father, Sir John Clay (John Clay, Gent.) of England. (New England Historic Genealogical Register, Vol. 37, page 202.) Other immigrants coming to Virginia, bearing the Clay name were: Jon Clay, (1646), Jno. Clay, (1643), James City County, Thomas Clay (1646) Lower Norfolk County, Edward Clay (1650) Northumberland County, (Probably a brother of Francis above.) Mrs. Francis Clay (1652) and John Clay (1654) Westmoreland County. (Early Virginia Immigrants, Greer.)

Now before proceeding with the genealogy of the descendants of Sir John Clay, just a word as to the form of the name Clay. We notice that the first immigrant spelled his name, or it was spelled for him, "Claye," while the first William's name was spelled "Clays." From the Otken Manuscript we take the following which appears to have been taken from 'The Clay Family by Frances Cowles" and is different from the "Clay Family" so often cited herein. Several localities in England were named because of the nature of the soil about them, and some of the people in these localities took the name as their own. So there arose families called Clay, Cley, Le Cley, Del Clay and De la Clay."

It is no uncommon thing to find the same name written with an "s" added to the termination and the fact that William Clays and John Claye were written differently, does not, I think, warrant us in disputing the fact that they were brothers. Quoting now from the Clay Manuscript of Mrs. Mary Clay of Americus, "The Clay name is an exceedingly old one in England, and many centuries ago the Clay families won the right to use Coat armour. The name appears in the Hundred Rolls of 1273 under some curious forms worth quoting, as Cley, Clai, Del Clay, de la Cley and le Clay. A still more singular form of it appears on a record of 1327 as att Cleygh—but by the time Yorkshire Poll Tax of 1397 was recorded, Clay or del Clay had become the established form. The name dates from the Saxon times, the Saxon equivalent being Claeg. As a family name it was said to have first been founded in the country of Nottingham, and was derived from the fact that the owner of it lived on Clay land, or at the Clay. The Clays were especially numerous in the Eastern part of England."

I have secured descriptions of three coats of arms of the Clay family. The first two are taken from the Otken MSS and are as follows: "One of them is blazoned: "Per pale vert and sable a lion rampant ermine between three escallops or "The crest is a lion's head per pale vert and sable, charged with an escallop argent. The other, which is blazoned: "Argent, three wolves sable, two in chief combatant, one in base passant." The third is taken from the "Clay Family" and is described as follows: "Arg, a chev, engrailed between three trefoils, slipt sable. Crest: Two wings expanded, Arg, semes of trefoils, slipped, sa." I have no means of determining the correct Arms and Crest for the Georgia Branch of the Virginia Clays, but show the one as given in the "Clay Family."

II.
The Clays In Virginia.

As stated in Chapter 1, the "Georgia Branch of the Virginia Clays" begins with the traditional Sir John Clay. The tradition assigning him the title of "Sir" is likely incorrect. He probably belonged to the lesser "Gentry" and was simply John Clay, Gent. This would entitle him to Coat Armour and is likely the grounds upon which the tradition rests. The title acquired by Francis Clay, at least, was that of Gentleman, and I therefore content myself in saying that John Clay, Gent, of the Eastern part of "Georgia Branch of the Virginia England was the ancestor of the Clays." Children were:

Richard Clay, with no record of his ever coming to America, but children Francis and Edward settled in Northumberland County, Va.

John Clay, who settled in Charles River County, Va., and who is the ancestor of the Georgia Branch

of the Virginia Clays.

William Clays settled in Charles River County, Virginia, and probably died without issue.

John Clay

John Claye above and wife Annie Clay, resided in Charles River County, Virginia. He is referred to as Captain John Clay, but by what authority, I fail to find. Children assigned to him and his wife were:

Francis Clay (Probably of Westmoreland County)
William Clay
Thomas Clay
Charles Clay
(Clay Family.)

Charles Clay

Our line begins with certainty with Charles Clay above, son of Cap. John Clay and wife Annie, of Charles River County, Virginia. He was born in 1638, married Hannah Wilson, daughter of John Wilson, senior, of Henrico County, Virginia. He fought under Bacon in Bacon's Rebellion in Virginia about 1673, when about thirty-five years of age, where he no doubt rendered faithful service. Ridpath says of Nathaniel Bacon as follows:

"His motives were as exalted as his life was pure, and his virtues as noted as his abilities were great. His ambition was for the public welfare, and his passions were only excited against the enemies of his country."

From the descendants of this couple came a line of descendants destined to wield a mighty influence in the great new nation which was shortly to arise from the next "Rebellion" and in which their descendants were so well represented. Before proceeding to our line proper, it is fitting to consider some of the related branches of the family here.

Charles Clay died in 1686, when only forty eight years old, without having made a will. His wife Hannah was appointed administrator of his estate and it is from the inventory and the will of Hannah made later, that we are able to determine the names of their children. One item in the will of Hannah Clay is illustrative of the period in which she lived. She willed to sons, "John, Thomas and Henry, each of them, one well-fixed gun." The question arises here, was

it from her that the Clays inherited
their courage, and tendency for pio-
neering? Children of Charles Clay
and wife, Hannah (Wilson) Clay:
1st. Mary Clay *
2nd. Elizabeth Clay *
3rd. John Clay, lived in Amelia
County *
4th. Thomas Clay
5th. Henry Clay
6th. Charles Clay
7th. Judith Clay*

Thomas Clay, Fourth Line.
Thomas Clay, son of Charles Clay
and Hannah (Wilson) Clay.
Information of Thomas Clay is incomplete. He lived in Prince George,
now Amelia County, where his will
bearing date of June 6, 1726, was
probated in the following November.
Name of his wife is not given. Children were:
1. Charles Clay, wife named Mary,
lived in Amelia County Virginia.
Children were, Peter Clay, Daniel
Clay, Jesse Clay, Charles Clay,
Eliza Clay Worsham, Hannah
Clay Avery, Pattie Clay Snead
and Anne Clay who married a
Clay. There is mentioned a William Clay with wife named Anne
in Clay Family and this may be
the Anne Clay here.
2. James Clay
3. John Clay
4. Dorothy Clay *
5. Phoebe Clay *
6. Hannah Clay *

John Clay (3 Above)
John Clay married Sarah Chappell,
daughter of James Chappell, leaving
her in his will 250 acres of land on
Deep Creek. Children were:
A. John Clay
B. Amey Clay Clement
C. Sarah Clay
D. Martha Clay
E. Dorothy Clay
F. Phoebe Clay

Henry Clay, Fifth Line.
Henry Clay, son of Charles Clay
and Hannah Wilson Clay.
Henry Clay was the first of this
name (Henry) we find in America. He
was born about 1672, married about
1708, Mary Mitchell, daughter of William and Elizabeth Mitchell. Mary
Mitchell was born January 1693, and
died 1777. We know very little about
this Henry Clay or his wife, as to
what their religious beliefs were or

of their activities in life or other facts
of a personal nature. Yet, when we
learn of the wonderful records made
by so many of their descendants thru
the next few generations we must conclude that they were Godly and that
their home and its examples exerted
a great influence for good on their
posterity. We now will give the
Will in substance of Henry Clay which
was probated at the September Term,
1760, Chesterfield Court.
"I, Henry Clay, of Henrico County,
being of perfect health, mind, and
memory, thanks be to God therefor,
and calling to mind my mortality, and
knowing that it is appointed unto all
men once to die, do make and ordain
this my last will and testament, that
is to say, princably and first of all I
give my soul into the hands of God
that gave it, and as for my body I
commend it to the earth, to be buried
in a Christian-like and decent form at
the discretion of my executors, nothing doubting but at the general Re-
surrection I shall receive the same
again by mighty power of God; and as
to touching my worldly goods where-
with it has pleased God to bless me
in this life. I give, devise, and dispose of the same in manner and form
following:
Primis. I give and bequeath unto
my son, William Clay, the land and
plantation whereon he now lives, and
my land and plantation on Deep
Creek, in Henrico County, whereon
Richard Belcher now lives, to him, his
heirs, and assigns forever.
Item. I give and bequeath to my
son, Henry Clay, the land and plantation he now lives on, and two hundred acres of land at Letalone, in
Goochland County, it being the Lower
Survey belonging to me at the said
Letalone, to him, his heirs and assigns
forever.
Item. I give and bequeath unto my
son, Charles Clay, the plantation
whereon he now lives and all of the
land on the north side of Swift Creek
and the lower side of Nuttree Run to
me belonging, and also four hundred
acres at Letalone, it being my Upper
Survey at Letalone, to him and his
heirs forever.
Item. I give and bequeath unto my
son, John Clay, the plantation whereon he now lives and all of my land on
the north side of Swift Creek and

upper side of Nuttree Run, to him and his heirs forever.

Item. I likewise give and bequeath my Grist Mill on Nuttree Run to be equally divided between my son Charles and my son John Clay, to be held in joint tenancy, to them and their heirs forever.

Item. I give to my daughter, Amey Williamson, five pounds, current money.

Item. I give to my daughter, Mary Watkins, five pounds, current money.

Item. I give to my grandson, Henry Clay (Dr. Henry Clay, of Ky.), 240 acres adjoinging the land of James Hill, etc.

Item. I give and bequeath to my granddaughter, Mary Clay, daughter of Charles Clay (afterwards Mrs. Stephen Lockett), one negro girl, named Phoebe.

Item. I give unto Mary, my well-beloved wife, the plantation whereon I now live, during her natural life, and my negroes, Lewis, Jo, Sue, Nann, Jenny and Sarah, during her natural life, and what stock and household goods she pleases to have or make use of, of mine.

Item. I devise that the rest of my slaves not heretofore given, and my stock and household goods, be given and equally divided among my four sons aforementioned, at ther discretion, and also the negroes above written, and gave my wife, may be equally divided after my wife's decease.

Item. I give to my four sons, above written, and to my wife, to be equally divided, all the ready money and money out at use, that I shall be possessed with at my death.

Item. After my wife's decease I give my plantation, whereon I now live, to my son John Clay and his heirs forever, together with the adjacent lands thereunto belonging, and I do hereby make, constitute and ordain my four sons, above written, to be my only and sole executors of this, my last Will and Testament."

Special attention is called to the bequest to William Clay, in that it mentions plantation whereon "Richard Belcher now lives," and also to bequest to wife in which is mentioned "Lewis," a negro. Both of these names are significant.

So far we have followed the "Clay Family" in our genealogy from Captain John Clay of Charles River County. Here we must supplement this by "Johnston." The "Clay Family" gives William Mitchell Clay as the first of the children of Henry Clay and Mary Mitchell. His name is given simply "William" in the will, and so I give it here. The children of Henry Clay and Mary Mitchell are given as in the "Clay Family," as follows:

1. William Clay
2. Henry Clay
3. Charles Clay
4. John Clay
5. Amey Clay *
6. Mary Clay *

1. William was probably the eldest son of the children. Beheathland Clay Rigsby stated in notes left that Pearce Clay, of Washington County, Georgia, was a son of a brother of her grandfather, which appears to have been an error. She probably meant that he was a son of a brother of her great-grandfather. If so, then Pearce Clay was a son of William Clay. Mitchell Clay is identified by statements made by "Johnston" as a son of this William, and Johnston further gives an account (Page 48) of the death of a Mr. Clay in Western Virginia, 1774, which everything indicates was William Clay.

"While Field's company was encamped on the banks of the Little Meadow River, a branch of the Gauley. two of his men, Clay and Coward, (other authorities spell Cowherd) were sent to hunt deer for the company and were attacked by the Indians. Clay was killed, but Coward made his way back to camp, having first killed one of the Indians." This was just before the battle of Point Pleasant, and I believe explains the lack of further information concerning William Clay. I give the name of Mitchell and Pearce Clay only, leaving blank space for other names and believing that William Clay of Franklin County, Virginia, and Obed Clay, of Virginia, were sons also, but not so listing for want of proof.

A. Mitchell Clay
B. Pearce Clay

....

Mitchell Clay (A. above)

(Johnston our authority here) was probably born about 1735. Johnston says "One brother, the father (should be grandfather), of Henry Clay, of Kentucky, a Baptist minister settled in the Slashes of Hanover; one, the ancestor of General Green Clay, settled in Powhatan, and was the ancestor of General Oden G. Clay of Campbell County, Virginia. The one who settled in Franklin county was the ancestor of the elder Mitchell Clay, who came from Franklin County to the Clover Bottom on the Bluestone, in 1775."

This statement by a process of elimination enables us to state definitely that Mitchell Clay was a son of William Clay. The genealogies are given later and substantiates this statement. Mitchell drew the land in then, Fincastle County, Virginia, for services rendered as a soldier in the French and Indian war, which began in 1754. Summers' History of Southwest Virginia (1746-1786) page 146 states that on April 25, 1774, Mitchell Clay had 1000 acres, both sides Bluestone Creek, Clover Bottom, according to a survey by John Floyd and others in 1774-1775, lying mostly in Kentucky. This land was acquired under the King's proclamation of 1763 for service in French and Indian war 1754-1763. The grant was made by Dunmore, Governor of the Colony and embraced 1000 acres. It is probable that both Mitchell and his father were in this war. Johnston says that Mitchell Clay married Phoebe Belcher in Franklin County, Virginia, in 1760. He is evidently in error, as Franklin County was not then created. Johnston obtained his information from a manuscript record made by two of the grandsons of Mitchell, and these are usually more or less elastic as to dates and places, though on the whole, fairly accurate. Mitchell Clay had been living on the Clover Bottoms only about one year when the war of the Revolution broke out. He was on the extreme frontier of civilization, and situated directly in the path of the red man. He appears to have rendered valuable service to his country by informing, aiding and guiding the body of scouts who were maintained in the section to guard against Indian attacks.

William Hutchinson in making affidavit (See Virginia Militia in the Revolutionary War, by J. T. McAllister, Section 44, page 75) said in substance that he, Hutchinson entered service in May, marched across New River, through the present county of Giles, then thinly peopled, and served as ranger, being on constant duty. He says that he enlisted under Archibald Wood to serve as long as the Indians might be troublesome, and in the fall his company marched up the Blue Stone to the settlement near its head to protect the people gathering fodder. There were some places traversed by him never before seen by white man. The country was wild and mountainous, frequently he could hear far off, the whistle, yell or tread of the savage, often sleeping at night with no covering but his blanket and no shelter but the forest, having for company only the scream of the panther or the yell of the Indian. He says that on one occasion after marching twenty miles, all of the company refused to go further, and that David Clay showed him the way. They were pursued by ten or twelve Indians, but hurrying along, sometimes in mud to their knees or water to their necks, hastened on the journey by the yells of the Indians, finally reached their destination, having travelled 40 miles that day.

Thus, is introduced the first of the Virginia Clays (David Clay) save one known to have come to Georgia. His surroundings in Virginia are vividly pictured in the foregoing affidavit and his life will be treated more fully in Chapter IV. Now we will continue the family of Mitchell Clay by giving the circumstances of what is commonly known as "The Clay Tragedy."

The Indians appear to have become angered at Clay and his family by reason of the aid given by them to the scouts and militia during the Revolution.

In August, 1783, after Clay had harvested his crops, and while he was absent from home on a hunting expedition to secure game for the family larder, a party of Indians crept in and attacked the family. At the time Bartley and Ezkiel were building a fence around some stacks of grain. The older sons had not returned from the Revolution. Tabitha and some of the girls were at the river washing, while Mrs. Clay and the smaller children seem to have been in the house. The first they knew of the Indians was when one of them shot Bartley from ambush. This frightened the girls, but Tabitha, seeing an Indian about to scalp her brother, rushed to his assistance and engaged the Indian in a hand to hand conflict, she being without any weapon. It seemed for a while that she might be victorious, but the Indian resorted to his hunting knife and literally cut her to pieces.

Mrs. Clay undertook to secure the aid of one Blankinship at this time, but he being a coward, ran off and left the family to its fate. After killing Tabitha and Bartley, the Indians captured Ezekiel Clay, and for some cause left the premises with him, perhaps in search of the elder Mitchell Clay.

Mrs. Clay with her small children, secured the bodies of Bartley and Tabitha and placed them on the bed, when she and her small children left home, going to the New River Settlements.

Mitchell Clay wounded a deer, which he followed for sometime and was late in returning home, when he found the bodies of his two children on the bed and his wife and small children gone. Imagine his horror and grief, not only for the dead children, but for those members of his family whose fate was as yet unknown to him. There being nothing he could do at home, he made his way to the New River Settlements, pursued by the Indians into the Settlements. Here the settlers appearing too strong, the Indians stole some horses and made their way back towards the Ohio River.

A party was soon made up to follow them, consisting of Charles Clay, Mitchell Clay, Jr., James Bailey, William Wiley, Edward Hale, Isaac Hare, John French and Captain James Moore. They first went to the cabin and buried the Clay children. The Indians had divided, which fact was not discovered by the pursuers until after they had come up with the party that had the horses. In the ensuing battle between the whites and the Indians, several Indians were killed. Charles Clay, only a mere boy, killing one of the Indians himself in the encounter.

Mitchell Clay, Jr., was at the time too small to handle a gun well, but shot at one of the Indians, but missed him, the Indian being killed by another member of the party.

The party of Indians carrying Ezekiel Clay were not overtaken. They took him down the West fork of the River, to their town, Chillicothe, where he was burned at the stake. The whites were so incensed at this conduct of the Indians that Edward Hale and William Wiley stripped the skin from the backs of two of the Indians and took the hide home and made razor straps form it, which were kept in the family for many years as a souvenir of the battle.

Children of Mitchell Clay and Phoebe Belcher Clay were:

a David Clay, moved to Georgia. See Chapter IV.

b William Clay, Juror Giles County, Virginia, 1806.

c Henry Clay, Constable Giles County, Virginia, 1806.

d Charles Clay, Juror Giles County, Virginia, 1806.

e Bartley Clay, killed by Indians on Bluestone, 1783.

f Ezekiel Clay, captured by Indians and burned at stake at Chillicothe, 1783.

g Mitchell Clay, probably Mitchell, Jr., and John who left MSS of above tragedy were sons.

h Tabitha, killed by Indians on Bluestone, 1783.

i Rebecca, married Col. George Pearis.

j Patience, married George Chapman.

k Sallie, married Captain John Peters.

l Obedience, married John French.

m Nannie, married Joseph Hare.

n Mary, married William Stewart.

Considerable genealogies are given of the descendants of these girls, by Johnston, but to repeat would be too tedious, in a sketch of the "Georgia Branch of the Virginia Clays."

Henry Clay (2 above)

Henry Clay, son of Henry Clay and Mary Mitchell, resided in Southam Parish, Cumberland County. His wife was Lucy Green, sister of Martha Green, who married Charles Clay and who was the mother of General Green Clay. His will was probated October, 1764, and from it we get the names of his children, but before giving their names I will briefly treat of the Green family. This Green family appears to have originated in one Thomas Green known as the Sea Gull, born on the Atlantic of an immigrant on her way to America. He was of Dutch ancestry, his father being Thomas Green, who settled near Petersburg, Virginia, and who married Martha Filmer, daughter of Major Henry filmer, who was a member of the House of Burgesses. Children of Henry Clay and wife Lucy (Green) Clay:

A Henry Clay, born 1736
B Charles Clay, moved to Kentucky, murdered on trip back to Virginia and record incomplete.*
C Samuel Clay, moved to North Carolina, where he was a member of the Legislature. *
D Thomas Clay, who remained in Cumberland County, Va. *
E Abia Clay, moved to Georgia. See Chapter VI.
F Marston Clay*
G Rebecca Clay*
H John Clay. See Chapter VI for probable descendants.
I Elijah Clay*
J Lucy Clay*

Henry Clay (A Above)
Henry Clay, son of Henry Clay and Lucy Green Clay, born in Cumberland County, Virginia, 1736, married Rachel Povall, 1754, moved to Kentucky, 1787, where he died, 1820. He was a physician and the records of his family are preserved in the public records and monuments of Bourbon County, Kentucky. The descendants of David Clay, of Georgia, bear a strong resemblance to the photographs of this branch of the family. Their children were:

a Elizabeth Clay, m John Bruce.*
b John Clay, m Patsy Ingram.*
c Rebekah Clay, m William Finch.*
d Samuel Clay, m Nancy Winn.
e Rachel Clay, m Barkley Martin, no issue.*
f Sally Clay, m Matthew Martin.*
g Tabitha Clay, m Benjamine Bedford.*
h Mary Ann Clay, m Thomas Dawson.*
i Henrietta Clay, m George M. Bedinger.*
j Mattie Clay, m Littleberry Bedford*

k Henry Clay, m Peggy Helm and became a man of much note in Kentucky (Not the celebrated Henry.)
l Letty Clay, m Archibald Bedford.*

Samuel Clay (Identified as d above.)
Samuel Clay, born May 10, 1761, served under General Green in the Carolinas during the Revolution, married Ann Winn, who was also known as Nancy. Will probated in Bourbon County, June 1810. Children:

1' Henry C. Clay, m Mary Grimes.*
2' Letitia Clay*
3' Samuel Clay*
4' George Clay*
5' Littleberry Bedford Clay.
6' Richard P. Clay. (See Chapter I for probable source of name)*
7' John Clay. Said to have come to Georgia.
8' Thomas Clay. Said to have come to Georgia.
9' Rachel Clay*
10' William Green Clay*

Having extended this line sufficient for our purpose, that is to illustrate "The Georgia Branch of the Virginia Clays" we will now return to Charles Clay, a brother of Henry No. 2, and a son of Henry Clay and Mary Mitchell Clay, who is No. 3 in our line. This is the Charles Clay so often mentioned as the ancestor of Cassius M. Clay.

Charles Clay (Identified by 3)
Charles Clay, son of Henry Clay and Mary Mitchell Clay, born Jan. 31, 1716, married Martha Green, Nov. 11, 1741 and died Feb. 25, 1789. She was a sister of Lucy Green who married Henry Clay No. 2. Children:

A Mary Clay*
B Eleazer Clay, was a Baptist Minister, thrice married, possessed considerable wealth and served in both the French and Indian War and the Revolutionary War.*
C Charles Clay,
D Henry Clay, died in service of his country during Revolution in Trenton, N. J.*
E Thomas Clay, married Polly Callahan, was a soldier of the Revolution and a member of the first Constitution Convention of Kentucky. Appears to have many descendants in Texas.*

F Betty Clay, married Alexander
   Murray.*
G Lucy Clay, married William
   Thaxton.*
H Matthew Clay. See Chapter III.
I Green Clay.
J Priscilla Clay*
K Martha Clay, married Hopkins
   Lewis*
Charles Clay (Identified as C above)
Charles Clay, born Dec. 24, 1745,
married Editha Davies, Jan. 15, 1767.
He was an Episcopal minister, or-
dained by the Bishop of London in
1769, served as Rector of St. Ann
Parish, Albemarle County. He was an
earnest patriot and created much en-
thusiasm in behalf of American Inde-
pendence. He moved from Albemarle
County to Bedford County, where his
Will is of record, in which he mentions his friend the Hon. Thomas Jefferson, late president of the United
States. His children were:
a Junius Axel Clay.*
b Odin Green Clay, The Odin G.
   Clay mentioned by Johnston, of
   Campbell County, Virginia, who
   served in the Virginia House and
   who was first President of the
   old Virginia & Tennessee Railroad.*
c Paul A. Clay, who was a minister of Manchester Parish, Manchester County. *
d Cyrus B. Clay.*
Green Clay(Identified as I above)
General Green Clay, who was the
first historian of the Clay family, was
born Aug. 14, 1757, married Sally
Lewis, March 14, 1795, and died Oct.
21, 1828. First Deputy Surveyor oi
Kentucky, delegate to convention that
ratified Constitution, served in Kentucky Legislature twenty years,
speaker of (Ky.) Senate, 1807, Revolutionary soldier and also war of 1812.
Children were:
a Elizabeth Lewis Clay*
b Paulina Clay*
c Sally Ann Clay*
d Sidney Payne Clay*
e Brutus Junius Clay*
f Cassius Marcellus Clay
g Sophia Clay*
Cassius Marcellus Clay (Identified
   as f above)
His life and career would fill a
volume within itself. His life is certainly an epic of the slavery quarrel.
He was appointed as minister to Rus-

sia by Abraham Lincoln. His "Memoirs" give his record and should be
secured and read by those interested
in his life.
We must here digress to take up another line, that is of the immortal
Henry. His line begins with John
Clay, son of Henry Clay and Mary
Mitchell Clay, if we are to accept the
verdict of genealogists. I am giving
his line in agreement with the authorities, but, however, without adding the
weight of my evidence to the mass.
John Clay (Identified as 4)
John Clay died about 1762 and his
Will is recorded in Chesterfield County. His wife was Mrs. Mary Bass
and they had children as follows:
A John Clay.
B Edward Clay, who went to
   North Carolina, served in North
   Carolina Legislature, where he
   was tried and expelled for crime.
   The evidence in this case ha:
   been reviewed by me and I believe
   that he was "framed" on the
   charge brought against him. He
   has been erroneously assigned to
   Alabama.
C Fanny Clay*
Rev. John Clay (Identified as A
above) is the John Clay assigned as
the father of Henry Clay. He married
Elizabeth Hudson, whose mother was
a Jennings as was the mother of William J. Bryan, both families of Virginia and it is entirely possible that
the two great commoners were cousins, if the lineage of the Jennings
were followed up. His Will is recorded in Hanover County, Virginia,
and the "Clay Family" contains a
copy of it. He was a Baptist minister
and is referred to in old records in
Hanover County as Sir John Clay.
This for a long time gave me no end
of worry, that is in trying to trace
title from Sir John Clay of England
to Sir John Clay of Hanover County,
Virginia, until I established the fact
to my satisfaction that the English
title was only that of Gentleman, after which is occurred to me that according to the English custom, titles
were frequently conferred by usage
without legality upon professional
men, much as J. P.'s receive the ap-
pellation of Judge, and attorneys of
Colonel, in this day. This I have been
informed, was frequently the case
with ministers and others on whom

were bestowed titles for taking literary degrees. I leave this question now for future generations to puzzle over.

Children of John Clay and Mary Bass Clay were:

a John Clay, who moved to New Orleans.*

b Henry Clay, whose name is so familiar, and his life has received such copious treatment that I will pass his record without further comment. Numerous biographies contain histories of his life from various angles and the reader is referred to them . The three outstanding things in his life are the Missouri Compromise, the Omnibus Bill and his candidacy for President of the United States, when he used the statement familiar to every school boy, "I had rather be right than President."

c Porter Clay.

Porter Clay (Identified as c above) is not so well-wnown as his distinguished brother, but for our purpose it is necessary to make a more extended study of his life as subject to throw light on our investigation. He has been treated of very briefly in the "Clay Family," which simply states that he was born in 1779 and died in 1850, that he married first Sophie Grosch, and had one child, a Mrs. Taylor, but her name is not given; second, a Mrs. Hardin, who left no issue. That he was auditor of Kentucky in 1822, later becoming a Baptist minister. That he was buried at Camden, Arkansas. To this I have been able, through the kindness of Miss Otken to add the following, substance of which is gathered from the Centennial Edition of a newspaper published in Camden, Arkansas, Oct. 16, 1924.

"While thousands annually visit the tomb of Henry Clay at Lexington, Va., to pay tribute to his memory, the grave of Porter Clay, his brother, is unknown except to a very few. It is marked with a slab of stone, covered with moss and well nigh forgotten. It lies in an old and unfrequented cemetery at Camden, Arkansas.

"Porter Clay was many years younger than his illustrious brother,

Henry. Though not inferior to the great statesman in intellect. Porter was without the inordinate ambition that history lays at the door of his brother. Porter Clay gave the best of his life to the service of religion. He died in poverty. Both boys were reared by a pious Baptist mother, but Henry was captivated by the glare of politics, while Porter followed the desire of his mother's heart and became a Baptist minister and revivalist.

."At the age of 21, in 1815, Porter Clay was admitted to the bar in Kentucky. He was appointed auditor c' state accounts by Governor W G. Slaughter.

Even at this time, he felt the call to the ministry and he hesitated long before he accepted the more lucrative position. Friends persuaded him to accept, however, insisting that he had a brilliant future before him. By this time Henry Clay had served two short terms in the United States Senate and had been the Speaker of the House of Representatives for four years. It was freely predicted that young Porter Clay would follow in the footsteps of his brilliant brother.

"Porter served the state as auditor for several years. During this time his wife died and he re-married to the widow of Senator M. D. Hardin, who before her marriage was a Logan. Mrs. Hardin was a woman of great wealth and burning ambition. She desired her husband to take his place with the great men of the nation.

"Mrs. Hardin was the mother of two sons at the time of her marriage. As these boys grew up they developed wild and unruly traits of character. They manifested an open contempt for their step-father, who entered the ministry shortly after his second marriage, and for his simple life, and one of them became notorious for his waywardness and profligacy. It was this stepson who distinguished himself later in life, during the war with Mexico, and who challenged Jefferson Davis to a duel for some fancied slight. The duel was never fought for President Zachary Taylor interfered and prevented it.

"About 1840 Mrs. Clay persuaded Porter Clay to move to Jacksonville, Ill., and reside with herself and the two step-sons in the house that had been the property of Senator Hardin. The mother and sons gradually came to treat Porter Clay as an outcast. So incessant was their abuse of him that he was eventually forced to leave their roof.

"He then became an evangelist, and travelled widely in this work. It was in this capacity that he came to Camden in the late 40s.

"After holding a revival at Camden he founded a church and became its first minister. He expected to spend the remainder of his life in ministering to the people of the little city on the banks of the Ouachita. He felt that he had reached the goal of his mission. But in 1850, two years before the death of his famous brother, Henry Clay, Porter Clay was stricken with fever and died after a short illness.

"His grave was unmarked for a number of years, but a small board was placed upon it finally by the members of the Baptist church. Several years ago the New Century Club of Camden, erected a slab of stone over the grave."

The author of this sketch is descended from a common ancestry with both Porter Clay and the first husband of his second wife. Mrs. Clay's first husband, had a son, Martin D. Hardin, who was much interested in his lineage and prepared a circular and sent out to Hardins trying to secure information relating to his family. His sister, Mrs. Elen (Hardin) Walworth, was one of the founders of the Society of the Daughters of the American Revolution, and I imagine that it was through the urge of his second wife that he (Porter) became interested in his family history and that the tradition given by him was given with no thought of the importance which might later be attached to it. Before passing on, we here give the Porter Clay tradition as contained in the "Clay Family."

"In the reign of Queen Elizabeth, Sir Walter Raleigh brought over to the Virginia plantations, among others, three brothers, sons of Sir John Clay, of Wales, England. He gave them ten thousand pounds sterling each. They were named Charles, Thomas and Henry. They settled on James River, near Jamestown. Charles and Thomas had large families. Henry had none, but the name has been handed down with great tenacity in both families ever since. Cassius M. Clay is a descendant of Charles Clay; Henry and myself from Thomas Clay."

Charles Clay and His Descendants

Who Setteled In Alabama, Mississippi, Louisiana and Missouri.

By Frences Powell Otken
Macomb, Mississippi
Sixth Line

CHAPTER III

Charles Clay, son of Charles Clay and Hannah Wilson Clay, resident of Dale Parish, Chesterfield, Va., signed his will January 28, 1754, which was recorded Aug. 1765. He gives his homestead to his beloved wife, Sarah. Mary, daughter of his son, Henry Clay, deceased, is to receive her father's part.

Issue of Charles and Sarah Clay:
1. Thomas Clay to whom father deeded, May 5, 1752, 250 acres of land in Amelia county.
2. Charles Clay to whom his father deeded May 5, 1752, 250 acres of land in Amelia county.
3. William Clay to whom his father deeded May 5, 1752, 250 acres of land in Amelia county.
4. James Clay.
5. Judith Clay received 50 acres of land adjoining her brother, Thomas Clay.
6. Henry Clay, vestryman of Dale Parish, Chesterfield county Va., 1751.

James Clay (4).

James Clay, born Hanover County, Va., died 1790 in Chesterfield Co., Va. He married Margaret (Peggy) Muse, b April 2, 1737, d Feb. 13, 1832 in Amite county, Miss. James Clay inherited the Homestead at his mother's death. A choice tribute has been paid to the memory of this sainted woman which is given in full in biography of Wilford Zachiariah Lea later in this chapter. Children:
A. William Clay.
B. James Clay. Land records show that James Clay in 1795 became a stockholder in the Mississippi Land Company, the old Georgia Company, and took 28,000 acres of land on the Mississippi River. On January 13, 1808, a patent was issued to James Clay for 350 Arpents on the Waters of the Mississippi in the St. Charles District. No further information. (Query —Was this the James Clay who performed the marriage ceremony for Lewis Clay and Judith Jones?)
C. Martha Clay, married Mr. Johnson and settled in North Carolina. No record.
D. Elizabeth Clay. No record.
E. Lydia Clay. No record.
F. Mary Clay. No record.
G. Jeremiah Walker Clay. Juror in Grainger county, Tenn., 1802. Took 450 Arpents in St. Charles District. (La.).
H. Eleazer Clay.
I. Nancy Clay.
J. Sabrina Clay.

William Clay (A).

William Clay, son of James Clay and Margaret Muse Clay, b Aug. 11, 1760, Chesterfield Co., Va., d Aug. 4, 1841 in Grainger county, Tenn. Dec. 30, 1788, he was married to Rebecca Comer in Halifax Co., Va. Rebecca Comer was a daughter of Samuel Comer, b 1766. William Clay enlisted in the Revolutionary War at the age of sixteen, applied for pension October 10, 1832, at which time he was residing in Grainger Co., Tenn. Pension granted for seven months service as private under Capt. Henry Cheatham, Col. Robt. Goode and Capt. Ed. Mosely and for one months service as s'gt. in Virginia troops. His wife, Rebecca Comer Clay was allowed a pension on application executed May 3, 1843, while a resident of

Grainger county, Tenn., age 77 years.
Issue:

a Clement Comer Clay.

b Margaret Muse Clay, b February 14, 1792, married John Bunch.

c Nancy Clay, b Sept. 18, 1794, m Mr. Hightower.

d William Clay, b July 18, 1797, d before 1830. No issue.

e. Cynthia Clay.

f Micajah Clay, b June 18, 1802, m Kendricks.

g Samuel Anderson Clay, b March 29, 1805.

Clement Comer Clay (a).

Clement Comer Clay, son of William and Rebecca Comer Clay, married Susannah Claiborne Withers in 1815. He was born Dec. 17, 1789 in Halifax Co., Va., died September 7, 1866, in Alabama. Mr. Clay attended college at Knoxville, Tenn., and read law under Hon. Hugh Lawson White receiving his license to practice his chosen profession 1809. Soon after being admitted to the bar he moved to Huntsville, Ala., where he resided till his death. He served in the war of 1812, represented his county in the territorial legislature in 1817, serving the only two sessions of that body. He also served his state as Supreme Court Judge, Congressman, United States Senator and Governor of the state. He "was of medium size, but erect and with dark and restless eyes. His bearing was naturally austere and although sociable with a few, he was intimate with none. He was honorable in all the relations of life and sensitive of the slightest imputation derogatory thereto." Issue:

1' Clement Claiborne Clay, b Dec. 1817, d Jan. 4, 1882, Madison county, Ala., m Virginia Caroline Tunstall, Feb. 1, 1843. No issue. After the death of Mr. Clay his wife married Gov. Clopton of Ala. Mr. Clay graduated at the State (Ala) University in 1840. He studied law at the University of Virginia and was licensed to practice, beginning the practice of his chosen profession at Huntsville, Ala. Public questions soon engrossed his attention. He was a member of the General Assembly of Ala., Judge of the County Court of Madison county, elected to the U. S. Senate when only 35, re-elected without opposition. Resigned in 1861, elected Senator to first Confederate Congress, offered office of Judge Advocate General for Alabama by Jefferson Davis, but declined. Commissioner with Hon. Jacob Thompson to Canada on secret mission in behalf of Southern Confederacy. Surrender at close of war to General Wilson at Macon, Ga. He was charged with complicity in the assasination of Abraham Lincoln and imprisoned with Jefferson Davis in fortress Monroe until 1866, when he was released through the efforts of General U. S. Grant and other prominent officials. His wife was constant in her efforts to secure his release and the case against him never came to trial.

(This is one illustration of the danger of rabid public sentiment. One of the family mobbed in Kentucky for his abolition sentiments, and later appointed as Minister to Russia by Abraham Lincoln and another member of the family charged with the assasination of Lincoln.)

2' John Withers Clay, b Jan. 11, 1820, m Mary Fenwick Lewis Nov. 11, 1847, issue: Caraliza Clay, John Withers Clay married Mary Saunders, Clement C. Clay, Clarence H. Clay, Ellen L. Clay, William Lewis Clay, Attorney, Huntsville, Ala., 1875, married Louisa Johnson 1878, Mary Lewis Clay, Susannah W. Clay, Elodia Clay, Virginia Clementine Clay b Feb. 17, 1862, d March 12, 1911, unmarried.

3' Hugh Lawson White Clay married Celeste Comer.

Cynthia Clay (e) Greene.

Cynthia Clay, daughter of William Clay and Rebecca Comer Clay, married Alston Hunter Greene, and had issue:

1' Mary Sledge Greene.

2' Clement Comer Clay Greene.

3' Elvira Cynthia Greene, b Sept. 17, 1832, d Feb. 9th, 1837.

4' William Augustine Greene.

5' Cordelia Elizabeth Greene.

Mary Sledge Greene (1'). Nelson.

Mary Sledge Green, b Aug. 17, 1827, d July 13, 1881. Dec. 1, 1840, she was married to Allison Nelson, who was born March 17, 1823, and died October 7, 1862. Issue:

A' Emma Cynthia Nelson.

B' Alice Sophia Nelson.

C' John Alston Nelson.

Emma Cynthia Nelson (A'), b Nov. 24, 1842, d Jan. 30, 1869, married John Bayless Earle, Dec. 15, 1857. Mr. Earle was born Sept. 17, 1833.

a' Allison Nelson Earle, b March 14, 1860, married Annie Babcock Hix, April 27, 1892. She was born Feb. 19, 1869. Issue: William Hix Earle, Allison Nelson Earle, Emma Cynthia Earle and Frances Elizabeth Earle.

b' Annie Elizabeth Earle, born April 5, 1863, married April 23, 1890, Paterick M. Farrell, born Feb. 17, 1855. Issue: Emma Nelson Farrell, Mary Farrell, Baylis Earle Farrell.

c' John Baylis Earle, b June 20, 1866.

d' Henry Sears Earle, b Feb. 22, 1869, m Mattie Rogers, b Aug. 6, 1872, d April 7, 1892. Issue: Charles Rogers Sears Earle, died in infancy.

Alice Sophia Nelson, (B'), born April 26, 1845, married June 8, 1865, John H. Harrison and had issue:

a' Mary Evans Harrison, b July 9, 1866, m Nov. 26, 1885, Daniel Stonewall Eddins and had issue: Daniel S. Eddins, Alice Eddins, and George Morse Eddins.

b' Allison Nelson Harrison, b Sept. 19, 1869, m Irene Dunklin.

c' John H. Harrison, b April 1, 1872, m April 21, 1898, Addie Earle.

d' James H. Harrison, b Oct. 6. 1874, d Jan. 3, 1877.

e' Guy Brown Harrison, b Nov. 1, 1876, m Feb. 12, 1898, Nora Wimple.

John Alston Nelson (C'), born July 22, 1848, died June 21, 1891, married Jan. 1, 1871, Georgia Alice Little, and had issue:

a' Mary Sledge Nelson, b Jan. 10, 1872.

b' Hiram Lucious Nelson, b Nov. 12, 1874, m Sept. 18, 1895, Hattie Hines and had issue: Henry Nelson.

c' Allison Nelson, b June 26, 1876.

d' Baylis E. Nelson, b March 19, 1878, d Nov. 19, 1898.

e' John Alston Nelson, b March 9, 1881.

f' Kate Nelson, b Jan. 1883.

g' Harvey Nelson, b March 1888.

h' Levie Nelson, b Oct. 1, 1891.

Clement Comer Clay Greene (2').

Clement Comer Clay Greene, son of Cynthia Clay and Alston Hunter Greene, was born June 13, 1829, died Oct. 26, 1889, married April 25, 1850, Mary Frances Godwin, born Oct. 17, 1833, died April 17, 1871. First Lieutenant Cobb's Cavalry Civil War 1861-65. Issue:

A' Alston Hunter Greene, b Feb. 9, 1851, m Oct. 17, 1883, Mary Lou Hunnicutt, b May 8, 1860. Issue: Edgar Laurence Greene, Fannie Letitia Greene, Calvin Clay Greene.

B' William Daniel Greene, b Oct. 8, 1852, m Aug. 30, 1892, Mrs. Edmonia Long Harney, b May 2, 1868. Issue: Evelyn Goodwin Greene, Carl Elkin Greene.

C' Julia Elizabeth Greene, b March 1, 1855.

D' Clement Clay Greene, b Oct. 7, 1857, m Nov. 18, 1891, Mae Rhodes, b March 2, 1870, d June 20, 1895.

E' Allison Nelson Greene, b April 9, 1860.

F' Anna Blanche Greene, b June 18, 1863, m Oct. 17, 1883, Forrest Adair, of Atlanta, Ga., b March 24, 1864. Mr. Adair has been prominently connected in the real estate business in Atlanta, where he has achieved a reputation which covers America. Issue: Elizabeth Adair, b Jan. 30, 1885; Frank Adair, b July 31, 1886; Forrest Adair, b July 6, 1888; Robin Adair, b Aug. 14, 1893.

G' Mary Frances Greene, b Jan. 9, 1867, m Feb. 28, 1889, George Townes Rowland, b Oct. 7, 1858. Issue: Hugh Rowland, Mt. Vernon, N. Y., and Mary Frances Rowland.

H' Robert Lee Greene, b March 21, 1870, d April 28, 1872.

Clement Comer Clay Greene, married second Louise Wilson, b Feb. 26, 1850. By this marriage, children:

I' Edna Earle Greene, b July 18, 1873, m Aug. 16, 1892, William Douglas Brannan, b July 22, 1870. Issue: Nell Brannan and Mary Greene Brannan.

J' Forrest Greene, b May 27, 1877.

K' Hubert Greene, b Aug. 7, 1880.

William Augustine Greene (4').

William Augustine Greene, born

March 1, 1835, died Sept. 27, 1856, married 1853, Louisa Susan Pitman, and had issue:

A' Mary Emma Greene, born November 9, 1854, died Nov. 14, 1892, married Oct. 7, 1873, McKinzie Obediah Thompson, b Feb. 1, 1850. Issue: Robert Lyle Thompson, b Nov. 3, 1874, married June 18, 1893, Eva Eugenia Hilburn, had issue, Lyle A. Thompson, Jennie E. Thompson; Allison McKinzie Thompson, b May 7, 1876; Leonard Olin Thompson, b June 12, 1878; Helen Louise Thompson, b Oct. 1879; William Hugh Thompson, b March 30, 1882, d Jan. 11, 1883.

B' Allison Lawson Greene, born Nov. 27, 1855, d June 3, 1893, married April 19, 1882, Susan Caryl Rosenbury, and had issue: Charles Allison Greene, Charlotte Louise Greene, Earle Rosenbury Greene, Caryl Greene, and Ward Storrs Greene.

C' William Augustine Greene, b Aug. 26, 1858, married Nov. 11, 1879, Margaret W. Thompson. Issue: William E. Greene, Lamar Greene, and Marion E. Greene.

D' Annie Laurie Greene, b May 3, 1857, died Aug. 3, 1886, married Nov. 22, 1877, Thomas Henry Jeffries, b April 16, 1854. Issue: Maybelle M. Jeffries, Warner Moore Jeffries, Clymer DeF. Jeffries, and Susan A. Jeffries.

Cordelia Elizabeth Greene (5').

Cordelia Elizabeth Greene, daughter of Cynthia Clay and Alston Hunter Greene, was born Nov. 10, 1840, married Aug. 16, 1857, Henry Holcomb Glenn, born Jan. 9, 1829, died Nov. 10, 1883. Issue:

A' Thomas Cobb Glenn.
B' Henry H. Glenn.
C' Henry Luther Glenn.
D' Mary Kate Glenn.
E' Robert M. Glenn.

ELEAZER CLAY (H)

Eleazer Clay (H), son of James Clay and Margaret Muse Clay, was born Oct. 14, 1778, died Feb. 18, 1863, Farmington. Missouri, married Mary Dunville, Jan. 19, 1802 (date of license issued and on file at Rutledge, Tenn.), born Dec. 26, 1784, died April 16, 1852. Issue:

a Mary Ann Clay.
b Ailcey Clay.
c Margaret Muse Clay.

d James Clay, twin to William, married twice. Issue by first marriage: Frank E. Clay, Robert Clay, William Clay, Caroline Clay, Bettie Clay, Katherine Clay, Nancy Clay. Issue by second marriage: Clara Clay, Luella Clay.

e William Clay.
f Nancy Clay.
g Eleanor Clay.
h Eleazer Greene Clay.
i Robert D. Clay, m Miss Hunt and had issue: Henry Clay, Robert Clay, Judge; William Clay; Edward Clay, Kansas City, Mo.; Romeo Clay; Phillip Clay; Thomas Clay; Waide Clay.
j Morgan S. Clay.
k Mahala M. Clay.
l Angeline Clay, m Rev. Rucker and had issue: One son, who became a Methodist minister, Farmington, Mo.
m Wade Hampton Clay.

Eleazer Greene Clay (h) married and had issue:

1' Clement C. Clay.

Clement C. Clay, (1'), married and had issue:

A' Mary Clay.

Mary Clay (A'), who married Mr. Lewis, had issue:

a' Kate Lewis.

Kate Lewis (a'), who married Hon. W. H. Arnold, of Texarkana, Ark., had issue: Richard Lewis Arnold, b 1905.

Wade Hampton Clay (m), pioneer settler of St. Francis Co., Missouri, near Doerun, Mo., married first, Miss Music, and had issue:

1' Henry M. Clay.
2' Volney C. Clay.
3' Orlena Clay.
4' Cordelia Clay.

Wade Hampton Clay (m)

Wade Hampton Clay married second, Mary E. Sutherland, and had issue:

5' Anna M. Clay.
6' Julia Clay.
7' Eva Clay, died 1919.
8' Benjamin M. Clay.
9' Wade Hampton Clay, lawyer, San Francisco, Calif.
10' John Suhterland Clay, Probate Judge 12 years, State Senator from Missouri four years, Farmington, Mo., married and had issue: Homer Tullock Clay, M. D.

36

Grand Rapids, Mich., Alva
Marie Clay, m Charles R. Wilson, Kansas. City.

Nancy Clay (1) Lea.

Nancy Clay, (1), daughter of James
Clay and Margaret Muse Clay, married David Lea, and had issue:
a Margaret Muse Lea.
b Wesley Wilson Lea., b Nov. 17,
   1804, d June 24, 1861, unmarried.
c William Dixon Lea.
d Winchester Muse Lea, b Aug.
   11, 1809, d Nov. 21, 1809.
e Landon Ludwell Lea.
f Melissa Lea.
g James Monroe Lea, b May 16,
   1815, d and is buried at Oakland
   College, Miss.
h Robert Montgomery Lea.
i Mary Reed Lea.
j David Clay Lea.
k Julia Clay Lea, b Oct. 16, 1823,
   d Dec. 5, 1840, unmarried.
l Charles Clinton Lea, b Nov. 12,
   1827, d and is buried at Oakland
   College, Miss.
Margaret Muse Lea, (a) above,
was born Jan. 2, 1803, married Agrippa Gayden, born 1779. Issue:
1' George Gayden, died 1861.
2' Frank Gayden, settled in Bolivar Co., Miss. Was the first prisoner.. exchanged.. between.. the
    North and South in the War of
    1861-65, captured in Missouri and
    exchanged the same day.
3' Minerva Gayden, died in girlhood.
4' Mary Gayden.
5' Elvira Gayden, died 1863, married A. C. Cage, sugar planter of
    Terre Bonne Parish, Louisiana.
6' Iverson Greene Gayden.
Mary Gayden (4') b March 17, 1830,
d Rpril 21, 1851. Married Dr. Joseph
Redhead, March 25, 1847. (He was
born Oct. 14, 1812, Northumberland
County, England, died Oct. 7, 1861,
Wilkinson county, Miss.) Issue:
A' Mary H. Redhead married first
    Dr. Hamilton, second, Mr. Merrill of Newburyport, Mass.
B' John A. Redhead born Oct. 28,
    1847, married Julia Norwood
    1878, issue: Joseph Redhead,
    John Redhead and Ella Redhead.
Iverson Greene Gayden (6'), married Octavia Perkins and had issue:
A' Julia Lea Gayden, m Col. E. L.
    Woodside, b Feb. 20, 1845, d
    Dec. 21, 1912, Baton Rouge, La.
    Issue: Robert I. Woodside, of

Greenville, S. C.
B' Agrippa Gayden, m Katie Perkins.
C' Octavia Gayden, m Robert Lee
    Tullis, Oct. 23, 1919, La. State
    University, Baton Rouge, La.
D' Margaret Gayden, m Donald
    Derickson, June 27, 1912, Prof.
    Cornell University, Ithaca, N. Y.
E' Percy Gayden, Gurley, La.
F' Iverson Greene Gayden, m
    Mamie Hands, Aug. 18, 1917; m
    second Dec. 23, 1919, Georgia
    Shands.
William Dixon Lea, (c) above, was
born Jan. 28, 1807, died May 4, 1849,
married Virginia Caroline Kemp, May
14, 1833, born Nov. 17. 1817, died
Jan. 19, 1894, at Clinton, La., buried
in family burying ground, Nettles
Place, on McAdams Bridge road four
miles east of Clinton, La. Issue:
1' David Merritt Lea, b July 19,
    1836, d Aug. 6, 1836.
2' Margaret Melissa Lea.
3' William Dixon Lea, b Feb. 5,
    1841, d July 12, 1863. Killed in
    War of 1861-65, Jackson, Miss.
4' Mary Elvira Lea, b July 29,
    1843, d Dec. 20, 1843.
5' Charles Monroe Lea, b Jan. 3,
    1845, d Aug. 31, 1864. Killed in
    War of 1861-65.
6' Anna Maria Lea, b March 23,
    1847, d Sept. 21, 1866.
7' Virginia Teresa Lea, b Nov. 5,
    1849, d Dec. 20, 1913, Jacksonville, Fla., m Charles H. Smith,
    July, 28, 1888, died Dec. 5, 1912,
    Jacksonville, Fla.
Margaret Melissa Lea, (2'), was
born June 18, 1838, died Feb. 3, 1888,
married Thomas J. Batchelor, March
27, 1859, he died Aug. 2, 1876. Issue:
A' William Dixon Lea Batchelor,
    b Dec. 30, 1859, d Feb. 1, 1879.
B' Riley Batchelor, b Jan. 20, 1862,
    married Elizabeth Hayes, March
    17, 1892.
C' Saluda Chapman Batchelor, b
    Nov. 15, 1865, married John A.
    C. Gordon, Feb. 15, 1893, died
    Oct. 5, 1917, issue: Virginia Gordon, b April 23, 1895; John Gordon, b Jan. 18, 1899; Vanita Gordon, b April 8, 1901; Ludwell Lea
    Gordon, b Jan. 9, 1903.
D' Virginia Lea Batchelor, b Sept.
    18, 1863, married Frank Drenning, Jan. 2, 1890, Wathena, Kan.,
    died Jan. 21, 1912, issue: Dudley

Lea Drenning, b Oct. 31, 1890, d July 31, 1892; Saluda Drenning, b May 4, 1893, m Oct. 15, 1921, George Turner Adams, of Akron, Ohio; Estelle Drenning, b Nov. 2, 1897 m W. N. Kerr, of Akron, Ohio; Beverly Drenning, b Nov. 27, 1902; Margaret Lyons Drenning, b June 16, 1903, d May 4, 1907.

E' Mary Lea Batchelor, b Dec. 25, 1867, d May 4, 1907, married David Lyons, 1901.

F' Maggie Batchelor, b Aug. 24, 1872, d Feb. 3, 1888.

G' Samuel Lea Batchelor, b Jan. 27, 1874.

Landon Ludwell Lea, (e) above, was born Oct. 16, 1810, died July 8, 1890, Amite Co. Miss., married Emily Robinson, Sept. 8, 1836, born Sept. 2, 1820, died May 8, 1841, married second, Charlsey Jane Edwards, Nov. 9, 1844, born Dec. 22, 1827, died June 30, 1862. Issue by first marriage:

1' James Monroe Lea.

2' William Jared Lea.

3' Emily Catherine Lea.

4' Mary Emily Lea, b Feb. 8, 1845, d Feb. 20, 1858.

5' Iverson David Lea, b April 6, 1847, d March 6, 1848.

6' Nancy Josephine Lea.

7' Ella Letitia Lea.

8' Roberta Eudora Lea, b Sept. 15, 1854, d Feb. 20, 1901, McComb, Miss., m William Franklin Holmes, Dec. 11, 1883, b May 31, 1854.

9' Eulalie Gertrude Lea, b Dec. 1, 1856, Amite Co., Miss., unmarried.

James Monroe Lea, (1'), was born Nov. 30, 1837, died April 3, 1891, married Florence McKnight, Oct. 17, 1865, born Oct. 2, 1847. Member of Company E. 22nd Miss. Regiment, War of 1861-65, Featherstone's Brigade, Stewarts Corp. Issue:

A' Fannie Emily Lea, b Aug. 19, 1866, d Oct. 23, 1890.

B' Julia Clay Lea, b March 29, 1868, married William Lafayette Deal, Dec. 20, 1888. Issue: Alexander Monroe Deal, b March 5, 1890, d Aug. 28, 1911; Ary Margaret Deal, b March 5, 1890, died Aug. 29, 1904; William Fay Deal, b Dec. 28, 1892, d Feb. 24, 1902; Susie Emily Deal, b Jan. 21, 1895, m Lee Blair; Henry Harville Deal, b June 5, 1898; Anna Lea Deal, b June 3, 1902; Cecil Homer

Deal, b Dec. 25, 1904; Julia Vera Deal, b July 21, 1907, d Oct. 5, 1911; Luna Lavelle Deal, b Jan. 5, 1911.

C' Landon Ludwell Lea, b May 5, 1871, d Sept. 19, 1878, Ladelle, Drew County, Ark.

D' Ary Florence Lea, b March 12, 1873, d June 19, 1879, Drew Co. Ark.

William Jared Lea (2'), born March 9, 1839, died Dec. 22, 1921, married Dec. 3, 1872, Ella Hension, born Feb. 6, 1854. Member Liberty Guards, Company E. 22nd Miss. Regiment War of 1861-65. Issue:

A' Charlie Lea, b Aug. 30, 1874, married Mrs Susie Van Norman, Nov. 4, 1902, born Aug. 21, 1874, issue: Ottilie Lea, b Dec. 25, 1903; Chas. Davis Lea, b July 19, 1905; Jewel Lea, b Aug. 31, 1907; Mildred Vaughn Lea, b July 18, 1910; Willam Jared Lea, b May 18, 1913.

B' Mary Emily Lea, b Feb. 22, 1877, d Sept. 12, 1884.

C' William M. Lea, b Nov. 30, 1878, disappeared in 1898 from Amite Co., Miss.

D' Van W. Lea, b July 1, 1881, married Ola Solley, issue: Eva Loraine Lea; Paul Lea; Georgia Lea; Phillip Lea.

E' Landon Ludwell Lea, b March 4, 1884, married Myrtle Jones, issue: Norman Jared Lea, b June 27, 1910.

F' Vaughn Lea, b Aug. 8, 1886, m Etta Haygood, issue: Margaret Elaine Lea.

G' Robert A. Lea, b Feb. 4, 1889.

H' Wallace J. Lea, b Oct. 19, 1891, m Sept. 26, 1915, Lola May Porter, issue: Barbara James Lea, b July 3, 1916; Virginia Lea.

I' Karl C. Lea, b Oct. 23, 1894.

Emily Catherine Lea, (3'), b May 8, 1841, d Feb. 3, 1887, Houston, Texas, married Charles William Harrell, Dec. 15, 1859, born May 1, 1837, Amite Co., Miss, d June 6, 1862, Osyka, Miss., m second Dec. 20, 1866, William Underwood, b Oct. 26, 1835, Shelbyville, Ky. Issue:

A' Landon Lea Harrell.

B' Charles Camelite Harrell, b Oct. 23, 1861, m William Gabe Martin, Dec. 22, 1880, died Oct. 1896, issue: Lea William Martin, b Oct. 3, 1881, d July 7, 1889; Charles Ellis Martin, b Feb. 19,

1896, issue: Lea William Martin,
b Oct. 3, 1881, d July 7, 1889;
Charles Ellis Martin, b Feb. 10,
1890; Oliver Louise Martin, born
July 19, 1891, d Jan. 19, 1919;
Edward Parker Martin, b Nov.
14, 1892, m Emmett Soleman;
Beulah Catherine Martin, b Jan.
17, 1895, m Mr. Creswell.

C' William Doss Underwood, (Ac-
tor, stage name "Lucifer"), born
Sept. 15, 1867, m June 1891,
Louise Alphonse Baptiste, Berke-
ley California. Issue: Emily Lea
Underwood, b May 8, 1892.

D' Fitzhugh Lea Underwood, b
Sept. 7, 1869.

E' Monroe J. Underwood, b July 8,
1871, m Aug. 27, 1897, Nancy
Lyle, d Oct. 11, 1901. No issue.
m second, Ida Barnhart, of Yoa-
kum, Texas, Dec. 24, 1905. Issue:
William M. Underwood, b Oct.
11, 1906; Thomas Monroe Underwood, b Nov. 5, 1907, d Sept. 5,
1911; Oscar Lea Underwood, b
May 9, 1912; Mary Avis Underwood, b Dec. 9, 1925.

F' Beulah Boyd Underwood, b
1874, m Sept. 14, 1901, Pitts
Montgomery, d March 1924,
Plantersville, Tex.

G' Mary Elizabeth Underwood, b
April 4, 1873, d 1875.

H' Kate C. Underwood, b 1877, m
D. A. Hoover, Pike county, Miss.,
Feb. 1901.

I' Roberta Gertrude Underwood, b
Nov. 7, 1878, m Nov. 5, 1898,
Douglas Abshier, married second
Oliver Earl Barker, of Texas,
Dec. 1, 1906, married third, Mr.
Pickerell, 1914.

J' Alma A. Underwood, b July 24,
1885, married Frank Perry, Jan.
17, 1906, married second, James
Corbett, July 10, 1914, married
third, Mr. Firth, Feb. 19, 1917.

Landon Lea Harrell (A'), was born
Feb. 29, 1860, Amite Co., Miss., died
Jan. 3, 1914, Los Angeles, Calif., married Veronica Donovan, Nov. 11, 1886,
born May 18, 1869, died March 20,
1913, Los Angeles, Calif. Issue:

a' Charles Donovan Harrell, b
Sept. 26, 1887, d Sept. 24, 1920.

b' Marguerite Harrell, b July 10,
1891, married Edward Locke, Dec.
25, 1908, b Sept. 19, 1887, m second, Cecil Nellis, issue: Edgar
Locke, b Oct. 2, 1909; Lea Harrell Lock, b Oct. 1, 1910; Cecil

Nellis, Jr.

c' Veronica Harrell, b June 23,
1894, m Clyde Perry, May 6, 1911,
issue: Mildred Marie Perry, b
Nov. 7, 1912.

d' Joe D. Harrell, b June 21, 1896,
d Oct. 12, 1919.

e' Cecile Harrell, b May 16, 1899,
married Earle Simmons, Washington, D. C.

f' Elizabeth Harrell, b Oct. 1,
1900, married C. Ponder Wood,
Houston, Texas, April 1920.

g' Anthony Harrell, died in infancy.

h' Annie Harrell, died in infancy.

i' Marie Harrell, b Sept. 19, 1904.

j' Michael Harrell, b May 13,
1901.

k' Emily Lea Harrell.

Nancy Josephine Lea, (6'), was
born Aug. 5, 1849, died April 4, 1911,
McComb, Miss., married Seaborn T.
Jones, Oct. 16, 1872, born Feb. 12,
1852, died Jan. 4, 1917. Issue:

A' Katie Lea Jones, b April 12,
1874, m William Franklin
Holmes, Dec. 25, 1901, b May 31,
1854, Lucedale, Miss. No issue,
but adopted daughter, Katie Nell
Holmes.

B' Alice Gertrude Jones.

C' Emily Ella Jones.

D' William Reed Jones, b April 6,
1880, d April 15, 1880.

E' Harry Aldridge Jones.

F' James Monroe Jones, b March
19, 1887, d Nov. 25, 1923, m June
12, 1911, Bertha Ott, of Osyka,
Miss., b Feb. 21, 1882. Issue:
Esther Ott Jones, b Sept. 22,
1914; Landon Lea Jones, b March
21, 1917; William Monroe Jones,
b June 22, 1920.

G' Leon Ludwell Jones, b May 19,
1881, m March 18, 1906, Hattie
Nix, of Houston, Texas, b Jan.
30, 1882, issue: Harry William
Jones, b Feb. 8, 1907, Houston,
Texas; Leonidas L. Jones, b Oct.
23, 1909; Addie Lea Jones, b
Nov. 3, 1913, d May 1920.

H' Viola Josephine Jones, b Feb.
2, 1890, m Clyde Wesley Brum-
field, June 29, 1915.

Alice Gertrude Jones (B'), was born
June 2, 1875, married Henry Clay
Fuller, Oct. 16, 1889, born June 14,
1867. Issue:

a' Francis Josephine Fuller, b

Dec. 22, 1892, d Jan. 16, 1893, Texas.

b' Diette Fuller, b April 19, 1894, Feb. 19, 1917, married Richard C. Cade. Issue: Lula Alice Cade, b Jan. 29, 1919, Texas.

c' Bernice Gertrude Fuller, b Sept. 8, 1895, d Sept. 22, 1895.

d' Bryan Holmes Fuller, b Oct. 10, 1896.

e' Braun Monroe Fuller, b Dec. 5, 1897, m July 21, 1917, Lois Blakely. Issue: Virginia Lois Fuller, b June 27, 1918.

f' Nellie Thomas Fuller, b March 21, 1899, d June 22, 1899, Swift, Texas.

g' Katie Lea Fuller, b Sept. 2, 1900, m Charles C. Thomas, Dec. 24, 1919. Issue: Norma Thomas, b Dec. 24, 1920.

h' Henry Clay Fuller, b Dec. 22, 1902.

i' Seaborn Tecumseh Fuller, b July 8, 1904.

j' Townsend Fuller, b Dec. 2, 1906.

k' Robert Travis Fuller, b March 8, 1911.

Emily Ella Jones (C'), was born Sept. 4, 1877, married Thomas J. Donahue, of Houston, Texas, March 23, 1897, born March 1, 1870, New York, Issue:

a' Thomas J. Donahue, b Aug. 7, 1899, Houston, Tex.

b' Katherine Donahue, b Jan. 13, 1898, married Dewitt Estess, Dec. 29, 1920, Issue: Emily Estess.

Harry Aldridge Jones (E'), born Jan. 11, 1884, married Annie Nix, March 20, 1919. Issue:

a' Louise Jones, b Feb. 4, 1920, Houston, Texas.

Ella Letitia Lea, (7'), was born March 15, 1852, died Aug. 22, 1894, married Dec. 20, 1870, McClung Webb, of Amite Co., Miss., born Feb. 27, 1850. Issue:

A' Annette Roberta Webb, b Nov. 22, 1872, d Jan. 20, 1893, married Charles Dixon, Jan. 21, 1892, born Aug. 19, 1870.

B' Alva Scott Webb, b Dec. 3, 1874, d Nov. 30, 1895, fell into Mississippi River at Chalmette, La., and drowned.

C' Frank Webb, b Sept. 5, 1876, d May 24, 1892.

D' Lea Webb, b Jan. 4, 1880, d May 4, 1881.

E' Clyde Rivers Webb, b Jan. 13, 1882, m Lena Elizabeth Berry-

hill, Dec. 23, 1900, b Nov. 26, 1882.

F' Clifford Webb, b Sept. 22, 1884, d Sept. 23, 1884.

G' Golda Holmes Webb, b Nov. 19, 1889, m William Alva Marsalis, Dec. 29, 1905, b Dec. 8, 1881. Issue: Hilda Lea Marsalis, b March 6, 1909; Emma Louise Marsalis, b Sept. 3, 1911. Married second, C. W. Briggs, May 27, 1914.

H' Robert Edward Webb, b May 7, 1892, d Jan. 22, 1893.

Melissa Lea (f), was born Feb. 18, 1813, died Sept. 19, 1882, married William McDuffy Matthews, Dec. 3, 1833, born May 15, 1808, died June 6, 1848, Bayou Gross Tete Parish, Point Coupee, La. Issue:

1' Mary Jane Matthews, b Sept. 12, 1834, d June 30, 1878, St. Helena Parish, La., m Jan. 30, 1851, Theodore Frederick Anderson, b Sept. 6, 1820, Sweden, Parish of Rogeta, England, Province of Helsendegland, d Nov. 1900. Issue: Edward McDuffy Anderson, b Dec. 30, 1853; William Eric Anderson, b April 16, 1857, d 1859; Laceland Co., Mo; Annie Julia M. Anderson, born in 1859; Lena Jane Anderson; Oscar Wallace Anderson; Frederick Lea Anderson, b Nov. 1872, d Feb. 22, 1904, Baton Rouge, La.

2' Julia Virginia Matthews, b Nov. 28, 1836, d April 10, 1886, St. Helena Parish, La., m Napoleon B. Calmez, of Hinds county, Miss., March 9, 1854, b Feb. 4, 1828. Issue: William Berry Calmez; Sarah Melissa Calmez; Mary Elizabeth Calmez; Myrtella Calmez; Julia Calmez; Rosa Wygelia Calmez; Octavia Calmez; Lilly Lea Calmez; William Berry Calmez, 2nd; Calhoun Caldwell Calmez; Napoleon Bonaparte Calmez.

3' William Wallace Matthews.

4' Wesley Lea Matthews, b Oct. 23, 1841, d May 6, 1842.

5' George McDuffy Matthews, b March 10, 1843, Bayou Gross Tete, La., d Aug. 16, 1850, Carrollton, La.

6' Nancy Clay Matthews, b Sept. 7, 1845, d Sept. 19, 1845.

7' Margaret Rosalie Matthews, b Oct. 31, 1846, Bayou Gross Tete,

La., d Aug. 19, 1850, Carrollton, La.

William Wallace Matthews (3'), was born June 10, 1839, died Dec. 24, 1911, buried Masonic Cemetery, New Orleans, La., married Catherine Lavinia Hutchinson, born April 6, 1846, died Jan. 4, 1889. Issue:

A' Charles Lea Matthews, b Aug. 26, 1876, married Sarah Elizabeth Easley, Nov. 29, 1897. Issue: Lorena Lavinia Matthews, b Dec. 17, 1898; William Davis Matthews, b Aug. 5, 1901; James Eric Matthews, b Jan. 6, 1908; Mamie Elizabeth Matthews, b Aug. 4, 1910.

B' Eulalie Matthews, m Dennis Mills, Louisiana.

Robert Montgomery Lea (h), was born Oct. 7, 1817, died Aug. 30, 1855, married Letty Edwards, of Wilkinson county, Miss., born Dec. 22, 1812, died Dec. 11, 1879. After death of R. M. Lea in 1855, Letty E. Lea, married Peter Graham Quin, of Pike county, Miss. No issue by first marriage, but adopted Eleanor Lombard, b Jan., 1852, married Nov. 21, 1872, Dr. W. W. Wroten, of Magnolia, Miss., b May 15, 1847. Issue:

A' Robert Lea Wroten, b Nov. 24, 1873.

B' Vincent J. Wroten, b Nov. 29, 1875.

C' Lillian L. Wroten, b July 14, 1878, married first, Jack Vaught. Married second, Grant Flippin. Issue: Lillian W. Vaught, b 1906, Magnolia, Miss.

D' Hugh William Wroten, b Oct. 29, 1880, m first, Annie Allen. m second, Alice Ott, Aug. 2, 1917, b 1887. Issue: William Hugh Wroten, b March 30, 1919.

Mary Reed Lea (i), was born Feb. 6, 1820, Amite Co., Miss., died Sept. 14, 1884, Magnolia, Miss., married first, Thomas Gorden, b Feb. 7, 1812, S. C. died Oct. 8, 1839, Amite Co., Miss. Married second, Samuel Lee, born May 9, 1796, S. C. died Oct. 9, 1876, East Feliciana Parish, La. Issue:

1' Julia Virginia Lee.

2' Mary Catherin Lee.

3' Charles G. Lee, b Aug. 4, 1850, m America Lucretia Smith, 1875. Issue: Mary Lee, b May, 1876.

4' Emily Smith Lee.

5' Jennie Clay Lee.

Julia Virginia Lee (1'), was born Jan. 25, 1844, E. Feliciana Parish, La., died April 24, 1920, Washington, D. C., married Heman Asbury Battles, Oct. 11, 1866, born Oct. 22, 1828, Lowell, Mass., died May 2, 1881, Colorado Springs, Colo. Issue:

A' Mary Morton Battles, b Aug. 10, 1867, Chatawa, Miss.

B' Julia Virginia Battles, b Sept. 4, 1869.

C' Samuel Lee Battles, b Aug. 4, 1871, m Katie M. Clough, of Amite, La., Nov. 21, 1894. Residence Washington, D. C.

D' Harriet Clay Battles, b Aug. 20, 1874, m Dr. Lyman James Clements, of Washington, D. C., Feb. 11, 1892. Issue: Julia Lea Clements, b Feb. 17, 1905, Washington, D. C.; William Heman Clements, b July 20, 1907; Samuel Clements, b Oct. 7, 1915.

E' Heman Asbury Battles, b May 1, 1876. Residence, Gulfport, Miss.

F' Nina Lea Battles, b Jan. 20, 1878, d Feb. 17, 1876, New Orleans, La.

David Clay Lea (j), born Nov. 4, 1821, Amite Co., Miss., died Oct. 4, 1847, married Nancy Edwards, Sept. 10, 1843, born Dec. 12, 1823, Wilkinson county, Miss. After the death of D. C. Lea, Nancy E. Lea married Murdock McCrain, on Sept. 23, 1850, born 1824, died 1871. Issue by first marriage:

1' Charles Edward Lea.

Charles Edward Lea (1'), was born April 6, 1848, died May 18, 1890, Greensburg, La., married Mary Hutchinson, born June 18, 1844, died Nov. 10, 1888, Greensburg, La. Issue:

A' Claud Lea.

B' Leila Lea, b Feb. 15, 1877, Greensburg, La., married Andrew Jackson Alford, Nov. 17, 1895, b April 10, 1874. Issue: Myrtis Lea Alford, b March 4, 1897; Mary Eliza Alford, b Feb. 15, 1898; Claudia Alford, (girl), b Dec 19, 1900; Daisy Irene Alford, b Aug. 2, 1903; Willie Allen Alford, b Feb. 3, 1906; John Dean Alford, b Dec. 13, 1912.

Sabrina Clay (J) Lea.

Sabrina Clay, daughter of James Clay and Margaret Muse Clay, married Zachariah Lea, who was a member of the Mississippi State Legislature, session of 1820, representing Amite County. Captain in Claiborne's

Regiment of Mississippi Militia, War of 1812. Reference, Adjutant General's office, War Department, Washington, D. C., No. 1637 159. Land records show Zacharia Lea settled in Amite County, Miss., July 15, 1807. Issue:

a Elizabeth Lea.

b Isabella (called Elceba) Lea, b March 1, 1805, Grainger county, Tenn., d Dec. 22, 1877, at Summitt, Miss., married first, Hon. Jehu Wall, 17 years a member of the Mississippi Legislature. No issue. Married second, Richard Bates. No issue.

c Lucinda Clay Lea.

d Hampton Muse Lea.

e Alfred Mead Lea.

f Nancy Lea.

g Wilford Zachariah Lea.

h James Everett Lea.

i Iverson Green Lea.

Elizabeth Lea (a), was born Nov. 22, 1802, near Lea Springs, Tenn., died Jan. 6, 1878, Amite Co., Miss., married first, John Frith, married second, John Everett in 1835, born July 31, 1793, Richland District, S. C., died Aug. 5, 1860, Amite Co. Miss. Issue:

1' Monroe Frith.

2' James Wilborn Frith.

3' Lucinda Lea Frith.

4' Amanda Frith, b Aug. 10, 1830.

5' Winchester Everett, son of Elizabeth Lea and John Everett, b Nov. 21, 1835, Amite Co., Miss., d June 14, 1920, Amite Co., Miss., unmarried. Member Judge Hurst's Company from Liberty, Miss., War of 1861-65.

6' Sabrina Everett, b Nov. 19, 1838, d Aug. 10, 1853.

7' Zachariah Lea Everett.

Monroe Frith (1'), born April 15, 1828, m Matilda Dickey. Issue: Robert Frith, Magnolia, Miss; married Floyd Atkinson. Issue: Clinton Frith, Monroe Frith; Robert Frith, Magnolia, Miss.; Eleanor Frith, married Mr. Brent.

B' Phoebe Frith, m Shadrack Young: Issue: Horace Young; Monroe Young, m Bessie Easley; Hugh Young; Myra Young, m Green Norman; Flora Young; Winchester Young.

C' Sallie Frith, b May 23, 1862, m June 15, 1881; Edward Paul Weirauch. Residence, 517 W. Daggett Ave., Ft. Worth, Texas.

Issue: Rowena Lee Weirauch, m Mr. Thorp, Dallas, Texas; Katie Weirauch, Ft. Worth Texas.

James Wilborn Frith (2') born 1833 died May 14, 1898, McComb, Miss., married Annie Harrell. Issue:

A' William Frith.

B' John Frith, m first, Julia Spurlock, married second, Miss Wyatt

C' Monroe Frith, m Maggie Sims.

D' Chris Frith, m Pearl Andrews.

E' James Dock Frith, m Eugenia Bonds.

F' Elu Frith.

G' Frances Frith.

H' Eva Frith, b 1872, d Aug. 13, 1879.

I' Lula Frith, m Zachariah Reeves.

J' Ary Frith, m Charles Wilkinson. No issue, but adopted daughter, Lucy Wilkinson.

K' Addie Frith.

Frances Frith, (G')), married J. Dudley Mcdowell, born 1859. Issue:

a' Edward Franklin McDowell, m Annie Elizabeth Godfrey, June 8, 1911.

b' Russell McDowell.

c' Golda McDowell, m Frank L. Butler, McComb, Miss., Issue Elwin Butler; Celeste Butler; Frances Elizabeth Butler; Frank Lea Butler; Wilborn Butler; Russell Butler.

d' Dudley McDowell.

Addie Frith (K'), married J. Emmett Wilkinson. Issue:

a' Katie Wilkinson, m Exba O'Mara. Issue: Junior O'Mara; Emmett O'Mara.

b' Maud Wilkinson, m Cecil B. Sauls. Issue: Cecil B. Sauls; Annie Lynn Sauls.

c' Annie Wilkinson, m L. M. Hicks Issue: Kathryn Hicks.

d' Myrtis Wilkinson, m Murray Quin. Issue: Murray Quin, Jr., Louie Quin.

e' Nellie Wilkinson, m Carleton E. Hunt., McComb, Miss.

f' Louie E. Wilkinson, m Elmer Hargrove.

Lucinda Lea Frith (3'), was born July 18, 1824, Amite Co. Miss., died July 17, 1909, Amite Co. Miss. Married Ivy F. Thompson, 1844, born Jan. 15, 1820, died July 28, 1860. Issue:

A' Wilborn Monroe Thompson.

B. Eunice Elizabeth Thompson, b June 20, 1848. Unmarried.

C' Ida Lucinda Thompson.

D' Eudora Holmes Thompson, b April 11, 1857, died Dec. 31, 1861.

William Monroe Thompson, (A'), born Aug. 17, 1853, died Aug. 20, 1891, buried at Orange Grove Cemetery, Lake Charles, La., married Almine R. Burris, Jan. 8, 1874, born April 22, 1852, died May 25, 1925. Issue:

a' Winchester Thompson, b Nov. 10, 1874, d Aug. 24, 1882.

b' Leslie Lea Thompson, b April 22, 1876, m Dec. 23, 1900, Lucy D. Creighton. Issue: William Monroe Thompson, b Sept. 21, 1902 m Lamar Davis, Nov. 5, 1925 Lake Charles, La.; Ida Pearl Thompson, b March 17, 1904, Long Beach Cal.

c' Ivy Finch Thompson, b Aug. 28, 1878, d Sept. 29, 1883.

d' Minnie Eudora Thompson, b Nov. 23, 1885, d Aug 21, 1887.

e' Bessie Ida Thompson, b May 31, 1889, m May 22, 1910, George Ashford, Lewis, La.

f' Augusta Allen Thompson, b May 11, 1891, d Dec. I, 1891.

Ida Lucinda Thompson (C'), born Aug 27, 1859, died Nov. 16, 1912, married George Godbold, March 7, 1888. Issue:

a' Minnie Clyde Godbold, b 1889, m Rev. Ivy K. Floyd. Address, Dallas, Texas. Issue: Lamar Floyd; Ray Floyd; F. G. Floyd.

b' Alma Lea Godbold.

c' Ivy Finch Godbold.

d' Carrie Lou Godbold, b July 10, 1894, m Jan. 30, 1920, John W. Mullins, Meadville, Miss. Issue: Aaron Wesley Mullins, b April 5, 1922; George Lester Mullins, b Dec. 9, 1924; Ida Pearl Mullins, b April 25, 1926.

Zachariah Lea Everett (7'), born 1842, died Dec. 22, 1912, Monroe, La. Member Company C 7th Mississippi Regiment, War of 1861-65. married Elizabeth Jourdan, Nov. 24, 1868, born Dec. 8, 1847, died March 20, 1913. Issue:

A' John William Everett, b Dec. 13, 1869, d May1, 1898, Ruston, La.

B' William Joseph Everett, m Lorena Fort. Issue: Nelle Everett.

Lucinda Clay Lea (twin of Elceba Lea), (c), was born March 1, 1805, Grainger Co. Tenn., died Dec. 17, 18-86, Amite Co. Miss., married John Richmond, born Nov. 5, 1801, died

June 24, 1882. Issue:

1' Elizabeth Richmond.

2, Seaborn Clay Richmond, b Nov. 30, 1829, died Dec. 19, 1853, of yellow fever, at Clinton, La.

3' Mary Bethany Richmond, b Nov. 30, 1844, d July 24, 1856.

4' Elceba Richmond, m Middleton Wicker. Issue: Frances and Elizabeth Wicker, twins; Seaborn Wicker; William Wicker.

5' Jane Richmond, m first, Mr. Shelton, m second Mr. Flannigan.

6' Iverson Green Richmond.

7' Emily Margaret Richmond Elizabeth Richmond, (1'), married Isaac Robinson. Issue:

A' Thomas Robinson, m Miss Sharpe.

B' John Robinson.

C' Wilford Robinson, b 1852, d March 2, 1918, Amite Co. Miss., m Frances Frith, Dec. 2, 1876. Issue: Wilford Robinson; W. E. Robinson; Winnie Robinson.

D' Erastus Robinson, m Elizabeth McMichale.

E' Lea Robinson.

F' Ella Robinson, married first, Mr. Terrell, m second, Jackson Williams, b Feb. 11, 1842, d Oct. 14, 1925. Issue: Myrtis Terrell, m Dr. Murray Quin, Amite Co. Miss.; George Terrell, unmarried; Howard Williams; Boyd Williams; Judge Williams; Carey Williams.

G' Emily Robinson, b 1860, d Aug. 23, 1923.

H' Janie Robinson, m Aug. 23, 1911, Dr. O. N. Arrington, Brookhaven, Miss.

I' Kittie Robinson.

J' Lucinda Robinson.

John Robinson (B'), born March 21 1850, m Dec. 18, 1872, Mattie Wilson, b1846, d June 14, 1920.. Issue:

a' Rosalie Robinson, m Ira S. Wyatt, Columbia, Miss. Issue: Edward Wyatt, m Willie Carr, Aug. 20, 1922; Eugene Wyatt.

b' Thomas Robinson.

c' Charles Ray Robinson, m Ruth Darville. Issue: Charles Ray Robinson, McComb, Miss.

d' Annie Robinson, m Harry Butler, Amite Co. Miss.

e' Edward L. Robinson, m Eva L. Hinton, Oct. 24, 1912. Issue: Evelyn Hinton, McComb Miss.; Edith Frances Hinton.

43

Lucinda Robinson (J'), married
Hamilton Ray McKnight. Issue:
a' Ethel McKnight, m Arthur C.
Truex, McComb, Miss. Issue: Elizabeth B. Truex, b April 29, 1905,
d Feb. 11, 1926; Mildred Truex;
Dorothy Truex.
b' Hettie McKnight.
c' Clyde McKnight, m R. A. Gulfe,
New Orleans, La., Jan. 19, 1913.
d' Hamilton Ray McKnight, m
Evelyn Martin, Oct. 12, 1915.
e' Julia McKnight, m Julian Ober-
schmidt, McComb, Miss., April
20, 1920.
Iverson Green Richmond (6'), was
born April 3, 1835, died Jan. 11, 1894,
lost his right arm at battle of Frank-
lin Tenn. War of 1861-65, married
Saint Helena Williams, born Oct. 22,
1842, died July 8, 1900. Issue:
A' John Richmond.
B' Dudley Richmond.
C' Seaborn Clay Richmond, b 1871
died Feb. 1926, Shreveport, La. m
Rosa McDaniel. Issue: Clarence
Richmond; Charles Richmond;
Alton Richmond; Harry Rich-
mond; Robert Lea Richmond.
D' Iverson Richmond.
E' Dolly Varden Richmond.
F' Burke Richmond.
G' John Richmond.
H' Myers Richmond.
I' Elizabeth Wheeler Richmond.
J' Nicholas Richmond.
Emily Margaret Richmond (7'), b
1841, died Sept. 17, 1914, married Dr.
W. C. Taylor, Issue:
A' Robert L. Taylor, m Elizabeth
Tate. Issue: Ozzie Vernon Taylor,
Kentwood, La.
B' Iverson Taylor.
C' John Everett Taylor, b Nov. 21,
1869, d Sept. 15, 1875.
D' Lula Taylor, m R. W. Draughn,
Jackson, Miss.
E' James Lea Taylor, b Oct. 27,
1864, d Aug 2, 1895.
Hampton Muse Lea (d), was born
Oct 5, 1810, "Travis Place", Amite
Co. Miss., died Aug. 19, 1886, Amite
Co. Miss,, married Maria Gordon, b
Oct. 13, 1810, died July 16, 1883, Is-
sue:
1' Alothea Ann Lea.
2' George Sylvester Lea, b June
20, 1836, d Nov. 30, 1864. Killed
at battle of Franklin, Tenn.,
War of 1861-65.
3' Jane Melissa Lea, b March 5,
1818, d Oct. 23 1862, m Dr. C. F.

Felder, b 1814, Miss., died 1875,
Texas. Issue: Alvie D. Felder,
b July 27, 1861, physician and
banker, Magnolia, Miss. Married
Ada Lenoir, 1886. No issue:
4' Cicelay Lea.
5' Marshall Thomas Lea.
Alothea Ann Lea (1'), was born
Oct. 17, 1834, died May 18, 1904, mar-
ried Thomas H. McDowell. Issue:
A' Cicely McDowell.
B' Edmund A. McDowell, b 1857,
Amite Co. Miss., d Apr. 14, 1924,
Beaumont Texas. Judge of the
60th District Court of Texas.
Married first, Minnie McDowell,
b May 19, 1858, d Aug. 25, 1898,
married second, Mrs. Laura Fer-
guson, daughter of Dr. Banks, of
Clinton Miss.
C' Elizabeth McDowell, Magnolia,
Miss.
D' Minnie McDowell, m Logan
Phillips of Jackson, Miss. Issue:
William Phillips; Doris Phillips.
Cicely McDowell (A'), married Hil-
lery Garner and had issue:
a' Hillery Garner, b 1883, d Jan. 5
1915, Magnolia, Miss., m A Thad
Leggett. Issue: Thad Leggett,
Jr.
Cicelay Lea (4'), born March 31
1843, died Feb. 19, 1906, married C.
Luke Guy. Issue:
A' Jefferson Davis Guy, m Geor-
gia Butler. Issue: Harry T. Guy,
m Hilda Wall.
B' Ada Guy, m Mr. Butler.
Marshall Thomas Lea (5'), born
Nov. 3, 1844, d July 5 1897, married
Dora Hitchcock. Issue:
A' George Lea, bJan. 17, 1875, d
Aug. 28, 1890.
B' Robert Lea, born Dec. 10, 1876,
died February 2, 1877.
C' Frank Lea, m Millie Reynolds.
D' Virgil A Lea, m Annie Rey-
onlds.
E' Elizabeth Lea, m Dr. Seaborn
Reynolds, Gloster Miss.
F' Lillian Lea, m Jan. 18, 1912
Daniel Hunter McLeod.
G' Muse Lea, m Ella Smith. Issue:
Hampton Lea; James Lea.
H' Clark Rice Lea.
I' Cary Lea.
J' Alvie Lea (girl)
Alfred Mead Lea (e), married Eliz-
abeth Garner. (Dr. T. S. Jones of
Baton Rouge, La., writes: "Some fif-
ty years ago Alfred Mead Lea and

family moved to Jackson, La. and I attended them as physician. I knew Clement Clay Lea, Also Clement Clay father and son, both of whom had been Governor and U. S. Senator of Alabama. I learned that Mrs. Elizabeth Garner Lea was a sister to the younger Clay and a daughter of the Elder one, and that Mr. Garner, her father, came from Madison County, Ala., and was a near neighbor to my father and mother".) Alfred Mead Lea moved from Amite Co. Miss. to Feliciana Parish, La. in 1849. Issue:

1' Clement Clay Lea.

2' James M. Lea.

3' Hampton Muse Lea, b Jan. 31, 1836, d Sept. 26, 1911, m Emma Jones, March 21, 1879, d April 8, 1880, m second, Rhoda Worthy, June 9, 1882, born Feb. 5, 1847. Member 4th Louisiana Regiment Co. A. Hunters Rifles, War of 1861-65. Issue,: Emma Lea, m April 19, 1899, Frank Morton Thompson, b 1872, d July 22, 1919 Slaughter, La; Alma Lea, d April 1897; Harry Lea, m Floretta Garcia, Jan. 27, 1904; Mabel Lea, m April 5 1907, Rev. W. L. Doss; Lillian Lea, m Charles L. Munson, March 23, 1921, attorney of St. Francisville, La.; Hampton Muse Lea.

4' Zachariah Lea.

5' Frank Lea, m and had issue: Belle Lea, Daisy Lea; Pryor Wilford Lea; Elizabeth Lea, m W. J. Johnson; Frank Lea; Myrtis Lea; Charles Lea; Florence Lea; Alec Ripley Lea; Zachariah Lea.

6' Pryor Lea, died in prison at Camp Chase, Ohio, War of 1861-65.

7' Sarah Elizabeth Lea.

Clement Clay Lea (1'), killed in battle, Atlanta, Ga. War of 1861-65, married Julia Cox. Issue:

A' Henry Alfred Lea, married and had issue: Henry Muse Lea.

B' Theodosia Lea.

C' Clara Clay Lea, m A. C. Ripley, Issue: Julia Ripley m D. S. Powell.

James M. Lea (2'), born 1835, in Amite Co. Miss. married Laura Armistead, born 1840, Wilkinson Co. Miss., died 1906, Coushalta, La. Issue:

A' Alfred Mead Lea, married and had issue: Walker Lea; Lilly Lea,

Leona Lea, m S. H. Vignes, Dec. 7, 1921; Alfred Mead Lea.

B' Kate Lea, m Henry Harvey. Issue: James Harvey; Dave Harvey; Henry Harvey; Emma Harvey, m Mr. Munson.

C' Lula Lea, m Keete Lockett, Coushalta, La.

Zachariah Lea (4'), born March 17, 1830, died Sept. 19, 1902, Jackson; La. Married Sallie Worthy, May 2, 1865, born Dec. 26, 1839. Issue:

A' Jessie Worthy Lea, b Oct. 5, 1868, m Grace Mardenbrough, Dec. 12 1899, born May 5, 1873, daughter of George Wright Mardenbrough (born St. Kitts, West Indies, and wife Jane Cecilia Riley, b Aug. 13, 1850, Mobile, Ala. Issue: Helen Mardebrough Lea, b Dec. 21, 1900, Jackson, La.

B' Estelle Lea, b Nov. 11, 1870, m Feb. 14,1895, Herbert H. Ferguson.

C' Ida Lea, b Feb. 5, 1873, unmarried.

D' Mary Coline Lea, b Jan. 24, 1877, Jackson, La. d April 5, 1907 when cyclone destroyed old family residence.

E' Evelyn Lea, b Dec. 12 1879, d May 11, 1881.

Sarah Elizabeth Lea (....., married D. C. Thompson, died January 24 1924, Slaugter, La. Issue:

A' Frank Morton Thompson, b 1872, d July 22, 1919, m Emma Lee, April 19, 1899.

B' Edna Earl Thompson.

C' May Belle Thompson, m F. M. Leguence, Abbeville, La. Issue: Frances M. Leguence; Miriam Elizabeth LeGuence.

D' John Scott Thompson, m and had issue: Bessie Morton Thompson.

Nancy Lea (f), was born March 7, 1814, died Feb. 6, 1846, Amite Co. Miss. Married Aaron Robinson, Issue:

1' Louisa Robinson, m Jared Jackson. Issue: James Lea Jackson, b Sept. 24, 1865, d Feb. 24, 1878.

2' Erastus Clay Robinson, b Dec. 31, 1833, d March 11, 1857.

3' Moses Robinson, disappeared from Centerville, Miss., in 1877.

4' Thryza Robinson, died in youth.

5' James Robinson, killed in War of 1861-65.

Wilford Zachariah Lea (g), was was born Dec. 27, 1816, near Liberty, Miss. Died Dec. 20, 1906, Liberty,

Miss. Married Rachael Powell, Jan. 27, 1842, born July 6, 1819, died on March 10, 1904, Liberty, Miss.

From "Some Men Of The Pew" by Z. T. Leavell, we take the following tribute:

"Wilford Zachariah Lea was born at Huron, Miss. Dec. 27, 1816. Huron is about thirteen miles East of Liberty, the county seat of Amite County, Mississippi. His father and mother, Zachariah Lea and Sabrina Clay, were married in Virginia, the state of nativity. After a short stay near the present city of Knoxville, Tenn. coming down the Tennessee and Mississippi rivers in a flat boat of their own construction, they reached Natchez, Miss. about 1805. Zachariah Lea had a number of brothers who came to Miss., with him, and the women would ply the oars while the men would ward off the Indians, with their rifles.

"Along with these emigrants came to our state, a woman of blessed memory, Mrs. Margaret Muse Clay, who was the grandmother of Wilford Zachariah Lea. She was born in Chesterfield County, Va. April 2, 1737 and died at Huron, Amite Co., Miss. Feb. 13, 1832. About one hundred and fifty years ago, she was accustomed in her native state (Virginia) to go and hear the persecuted Baptist preachers preach from the prison windows to those who would congregate outside jail. She became a convert, and to avoid persecution, was baptized in the night in James River, near Richmond. The ice was broken to make a place for the solemn ceremony, witnessed by the stars, and the few whose love for their Master cast out fear of the tribunal of men. But they could not elude the watchfulness of the enemies of religious liberty, and being apprehended were sentenced, to pay a considerable fine or be publicly whipped at the post. Margaret Muse Clay could not pay this fine, and the public flogging for being a Baptist would have been administered to her, but for a kind-hearted one who paid the fine for her.

"Margaret Muse Clay lived with Zachariah Lea, the father of Wilford Zachariah Lea. She gave thanks at the table and conducted family worship. She would sometimes have young Wilford kneel by her side, and placing her hand on his head, would pray Heaven's blessing on the youth of tender years. What a benediction on the boy! Ah, how lovely the grandmothers who speak to the dimple-cheeked flaxen haired little boys of the light they see coming over the Jasper Walls from the Throne of One whose "years shall not fail". Mr. Winchester Everett, of Amite county, Miss. has the old arm-chair (made of hand hewn hickory and brought with her from Virginia) and the hymn book that belonged to Grandmother Clay, which he prizes for memories that cluster about them. Her remains rest in peace in the family burying grounds of the Leas at Lea Hall, Amite Co. Miss.

"Virginia has in Hollywood, at Richmond, the mortal remains of our Southern Chieftain, Mississippi's pride—Jefferson Davis. May his ashes rest there in peace! Mississippi's genial soil holds the sacred dust of one of Virginia's noblest daughters— Margaret Muse Clay, born so near Richmond as within the sound of a cannon shot, and our generosity is not called upon to yield anything to the "Mother of Presidents" in exchange of the ashes of a Statesman for the sacred dust of a saint.

"Zachariah and Sabrina Clay Lea first settled on the Amite River, ten miles east of Liberty, Miss. about 63 miles southeast from Natchez, Miss. After laboring through the day, at night he pounded his corn in a mortar for meal. He brought salt and flour for his family on a pony from Natchez, Miss. along the Indian trails. The old Salem Church of Cole's Creek had then been in existence fourteen years.

"After remaining a few years on the Amite River, Zachariah Lea moved to Huron, three miles further east, where Wilford Zachariah Lea was born, and where James Everett Lea, Sr., grandson of Zachariah Lea, is now living. Here Dr. Charles H. Otken found his wife (Miss Emily Jane Lea) and Elder A. J. Miller followed his example, and Elder Robert W. Merrill got a good wife when he married the sister of the wives of these two noble men, the three being the sisters of James Everett Lea, Sr. My head would grow dizzy should I climb higher up this Genealogical Tree, and I trust I shall be excused from any further demonstration of my agility in the ancestral garden.

"Wilford Zachariah Lea joined the Liberty Bell Baptist Church when he was twenty-years of age, and was baptized by Elder W. B. Hall. This was about 1841. He has continued his membership at Liberty until the present time. He moved to his home three miles east of Liberty in 1842. He has been going over the same road to church for fifty-eight years. For more than half a century he has been a faithful and constant attendant at church. For thirty years he did not fail thirty times to attend the conference meetings of his church. He has not in the fifty-nine years of his connection with the Liberty church been asked for his contribution to his pastor's salary, it is always paid promptly. For fifty-nine years a member of a church and not once necessary under the most trying financial conditions of his church, to ask him for money to pay the pastor. Ah! That some people in our state would read this. Such statements are far too prosy for them.

"Mr. Lea had been a Deacon for 47 years, and served as clerk of his church 30 years. He was treasurer of the old Mississippi Association twenty-five years. The Mississippi Association is the Mother Association in the State, constituted Sept. 1806. It has had many great laymen, and to be treasurer of it for twenty-five years is no mean compliment.

"Mr. Lea had in his long life, been a man of great hospitality. His residence is a typical southern rural house, two stories high, with spacious rooms, broad halls, and with a wide inviting front veranda. In passing such a home, anyone feels as if he is doing violence to his love of ease not to turn in and enjoy the cool shades or enter its open doors. Here Baptist preachers have been entertained for more than fifty years, and the doors are wide open yet. It used to be said, if a Baptist preacher went to South Miss. to preach, he must go to see Wilford Z. Lea and get him to sign his credentials. The first time I ventured to preach in the Mississippi Association was at New Providence church, I asked him to do the usual favor. With a merry laugh, he said the people would take my word for it that I had met him and gotten his approval. Dr. J. R. Graves was very fond of Mr. Lea. During Dr. Graves' last days, he visited this gen-

erous host and remained with him a fortnight or more to recuperate his failing health. It was Dr. Graves who gave Mr. Lea's home the name of "The Free Baptist Hotel." Perhaps the good old deacon has not at any time heard the flapping of the wings of Angels, but doubtless he has often felt after his visitors had left his hosptiable home he had gotten more than he had imparted.

"Wilford Zachariah Lea is a ripe Christian character. His pastor, Elder T. C. Schilling says, "Bro. Lea is one of the most consecrated christians that I have ever known." In speaking in view of the approaching Graves' last days, he visited this genend of his life, Mr. Lea said: "My mother was a good woman. I hope to see her before long. I am as a man on his way home, waiting at the depot for the coming train. I am listening for the whistle." His soul may be happy when he hears the shriek of the engine down the way, but many will mourn his loss and the world will be poorer when the Heavenly Train pulls out with Wilford Zachariah Lea aboard.

"Mr. Lea is a correct man. He inherited from his old grandmother the feeling that what is right is worthy to be observed, and that the demands of conscience are final. The pleading of policy and the proffer of a bribe are as sounding brass to such people, they are a positive annoyance, and rejected with scorn. I have it in my mind that Margaret Muse Clay and Henry Clay were related by blood. Henry Clay, the son of a Baptist minister, was born and reared in the "slashes" of Hanover county, Va. near Richmond, on the north side of the James River. Henry Clay said, "I would rather be right than be President." Margaret Muse Clay was ready to bear the lash for conscience sake.

"Wilford Z. Lea was born in this strain of blood. His life has been ordered by the plummet of truth, his edges have been cut by the ledger line of Holy Writ. He has always aligned himself with the good, the true, the progressive, and no spectres of wronged widows and orphans haunt him in his declining years. He has lived for God and Humanity, Grateful humanity honors and reveres him and God is ready to receive and reward him.

Issue of Wilfor Zachariah Lea and Rachel Powell Lea are as follows:

1' Josiah Powell Lea, b Aug. 30, 1843, d June 17, 1864 d Atlanta, Ga. War of 1861-65.

2' Cornelia Lea, b 1847, m James G. Dixon, b Dec. 29, 1845, d Nov. 26, 1894. Issue: Myrtis Dixon; New Orleans; Annie Dixon, m James Howell; Lea Dixon, m Miss Wahl, of New Orleans; James Dixon, New Orleans.

3' Jefferson Davis Lea.

4' William Alfred Lea.

5' Iverson Green Lea.

6' Sabrina Jane Lea, b Nov. 20, 1856, d Dec. 26, 1900.

7' Mary Emma Lea.

8' Wilford Zachariah Lea, b Dec. 7, 1860, Liberty, Miss. married Mollie Garrow, Dec. 5, 1887, born March 30, 1866. Issue: Nathaniel G. Lea, b Oct. 12, 1888, died April 30, 1890; Janie Lorena Lea, b Feb. 10, 1892, m March 14, 1921 James S. Goodwin, of Marvell, Ark; John Carl Lea, b Nov. 19, 1893; Gertrude Howe Lea, b Jan. 8, 1897, d May 5, 1901; Mary Lea, b Sept. 11, 1899; Wilford Zachariah Lea, b March 5, 1904.

Jefferson Davis Lea (3'), born July 13, 1850, married Dec. 29, 1875. Janie Going. Issue:

A' Howard G. Lea, b Sept. 26, 1876, married Ella Inman, New York City.

B' Elizabeth Lea, b Aug. 6, 1878, Memphis, Tenn.

C' Emma Lea, b Nov. 2, 1884.

D' Joseph D. Lea, b Dec. 5, 1880, m Nellie Henson, had issue: address, 5530 S. Liberty St., New Orleans.

E' Edna A. Lea, b Dec. 6, 1885, m Dr. E. D. Butler, Oct. 6, 1914. Address, Wilmer, Ark.

F' Georgia D. Lea, Memphis,Tenn.

G' Perla Lea, Brookhaven, Miss.

H' Memie R. Lea, m Lawrence L. Simpson, Feb. 14, 1918. Stevensville, Mont. Issue: Lawrence L. Simpson.

I' Henry Lea.

William Alfred Lea (4'), born April 28, 1852, married Jan. 2, 1878, Ella Anderson, b Dec. 11, 1860, d April 28, 1917, Amory, Miss. Issue:

A' Ernest Linwood Lea, b Oct 17, 1878, d Jan. 26, 1926, Byhalia, Miss. married Dec. 18, 1917, Lillie Bertha Roper.

B' William Edgar Lea.

C' Eugene Scott Lea, b Dec. 14, 1882, Ft. Worth, Texas. Married Hazel Ward, June 24, 1911.

D' Thomas Stockdale Lea, b June 6, 1885. 4318 Madison St., Chicago.

E' Mary Edith Lea, b Sept. 22, 1887, m Eugene Runion, Commerce, Ga., Feb. 19, 1907.

F' Ralph Monette Lea, b March 12, 1890, d June 14, 1918.

G' Hoyt Clay Lea, b June 26, 1892, Atlanta, Ga.

H' Curry Lea, b Mar. 10, 1895, 195 Broadway, N. Y.

I' Theodore Emerson Lea, b June 7, 1898, 4140 W. Madison St., Chicago.

William Edgar Lea (B'), born Aug. 25, 1880, married June 14, 1899, Gertrude Swinwood, born Sept. 2, 1880, New Castle, England. Issue:

a' Velma Mae Lea, b April 15, 1900. Lula, Miss.

b' Thomas Edgar Lea, b April 18, 1902. No. 1400 East 53rd. St., Chicago.

c' Lena Mildred Lea, b April 20, 1905, m James Rollen Scribner, Feb, 11, 1925. Amory Miss. Issue: Sarah Nell Scribner, born March 25, 1926.

d' Edith Nell Lea, b July 11, 1914.

Iverson Green Lea (5'), born Oct. 30, 1855, Liberty Miss, married first, Perla Swearingen, Jan. 8, 1879, born Oct. 26, 1857, married second, Elizabeth White, Sept. 10, 1913. Issue by first marriage:

A' Van Swearengen Lea, b March 5, 1880, d 1881, Liberty, Miss.

B' Rachel Annie Lea, b June 30, 1883, m Rev. J. R. Johnston, Sept 1, 1912. D'Le, Miss. No issue.

c' Ella Anderson Lea, b Nov. 22, 1886, m James Samuel Bennett, Dec. 18, 1906. Address, 1434 S. Driver St., Memphis, Tenn. Issue: Lenera Claire Bennett, b Sept. 29 1907; Majorie Pearl Bennett, b May 10, 1910; James Swearingen Bennett, b Jan. 3, 1913; Ella Lea Bennett, b Sept. 3, 1914; Jean Edward Bennett, b Sept. 29, 1916; Donald Bennett, b July 28, 1918.

D' Carey Lea, b Sept. 27, 1888, d Oct. 17, 1892.

E' Stella Lea, b Jan. 24, 1890, m David Morgan Williams, May 1, 1918. Address, 714 E. Elm St., Eldorado Ark. Issue: David Mor-

gan Williams, b Sept. 25, 1919;
Milton Lea Williams, b March 15,
1921; Pearla Annie Williams, b
Oct. 31, 1924.
F' Iverson Norris Lea, b Sept. 20,
1897, died at age of five weeks.
Mary Emma Lea (7'), born Nov. 9,
1858, Liberty Miss married Rev. Robt.
N. Hall, Dec. 2, 1885, died Oct. 2, 1894,
Woodlawn, Harrison Co. Texas. Issue:
A' Rosa Hall, b Dec. 29, 1889, m
Louis Clark Brown, Jan. 19, 1907,
born March 10, 1886, druggist,
Rosedale, Miss. Issue: Rosa Lee
Brown, b Feb. 2, 1908; Maurine
Brown, b July 20, 1910.
B' Fay Hall, b March 14, 1891, d
April 17, 1926, m Franklin How-
ard Butler, McComb, Miss. Issue:
Howard Lea Butler, b 1916; Mc-
Dowell Butler; Franklin Hall
Butler, b July 4, 1923.
C' Robert N. Hall, b Feb. 17, 1893.
Address, San Francisco, Calif.
James Everett Lea (h), born July
28, 1819, Amite Co. Miss. died April
25, 1878, married Frances Powell, sister to Rachael Powell Lea, Jan. 15,
1846, born Aug. 22, 1827, d Feb. 12,
1886, Amite, Co. Miss.
From resolution adopted by Grange
No. 31 P. of H., Amite Co. Miss. we
take the following:
"Whereas the messenger of death
has again visited our midst and we are
called to mourn the loss of our highly
esteemed citizen and much beloved
Brother, James Everett Lea, who departed this life on the 25th, ult., in
the 59th year of his age, and it is
with melancholy satisfaction, and under a sacred sense of duty, that we
beg to lay a simple tribute on his
grave, to aid in honoring the memory
of one who was among the first in our
county to advocate the cause of the
Patrons of Husbandry, and who possessed so many shining virtues that
his life should be exemplified and his
memory fondly cherished, Therefore:
"Resolved, That in the death of
Brother Lea, a member of Sylvan
Grange, and for several years a delegate to this county Grange, our Order has lost one of its most zealous
and prominent supporters, one who
placed faith in God, nurtured hope,
dispensed charity, and was noted for
his fidelity, while the church and society have lost a true christian, an
honest and useful citizen, and a pure

and genial associate.
"As a husband and father, he had
but few equals, and none but those of
his household can appreciate his merit in this respect. Much of his life
was spent in adding to the comforts
and attractions of his home, for here
was the center of his purest happiness
where the music of his heart swelled
its notes in one perpetual anthem of
good-will. Unassuming in his man-
ners, cheerful in disposition, liberal
in his opinions, just in his dealings,
sincere in his attachments, manly and
generous towards all, he made many
warm friends, who, with a numerous
and devoted connection deeply mourn
his loss. It is a relief to know, however, that before his death he became
perfectly resigned to his fate, believed his sins were all forgiven, and died
in the triumphant hope of a glorious
immortality. Let his fond wife and
children, and others near and dear to
him, to whom we extend our warmest
sympathy, be consoled by this and
confidently hope that
"His pure thoughts were borne,
   Like fumes of incense o'er the
   clouds,
And wafted thence on angels' wings
   through ways
   Of light to the bright Source of
   All."
Issue:
1' Emily Jane Lea.
2' Dewitt Clinton Lea.
3' Mary Virginia Lea.
4' Rosa Frances Lea, b March 5,
1853, d Aug. 26, 1924, married
Rev. Aaron John Miller, Dec. 24,
1879, born Nov. 12, 1847, died
March 11, 1912. No issue.
5' Charles Clay Lea.
6' Ella Louisa Lea.
7' James Everett Lea.
8' Jula E. Lea.
9' Myrtis Leona Lea, b Sept. 16,
1867, d May 21, 1909, Elpaso,
Texas, married Rev. Robert W.
Merrill, b Sept. 13, 1860. Issue:
Robert Winfred Merrill, b Dec.
24, 1889, m Sept. 3, 1922, Leah
Buster, address, 910 Chester St.
Dallas, Texas; Lea Warren Merrill, b Sept. 3, 1891, m Luelah
Williams, June 1, 1916. Address,
1065 Peralta Ave., Berkeley, Cal;
Herbert Vassar Merrill, born
July 21, 1893, died December 20,
1893; Arthur Kenneth Merrill, b
Dec. 25, 1894, m Margaret Corco-

ran, June 10, 1925. Address Philadelphia; Mildred Young Merrill, b Jan. 17, 1897, m John W. Blake Sept. 1914. Address, Putnam, Texas; Edward Everett Merrill, b Oct. 10, 1900. Residence, 130 W. 12th St., Dallas, Texas; Myrtis Leona Merrill, b Aug. 4, 1903. Residence, Kerrville, Texas.

Emily Jane Lea (1'), born Jan. 15, 1847, Amite Co. Miss. died Dec. 6, 1918, McComb, Miss. married Charles Henry Otken, born Feb. 26, 1839, New Orleans, La. died Feb. 12, 1911, McComb, Miss. He was Principal Peabody Public School, Summit, Miss., 1867-77, President and founder Lea Female College, Summit, Miss. 1877-94, President McComb Female Institute, McComb, Miss. 1894-99, County Superintendent Education, Pike Co., Mississippi, to 2-12-1911.

A Tribute.

From "The Life And Character Of Charles Henry Otken," by Henry P. Hughes we take the following.

"On Sunday morning, February 12, 1911, at his home in McComb Mississippi, after a brief illness, Dr. Charles Henry Otken, distinguished as soldier, educator, minister and writer, answered the last roll call. He has passed "over the river to rest under the shade of the trees."

"Dr Otken was born in the Parish of Orleans, Louisiana, February 26, 1839. At the age of six he lost his mother, a woman of rare intellect and great force of character. The home being broken up, the boy was placed in charge of his uncle at Carrollton, where he attended school until he reached his eleventh year, when he entered a store as clerk, where he remained for five years. At the age of sixteen he was converted under the influence of Rev. Mr. Duncan, a Baptist minister, and on his suggestion soon after enrolled as a student in Mississippi College at Clinton, Miss. While in his junior year, the Civil War broke out; answering the call of patriotism, he entered the army as a private soldier. After two years of active service, while stationed at Mobile, Ala. he was ordained as a minister in the Baptist Church. During the remainder of the war he served as Chaplain of one of the regiments commanded by General M. P. Lowrey, father of Dr. W. T. Lowrey, now President of Mississippi College.

"At the close of the war, Dr. Otken located at Liberty Miss., at that time one of the most promising towns in the state. Here he was pastor of the church and teacher of the village school—at that time it not being considered the proper thing for a minister to accept money for his services.

"Moving to Summit, Miss., Dr. Otken became the intimate friend and associate of such well known men as Colonel Garland, Colonel T. R. Stockdale, and Judge Hiram Cassedy. Here in 1866, two years before the organization of the common school system, he opened the Peabody Public School, the first beneficiary in the state of the Peabody Fund.

"Recognizing the need for higher education, in 1877 Dr. Otken founded the Lea Female College, which for a number of years was a prominent institution, supplying a majority of the teachers for this portion of the state.

"In 1895 Dr Otken was chosen the first President of the McComb Female Institute, a newly organized, non-sectarian institution of McComb Miss.

"In 1903 he was elected Superintendent of Education for Pike County, Mississippi, which position he so ably filled up to the very day of his death.

"The doctor was a valuable contributor to the press . In 1895 he was awarded second honors by the Times Democrat , of New Orleans, for a thesis on "The Agricultural Crisis in the South." There were ninety-three contestants from ten Southern States, the first prize being won by Dr. Walter Maxwell, a Ph. D. of the University, of Zurich, and an A. M. of Harvard. In 1894 Dr. Otken published his most portentious work, "The Ills of the South," being a critical analysis of the operation of the Lien Law, based on personal observation. In recognition of its merit the author was invited to address an assemblage of scholars in Ottawa, Canada.

"Upon the resignation of Hon. Thos Gathwright, State Superintendent of Education, the position was tendered Dr. Otken by Governor Stone, but he chose rather to serve his own people than to yield to the allurements of political life. For a number of years he was trustee of the University of Mississippi, and of Mississippi College. He was twice honored by his Alma Mater, receiving the A. M. and

Ph. D. as honorary degrees. He was the first Vice-President of the first Mississippi Teachers' Association.

"As a minister Dr. Otken was widely known and highly esteemed. He declined numerous calls from leading churches, among them being the First Baptist Church of New Orleans. On invitation of Col. McComb, the founder of the town, he delivered in the rail road roundhouse the first sermon ever preached in McComb Miss.

"Possibly Dr. Otken's greatest effort was in behalf of prohibition. While President of Lea Female College, he secured the passage of an Act by the Legislature, forbidding the sale of liquor within five miles of the town of Summit, Miss. This was the first restriction placed upon the sale of liquor in the state. However, it was but the beginning of the battle which Dr. Otken waged with unrelenting vigor till statutory prohibition became an accomplished fact.

"Dr. Otken was buried from the First Baptist Church in McComb, the service being conduced by Rev. Theo Whitfield, ably assisted by Dr W. T. Lowrey, President of Mississippi College, whose touching address will long linger in the minds of his hearers. The body was laid to rest with Masonic ceremony in the cemetery at Summit, where a large number of friends representing three generations, were assembled to pay their last tribute of respect.

"We of this day cannot realize the condition of affairs when Dr. Otken began his labors in the pine hills of South Mississippi. The ship of state had been swept from her mooring, social and political institutions were wrecked, the doors of the University were closed, the system of free schools was not yet established. Colleges and Universities may shape the opinions and mould the sentiment of men, but here was a people standing in the dark shadow of destiny, whose thoughts and actions must be given immediate direction. A new civilization adapted to new conditions must be built upon the ruins of the old; facts not theories must engage attention.

"Again Dr. Otken answered his country's call; quiet and unassuming, with brilliant intellect, and broad perspective, with unflinching courage and unfaltering devotion, he gave of all gifts the most priceless—not money

but himself. Thru the press, from the pulpit, and on the rostrum, a true Gamaliel that he was, he proclaimed the gospel of humanity to a bewildered people, filled their hearts with a new hope and pointed them to higher ideals and nobler purposes.

"For more than forty years the intellect and the genius which dared in public print to match the philosophy of Zurich and the logic of Harvard expended itself in behalf of the people of his community.

"His labors were not in vain. Thruout the commonwealth of Mississippi, teachers, lawyers, statesmen, yeomen, all, proudly bear his mark; while a purer, nobler motherhood softly sings his praise in the ear of a rising generation.

"The real measure of a man's greatness is the service and sacrifice he has rendered in humanity's cause; with this as a standard, we solemnly declare there is none more worthy than Charles Henry Otken. He was true; true to his God that he worshipped, true to his country that he loved, and true to his fellowman, whom he served."

A Tribute.

"On Friday morning, December 6th, 1918, the gentle, noble spirit of Mrs. Emily J. Lea Otken entered into its Eternal rest.

It was a beautiful and tranquil life which ended in the early dawn of Friday morning. A life not full of shining deeds, but one from which eminated gentleness, patience and sweet unselfishness. The usefulness of her life was measured by the happiness she scattered along her pathway, and the pure example her life impressed. Noble in the gentle purposes of her sex, refined in thought and pure in its expression, this was a life which typified in its even course the sweet and tender mission of a woman-to minister, to cheer, to elevate and to point the way by good deeds and a triumphant faith, to heaven.

Like a weaver's shuttle have slipped by the years which made up her earthly pilgrimage, and yet, each day was filled with deeds of kindness and acts of love that shall live when we have passed away. For after all it is the life we live that counts for most. No grandeur of eloquence or beauty of thought can paint with words that which in life is truest and best, for life is the index of actions that speak louder than words, and eloquence loses its charm when we attempt to portray the elements of such a character as hers. Such souls do not die. The tenement of clay enveloping the spark of life may lie cold and still in death, but that which made her a noble, useful woman and her life a benediction and a blessing to mankind, will live on forever.

Her life was the embodiment of the highest virtues of true womanhood—Consecrated, pure and true—none knew her but to love her. Unselfish and loyal, hers was a life of service, and thus throughout Life's Day, she lived and wrought among us, until at eventide she heard the chimes of Eternal Peace and her gentle spirit passed into the realms of everlasting life.

By loving friends, the sleeping form was borne to Summit, Miss., and her mortal body was laid to rest close beside the loved ones who had gone before, beneath a mound of fragrant flowers, loving tributes from devoted friends and sorrowing relatives, but her soul on bright wings of Promise has entered the Heavenly portals and awaits us Over There."

Their children are:

A' Mary Frances Otken, m Rev. Benjamin Franklin Lewis, address, 320 Alexander Ave., Jackson, Miss. Issue: Benjamin Franklin Lewis, died 1895; Evelyn Lewis; Robert Leroy Lewis; married Mary Rite; Arthur Beverly Lewis

B' Katie Henrietta Otken, d June 2, 1892,, Summit, Miss.

A Tribute.

"Like a clap of thunder from a clear sky, death has suddenly stricken down one of the noblest, purest beings in our midst, as you have seen the storm uproot the straightest, most beautiful tree of the forest. The sunny head that the mother so loved is resting beneath the green sod; the scintiliating brain that compelled all to admire who felt its power will nevermore be restless or disturbed; the heart that knew no selfishness, but beat for others only, is still forever, but the name of Katie H. Otken is not dead, and futurity cannot lay it under the dust, for it is linked with her life and influence, and the good she did is eternal.

"The vacancy she left must remain.

None can fill it, and it must ever remind us of the work of her hands and heart. She lived for home, for humanity and for God. If, in future years, mothers point their daughters back to her life and tell them there was one who did her every duty faithfully—one who, in the purity of her nature, would not consent to lower tone of true womanhood by countenancing anything that was trivial, low or base—one who never uttered weak or careless sentiments, but one whose language showed a bright pure mind; and if the girls of the coming years shall, by the inspiration of her name, live true, womanly and useful lives, can we not say that her life has accomplished glorious results?

It is hardly needful for me to repeat the history of her life it is too well known.

She was educated in her father's school, Lea Female College, where she has been teaching since her graduation. She was converted and united with the Baptist church, in Summit, at the age of sixteen. She died June 2, 1892.

These are the bare records, but those who knew her can read much between the lines—much that tells of her love for God, for her fellow-man, for her State and her love and anxiety for Summit.

She, no doubt, found misplaced sharps and flats in musical exercises, and, perhaps, some sharps may have jarred upon her life, and some flats may have disappointed or wearied her but now she has found that perfect music with no discord, whose pure notes shall resound through all the spaces of eternity on harps touched by angel hands, for she knew the Lord and loved the Son of God, and she now joins in the symphonies of praise that roll and reverberate around the great White Throne.

Her life speaks this to you, girls of Summit, and of Mississippi: Make your kindred happier, make the world better, guard your speech at all times and live each day as if it were your last.

We miss the bright star that has set to rise no more, and we search the Heavens in vain for its counterpart, but we find nothing there save clouds now, for we are passing under the rod. But God is merciful, and that rod shall be lifted and we shall meet

her some great day, when human life
and human mysteries shall be no
more.
"Blessed be God, for He created death,
And death is rest and peace,
And giveth life that nevermore shall
Cease."

A FRIEND.

In Memory of Katie H. Otken.

Bring here your fairest flowers, O,
my friends!
And heap them high above this peace-
ful bed,
Fairer than any flower our lovely
dead,
Sweeter than any flower the life which
ends.

Give me a lily for these folded
hands,
Give me a chaplet for this marble
brow;
Give her your full appreciation
now—
Perhaps, in heavenly lands, she un-
derstands!

A sound of mourning comes from
every room.
Twice twenty girls lament their un-
told loss.
Teachers and friends are bowed beneath the cross;
The news spreads, the town is filled
with gloom.

A dimpled child once played about
these grounds,
With dancing eyes and tangled flaxen
curls,
She ruled us even then, we little
girls,
Thronged after her in all her merry
rounds.

The years passed by, I saw a woman
bright,
Ruling with gentle sway a host of
girls,
Above that lofty brow her baby
curls
Still rested like a diadem of light.

Her voice was grand! It was both soft
and deep.
She could command, and she could
gently woo:
Her noble accent thrilled me through
and through
Like some great organ tone suppres-
sed and sweet.

The aloe blooms once in an hundred
years.
Our family tree at last burst into
flower!
But while we gazed thereon, mysteri-
ous power
Chilled the fair flower and dimmed our
gaze with tears.

Are those indeed, the brave who rush
to strife,
And fight with sword, and face the
cannon's breath.
The coward flies into the arms of
death—
The hero grapples with the foes of
life.

No warrior ever bore a braver
heart
Into the very thick of battle
smoke,
Than my dead friend, hers was a
heart of oak,
In life's great strife, she played a
hero's part.

Ye soldiers of the Cross, fight on
'till death,
Nor fear the allied legions which
oppose,
Our fallen comrade conquered all her
foes,
And lived and died triumphant in the
faith.

O, many millioned man! Can all thy
gold
Outweigh one gracious deed of this
brave life.
Is there no high regard for noble
strife,
Can characters like hers be bought
and sold!

A soul like hers is worth a thousand
spheres
Rolled into one, and sown with dia-
monds bright,
Strewed with fair flowers, and bathed
in fadeless light,
Flashing with splendor through
eternal years.

O, lovely friend! I know that thou art
free
From every pain and crowned with
glory bright,
I would not call thee back into the
night,
I only wish that I were there with
thee!

By Maggie Tate Lea.

C' Emily Lea Otken, d 1873, Summit, Miss.

D' Infant son died 1876.

E' Perla Clay Otken.

F' Charles Henry Otken, M. D. Asst. Camp Surgeon, Camp Leach Washington, D. C. World War.

G' Lea Gidiere Otken.

H' Lois Bridgeforth Otken.

I' Frances Powell Otken.

J' Luther Boyce Otken, M. D. Capt Base Hospital 22 Bordeaux, France, World War, m Frances Mae Hodges. Issue Emily Jane Otken, Greenwood, Miss; Mary Frances Otken.

Dewitt Clinton Lea (2'), born Jan. 3, 1849, Amite Co. Miss. died Jan. 20, 1918, Hattiesburg, Miss. m Catherine T. Strickland, on Feb. 29, 1872, died June 27, 1922, Hattiesburg, Miss. Issue:

A' James S. Lea, m Ruby Hosmer. No issue, but an adopted daughter, Rosa Lea.

B' Lila Burton Lea, b 1875, d Dec. 4, 1912, m William R. Easterling. No issue.

C' Samuel C. Lea, m Charlena Tessie Norwood, June 1, 1911, married second, Annie Galvanie, Aug. 10, 1911. Issue by first marriage: Ethlyn Lea. Issue by second marriage: Annette Lea.

D' Laurence M. Lea, unmarried. Hattiesburg, Miss.

E' Emmett W. Lea, d March 30, 1910, m and had issue.

F' Hollis Lea, Jacksonville, Fla.

G' Dewitt Clinton Lea, m April 23, 1923, Hattie Pearl Langford, Hattiesburg, Miss.

H' Ruby Marguerite Lea, m Walter Thomas Herren, Canton, Miss.

Mary Virginia Lea (3'), born March 15, 1851, died May 11, 1910, married William Atkinson, born July 1, 1847, Columbia, Miss., died 1909, New Orleans, La. Member Forrest Cavalry War of 1861-65. Issue:

A' Howard Atkinson, died in youth

B' Mary Lea Atkinson, died in youth.

C' William J. Atkinson, m Gertrude Creswell, in 1913, Address, Mobile, Ala.

D' Luther See Atkinson, Los Angeles, Cal.

E' Hilda L. Atkinson, m Charles Carroll Miller, Nov. 1912. Address, Meridian, Miss. Issue: 1 son, borned 1925.

F' Edward C. Atkinson.

Charles Clay Lea, (5'), born Aug. 19, 1855. died May 23, 1913, Magnolia, Miss., married Jan. 29, 1884, Laura Lee Hanes. Issue:

A' Thomas J. Hanes Lea, m Oct. 2, 1913, Mrs. Ethel Losey, Bogalusa, La.

B' Charles Clay Lea.

C' Lois Lea.

D' Alice Lea, m Robert Hardison, Birmingham, Ala., July 21, 1920.

E' Florence Lea' m Robert H. Russel Aug. 29, 1919, Holyoke, Mass. Issue: Dorothy Lea Russell, born Aug. 1920; Jean Florence Russell, born Jan. 2, 1925.

F' Hampton Lea, Magnolia, Miss.

Ella Louisa Lea (6'), born April 27, 1858, married S. B. Webb. Address Osyka, Miss. Issue:

A' Myrtle Webb.

B' Herbert Webb, m Harritt Brigham, Sept. 19, 1917. Issue: Josephine Webb; William Brigham Webb.

C' Julia Webb.

D' Hollis Webb, m Susie Varnado, Magnolia, Miss. Issue: Sue Evelyn Webb.

E' Loyette Lucile Webb.

F' Allie Webb.

James Everett Lea (7'), born Jan. 16, 1861, married Maggie Tate, Jan. 2, 1887, born 1867, died April 22, 1893. Married second, Elizabeth Westmoreland, Clarksdale, Miss. Issue:

A' James Everett Lea, Washington, D. C.

B' Myrtis Lea, m Dr. Benjamin Lampton Crawford, Dec. 29, 1909, Tylertown, Miss. Issue: Dorothy Lea Crawford; Walter W. Crawford; Benjamin Lampton Crawford; Everett Howell Crawford.

C' Alma Clay Lea, m Albert McCrary, Jan. 1, 1913, Philadelphia, Tenn. Issue: Hannah Margaret McCrary, b Dec. 9, 1919.

D' Maggie Lea, b April 4, 1893, d Jan. 20, 1895. Issue by second marriage.

E' Mary Atkinson Lea, m John J. Duke, June2, 1917, address, Memphis, Tenn. Issue: Mary Lea Duke.

Jula E. Lea (8'), b Dec. 6, 1863, m Sidney C. Lenoir, Greenwood, Miss., M. D. Issue:

A' Sidney C. Lenoir— Residence, Memphis, Tenn.

B' Lucille Loyette Lenoir, m Aug. 23, 1924, Mayes Lively Berry, of Crockett, Texas. Issue: Beth Berry.

C' Alton Lenoir.

Iverson Green Lea (i), born Aug. 16, 1822, died April 16, 1864, married Lemanda Elizabeth Martin, born Mch. 3, 1833, died Oct. 26, 1901. After the death of I. G. Lea, Lemanda E. Lea, married James N. Little. Issue:

1' Warren Eugene Lea, b Sept. 19, 1855, m Jan. 1, 1879, Lucy McKnight, b April 1, 1861, d July 8, 1900. Married sec., Rosa Cockerham, April 24, 1901. Address, McComb, Miss. Issue: Pigot Hamilton Lea, b Dec. 10, 1879, m Annie Allen, 1037 S. 31st St., Birmingham, Ala; Curtis Byron Lea, b Dec. 24, 1881, m Myrtis Newman, Hattiesburg, Miss; Myrtis Alma Lea, b April 28, 1884; Nancy Amanda Lea, b Dec. 31, 1885, d May 31, 1904; Grover Cleveland Lea, b April 5, 1888, d Sept. 22, 1900; Mamy Florence Lea, b Dec. 19, 1890, m Needham Yarbrough, Dec. 12, 1914; Julia Lea, m Clyde E. Smith, Aug. 21, 1921, address, Franklinton, La; Iverson Green Lea; Luther Lea; Warren Eugene Lea.

2' Sallie Lucinda Lea.

3' Erastus Clay Lea.

4' Lou Ella Graves Lea, b May 27, 1861, d March 20, 1919, unmarried

Sallie Lucinda Lea (2'), was born Aug. 1, 1857, married W. G. Cockerham, Dec. 25, 1878. Issue:

A' Howard Lea Cockerham, b 1881 m Evelyn Spinks. Address, Gunnison, Miss. Issue: Howard Lea Cockerham; Odessa Cockerham; Doris Cockerham; Frances Cockerham; Evelyn Cockerham.

B' Maude Elizabeth Cockerham, b 1883, m Forest White. Issue: Wexler White; Davis White; Sidney White; Edwin White; Cecil White; Raymond White.

C' James Ellison Cockerham, b Feb. 2, 1886, m Freddie Pell. Issue: Katherine Cockerham, New Orleans, La.

D' Iverson Grady Cockerham, b Dec. 14, 1890, d Oct. 11, 1922, unmarried.

E' Mable Alma Cockerham, b Dec. 29, 1892, m Howard Brashears. Issue: Ottie Lea Brashears, Gunnison, Miss; Clara Brashears; Howard Brashears.

Erastus Clay Lea (3'), was bron May 17, 1859, married Ludie Powell, Nov. 11, 1880, born April 15, 1860, d March 1, 1882. Married second, Willie Davis, Nov. 14, 1887, born May 31, 1861, died May 17, 1916. Married third, Mrs. Dora Sandifer, Jan. 21, 1917. Issue by third marriage:

A' Erastus Clay Lea, b Dec. 18,, 1917, Osyka, Miss.

B' Norma E. Lea, b Aug. 11, 1919, Osyka, Miss.

(By the Editor)

This chapter would not be complete without mention of Matthew Clay who was a son of Charles Clay and Martha Green Clay, and is identified as (H) in his line.

MATTHEW CLAY (5th Line 3H) CHAPTER 2.

Matthew Clay, son of Charles Clay and Martha Green, is said to have had a splendid personality. His eyes and hair were dark. He married a Miss Williams first, and second a Widow Saunders. His children, all by his first wife, were:

a. Mary Clay, lost her life in the destruction of the Richmond Theatre by fire in 1811.

b. Amanda Clay, was an invalid, but m George P. Kezee, said to have been a man of great sagacity.

c. Joseph Clay.

d. Matthew Clay.

Joseph Clay (c) did not resemble his father, having blue eyes and light hair. He married Margaret Bowen in East Tennessee. She was living as late as 1887. Children were:

1' Amanda Clay, m Norman Cherrie and had two children who died unmarried.

2' Clement C. Clay, m the only daughter of Rev. Phillip Tuggle. He moved to California where he became quite wealthy. He had two children in 1887. Was Major in Civil War and had two children who died in infancy.

Matthew Clay (d) moved to Madison county, Alabama, in 1816. A few years later he moved to Lawrence county, Ala., where he built a double pen log house. He married Frances A. Saunders. Their children were:

1' Thomas F. Clay.

2' Matthew Clay.

Thomas F. Clay (1') was born in Memphis, Tenn.

1825, died 1856. His wife was Miss Caledonia Anne Oliver, and was a daughter of John Oliver, who married Ruth Ann Weedon. Children were:

A' Alice Clay, who m Wheeler Watson.

B' John Oliver Clay, m Fannie Wilson Lawler 1884.

C' Fannie Lou Clay, m Henry D. Watson in 1881.

D' Child who died in infancy.

Matthew Clay III, (2') second son of matthew Clay and Frances A. Clay, was born February, 1827. He married Mary Harrison, daughter of Isham Harrison.

CHAPTER IV.
David Clay 5th line 1Aa.

David Clay, who is identified as 1Aa in Chapter II, after acting as guide as recounted in affidavit of Hutchinson, soon entered the War of the Revolution. North Carolina was hard pressed by the British and called on Virginia for aid. David Clay had several relatives in the Old North State and was one of the many native Virginians who responded to the distress call of their sister state. He enlisted in Evan's Company, 10th Regiment, N. C. Line (Col. Abraham Shepard, Capts. Hall and Kornegay. Hathaway's Register-Vol. 11, No. 4, page 580, also Colonial Records of North Carolina, Vol. 15, page 1038.)

His widow applied for and received a pension. After the close of the Revolution, David Clay came to Georgia where he drew land as follows: 1786, 200 acres in Washington County, Georgia, Book KKK, page 384; 1794, 196 acres in Washington County, Georgia, Book LLLL, page 593; Office Secretary of State, Atlanta, Georgia.

September 26, 1792, he was married to Eve Harden in Warren County, Georgia. (See Harden Hints and Genealogies.) He later acquired land in Wilkinson County, Georgia, but retained a plantation in each county until his death and spent a portion of his time on each plantation. He was an industrious, thorough-going man and accumulated considerable property before his death, which occurred in Wilkinson County, Georgia, about 1818. He was buried at the Passmore Cemetery which lies between the place where Mrs. Susie Gilbert lived, 1925, and the Peyton Clay cemetery. The only other people buried in this cemetery are said to have been Passmore and his seven wives. Children of David Clay and Eve Harden Clay were:

1' Lewis Clay
2' Adam Clay
3' Pearce Clay
4' Sarah Clay
5' Robert Clay
6' Peyton Clay
7' Edmund B. Clay
8' Mahany Clay

Tradition says that two of the above were twins and I am under the impression that they were Pearce and Robert, but am not sure.

Lewis Clay's Line of Descent
5th Line 1Aa1'.

Lewis Clay, No. 1' above, was either the oldest or next to the oldest of the children. He is not mentioned in the Pension Record of Eve Clay, for the reason that he opposed her application for pension on the ground that she had remarried, and was not entitled to a pension. Notes of Beheathland Clay Rigsby are as follows:

"Judith Clay died September 24, 1872, Lewis Clay, December 24, 1874. Lewis Clay was eighty years old, Judith Clay was 74. My grandfather was David Clay. He had a plantation in Washington County (Ga.) and one in Wilkinson County (Ga.) He was one eyed, one eye having been put out by the Tories. He was a soldier in the Revolutionary War. He married Eve Harden. After Grandfather's death, she married a man, I think, by the name of Pearson, but am not sure. That kept her from getting a pension which she was often talking about and trying to get." (She evidently never knew that Her grandmother, Eve, secured her pension.)

"My grandfather had a brother. I don't know his name. He had a son Pearce who lived in Washington County." (She evidently meant her great-grandfather.)

"There were two Clays who came from England, they have descended from them. I am not certain about their names. It seems their names were John and Lewis, but not certain."

"They lived ten miles South of Milledgeville. Their farms were between Commissioner's Creek and Oconee

River. I have been in the house that
my mother was married in. It was
a large log house. They were
wealthy."

The public records of Washington
County and Wilkinson County have
long since been destroyed by fire, as
well as the old family Bibles of many
members of the Clay family, and with
but few exceptions we must rely on
tradition. For this reason, I will
elaborate to some extent upon Lewis
Clay, so as to establish the probative
value of the traditions coming down
through him and his daughter as preserved in her notes.

He was probably born in Washington County, Georgia, 1783 or 1784. His
father in the next few years moved
with him to Wilkinson County, Georgia, from territory adjacent to Buffalo Creek to that adjacent to Commissioners Creek on opposite sides of the
Oconee River. Here he grew up and
received a common school education.
(I now have in my possession a partial set of accounts kept by him at
Dawson, Georgia, before and during
the Civil War.) He was living near
Milledgeville, in 1818, which was then
the Capitol of Georgia, when Early,
Irwin and Appling Counties were
opened for settlement and secured a
position with surveyors and helped
to survey the Counties and Lots. Upon one occasion the party of surveyors
were encamped on a ridge between a
lake or lagoon and a stream of water.
During the night while they were
asleep an alligator passing from one
body of water to the other, ran over
the face of one of the party and gave
him such a fright that he sat up all
the rest of the night.

His surveying over, he returned to
Wilkinson County, Georgia, where he
married Judith Jones, December 20,
1820. The Rev. James Clay performing the ceremony. (See Jones Genealogies.)

Lewis Clay lived in Wilkinson Coun-
ty until his oldest child had married
and his youngest child was born.
While there the Legislature of the
State named him and his brother-in-
law, James M. Hatcher, together with
Ratliff Brown, John Meredith and
Daniel Price, trustees of Liberty Hill
Academy. (Georgia Laws 1836, page
10.)

While living in Wilkinson County
he owned a large herd of cattle that

ranged in the Oconee River Valley, except for a few winter months. It was
Lewis Clay's custom to keep these
cows gentle by feeding them salt at
stated intervals, placing the salt on
a "lick log" and calling the cows "Co
wench, Co wench, salt, salt, salt!" The
cows, hearing the call, would come for
the salt. Reeves, a neighbor, was
plowing one day when Clay began
calling cows in the river bottom. Of
magnificient physique and powerful
voice, the call "Co wench, co wench,
co wench, salt, salt, salt!" heard by
Reeves in the distance became "Oh
Reeves, Oh Reeves, Oh Reeves, help,
help, help!" Reeves dropped his plow
and dashed to the call, stopping at intervals to listen when the cry for help
became more distinct, and urgent, it
appeared to him at each stop, until he
came to the hill dipping down to the
river. Here he stopped, almost exhausted to get his final directions. He
then recognized the voice and call,
and used the expression that has become tradition in the Clay family, because of its originality and because it
illustrates the power of the Clay voice,
"Goddurn Lewis Clay, Hell ought to
have him for a blowing horn."

While a resident of Wilkinson County he accomodated a friend by endors-
ing a note for several thousand dollars, which he had to pay, and as a
result of this he became financially
embarrassed.

Remembering now, the country
which he had assisted in surveying,
and hearing glowing accounts of its
fertility, he moved from Wilkinson
County to near Americus, Georgia,
where he lived only a short time before selecting a choice tract of land in
Lee County (Now Terrell County)
which he purchased and moved to it,
soon clearing and settling a splendid
farm. Here he and his wife became
active in their religious efforts. They
belonged to the Missionary Baptist
Church, while most of the other residents were of the Primitive or Hard-
shell branch of the denomination. They
soon gathered around them a few people of their belief and with the help
of their children and their neighbor's
children, started a Sabbath School.

The Legislature soon created Terrell County, and out of this beginning
came the first Missionary Baptist
Church constituted in Terrell County.
So much opposition developed against

1. Mrs. Sidney J. Jones
3. Col. Henry Clay, Sr. (Ky.)
   Clay Crest and Arms, Centre.
2. Mrs. Beheathland Clay Rigsby and
   Grandson Lewis Wilton Rigsby.
4 Lewis Clay.

the new church, which was called in derision, Clay's Church, that eventually after the material had been hauled to build the church (the church having been constituted under a brush arbor) that some one set fire to it and burned the lumber. They persisted, however, and the church was finally built. After the railroad came and Dawson grew up, the church was moved there and is now the First Baptist Church of Dawson.

Lewis Clay lived in Dawson until the Civil War, when he moved to Decatur County, Georgia, where he lived for only a few years, moving again to Thomas County, Georgia, where he lived for only about one year. This last year of his life is important from our view point. He lived about six miles north of Cairo, on the place now known as the Bennett Place and on the east side of Little Tired Creek. No sign of the settlement now exists. He cultivated a farm at this place in the eightieth year of his life. Warren Clay, then a widower with one child, lived on the place and helped with the farm. Milly Hester, nee Clay, a widow with several children and her mother Sallie Clay, nee Griffin, widow of John Clay, a son of Pearce Clay of Washington County, cooked and kept house for him. He was living on this place when taken with his last illness and Warren Clay brought him to my father's where he died. Milly Hester is the only one now living of those mentioned and she is nearly a hundred years old. I have consulted her frequently and she says that her father and Lewis Clay were cousins. Children of Lewis Clay and Judith Jones Clay were:

A' Lucy Clay Etheridge
B' Hardin Clay
C' Sarah Frances Clay Wadsworth
D' John Benjamin Clay
E' Lucius Augustus Clay
F' Peyton Clay
G' Ella Fair Clay Kilpatrick
H' Beheathland Luvinia Clay Rigsby

Lucy Cla yEtheridge 5th line 1Aa1'A'
Lucy Cla, A' above, married Harrison F. Etheridge, March 12, 1839, in Wilkinson County, Georgia, the marriage ceremony having been performed by James M. Hatcher, J. P.. Children were:

a' Rebecca Collier, who was twice married, first to James M. Kilpatrick, second to Bishop. A

great-granddaughter, Agnes Rebecca Bishop, married her cousin, Thomas Henry Clay, son of John Benjamin Clay, above.
b' Lucy Carolyn, b Oct. 7, 1844.
c' Joel H. b June 6, 1846.
d' James Lewis, b Nov. 30, 1847.
e' Milly Judie, b Aug. 12, 1848.
f' Shelley F. b Jan. 24, 1855.
g' Robert T. b June 30, 1856.
h' Martha E. b July 7, 1857.
i' Nicy C. b Nov. 13, 1858.
j' Edmund A. b May 30, 1859.

Edmund A. Etheridge, j' above, married Ella Nora Asberry Morgan, daughter of Asberry Morgan and his wife, Anna B. (Brown) Morgan and to them were born children as follows:

1" Anna Clay Etheridge, married a Houston and lives at Damascus, Ga.
2" Ruby Etheridge, married a Walker and lives at Elmodel, Ga.
3" Wheeler A. Etheridge, P. O. Hicox, Ga.
4" Cecil M. Etheridge, P. O. Center Hill, Fla.
5" Eula A. Etheridge, married Hammill, dead, son Herschell, P. O. Milford, Ga.
6" Leila Etheridge, married Wallace Boon Griffin, June 14, 1908, in Baker County, Georgia, the Rev. L. L. Lyons performing the ceremony. Mrs. Griffin and Mrs. Clay have supplied me with the above information. Mrs. Griffin's children are:
A" Grace Ione, b June 2, 1909.
B" Cordelia, b March 7, 1912.
C" Edmond Wallace, b Nov. 1916.
D" Rubye Abbiegail, b Aug. 3, 1920.

Hardin Clay, B' above, married Lucy Haden, moved to Arkansas before the Civil War. Was a soldier in the Confederate army, was captured and died in a hospital at Little Rock. Children:
a' Edmond Clay
b' Melissa Clay
c' Martha Clay
d' Robert Clay
e' James Clay
f' John Clay
g' Teresa Clay

Some of the children went to Texas. I have given notice through Arkansas papers, but failed to locate any member of the family.

Sarah Frances Clay (called Frankie) born Nov. 22, 1828, in Wilkinson County, Georgia, married William Hiram Wadsworth, but date of marriage unknown. With the exception of my mother she was best known to me of all the members of the family and she was a frequent visitor in our home. Her husband was familiarly known to the people throughout the section where he lived as Uncle Hiram. He was a soldier in the Civil War, serving at St. Marks, Fla. He was a son of Daniel Wadsworth and Lucy (Freeman) Wadsworth, of Bibb County, Georgia, and was of Scotch descent. Daniel Wadsworth was caught in the swindle in connection with the Yazoo fraud, went west and never returned to his family, no one knowing what finally became of him. Other children were: Eli, who was the father of Burton Wadsworth, of Madison County, Florida, long a State Senator and a member of the Constitutional Convention of Florida; Melsh, Scott, Sepp, Joseph, moved to Texas, William died near Macon, leaving children, and Margaret married a Hayes and moved to Cedar Keys, Florida. Children of Sarah Frances Clay Wadsworth and W. H. Wadsworth were:

a' Lewis Daniel, b July 23, 1847, d in Civil War.

b' Francis Marion.

c' Salema Luvinia, b Dec. 13, 1850, m first Nelson, second, Wm. Connell, brother of Rebecca who married John H. Wadsworth.

d' Judith Lucindy, b April 3, 1853.

e' John Hiram Wadsworth.

f' William Hardin Wadsworth, m Sallie Kilpatrick, lives at Girard, Ala., wife dead.

g' Lucy Ann Beheathland Wadsworth.

h' Charles Eliot, b March 21, 1866.

Francis Marion Wadsworth, b' above was born March 11, 1849, married first, Charity Ferrell, aunt of D. K. Ferrell and daughter of Jabez Ferrell, one of the first jurors of Thomas County Superior Court, and second, Mrs. Susie Carlisle, a widow who is the mother of Ira Carlisle, present State Senator from this District. Children by first marriage:

1" Robert Marion Wadsworth, only child, born Nov. 2, 1872, married Mollie Johnson, Oct. 9, 1897. She is dead, her father was named James Johnson and her mother

Rebecca Johnson. Before her marriage she was Rebecca.............. .... "Bob" as everybody calls him, is a Baptist, Mason and Democrat. Children:

A" Hiram Burton Wadsworth.

B" James Marion Wadsworth, b July 29, 1900.

C" Olif Charity Wadsworth Hudson.

D" J. T. Wadsworth, b Aug. 10, 1903.

E" R. D. Wadsworth, b Aug. 6, 1906.

F" B. C. Wadsworth, b March 18, 1908.

G" Follis Jewell Wadsworth, b Dec. 31, 1910.

H" Mary Gladis Wadsworth, b Jan. 31, 1912.

Hiram Burton Wadsworth, A" above, born Oct. 4, 1898, Res. 2222 N. W. 5th Ave., Miami, Fla. Married Jan. 28, 1923, Lila Fay Dekle, and to them has been born one child.

a" Virgil Marion Wadsworth, b July 4, 1924.

Olif Charity Wadsworth, C" above, born March 29, 1902, married Norman T. Hudson April 10, 1919 and to them have been born two children.

a" James Elwood, b Feb. 17, 1920.

b" Susie Elaine, b Aug. 22, 1922.

John Hiram Wadsworth, identified as e' above, married Rebecca Connell, who was a daughter of Peter Connell and his wife. A sister married Daniel Ponder and was mother of the Ponders of the Northwestern part of the co. John and wife live at Pelham, Ga., and have children as follows:

1" Underwood

2" Ammie, deceased.

3" William

4" Daniel

5" Lewis

6" Lizzie

7" Minnie

8" Charlie, who is in newspaper work at Albany, Ga.

Lucy Ann Beheathland Wadsworth, g' above, married D. K. Ferrell and to them have been born children as follows:

1' Luther R. Ferrell, res. Pelham, Ga.

2' Naomi Ferrell, m R. L. Levar, res. Cairo, Ga.

3' Shelton E. Ferrell, m Cora Taylor, who is the daughter of John H. Taylor and his wife, Mrs. Howell Talyor. John H. Taylor was a son of Rev. John Taylor and his wife Sally (Parker) Taylor who are mentioned on page 16 of the Sketch of the Rigsbys of Georgia, published July 4, 1925.

4' Micajah Ferrell, married first Della Gainous and second Lula Barrett. Both of these families are descended from some of the early settlers of Grady County. Lula Barrett, a daughter of James Barrett and his wife Mrs. Mary (McClelland) Barrett.

Just a word here about this Barrett family before proceeding. The oldest one of the children, Molly Barrett, married Henry J. Willis and they had numerous children, one of which is B. L. Willis, the present Tax Collector of Grady County. Another, Guy Willis, has charge of the street force and the sanitation work for the City of Cairo. Another, Alfred Willis, married Lilla Ferrell, sister of Micajah Ferrell above.

5' Lilla Ferrell, m Alfred Willis.
6' Ithael Ferrell, unmarried.
7' Kedar M. Ferrell, m a Lane.
8' Watson Ferrel, m Essie Tomlinson, a daughter of Rev. A. J. Tomlinson, res. Cairo, Ga.
9' Lucy Ferrell, unmarried.
10' Judson Ferrell, m in Baker County, Ga.

John Benjamin Clay, son of Lewis Clay and Judith Jones Clay, (Identified as D' above) born Dec. 2, 1829, in Wilkinson County, Georgia, was converted and joined the Baptist Church at an early date, and receiving a call to the ministry, spent the last few years of his life in active ministry of the Baptist Church. He was sent by his association as a missionary to the territory further south, where he served during the war and for some time after the war, organizing and constituting churches, being largely instrumental in establishing the Baptist denomination so strongly in this section of the state. He married Feb. 6, 1855, his wife before her marriage was Appy Eliza Bass (b July 20, 1837), who was a daughter of Abel Bass of Randolph County, Georgia, and his wife who before her marriage was Miss Cherrie Pope. The children of this Bass family were named as follows: William Bass, Deacon in the Baptist Church; James Calvin Bass, a Baptist minister; Bennett Bass, Benago Bass, the last two being active

members of the Baptist Church; the girls were named Jane Bass, Jennetty Bass, Matilda Bass, Annie Bass, who married Peyton Clay, and Appy Eliza Bass, above. Children of John Benjamin Clay, above, and his wife were:

a' Cherrie Annie Clay, m Henry H. Etheridge, Dec. 30, 1875, in Randolph County, Ga. Born May 26, 1856.
b' Endora Fannie Clay
c' Mary Esther Clay
d' Emma Eliza Clay, born Jan. 20, 1861, d Dec. 2, 1889.
e' Samuel Clay, b Nov. 15, 1862, d Dec. 16, 1862.
f' William B. Clay, b Nov. 3, 1863, d Oct. 7, 1884.
g' Laura J. Clay
h' John Bunyan Clay, b Sept. 3, 1867, d Oct. 14, 1868.
i' Joseph S. Clay
j' Thomas Henry Clay
k' Ella Ophelia Clay

Endora Fannie Clay (Identified as b' above) born June 2, 1858, in Calhoun County, Georgia, married Aug. 19, 1890, George Sydney Commander in Terrell County, Georgia. Children:
1" Fannie May Commander, b Aug. 25, 1891, married June 22, 1911, J. A. Tooley, one adopted girl, Margaret May.
2" George Otis Commander
3" Nancy Clay Commander, b Aug. 23, 1898, P. O. Graves Station, Georgia, married Jan. 18, 1920, Emmett S. Randall, Dawson, Ga., one child, William Emmett Randall, b Oct. 27, 1920.

Mary Esther Clay (Identified as c' above) b Jan. 2, 1860, Calhoun County, Post Office, Parrot, Ga., married John Thomas Thornton, Randolph County, Georgia, Nov. 1, 1883, children:
1" Shelly Clay Thornton, b Sept. 8, 1884, m Miss Alma Watkins, Dawson, Georgia, April 23, 1905, resides 722 S. 20th St. Birmingham, Ala. One child, Jennett Mary Thornton, b Feb. 21, 1908.
2" Lucy Mae Thornton, b Dec. 10, 1890, d Aug. 4, 1891.
3" John Thomas Thornton, Jr., b Feb. 16, 1900, m April 4, 1919 Miss Jimmie Horn, at residence of bride's parents. Resides at Parrott, Ga. Children: J. T. Thornton, Jr., being the third J. T. Thornton in line, b July 31, 1921, and Willie James Thornton, b March 6, 1924.

60

Laure J. Clay (Identified as g'
above) born July 20, 1865, in Decatur
County, Georgia, married Jan. 1, 1884
to Willim L. Miller, in Dawson, Ga.,
where the family has resided ever
since. Children:
1" Maud Kathleen Miller, b Nov.
28, 1884, married June 10, 1900,
William Franklin Watkins, Terrell County, Ga. Residence 313
Price St., Savannah, Ga. Children: Laura Lucille Watkins, b
June 23, 1901; William Alfred, b
June 14, 1906, Alma Marie, b Feb.
2, 1904.
2" Ufa Lee Miller, b March 24,
1887, married Sept. 16, 1906, Willie Dean Grubbs. Children: William Edward Grubbs, b Aug. 9,
1907, James Wade Grubbs, b
March 24, 1909.
3" Russia Iva Miller, b May 7,
1889, married June 7, 1908, Steve
David Fulford res. Dawson, Ga.
Children: Ivey Stephens Fulford,
b May 25, 1909, Jim Henry Fulford, b Jan. 2, 1911, William G.
Fulford, b Sept. 26, 1913, Annie
Laura Fulford, b Oct. 26, 1915,
Mary Amanda Fulford, b Oct. 6,
1917, Thomas Ed. Fulford, b July
22, 1920.
4" Jim Clay Miller, b April 11,
1892, married Nov. 24, 1912, resides at Dawson, Ga., wife before
her marriage Edna Kelley, marriage occuring in Randolph County, Ga. Children: Harry Miller,
b July 25, 1917, Anderson Miller,
b July 31, 1922.
5" Annie Will Miller, b April 20,
1897, married April 25, 1917,
Warren Williams McGraw, resides
in Dawson, Ga.
Joseph Sidney Clay (Identified as
i' above) born April 6, 1871, res. 609
Main St., Dawson, Ga. Dec. 3, 1893
he married Miss Annie Evarts. He
was engaged in the plumbing and elec-
trical business until a few years ago
when, because of his health he was
forced to abandom that business.
Children are:
1" Zuleita Clay, b Oct. 18, 1894, m
W. R. Melton, July 6, 1918. One
child, William Robert Melton, b
March 23, 1920. Res. Cuthbert,
Ga.
2" Marvin Cornelius Clay, b June
17, 1905.
3" Mary Frances Clay, b Nov. 7,
1908.

4" Clyde Anderson Clay, b April
10, 1913.
5" Joseph Lamar Clay, b Dec. 29,
1901, d May 1, 1902.
Thomas Henry Clay (Identified as
k' above) b Jan. 2, 1874, married
Agnes Rebecca Bishop, great-granddaughter of Lucy Clay Etheridge, Aug
8, 1897, res. Shellman, Ga., where he
operates a plumbing business and is
also engaged in farming. Both Thomas Henry and Joseph Sydney are
Methodists, although their father was
a Baptist minister, brought about I
understand, through the neglect of the
Baptists towards their father's orphans after his death and the fact that
their Methodist friends occupied the
position that they had a right to expect their father's church to occupy.
Children:
1" Howard Bunyan Clay, b Feb.
20, 1904.
2" Thomas Merrell Clay, deceased,
Nov. 11, 1908.
3" John Paul Clay, b Oct. 2, 1910.
Ella Ophelia Clay, (Identified as 1'
above) b Sept. 26, 1875, m A. C. Howard, July 6, 1897, resides in Madison,
Fla. Children:
1" Alfred Sidney Howard, b June
3, 1898, m Mary S. Clay, Aug 18,
1918, res. Madison, Fla. Children: Mabel, b May 13, 1919, d
May 13, 1919, Robert Alfred, b
April 16, 1920, Ray Edwin, b
Dec. 16, 1921.
2" Ruth Howard, b July 24, 1905,
d March 16, 1912.
3" Thomas Watson Howard, b
Nov. 20, 1906.
4" Harry Oliver Howard, b March
12, 1908.
5" Ralph Richard Howard, b Oct.
3, 1909.
6" Phillip Maxwell Howard, b Sept
20, 1912.
7" Norman Gahagan Howard, b
Feb. 4, 1914.
Lucius Augustus Clay (Identified
as E' above) born in Wilkinson County, Ga., Jan. 22, 1832 served in Civil
War, and he was wounded at Gettys-
burg, married Isabelle M. Stegall and
lived near Cairo until his death, which
occurred June 17, 1909, he being
buried at Long Branch cemetery, third
grave north from monument of Adella
White. Children:
A" Elizabeth J. Clay.
B" Mary L. Clay, b June 17, 1858.
C" Augustus M. Clay, b Jan. 3,

1862, d July 11, 1871.

D" Robert E. Clay.

E" John Lewis Clay, b Dec. 6, 1867, d April 14, 1887.

F" Alice B. Clay, b June 26, 1869, d July 11, 1871.

G" Martha Frances Clay, b Nov. 25, 1871.

H" Adella Clayton, Clay b July 25 1874, m William White and died without issue.

Elizabeth J. Clay (Identified as A" above) married Benjamin R. Harrison, Jan. 29, 1875, and died Nov. 23, 1912. Her husband still resides on the old homestead near Cairo, one of the largest and finest farms in the county, with his family of children with two exceptions living around him on choice farms of their own. Mr. Harrison is a descendant of one of the first settlers of this section, Benjamin Harrison, who was a soldier in the war of 1812 and from whom Mr. Harrison received his name. He has numerous relatives thruout this section and a very creditable biography of his life is contained in the History of Savannah and South Georgia, by Colonel Harden of Savannah. Children:

a" Martha Harrison, b Oct. 9, 1875, d Dec. 1, 1875.

b" Mary Malinda Harrison.

c" Leona J. Harrison.

d" W. Robert Harrison.

e" Benjamin F. Harrison.

f" Evie E. Harrison.

g" Jackson L. Harrison, b Nov. 27, 1890, d Oct. 24, 1905 as a result of an accident.

h" Gussie Belle Harrison, b April 8, 1894, d Nov. 28, 1894.

i" Eula Jane Harrison.

j" Alexis Smith Harrison, b April 14, 1897, d Sept. 13, 1897.

k" Otis Harrison, b July 28, 1899, d Sept. 22, 1899.

Martha Malinda (Linnie) Harrison, (b" above) born Aug. 22, 1877, Thomas County, Ga., married Seaborn H. Sutton, Dec. 3, 1896, res. Cairo, Ga. Mr. Sutton owns and operates a large farm about three miles from Cairo and is one of the reliable and progressive farmers of Grady county. Children:

1'" Mattie Bell, b Dec. 25, 1897, m Arthur Perry Singletary, July 16, 1916. He was a son of Edward Singletary and a brother of

Charley Singletary who married Fannie Clay. His uncle, John R. Singletary, is the present Ordinary of Grady County. Mr. Singletary died July 7, 1921, leaving two children, Horace Wayne, born Jan. 5, 1920, and Myrtle Katyline, b May 20, 1917, d July 26, 1918.

2'" Paul H., b Sept. 14, 1899, d May 7, 1900.

3'" John Benjamin, b Jan. 5, 1904.

4'" Seaborn Augustus, b March 2, 1907.

5'" Edna Jane, b Nov. 2, 1911.

Leona J. Harrison (c"above) born March 8, 1880, res. Miami, Fla., married July 5, 1900, Charles William Connally. Children:

1'" Ruth Foster Connally, b Sept. 4, 1901, m J. S. Chastain, Oct. 30, 1923.

2'" Mary Elizabeth Connally, b Feb. 4, 1904, m Ray Spence Singletary, June 24, 1924.

3'" Charlie Roberta Connally, b Sept. 29, 1907.

4'" William Clower Connally, b Nov. 17, 1913.

W. Robert Harrison, (d' above) b Dec. 23, 1882, married Brownie Wright May 28, 1915. He is a prosperous farmer living about two miles from Cairo. His wife was a Tenessee girl and prominently related in that state, her sister, Alma, married a brother of W. Robert. Children are: Mabel Harrison, b June 12, 1916 and Robert Leland Harrison, b Oct. 4, 1918.

Benjamin F. Harrison, e" above, b Feb. 24, 1885, married Alma Wright, April 18, 1913. His wife is a sister of the wife of W. R. Harrison. Only one child, Alton Wright, b Sept. 19, 1915. Mr. Harrison is occupying the old homestead with his family and his father lives with him. Mr. Harrison gives promise of keeping alive the progressive spirit of thrift and industry of his father.

Evie E. Harrison, (f" above) b Oct. 26, 1886, married Levy J. Harper, Feb. 3, 1907, and they reside near Mr. Sutton, who married Linnie Harrison. Mr. Harper is a son of Levy Harper, now deceased many years. His mother before her marriage was Miss Missouri West, both the Harper and West families being among the early settlers of what is now Grady County. Mr. Harper is a thrifty, industrious and prosperous farmer and his home setting back from the road with a native growth of pine in its virgin condition between the house and the highway never fails to attract comment from the passer-by. Children: Paul Herman Harper, b Nov. 14, 1914 and Hazel Virginia, b July 22, 1922.

Eula Jane Harrison, i" above, b Jan. 24, 1896, married Marion A. Barber, Feb. 3, 1918. They now reside in Miami, Fla. Mr. Barber is the second son of the Hon. W. D. Barber, a former representative in the Legislature, from Grady County. No issue.

Robert Edward Clay, D" above, born July 3, 1864, married Sarah Malinda Singletary, daughter of Harry Singletary. Mrs. Clay is now living at Thomasville, Ga. She is descended from one of the earliest settlers and hers is one of the largest connections in Grady County. Mr. Clay died Jan. 28, 1918, and is buried at the Cook Cemetery between Cairo and Pine Park. Children:

a" Florence Madel, b March 27, 1890, m B. C. Blanton, Jan. 30, 1910. Resides in Thomasville, Ga., where Mr. Blanton is engaged in the mercantile business. Children: Leslie Romell Blanton, b Nov. 14, 1910, Daniel Clayton Blanton, b Dec. 14, 1913, Edith Mae Blanton, b April 24, 1916, Robert Edward Blanton, b May 1, 1920, Jess William Blanton, b May 26, 1923.

b" Foster Goodman Clay, b June 22, 1890, married Mrs. Ida M. Brinson, Aug. 12, 1923. Resides in Thomasville, engaged in mercantile business. No issue.

c" Lilla Estelle Clay, b June 7, 1892, married Earl Stewart, March 1, 1914. Mr. Stewart has been engaged in farming until recently, but has moved to Florida. Children: Carlton Eugene Stewart, b Feb. 10, 1915, Sarah Agnes Stewart, b Aug. 10, 1918, d Oct. 7, 1919, Edna Odene Stewart, b Dec. 10, 1921.

d" Crawford Clay, deceased.

e" Harvey Harrison Clay, recently married a Miss Knight.

f" Nepsy Jane Clay. A trained nurse.

g" Robert Earnest, in U. S. Navy.

h" Millie Corene, deceased.

Martha Frances Clay (Identified as G" above) b Nov. 25, 1871, Miller County, Ga., married Charlie T. Singletary, Dec. 23, 1896, moving to Florida soon after marriage where they raised a family. Mr. Singletary has been dead for several years and Mrs. Singletary now resides in Tampa. Children:

1'" Ruby Arline Singletary, b March 29, 1898, married Joseph E. Davis, March 15, 1916. Residence Tampa, Fla. Children: Essie E. Davis, b April 22, 1917, Joseph Price Davis, b June 1, 1920, Charles Henry Davis, b Aug. 11, 1922, Frances Pauline Davis, b March 18, 1925.

2'" Russell O. Singletary, b April 29, 1900, married Irene Dubose, resides at Tampa, Fla.

3'" Rosa Ethel Singletary, b Dec. 9, 1901, married Lewis Bates, Feb. 10, 1923. Residence Bartow, Fla.

4'" Pauline Singletary, b June 27, 1907.

5'" Edward Augustus Singletary, b Sept. 7, 1911, d Dec. 11, 1913.

Peyton Clay, son of Lewis Clay and Judith Jones Clay and identified by F' was born in Wilkinson County, Ga., June 23, 1835, and died at Ashford, Ala., June 2, 1913. He was married three times, first to Miss Annie Bass, sister of the wife of John B. Clay, second to Miss Mattie Knowles and third to Miss Orpha Jane Newton. Mr. Clay was a soldier of the Confederacy, he was capture at Cumberland Gap, and served twenty-one months as a prisoner of war at Camp Douglas, Chicago, Ill. He was a very pious man and a strict member of the church, first joining the Baptist church, but later in life affiliating with the Christian church. By his first wife he had the following children:

a' William Dennis, b Nov. 10, 1857, never married, now deceased.

b' Martha Hassie, b Jan 15, 1856, died without issue.

c' Mary Della Clay.

d' Robert Henry Clay.

e' Edmund Peyton Clay.

f' Elton Abel Clay, b April 1870, died without issue.

g' Minnie Clay.

h' Sarah Frances Clay, died in infancy.

By second wife, Docie Clay, married Lovelace Grant, died leaving issue.

Mary Della Clay, c' above, born Nov. 27, 1860, died Jan. 13, 1892, and was buried at New Hope Church. Married Josie Brown in Calhoun County, Ga. Children:

1" Mary Brown, b Jan. 10, 1876, in Mississippi, lives now in Randolph County, Ga. P. O. Cuthbert, Ga. Married J. M. Mayfield, July 30, 1898. Children: Eva Mayfield, b Oct. 19, 1899, Myrtle Mayfield, b April 9, 1910, Elton Mayfield, b Oct. 4, 1907, Louise Mayfield, b Nov. 28, 1915.

2" Richard Elton Brown, b Feb. 11, 1885, Como, Miss., married Miss Natalie Birdie Barnes, June 30, 1912, and live at Thomasville, Ga. Mr. Brown has been for a number of years superintendent of the Thomas County system of highways and also of a large farm operated by the county. Children are Edward Ralph Brown, b May 24, 1913, Natalie Carolyn Brown, b Feb. 11, 1915, Joe Barnes Brown (Joseph) b Jan. 11, 1917, Richard Elton Brown, Jr., b March 26, 1919.

Eva Mayfield, daughter of J. M. Mayfield and Mary Brown Mayfield, married a Ragan, April 21, 1915, and has two children, Nettie Roselind, b Nov. 25, 1917, and James William Ragan, b July 19, 1922.

Robert Clay, d' above, b Randolph County, Ga. April 15, 1866, married Rachel Culbreth, Dec. 18, 1887, and resides in Cuthbert, Ga., R. F. D. No. 3. Children:

1" Infant, died Feb. 17, 1891.

2" Annie Clay.

3" Mary Clay, b Nov. 25, 1895, married her cousin, Sydney Howard. (See John B. Clay's line.)

Annie Clay, 2" above, born July 4, 1892, in Randolph County, Ga., married Earl Worthy, May 1, 1910. P. O. Edison, Ga. Children: Lucile Worthy, b Dec. 18, 1911, Estelle Worthy, b May 16, 1916, Ella Worthy, b May 16, 1916, (Twins), Frances Worthy, b Aug. 13, 1919.

Edward Peyton Clay, e' above, born May 9, 1867, in Randolph County, Ga. Married July 5, 1891, Miss Willie Louisa Edwards, marriage occuring in Newton Dale County, Alabama. Mrs. Clay is a member of the Edwards family of whom there has been so much newspaper talk in regard to an estate valued at several billion dollars in the City of New York.

She is a daughter of James S. Edwards and Sarah Ann (Kelly) Edwards. James S. Edwards was a son of Isaac Ovelton Edwards and Frances (Wyche) Edwards. Isaac Ovelton Edwards was a son of Thomas Edwards who was a brother of the Robert Edwards of New York who immigrated to America from Edinburgh, Scotland. Sarah Ann Kelly, mentioned above, was a daughter of Ezekiel Kelly and Elizabeth (Smith) Kelly.

Mr. Clay was for a long time engaged in farming, but in 1906 he was employed by Thomas County as Superintendent of Roads, which position he held for several years. He gave the training in road contruction to his nephew and retired. Later he accepted the same position with Colquitt County, but finally retired and is now living in Thomasville, where he owns some valuable property, including pecan groves and a young pear orchard. He is a member of the Baptist Church, a Mason, and a Democrat in politics. He and his wife have only 3 children ,all boys, and bear the distinction of having given all three to the World's War and having received them back into the family circle. The boys are:

1" Arvah Edward Clay, b April 14,1892, Newton, Ala. First held a position with Peninsula & Occidental Steamship Co., next with a wholesale business in Thomasville, later with a construction company in Bainbridge, Ga. From here he entered the World War, where he obtained the rank of Lieutenant and was one of the last to be discharged. After securing his discharge he accepted a position with the Phillipine Government as Assistant Purchasing Agent, resigning to go with the Y. W. C. A. now being in the auditing department in New York City. Married Miss Pattie Edith Gandy, daughter of Thomas Gandy of Thomasville. Dec. 29, 1920. No issue. Address 246 Summitt Ave., Jersey City, N. J.

2" J. P. Clay, b July 26, 1895, Thomas County, Ga., married Allimae Bowen of Thomasville, May 9,1919. He enlisted in the famous Chatham Artillery and did his bit in France, ranking as Sergeant. He and his wife reside at Thomasville, Ga., and have one living child, Mildred Clay, b April 9, 1920. They have lost one infant.

3" T. H. Clay, b May 25, 1897, married Miss Edith Rice, daughter of Charles Henry Rice, County School Superintendent, Thomas County, Ga., and his wife Annie Lou McKinnon Rice. He also did his bit in France, being in the Motor Transport Service. Res. Thomasville, Ga. No issue.

Minnie Clay, g' above, born May 27, 1876, in Randolph County, Ga., married W. A. Webb, April 16, 1891, and resides at Columbia, Alabama. Children:

1" Florence Webb, b March 17, 1892, m arried Roy Culbreth, March 1, 1914, Houston County, Ala. Res. Headland, Ala. Children are, Ethel Culbreth, b Nov. 28, 1914, Margaret Culbreth, b Sept. 28, 1917, Sarah Elizabeth Culbreth, b Oct. 24, 1919, and Florence Kathrine Culbreth, b Feb. 6, 1925.

2" Etta Mae Webb, b Dec. 18, 1894, Houston County, Ala., married Jesse A. Culbreth, Feb. 20, 1915, res. Columbia, Ala. Children: Minnie Maud Culbreth, b May 19, 1916, Jesse Earl Culbreth, b June 23, 1920, Rayward Bill Culbreth, b Dec. 17, 1921 and Robert Elton Culbreth, b July 9, 1924.

3" Verna Webb, b Sept. 28, 1896, married Mamie Lois Carrol, res. Quitman, Ga.

4" Lottie Webb, b Sept. 18, 1898, married Quinn C. Goodman, Oct. 20, 1921. P. O. Columbia, Ala. Children, Mary Quinn Goodman, b Oct. 12, 1922, James Webb Goodman, b Dec. 16, 1923.

5" Bill Webb, b Dec. 30, 1899.

6" Jessie Webb, b Sept. 14, 1902, d May 9, 1903.

Ella Fair Clay (Identified as G' above) daughter of Lewis Clay and Judith Jones Clay, married Andrew Wade Kilpatrick, who was a son of Andrew Wade Kilpatrick and Jennie (Scott) Kilpatrick. Andrew Wade Kilpatrick had a brother, James, who founded the little city of Sasser, Terrell County, Ga. A sister married John Bennett and they were the ancestors of the Bennett Family of Grady County, Ga. Andrew Wade Kilpatrick enlisted as a private in Company H, 64th Regiment, Georgia Infantry, September 18, 1863; was severely wounded at Crater near Petersburg, Va., July 30, 1864. Surrendered at Appomatox, Va., April 9, 1865. The family lived near Dawson, Ga., until the death of the wife which occurred about 1884, but do not have dates. Children:

a' Henrietta Kilpatrick.

b' Almeda Kilpatrick.

c' Taliaferro Kilpatrick.

d' James Kilpatrick.

e' Sallie Kilpatrick.

f' Mollie Kilpatrick.

g' Laura Kilpatrick, b Nov. 22, 1870, d Feb. 28, 1901. Married J. H. Brady. No issue.

h' Cora Kilpatrick, b Dec. 13, 1872, married Albert N. Davis, formerly a builder and contractor, now circulation manager of paper at Moultrie, Ga.

i' Viola Kilpatrick.

Henrietta Kilpatrick, a' above, married A. P. Bragg, children are:

1" William A. Bragg, b July 25, 1877, married Susie Henderson, reside at Meigs, Ga. Children. Pearl Bragg, b Aug. 29, 1901 Earl Bragg, b Dec. 11, 1904, Andrew Bragg, b Jan. 18, 1907, Jim Bragg, b Dec. 31, 1909, Ruby Bragg, b July 19, 1913, Katielou Bragg, b March 25, 1916, Emory Bragg, b Oct. 1, 1919, Robert Bragg, b June 8, 1921, Susie Bragg, b Oct. 8, 1923.

2" Thomas Wade Bragg, b July 25, 1871, married Sarah Josie Justice, Aug. 20, 1900. Res. Tarpon Springs, Fla. Children are: Andrew Lit, b Dec. 4, 1901, Leland Thomas, b May 7, 1905, Herbert, b Feb. 25, 1908, Wallace, b Sept. 14, 1911, Essie May, b May 2, 1914, Sara, b Dec. 24, 1917, Glorean, b Nov. 10, 1920.

Almeda Kilpatrick, (Identified as b' above) married James A. Miller, whose first wife was also a Kilpatrick, and whose son, William, married Laura Clay, daughter of the Rev. John B. Clay. I have no dates. Both dead. Children:

A" Dora Miller. No Further information.

B" Lloyd Douglas Miller, was a soldier in the Spanish-American

65

War, never returned and family was never able to learn his fate. Simply one of the great army of missing.

C" Ellie Miller.

D" Lillie Miller, married Benjamin Overstreet. No issue.

E" Mary Lizzie Miller.

F" Walter Miller, never married.

Ellie Pearl Miller, (C" above) b May 10, 1884, married Guy A. Cox, July 2, 1903. Res. Tifton, Ga. Children are: L. Frank Cox, b Feb. 2, 1905, Lillie Pearl Cox, b Nov. 19, 1906, Henry Miller Cox, b Sept. 17, 1908, Robert Anderson Cox, b Feb. 8, 1910, Mary Helen Cox, b Aug. 21, 1912, Guy A. Cox, Jr., b Feb. 12, 1916, Marcus Lafayette Cox, b March 10, 1921.

Mary Elizabeth Miller, (Identified as E" above) b June 11, 1892, Terrell County, Ga., married Dr. Marus L. Webb and reside at Mayodan, Rockingham, N. C., marriage was at Albany, Dougherty County, Georgia, April 30, 1911. No issue.

Taliaferro Kilpatrick, (c' above) m Jennie Waller at Dawson, Terrell County, Ga. Both are dead. Children:

a" James Wade Kilpatrick, b Feb. 3, 1890, married Ida George Dean, Manchester, Ga., May 4, 1924. Res. Atlanta, Ga. No issue.

b" Sara Lou Kilpatrick, b March 19, 1894, res. Georgia Experiment Station, Experiment, Georgia.

c" William B. Kilpatrick. Deceased.

d" George Kilpatrick, unmarried. Res. Atlanta, Ga.

e" Vera Kilpatrick, Atlanta, Ga.

f" Ralph Kilpatrick, Atlanta, Ga.

g" Mary Ella Kilpatrick, b Nov. 27, 1905, married L. Curtis Reed, Sept. 30, 1922. Res. Atlanta, Ga. No issue.

h" Oscar Kilpatrick. Res. Atlanta, Ga.

James Kilpatrick, (Identified as d' above) married twice, first Julia Pickett, second Lizzie Passmore, children by first wife, Lee Roy (Deceased), Kate, Bessie and Dave. No information in regard to second wife.

Sallie Kilpatrick (Identified as e' above) married W. H. Wadsworth, her first cousin. She is dead, leaving several children. No further information.

Mollie Kilpatrick, f' above, married Charles Fletcher Suggs, who was accidentally killed in Florida, several years ago. His widow lives at Manchester, Ga. Children are:

1" Annie May, who married Jesse Suggs, her cousin.

2" Carl Hammett Suggs, Atlanta, Ga.

3" Catherine Floyd Suggs, married Lee Martin and lives at Port Arthur, Texas.

4" Kate Suggs, b Nov. 27, 1898, Tifton, Ga., married Charles Leffew, May 4, 1915. Res. Atlanta, Ga. Children are: Grace Leffew, b June 27, 1916, and Charles Winston Leffew, Jr., b May 9, 1918.

Viola Kilpatrick, youngest child of Ella Fair (Clay) Kilpatrick, married Jefferson J. Stokes, who has been dead for some years, now. Mrs. Stokes has never married again. She has one child, Edward Wade, and they live at Manchester, Ga.

This brings us now to Beheathland, Luvinia Clay, the youngest child of Lewis Clay and Judith Jones Clay, and who is identified as H' in this Sketch. She was the mother of the writer and her line is continued in Sketch of the "Rigsbys of Georgia" published July 4, 1925, and a short biography will be appended to this Sketch, which see.

5th Line 1Aa2'

Adam Clay, son of David Clay and Eve (Harden) Clay, is identified as 2' under David Clay's line, married probably in Washington County, but his wife's name is not known. He was a hard working farmer who resided in that section for some time. Tradition says that he stammered. He and his wife moved to Jackson county, Florida, and nothing further is known of his family.

5th Line 1Aa3'

Pearce Clay, a son of David Clay and Eve (Harden) Clay, and who is identified as 3' under this line, evidently married and raised a family, but I have been unable to discover any descendants.

5th Line 1Aa4'

Sarah Clay, daughter of David Clay and Eve (Harden) Clay, and identified as 4' in this line, married James M. Hatcher, and their children were:

A' Green Hatcher.

B' John Hatcher.

C' Robert Hatcher.

D' Edward Hatcher.

E' Sallie Hatcher Shinholster Daniels.

F' Obedience Hatcher Jones. (See

Jones Genealogies.)

G' Mahany Hatcher Shepherd.

H' Harriet Hatcher Pace.

Note: Tradition assigns to James M. Hatcher, brothers and sisters as follows: Nancy Hatcher, married a Hancock of Crawford County, Ga., Betsey Hatcher married John Tharp, of Crawford county; Robert Hatcher, who lived in Crawford county, and Reuben Hatcher, who died in Wilkinson county, Ga.

From "The King's Mountain Men" by White, page 213, I find that Flayl Nicholas, was a son of Nancy Hatcher, a cousin to Henry Clay. This Nancy Hatcher must have been a daughter or granddaughter of William Clay, who was the father of Mitchell Clay. Several Hatchers resided in Bedford county, Virginia, before 1800 and their wills are recorded in that county. Major John Hatcher was a resident of Wilkinson county, Georgia. He and Dr. John Taliaferro were members of the Mt. Nebo Church. John Hatcher's wife is supposed to have been named Mary Brady and the known children are: John, Elizabeth, Robert, James and William Green.

5th Line 1Aa5'

Robert Clay, son of David Clay and Eve (Harden) Clay, and who is identified as 5' under this line, was guardian for Peyton Clay and Edmund B. Clay after the death of David Clay, according to the records of Wilkinson county, Georgia, which were preserved from fire.

5th Line 1Aa6'

Peyton Clay, son of David Clay and Eve (Harden) Clay, and who is identified as 6' of this line, was born December 25, 1800, in either Washington or Wilkinson county, Ga. On December 19, 1830, was married to Nancy M. Jones, a sister of Judith Jones, who married Lewis Clay. She was born December 31, 1805, died September 19, 1851. Peyton Clay was a man of unusual business ability and appears to have been the only son of David Clay, who died in Wilkinson county, Ga. He was a large slave holder, one of the stock holders in the construction of the Central Railroad through that section of the state, and the largest land owner in Wilkinson county at the time of his death, which occurred on the 11th day of November, 1880, in Wilkinson county, Ga.

He and his wife are both buried in the Peyton Clay Cemetery, northwest of Toomsboro and their graves are marked by a handsome monument. Children:

A' Lawrence W. Clay.

B' Martha Clay.

C' David Melton Clay.

D' Edmond William Clay.

E' Narcissa Clay.

F' Sarah Clay.

Lawrence W. Clay, A' above, was born Jan. 2, 1832, in Wilkinson county, Georgia, married Miss Jane Jackson, and to them were born children as follows:

a' Henry Clay, b Oct. 10, 1850, d Oct. 1, 1898. He never married, and lived and died in Wilkinson county, where he was a well known character.

b' Ella F. Clay, b Sept. 1, 1858, married Elwood G. Robinson. A daughter, Mrs. Mae Robison Lawson, lives in Dublin, Ga., and is prominent in D. A. R. Circles.

Martha Clay, C' above, born April 9, 1834, married Stephen Lord and resided in Wilkinson County, Ga. Children were:

a' Mary Hall Lord.

b' Talullah (Annie) Lord.

c' Peyton Clay Lord.

d' Narcissa Lord.

e' Mattie Lord.

f' William Lord.

g' Charles Lord.

h' Dock Lord.

Mattie (Martha) Lord, born Aug. 9, 1863, m James W. Vaughn, (born Nov. 14, 1855) Dec. 10, 1879. She died Jan. 24th 1898. Children are:

1" Bartow Vaughn.

2" Nelle Cora Vaughn.

3" James W. Vaughn, Jr.

4" Nannie Elizabeth Vaughn.

5" Martha Vaughn.

6" Mary Bell Vaughn.

7" Lena Inez Vaughn.

8" Jeffie Jeynelle Vaughn.

Bartow Vaughn, 1" above, married Jennie Tippens. Children are:

A" Lena Mae.

B" Mattie Lou.

C" Katherine.

Nellie Cora Vaughn, 2" above, married Eulice Beck Joiner. Children are:

A" Baby Nele Joiner (dead).

B" Martha Frances.

James W. Vaughn, Jr., married

Pearl .... Their children are:
A" Elizabeth.
B" Jeynelle.
C" Jim, Jr.
D" Nellie.

Nannie Elizabeth Vaughn, 4" above, born at Toomsboro, Ga., Oct. 14, 1887, married Edgar Eugene Steed, Toomsboro, Oct. 21, 1906. Residence 368 Moreland Ave., Atlanta, Ga. Mr. Steed is a son of Virgil Augustus Seed, of Talbotton, Ga. Mr. E. E. Steed has been twice married. He was married first to Olive Bryant. To them one child was born, Virgil Samuel Steed, born Jan. 18, 1904. Mr. Steed's first wife died 1904. Children by second wife are:
A" James Eugene Steed, b Oct. 10, 1907, d Nov. 27, 1907.
B" Joseph Elizabeth Steed, b May 31, 1909.

. Martha Vaughn, 5" above, was born at Toomsboro, June 26, 1890, married Fred Kendall Johnson. Residence 400 N. W. 17th Ave., Miami, Fla. Mr. Johnson's parents were John S. and Sarah Johnson, maternal grandparents, Purdy and Elizabeth Price, paternal grandparents, Jacob and Martha Johnson. All lived near Elizabethtown, N. C. Mr. Johnson is a W. O. W. and member of the Methodist Church and Mrs. Johnson of the Christian Church. Children:
A" Frederick Vaughn Johnson, b Aug. 14, 1911.
B" Martha Elizabeth Johnson, b Mar. 8, 1919; fifth in line to be named Martha.

Lena Inez Vaughn, identified as 7" above, was educated at Bessie Tift College, Forsyth, Ga., and was married to Dr. Harry Reeves Oliver, October 1, 1921. Dr. Oliver is a Physician and associate Professor of Clinical Pathology of Stanford University; a Sigma Xi and Phi Beta Pi. He served during the war as Major, Medical Corps, United States Army, and until 1923, when he resigned from service. Dr. Oliver is the son of John Meredith Oliver, who was born in Virginia and was a soldier in the Confederate Army. His wife Mary Llewelyn Trible, was born in Missouri.
Residence 2749 Union St., San Francisco, Cal. No Issue.
Jeffie Jeynelle Vaughn, 8" above,

married Howard Buford Nash. One child.
A" Dorothy Jeynelle.
David Melton Clay, identified as C' above, was born Dec. 25, 1837, married Fannie O'Bannon. Children:
a' Fannie Clay.
b' David Clay.
c' Velpo Clay.

Edmund William Clay, D' above, .was born Jan. 29, 1839, died June 4, 1898. His wife before her marriage was Miss Elizabeth Stevens, who was born Nov. 25, 1845, and died Jan. 9, 1923. They both are buried in Toomsboro, Ga. Mrs. Clay kept a hotel in Toomsboro, Ga., for many years after the death of her husband and was well known to the general travelling public. They left no children.

Narcissa Clay, E' above, married William M. Carswell. Children:
a' Leila Carswell was married to Weems J. Wood, who was a son of Benjamin A. Wood and his wife, who before her marriage was Miss Annie B. Darby, whose mother before her marriage was Miss Coatney Irwin, a sister of Gov. J. I. Irwin, of Washington county Ga. Children were: Leon, Judson, Lela Thelma, Robin Hudson and William Carswell.
b' William B. Carswell, born and reared in Wilkinson county, Ga., and was partially educated at Old Talmadge Institute, at Irwinton, Ga. The family moved to Pulaski, Ga., near Cochran, where he finished his literary education. He graduated in medicine at John Hopkins University, in 1885. He located at Cochran where he did a very lucrative practice. He married Miss Ida Overby, of Cochran, Ga., who was the daughter of W. H. Overby, who came from Virginia.
P. C. Carswell, is a resident of Macon, where he is connected with the Virginia-Carolina Chemical Co.
Sarah Clay, F' above, was born Jan. 7, 1845, at Toomsboro, Ga., died Nov. 13, 1923, was buried at Cochran, Ga. She married Thomas Jefferson Jordan, Feb. 11, 1864. He was born Oct. ,8 1836, died Nov. 25, 1891, marriage occurred in Wilkinson county, Ga. Children:
a' Minnie Jordan.
b' Evelyn Jordan.
c' Jeffie Jordan.
Minnie, a' above, married Emmett

Lee Coleman, June 3, 1885. He was born July 30, 1881. They have one child, Emmett Lee Coleman, Jr., born March 18, 1885, married Mary Laetitie Kelley, Oct. 30, 1918. Res. Barnesville, Ga.

Evelyn Jordan, b' above, was born Feb. 22, 1865, married Evan Holmes, Jan. 1890, d Oct. 1st following.

Jeffie Jordan, c' above, was born March 25, 1885, married Thomas Wilmore Fisher, Oct. 26, 1906. Children: Sarah Elizabeth Fisher, born July 23, 1907; Joseph Jordan Fisher, born April 3, 1909; Thomas Wilmore Fisher, born Nov. 28, 1913; Minnie Fisher, born Nov. 9, 1918.

5th Line 1Aa7'

Edmund B. Clay, 7' above, was evidently the youngest son of David Clay and Eve (Harden) Clay. (Records of Wilkinson County show that Robert Clay, as his guardian, paid tuition to his teacher, David S. Pearce Query. Was he a relative?) He married Sallie or Sarah Jones, a daughter of John Lawrence Jones and Lucy Taliaferro Jones, who was a sister of Judith Jones, who married Lewis Clay, to Nancy Jones, who married Peyton Clay, and to Richard Jones, who married Obedience Hatcher, a granddaughter of David Clay and Eve (Harden) Clay.

Edmund Clay moved to Lee County, Ga., together with Lewis Clay, where he died, leaving children as follows:

A' David Clay.
B' John W. Clay.
C' Nanny Clay.

The administration of the estate of Edmund B. Clay was begun in Lee county, Ga., but was finally disposed of in Terrell county, after Terrell county was made from territory embraced in Lee county.

David Henry Clay, identified as A' above, was born in Wilkinson county, Ga., April 1, 1841, and died Dec. 16, 1904, in Decatur county, Ga., and was buried in Durham cemetery situated in the Northwestern part of the county. He married in 1876, Mrs. Guest, who was the widow of James Guest. Mrs. Guest before her marriage was Miss Martha Jane Fiveash, a daughter of John Fiveash and his wife, Nanny (Knight) Fiveash. David Henry Clay was a member of the Missionary Baptist Church, a Master Mason, and was wounded in the Confederate service. Their children were:

a' Edmund Fiveash Clay, b Feb. 14, 1877, m Roberta Lane. Res. West Frostproof, Fla. Children: David Hay Clay, b June 14, 1916, and Earl Fiveash Clay, b June 12, 1918.

b' Cora Estelle Clay, b Sept. 16, 1878, m James B. Lane, Jan. 10, 1904, res. Brinson, Ga.

c' Nancy Sarah Clay, b Oct. 30, 1883, m Homer Powell. Mrs. Powell is deceased, but her husband lives near Brinson, Ga.

d' Julia Petronia Clay, died quite young, Sept. 23, 1880.

John W. Clay, identified as B' above, married twice, first to Gusta Ann Powell, a sister of Jesse Powell, who married Nanny Clay, second a Mrs. Helms.

Just a word, as to the Powells here. The Powells who have married so often into the Clay family appear to have been descended from John Powell and Martha (Wall) Powell, who lived in Terrell county, Ga. They evidently came from Washington county into Lee county, before Terrell county was created. John Powell was a son of William Powell who immigrated from England to America. We have no record of children of John W. Clay by his second wife, but children by his first marriage were:

a' Amanda Clay, m John Holder, both dead.

b' Edmund Clay.

c' James B. Clay.

d' and e' Beulah and Lula Clay, twins.

f' Nannie Clay.

g' Thomas Clay.

h' David Clay.

i' Leila Clay.

This family moved to Texas sometime in the 80's, where Mr. Clay was stung by some kind of an insect, from which he died.

Nanny Clay, identified as C' above, was born Feb. 9, 1843, died 1920, married first, Charles Haynes, Feb. 1864, second, Jesse H. Powell, 1868. By her first husband she had one child, Salley Haynes, who married E. S. Perry, now deceased. Mrs. Perry resided in Bainbridge, Ga., until recently when she married a second time. By her second husband she had children as follows:

a W. G. Powell.

b Mrs. J. B. Donalson, Cyrene, Ga.

c Mrs. E. Rich, Bainbridge, Ga.

d Mrs. E. G. Rich, deceased.

e Mr. J. T. Powell, Brinson, Ga.

f Mrs. A. J. Rich, Bainbridge, Ga.

g Mrs. W. W. Lane, Jacksonville, Fla.

h Mrs. P. D. Rich, Bainbridge, Ga.

i Johnnie Powell, deceased.

j Mrs. W. C. Simms, Bainbridge, Ga.

k Mrs. J. B. L. Barber, Bainbridge, Ga.

Mahany Clay, identified as 8' above, the youngest child of David Clay and Eve (Harden) Clay, evidently married Thomas H. Wynn. She was for a long time unknown to the other descendants. The following records from the Court of Ordinary of Wilkinson county, Georgia, which by chance was saved from the many fires, established her relationship. It being of general interest as giving an example of a bride's trousseau of that time, is given in full.

Page 29, Book of Returns, 1818-28.

"Rec'd of Adam Harden, guardian for Mahany Clay, formerly minorof David Clay, dec'd, now my wife, payment in full for her legacy of the estate of the said David Clay, dec'd. Dec. 30, 1822.

Signed
Thomas H. Wynn."

Test,
Solomon Worrill, Clk.
.... ******* ***** ....
* * * * * * * * * * *

Page 52, Book of Returns, 1818-28.

"The expenditures of the Estate of Mahany Clay, minor of David Clay, dec'd for the year 1821. By Robt. Clay, bot of Fanandet Adkinson & Co.

1 fine drest Straw Bonnett $13.00

1 fine Canton Crepe Shawl 10.00

1 pr. Stockings 1.00, 1 Trunk 5.00 .... 6.00

4 yd. dimity 2.00, 1 parasol 7.00 9.00

1 pr. Shoes 1.50, 2 yds. Book Muslin 2.00 .... 3.50

1 Side Comb 75c, 1 pr. silk Gloves, 75c, 1 belt 50c 2.00

5 yards Muslin 62½c, 1 tucking comb 1.00 ....4.12½

1 Large Shawl 1.50, 1 Blk Crepe Dress 9.00 .... 10.50

1 Yd. Satin 1.50 .... 1.50

Jan. 1st, 1821. Sundrie Articles $79.50
Adam Harden.

Sworn to and subscribed, Jan. 1st, 1821.

S. Worrill, C. O. "

It appears that the above was her trousseau. The total cost is not given, but appears to have been $139.12½, and indicates well the condition of the family's finances and position.

———— ———— ————

PEARCE CLAY AND SOME DESCENDANTS.

SENATOR A. S. CLAY'S LINE.

CHAPTER 5.

Pearce Clay, son of William Clay, an uncle of David Clay, was probably born in Henrico County, Virginia, quite early (in 1730 or 1740). I am unable to determine the correct way of spelling this name. Perceble Clay drew two hundred acres of land in Wilkes county, Ga., in 1794. Book DDDD, page 577.

Percibal Clay drew one hundred acres of land in Washington county, Ga., in 1799. Book CCCCC, page 163.

Pierce Clay test will of Capt. John Taliaferro in Wilkinson county, Ga.

Above is the only record I have found mentioning his name. The family has uniformly spelled it Pearce Clay and so shall I. The name of his wife is not known with certainty, although all the evidence indicates that it was Martha. We must rely upon conclusions entirely as to this. We know definitely that he settled on Buffalo Creek, on the East side of Oconee River, probably before the year 1800. This was in Washington county, Ga. He was a large slave holder and his plantation was like a little kingdom within itself. Cabins surrounded the homestead, populated with slaves, and the farm was teeming with industry; farming operations, shops for repairing tools, and sheds wherein thread was spun and woven into cloth.

His cribs were well supplied with grain and his hogs, cattle and colts roamed over the range. His loom house always had a supply of cloth to satisfy the needs of his slaves, as well as the members of the family. He probably had several children, but we know only the names of the following:

a William Monroe Clay.

b John Clay.

c Patsy Clay.

William Monroe Clay is said in "Memoirs of Georgia" to have been born in 1764 in Virginia. I doubt that this date is correct, because a great many other statements made therein in regard to the Clay family are not correct. He was probably born between 1780 and 1790. He died in Washington County, Georgia, about 1857. He was a very large man weighing something like three hundred pounds, and was able to work up until the time of his death, which does not seem to have been probable if he was born as stated in "Memoirs of Georgia." I have talked with those who remember him and this statement I think is correct. He married Mary, called Polly, Hardin, who was a daughter of Nicholas Hardin and a niece of Eve Hardin, who married David Clay. (See Hardin Sketch.) William Clay was a large land owner in Washington County. He had many children.

1' Pearce Clay, m Susan Ray. They had two children, John and William, who were born in Washington County, Georgia, afterward the family moved West and were lost sight of.

2' Adam Clay, wife was named Georgia, but do not know her maiden name. They are supposed to have descendants in Baldwin County, Georgia, but I have been unable to discover any.

3' Millie Clay.

4' Sarah Clay.

5' Martha Clay. No further information.

6' Nancy Clay. No further information.

7' Mary Clay, m a Perkerson, but I have not been able to find any descendants.

8' Lydia Clay. No further information.

9' Nicholas Clay.

10' William James Clay.

11' Thomas Clay; wife was named Julia. It is known that they had children, Molly and Thomas, and

descendants are supposed to be living in Baldwin County, Georgia, but I have been unable to learn of them.

Millie Clay, identified as 3' above, married Joseph Harris in Warren County, Georgia and to them were born a large number of children:

A' Benjamin F. Harris, Sandersville, Ga.

B' Elizabeth Harris married Dan Chambers.

C' Wiley Harris, married Tresia Walker, Sandersville, Ga.

D' Molly Harris, married B. F. Gladden.

E' Tresia, marrried A. H. Ainesworth, Tennille, Ga.

F' Church Harris, unmarried, Sandersville, Ga.

G' Joseph Harris, married Annie Goss.

H' Martha Harris, married J. W. Pool, McRae, Ga.

I' Lydia Harris, married Sam Hall.

J' Thomas Harris, married Minnie Hood.

K' U. L. Harris, married Lena Roughten, Sandersville, Ga.

L' Ida Harris, married Jessie Doolittle, Sandersville, Ga.

M' Effie Harris, married James Renfroe, Sandersville, Ga.

Sarah Clay, identified as 4' above, married Turner Hitchcock and to them were born:

A' Mary Hitchcock, m Offie Trawick, Tennille, Ga.

B' Lucy Hitchcock, m John I. Renfroe, Harrison, Ga.

C' William Hitchcock, m Sarah Swint.

D' Hattie Hitchcock, m William Underwood.

E' Ella Hitchcock, m George Veal. Nicholas Clay married three times, first to Sarah Trawick, who was born May 13, 1827, second to Kizzie King, who was born May 9, 1830, and third to Naomi Swint, who was born July 3, 1833. Children:

First Marriage:

A' Ella Clay, m Rayburn Hall, Sandersville, Ga.

B' William Clay, deceased.

C' Bossie Clay, deceased.

D' Molly Clay, deceased.

Second Marriage:

E' Sally Clay.

F' Nicholas H. Clay, Macon, Ga.

G' Jesse Clay

H' Manassas Clay, deceased.

Third marriage:

I' Samuel Clay, deceased.

J' Pattie Clay, m Marion Veal, Sandersville, Ga.

K' Kizzie Clay, m a Garland, Sparta, Ga.

L' Virginia Clay, m a Griffin.

William James Clay, identified as 10' above, born Oct. 29, 1829, in Washington County, Ga., married Edna Ann Peek, Nov. 28, 1852. He died May 22, 1911, in Cobb County, near Marietta, Ga. Children:

A' Alexander Stephens Clay.

B' William Monroe Clay, b Feb. 14, 1856.

C' Sarah Thomas Clay, b Oct. 31, 1861.

D' Robert Lee Clay, b June 15, 1869.

E' Mary Elizabeth Clay, res., Austell, Cobb County, Ga., m Drewery Morgan Davis, April 6, 1877. Mrs. Davis has given me considerable information in regard to her family.

Alexander Stevens Clay, identified as A' above, is the best known of all the Georgia Branch of the Virginia Clays. He was born in Cobb County, Georgia, Sept. 25, 1853. Died at Atlanta, Ga., Nov. 13, 1910. He was largely a self-made man and graduated from Hiawassee College, in 1873, taught school two years, studying law in the meantime, and was admitted to the bar in 1877.

He was elected to the General Assembly in 1884 and again in 1886, and during his second term was Speaker of the House. In 1882 he was elected to the State Senate and was President of that body for two years. He was Chairman of the State Democratic Executive Committee in 1894, and conducted the campaign of his party that year; was chosen U. S. Senator in 1896, to succeed General John B. Gordon, and was re-elected for its full term, beginning March 4, 1903. (The above is taken from Cyclopedia of Ga., Vol. 1, page 399.)

November 25, 1880, he married Sarah Frances White, a daughter of Andrew Jackson White and Margaret (Butner) White. To them was born children as follows:

a' Eugene Herbert Clay, b Oct. 31,

1881. He was a graduate of the University of Georgia, and also of Mercer, was Mayor of Marietta, Solicitor of Blue Rdige Circuit, member of Legislature, President of the State Senate. He died June 22, 1923, leaving one child, Eugene Herbert Clay, Jr., now 14 years of age.

b' Alexander Stevens Clay II, was born April 1, 1896, at Marietta, Ga. He married and has one child, Alexander Stevens Clay III, who is now studying in the Law Dept. of the University of Ga., age 21.

c' Frank Butner Clay, b Oct. 19, 1888, student at University of Ga., graduate of West Point, Major U. S. Army, died at Walter Reed Hospital, Aug. 22, 1920.

d' Ryburn Glover Clay, b Jan. 20, 1891, P. O. Address, Atlanta, Ga., married; Vice-President of Fulton National Bank, Atlanta, Ga. One child, Zarda, age 2 years.

e' Evelyn Clay Everett, b June 8, 1897. Resident 596 Riverside Drive, New York City, N. Y., m Roberts Everett, May 31, 1917. To them was born one child, Helen Roberts Everett, b Sept. 13, 1918.

John Clay, identified as b, son of Pearce Clay, was evidently born in Washington County, Ga., where he married Sally Griffin, about 1818. Sally Griffin was a daughter of Lewis Griffin and Martha Boyett and was one among the early setlers of what is now Grady county. John Clay evidently came to Grady County, then Thomas, but the family moved from Grady County to Miller county, where he died, his family later returning to Grady county. Children

1' David Clay, m Sallie Sasser, April 10, 1850, died in Civil War.

2' Martha Clay.

3' Pearce Clay, m a widow Porter.

4' Warren Clay, m his first cousin, a daughter of Frank Griffin.

5' Millie Clay, m Dave Hester, brother of Hardy Hester, who married Martha Clay.

Martha Clay, identified as 2' above, married first Hardy Hester, second a Mr. McWilliams. Hardy Hester was

a son of Thomas Hester, who was a
soldier in the war of 1812, and his
wife, Millie Hester. Thomas Hester
and his wife were among the earlier
settlers in what is now Grady county,
Ga., and left a large number of children.

Hardy Hester and his wife Martha
(Clay) Hester had children as follows:

A' Mary Hester, m Jefferson Collins.

B' Sallie Hester, m Jim Cone.

C' George W. Hester.

D' Malinda Hester, m Frank Jordan.

E' Thomas Harden Hester.

F' Missouri Hester, m Charlie Ne-
smith.

H' Zenobia McWilliams.

G' Joseph W. Hester.

Second marriage:

George Hester, married Callie
Roads. She is now deceased. He re-
sides at Pelham, Ga. Two children:
Marshall Hester, married Lella Swann
(See Watson-Swann Sketch.) Ruth
Hester, married Jesse L. Ragan. P. O.
address, Cairo, Ga.

Thomas H. Hester, married Susan
Elizabeth Wilder. He is now deceased.
Their children are:

a' Henry Hester.

b' Martin Hester, m Arthur W.
Mills.

c' Susan E. Hester, m David Brock

d' Thomas Lee Hester, m Dollie
Brock.

e' Clara Belle Hester, m Claude
Owens.

f' Ruby Hester, m J. W. Tuggle.

g' Hansel Hester, m Miss Black.

h' Annie May Hester, m A. T.
Johnson.

i' William B. Hester, unmarried.

j' Hilda Hester, m Raymond Johnson.

k' Robert Hester, unmarried.

Henry Hester, identified as a' above
was born Feb. 7, 1889 in what is now
Grady county, Ga. He married Daisy
Elinor McIver, May 16, 1912.

Mr. Hester is a resident of Cairo,
Ga., holding the position of Cashier
of the Cairo Banking Co. His wife
is a member of the Baptist Church
Mr. Hester is one of the Board of
Councilmen of the City of Cairo, and
is considered one of the safest business men of this section of the State.
Children: Daisy Hester, deceased;

Dorothy Marion Hester; Henry Hester, Jr.; Thomas Roderick Hester
(named for each of his grandfathers);
David Clay Hester.

Joseph W. Hester, identified as G'
above, son of Hardy Hester and Martha Clay Hester, was born in Thomas
county, Ga., Dec. 14, 1857, married
Addie Belle Moore, of Randolph
county, Ga., Dec. 12, 1889. Mrs. Hester is deceased. Residence of Mr.
Hester is Cairo, Ga. Children:

a' Anderson Hester, b July 6,
1893, m Miss Lilla Cone, May
13, 1917. Res., Cairo, Ga. Children: Leland Wright Hester, b
Feb. 2, 1919; Wayne Bernard
Hester, b Aug. 19, 1924.

b' Harvie Hester, b Aug. 23, 1896,
died in the service of this country at Charleston, S. C., Oct. 18,
1918.

c' Pearl, b June 1, 1910.

d' Eula Grace, b Jan. 19, 1912, m
Paul Bond, Feb. 28, 1926.

RANDOM NOTES RELATING TO THE CLAY FAMILY.

CHAPTER 6.

It has been said that the Clays of
America are all descended from a
common ancestor. There appears to
be no foundation for this statement.
In addition to the Clay immigrants
as given in Chapter I we find that
there was another family of Clays
quite prominent in American history,
who settled in Philadelphia early in
the history of our country. These
appear to have been descended from
Robert Clay and Hannah Slater,
whose marriage was celebrated in
England in 1678.

Another family of Clays came to
North Carolina, where we find in the
North Carolina State Records, Vol. 1,
page 39, that Henry Clay, Sr., Henry
Clay, Jr., Mary Clay and Priscilla
Clay came to North Carolina in 1693.

Another family of Clays came to
Georgia direct from England. This
family appears to have been descended from Ralph Clay and his wife
Elizabeth Habersham, of Yorkshire,
England. Their son, Joseph Clay,
came to America, where he became a
member of the council of safety, a
member of the Provincial Congress, a
member of the Executive Council and

also a trustee of the State College. He married Anne Legardere. Their children were:

1. Hon. Joseph Clay.
2. James Clay.
3. William LeConte Clay.
4. Parnell Clay.
5. Ralph Clay.
6. Catherine Clay
7. Sarah Clay.
8. Elizabeth Clay.
9. Ann Clay.

If the above Clays were descended from a common ancestor it must have been at some period of time very remote from the settlement of Georgia.

Before proceeding to our notes relating to Georgia proper, it is fitting that we give the following extract, from Warrants of land in South Carolina, 1672-79, by Salley.

To Mr. John Yeamens, Surveyor:

In Pursuance of an order of Council dated ye 20 day of septr. Instant you are furthwith to cause to be admeasured and layd out for Steven Clay marriner foure hundred acres on land in some place not yet layd or marked to be layd out for any other or use and if ye same happen upon any Navigable river or any river capable of being made Navigable you to allow only ye 5th part of ye depth thereof by the water side and a Certificat fully specifyeing the scituacon and bound thereof you are to return to us with all convenient speed And for your so doing this shalbe sufficient Warrant Given under our hands att Charles Towne this 10th day of September 1676.

Joseph West."

Goodspeed's Memoirs of Mississippi Vol. 1, page 957, says that James Houston, 1886, married Miss Mary C. Clay, daughter of H. P. Clay and Catherin (Milligan) Clay. H. P. Clay was a native of South Carolina, born 1812, and a son of Simon Clay. He came to Lauderdale County, Mississippi, 1842, residing there until 1851, when he moved to Kemper county. There he passed the remainder of his days, dying in 1879.

Records in the office of the ordinary of Elbert County, show that Simeon Clay married Mary Lockhart, Feb. 21, 1818.

Jan. 11, 1836, John Clay deeded to John L. B. McCrone, 125 acres of land in the eighteenth district, lot 182

of Thomas County, Georgia, now Grady County, Georgia.

There was recorded in Thomas Co., Georgia, December 24, 1863, the following instrument, which is given because of the interest which may attach to the peculiar document.

"Rec'd. of Joseph Clay his substitute papers bearing date of April 16, 1863. The name of the substitute, Nelson Rayfield, age 52 years, and received of Captain Martain's Company, Light Artillery.

D. L. Pitts, E. O. of Thomas Co.,

T. C. Braswell, D. C.

"Recorded Dec. 24, 1863."

Augustus Clay drew land in Columbia County, Georgia.' The name indicates that he was related to the Georgia Branch of the Virginia Clays. His relationship is not known, nor is it known as to whether or not he left descendants, although Mr. Robert Augustus Clay, a resident of Lee County with his post office address at Desoto, Georgia, is a great grandson of an Augustus Clay, who came tn Georgia quite early, the line being as follows:

Augustus W. Clay, (son of Augustus Clay, who was born in Virginia,) was born in Columbia County, Ga., Oct. 7, 1828, died Aug. 16, 1904, Walnut Grove, Ga., married Elizabeth P. Wilkerson, of Walton County, Ga., Mr. Clay represented Walton County in the Legislature about 1876, was an officer in the civil war. Children were:

1. Janie Clay.
2 Reuben P. Clay.
3 Augustus C. Clay.
4 Adolphus C. Clay.
5 Altha K. Clay.
6 Effie Clay.
7 Jesse O. Clay.
8 Bessie Clay.

Reuben P. Clay, identified as 2 above, was born July 26, 1855, at Walnut Grove, Ga., married Dora E. O'-Kelley, at Covington, Ga., Nov. 23, 1881. Their children were:

A Pearl E. Clay, b Oct. 16, 1884, res., Hapeville, Ga.
B Robert A. Clay, b Oct. 4, 1884, m Eddye L. Hooks, De Soto, Ga., Aug. 27, 1925. She is the daughter of Mr. and Mrs. James T. Hooks. No issue.
C Thomas P. Clay, b June 8, 1886, res., Miami, Fla.
D Nobie E. Clay, b Feb. 1888, res.

Decatur, Ga.

E Marvin C. Clay, res., Miami, Fla.

F Marie A. Clay, res., Miami, Fla.

Jefferson Clay drew land in Jasper county, but I have not been able to secure any further information in regard to him.

Greenberry Clay drew land in Morgan county, but I have been unable to get any trace of descendants or any further recorded information.

Green Clay drew land in Habersham County, Ga.

John Clay drew land in Washington county, Ga.

Edmund Clay drew land in Talbot county, Ga. This Edmund Clay was probably the same Edmund Clay who later moved to Jackson county, Fla., and who had a son, John or Jack Clay, long a resident of Concord, Fla., and whose son, Henry I. Clay, is now a resident of Grady county, with Post Office address at Calvary, Ga.

William Clay drew land in Washington County, Ga.

Silas N. Clay drew land in Campbell County, Ga.

Samuel Clay drew land in Harris County, Georgia.

These lands were drawn between 1827-1838, and the most of the Clays named were evidently children of the early settlers of Georgia or near relatives who came into the state later.

Jesse Clay drew several tracts of land in Wilkes county, Georgia, and appears to have been later cut off into Oglethorpe county, where he drew land on Little River and where he is mentioned as being one of the first jurors of the county. We find that Jesse Clay married Hannah Coleman, of Amelia county, Va., in 1790.

I have frequently been asked as to Mr. C. C. Clay of Americus, Ga., and what relation his line is to the other Clays. His line begins in one John Clay of Virginia. It is uncertain as to whether this John Clay was a son of William Clay or the John Clay, who was a captain in the Revolutionary war and who was the eighth child of Henry Clay and Lucy Green. John Clay died in Rutherford County, Tennessee in 1835 at the age of ninty six, which would have made his birthday in 1739. I have learned nothing of the other children of this John Clay, but his wife before her marringe was Miss Millicent Epps, of Rich-

mond, Virginia, and she was a cousin of the wife of Thomas Jefferson. They had one child, Joshua Clay, born probably in Dinwiddie County, Virginia. He married Miss Sarah Elizabeth Jennings, said to have been related to Henry Clay's grandmother. Joshua Clay served four years in the Revolution, moved to Rutherford Co., Tennessee, and owned fifty acres of land in what is now the heart of Nashville. His old mansion, if not there now, was standing a few years ago. Joshua Clay and his wife had one son, John William Clay.

John William Clay married Sarah Mariah McRee, who was of Scotch descent.

C. C. Clay appears to have had brothers and sisters, but I have not been able to secure information in regard to any of them, or details of his early life. He appears to have moved to Macon, where he took a business course, moving from Macon to Sumter County, Georgia near Americus, where he spent the rest of his life, being a very successful business man and planter in that community. He was a Democrat in politics and a member of the Elks organization and of the Methodist Church.

October 3, 1877, he married Miss Mary Bryan, daughter of Thomas Green and Martha (Hooks) Bryan, descendants of prominent North Carolina families, their children are: Clifford C. Clay and Henry Clay.

(Above information from Clay manuscript, furnished by Mrs. Mary Clay of Americus, Georgia.)

Marriage Records, Decatur Co. Edmond Clay and Liza Riggan, married Aug. 26, 1852.

Edmond Clay, Sr., and Elinor Glover, married December 17, 1852

Decatur Book of Deeds B p 151, Avy Clay, May 28, 1831 conveys to granddaughter Mahany Brown, the daughter of Robert Brown, Territory of Florida, and Matilda Clay Brown, personal property, including one negro woman.

The last of the Clays to be mentioned by us needs to have mention of him prefaced by a little Georgia history. At the close of the War of the Revolution in 1783, it appears that Virginia had more soldiers than she had land to reward them for their services, and that the State of Virginia petitioned the State of Georgia asking that two hundred thousand acres of land be set aside by the state for such immigrants as might wish to settle down in one solid community; in response to this the State of Georgia, in 1784, acceded to this request from the State of Virginia and orgnaized the Counties of Washington and Franklin. Immediately after this we find that the Virginians came "not scatteringly and wide apart, but in quick succeeding throngs, bringing along with them their wives, children and servants, and their household goods and gods. Whitney had not then invented the cotton gin and the cultivation of tobacco was the principal industry in this section of Georgia, as well as in Virginia." See Miscellanies of Georgia.

At this time these counties adjoined each other and the Oconee River on their west was the boundary separating the whites from the indians. This territory was claimed by both the Whites and Indians, and frequently there were conflicts and trouble. This being true, the settlers came principally from the Southwestern part, or frontier settlements of Virginia, because they were more used to the Indians, and better capacitated to stand the life on the frontier with its dangers. This was the time and occasion when Lieutenant Abia Clay of Virginia first made his appearance in Georgia, where we find that he was appointed tobacco inspector for the State of Georgia, probably for the purpose of aiding the Virginians in the growth of tobacco in the territory just organized. (Revolutionary Records of Georgia, Vol. II, page 728.)

Abia Clay is also listed as a Revolutionary soldier, page 378, of the Georgia Roster of the Revolution. Abia Clay evidently did not live long to enjoy his life in the new territory, for we find that his will was executed on Nov. 20, 1791, which we give as follows:

State Of Georgia,
Richmond County:
In the name of God, Amen.

I, Abia Clay, of the State and County aforesaid, being sick and weak in body, but of perfect mind and memory, make this, my last Will and Testament, in manner and form following, viz: First, I recommend my soul to God who gave it, and my body to the earth from whence it was taken, to be decently buried at the discretion of my Executor, hereafter named

Item. I give and bequeath to my son, Samuel Clay, and to his heirs, forever, the following negroes, viz: Tom, Rachel and her children; but in case the said Samuel Clay should die without heir, then it is my desire that the negroes aforesaid shall be equally divided among the children of Robey Cocke, of York County, Virginia.—the residue of my Estate, viz: Phebe, my stock of horses, cattle, hogs and household furniture, I desire may be sold to discharge my just debts.—Lastly, I nominate and appoint William Freeman, Esquire, Executor to this my last Will and Testament. In testimony whereof I have hereunto set my hand and seal this 20 day of November, in the year of our Lord, 1791.

ABIA CLAY (Seal)

Signed, sealed and acknowledged in presence of—
John Fury
Chs Statham
William Jones

Jones Genealogies and Notes Indicative
of the Lineage of
John Lawrence Jones
of Virginia, North Carolina and Georgia.

CHAPTER VII

John Taliaferro, son of John Taliaferro and Sarah Smith Taliaferro, who was the daughter of Major Lawrence Smith, married Mary Catlett and their children were:

1 Lawrence Taliaferro, b Sept. 8, 1721, m Susanna Powers.
2 Martha Taliaferro.
3 William Taliaferro, b Aug. 9, 1726, m twice; first Mary Battaile who was a daughter of Nicholas Battaile and Mary Thornton Battaile.
4 Lucy Taliaferro, m Col. Charles Lewis.
5 Mary Taliaferro, b about 1730, m Joseph Jones about 1748. Joseph Jones and his wife were sponsors for Samuel Lewis, son of Fielding Lewis, and Joseph Jones and Edward Rice were sureties on bond of William Taliaferro, as guardian for minors of William Hunter. (Nicholas Taliaferro Manuscript.)

John Lewis of Warner Hill, son of Counciller John Lewis and Elizabeth Warner, born in Gloucester county, Virginia, in 1682, married Frances Fielding and to them were born:

1 Warner Lewis, b 1720.
2 Fielding Lewis, b 1725.
3 An unknown child.
4 Col. Charles Lewis, m Lucy Taliaferro.
5 John Lewis.

Fielding Lewis, 2 above, married first Katherine Washington, daughter of John Washington and Katherine Whiting Washington. Second Betty Washington, who was a first cousin of his first wife and a sister of Gen. George Washington. He had a son, John Lewis, who was married five times. John's third wife was Elizabeth Jones, daughter of Gabriel Jones, a distinguished lawyer of Virginia and known as the "Valley Lawyer." His fourth wife was a widow Armestead, who before her first marriage was Mary Ann Fountain. (See "Lewis and Kindred Families" by McAllister and Tandy.)

Fielding Lewis, but not the one above, drew land in Pitts District, Baldwin County, Georgia, about 1838. Lewis Jones drew land in Wilkinson county, Ga. Taliaferro Jones drew land in Wilkes county.

Mentioned in connection with claims under Yazoo Fraud are Valentine Jones and Seaborn Jones. Joseph B. Jones is mentioned as receiving a fraudulent grant of a hundred thousand acres of land in Franklin County, 1794. See History of the Public Domain of Georgia, by S. G. McLendon.

Dr. John Taliaferro of Georgia, willed lands to his daughter, Lucy, next to lands of Joe Jones and names John Jones, husband of his daughter, Lucy Taliaferro Jones, executor of his will. For copy of this will see forthcoming sketch of Taliaferro family by Miss Willie Ivey, of Tennille, Ga.

To prevent confusion as to the two Col. Charles Lewises and also because of the interest to the Clay family, the following information is given:

John Lewis, who was known as Irish John Lewis, married Margaret Lynn, in Ireland. They settled in America and had the following children:

1 Samuel Lewis, b 1716.
2 Thomas Lewis, b 1718.
3 Andrew Lewis, b 1720. He was the Gen. Andrew Lewis who was the commander of the army at the Battle of Point Pleasant.

4 William Lewis, b 1724.
5 Margaret Lewis, b 1726.
6 Ann Lewis, b 1728. Margaret and Ann are said to have never been married. This information has not been verified to my satisfaction, however.
7 Charles Lewis, b 1728. He was a Colonel in the army and was killed at Point Pleasant. A Mr. Clay was killed in this battle, who I think was William Clay, the father of Mitchell Clay.

In making a careful study of the Jones family in Wilkinson County, Ga., I found from the oldest settlers that one Gabriel Jones and Nancy Jones, who married Peyton Clay, were cousins, but whether first cousins or second cousins, I was unable to learn. This Gabriel Jones was a son of Joseph Jones, who lived next to Dr. John Taliaferro, and his wife (probably a second wife) before her marriage was an Anderson. Their children were:

1 John Jones, who was also called Jack, married a Deason and moved to Texas.
2 Hiram Jones.
3 Frank Jones, married Fannie Burk and moved to Texas.
4 Martha Jones, also known as Polly, married Ambrose Nelson.
5 Gabriel Jones, who appears to have been the youngest son of Joseph Jones, was born in 1801. He married first, Nancy Underwood, who was a sister of Thomas Underwood, who was killed by being stabbed in the dark in the Courthouse in Wilkinson county, Ga., very early in the history of the county; he married second, Mariah Carr.

Gabriel Jones, 5 above, had by his first wife the following children:
A Joseph Jones, m Mary Jane Deason, went to the Civil War, from which he was reported as missing, and never returned.
B Matthew Jones, m Evelyn Ballard, died in the Civil War.
C Hiram Anderson Jones, died in Civil War, without issue.
D William Franklin Jones, m Elizabeth Slade.
E James Gabriel Jones, died in Civil War, without issue.
F Mary Jones, m W. B. Carr.
G Matilda Jones m Joseph Martin.

H John Washington Jones, killed in battle in Civil War.

By his second wife he had children as follows:
I Frances Rebecca Jones, m Morgan Bloodworth.
J Joseph Taliaferro Jones unmarried.
K Madison Monroe Jones, m Lefa Temple, who was a daughter of Dr. John Temple and Sarah Temple, who were first cousins. They have a son, John Gabriel Jones, Milledgeville, Ga., Route No. 1.

The above information was furnished me by Mr. Madison Monroe Jones, and is given as suggestive and will indicate to a trained genealogist, lines along which to make further search or investigation for the ancestry of John Lawrence Jones.

John Lawrence Jones.

John Lawrence Jones, whose posterity we are about to trace has been an enigma to those genealogists who have undertaken to identify him with any line. Many members of the family are under the impression that he was born in Surrey County, North Carolina. He married Lucy Taliaferro, daughter of Captain or Dr. John Taliaferro, and genealogists have indicated that he was a son of John Letton Jones, of Surrey County, North Carolina.

John Lawrence Jones was evidently born in Virginia, raised in some of the more settled provinces and came from a family of considerable culture and distinction. He was highly appreciative of the finer things of life and was to some extent out of joint with the rougher elements with which he came in contact in his Georgia environment. That he was a man of intelligence and integrity is proven by the fact that he was named executor of the will of Dr. John Taliaferro. That he was a man of courage is proven by the fact that he took up arms in defense of the people of his community from the depredations of the Indians, serving as a soldier in the Indian war. (My Mother's Notes.) That he was a man of good breeding and culture is shown by the records of his descendants, and it is patent to me from the traditions of my mother and from the evidences in hand, that John Lawrence Jones was a worthy mate for his wife, LucyTal-

iaferro, and that his children were
worthy mates for the Clay descendants, with whom so many have united
in marriage.

John Lawrence Jones, born Dec. 8,
1776, married Lucy Taliaferro, daughter of John Taliaferro and Mary
Harden, in 1797. He died March 1,
1830. His wife, Lucy (Taliaferro)
Jones, was born May 29, 1780, and
died Feb. 28, 1842. Children were:

1st Judith Jones, b Sept. 19, 1799,
m Lewis Clay. (See Georgia
Branch of the Virginia Clays.)

2nd Elizabeth Jones, b Sept. 23rd,
1801, m first, a Nelson, and second Robert Cameron. She had
one son, Robert Cameron, Jr.,
and probably others, but have
been unable to secure further information.

3rd Nancy Jones, b Sept. 31, 1805,
m Peyton Clay. (See Georgia
Branch of the Virginia Clays.)

4th Craven Jones, b Sept 16, 1805
is said to have died young and
without issue.

5th Sarah Jones, b Sept. 15, 1808,
m Edmund Clay. (See Georgia
Branch of the Virginia Clays.)

6th Frances Jones, b July 5, 1810, is
said to have died young and without issue.

7th Beheathland Jones.
8th John Richard Jones.
9th Mary Jones, b Oct. 30, 1817, is
said to have died young.
10th Dr. Taliaferro Jones.
11th Frances M. Jones.
12th Seaborn Jones, b Jan. 22, 1824.

Beheathland Jones, 7th Line.

Beheathland Jones, was born Nov.
1, 1812, in Wilkinson county, Ga.,
m James H. Fountain, Nov 16, 1836,
who was born Jan. 8, 1799; d Aug. 12
1863. Mrs. Fountain died July 12,
1876, in Wilkinson County, Georgia,
and is buried at Armah Cemetery.
Children:

1 Augustus J. Fountain, b Sept.
27, 1837, married Louisa Stevens,
1860, and died Nov. 22, 1862, in
Confederate service. Children:
Beheathland Fountain, m a Daniels, died soon after; Annie Fountain, m John Whittaker.
2 Israel Jackson Fountain.
3 Lucy Ann Fountain.
4 Seaborn Jones Fountain.
5 Thomas Franklin Fountain.
6 Nancy Caroline Fountain.

Israel Jackson Fountain (2) born
June 17, 1839, married Rebecca J.
Hatsfield, Aug. 11, 1865, and died
Feb. 17,1901. Children were:
A Mary Lucy Fountain.
B Ida Nancy Fountain, b Nov. 7,
1868, d May 22, 1911.
Mary Lucy Fountain, identified as
A above, was born Nov. 16, 1866, mar-
ried T. H. Bragg, Sept. 24, 1885. Res.
Irwinton, Ga. Children were:
a Willard A. Bragg, residence 2111
Oak St., Vicksburg, Miss.
b Otis Bragg, res. 911 Atlanta,
Ave., Decatur, Ga.
c Mamie Bragg. (Mrs. R. A.
Maddox, res. Irwinton, Ga.)
d Jennie Bragg.
e Earnest E. Bragg, res. Pearl
Ave., Spartanburg, S. C.
f T. H. Bragg, Jr., res., Peachtree
Road, Atlanta, Ga.
g Ethel Bragg. (Mrs. B. W. Lee,
121 Church St., Decatur, Ga.)
h Wilmer Bragg.
i Olan Bragg.
Lucy Ann Fountain (3), born May
19, 1843, seventh line, married Rich-
ard E. Hatfield, who was a son of S.
W. Hatfield, m July 1860. Both fath-
er and son served in the Civil War.
Richard E. Hatfield was in the 57th
Ga. Regiment, Company I, and S. W.
Hatfield was in the 2nd Ga. Militia,
last call. Issue:
A James Ira Hatfield.
B Lucy Beheathland Hatfield.
C Clara Frances Hatfield.
D Mattie Annie Hatfield.
E Samuel Eugene Hatfield, res.
Irwinton, Ga.
F Sidney Ware Hatfield, res. Mac-
Intyre, Ga., b Jan. 1st, 1877, in
Wilkinson, county, m Jan. 20,
1903 Winnie Cornelia Smith who
was born in Wilkinson County,
Ga. Issue: James Ira Hatfield b
Oct. 31, 1903; Sidney Johnson
Hatfield b March, 17, 1906; An-
nie Lou Hatfield, b March 9, 1909;
Emory Smith Hatfield b April 21,
1915; Edna Winifred Hatfield b
Jan. 2, 1917.
James Ira Hatfield, A above, born
Dec. 14, 1861, died Aug. 10, 1920, mar-
ried first Fannie Stuckey, Dec. 10,
1885, and second Christie Ann Vickers, July2, 1893. Issue by last marriage:
a Christie Ann Hatfield.
b Elizabeth Hatfield.
c Stella Lee Hatfield.

d Mattie Aurora Hatfield.
e Nanny Inez Hatfield.
Lucy Beheathland Hatfield, B above, born March 26, 1866, married Isaac T. Davis, Dec. 16, 1885. Children:

a Thomas Ivey Davis.
b Annie Gertrude Davis.
c Isaac Watson Davis.
d Maxie Lucy Davis., Mrs. I. T. Etheridge, Haddock, Ga.
e Laura Almeta Davis.
f Terry Ellis Davis.

Clara Frances Hatfield, D above, born March 30, 1868, taught school several years prior to her marriage to John Seaborn Davis. John Seaborn Davis graduated from Mercer University, in 1893, and taught school several years before and after graduating. He was State Senator from his district in 1911-13, and is now practicing law at Irwinton, Ga. He also served as Ordinary of Wilkinson County, Ga., for eight years. Children:

a Clara Izetta Davis, principal of the High School at Toomsboro, Ga.
b Willie Lee Davis.
c Curry Davis.
d Sarah Lucy Davis.
e John Ellis Davis.
f Jameson Grady Davis.
g James Cecil Davis.

Sarah Lucy Davis, m J. T. Youngblood, and she left a daughter, Sarah Youngblood, born May 8, 1925. Izetta, Willie, and Sarah L. (Sadie), are graduates of G. S. C. W., Milledgeville, Ga. Willie Davis has been teaching high school in the Wilkinson county high school at Irwinton, Ga., for the past six years. John Ellis and Jameson are farmers, and Cecil is in school at Irwinton, Ga., Sarah L. (Sadie), taught for the four years following her graduation, 1921, as Principal of McIntyre High School, McIntyre, Ga.

Mattie Annie Hatfield, (D) born Aug. 18, 1870, married James Robert Torrence, June 10, 1891. Res. Milledgeville, Ga .Children:

a Ellis Watson Torrence.
b Robert Guy Torrence.
c Annie Winifred Torrence.
d Clara Belle Torrence.
e Mamie Elizabeth Torrence.
f Lillian Torrence.
g Charles Gresham Torrence.

Samuel Eugene Hatfield, identified as E above, born July 22, 1873, married Sara Emily Gibson, Dec. 28, 1898. Children:

a Eugene Fountain Hatfield.
b Ann Lanetta Hatfield.
c Alma Lillian Hatfield.
d Samuel Evans Hatfield.
e Lucile Amanda Hatfield.
f and g Millard and Willard Hatfield, twins.
h Buena Vista Hatfield.
i Alice Gibson Hatfield.

Sidney Ware Hatfield F above, born Jan. 2, 1877, married Winnie Cornelia Smith, Jan. 20, 1903. Children:

a James Ira Hatfield.
b Sidney Johnson Hatfield.
c Annie Lou Hatfield.
d Emory Hatfield.
e Edna Hatfield.

Seaborn Jones Fountain, 4 above, Dec. 27, 1866, married Margaret Irwin, born April 7, 1841. Children:

A Thomas Chandler Fountain.
B Leilla Augusta Fountain.
C Augustus Theodore Fountain, b in Wilkinson county, Ga., Sept. 7, 1871, m Dec. 25, 1895 Minnie Lavendar, daughter of W. B. Lavendar and Pennie Lavendar, Issue: Clara Fountain Wood b Oct. 21, 1897. Ernest Fountain b Sept. 7, 1899, Gordon, Ga. Rt. 2, m June 16, 1918; Irwin Jones Fountain, b June 28, 1904; Royce Fountain, b March 16, 1907, Gordon, Ga; Clayton Fountain, b Oct. 8, 1910, Gordon, Ga; Mary Fountain, b Oct. 8, 1910, Gordon, Ga. Mary Fountain b July 7, 1915, Gordon, Ga.
D Bessie Fountain.
E Annie Maebelle Fountain.
F Seaborn Fountain, res. Gordon, Ga., Rt. No. 3.
G William Fountain, b Sept. 14, 1879, died July 12, 1882.
H Avarilla Fountain.

Thomas Chandler Fountain, A above, born Oct. 2, 1867, died May 14, 1905, married Frances Newby Dec. 16, 1888. Children:

a Roberta Fountain. (Mrs. C. W Robinson, 851 Oak St., Macon. Ga.)
b Clara Edna Fountain. (Mrs Thomas A. Drew, 126 Cole St. Macon, Ga.)
c Willie Augusta Fountain. (Mrs J. W. Housley, 109 Plant Ave. Tampa, Fla., born Sept. 26, 1892

Wilkinson county, Ga. m 1st. Aug
22, 1909 to Frank H. Powers, Jr.
son of Ella Drake and Frank H.
Powers, 2nd; October 10, 1917.
James Washington Housley. Is-
sue by first marriage; Donald
Chandler Powers, b Oct. 17, 1910,
Bibb County, Ga.

Leila Augusta Fountain, B above,
born July 16, 1869, married first Dec.
1888, Thomas Davis, second July 26,
1896, W. H. Singletary, res. 165 Fair-
mont St., Atlanta, Ga. Children by
first marriage:

a Lucia Leona Davis, b Gordon,
Ga. Sept. 1, 1890, m Aug. 13, 1919
W. M. Clement: Res, Mod. School
Rome, Ga. Issue: Emily Clement.
b Alvah Davis.
c Thomasine Davis.
Children by second marriage:
d Ellis Singletary, res. Tampa,
Fla.
e Kathleen Singletary.

Augustus Fountain, C above, born
Sept. 7, 1871, married Mary Allie
Lavendar, Dec. 25, 1895. Children:
a Clara Fountain.
b Ernest Fountain.
c Irvin Fountain.
d Royce Fountain.
e Clayton Fountain.
f Mary Fountain.

Bessie Fountain, D above, born
Oct. 9, 1873, married W. Hawkins, March, 1893, res. 1820 Marion
St., Columbia, S. C. They had only
one child, Leila, who is dead.

Annie Maebelle Fountain, E above,
born Dec. 4, 1875, married R. W.
Ross, 1897. Res. 111 A Richardson
St., Atlanta, Ga. Children:
a E. B. Ross.
b S. J. Ross.
c Bascom Ross.
d Eloise Ross.
e Ernest Ross.
f Clio Ross.
g R. W. Ross.
h Woodrow Ross.

Seaborn Fountain, F above, born
Aug. 9, 1877, married Minnie Smith,
1899. Children:
a Lizzie Fountain
b Archie Fountain.
c Chandler Fountain.
d Bessie Maude Fountain.
e Marvin Fountain.
f Robert Fountain.
g Minnie Jewel Fountain.

Avarilla Fountain, G above, born
May 30, 1882, married R. S. Sanders,

Aug. 7, 1922. Res. Gordon, Ga., Rt.
No. 3. No issue.

Thomas Franklin Fountain, No. 5,
seventh line, born Feb. 29, 1848, mar-
ried Epsie Dean, Nov. 8, 1866, and
died Sept., 1893. Children:
A Luke Fountain.
B Mattie Fountain.
C Annie Fountain.
D Lillie Fountain.
E Thomas Fountain.

Nancy Caroline Fountain, No. 6,
seventh line, born March 31, 1852, in
Wilkinson County, Ga., married La-
fayette Balkcom, March 5, 1868. Mr.
Balkcom was born Jan. 16, 1840,
served in the Confederate army thru-
out the war between the states, and
died April 25, 1921. Mr. Balkcom
and his wife were married in Wilkin-
son County, Ga., the ceremony hav-
ing been performed by Rev. Charles
Johnston, Methodist minister. Mrs.
Balkcom resides at Griswoldville, Ga.
Children:
A Carrie Tallulah Balkcom.
B Alonzo Eugene Balkcom, res,.
Griswoldville, Ga.
C Annie Irene Balkcom.
D Estelle Beheathland Balkcom.
E Clarence Lafayette Balkcom,
res. Griswoldville, Ga.

Carrie Tallulah Balkcom, A above,
born Feb. 1, 1869, married Dr. Schiller
B. Poland, Sept. 16, 1886. She died
Oct. 9, 1916. Their children are:
a Sadie Poland. (Mrs. Manuel H.
Jones, Orlando, Fla.)
b Carl Poland, died in World War.
c Annie Estelle Poland.
d Eugene Poland, 112 New Orleans St., Hattiesburg, Miss.
e Hugh Poland.
f De Witt Poland.

Alonzo Eugene Balkcom, B above,
born July 29, 1871, married Leila
Sketoe, April 15, 1894. Children:
a Lucile Balkcom. (Mrs. R. H.
Stevens, 669 2nd St., Macon, Ga.)
b Thomas Balkcom, res. Griswold-
woldville, Ga.
c Nannie Balkcom, (Mrs Eugene
Gibson 8277 Chamberlain St., De-
troit, Michigan.
d Ava Balkcom. (Mrs. Robert
Christian, Gray, Ga.)
e Alice Balkcom.
f Fred Balkcom.
g Agnes Balkcom.
h Albert Balkcom.
i Milton Balkcom.
j Henry Balkcom.

k La Verne Balkcom.

Annie Irene Balkcom,, c above, born July 11,, 1874, in Jones County, Georgia, married Simeon Lafayette McWilliams, on June 18, 1891. Mr. McWilliams was born March 4, 1860, d Nov. 13, 1913. His father was Simeon McWilliams, a Confederate soldier. Mr. and Mrs. McWilliams were married in Jones County, Georgia, the ceremony having been performed by Rev. Joseph Carr, Methodist minister. They have only one child:

a Olive McWilliams, b April 20, 1892, whose address is 105 Buford place, Macon, Ga. She married Dec. 5, 1914, Sidney William Hatcher, who is a prominent lawyer in Macon. Mr. Hatcher was born Jan. 25, 1882, and is the son of Sidney W. Hatcher, who was a Confederate soldier and also a descendant of Major John Hatcher, Revolutionary soldier of Wilkinson county, Georgia. Mr and Mrs. Hatcher were united in marriage by the Rev. W. N. Ainesworth, now Bishop of the M. E. Church, South. Mrs. Hatcher has been a great aid in collecting this information and assisting in this work:

Estelle Beheathland Balkcom, D above, born March 22, 1877. married Porter Henderson, May 24, 1895. She died April 30, 1898, leaving one child:

a Shelton Henderson, res. Gordon, Ga., Rt. 3.

Clarence Lafayette Balkcom, E above, born Sept. 7, 1880, married Mamie Smith, Dec. 23, 1902. Children:

a Ernest Balkcom.

b Harry Balkcom.

c Ralph Balkcom.

d and e Marian and Raymond Lafayette Balkcom, twins.

John Richard Jones, 8th Line.

Dr. John Richard Jones, son of John L. Jones and Lucy Taliaferro Jones, his wife, was born in Wilkinson county, Ga., Dec. 20, 1814. On March 12, 1839, he was married to Obedience Hatcher, daughter of James M. and Sarah (Clay) Hatcher, of the same county.

Early in their married life they left Georgia for Marianna, Fla., in which vicinity they bought a farm.

Dr. Jones was an ordained minister of the Baptist church and was also a homeopathic physician, finding many instances where he could serve the physical as well as the spiritual needs of the people. He was a member of the Masonic order, his apron being now in the possession of one of his grandsons.

His death in the early part of March, 1852, came as a distinct shock to his family. He had goine to Apalachicola to preach and while conducting services there he was striken with pneumonia and died shortly after. His body was accompanied to his home by a representative of the church which he was serving at the time. He was survived by a wife and six children, viz:

1 William Marian Jones.

2 James Taliaferro Jones.

3 John Mallory Jones, b Dec. 16, 1845, d July 10, 1857.

4 Seaborn Henry Jones, b April 22, 1847, d Aug. 25, 1889.

5 Esther Kitturah Jones, b Aug. 22, 1849, d June 27, 1862.

6 Sarah Ellen Jones.

William Marion Jones, identified as No. 1, eighth line, was born Sept. 8, 1841. He entered the Civil War, and died Feb. 12, 1863.

James Taliaferro Jones, identified as No. 2, eighth line, was born June 18, 1843, married Sarah Eunice Law, April 20, 1871. She was born October 16, 1846. Mrs. (Law) Jones, was descended from the Christian, Walton, Law, Washburn, Cobb and Massingale families, of Virginia, South Carolina, and Tennessee. James Taliaferro Jones was a Confederate veteran, serving from 1862 to 1865 in the War between the States, died Jan. 28, 1915 at West Hickory St., Denton, Texas, the funeral services being conducted by the Rev. M. E. Hudson. James Taliaferro Jones, was born in Wilkinson county Ga., but his parents moved, when he was only two years old, to Florida, where he grew to young manhood. His principal service in the War between the States was in the 2nd Cavalry. He was discharged at Quincy, Fla., May 16, 1865. Soon after his discharge he moved to Texas with his mother and family, and settled in Grimes county, later moving to Madison county, Texas. Mr. Jones went to Denton in 1873 and soon became identified with the public interest of Pilot Point. He entered into partnership with D. J. Moffet, as senior

Editor of the Pilot Point Post, one of the pioneer newspapers of North Texas. The fact that this paper survived the indignant protests of the lawless element, then in power, is no small compliment to its founders.

Mr. Jones was a staunch man, a deacon in the Baptist Church for nearly forty years, and stood fearlessly for law, order and Christian citizenship. Children were:

A Clara Bell Jones, b Feb. 17, 1872, died young.

B Lenora Ellen Jones.

C Mamie Law Jones.

D Albert Sidney Jones, b Sept. 15, 1878, died young.

E Richard Taliaferro Jones.

F Victor Christian Jones.

G Willie Jones.

Lenora Ellen Jones, who is identified by B, eighth line, married Sidney Johnston Jones, No. 8, tenth line, which see. Res. 721 W. Hickory St., Denton, Tex.

Mamie Law Jones, identified as C above, was born Jan. 13, 1876, married Samuel Houston Sullivan, Oct. 26, 1898. Res. Box 24, Sanger, Texas. Children:

a Jack Taliaferro Sullivan.

b Frances Marion Law Sullivan.

c Eunice Douschka Sullivan.

Richard Taliaferro Jones, identified as E above, was born Aug. 26, 1880, married July 5. 1916, May Ree Hunt, res. 625 East Park Ave., San Antonio, Texas. One child:

a Roland Taliaferro Jones.

Victor Christian Jones, identified as F above, was born Dec. 29, 1882, married Sept. 15, 1915, Carrie McCraran, res. 140 E. French Place, San Antonio, Tex. No issue.

Willie Jones, identified as G above, was born Jan. 8, 1887, married Herman Carl Schultz, Jr., June 15, 1910. Res. 367 South Rugby Ave., Hunting Park, California. Children:

a Herman Carl Schultz.

b Charles Frederick Schultz.

Sarah Ellen Jones, No. 6, 8th line, was born May 1, 1851, married Solomon H. Bryant, who was a son of Capt. Alex Bryant and Mrs. Kate Bryant, in 1881. Mr. S. H. Bryant died Jan. 11, 1897. Mrs. Bryant was born in Marianna, Fla., and died at Dallas, Texas, Nov. 7, 1921. Children:

A Alvin Cleveland Bryant, Au-

brey, Texas.

B Bertie Bryant. (Mrs. R. C. Hames, 2226 Garrett Ave., Dallas, Tex.)

C Vera Bryant, Dallas, Texas.

Alvin Cleveland Bryant, A above, born July 26, 1883, married May Smith, June 24, 1911, the daughter of James and Fannie Smith, of Aubrey, Texas. Children:

a Alton Morris Bryant, b Nov. 10, 1913.

b Norman Dale Bryant. b Dec. 10, 1925.

Bertie Bryant, B above, was born Nov. 8, 1888, married Rollie C. Hames, May 27, 1916, res 2226 Garrett, Ave., Dallas, Texas. Children:

a Elaine Hames, b and d Jan. 2, 1919.

b Ellen Kathleen Hames, b June 14,1921.

Rollie C. Hames, parents were Thomas and Elizabeth Hames, of South Carolina.

Vera Bryant, C above, was born Oct. 8, 1892, 2226 Garrett Ave., Dallas, Texas.

Dr. Taliaferro Jones, Tenth Line.

Dr. Taliaferro Jones was born in Wilkinson County, Ga., Dec. 24, 1818. Soon after completing a course at Augusta Medical College, Augusta, Ga. married Caroline Jane Saxon, daughter of Benjamin Saxon, of Twiggs County, April 23rd, 1845. In 1856 they moved to Dougherty county, settling on the East side of the river, two miles from town. During the war between the states he joined a cavalry troop, but before his company left for the front, was requisitioned by the Government to remain at home to care for the sick in the Eastern part of the county.

He led an active life in the pursuit of his profession until 1873, when ill health forced his retirement from practice. He moved with his family the same year to Albany, where he continued to reside until his death in May 1891. Dr. and Mrs. Jones had the following children:

1 Mary Tallulah Jones Massey.

2 Paul Eve Jones, died young.

3 Laura Cornela Jones Alfriend.

4 Henry Clay Jones.

5 Benjamin Taliaferro Jones, b Nov.1, 1855, died young.

6 Frances Esther Jones Boon.

7 Francis Bartow Jones, b Aug.

26, 1859, d Mar. 15, 1914.

8 Sidney Johnston Jones.

9 Annie Lee Jones Dasher.

Mary Tallulah Jones, identified as No. 1. 10th line, was born Aug. 14, 1846, married Benjamin Massey, Apr. 7, 1868. Issue:

A Caroline Massey.

B Talaferro Massey, d unmarried.

C Mabel Massey.

D Daisy Massey.

Caroline Massey, A above, married Phillip Everett Pearce. Children:

a Louise Creswell Pearce, m Humphrey Tomkins. Children: Humphrey Tomkins, Jr.; and Jane Massey Tomkins.

Mabel Massey, C above, married Walter Britt Rogers. Children:

a Caroline Rogers, m Wiley S. Whitehead. Issue: June Whitehead.

b Walter Britt Rogers, Jr., died young.

c Elizabeth Rogers, m Frank A. Bowers. Mrs. Bowers was born July 14, 1906 at Manassas Va. Mr. Bowers is a son of Estelle Todd and James Andrew Bowers. Marriage occurred Aug. 29, 1923. Frank Andrew Bowers, Jr., born, Feb. 12, 1922.

d Lewis Rogers.

e Eleanor Rogers.

Daisy Massey, D above, married Elmo Peyton Nowlin, they have one child:

a Elizabeth Nowlin.

Laura Cornelia Jones, born Aug. 9, 1850, identified as 3, 10th line, married James E. Alfriend, Nov. 20, 1867. They had one child, Lillian Pauline Alfriend.

Henry Clay Jones, No. 4, 10th line, was born March 12, 1852, married Camilla Sims, Nov. 6, 1879. No issue.

Frances Esther Jones, No. 6, 10th line, was born June 20, 1857, married first, S. Jerome Harris, March 10, 1880, second, B. F. Boon. By her first husband she had one child, Hugh Harris, who died young.

Sidney Johnston Jones, who is No. 8 of the 10th line, was born Sept. 3, 1861, married his cousin, Lenora Ellen Jones, of Denton, Texas, on Feb. 21, 1895. Mrs. Jones is identified as B, 8th line.

Sidney Johnston Jones, was born and reared in Dougherty County, Ga. He attended the schools at Al-

bany until the age of 17 when he entered the law office of Wooten & Jones, where he read law for two years under Judge W. T. Jones, and was admitted to the bar on April 23, 1880. During the next two years he practiced with Judge D. A. Vason, one of the foremost lawyers of Georgia. On Jan. 1, 1887, Mr. Jones formed a partnership with Judge Samuel W. Smith, which continued until the death of Judge Smith in 1915. They specialized in Title abstracting and in conveyancing, and in this line of work, enjoyed for years, the largest practice in the section. Mr. Jones was a member of the Albany City Council, 1891, served as solicitor of County Court, now the City Court of Albany, from 1892 to 1896. At the time of his death, Mr. Jones in the point of service was the oldest member of the Albany bar. The author knew him for a few years before his death, but the relationship was quite pleasant for the short time of the acquaintance. His death occurred in 1925, funeral services were conducted by Rev. J. N. Peacock, pastor of the First Methodist Church and Dr. J. B. Turner, pastor of the First Baptist Church. Pall bearers were: Messrs. John H. Clark, W. H. Warren, Sr., H. H. Tarver, S. S. Bennett, Judge Clayton Jones and Cruger Westbrook. The above information was obtained from the notice of the death as published by the Albany Herald.

His wife was a daughter of James Taliaferro Jones, and was born at Pilot Point, Texas, June 16, 1873. She soon entered Franklin Seminary, later attending the public schools of Denton, Texas, she also attended the North Texas State Normal. Afterwards, she attended Baylor Female College, Belton, Texas, two years, graduating from the Art department of the Institute in 1892. On moving to Albany, she promptly identified herself with the religious, literary, civic and patriotic activities of the city. She was a charter member of the Albany Woman's Club, and of the Hospital Aid Association, serving both organizations as recording secretary. Until leaving Albany, after the death of her husband, she was an enthusiastic member of the Chautauqua, Literary and Scientific circles, graduating in 1915. By her regular and systematic study she earned forty-nine seals for her diploma. During the World War she gave herself completely to the service of her country, which she served as Director in the Surgical Training Department of the local Red Cross, and also as Director of publicity for the Woman's organization of the Dougherty County Red Cross Association. She also conducted the Navy knitting club under the auspices of the Thronateeska Chapter, D. A. R. She was for many years historian for the local Chapter, U. D. C's of Albany and was Regent from May, 1916 to May, 1918, during which time the Chapter grew in membership and efficiency and met every obligation imposed by the great War. In 1920, Mrs. Jones was elected to the office of Librarian of Georgia, D. A. R., in which she was eminently successful, due to her great love of books and her interest in genealogies. Mrs. Jones has a wonderful collection of scrap books which she has compiled. She rendered the people of Dougherty county invaluable service in connection with the History of Dougherty County which was issued under the auspices of the Thronateeska Chapter D. A. R. Mrs. Jones is a genealogist of no mean quality and has done some very valuable genealogical research work. In her manuscript of the Taliaferro family which was published a few years ago by the Lookout Magazine of Chattanooga, Tennessee, she attracted considerable attention and has been of invaluable aid to those interested in this work since.

She has been of wonderful help to the author in this work and it is to be regretted that because of the loss of her husband and family cares and her financial interests which require so much of her time, she has not been able to take over this Sketch which would have been so much better if she could have prepared it.

Annie Lee Jones, identified as 9 of the 10th line, was born March 7, 1864, married Arthur Lee Dasher, Dec. 7, 1886, res. 528 Broad St., Albany, Ga., children:

A Myrtice Dasher, married Dr. Mark E. Perkins, March 4, 1916. They have one child, M. E. Perkins, Jr.

B Capt. Arthur Lee Dasher, soldier in the World War, married

Lois Elizabeth Wright, daughter of Mr. Harry Wright and Harriet (Bullock) Wright and granddaughter of general Robert Bullock, of Fla., April 2, 1913. Mrs. Dasher died Nov. 1925. Mr. Dasher was born May 10, 1890. Issue: Arthur Lee Dasher, Jr., Elizabeth Care Dasher and Harriett Ann Dasher.

C Gladys Dasher.

D Mark Dasher.

E Lois Dasher, married William Robinson Pate, March 22, 1917. Their residence is 188 37th, St. Milwaukee, Wis. They have two children: Lois Elizabeth Pate and James Saxon Pate.

F Frances Dasher, married Leonard Bailey, children: Leonard Bailey, Jr., Lanier Bailey and Ann Celeste Bailey.

G Sidney Jones Dasher.

H Saxon Lanier Dasher.

Francis Marion Jones, 11th Line.

Francis Marion Jones, was born Aug. 11, 1822, was the son of John Lawrence and Lucy (Taliaferro) Jones, married Rebecca Etheridge. Children:

1 Marcellus Jones, b 1843, died when 14 years of age.

2 George N. Jones, b Jan. 3, 1844, served in Civil War, married Hopie Thomson, res. Pine Hurst, Ga. Issue: Sallie Jones, Richard Jones, killed in railroad accident, Cordele, Ga., 1910; William Jones. George N. Jones married second, Cora Mask, issue: Eva Mildred Jones; others died young.

3 John Thomas Jones, born Nov. 3, 1848, married Sarah Collins. Issue: Anna Roe Jones, David Jones, Zebulon Burdette Jones, Fort Gaines, Ga., Orrie Mella Jones, Sidney Johnston Jones, killed in railroad accident, Birmingham, Ala., Sallie Jones, Samuel Porter Jones, Henry Clay Jones, 1913 Crenshaw Boulevard, Los Angeles, Cal., Taliaferro Jones, Mabel Jones, Aaron Jones, killed by breaking of telephone pole, two infants deceased.

4 Hopie Ann Jones, married first S. J. Monk, second J. F. Scaif, Mrs. Scaife was married to Mr. Monk, Feb. 1, 1887, upon his death which occurred, Nov. 5, 1893, she married J. F. Scaife in Baker County, Georgia, Dec. 23, 1894.

No issue.

5 Taliaferro M. Jones, married Augusta Jenkins. He was born June 15, 1857, died May 28, 1903. Issue: Homer, res. 99 Jeff Davis St., Macon, Ga. Bycie, Benniah H., res. New York City, Paul Talliaferro Jones, b Oct. 28, 1887, at Smithville, Ga. m Bertye Chitty, Jan 16, 1914, daughter of Wm. H. Chitty and Rachael Moore. Their children are, Hachael Augusta Jones, b March 23, 1923; Pauline Jones, b Aug. 28, 1925. Talliaferro M. Jones has 2 other children, Mamie and Beff. Beff deceased.

6 Benniah H. Jones, born July 15, 1857, married Lula Rakestraw. Issue: Alma Jones and Bertie Jones.

7 Gertrude Jones, born Aug. 31, 1860, married Henry Taylor.

8 Georgia Rebecca Jones, born July 8, 1863, married "Dock" Sanders. Issue: Bessie Brown Sanders, Carrie Rebecca Sanders, Benniah Sanders, Grady Sanders, Otis Sanders, Ethel Sanders, Edith Sanders, Eva Sanders.

Seaborn Jones, 12th Line.

Seaborn Jones, born Jan. 22, 1824, son of John Lawrence and Lucy (Taliaferro) Jones, married .... Issue:

1 Thomas Jones.

2 Robert Jones, married ....

3 Taliaferro Jones.

4 Seaborn Jones, married ....

5 Alice Jones, married Marion Helms. Issue: Two sons.

6 Ida Jones.

HARDEN HINTS AND GENEALOGIES

MARK HARDIN

BY L. W. RIGSBY

CHAPTER VIII

There has been much confusion in regard to the early history of this family. A great many immigrants have come to America bearing the name of Hardin, Harden and Harding. The tendency among geneaiogists has been to get these various families of Hardins confused and connect them up, although no actual relationship exists.

In my work in connection with the Jones, Clay and Taliaferro families I have succeeded in discovering information which I think will be of importance to those interested in the Hardin family and this sketch is writ-*en, first, to supply information to Taliaferro and Clay descendants who are also descended from the Hardin family, and, second, to be a guide for future study for the history of this family. Lack of space and expense of printing forbids my giving documents in support of these genealogies. The reader is referred to Collin's "History of Kentucky", "Life of Col. Ben. Hardin", "History of Savannah and South Georgia" by Col. Hardin, "History of Georgia Baptists", Bench and Bar of Georgia", "History of Thomas County" and numerous documents of county records still extant.

Mark Hardin was born in Rouen, France in 1660. When he was aout twenty five years old Louis XIV issued the edict of Restoration, October 20, 1685, which had the effect of revoking the edict of Nantes. Mark Harden was a Huguenot and immediately fled from France, settling either in England or Wales. He married Mary Hogue, also spelled Hoge, but whether the marriage occurred before he fled from France or after is uncertain. Residing for a short while in England or Wales, he later moved to Canada with his family, but because of the rigid winters, came south and setttled in Virginia about 1706, where he resided in Prince William County until the time of his death about 1734.

It is possible that his residence was in that part of Prince William county which was cut off and organized into Fauquier county in 1759. It is probable that Mark Hardin had brothers who also came to America and settled. Evidence indicates that William Harden, who settled in South Carolina, and who was the ancestor of Gen. William Hardin of Marion'e Command and also Major Edward Harden, of Athens, Ga. was a brother. Children of Mark Hardin and Mary Hogue Harden were:

1st.   John Hardin
2nd.   Martin Hardin
3rd.   Mark Hardin
4th.   Henry Hardin
5th   Martha or Polly Hardin
6th   Abagail Hardin
7th.   Anne Hardin
8th.   Elizabeth Hardin
9th.   Alis Hardin

See will of Probate, Prince William County, Va.

HENRY HARDIN (4th Line)

Henry Hardin married Judith Lynch a near relative of Charles Lynch. He is said to have assisted at the Battle of King's Mountain, but was probably not a member of any regular organization because of his age. He was living in Pittaylvania Counjty at the time of his death, which occurred about 1796. Date of his birth is not known, but it was probably about 1710. Children were:

1. Avarillah Hardin, m a Wright.
2. Mary Hardin, m Capt. John Taliaferro. (See Taliaferro, Clay and Jones sketches for descend-

ants.

3. Mark Hardin.
4. William Hardin.
5. Elizabeth Hardin, m a Wilson.
6. Judith Hardin, m a Burgess.
7. Martin Hardin.
8. Henry Hardin.
9. Sarah Hardin, m a Burkhalter

Mark Hardin (3) moved from Virginia to North Carolina, where he resided for a good many years. He was twice married, first to Mary Hunter and second to Frances Newsome, the last marriage occurring in Warren County, Georgia. He was a soldier in the French and Indian War, serving under Gen. Washington at Braddock's Defeat. Many have thought he served in the Revolution, which is entirely proboable, but the service record assigned to him probably belonged to another Mark Hardin, who died in Kentucky. (See will, Warren County, Ga. Children by his first wife were:

A. Henry Hardin .
B. Mark Hardin, m Frances Hill in N. C. served as major in war of 1812, and had children: William Hill Hardin, b 1794, d 1884; John Hardin, died while Cadet in West Point; Lauriston Hardin, b 1803, d 1858; Pleasant H. Hardin; Mark Hardin; Cynthia Hardin; Harriet Hardin; Susan M. Hardin.
C. Martin Hardin, d unmarried about 1847 in Decatur County, Ga where he left a considerable estate and much of the proceedings of his adminstration is on record in Bainbridge, Ga.
D. James Hardin.
E. John Hardin.
F. Polly or Mary Hardin, m Jas. George and they were ancestors of the late U. S. Senator George from Mississippi.
G. Georgia Hardin.
H. Judith Hardin.
I. Willis Hardin.
J. Sallie or Sarah Hardin.
By second wife:
K. Martha or Patsy Hardin, m Jacob Garrard and resided at Columbus, Ga , and were ancestors of the late Louis Garrard of that place.
L. Nancy Hardin, m Clark Blandford. They also resided at Columbus, Ga., and their son, Mark Blandford was one of the Supreme Court Judges of the State of Georgia.
M. William S. Hardin, attorney at

law, d unmarried.

Henry Hardin (A) married first Sarah or Effie Cook, and second Matilda Jones. Children are said to have all been by his second wife. Henry Hardin was a soldier in the Revolutionary war, enlisting from Surrey Co. N. C. His pension record shows that he was born April 12, 1761, Johnston County N. C. (See will Walton County, Ga.) Children were:

a Effie Hardin, b Dec. 9, 1781, m Richard Fletcher, Warren County Ga., 1803. They were ancestors of U. S. Senator Duncan U. Fletcher, of Florida.
b Judith Hardin, b Sept. 14, 1783, m Thomas Stephens.
c Elizabeth Hardin, b Oct. 1, 1785 m first, Eads, 3children by Eads, m second Taylor.
d Mark Hardin, b March 8 1789, m Mary Hadley, one child.
e Benjamin Cook Hardin, b Nov. 16, 1792, d Dec. 10, 1847.
f Edward Jones Hardin, b Jan. 3, 1795.
g Rebecca Thomas Hardin, b Dec. 12, 1798, m Rice Green.
h Claressa Warren Harden, b Sept. 12, 1801, m Fen Gordon.
i Harriet Hargrove Hardin, b July 11, 1804, m Wiley Thornton.

Edward Jones Hardin (a)

Edward Jones Hardin, b 1795, d 1856, at Columbus, Ga., m Miss Jane Louisa Barrett in Augusta, Ga. She was born in 1803 and died at LaGrange, Ga., 1886. Mr. Hardin appears to have moved quite early to Port Saint Joseph, Fla., where they resided for a time, later moving to Columbus, Ga. Children were:

1' Ellen Jane Hardin, d unmarried
2' Georgia W. Hardin m Samuel Law.
3' Martin Benjamin Hardin m first Susie Taylor, second Josephine Law. Was a celebrated Baptist minister. A biographical sketch of his life is published on page 249, "History of Georgia Baptists."
4' Edward Henry Hardin, m Ellen S. Rodgers in Augusta, Ga., 1861.
5' Clara Hardin, deceased, never married.
6' Henrietta Matilda Hardin, b May 1, 1827, m first James Henry Carter, 2nd, Gen. James E. Harrison. She died July 30, 1909, in Waco, Texas. A son, Mr. James M. Carter resides in Waco and

has supplied considerable of the information necessary for the foregoing.

MARTIN HARDIN

There appears two Martin Hardins in Fauquier County, Va., information relating to Martin Hardin the first is rather meager. It appears that he had children as follows:

1. Martin Hardin, b 1720.
2. William Hardin, b 1722.
3. Mark Hardin, b 1723.
4. John Hardin, b 1724.
5. Benjamin Hardin, b 1726.

The name of his wife is uncertain. It has been stated that he married Lydia Waters, but the truth of this statement has not been established. This Martin Hardin was evidently the son of Mark Hardin and Mary Hogue of Prince William County, Va.

MARTIN HARDIN II.

Martin Hardin, II, of Fauquier county, Virginia, is said to have married Lydia Waters. He was evidently a grandson of Mark Hardin and Mary Hogue Hardin. I do not have sufficient information to determine as to which it was that married Lydia Waters. The wife of Martin Hardin II was certainly named Lydia, but as to whether or not her maiden name was waters, Hardin or some other name I am unable to say at this time. Children of Martin Hardin II were:

1. Sarah Hardin, b April 10, 1743.
2. Lydia Hardin, b April 10, 1748.
3. Mark Hardin b Dec. 1, 1750.
4. John Hardin, b Oct. 1, 1753.
5. Martin Hardin, b Feb. 1, 1757.
6. Rosannah Hardin, b March 9, 1760.

John Hardin (4), married Jane Davis Hardin and had four children:

A. Sarah Hardin, b 1774.
B. Martin Hardin.
C. Mark Hardin, b 1780.
D. Mary Hardin, died young.
E. Lydia Hardin, died young.
F. Rosannah Hardin b 1791 m Curtis Fields.

Martin Hardin (B) married Elizabeth Logan, daughter of Gen. Logan. This was Gen. Martin D. Hardin, who served as a major in the war of 1812 under Gen. Harrison. He served as Senator of Kentucky and died in 1823. Children were:

a. Gen. John J. Hardin, of Ill.
b. Gen. Martin D. Hardin, of the Civil War, d at St. Augustine, Florida.

c. Mrs. Ellen Hardin Walworth, one of the organizers of the D. A. R. and who died in 1915.

N. B. It was the mother of these three children who as a widow married Porter Clay, as shown by the Clay family. Chapter II.

JOHN HARDIN

This John Hardin is largely traditional and no records have been found extant relating to him. The cumulative evidence, however is that he was a resident of Virginia and circumstantial evidence indicates most strongly that he moved from Virginia to North Carolina where he died about the time of the Revolutionary War. No definite proof has been found to connect him with the Mark Hardin line. However, the facts and circumstances indicate that he was so connected. It is not known who he married, but it is thought that his wife and the wife of Mark Hardin, the 1st, of Georgia were related in some way. Children:

1. Adam Hardin.
2. Nicholas Hardin.
3. Eve Hardin, m David Clay, and for her descendants reference is made to Chap. IV. of the Georgia Branch of the Virginia Clays.
4. Lois Hardin, m Turnel Hayden. Tradition says that there were 3 other sons as follows: John, Mark and William, but I have been unable to clearly establish this.

Adam Hardin, son of John Hardin, above, was one of the first of the Hardins of whom we have any record in Georgia. He evidently came to Georgia when quite a young man, but the name of his wife is not known. He drew land in Wilkes County in 1789 and in Washington County in 1790, later moving to Putnam County where he died and where his will is probated. Children were:

1 John Harden, who m Elizabeth Spivey, sister of Moses Spivey, whomarried Sarah Harden.
2 Adam Harden, Jr. m first, Priscilla Adams, Nov. 2, 1818, and m second, Ann Elizabeth Flemming, by whom there are children.
3. Hutson Harden. No furhter information.
4. Mary Harden, m Abraham Roberts. This family lived in Coweta County, where they were pioneers of that section.

5. Sarah Harden, m Moses Spivey, and they were ancestors of Jessie Spivey who married Gov. Jos. M. Terrell.

6. William Henry Harden, is said to have moved to Florida and was killed by Indians.

7. Atkinson Tabor Harden, m Rebecca Cloud, lived at Rome, Ga., but have no descendants living.

8 Sandlin Harden, m Polly Stevenson ,had one child, Rhoda Harden, who married a Carlisle, of Troup County, Ga. and died probably without issue.

9. Lennie Harden, m Moore Stevenson. This family originally lived in Coweta County, Ga. Most of the children moved to Texas. The children were named: William Stevenson, Thomas Stevenson, Franklin Stevenson, Joseph Stevenson, James Stevenson, Augustus Stevenson, Elizabeth Stevenson and Emma Stevenson.

Nicholas Hardin (2) son of John Hardin, died in Washington County, Ga. The name of his wife is not known. Children were.

A James Monroe Hardin, b 1797, d Aug. 6, 1862, m first Polly Reeves, name of second wife, not known.

B John Hardin, served as clerk of Baptist Church, Washington Co., and later moved to Ala.

C Thomas Hardin.

D William Hardin, d a bachelor.

E Nicholas Hardin, d a bachelor.

F Adam Hardin, moved to Sumter County, Ga., and resided near Americus for a time, later moving to Florida or Alabama.

G Mary, or Polly Hardin, m William Monroe Clay. See "Georgia Branch of the Virginia Clays" Chap. V.

H Elizabeth, or Betsy Hardin, m a Glenn.

I Sallie Hardin, m Richard Smith.

VALENTINE HARDIN

Valentine Hardin is said to have been a nephew of John Hardin above, and the first cousin of Adam Hardin, the first. Tradition is that he was born in 1770. He married Margaret Castlebery about 1790 or 91, died in 1800, age thirty years. He is buried in Washington County, Georgia. His childen were:

1. Betsy Hardin m William Barton
2. Sallie Hardin, m James Dowdy.

3. Rosa Hardin, m Carter Crew, and lived near Dallas, Ga.

4. William Henry Hardin.

William Henry Hardin, (4) was b Jan. 29, 1798, married Nancy Cloud, Sept. 21, 1820. Children were:

A Martha Hardin, b Dec. 3, 1821, m Dr. Swan Burnette, at Cassvill, Ga., Sept. 8, 1835, d on plantation in Clay County, Ga., 1841, buried at Fort Gaines.

B Elizabeth Amanda Hardin b in McDonough, Ga., Nov. 22, 1823, m James M. Spurlock, Nov. 25, 1838, at Armurchee plantation, in Floyd County, near Rome Ga.

C Mary Blanche Hardin, b June 10, 1828 at McDonough, Ga., m William Johnstone at the Armuchee Plantation, Aug. 9, 1843, d at Rome., Ga. 1853.

D Mark A. Hardin, b at McDonough, Ga., Sept. 21, 1830, d at Atlanta, Ga., m Emma Sullivan, of Greenville District, S. C., Jan. 15, 1851. Legislator from Bartow County, Ga., and Reading Clerk, Georgia House of Representatives for several years.

E Josephine Hardin, b at Armuchee Platation, Feb. 21, 1839, d at Kingston, Ga. m John A. Beck, of Griffin, Ga., 1858.

F John Forsyth Hardin b at Armucheo plantation, Oct. 9, 1842, m Mary Roper, at Kingston, Ga. Sept. 31, 1872, d in Atlanta, Ga., Aug. 3, 1887. There were two girls who died young.

WILLIAM HARDIN

One William Harden settled in South Carolina some time before 1720 He is supposed to have gone from Kent, England to the Island of Barbadoes, and from there to South Carolina. Very little is definitely known of this William Harden, but it is quite likely that he was a brother of Mark Harden, of Prince William County, Va. He had a son, William Hardin, b Nov. 22, 1720, who died in Prince William Parish, S. C., Sept 12, 1760. This William had a son, William Harden, who was a colonel of a regiment under Gen. Frances Marion during the war of the Revolution. He was born in Prince William Parish, S. C. Sept. 8, 1742, and died there Nov. 28, 1785. This William Harden was the father of Thomas Hutson Harden and brother of Edward Harden, and from these two, Thomas Hutson Hardin and Edward Harden, the Hardens, of Athens Ga., and Savannah, Ga., originated. Col. William Hardin and Major Edward Harden had a sister, Rebecca. who married a White and they are the ancestors of the Stillwells, of Rome, Ga.

Other Hardens that should be mentioned in this connection are Henry Harden and Joel Harden, both of whom married Crabtrees. From these are descended the Hardens of Stewart and those around Andersonville.

There are several other Hardens mentioned in the early records of Ga. most of whom probably belong to the family of Mark Harden of Prince William County, Va. To trace them out and connect them up is beyond the scope of this work. Later, if sufficient interest should be manifested this may be done.

BEHEATHLAND LUVINIA (CLAY) RIGSBY.

The subject of this brief sketch was the mother of the author of the foregoing sketches. They were prepared in response to an oft repeated request made before her death. The author had intended to delay their preparation and publication until he had reached a more advanced age and demand for the work had become more insistent. But upon having been brought rather close to death in 1921 and having been made to realize the uncertainty of life and the danger of dying without having fulfilled my mother's request I began the work. The work is therefore really my mother's and I have been only the instrument in executing her designs. I have been placed under obligation to so many of my kindred that it is impossible to enumerate and give credit to all, but in addition to my mother, all kindred whose names appear in the foregoing sketches are gratefully thanked, and every mention is honorable. My mother was known in her girlhood as "Hettie" or "Hetthie" Clay and it was this name that she liked best. She was the youngest child of Lewis Clay and Judith (Jones) Clay, and was born Oct. 31st, 1839 in Wilkinson Co. Georgia. Her parents moved to Sumter county, Georgia while she was quite young. Remaining there for only a few years the family moved to Lee County, Georgia. She was living

in Lee County near where Dawson, Georgia is now situated when Terrell County was organized.

She was educated under Professor McNulty at Dawson and taught for several, years, teaching in several counties of the State. Her methods were in advance of the period in which she taught and many of the boys and girls taught by her have made a success of their lives.

December the 11th 1866 she was married to Lewis Johnson Rigsby, the ceremony having been performed in Decatur County, Georgia, by her brother the Rev. John B. Clay.

Her complexion was fair, eyes gray, hair auburn and her height about five feet and six inches and she weighed from one hundred forty pounds when young to one hundred eighty when older. Her features were agreeable and her face the most expressive of her emotions of any that I have ever seen. Grief, pain, suffering, pleasure, or anger stamped themselves unmistakably on her features.

Her mentality was well developed along lines of literature and science. Her memory, imagination, reason and judgment was all of a high order. For several years her health was poor but it was due to no organic cause, rather of a nervous character.

Her ideals were high, her morals above criticism and her temperament religious. She had some musical talent and sometimes had premonitions of coming events.

She joined the Baptist church when quite young at Dawson Ga., and remained a consistent Christian during her entire life, her membership having been at various times with New Hope, Cairo, Pleasant Grove and Capel Churches. She took an active interest in Sunday Schools and Missionary activities. It was probably a Sunday School organized and taught by her that laid the foundation for the organization of the Capel Baptist Church.

Her interest in the unfortunate was always sympathetic and she extended the helping hand to alleviate the suffering of many such.

During the last term of school she taught she became attached to one of the pupils in her school, the daughter of a widow, Mrs. Subrina Hesters, and the attachment being mutual, and the child's mother consenting thereto, the child was taken as an adopted daughter. Between these two there existed a mutual bond of affection equal if not superior, to most mothers and daughters. This extended to and lasted until the death of my mother.

She was a faithful wife and devoted daughter, providing a home for her aged father and mother until their death. She was also one of the wisest and kindest of mothers.

Her death occurred at Cairo, Ga., Oct. 28th, 1916 and her grave is by that of her husband at Long Branch Cemetery, one head stone marking both graves.

Children were Istalina Attwood who died at ten years of age; Lewis Wiley author of this Sketch and Jennie the adopted daughter who married Robert M. Mott, December 1888. Mrs. Mott is now a resident of Cairo, Georgia, her husband having died a few years past.

Ancestry and Posterity of Dr. John Taliaferro and Mary (Hardin) Taliaferro

WITH NOTES ON---

Berryman, Newton, Beheathland, Franklin, Lingo and Other Southern Families. Compiled by Willie Catherine Ivey and dedicated to the memory of Dr. John Taliaferro. His name shall be as lasting as the country he honored.

❧★❧

A union of hearts, and a union of hands,
Of life's sweetest joys that time cannot sever;
Where love abounds, true fellowship stands,
His name shall abide forever.

❧★❧

Foreword

This sketch has been compiled for the purpose of preserving the family history and heritage of Dr. John Taliaferro and his beloved wife, Mary Hardin. When I began this work, I had no idea that their descendants were so numerous and the families so widely scattered; I have found that the task of completing the rolls of descendants lies beyond the limits of my pen, and depends largely upon the interest manifested by the various branches of the family. There are more than one hundred and fifty families who have failed to send me their lines of descent and I have been unable to record their names in the lineage. I desire to make acknowledgements to those, who from the start, have given me not only sympathetic encouragement, but substantial help. I desire especially to thank Judge Lewis Wiley Rigsby, Cairo, Ga., who has fostered the publication of this work; his unceasing co-operation and his careful management, have made an otherwise arduous task, comparatively light; and without his unnumbered courtesies, this sketch could never have been compiled. And to those who have lent me a helping hand by going through old files and papers, old church records, old state records, family Bibles, and various other documents to secure dates and records which soon, perhaps, would have passed into oblivion; for their substantial help and co-operation, I feel myself a lasting debtor. The list includes: Mrs. Minnie Bagley Bradshaw, Judge Ira Stanley Chappell, the late Mr. Clifton Thomas Chappell, Miss Judy Franklin, Mr. Shadrack C. Franklin, Mr. Alfred L. Holman (Genealogist), Mr. Joseph Edward Hendrix, Mrs. Olive McWilliams Hatcher, Miss Adelene Ivey, Mrs. Coral Beville Jones, Mrs. Lenora Jones (Mrs. Sidney J.), Mrs. Mayme Callaway Jones, Mrs. Julia Porter Kitchens, Mrs. Winifred Stewart Kent, Mr. Walter Wylie Lovill, Judge Lewis Wiley Rigsby, Mrs. Fannie Johnson Shelverton, Mr. Charles P. Taliaferro, Mrs. Louise Ivey Whitehurst, Mrs. Bettie Brantley Wright, Mrs. Pattie Franklin Taliaferro and numerous others, who have helped preserve the records of this family. The short- comings of the work are mine. May there yet be some other descendant better qualified for this work than I, who will undertake and complete the task which I have begun.

WILLIE CATHERINE IVEY.

Tennille, Ga.,
July 31, 1926.

CHAPTER I.

EARLY ACCOUNTS OF THE TALIAFERRO FAMILY

The Taliaferro family has been so very numerous and widely spread throughout the South and West that it would be now, perhaps impossible to prepare a pedigree including all its branches. This sketch records only such portions of the family that bear directly upon the life, the ancestry, and posterity of Dr. John Taliaferro. Accounts of the earlier portion of the Taliaferro family have been derived chiefly from records at Court House, Essex Co., Va., and from the correspondence of Thomas Jefferson in the Archives Dept. of the Congressional Library at Washington, where there are some letters of George Wythe to Mr. Jefferson, which are interesting in connection with the history of the origin of the family; Mr. Wythe's interest in the matter being due to the fact that his wife at that time (his second wife) was Elizabeth. daughter of Col. Richard Taliaferro of James City County, Va. During Mr. Jefferson's stay in London and Paris in 1786-87 he secured for his friend, George Wythe, a copper plate engraved with the Arms of Taliaferro, and the best editions of "Vitruvius" and "Polybius" containing much of the early history of this family.

The correspondence of Mr. Wythe and Mr. Jefferson accepts the Italian origin of the family; the name originating from the Latin "tutum ferre," meaning "to bear a sword or dart." Tradition says that this name was bestowed upon a barbarian during Cæsar's campaign in Gaul 58 B. C., when a barbarian who saved the life of Cæsar was rewarded for his bravery by being made Armor Bearer to Cæsar; this being a great privilege, in as much as it was contrary to custom in the Roman Camps to allow a barbarian to carry arms, Mr. Wythe supposes the Italian Emigrant to be Lawrence Taliaferro, who came to Scotland in 1500; but there are grounds for even an earlier origin, and there is no doubt that the family had been long seated in England before their emigration to Virginia.

A branch of the Taliaferro family wandered into Normandy; Taliofor of Talafer being the name of a Norman

knight who came over to England with William the Conqueror in 1060; he being called the hero of Hastings. He received large grants of land for his bravery in County Kent, which descended to his posterity, who became the Earls of Pennington.

In Bulwer's novel, "Harold," there is the story of a troubadour named Taliaferro who was a personal friend of William the Conqueror. This Taliaferro died a gallant death at Hastings.

In 804 A. D., a Taliaferro was created Duke de Angouleme by Charles the Bold of France, and in Hume's History of England there is a record of the marriage of Isabelle Taliaferro, daughter of Count de Angouleme to King John of England; and from them descended a long line of kings and queens. They were also dukes of the Plantagenet line, thus linking not only with the Norman King, but with the old line of English rulers, Edward the Confessor and others.

Be that as it may, the first of the family in Virginia was the Emigrant, Robert Taliaferro, Gentleman. It is not known from what country Robert Taliaferro came, but as he and his sons were Protestants, it is supposed that religious freedom was the cause of the emigration. He first resided in York County; the records showing that his name first appears about 1645. He was a man of consequence; for he had large grants of land in Gloucester County and on the Rappahannock River, including one of 6500 acres, which he patented jointly with Major Lawrence Smith. The grant in Gloucester is dated 1655, and in the document the name is written "Toliver," thus showing that the pronunciation is the same as it is to-day. He married Sarah, daughter of Rev. Charles Grymes of "Brandon," and aunt of Hon. John Grymes, receiver general of Virginia. He died about 1682.

From the Emigrant, Robert Taliaferro, there has come a long line of descendants, some of whom remained in Virginia, while many others moved with their families South and West, settling in Kentucky, Tennessee, North and South Carolina, Alabama and Georgia. Among these worthy descendants of the Emigrant, Robert Taliaferro, there was one Dr. John Taliaferro, a physician, a soldier, and a Baptist minister, who moved from his home on Bannister River, Pittsylvania Co., Va., in 1779 to Surry County, North Carolina, settling on Fisher's River; and later, about 1790-91, he removed to Wilkinson County, Georgia, where he has to-day some worthy descendants who feel a pride in his name and service. From this good man there has descended a number of prominent Baptist ministers, physicians lawyers, and statesmen, residing in this and other Southern States.

CHAPTER II.

THE TALIAFERRO ARMS AND FAMILY TRAITS

The crest of arms that was adopted by the English branch of the Taliaferro family bears the motto "Viresco," meaning "I Flourish"; thus signifying the unison of the Plantagenet and English line of rulers.

The Italian crest, which is generally accepted as the most authentic, has been adopted by the Virginia branch of the Taliaferro family and is the one that is pictured in this sketch. It is as follows:

"It is a shield with a bar of iron crossing from the sinister chief to the dexter base, a sword of gold cutting through the bar of iron; handle of sword in dexter chief; point in sinister base; one gold rowel for a spur, or mullet, in honor point; another in pacific middle base. Colors: Pure ruby in right shield, pure silver in left, bar of iron brown, sword gold, rowels gold. Crest above the shield is an ancient helmet of blue. Motto: "Fortis et Firmis."

To give an accurate and comprehensive account of the personal traits and characteristics of the Taliaferro family is no easy task; for it is only after years of association, observation, and

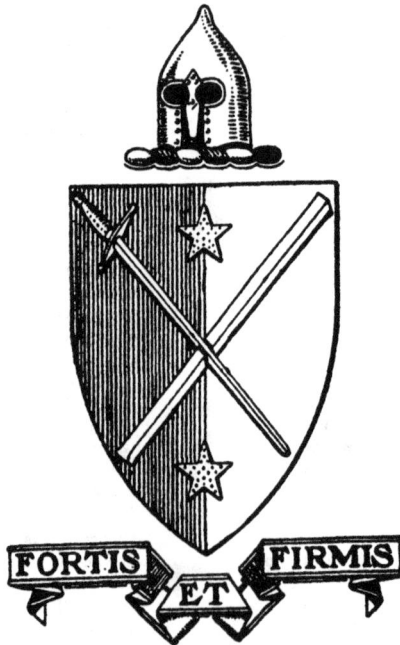

Taliaferro Crest and Arms

experience that one can truly appreciate their many virtues and discount their shortcomings. It is only here and there that one finds a descendant of the present generation who still clings to the old personalities which predominated this people; the old customs and ways of living which guided their lives in their home, in politics, in war and in religion; yet to fully grasp the context of this sketch, it is essential to know something of their family life and the principles for which they stood; to know that they ranked first in war and first in peace; were loved by friend and admired by foe; and surmounting all else was their unchanging faith and trust in the Almighty God.

The earliest traditional accounts of the Taliaferro family, dating back to 58 B. C., show them to be a tribe of barbarians, living about twelve miles from the present site of Florence, Italy. The old legend states that they excelled in music and in warfare; being born to the one they achieved the other and history as well as tradition shows that they sang as they entered into battle.

Wace, the chronicler describes the brave minstrel thus:

"Taillefer, who sang very well,
On a horse that ran swiftly,
Went before the duke singing
Of Charlemagne and of Roland,
Of Oliver and of the Vassals
Who died at Roncesvalles."

Their lives were marked by courage, bravery and a desire for leadership. From the earliest period they have fought, bled and died for their country's cause; thus proving the truth of the words of the late Theodore Roosevelt, "Only those are fit to live who are not afraid to die."

Other features which characterized this family are ambition, influence and power. They also possessed a marked degree of culture and education. During the Medieval Age a branch of this family married into the Royal household; and children of their flesh and blood have held in their hands the destiny of nations. They threw aside the bonds of barbarism and achieved the highest honors that God has bestowed upon mortal man. They were men whom power could not corrupt; death could not terrify; defeat could not dishonor.

As to personal appearance, they are said to have possessed to a marked degree the Italian type of brunette beauty, being tall and stalwart of form. As to religion, they were no doubt of the Roman Catholic faith, but after the emigration of the family to England, they adhered to the Church of England and the old church records of Virginia show that during the Colonial period they were still of the Episcopal faith. It was no doubt desire for religious freedom and conquest which caused the emigration of the family to America. Dr. John Taliaferro and his children were of the Baptist faith. But regardless of the sect or creed, one seldom found a Taliaferro who failed to manifest the utmost faith and trust in God. The church and state records indicate that the descendants of the Emigrant, Robert Taliaferro, were men of honor and of trust; holding high social, political, and religious offices in the old Virginia Colony.

In the family of Dr. John Taliaferro there predominated certain characteristics so marked as to be termed by some members of the family the "Taliaferro Trademark." Among the present day descendants one seldom finds these characteristics combined in one personality; however, it is still in

evidence among some branches, the most noticeable being the Tennessee branch of the family. Mr. John Dickerson Rose, Kingston, Tenn., in describing these characteristics says: "As to family traits, our people are very clannish, they will scrap with themselves, nothing serious; but for an outsider to interfere and impose on any member of the family, the whole bunch resents it, and it means a sure enough fight. As to religion, they are all Baptists and as to politics, they are all democrats, and I mean sure enough ones at that. My mother is still an unconquered rebel and she doesn't mean Confederate either, just a plain rebel. Our Kentucky kinsmen are feudists. They have been killing and being killed for about one hundred years, but civilization is finally overcoming that." A vivid description of these Kentucky feudists, referred to by Mr. Rose, may be found in the "Trail of the Lonesome Pine."

These boys were reared according to the best standards of their day, but they evidently inherited a double portion of the fighting spirit which so characterized those of the early Christian Era. Their fellow kinsmen are gratified to know that these feudists have laid aside the armor of warfare and have returned to civilization and to God.

In speaking of family traits, Mrs. Luvenia Taliaferro, wife of the late Richard Dickerson Taliaferro, says that the Taliaferro by-word is "By Blood." Her husband served with honor and distinction during the War Between the States; he and his brothers singing as they entered into battle. He was present when Lee surrendered to Grant at Appomattox and said, "I would rather die than surrender." His wife relates an amusing incident which occurred when Mr. Taliaferro had already passed his three score years and ten. He and his good wife attended a circus at Leon, Oklahoma, during which the band played "Dixie." He felt the old southern blood tingling in his veins; waving his hat high in the air, he entered the ring amidst the cheers of spectators and cried, "Play it again! Play it again!" His wife rushing to his side, tapped him on the shoulder and said, "Hush Papa, you'll get arrested." Paying no attention to her entreaty, he shouted, "By blood, there aren't enough men under this tent to arrest me." He continued to wave his hat and sing, while the band continued to play the old southern melody and the crowd laughed and cheered.

Family tradition credits the home of Dr. John Taliaferro with being a home where love and religion walked hand in hand. It is said that the love they bore for one another surpassed all understanding; friends and visitors found the welcome of true southern hospitality awaiting them; and the stranger within their midst found the latch-string on the outside of the door. Their hearts were kind; they delighted in relieving the wants of their fellow creatures, and cultivated that divine pleasure by the most liberal and unpretending methods; to the poor they were benefactors; to the rich, examples; to the wretched, comforters; their piety went hand in hand with their benevolence, and they thanked their Creator for being permitted to do good.

CHAPTER III.

THE TALIAFERROS IN VIRGINIA

The known lineage of the Virginia branch of the Taliaferro family begins with the Emigrant, Robert Taliaferro, who came to Virginia in 1645. He was a man of prominence; he and his sons holding high state and church offices in the Colony. He owned large tracts of land including one of 6,500 acres, which he patented jointly with Major Lawrence Smith. His children and grand-children were related by blood and marriage to the first families of Virginia; their names being mentioned in "The Genuine Aristoc of Virginia" and in The Richmond Critic as "The First Families of Virginia." Robert Taliaferro was married to Sarah Grymes, daughter of Rev. Charles Grymes of "Brandon," then of Gloucester, now of Middlesex County. Robert Taliaferro and Maj. Lawrence Smith, being great friends and intimately associated in business, were drawn still closer together by the intermarriage of their children, John Taliaferro and Sarah Smith. The terms of the treaty at Yorktown were arranged in the Moore House which, at one time, belonged to Maj. Lawrence Smith, and at this time was owned and occupied by his great-granddaughter, Lucy, the wife of Col. Augustine Moore. Nicholas Taliaferro, the great-great-grandson of Major Lawrence Smith, was present when the treaty was made. This estate is now known as "Temple Farm." (See William and Mary College Quarterly, Vol. II., Nos. 1, 4; Vol. IX, No. 1; Vol. X, No. 4; Vol. XX, No. 4; Vol. V, No. 3; Vol. VIiI, No. 2; Vol. X, No. 1; Vol. XII, Nos. 1, 2; Second Series, Vol. I, No. 3.)

If it were possible to prepare a pedigree including all the descendants of the Emigrant, Robert Taliaferro, the lineage would probably be of such magnitude that the average person could not comprehend it. With the exception of the first John Taliaferro, who married Sarah Smith, the descendants of Robert Taliaferro and his wife, Sarah Grymes, are not continued further than this chapter. For convenience the descendants of John Taliaferro and Sarah Smith have been arranged in a separate chapter. (See Chapter IV.)

Robert Taliaferro and his wife Sarah (Grymes) Taliaferro had issue: First, Robert; second, Francis; third, John; fourth, Richard; fifth, Catherine; sixth, Charles.

POSTERITY

I. Robert Taliaferro (son of the Emigrant Robert Taliaferro and Sarah (Grymes) Taliaferro). Authorities: In 1672-3 Robert Taliaferro, Jr., "Son of Robert Taliaferro," had a grant of land on the Rappahannock River, adjoining the land of Henry Corbin and Mr. Grymes, which was due him, the said "Robert Taliaferro Jr.," as "the grandson of Mr. Grymes." On June 1, 1687, Robert Taliaferro gave bond for the estate of Robert Taliaferro, deceased. He married Sarah Catlett, daughter of Col. John Cattlett and Elizabeth Underwood. (Elizabeth Underwood was one of the step-daughters of Capt. John Upton of Isle of Wight County. She married first Capt. Francis Slaughter of Rappahannock County; second, Col. John Catlett; third, Rev. Amory Butler.) A deed in Essex County, dated 1687, shows that Robert Taliaferro and Francis Taliaferro and their wives, Sarah and Eliza-

beth, sold 300 acres, part of the
land bequeathed to said Sarah and
Elizabeth by John Catlett, their
father. Robert and Sarah (Catlett) Taliaferro had issue:
A. Robert Taliaferro (In 1711-12
Robert Taliaferro, calling himself "only son and heir apparent
of Robert Taliaferro, de-
ceased," made a bond to Augustine Smith.) He married Margaret (Buckner?). Margaret
Taliaferro, on Aug. 7, 1711, ap-
points R. Buckner, Attorney, to
relinquish dower in 100 acres
sold by her husband, Robert
Taliaferro. Robert and Margaret (Buckner?) Taliaferro had
issue:
1. Robert Taliaferro.
2. Ann Taliaferro.
3. Elizabeth Taliaferro.
In Jan., 1724, Robert Taliaferro, the
elder, gave his two daughters, Ann and
Elizabeth, a negro apiece.
II. Francis Taliaferro (son of Emigrant Robert Taliaferro and Sarah
(Grymes) Taliaferro). In 1688,
John and Francis Taliaferro gave
bond for Mrs. Sarah (Grymes)
Taliaferro, widow of Robert Taliaferro. Francis Taliaferro of
Gloucester made a deed to his
brother, John, son of Robert Taliaferro, deceased, of Rappahannock
County, Sept. 28, 1682. On the
same day Francis Taliaferro made
a deed to brothers Richard and
John, Francis Taliaferro was living in Gloucester County in 1682;
Justice of Essex Co . 1690-1700;
married Elizabeth Catlett, daughter of Col. John Catlett. In 1701
Francis and Elizabeth (Catlett)
Taliaferro sold 416 acres in Essex
Co., half of a tract granted to Col.
John Catlett Sept. 10, 1000; and
by his will given to his two daughters, Elizabeth and Sarah, "The
said land was surveyed and perfected for Mr. Francis Taliaferro,
as marrying Elizabeth, daughter
of Col. John Catlett, May 4, 1691.
Per Will Moseley, Surveyor."
Francis Taliaferro died 1710. In
1710, Elizabeth, as admx. of Francis Taliaferro, presented an inventory of estate. On March 20,
1716, John Taliaferro of "The
Mount," and Thomas Catlett go on
Elizabeth Taliaferro's bond as
admx. Francis and Elizabeth
(Catlett) Taliaferro had issue:

A. Francis Taliaferro; mentioned
in the Will of his uncle, William
Catlett, dated 1697, proved 1699;
nothing further is known of him.
B. John Taliaferro of "The
Mount." (Aug. 17, 1725, in a
lease and release of land to Robert Taliaferro of Stafford, his
brother, he says the land was
taken up by his father, Francis
Taliaferro, in co-partnership
with Henry Brice.) John Taliaferro of "The Mount" married
Agatha ——?, and had issue:
1. Francis Taliaferro.
2. John Taliaferro.
C. Robert Taliaferro "of Stafford
County." His will recorded in
Essex County, Dec. 3, 1725; he
names his brothers and sister,
Eliza, wife of Thomas Stribling,
and their children, and sister,
Agatha Taliaferro, as his heirs.
He had no children.
D. Eliza Taliaferro married Thomas Stribling.
E. Col. Richard Taliaferro. Virginia Gazette, July 3, 1779, "died
Richard Taliaferro, Esq., in the
74th year of his age, with the
gout in his head." He lived in
James City County, Virginia;
married Elizabeth Eggleston.
His Will dated Feb. 3, 1775, was
proved Aug. 19, 1779. Issue:
1. Richard Taliaferro; a scholar
at William and Mary College
in 1754; married Rebecca
Cooke, daughter of Richard
Cooke of Surry County. Issue:
a. Richard Taliaferro; died
without issue before 1787.
b. Elizabeth Taliaferro; married Daniel Call, the celebrated lawyer.
c. Ann Taliaferro; married
Carter Nicholas.
d. Rebecca Taliaferro; married William Browne.
e. Sarah Taliaferro; married
William Wilkinson of James
City County.
f. Lucy Taliaferro.
g. Benjamin Taliaferro; married a Miss Tazwell.
h. Robert Taliaferro; b. Nov.
1, 1783; married Miss Wilkinson.
2. Elizabeth Taliaferro; married
George Wythe. George Wythe
was Professor of Law and
Police of William and Mary
College; also one of the sign-

ers of the Declaration of Independence. Elizabeth Taliaferro was his second wife.

F. Capt. William Taliaferro; b. Jan. 17, 1707-08; Justice of Essex County; married Ann Walker. Issue:

1. Walker Taliaferro; member of House of Burgesses from Carolina Co. 1765-1773; member of the County Committee 1774-76. He had issue:
   a. William Taliaferro; married Elizabeth Hartwell.
2. Christopher Taliaferro.
3. Lucy Taliaferro; married 1st, Col. Charles Carter of Cloves; 2nd, William Jones.

III. John Taliaferro (son of Emigrant Robert Taliaferro and Sarah (Grymes) Taliaferro); was the first of the family to bear the name of "John" in Virginia and it was from him that Dr. John Taliaferro descended. (For his descendants see Chapter IV.)

IV. Richard Taliaferro (son of Emigrant Robert Taliaferro and Sarah (Grymes) Taliaferro); very little is known of him. Records in Essex Co. show that he and his brother, Charles, were under age in 1682.

V. Catherine Taliaferro. (Daughter of Emigrant Robert Taliaferro and Sarah (Grymes) Taliaferro.) In 1686 Charles and Catherine Taliaferro chose brother Robert as guardian. In 1687 a deed shows that Capt. John Battaile Sr. married Catherine, daughter of Robert Taliaferro, deceased. There is no record of issue by this marriage. John Battaile was a captain of rangers in active service against the Indians in 1692. He was a burgess from that same county in the same year and again in 1696. At the time of his death he was colonel of the militia. He married I. Catherine Taliaferro; II. Elizabeth Smith. That his second wife was a daughter of Major Lawrence Smith is proved by a deed recorded in Essex, February 1707-08. The legatees of his will were his wife, Elizabeth, his sons, John, who was under seven years at the time of his will: Hay, Lawrence and Nicholas, and his daugh-

ter, Elizabeth. On account of the destruction of most of the records of Caroline County, where the family afterward resided, it is difficult to trace the descendants. Capt. Nicholas Battaile, youngest son of John Battaile, resided at "Hay" in Caroline County. He married I. Mary Thornton; II. Hannah Taylor, sister to Zachary Taylor, grandfather of President Taylor. She had a son, Hay Battaile, who went to Kentucky in 1819.

VI. Charles Taliaferro. (Son of Emigrant Robert Taliaferro and Sarah (Grymes) Taliaferro). Living in Essex 1724; married ——? Issue:

A. Charles Taliaferro; he predeceased his father; married Sarah, who probably was Sarah Slaughter. Issue:

1. Mary Taliaferro; married Thomas Turner.
2. Sarah Taliaferro; b. 1727; d. 1784; marred 1st, 1744, Capt. Francis Conway II; 2nd, 1767, Col. George Taylor. Issue by first marriage, at least one child.
   a. Sarah Conway, who married her step-brother, Charles Taylor, son of Col. George Taylor and his first wife, Rachel Gibson.
   Issue by second marriage:
   b. ——Taylor (a son, who was born in 1769).
3. Catherine Taliaferro.

The Will of the elder Charles Taliaferro (1734) devises his estate to three grand-daughters, Mary, Sarah and Catherine Taliaferro, with reversion to daughter-in-law, Sarah Taliaferro. Hayden quotes the Will in full. In 1749 Thomas and Mary (Taliaferro) Turner and Francis and Sarah (Taliaferro) Conway convey the same property by deed. In passing, it is interesting to note that one of the Excrs. to the Will of the elder Charles Taliaferro was Francis Thornton, whose wife was Mary, the sister of John Taliaferro of "Snow Creek," and a niece of the decedent; one of the witnesses to the Will was Thomas Slaughter, whose wife was Sarah, Francis Thornton's daughter. The grouping of these people in this connection may give a hint as to the identity of Sarah Taliaferro, the daughter-in-law; she was probably a Slaughter.

CHAPTER IV.

THE FIRST JOHN TALIAFERRO

John Taliaferro, son of the Emigrant Robert Taliaferro and his wife, Sarah (Grymes) Taliaferro. (See Chapter III, No. III), was the first of the family to bear the name of "John" in Virginia. He and his children played an important part in the social, state and church life of the Colony, but owing to the destruction of the records in Caroline County, where most of the family resided, it has been impossible to obtain a complete record of the lives of his children. Because of this fact there has existed for some time a false idea as to the parents of Capt. Richard Taliaferro, who married Rose Berryman. Some historians have claimed that he was a son of Zachariah Taliaferro (b. 1683; d. 1745); but the Will of the first John Taliaferro, dated 1715, proved 1720 in Essex County, discloses the fact that Captain Richard Taliaferro was a son of the first John Taliaferro and his wife, Sarah (Smith) Taliaferro. The records contained in this chapter are proved by the original court records of Essex, Spotsylvania and Orange Counties; the parentage of Captain Richard Taliaferro has the personal endorsement of Dr. Lyon G. Tyler, the former President of William and Mary College and Editor of the College Quarterly, and who is the present Editor of Tyler's Historical and Genealogical Magazine.

The first John Taliaferro was a lieutenant commanding a company of rangers against the Indians in 1692; Justice of Essex, 1695; Sheriff; member of House of Burgesses, 1699. He married Sarah, daughter of Major Lawrence Smith (see deed of Francis Taliaferro to brother, John, who is about to marry Sarah Smith, 1682.) He was a large land holder in Essex County and the bricks for building his beautiful home, "Powhattan," were brought over from England. John Taliaferro died in 1720, and his Will, dated June 1, 1715, was proved in Essex County June 21, 1720. It names his wife, Sarah, and his children, Zachariah, Lawrence, John, Mary, Elizabeth, Charles, Robert, Catherine, Richard, and William.

John and Sarah (Smith) Taliaferro had issue:
First, Zachariah Taliaferro.
Second, Lawrence Taliaferro.
Third, John Taliaferro of "Snow Creek."
Fourth, Mary Taliaferro.
Fifth, Elizabeth Taliaferro.
Sixth, Charles Taliaferro.
Seventh, Robert Taliaferro.
Eighth, Catherine Taliaferro.
Ninth, Richard Taliaferro.
Tenth, William Taliaferro.

First Line.

Zachariah Taliaferro.

Zachariah Taliaferro, son of John and Sarah (Smith) Taliaferro, was born in Essex County, Virginia, 1683; died in Caroline County 1745. He was one of the executors of his father's will. The name of his wife is unknown. Issue:
I. Catherine Taliaferro.

Second Line:

Lawrence Taliaferro

Captain Lawrence Taliaferro, son of John Taliaferro and Sarah (Smith) Taliaferro; Sheriff of Essex Co. 1720; married Sarah Thornton (b. Dec. 17, 1680), daughter of Francis Thornton Sr. and Alice Savage. His Will dated May 7, 1726, was probated in Essex Co., June 27, 1726. Capt. Lawrence and Sarah (Thornton) Taliaferro had issue:

I. Francis Taliaferro of "Epsom," Spotsylvania; vestryman of St. George Parish; married 1730, Elizabeth Hay; died 1757. Their estate, still known as "Epsom," lies four miles below Fredericksburg, one mile above Massaponax Run. Its present owner is Mr. J. A. Jones. All the improvements on the place were destroyed during the Civil War. It was an extensive plantation in the early days and still is one of note. Francis and Elizabeth (Hay) Taliaferro had issue:

A. Elizabeth Taliaferro who married first her cousin, Col. William Taliaferro of Newington; 2nd, Captain Benjamin Hume. Col. William and Elizabeth (Taliaferro) Taliaferro had is-

sue, one child, Ann Hay Talia-
ferro, who died in infancy.
There was no issue by her sec-
ond marriage to Capt. Benjamin
Hume.
B. Hay Taliaferro of "Cheerful
Hall"; married Lucy Mary
(Taliaferro) Thurston, her sec-
ond husband.
C. Francis Whitaker Taliaferro;
married Jane Taliaferro of
"Blenheim." He inherited "Ep-
som."
D. Col. Lawrence Taliaferro of
"Rose Hill" (b. Dec. 9, 1734; d.
Apr. 8, 1798); served in the
Revolution as Colonel command-
ant of the minute men raised in
Orange, Culpepper and Fauquier
Counties. Married 1st, Mary
Jackson; 2nd, Sarah Dade.
Issue by first marriage:
1. Mary Taliaferro; died young.
2. Anna Taliaferro; married
William Fitzhugh.
3. Sarah Taliaferro; married 1st
Capt. Francis Dade; 2nd,
Capt. William Dade. Captain
William Dade was born 1760;
was an officer in the Revolu-
tion; removed from Orange
County to Kentucky and died
there July 23, 1840.
Issue by second marriage:
4. Hay Taliaferro of "Rose
Hill"; b. 1775, d. 1834; married March 16, 1797, Sukey
(Susanna), daughter of Capt.
Catlett Conway of "Haw-
field."
5. Baldwin Taliaferro of "Wood-
park," afterwards removed to
Tennessee; married, 1797,
Anne, daughter of Gen. Alexander Spotswood of "New
post," Spotsylvania.
6. Lawrence Taliaferro; never
married.
7. Francis Taliaferro; married
Henrietta Thornton and removed to Kentucky.
8. Elizabeth Taliaferro; married Battaile Fitzhugh, of
"Santee," of Caroline County.
9. Patsy Taliaferro; married
Dr. William Fitzhugh, of
"Fauquier."
10. Verlinda Taliaferro; married Catlett Conway Jr. of
Greene County.
11. Georgina Taliaferro; never
married.
E. John Taliaferro of "Hagley,"
King George Co., married Eliza-

beth, daughter of James Gar-
nett of Essex.
F. Ann Hay Taliaferro; married Richard Brooke of
"Smithfield," Spotsylvania. Issue:
1. Lawrence Brooke; surgeon,
United States Navy, was with
Paul Jones on the "Bon
Homme Richard"; he died
after 1799.
2. Robert Brooke; cavalry officer in the Revolution; member of the House of Delegates
from Stafford; father of Lieut.
Francis J. Brooke, U. S.
Army, killed in action in Florida, 1837; and of the distinguished lawyer, Henry L.
Brooke.
3. Francis T. Brooke; captain of
artillery in Revolution; married 1st, Mary Randolph Spotswood, daughter of General
Alexander Spotswood; 2nd,
Mary Champe Carter, daughter of Col. Edward Carter of
"Blenheim," Albemarle.
4. ——— Brooke; (daughter)
married Fontaine Maury and
was the mother of Richard B.
and Butler Maury.
There were several Hay Taliaferros
in the immediate neighborhood. Hay
of "Piedmont" called "Blenheim Hay"
to distinguish him from Hay of
"Cheerful Hall," whose brother, Francis Whitaker Taliaferro, had married
Jane Taliaferro of "Blenheim," the sister of the first named Hay. Elizabeth,
the step-mother of Nicholas Taliaferro,
was the sister of Hay of "Cheerful
Hall," of Francis Whitaker (who inherited "Epsom") and of Col. Lawrence Taliaferro of "Rose Hill." Hay
Taliaferro Jr. was the son of the latter and is the one mentioned in Col.
Taylor's diary—"March 16, 1797; Hay
Taliaferro married Sukey Conway and
my son and daughter went to the wedding; the horses ran away and they did
not get back." Hay Taliaferro of
"Cheerful Hall" was the second husband of Nicholas Taliaferro's sister,
Lucy Mary (Taliaferro) Thurston.
II. John Taliaferro Sr., Lieutenant
Colonel. Spotsylvania Militia;
Sheriff 1741; afterwards of "Dis-
sington" King George County;
married Ann Champe; died 1750.
Issue:—
A. Col. John Taliaferro, II, of "Dis-
sington"; married Elizabeth
Thornton, daughter of Col. John

and Mildrad (Gregory) Thornton.

B. Ann Taliaferro; married Nicholas Taliaferro. (See "Family Register of Nicholas Taliaferro" for names of their children).

III. Sarah Taliaferro; married William Brooke.

IV. William Taliaferro; of King and Queen County; sheriff 1742-3; vestryman of Stafford Major Parish.

V. Elizabeth Taliaferro.

VI. Mary Taliaferro.

VII. Alice Taliaferro.

Col. John Taliaferro, Sr., of "Dissington," King George, married Ann Champe, the daughter of Col. John Champe, Sr., of Lambs Creek, King George, one of the wealthiest and foremost men of the colony. Col. Champe had six daughters, all noted beauties. Elizabeth married Judge Fleming. Jane married Col. Samuel Washington; Mary married Col. Lewis Willis; Lucy married Austin Brockenbrough; Ann married Col. John Taliaferro of "Dissington," and Sarah married Col. Edward Carter of "Blenheim," Albemarle County.

Third Line.

Col John Taliaferro of "Snow Creek," son of the first John and Saran (Smith) Taliaferro, was born in 1687; and died May 3, 1744. John of "Snow Creek" is the Major John, who was requested "to bring up the Surplice" in 1730 to the newly established church at Germana; he was a man of note in the Colony. He was married Dec. 22, 1708 to Mary Catlett, daughter of Col. John Catlett, Jr., and Elizabeth Gaines, his wife. The Catletts owned a large estate at the mouth of Golden Vale Creek in present Caroline County. Col. John Catlett, Jr., (b. 1658), was a son of Col. John Catlett, Sr., and his wife, Elizabeth Underwood, who had been previously married to the first Francis Slaughter. According to the Westover Papers, Col. John Taliaferro settled at Snow Creek in 1707. Snow Creek flows into the Rappahannock River a short distance from Fredericksburg. When John Taliaferro and Francis Thornton settled there, that section belonged to Essex County, and they were near neighbors and brothers-in-law, the latter having married the former's sister, Mary. The Act creating Spotsylvania Co. (1720) specified Snow Creek at its southern

boundary. This threw John Taliaferro into the new county and left Francis Thornton in the old. John Taliaferro, a Justice of Spotsylvania 1720; a vestryman of St. George's Parish, 1725.

Col. John of "Snow Creek" (1687-1744) and his son, Lawrence Taliaferro (1721-1748) were buried at Old Hickory Neck Church, in James City Co., near the present village of Toana; up to some thirty-five or forty years ago their tombs were well preserved. At the present time no trace of them remains, except that a few fragments of the stone of Lawrence Taliaferro have been discovered and have been embedded in the cement floor of the small entrance porch which has recently been added to the venerable little building. A description of these tombs can be found in Vol. IX., Virginia Historical Collections. Bishop Meade has but little to say about Old Hickory Neck Church: "The building is the original one," he records, "now much out of repair and used indiscriminately by various sects." It was for many years used as a school room. No one knows when it was built, but it must have been some time prior to 1744.

Col. John and Mary (Catlett) Taliaferro had issue:

1. Lawrence Taliaferro (b. Sept. 8, 1721; d. May 1, 1748). He married Susanna Power, youngest daughter of Major Henry Power of the family of Lord Power of Remaine, Ireland, and had issue:

A. Sarah Taliaferro; b. Oct. 13, 1746; married Capt. William Dangerfield.

II. Martha Taliaferro (b. June 24, 1724); married William Hunter and had issue by him:

A. James Hunter; b. Nov. 6, 1746.

B. William Hunter; b. Aug. 24, 1748.

C. Martha Hunter; b. Oct. 29, 1749. The elder William Hunter of Fredericksburg, who married Martha Taliaferro, died Jan. 25, 1754. His Will Nov. 5, 1753, names Exers. Cousin James Hunter, brother-in-law William Taliaferro, of Orange Co., Mr. Fielding Lewis, Mr. Charles Dick.

III. Col. William Taliaferro; born at "Snow Creek" Spotsylvania, Co., Rappahannock, Virginia, Aug. 9, 1726; died at "Newington," his seat on Mountain Run, Orange County, Va., after a painful illness without a groan, the 21st of April, 1798, aged 72 in August, 1798. He was lieutenant-colonel of Orange

County Militia; his commission was dated May 5, 1756. (Order Book 1755 to 65, (See Vol. II. Va. Co. Records, p. 126—Crozier). As "Col. William Taliaferro," he is mentioned as one of the sponsors (1758) of Catlett Madison, a brother of the President. He is sometimes confused with Col. William Taliaferro of the Revolution. He lived at "Newington," which is located on Mountain Run, some twelve miles to the southeast of the town of Orange, and was for more than seventy years, prior to 1910, owned by Mr. Lawrence Sanford, who purchased it from Elizabeth, the second wife and relict of William Taliaferro; and later the wife of Capt. Benjamin Hume. "Newington" is now the property of Mr. E. Clay Pannell; a part of the house remains as originally constructed, about 1753. The old burying ground lies about one hundred yards distant, while the site of the first Court House erected in Orange (of which merely a trace can be located) is but another hundred yards removed. A feature of "Newington" is its striking hall and stairway.

Col. William Taliaferro was married first to Mary Battaile on Oct. 4, 1751, by the Rev. Musgrove Dawson. Mary Battaile, b. Sept. 18, 1731; d. Nov. 9, 1757, was the daughter of Capt. Nicholas Battaile and Mary Thornton. Capt. Nicholas Battaile was a son of Col. John Battaile, Sr., (d. 1708) and his second wife Elizabeth, daughter of Major Lawrence Smith. Mary Thornton was the daughter of Francis Thornton, II, and Mary Taliaferro, his wife; and a granddaughter of Francis Thornton and Alice Savage.

Col. William Taliaferro was married second to Elizabeth Taliaferro, daughter of Francis and Elizabeth (Hay) Taliaferro of "Epsom," Spotsylvania Co., on Dec. 5, 1758, by Rev. Musgrove Dawson. She was born Oct. 4, 1741 and before her marriage lived at "Epsom."

Col. William and Mary (Battaile) Taliaferro had issue:

A. John Taliaferro; b. July 31, 1753, and was baptized by the Rev. Musgrove Dawson; his sureties were Col. John Thorn-

ton, Col. Henry Fitzhugh's lady, Mr. Charles Lewis and his lady, the 24th of August 1753. (Col. John Thornton was the infant's maternal great-uncle. His wife was Mildred Gregory, one of the three Gregory sisters, who married Thornton brothers. They were daughters of Roger Gregory and Mildred Washington, aunt and god-mother to the President. After Roger Gregory's death she married Col. Henry Willis of Fredericksburg, his third wife.)

Henry Fitzhugh married Sarah Battaile, daughter of Capt. Nicholas Battaile and sister of Mary (Battaile) Taliaferro, the infant's mother.

Col. Charles Lewis married Lucy, daughter of Col. John Taliaferro of the Manor Plantation "Snow Creek," Spotsylvania Co., Va., about 1750. He was a brother of Col. Fielding Lewis, who married 1st, Catherine Washington; 2nd, Betty Washington; the former a cousin and the latter an only sister of the President. Col. Charles Lewis' lady, the sponsor, was the infant's paternal aunt.

B. Lucy Mary Taliaferro; (b. Dec. 13, 1755) was baptized by the Rev. Mungo Marshall; her sureties were Mr. Reuben Thornton, Mr. Henry Willis for Mr. Henry Heath, Mrs. Elizabeth Thomas and Miss Mary Waugh.

Before the birth of Lucy Mary Taliaferro, the family had removed from St. Mary's Parish, Caroline, to what had been St. Mark's, and was then, as now, St. Thomas' Parish, Orange Co. She was married first, June 11, 1773, to William Plummer Thurston; and second, April 5, 1791, to Hay Taliaferro of "Cheerful Hall." (Orange County marriage records).

C. Nicholas Taliaferro was born Oct. 30, 1757; his sureties were Col. George Taylor, Mr. Erasmus Taylor, Mrs. Sarah Slaughter, Miss Betty Slaughter and Mrs. Mildred James. (See Chapter V. "Family Register of Nicholas Taliaferro").

Col. George Taylor, b. 1711, was the great-uncle of the President. He married for his second wife, Sarah Taliaferro, the widow of Francis Conway, II. She was the granddaughter of Charles Taliaferro by an only son, who predeceased his father and was also named Charles. (Chapt. III.).

Erasmus Taylor was the brother of Col. George Taylor. He married Jane Moore. Jane Moore was the daughter of John and Rebecca (Catlett) Moore, who was the widow of the first Francis Conway, and whose daughter, Nellie Conway, half-sister to Jane Moore, married Col. James Madison. They were the parents of the President. Col. Frank Taylor in his diary quoted by Dr. Slaughter records, "July 19, 1794, died Erasmus Taylor, eighty-three years old.'

William Taliaferro of "New-ington" was married to Eliza-beth Taliaferro, a second wife, on Dec. 5, 1758, by the Rev. Mus-grove Dawson. She was the daughter of Francis and Eliza-beth (Hay) Taliaferro of "Ep-som." Issue:

D. Ann Hay Taliaferro; b. Feb. 27, 1760, and had private bap-tism by the Rev. James Marye, and died March 2, 1760. She was the only issue of Col Wil-liam and Elizabeth Taliaferro.

Nicholas Taliaferro's mother, Mary (Battaile) Taliaferro died at his birth and the only mother he ever knew was Elizabeth, whom family tradition credits with being a mother indeed. Elizabeth inherited a tract of 1000 acres adjoining "Newing-ton," and was therefore a near neighbor of her distant cousin, William Taliaferro, whom she later married.

IV. Lucy Taliaferro; married Col. Charles Lewis of Cedar Creek, a brother of Col. Fielding Lewis of Kenmore, who married 1st, Catherine; 2nd, Betty Washing-ton.

V. Mary Taliaferro; married Joseph Jones.

The Sponsors for Augustine Lewis, one of the sons of Col. Fielding and Betty (Washington) Lewis 1752, were "Charles Lewis and Charles Washing-ton, uncles, god-fathers; Aunt Lucy Lewis and Mrs. Mary Taliaferro, god-mothers"; the latter was the mother

of Lucy Lewis and the widow of Col. John Taliaferro of "Snow Creek." She died in 1771, over eighty.

Fourth Line.

Mary Taliaferro.

Mary Taliaferro, daughter of the first John Taliaferro and his wife, Sarah (Smith) Taliaferro, married Francis Thornton, Jr., son of Francis Thornton Sr., and Alice Savage, and grandson of William Thornton, the Emigrant. The record of the grand-children of Mary (Taliaferro) Thorn-ton is incomplete. Francis and Mary (Taliaferro) Thornton had issue:

I. Francis Thornton, III, of "Fall Hill," Married Frances Gregory. Issue:

A. Mildred Thornton; married Charles Washington.

B. John Thornton; married Jane Washington, daughter of Col. Samuel Washington and his first wife, Jane (Champe) Washing-ton.

C. Mary Thornton; married Wil-liam Champe.

II. Col. John Thornton; married Mildred Gregory. Issue:

A. Mildred Thornton; married Col. Samuel Washington, his second wife. His first wife was Jane Champe, who was the mother of Jane Washington; she was also a sister of Ann Champe.

B. Elizabeth Thornton; married Col. John Taliaferro, II, of "Dis-sington."

III. Mary Thornton; married Cap-tain Nicholas Battaile of "Hays." Issue:

A. Mary Battaile; married Col. William Taliaferro of "Newing-ton."

B. Sarah Battaile; married Oct. 23, 1746, Henry Fitzhugh.

IV. Reuben Thornton; married Eliza-beth (Gregory) Willis, widow of Henry Willis.

V. Sarah Thornton; married Thomas Slaughter.

VI. Elizabeth Thornton; married Thomas Merriwether. Issue:

A. Nicholas Merriwether, married Margaret (also called Peggy) Douglas, daughter of Rev. Wil-liam Douglas. Rev. William Douglas came to Virginia in 1748-9 as a teacher in the fam-ily of Col. Monroe of Westmore-land; President Monroe was one of his pupils; so also at a later date was Jefferson.

Ninth Line.
Richard Taliaferro.

Captain Richard Taliaferro of Caroline Co., son of the first John Taliaferro and his wife, Sarah Smith, was born before 1706; James Taliaferro in his sketch of the Taliaferro family places the date of the birth of Capt. Richard Taliaferro in 1703, which is probably correct. He was a man of consequence; patented more than 10,-000 acres in the present counties of Amherst and Nelson, Virginia; also patented land in Patrick County, 1745. On account of the destruction of most of the records of Caroline County, where he resided, it has been difficult to learn much concerning his life in the Colony. He served as a colonel in the English or Colonial Armies and also attained the rank of Captain; and family tradition states that he met his death while he and his men were crossing the Potomac on a flat-boat but the date of his death is recorded as Sept. 27, 1748. On June 10, 1726 he was married to Rose Berryman, daughter of Major Benjamin and Elizabeth (Newton) Berryman. Capt. Richard and Rose (Berryman) Taliaferro were the parents of Dr. John Taliaferro, to whose memory this sketch has been dedicated. (For ancestry of Rose Berryman see Chapter VI., of this sketch).

Capt. Richard and Rose (Berryman) Taliaferro had issue:

I. Sarah Taliaferro; b. June 7, 1727; married John Lewis. Issue:
- A. Robert Lewis.
- B. Taliaferro Lewis.
- C. John Lewis.
- D. Mildred McCoy Lewis.
- E. Charles Lewis.
- F. Jesse Lewis.
- G. Richard Lewis.
- H. Henry Lewis.

II. Benjamin Taliaferro; b. Nov. 1, 1728; d. about 1751; his land in Amherst was inherited by his brother Zachariah.

III. Zachariah Taliaferro; b. Aug. 29, 1730; d. in South Carolina in April, 1811; was early in life a captain of a ship; Justice and sheriff of Amherst; member of Amherst Committee of Safety 1775-6; married 1749, Mary Boutwell. Issue:
- A. Col. Benjamin Taliaferro; b. 1750; d. Sept. 3, 1821; entered Revolution a lieutenant; served in campaign in Jersey 1777-8; promoted to captain; volunteered

for the Southern Army under Lincoln, and saw active service under Lee's command; captured at Charleston. He removed to Georgia in 1784, where he played an active part in the annals of Georgia History. He was President of the State Senate, member of the United States Congress, 1790-1800; of the Georgia Convention 1799; and Judge Superior Court. He died in Wilkes County, Georgia, and during his thirty-five years residence in the State of Georgia, no citizen was more generally esteemed. Taliaferro County, Ga., was named in his honor. He married 1st, Martha Merriwether, daughter of Daniel Merriwether; 2nd, Miss ——— Cox. Issue by first marriage:
1. Louis Bourbon Taliaferro; married Betsy Johnson.
2. Betsy Taliaferro.
3. Emily Taliaferro; married Isham Watkins.
4. Benjamin Taliaferro; married Martha Watkins. Will of James Watkins, Sr., (1824) of Elbert County, Ga. (3rd Item) "I give to my daughter Martha Taliaferro, a negro man by name Bowling."
5. David Merriwether Taliaferro; married Mary Barnett.
6. Col. Thornton Taliaferro.
7. Nicholas Taliaferro; married Malinda ———?
8. Martha Taliaferro.
9. Margaret Taliaferro.
10. Mary Taliaferro.

Issue by second marriage:
11. Zachariah Taliaferro.

B. Zachariah Taliaferro; b. April 28, 1759; d. April 14, 1831; served in Revolution; settled in Pendleton, S. C.; married 1802 Margaret Chew Carter, descendant of King Charter. Issue:
1. Sarah Ann Taliaferro; b. June 2, 1803; married Dr. O. R. Broyles, of Anderson, S. C.
2. Lucy Hannah Taliaferro; b. May 5, 1805; married Col. D. P. Taylor, Anderson, S. C.
3. Mary Margaret Taliaferro; b. May 5, 1808; married Major R. F. Simpson of Laurens, S. C.
4. Caroline Virginia Taliaferro; b. Nov. 5, 1811; married Dr. H. C. Miller, Abbeville, S. C.

C. Sallie Taliaferro; m a r r i e d Daniel Harvey and removed to Georgia. Issue:
1. Mary B. Harvey; married Presley Gilmer.
2. Martha Harvey; m a r r i e d Thompson Gilmer.

D. Richard Taliaferro moved to Georgia and never married.

E. Warren Taliaferro; m a r r i e d Mary M. Gilmer. Issue:
1. Nancy Taliaferro; married Thomas Rainey.
2. Charles Boutwell Taliaferro; married Mildred Merriwether; of their eight children was the late Dr. Valentine H. Taliaferro of Atlanta, Ga.
3. Sophia Taliaferro; married James Merriwether.
4. Polly Taliaferro; married a Mr. Landrum.

F. Burton Taliaferro; married 1st, Sallie, daughter of John Gilmer, and moved to Ga.; married 2nd, Lucy Carter of Va.

G. Nancy Taliaferro; m a r r i e d Thompson Watkins and removed to Ga.

H. Frances Taliaferro; married Moses Penn, and removed to Ga. Issue:
1. Richard Penn.
2. ——— Penn; (a daughter); married Rev. Dabney Jones.
3. ——— Penn, (a daughter) married Edward Jones.

I. Charles Taliaferro; was twice married. No record.

J. Boutwell Taliaferro. No record.

IV. Richard Taliaferro; b. Feb. 15, 1731; d. Feb. 26, 1731.

V. Dr. John Taliaferro, (See Chapter IX, part II. of this sketch).

VI. Col. Charles Taliaferro; b. July 17, 1735; removed to Amherst in 1758; married Isabelle McCullough of Westmoreland County. Issue:
A. Richard Taliaferro; b. in Amherst, May 23, 1759; d. 1806; served in the Revolution as captain in the Continental Line; removed to South Carolina and was Clerk of Chester Co., and afterwards lived in York Dist. S. C.; married Mildred, daughter of Lucas Powell. Issue:
1. William Taliaferro.
2. Rebecca Taliaferro; married 1st, Mr. Brown; 2nd, James Black.
3. Elizabeth Edwards Taliaferro; married John Pilcher.

4. Benjamin Taliaferro; married Rhoda Carter.
5. John Taliaferro; married Clementine McKinstry.
6. Dr. Roderick Taliaferro; married Nancy Bell.
7. Isabella Taliaferro; d i e d young.
8. Emily Taliaferro; married Wesley Terry.
9. Dr. James Powell Taliaferro; the youngest son, never married. He located in Alabama and was a very successful and popular physician.

B. Charles Taliaferro of Amherst; b. March 29, 1761; served in several campaigns in the Revolution; was at the siege of Yorktown; appointed Justice of Amherst, 1798; several years a member of House of Delegates and State Senate; married Lucy Loving.

C. Peter Taliaferro; b. March 4, 1763; died unmarried, July 4, 1785.

D. John Taliaferro; b. May 4, 1765; d. Nov. 24, 1809; married Elizabeth Loving.

E. Zachariah Taliaferro; b. Sept. 3, 1767; d. Sept. 12, 1823 in Louisiana; married Sallie Warmuck and had one son, James Govan Taliaferro, who at the time of his death, in 1880, was chief justice of that state.

F. Benjamin Franklin Taliaferro; b. June 9, 1770; married Mildred Franklin of Amherst. The late Capt. Patrick Rose Taliaferro of Sandersville, Ga., was one of their descendants.

G. William Taliaferro; born March 16, 1772; died 1805.

H. Sarah Beheathland Taliaferro; b. Aug. 16, 1774; married William Loving and died in Logan Co., Ky., in 1844.

I. Roderick Taliaferro of Lynchburg; b. May 16, 1777; married a Miss Price.

J. James Taliaferro; b. April 12, 1779; moved to Tennessee; married 1st, Lucy Rice; 2nd, Susan Prockman.

K. Rose Berryman Taliaferro; b. Jan. 2, 1783; married Josephus Loving and moved to Tennessee.

VII. Beheathland Taliaferro; b. Aug. 20, 1738.

VIII. Peter Taliaferro; b. Feb. 12, 1740; married Anne Hackley.

IX & X. Elizabeth and Rose Taliaferro (twins) b. Nov. 2, 1741.
Elizabeth Taliaferro married Zack
Hawkins and they had sons, one
of whom was John Hawkins. No
record.

XI. Mary B. Taliaferro; b. Oct. 6,
1743; married —— Wortham.

XII. Francis Taliaferro; b. Dec. 9,
1745.

XIII. Richard Taliaferro; b. Sept.
2, 1747. He served in the Revolution.

Tenth Line.
William Taliaferro.

William Taliaferro, son of the first
John Taliaferro and his wife, Sarah
(Smith) Taliaferro, patented land in
Patrick County in 1745. No further
information.

An interesting sketch of the life of
Col. Benjamin Taliaferro, son of
Zachariah and Mary (Boutwell) Talia-
ferro, is contained in "Georgia's Land
Marks, Memorials and Legends," by
Lucian Lamar Knight, Vol. 1, page
941; Vol. II, pages 12-13.

CHAPTER V.

FAMILY REGISTER OF NICHOLAS TALIAFERRO

The Family Register of Nicholas
Taliaferro (son of Col. William Taliaferro and Mary (Battaile) Taliaferro
of Newington), was written by Nicholas himself; and has been transcribed literally from "OLD BUCHAN,"
by Thomas A. Marshall of Vicksburg,
Miss., for his sister, Mrs. Mary A. P.
Doniphan of Augusta, Ky., on 21st day
of June, 1849. "Old Buchan," was a
family medical recipe book on the
blank pages of which Nicholas Taliaferro had transcribed his "Family
Register." This book was carried to
Vicksburg, Miss., from Kentucky by
Judge Marshall and it was lost in the
fire which destroyed "Openwoods," the
Marshall family home, during the
siege of that city in the Civil War.
Judge Thomas A. Marshall was the
son of Nicholas Taliaferro's daughter,
Matilda Battaile, whose husband, Martin Marshall, was the son of the Rev.
William Marshall and his wife, Mary
Ann Pickett; he was a first cousin to
the Chief Justice. The Register fol-
lows:

"My Honored Grandfather, John
Taliaferro, was married to my honored
grandmother, Mary Catlett, the 22nd
day of December, 1708; my honored
grandfather departed this life the 3rd
of May, 1744. My Uncle, Lawrence
Taliaferro was born the 8th of September, 1721; he married Susanna Power,
youngest daughter of Major Henry
Power, and had issue, Sarah Taliaferro, born 13th October, 1746, O. S.,
now the wife of Captain William
Dangerfield. He died the first of May,
1748.

My Aunt, Martha Taliaferro, was

born the 24th of June, 1724 and married Mr. William Hunter, and had
issue by him, James Hunter born 6th
November 1746, William Hunter born
24th of August, Anno 1748 O. S.,
Martha Hunter born 20th October 1749
O. S., Mr. William Hunter died the
25th of January 1754.

My honored father, William Taliaferro, was born at "Snow Creek,"
Spotsylvania County, Rappahannock,
Va., the 9th of August, 1726 and departed this life at "Newington," his
seat on Mountain Run, Orange County,
Va., after a painful illness without a
groan the 21st of April 1798, aged
seventy-two in August 1798.

My honored father William Talia-
ferro was married to my honored
Mother, Mary Battaile, the 4th of
October, 1751, by the Rev. Musgrove
Dawson. She was born the 18th of
September, 1731, and died the 9th of
November, 1757, the daughter of Cap-
tain Nicholas Battaile, of "Hays,"
Caroline County, Rappahannock,
Virginia. My grandmother's maiden
name was Thornton.

John Taliaferro, son of William and
Mary Taliaferro, was born Tuesday
morning, seven o'clock, the 31st of
July, 1753 and was baptized by the
Rev. Musgrove Dawson; his sureties
were Colonel John Thornton, Colonel
Henry Fitzhugh's lady, Mr. Charles
Lewis and his lady, the 24th of August,
1753.

Lucy Mary Taliaferro was born the
13th of December Anno 1755, Tuesday
nine o'clock at night and was baptized
by the Rev. Mungo Marshall; her
sureties were Mr. Reuben Thornton,

Mr. Henry Willis for Mr. Henry Heath, Mrs. Elizabeth Thomas and Miss Mary Waugh.

Nicholas Taliaferro was born the 30th of October, A. M., 1757; his sureties were Col. George Taylor, Mr. Erasmus Taylor, Mrs. Sarah Slaughter, Miss Betty Slaughter and Mrs. Mildred James.

My honored father was married to Miss Elizabeth Taliaferro, a second wife, on Tuesday the 5th of December 1758 by the Rev. Musgrove Dawson. She was the daughter of Francis and Elizabeth Taliaferro, of "Epsom," Spotsylvania County, Rappahannock, Virginia, and was born the 4th of October 1741.

Ann Hay Taliaferro was born Wednesday the 27th February 1760 at three-quarters after eleven o'clock at night and had private baptism by the Rev. James Marye, Jr., and died the 2nd of March, 1760 at seven o'clock A. M.

Family Register

Nicholas Taliaferro was married to Ann Taliaferro on Saturday the 3rd of November, 1781, eleven o'clock, by the Rev. James Stevenson. My beloved wife, Ann Taliaferro, was the daughter of Colonel John and Ann Taliaferro, of "Dissington," was born the 7th of April, 1756, and departed this life the 3rd of February, 1798.

Lucy Mary Taliaferro, daughter of Nicholas and Ann Taliaferro, was born Tuesday morning, nine o'clock, 6th of August, 1782, and was baptized by the Rev. William Douglas the 18th of January, 1783; her sureties were Mr. Winslow Parker, Mrs. Lucy Mary Thurston, Miss Ann Thurston, my wife and self.

John Champe Taliaferro was born Tuesday morning 7 o'clock the 12th of October 1784 and was baptized by the Rev. James Stevenson the 27th of April, 1786. His sureties were Mr. John Grinnan, Mr. Joseph Stewart, Miss Frances Willis Stewart, and his mother and departed this life 26th of February, 1811 after a painful illness.

Matilda Battaile Taliaferro was born Sunday morning, eight o'clock, the 30th of September Anno 1787, and was baptized by the Rev. James Stevenson the 24th of August, 1788; her sureties were Mr. John and Miss Ann Grinnan, and her mother.

Mary Willis Taliaferro was born One o'clock the 11th of August, 1789 and was baptized by the Rev. James Stevenson the 15th of November, 1789.

Her sureties were Mr. John Stevens, Mr. Joseph Morton, Miss Elizabeth Taliaferro, Miss Ann Hay Taliaferro and her mother. She departed this life the 25th of January, 1797 and was buried in Pennsylvania, where General Braddock was defeated, Alleagney County.

George Catlett Taliaferro was born Wednesday evening, four o'clock, the 21st of March Anno 1792 and was baptized by the Rev. Mr. Woodville the 23rd of December, 1794; his sureties were Mr. John Grinnan, and wife Lucy and Myself.

William Thornton Taliaferro was born Friday, January 16th, 1795, at eleven P. M. and was baptized by the Rev. Mr. O'Neal; his sureties were his grandfather who named him, Mr. Hay Taliaferro and Hay Taliaferro, Jr., his grandmother, mother and Miss Abby Gibson.

Nicholas Taliaferro was a second time married, to Miss Frances Blasingame, daughter of Mr. James and Mary Blasingame, and had issue:

Carr Blasingame Taliaferro who was born Tuesday 13th, August, 1799, half after two in the evening.

Lawrence Washington Taliaferro was born Tuesday, nine o'clock, 28th of October, 1800.

Ann Patterson Taliaferro was born Friday night ten o'clock, 29th of October, 1802, and departed this life Tuesday night about twelve o'clock, 25th of November, 1803, she was cutting teeth and was taken with epilepsy fits; her two eye teeth came through the gums before she died.

James Hay Taliaferro was born the second day of September, 1804; very warm sunshiny day.

Nicholas Taliaferro was born Thursday, half after eight o'clock the 14th of August, 1806, in the morning.

Marshall Howe Taliaferro was born the ninth of March, 1809, eleven o'clock at night.

Carr Blasingame Taliaferro departed this life Thursday morning, half after nine, 1806.

James Hay Taliaferro departed this life Thursday night twelve o'clock 18th of August, 1808.

John Champe Taliaferro died 26th of February, ten minutes after two in the morning, 1811.

Frances Ann Taliaferro was born Saturday, eleven o'clock P. M., ninth November, 1811.

William Buckner was born the 19th of June, 1780, and was married to Lucy Mary Taliaferro, 26th of June, 1799, and had issue:

Philip Johnson Buckner, born 8th of August, 1800.

Ann Whitaker Taliaferro, born 8th of January, 1803.

Nicholas Taliaferro Buckner, born 29th of June, 1805.

My Brother, John Taliaferro, married Ann Stockdell, daughter of Captain John and Mary Stockdell of Orange County, Virginia, and had issue:

Mary Taliaferro, Born 17th of June, 1773, married Robert Reynolds and died with her first child which is called Thornton.

Elizabeth Hay Taliaferro was born 4th of May, 1778.

Lucy Mary Battaile Taliaferro was born 14th of May, 1780.

William Taliaferro was born 23rd of March, 1782.

Sarah Taliaferro was born 20th of February, 1784.

John Taliaferro was born 6th of April, 1786.

Martha Taliaferro was born 22nd of January, 1789.

Nicholas Hay Battaile Taliaferro was born 15th of June, 1793.

Lawrence Wesley Taliaferro was born August 5th, 1796.

A Register of the Names and Ages of My Negroes.

1. James, born in March 1756.

2. Rachel was born in November, 1773.

3. Clementina was born in February, 1781.

4. Anthony born 12th of March. 1784, 9 o'clock in the morning.

5. Billy was born 9th of December, 1785, eleven o'clock at night.

6. Hannah born 19th of August, 1786, four o'clock in the morning.

7. Sarah born 10th of June, 1773.

8. Betty born 15th of September, 1788.

9. Sally born 10th of July, 1788.

10. Phil. born 5th of August, 1789.

11. Daniel born the 12th of January, 1792.

12. Jenny was born the 6th of November, 1749.

13. Sharlotty was born the 10th of February ——.

14. Ben was born the 25th of October. 1798.

15. Nelly was born the 5th of January, 1801, in the morning.

16. Mary was born 12th of March, 1803, half after eleven, apparently still born.

17. Lucy born 11th of August, 1805, three o'clock in the afternoon.

18. Joe, born 9th of November, 1806, twelve o'clock, Sunday.

19. Prissy, born Sunday night 11th of December, 1808.

20. Caroline, born Tuesday morning 28th of September, 1809.

21. Simon, born Sunday morning 2nd of September, 1810.

22. Henry born 22nd May, 1811.

23. Charles, born 1810.

I left "Totter-down-hill," my seat on Cedar Run, Culpepper County, State of Virginia on the 11th of October, 1796 and landed at the Lower Brooks at Limestone, in the State of Kentucky on the fifth of February, 1797 and bought a lease of Lewis Day on John Craig's land where I lived till the 15th of March, 1798 and then moved to Bracken County, my present seat, the Grampian Hill.

NICHOLAS TALIAFERRO.

15th of March. 1811.

This seat I bought of Mr. James Blasingame, three hundred and thirty-seven and one-half acres at twenty-four dollars per acre, and paid the whole money.

"N. T."

CHAPTER VI.

THE ANCESTRY OF ROSE BERRYMAN

Rose Berryman was born in the historic County of Westmoreland, Virginia probably in the year 1708. She came of distinguished ancestry, her father, Major Benjamin Berryman, being a man of prominence in the Colony. Her maternal grandfather, John Newton, was a son of the celebrated Thomas Newton, Esq., of Charleston Manor and Kingston-on-Hull, Gentleman, of England, and came to America in 1660. John Newton held large estates at Carleton as well as a large tract of land in Virginia.

Rose Berryman was one among a family of seventeen children, and she spent her girlhood days on the Berryman estate in Westmoreland County. On June 10, 1726, she was united in marriage to Captain Richard Taliaferro of Caroline County. Their home was blest with thirteen children, one of whom died in infancy. This family resided in Caroline County and probably belonged to St. Thomas' Parish, the records of which have been destroyed. Captain Richard Taliaferro was a large landholder and patented 10,000 acres in the present counties of Amherst and Nelson. He passed away on Sept. 27, 1748. The cause of his death is unknown; although traditional accounts in the family of his granddaughter, Anna (Taliaferro) Mc-Crary, state that he was killed while crossing the Potomac on a flatboat, and only a few of his men escaped death.

The sad loss of her husband left Rose (Berryman) Taliaferro with entire responsibility of her home and the rearing of twelve children. She reared and educated them according to the standards of the old Virginia Colony; breathing into their lives love in its truest form; love for one another; love for their fellowman; love for their country; and love for their God. Several of her sons and grandsons served with honor and distinction in the Revolution; one son, Dr. John Taliaferro, being not only a soldier, but a prominent physician and a Baptist Minister. In her declining years she could have pointed to these boys with pride and said. "These are my Jewels." Her parents could not have chosen a more fitting name for her than Rose. In the garden of life she lived and grew and bloomed, not for herself, but for the pleasure of others. Her memory reflects the beauty of the name she bore; her love the sweetness; her life the purity of the rose. Though she sleeps today in an unmarked grave, she is not forgotten. She was the mother of Dr. John Taliaferro. She cared for him through the tender years of childhood and moulded his character into a life of usefulness and good deeds. It was at her knee that he prayed his first prayer, and it was doubtless through her Christian influence and training that he became the great physician, soldier and minister that he was. How precious are the memories that around her dead name play! And love, like incense rises for his mother. She found a way to pass all barriers to her own; her love could bridge the distance that years and space had made; her prayers have opened Heaven's door for those whom she pled; she knew their weaknesses and strength, and their deepest needs.

The following is the ancestry of Rose Berryman; it will be remembered that she was Berryman on one side and Newton on the other.

BERRYMAN

Devonshire Pedigrees state that Arms were granted to the Berryman family in 1575.

John Berryman, of Berri, and his wife, Eleanor Dare of Upcott, had a son, John de Berrie, (John Berryman) who married in 1605, Elizabeth, daughter of Sir Thomas Fulford de Fulford, who traced his lineage to Robert Challons.

John Berryman, grandson of John and Elizabeth, was the first of the family to come to America from England, settling in Westmoreland Co., Va. in 1654. (See Va. Hist. Mag. Vol. 6, P. 119.) He married Miss Tucker of Va. and had an only child, Benjamin Berryman.

Benjamin Berryman held many offices in the Colony, being Gentleman Justice, Attorney in Stafford and King George Counties, Sheriff of Westmoreland Co., Captain and Major. He married Elizabeth Newton, only daughter of John Newton and his second wife, Rose Tucker Gerrard, of Westmoreland Co., Va. (Benjamin Berryman's will dated Aug. 4, 1729; probated Aug. 27, 1729; Elizabeth Berryman's will dated June 14, 1762; probated Feb. 22, 1763.)

Benjamin and Elizabeth (Newton) Berryman had twenty-two children, seventeen of whom lived to reach the age of maturity. Among this large family of children were: James William and Maximilian Berryman; John Berryman, who married Beheathland Gilson, and died before he became of age, leaving an only son, Gilson Berryman; Newton and Henry Berryman; Benjamin Berryman, who married Sarah Bushrod; Rose Berryman, who married Capt. Richard Taliaferro on June 10, 1726; Frances Berryman who married George Foote; Ann, Elizabeth, Sarah and Catherine Berryman.

The Berrymans, through the marriages of their children have become connected with many distinguished families of Virginia: Randolphs, Ishams, Woodsons, Taliaferros, etc.; and with the Allertons of Massachusetts, through the descendants of Isaac Allerton, born Plymouth, 1630, moved to Wicomico Co., Va., and married there.

NEWTON

John Newton, son of Thomas Newton, Esq., of Carleton Manor and Kingston-on-Hull, Gentleman, came to America in 1660. (See William and Mary Quarterly Vol. 4, p. 3; Vol. 5 p. 69. "Soldiers of Virginia." Vol. 2, p. 487-489; Newton Gen. p. 808.) He married first, Joan Barr of England, and had issue: 1. John Newton; 2. Joseph Newton. He married secondly Mrs. Rose Tucker Gerrard, widow first, of John Tucker of Virginia, and secondly, of Thomas Gerrard, of St. Clement's Manor, St. Mary's County, Md. and of Westmoreland Co., Va. John Newton had issue by his second marriage; 3. Thomas Newton, who married Elizabeth Storke; 4. Benjamin Newton; 5. Elizabeth Newton, who married Benjamin Berryman; 6. Gerrard Newton. (John Newton's will dated Aug. 19, 1695; probated July 28, 1697 in Westmoreland Co., Va.; Rose Newton's will dated Dec. 1, 1712; probated Feb. 3, 1713 by Thomas Newton.)

Through the Newtons the Berrymans trace their lineage back 2000 years to Prince Caractacus, who became King Caradoc of Britain A. D. 53. In this line one of their ancestors distinguished himself at the Crusade under Richard, Coeur de Lion, against the Saracens at the Battle of Escalon in 1192. Later another, Sir John Newton, was sword-bearer to Richard I, King of England.

BERRYMAN-NEWTON LEGAL DOCUMENTS.

(Abstract)

BENJAMIN BERRYMAN'S WILL,

Aug. 4, 1729.

Westmoreland County, Va.

Book of Deeds and Wills.

No. 8—page 366.

In the name of God, Amen: I, Benjamin Berryman of ye county of Westmoreland......give to my son James my house and land whereon I now live......alsoe my watter Grist mill to him, the said James Berryman, and the heirs male of his body, and for want of such heirs to my son William Berryman, etc. (and in case of death of each and his male heirs to descend in order to) Maximillian,......John, Newton.......Henry ....Benjamin Grandson Gilson......then to my right heirs at law.

2. I give to my son Henry Berryman, two hundred ackers of land....

3. I give to my son William the rest of my first land....

4. My land in King George County ....I have given by deed to my son Benjamin....and the remaining two hundred ackers I give to my son John....

5. I give to my son Newton Berryman and to my son Maximillian Berryman Six hundred and sixty-three ackers of land att a place called the marsh in King George County to be equally divided between them....

6. My son Benjamin Berryman hath his parte of negroes and is possessed of them and I doe by this will confirme them to him he hath alsoe had his share of cattell hogg household goods etc. Alsoe my daughter Rose hath had her parte and my daughter Anne her parte and my daughter Elizabeth her parte soe that I give them noe more and need not say any further of them...........................
....
....

Memorandum:....I make my sons William Berryman and James Berryman to be my executors with my son Benjamine Berryman.... forasmuch as I have entailed my land on my sons and theire male heirs....in case of faillure of the male heirs of my sons, then I give to my four daughters Rose, Sarah, Frances, and Catherine and the heirs male of their bodys and for want of such I give to my sons and daughters and heirs forever. As witness my hand and seal this fourth day of August ye year 1729.

BENJAMIN BERRYMAN.

Test.

Thomas Sharpe.

Thomas Stonehouse.

Moses Caddy.

Will Book No. 14, page 179.

ELIZABETH BERRYMAN'S WILL
June 14, 1762.
prob. Feb. 22, 1763.

....I, Elizabeth Berryman of the County of Westmoreland....appoint this my last will & Testament in manner Following. Whereas my husband Benjamin Berryman by his last Will authorized me to make distribution of all his slaves to his six sons or the survivors of them, and whereas three of the said sons, Viz., Newton, John and Henry died before they came of age and was not possessed of any of their father's estate, and whereas William, James and Maximillian are the surviving sons I give all the slaves with their increase to be divided as follows, Imprimis I give my son William Berryman old negro Jack and Grace and thirteen children etc....

Item, I give to my son James Berryman, Negro George, Jack etc....Item, I give to my son Maximillian fourteen Negroes which he has in his possession as also etc.....Item, my will and desire is that my stock and household stuff of what kind soever....shall be equally divided between three children ....William, James and Katherine Knowles.

Item: my son Benjamin Berryman had his part of his fathers estate before his death,

Item: my daughter Rose Taliaferro had her part of her fathers estate before his death,

Item: my daughter Frances Foote ....Sarah Douglas....K a t h e r i n e Knowles have had their parts etc....

Item: I appoint my sons William and James Berryman executors to this my last Will and Testament:

In witness whereof I have hereunto set my hand and seal this 14th day of June, 1762.

her

ELIZABETH X BERRYMAN.

mark

Signed Sealed and delivered in presence of:

Gerrard Blackstone Causeen.

William Staples.

Josias Causeen.

Thomas Clark.

(Abstract)

WILL OF JOHN NEWTON
Westmoreland County, Va.
Aug. 19, 1695.
prob. July 28, 1697,
(Book 2 p. 104).

I John Newton of lower Machodock, in West Co.....give unto my eldest son John and his heirs forever what land I have at Carleton (etc.) I give unto my son Joseph Newton and his three sons 1,000 lbs. of tobacco apiece, (the same) to my son Benjamin Newton and his daughter....Item: I give to my son Gerrat that 1,000 acres I bought of Thomas Short....To my daughter Elizabeth one-half of tract of 2150 acres, & 1 negro....To Rose Newton my wife all my plate for life, & then to my daughter Elizabeth.

WESTMORELAND COUNTY RECORDS—MONTROS, VA.
Book 8, page 2.

Berryman's Bond to Thomas Newton.

Know all men by these presents that I, Beheathland Berryman do owe and stands justly indebted to Thomas Newton of the County of Westmoreland to him his heirs executors & the full and just sum of two hundred pounds Sterl. money of Great Britain to be paid on demand for which payment well and truly to be made I bind myself my heirs &c firmly in these presents—Witness my hand and seal this 17th day of July, 1723.

The condition of the above obligation is such that whereon a right title and property of in and to one certain parcel of land lying and being on the South side of Rappahannock River containing one thousand and fifty acres of land whicn is given by the Last Will and Testament of Beheathland Storke dated ye second day of October, 1698 to her two daughters Elizabeth and Catherine as by ye said Will, will appear and also by patten granted to the said Beheathland Storke then Gilson from Sir. William Berkley then their Governor dated 1667, which said land supposing to be leased and afterward granted to Thomas Gilson by patten dated as is supposed in the year 1670 which sd. land to him we granted is Come to and descended to me ye said Beheathland by being only daughter and heiress at law to the said Thomas now so it is that upon the making over of what right I may have to the said land to Capt. Newton or his Assigns by good and sufficient deeds without warranty except from myself and my heirs or those

that may claim under me provided it
be done at his charge and when I be
thereunto required by him his heirs
&c and that I be att no trouble in
travelling to signe ye sd. deeds that
then this obligation to be void and of
no effect other ways to stand in full
force power and virtue as Witness my
hand and seale the day and year above
expressed.

BEHEATHLAND BERRYMAN.
(Seal).

Signed, sealed and delivered in the
presence of us:
Orlanda Paying.
Benjamin Berryman.

Westmoreland:

At a Court held for the said county
the 30th day of March, 1736.

Willoughby Newton, Gent. presented
to this Court this Bond passed from
Beheathland Berryman decd. unto
his rather Thomas Newton Gent. also
decd. which at the Instance of the
said Willoughby is admitted to Record.

Test, G. TURBERVILLE, C. C. W.

Recorded the eighth day of April, 1736.

Pr. G. T., C. C. W.

CHAPTER VII.

ORIGIN OF THE NAME "BEHEATHLAND" AND ITS DESCENT INTO THE BERRYMAN FAMILY

Beheathland (Behethland).

In a rare book at the Congressional
Library, printed in England in 1819,
from the MSS. of Capt. John Smith,
"Travels and Adventures" Vol. 1, p.
166 (1593-1629), in a list of "Gentle-
men" who went with Capt. Smith and
Capt. Newport to visit the Indians of
Pohatan at Weremocomoco, were:
Capt. Robert Beheathland, Thomas Coe,
William Dyer, Anthony G o s w e l l,
Thomas Hope, Nathaniel Powell,
Mitchell Phittiplace, William Phittiplace, Richard Wyffian, John Tavener,
and Anas Tedkill, "All Gentlemen."
(p. 153, is list of 100 planters, among
whom is "Robert Beheathland"). In
the "Southern Historical Association,"
Vol. 2, p. 162, similar account.
Va. Hist. Mag. Vol. II, p. 263. See
"John Beheathland." "About to go to
my mother in Va., having small means
coming to me from my grandfather,
Richard Beheathland, (deceased), wish
to leave all to Chas. Beheathland, my
guardian." Prob. Oct. 22, 1639. This
unusual surname was represented at
the time of the first settlement.
Robert Beheathland, Gentleman, came
in the first ship which landed at
Jamestown in 1607. During the period
1607-1609 his name appears frequently
in Smith as taking an active part in
the affairs of the Colony. In 1620 a
petition was presented to the Royal
Council for Virginia by many of the
first personal adventures and planters
(who were ready to return if a favor-
able response was made) asking that
some person of distinction be appointed

Governor of Virginia to succeed Lord
Delaware, among the signers was Capt.
Robert Behethland.

Capt. Robert Behethland had a
daughter, Ann Behethland, who married, either, William or, Thomas Bernard of Warwick Co., Va.

Ann (Behethland) Bernard had
daughter, Beheathland Bernard, Who
married 1st, Francis Dade, who died
1663. (In 1655, a deed from Francis
Dade and Behethland, his wife.) By
Dade, she had two children:
I. Ann Dade, who married ———
Massey, and had Dade Massey.
II. William Bernard Dade.
She married 2ndly, Maj. Andrew
Gilson, of Stafford Co., Va.,
(Colonial Officer in 1680). By
Gilson she had two children:
III. Thomas Gilson, who had issue:
A. Behethland Gilson, (deed made
July 17, 1723, who married John
Berryman, brother of Rose
Berryman, and had issue:
1. Gilson Berryman (d. Apr. 4,
1749, St. Paul's Parish Reg.)
He married his cousin, Hannah
Berryman (d. before 1748).
Gilson Berryman's will dated
July 23, 1748; probated June
12, 1750. They had one son,
John Berryman, and daughter,
Behethland Gilson Berryman,
who married Francis Thorn-
ton. (Probably a son of one
of the Thornton brothers, who
married Gregory sisters.)

B. Dorothy Gilson; married ——
Spiller.

IV. Betheland Gilson; (William
and Mary Quarterly Vol. 4, p. 37.)
b. 1666; d. 1693; married Nehemiah
Storke. (d. 1692) and had issue:
A. Elizabeth Storke; b. 1687; d.
Apr. 1759; married 1702, Thomas
Newton (d. 1736), son of John
Newton. They had issue:
1. Willoughby Newton (b. 1702
Westmoreland Co., Va.; will
dated Dec. 27, 1766; probated
May 28, 1767) married Sarah
Eskridge, (b. 1727; d. 1753).
B. William Storke.
C. Catherine Storke.

NOTE: "Dade, Francis (d. 1663),
Stafford county, 1654 &c.; sixth son of
William Dade, Esq., of Tannington,
Suffolk, and his wife Mary, daughter
of Henry Wingfield, Esq., of Crofield,
Suffolk. When Francis Dade came to
Virginia he called himself for several
years Maj. John Smith. The reason
is unknown; but it was evidently noth-
ing which prevented him from visiting
England later, as he was returning
from a visit to England when he died
at sea in 1663." (Some Emigrants to
Va., 2nd Edition, by W. G. Stanard).

Rose Berryman brought the name
"Behethland," into the Taliaferro
family; showing her affection for her
sister-in-law, Behethland (Gilson)
Berryman, by naming No. seven child
Behethland, b. Aug. 20, 1738; (p. 35-6
Marshall).

Rose (Berryman) Taliaferro's son,
Dr. John Taliaferro, b. April 7, 1733,
married Mary Hardin; he named one
of his children Behethland.

Rose (Berryman) Taliaferro's son
Charles, b. July 17, 1735, married
Isabelle McCullough, and one of his
eleven children was named, Beheathland.

Benjamin Berryman's daughter,
Frances, married Dec. 31, 1731, Geo.
Foote; and she named one of her
children Behethland, who married Dec.
11, 1766, Benjamin Pope.

Benjamin Berryman's son, Benjamin
(2nd), who married Sarah Bushrod
had a daughter Hannah, who married
her cousin, Gilson Berryman; her
daughter was named Behethland.

It is through the intermarriage of
the descendants of Behethland (Bernard) Gilson into the Berryman and
Newton families that this unusual surname, "Behethland," has descended into
the Berryman family and in turn has
been passed for many generations into
the family of Rose (Berryman) Taliaferro. Some branches of the family of
Dr. John Taliaferro have retained this
name in its original form; while
others for convenience in pronunciation have shortened it. Dr. John
Taliaferro called his daughter "Bethland," and Elijah Lingo called his
daughter "Hethy." In the Clay and
Jones families the name is called
"Hettie," and in the family of Charles
Taliaferro, it is "Bathilda" and
"Bathilda-Ann."

CHAPTER VIII.

COLONIAL SERVICES WITH PROOFS OF ELIGIBILITY OF DESCENDANTS FOR MEMBERSHIP IN COLONIAL DAMES SOCIETY

Richard Taliaferro.

Services: Colonel in Colonial or English Army. Patented 10,000 acres in present Counties of Amherst and Nelson, Va.

Proofs: Richmond Critic of Va., Feb. 1, 1890.

Historic Sketch of Randolph, p. 450.

Historic Sketch of Taliaferros, p. 899.

M. C. Pilcher's—Cambell and Pilcher Families, p. 399-405.

Wm. M. Paxton's—Marshall Family, p. 85.

Louisville Courier Journal, Aug. 30, 1896.

Louisville Courier Journal, May 2, 1897.

Lookout Mag. Chattanooga, Tenn., May 20, 1916.

William and Mary Quarterly Vol. XX., No. 4.

Richard Taliaferro, b. before 1706; died Sept. 27, 1748; married June 10, 1726, Rose Berryman.

Benjamin Berryman.

Services: Captain, Major, Sheriff, Gentleman Justice.

Proofs: In Westmoreland Court, 1705-1721, Benamin Berryman, Gentleman Justice.

Va. County Records, Vol. I, p. 14-37, Captain, then Major in Colonial or English Army.

Tyler's Quarterly, Vol 4, 1923, p. 82-91-176-199, "Commissioner of Peace for Westmoreland Co., Va., 1703;"

P. 185, "June 12, 1712, Gentlemen Justices for Westmoreland Co.," see, Benjamin Berryman and Henry A. Ashton.

P. 199, "Feb. 20, 1720, Justices in Queen Anne's Reign, Augustine Washington and Benjamin Berryman."

Gov. Alex Spottswood, in 1719, appointed Benjamin Berryman Sheriff of Westmoreland Co.

Benjamin Berryman married Elizabeth Newton, daughter of John Newton and Mrs. Rose Tucker Gerrard of Westmoreland Co., Va.

JOHN NEWTON

Services: Justice and Land Proprietor.

Proofs: In William and Mary Quarterly, Vol 2, p. 48, "July 24, 1677; Sept. 29, 1677, in List of Justices for Westmoreland Co., Va., to decide on a Petition for Col. Isaac Allerton," see, "John Newton."

John Newton came to America in 1660; married 1st, Joan Barr of England; married 2nd, Mrs. Rose Tucker Gerrard of Westmoreland Co., Va.

In Bulletin of Va. State Library, Vol. 14, No. 3 and No. 4, April, July 1921, p. 25.

"Justices of Peace, in position of honor and service, represented the Genuine Aristoc of Colonial Virginia." "They were the most able, honest and judicious persons of the Country."

CHAPTER IX.

DR. JOHN TALIAFERRO—HIS LIFE, WORK AND POSTERITY

Dr. John Taliaferro, to whose memory this sketch is dedicated, was a son of Capt. Richard Taliaferro and Rose (Berryman) Taliaferro. He was born in Caroline Co., Va. on April 7, 1733. Of his childhood and early life but little is known; he was one among a large family of children. He lived in Historic Virginia, with its stately customs and traditions, and surrounded by a wide circle of kinfolk. He was educated no doubt in Caroline County in an environment, which influenced his young life and indelibly impressed on his heart a love for religion that caused him in later years to develop into the good man that he was. At the age of fifteen, his father was called by death, thus leaving his mother with the great responsibility of business and home cares. Dr. John and his older brother, Zachariah, doubtless helped to bear this burden and relieved her of much of the responsibility.

The exact time that Dr. John received a call to the ministry is unknown, but it was probably during early manhood. He studied medicine and became a great physician in the Colony. His friends called him by the familiar term "Dr. John," this to distinguish him from the many John Taliaferros, who lived in Virginia at that time. He was married about 1755 to Mary Hardin, daughter of Henry Hardin and Judith (Lynch) Hardin. Henry Hardin was the son of the French Emigrant, Mark Hardin, (b. 1660) in Rouen, France; d. 1734 in Prince William Co., Va.) and his wife, Mary (Hogue) Hardin. The will of Henry Hardin, dated May 25, 1796, recorded in Pittsylvania Co., Va., names his wife, Judith, and daughter, Mary Taliaferro; (see Sketch of Hardin Family by L. W. Rigsby). Family tradition says that Judith Lynch came from Lynch Settlement, which is now Lynch Station, near Lynchburg, Va.; these places being named for her family. Her brother, Capt. "Bill" Lynch, served in the Revolution. She is said to have been closely related to the Charles Lynch, who originated the famous "Lynch Law," and the Lynch who founded Lynchburg and owned the ferry at that place but the degree of relationship is unknown.

Dr. John Taliaferro first patented land in Pittsylvania Co. in 1769. At the outbreak of the American Revolution, he bravely responded to his country's call; and on Sept. 12, 1776, he organized a company of minute men. of which he was made captain. (Va. State Library Rept. Vol. 8, p. 426; National Society Daughters of American Revolution, Natl. No. 139572). The Pittsylvania Co. records show that in 1779 he sold his property, spoken of as "his home," and moved to Surry Co., N. C. With a heart filled with love for his fellowman, his country and his God, he left his home and relatives in the Old Dominion State and crossed the Blue Ridge Mountains into Surry Co. to do a greater and nobler work that God had planned for him. With the family of Dr. John Taliaferro, came his beloved friend, Bernard Franklin, and his family, to Surry, where they settled on Fishers River.

Surry County is one of the northwestern counties of North Carolina, and joins Grayson, Carroll, and Patrick counties, Virginia. It is a romantic section, and produces a people equally romantic. The highest part of the majestic Blue Ridge, a branch of the great Alleghany, stands in bold view, overlooking the whole country. From its base flow many crystal streams as cold as ice water can be made in Southern cities. Some of them are dignified with the name of "river." Thus there are "Mitchell's River," "Big Fisher's River," and "Little Fisher's River;" and of creeks there are "Stewart's Creek," "Ring's Creek," "Beaver Dam Creek," and so forth. All these streams, with branches and springs constantly pouring into them, after running a short and swift course, precipitate themselves into the pure, clear, and rapid Yadkin. Near the foot of the Blue

Ridge, on its spurs and ridges, and on those rivers and creeks, lived the families of Dr. John Taliaferro and Bernard Franklin.

But "Shipp's Muster-Ground," on Ring's Creek, lying between Big Fisher's and Little Fisher's Rivers, was the common centre of rendezvous for the whole country. These two rivers took their names from the loftiest peak of the Blue Ridge chain of the Alleghany, called "Fisher's Peak." It is a peak of overwhelming beauty and grandeur. It was named after Colonel Daniel Fisher, who ran the line between Virginia and North Carolina to the top of this peak. The line crosses this lofty point near its centre. The tradition of the country says—and it is supposed to be true—that, Mr. Fisher being a fleshy man, the ascent of the mountain overcame him; he fell sick, died, and was buried on its height.

Near the base of the mountain, and a few miles east, south, and southwest of it, lived a healthy, hardy, honest, uneducated set of pioneers, unlike, in many respects, any set of pioneers that ever peopled any other portion of the Lord's globe. They came mostly from Virginia, and a portion of them from the middle and lower parts of North Carolina, and a few from other sections—a sufficient number from all parts to make a singular and pleasing variety. The emigrants from Virginia furnished exceptions to the general claims of Virginians, most of whom claim to belong to the "first families;" but it was honor enough for them that they came from "Fudginny." This section was settled between the years 1770 and 1780. They had stirring times during the Revolution. The early settlers were pretty equally divided between Whigs and Tories. A majority were probably Tories, but the Whigs, headed by a few daring spirits, held the Tories in check and drove them to the mountain fastnesses.

Dr. John Taliaferro was a teacher and Baptist preacher and the only physician in Surry County at that time. He followed Greene's army as surgeon, and administered to the sick and wounded soldiers; giving to them such comfort and physical relief as only skilled hands can offer; and pouring forth his very soul in words of spiritual comfort to the dying upon the field.

Richard Taliaferro, eldest son of Dr. John Taliaferro, following his father's

example, joined the Volunteer Riflemen from Wilkes, Surry, Stokes, Forsyth. and Guilford Counties. He enlisted at the same time with his cousin and brother-in-law, Jesse Franklin, North Carolina's distinguished son and governor. Richard Taliaferro, who was twenty-five years of age at the time of the Battle of Guilford Court House, went into the battle with his cousin, Jesse Franklin (seventeen years old, who was scout of his cousin, Capt. Ben Cleveland.) Jesse and Richard rode down from Surry to join Greene's forces and fought as privates, side by side; Jesse loading their two old flint locks and Richard doing the firing. Richard killed several British and was killed after the order was given to retreat. The North Carolina troops were the last to leave the field.

Richard Taliaferro was the last man in the field at Guilford; he died from a saber thrust from one of Tarleton's dragoons, March 15, 1781. He gave his life and blood that the American People might find rest in the folds of that grand old flag, the Red and White and Blue; he pledged his life, his heart and his soul of honor, to love and protect the liberty for which it stands. He shed his blood that its stars and stripes might be our dreams and our labors, that they may ever be bright with cheer, brilliant with courage, firm with faith, because he. Richard Taliaferro, the hero of Guilford's Battle ground has helped to make them so. May his descendants never forget these things else how can we hope the future will grant our prayer, "Long may it wave o'er the land of the free and the home of the brave!"

Lord Cornwallis had three horses killed from under him during the battle; the first, a large iron grey. killed near the Ross house on southwest portion of grounds. The second, a dragoon's horse improvised for the occasion, shot near the Battle Ground line north of present restaurant; the third. a celebrated stallion named "Roundhead," which Tarleton had stolen from the farm of Judge Moore in Chatham County. Those who desire to study the Battle of Guilford Court House should read Schenck's History. "North Carolina 1780-81," chapters seven and eight. as it is the most comprehensive description ever attempted. This history records page 301, the following: "It is not only true that these riflemen of Surry were present, but they were the very last to leave the field, after Tarleton's final charge which dispersed the American forces on the left; for in that charge Taliaferro, of Surry, was killed, and Jesse Franklin, afterwards Governor of North Carolina and United States Senator from this State, made a very narrow escape. The narrative of these occurrences is given by Caruthers, in his Sketches of North Carolina, second series, upon the authority of the present Judge Jesse Franklin Graves, a grandson of Gov. Franklin, than whom no better man or purer Judge now adorns the bench of the "Old North State."

Dr. John Taliaferro, who was surgeon in Gen. Greene's Army was doing all he could to relieve suffering soldiers the day Richard was killed. After his son was buried, where he fell, the wounded were moved to the Quaker Settlement, four miles away, New Garden, now Guilford College and he worked among the wounded as long as his services were needed, burying many in the graveyard there. He did all he could for the British that were left on the field and rebuked his daughter, Judith, who was helping him, for wishing to favor the Americans.

Richard Taliaferro was buried on the field at Guilford Battle Grounds; where on the crest of the hill beyond Lake Wilfong, there is a monument erected by Gov. Thomas M. Holt in 1893 to the memory of three heroes of the battle, Major Joseph Winston. Captain Jesse Franklin and Richard Taliaferro. The tablet reads: "In memory of North Carolina Troops under Major Joseph Winston, who were fighting the Hessian and Tarleton's cavalry near this spot after the Continental line had retreated from the field of battle, March 15, 1781."

On the side of the stone are inscribed the names:

Major Joseph Winston
Captain Jesse Franklin.
Richard Taliaferro.
Palmam qui meruit ferat.

A poem by Harry Jerome Stockard read at the dedication of this monument is as follows:

"This is the ground where Patriots bled;
Wide scattered here are Guilford's dead,

Peace! come with slow and reverent tread,
And voices all subdued,
Break not their long, deed love engendered solitude.
Where silence reigns above this field,
Once wild the thundering squadrons wheeled,
Earth jarred, and armies swerved and reeled."

"Me seems I hear that volley's roar,
And see—but now I see no more!
Lo! through the clouds of smoke they pour,
Dragoons and Hessian slaves,
And Winston's level flame rolls back their circling glaives.

"But that fierce onset is not stayed,
They fought those legions undismayed,
They meet; they mix; blade rings in blade
Till but the dead and he remain
Brave Taliaferro could die, but never flee!

"Dead is that soul that does not flame
At sight of Guilford's Deathless name
And her three children's—heirs of fame!
By Alamance's Child
Graven on that fair memorial to their dead up-piled."

The graves of Ex-Governor Jesse Franklin and Joseph Winston are beside this monument, the former having been removed from Surry County. The headstone says: "Born 1764; died 1824." Joseph Winston's remains were removed from Forsyth County. The old stand-stone headstone, so moss grown it can scarcely be deciphered, bears the dates; "Born June, 1740; Died April, 1815."

Beyond the hill by the Winston monument lies the old site of the Court House. All traces of the town are not yet obliterated. One handsome oak stands sentinel there, known as Battle Ground Oak. Tradition says General Greene tied his horse to it during the battle. Slight indentation of the old roads known as Adams Street, Greene Street, and Battle Street can be seen. Andrew Jackson lived at this village for awhile and there was admitted to the practice of law in the county court.

It is stated by members of the family that when Jesse Franklin brought Richard Taliaferro's horse and trappings home from the battlefield, that his dogs recognizing his clothing, whined and moaned for him. This scene was so pathetic that it was indelibly impressed upon the hearts of all who witnessed the return of the horse without his master. The memory of Richard Taliaferro is long cherished among the descendants, especially those living on the old plantation in Surry. The old estate lies on Fisher's River, for four miles up and down it. The place where Dr. John Taliaferro lived is now owned by Mr. Walter Wylie Lovill and his son, William Shadrack Lovill; it having never gone out of the family. There are 778 acres in this tract. The old house sites, where Dr. John and his son. Richard, lived, are still in evidence. Mr. W. W. Lovill speaks of "Uncle Dick" as though he knew him personally; and loves and cherishes the memory of this brave boy. He takes pleasure in pointing out to visitors the Poplar tree where Uncle Dick killed a panther; he tells them how he loved his dogs and what a good workman he was. In speaking of this Poplar Tree, Mr. Lovill says, "There stands a Poplar tree that my grandfather has pointed out to me time and again, where Uncle Dick killed a panther. When logging the place I had the tree preserved and it yet stands."

Dr. John also owned a considerable tract of land on "Big Fisher's River," about six miles from the place that he lived on and that Mr. Lovill now owns; also a hundred acres on Moores Fork, just two miles from the old home place.

After the death of Richard Taliaferro his widow, Dorcas (Perkins) Taliaferro, went on horseback with three small daughters, Jean, Mary Hardin, and Judy, from their home in Surry to the home of Dr. John Taliaferro, where she made her home. Court records at Dobson, Surry Co., N. C., show that on Nov. 12, 1781, Dorcas Taliaferro was appointed administrator of estate of Richard Taliaferro, who fell in his country's cause. She was made exempt from paying taxes, and she went under bond with John Taliaferro and Willliam T. Lewis in the sum of 500 pounds apiece. Dr. John Taliaferro's devotion to his daughter-in-law Dorcas, was without a parallel, the two families living happily under the same roof for many years. He was a very just man and often settled disputes in the neighborhood. He is said to have been very proud of his name; always insisting on it being spelled in the original form, "Taliaferro." It is said that a man by the name of Oliver committed a crime in Surry Co. just after the Revolution and to escape punishment, he fled to Tennessee; prefixed the letter "T" to his name, thus making it "Toliver." Dr. John impressed it upon his children not to recognize any relationship with this family.

In 1790-91 Dr. John Taliaferro and his daughter-in-law, Dorcas Taliaferro, were offered government land in Georgia, which they accepted; Dorcas receiving a tract of 3000 acres on Fishing Creek in Baldwin Co., Georgia; and Dr. John a similar tract in the adjoining county of Wilkinson. He divided his land in Surry County among his children who wished to remain there; the records showing deeds made by Dr. John Taliaferro. 1790-91 to his son Charles Taliaferro. with his sons-in-law Levi Pruitt, Joseph Porter and a party by the name of ———— Lay, as witnesses. His daughter, Anna (Taliaferro) McCrary, had already previously moved from Virginia to Baldwin County, Ga., settling near the home of her brother-in-law, Bartley McCrary, Sr., Dr. John with his own family and his son Richard's family, made their home in Wilkinson Co., Georgia. Here he spent the declining years of his life; years of usefulness and of service to humanity and God. Doctors were scarce and the churches were scattered, but he lost no time in doing what he could. Religious gatherings were often held in the homes, people coming from a long distance to worship and attend the preaching services conducted by Dr. John Taliaferro.

This record is taken from the church book of Mt. Nebo Church, Wilkinson Co., Ga., and is in the possession of J. Reddick McCook: "John Taliaferro, Rec'd. by letter Aug. 24, 1816. Died Apr. 7, 1821. Lydia Taliaferro, Rec'd by letter Aug. 23. 1817. Dismissed July 21, 1821."

In 1819 there was a land grant issued by Gov. John Forsyth to Dr. John Taliaferro for Revolutionary services; this together with his other property being located in Wilkinson County. A few years after his removal to Georgia, his sons-in-law, Levi Pruitt and Joseph Porter, settled with their families in Warren and Wilkinson Counties. His son Charles and his daughter, Judith, remained with their families at the old home place, in Surry, N. C. For many years letters passed between relatives in Georgia and North Carolina; and although the postage was twenty-five cents per letter and the mails very slow and uncertain, these families managed to keep in touch with one another.

Dr. John Taliaferro passed away at his home in Wilkinson County, Georgia on his eighty-eighth birthday, April 7, 1821. His will was probated in said county July term of court of the same year.

The life of Dr. John Taliaferro is remarkable in many ways. The keynote of love which shed its rays of gladness upon his heart and life told of the nature of God, who is love; it told of the human and divine love which answers to each other and like reflecting mirrors, act and react on each other endlessly. His home is credited with being an institution of religion and love, the one merging into the other; for what is religion but the embodiment of love? His beloved wife and children were the inspiration of his very being; the love he bore for them, and they for him, surpassed all understanding. The sad loss of the eldest son, Richard Taliaferro, who fell on Guilford's Battle Ground, cast a shadow over his life which followed him to the grave. This brave boy was the pride of his heart; the light of his life; the embodiment of the truth, honor and trust which filled his soul with joy. Through the remaining years of the life of Dr. John Taliaferro grief and pride were thus mingled in his heart, drawing him closer by the ties of family love, making his life work among his fellow man even sweeter and greater than ever before. The preservation of family names seems to have been unwritten law in his home; and it has descended unto his posterity, and is still in evidence among the present generation. Lucy is said to have been his favorite child; but this was nothing more than his paternal love for his baby child; she being several years younger than his other children. When he removed to Georgia, he gave his property in Virginia and North Carolina to his older children; this explaining why they received such a small portion at his death. It has been said of him that his heart was kind, his disposition smooth and temperate; his manner gentle; his

tact for making friends remarkable. His impartial nature, his many deeds of benevolence, his marked degree of pride were, in the communities where he resided, without parallel.

In addition to the great love which he bore for his family, there lies in the life of Dr. John Taliaferro three outstanding virtues; three noble qualities that one seldom finds combined in the heart and soul of mortal man. Dr. John Taliaferro was a doctor of medicine; he was a soldier; and he was a minister of the Gospel. He served his fellow man; he served his nation; and he served his God. In him his fellow man found such ministering service as only skilled hands can offer; in him his country found one of the loftiest virtues which the Almighty has implanted in the heart of man—true patriotism, which is only founded on exalted principles and supported by great virtues; and lastly, in him his Creator found a meek and thankful heart, a heart that responded to his Master's bidding, a soul devoted to His service. May the descendants of Dr. John Taliaferro remember with great pride his glorious examples that they may imitate them. Through the years to come may in their lives there shine some of his reflected glory, such as only comes from high and noble characters; may they ever perpetuate his memory, and in so doing, build unto him a lasting monument; for in the words of Daniel Webster, "If we work upon marble it will perish; if we work upon brass time will efface it; if we rear temples they will crumble into dust; but if we work upon immortal souls, if we imbue them with principle, with the just fear of God and love of fellow man, we engrave on those tablets something which will brighten all eternity."

Then with apologies to John Oxenham, well might we in reverence bow our heads and say:
"Dr. John is dead, they said!
   Dr. John the Teacher,
   Dr. John, Doctor, Soldier, Preacher.
"Dr. John is dead they say!
   Fighting the fight
   Holding the light,
   Into the night.
"Dr. John is dead they say!
   But the light shall burn the brighter,
   And the night shall be the lighter,
   For his going;
   And a rich, rich harvest for his sowing.

"Dr. John is dead they say!
What is death to such a one as
Dr. John?
One sigh perchance, for work un-
finished here,
Then a swift passing to a mightier
sphere,
New joys, perfected powers, the
vision clear,
And all the amplituae of Heaven
to work,
The work he held so dear.
"Dr. John is dead they say!
Nor dead, nor sleeping! He lives
on! His name
Shall kindle many a heart to
flame,
The fire he lighted shall burn on
and on,
And all the kingdom of the earth
be won,
And won.
"A soul so fiery sweet can never die,
But lives and loves through all
eternity."

NOTES

For several years there has existed
among the descendants of Dr. John
Taliaferro a difference of opinion as
to whether he was twice married.
Tradition in Surry Co., N. C., states
that his wife, Mary Hardin, who was
the mother of his children, lies buried
in an unmarked grave in the old
Taliaferro-Franklin burial ground in
Surry; other traditions say that she
is buried in the same grave with a
daughter Sallie, who was a dwarf, and
died at the same time her mother
passed away. However, the will of
Henry Hardin, dated 1796, disproves
the claim that his daughter Mary,
died prior to the removal of Dr. John
Taliaferro to Georgia in 1790-91; and
this will, indicating that she was still
alive in 1796, establishes beyond all
doubt that she was the mother of all
of Dr. John Taliaterro's children.
History of Baldwin County, Georgia,
page 261 shows that John Taliaferro
married Lydia Howard in 1814. Lydia
Taliaferro whose name appears on the
old records of Mt. Nebo Church was
probably the second wife of Dr. John
Taliaferro.

Mr. Shadrack C. Franklin, formerly
of Mt. Airy, N, C. Member of Legislature 1887, secured this paper:

"On one of the old records of Surry
County I find the following entry on
page 13. State of N. C., Surry Co.
At a court of Pleas and Quarter Session begun and held in and for the
said County of Surry. At the Court

House in Richmond on the second
Monday in November, being the 12th
day in the year of our Lord 1781 and
in the six years of American Independence. Present Martin Armstrong
Esq. Adjourned till tomorrow morning, 9 o'clock.
Tuesday 13th, November Court met
according to adjournment.
Present Martin Armstrong, Gibson
Woolridge, Esqs., Administration of
the Estate of Richard Taliaferro dec'd
is granted to Dorcas Taliaferro wife
and relict of said dec'd who entered
into Bond with John Taliaferro and
William T. Lewis in the sum of 500
specie. Ordered that letters of adm.
issue accordingly administratrix quali-
fied according to law.
"Ordered by the court that Dorcas
Taliaferro wife and relict of Richard
Taliaferro, who fell in his country's
cause be recommended to the General
Assembly as a proper person to be
exempt from paying taxes etc. She
having a helpless family to support."
Witness my hand and official seal at
office in Dobson, N. C., Aug. 1, 1912.
W. W. Hampton, Clerk Superior Court,
Surry Co., N. C. An old Country
Seat. A true copy.
(The above mentioned William T.
Lewis was evidently related by blood
or marriage to the family of Dr. John
Taliaferro. Mark Hardin Taliaferro
in "Fisher's River Scenes" refers to
him as "Uncle Billie Lewis." "Uncle
Billie" was probably a great uncle of
the author, and married a sister of
Dr. John Taliaferro.)
Gov. Jesse Franklin and Richard
Taliaferro were close friends and
brothers-in-law; Richard married
Dorcas Perkins and Jesse married
Meekie Perkins.
Family tradition says that Henry
Hardin helped to keep the camp fires
burning on the night before the Battle
of Kings Mountain.
Mark Hardin, brother of Mary, was
a close friend of Col. Cleveland, who
was one of the four Colonels who
fought the battle at Kings Mountain.
He helped Cleveland arrest Tories
during the Revolution and lived in
Alleghany County across the Blue
Ridge from Surry. Col. Cleveland
was an uncle of Jesse and Shadrack
Franklin.
Schenck's History "North Carolina
1780-81" in describing the Battle of
Guilford Court House, p. 309-310 says,
"The next volunteer corps of Virginia
was a battalion of riflemen under Col.

Charles Lynch. I have not been able to find in Johnson or Lee, who give particulars, or in any general history, an estimate of their number. In a note, p. 269, Lee says: 'Colonel Lynch had lately joined, commanding one of the battalions of Virginia militia which arrived' (on the 11th March) 'under Brigadier Lawson,' and Johnson says they were all volunteers and riflemen. It may be safe to estimate them between one and two hundred men, say 150.

"This was the Col. Charles Lynch who gave the name of 'Lynch Law' to the summary punishment of violent and desperate criminals. He was of Quaker descent and an ardent Whig; he folded up his non-combatant principles when they were in the way of his patriotic impulses. He inflicted these punishments generally on the worst class of Tories; but to his character for mercy, be it said, he did not take human life. In Judge Lynch's court there generally sat as associates Robert Adams and Thomas Calloway, and an old song commemorating their judgments ran thus:
"Hurrah for Colonel Lynch, Captain Bob and Calloway,
They never turned a Tory loose
Until he shouted liberty."
Colonel Lynch died October 29th, 1796, aged 60 years."

WILL OF JOHN TALIAFERRO

Records of Returns—Wilkinson County —1820 to 1828—Page 21.

In the Name of God, Amen. Whereas, knowing all flesh to be subject to death, and being anasarcal and looking shortly for a change, have a desire to distribute my worldly property while sound in mind. My first request is that my body be decently buried without superfluity. The next, that my debts be justly paid, that are just, and then as my wife and myself drew a contract before marriage, that is, that she set up no claim to my property nor I myself as heir set up any right to hers, but at my death deliver all her property to her and then I lend her during life and her widowhood the land from the cutoff along this side the lane next the house, with the use of the spring and all the houses and cleared land, and also Jack and Arey and family, with cattle, hogs, corn and fodder to serve the first year, or her hundred dollars as the contract called for, but the land is not to be rented nor the negroes to be hired, but the whole of my property left together until my wife's death, then to be divided as follows: I give my son Richard's three daughters Jean, Mary and Judy, one hundred dollars, each of them. My daughter Rose, I give the young mare I left with her, and ten dollars. My daughter Elizabeth, I give the horse I left with her, and ten dollars. My daughter Anne, I give ten dollars. My sons, Charles and Benjamin I give to each of them ten apiece.

Now for the remainder of my children, Judith, Mary, Behethland and Lucy, I lend during their natural lives, but to be divided as follows: Lucy is to have the land from the cutoff down each branch to the lines next to Joe Jones, then from the cutoff along the lane next to their house to the Spring, with the care of my old wench Sabina, then I lend her during natural life my wench Betty and her children, but give the whole of the property at her death that is mentioned to her children, except Sabina, which is to possess her house and property. As for the remaining part of my property, I lend during life to my other three daughters, Judith, Mary and Behethland, but the property I give to their children. After the death of my wife, the whole of my property is to be sold by giving such credit as it will bring the most and after collected equal distribution made to the legatees.

Now for the true performance of my last Will and Testament, I leave my beloved friend, Gen. John Scott, John Jones and Elijah Lingo, and I do revoke all other wills and leave this as my will and testament.

In witness whereof, I have set my hand the third day of April, in the year of our Lord, one thousand eight hundred and seventeen.

JOHN TALIAFERRO.

Test:
James Rabb.
Robert Hatcher.
Thos. Boazman.
Pierce Clay.

The will of John Taliaferro was probated in July, 1821 term of Ordinary's Court, Wilkinson Co., Ga., and on Pages 37 and 38 Record of Returns Ordinary's office appears record of sale of his property and appraisers returns of Estate of John Taliaferro.

CHILDREN OF DR. JOHN TALIAFERRO

The children of Dr. John Taliaferro were born in Virginia; some of them in Pittsylvania Co., Va., between the years 1769 and 1779, while the older ones were born probably in Caroline County, prior to Dr. John's removal to Pittsylvania. Lucy the youngest child, was born in Surry County, N. C. His children named in the same order as mentioned in his will are as follows:

I. Richard Taliaferro; b. 1756; killed at Guilford Court House March 15, 1781; married in Buckingham County to Dorcas Perkins. (See Chapter 10).

II. Rose Taliaferro; married Joseph Porter. (See Chapter 11).

III. Elizabeth Taliaferro; married Levi Pruitt. (See Chapter 12).

IV. Anna Taliaferro; married Johnathan McCrary. (See Chapter 13).

V. Charles Taliaferro; married 1st., Sallie Burroughs; 2nd, Dicie Tucker. (See Chapter 14).

VI. Benjamin Taliaferro; married Ada Snow. He moved to Georgia with his father when just a lad and his marriage probably occurred in Wilkinson Co., Georgia.

The Snow family was very numerous in Surry Co. and some of them moved to Georgia. There still exists in Wilkinson County a settlement known as "Snow Hill," and a school house that bears the same name. Benjamin and Ada (Snow) Taliaferro had several children but they removed to Bedford County Tennessee and probably to Texas. There is no trace of their descendants so far as the writer knows.

VII. Judith Taliaferro; married Shadrack Franklin. (See Chapter 15).

VIII. Mary Taliaferro; married probably a Mercer. No further information.

IX. Bethland Taliaferro; no information.

X. Lucy Taliaferro; b. in Surry County, N. C., May 29, 1780; d. Feb. 28, 1842; married 1797, John Lawrence Jones, (b. Dec. 8, 1776; d. Mar. 1, 1830.) She is said to have been very beautiful and her father's favorite child. For the descendants of Lucy (Taliaferro) Jones see the accompanying Sketch of the Jones Family, compiled by Judge L. W. Rigsby, of Cairo, Ga.

CHAPTER X.

RICHARD TALIAFERRO

Richard Taliaferro, eldest son of Dr. John and Mary (Hardin) Taliaferro, was born in Virginia in 1756; married Dorcas Perkins in Buckingham Co., Va. During the Revolution he moved with his family to Surry County, N. C., settling on Fisher's River, near the home of his father. An account of his death at the Battle of Guilford Court House has already been given in Chapter 9. After his death, his widow went on horseback with her three small daughters, one an infant, to the home of her father-in-law, Dr. John Taliaferro. These two families lived many years in the same home and they both moved to Georgia at the same time. Richard and Dorcas (Perkins) Taliaferro had three daughters; Jean Taliaferro, who married a Lokey in Wilkinson County, Ga.; Mary Hardin Taliaferro, (b. 1779), who married Elijah Lingo in Wilkinson County, Ga.; and Judy Taliaferro, whom circumstantial evidence indicates, married Rhodan A. Greene of Baldwin Co., Ga. This chapter records only the descendants of Richard Taliaferro's second daughter, Mary Hardin Taliaferro. There is no trace of the descendants of her sisters, Jean and Judy.

After the Widow Dorcas moved her family to the home of Dr. John Taliaferro, there were two girls in this home bearing the name of "Mary Taliaferro." To avoid confusion, Richard's daughter, Mary Hardin Taliaferro, was given a nickname, "Nancy," by which she was called as long as she lived; however, she signed her real name in writing.

Mary Hardin Taliaferro (called Nancy) was married to Elijah Lingo in Wilkinson County, about 1795. The great love which she bore for her family is evidenced by the names which she bestowed upon her children. The family Bible, Court records, Land Grants, etc., show that three of her sons bore the name of Taliaferro and two of them, Richard Taliaferro. After the death of her husband in 1830, she moved to Clopton, Ala. Her eldest son, Richard Taliaferro Lingo, built a home for her and her daughter, Elizabeth (Lingo) Rogers, who

was also a widow at that time. After the remarriage of Elizabeth to a Baptist minister by the name of Loften, Mary Hardin (Taliaferro) Lingo came back to Georgia and made her home with her youngest son, Taliaferro Lingo, near Americus, Ga., where she died in 1850. She is buried in the old Lingo graveyard near Americus. Her children inherited her portion of the land on Fishing Creek in Baldwin County, Ga., which was given to her mother, Dorcas Taliaferro, "as widow of Richard Taliaferro, who fell in his Country's cause."

The Lingo family is of Italian origin, the name being originally spelled 'Lingot;" but the pronunciation of the letter "t" is silent. This family emigrated to Ireland, probably about 1600. The Irish emigrant, who came to America, was John Richard Lingo, who settled at Lewiston, Delaware about 1750. His son, William Lingo, was born at Lewiston, Del, in 1753; died in Maury Co., Tenn., 1836; married 1773. Sussannah ———? William Lingo served in the Revolution as a Private in Battle of Guilford and Eutaw Springs. He enlisted in 1779. (Verified by original Pension Application on file in Pension Bureau: see National Society D. A. R. Nat'l. No. 139572). William Lingo had sons, Elijah Lingo (b. in Lewiston, Del., 1774), married Mary Hardin Taliaferro; and John A. Lingo, who was born about 1776 and moved to Cumberland, Md. in 1810. John A. Lingo had sons, E. A. Lingo, Uniontown, Penn.; William H. C. Lingo, b. 1802; d. 1842, of Lebanon, Ohio. John A. Lingo has many descendants living in Ohio, Pennsylvania, Missouri and Texas. The Texas branch of the family are quite wealthy, having amassed a large fortune in the lumber business at Dennison, Texas.

Elijah Lingo moved from Lewiston, Del. to Cumberland, Md.; later moving to Wilkinson County, Ga. about 1793-94. It was here that he met and married Mary Hardin Taliaferro. They resided for several years in Wilkinson County, near the present site of Lewiston, Ga.; this small town being named for his old home in Delaware.

Behethland Berryman Lingo Johnson   Henry Rogers Johnson, Sr.

Lillian Ivey Davis   Monument to Richard Taliaferro

They later moved to Hancock County; from Hancock, to Twiggs County, returning to his old home in Wilkinson Co. in 1815. He was a man of trust and executive ability and was made one of the executors of the will of Dr. John Taliaferro. Dr. John loved him as though he were his own son and had great trust and confidence in him. He died in 1830 and is buried in the old Lingo family burial ground in Wilkinson County. The writer has no proof of the military services of Elijah Lingo, but as his children drew bounty land in Baldwin and Twiggs Counties, which gives evidence that he served, either in the Indian War or the War of 1812. Elijah and Mary Hardin (Taliaferro) Lingo had issue:

First, William Lingo; married Margaret Moore, 1819.

Second, Behethland Berryman Lingo.

Third, Elizabeth Lingo.

Fourth, Richard Taliaferro Lingo.

Fifth, Martha Lingo.

Sixth, John Richard Taliaferro Lingo.

Seventh, Mary Hardin Lingo.

Eighth, Patsy Lingo.

Ninth, Elijah Lingo.

Tenth, Taliaferro Lingo.

Eleventh, Nancy Lingo.

Twelve, Lucy Ann Lingo.

Second Line.

BEHETHLAND BERRYMAN LINGO

Behethland Berryman Lingo (called Hethy), daughter of Elijah and Mary Hardin (Taliaferro) Lingo; b. Dec. 28, 1797; d. Nov. 28, 1870; married 1820, John Clark Johnson (b. May 5, 1794; d. Jan. 8, 1856), of Macon, Ga. A photo of her is reproduced in this sketch. John Clark Johnson served as a private in Capt. Shiver's Co., of Georgia Militia in the War of 1812. He was stationed in Savannah. For said services he was given Land Warrant No. 6492, dated Sept. 17, 1855, for 80 acres of land in Georgia, to be selected by him. He died before this warrant was taken up. Issue:

I. Nancy Johnson: died unmarried.

II. William Lingo Johnson, b. Sept. 7, 1822 in Twiggs Co., d. Jan. 12, 1906 in Macon, Ga.; married in Augusta, Ga., 1847, Ann Elizabeth Kunze (b. July 24, 1825), in Augusta, Ga., d. Mar. 25, 1913), daughter of Lewis Kunze. William Lingo Johnson served as

captain in the War between the States. Issue:

A. Lewis Bernard Johnson.

B. Clara Ella Johnson; married J. T. Jossey. P. O., 852. First Street, Macon, Ga. Issue:
1. William Johnson Jossey.
2. James Thomas Jossey.
3. Clara Ella Jossey; married Domingo Carlos Acosta (died July 26, 1926). P. O. address, Tulsa, Okla. Issue:
   a. Catherine Acosta.
   b. Margaret Acosta; married James Dwen. P. O. address, Tulsa, Okla. Mr. Dwen's relatives in Ireland have compiled a family history and his wife's Taliaferro ancestry is included in this book. Issue: Margaret and James Dwen.
   c. Marion Acosta.
   d. Naomi Acosta.
   e. Domingo Acosta.
   f. Marcia Acosta.
4. Minnie Eloise Jossey; married W. A. Capps. P. O. address, Box 119, Athens, Ga.

C. Julia Johnson; she lives with her sister, Mrs. Shelverton. P. O. address, 852 First Street, Macon, Ga.

D. Benjamin Franklin Johnson.

E. Davis Beauregard Johnson.

F. Fannie Belle Johnson; married April 8, 1891, William Edward Shelverton, son of Josiah B. and Susan (Cawley) Shelverton. P. O. address, 852 First Street, Macon, Ga. Mrs. Shelverton is a fine musician and has for several years served as organist for the First Baptist Church, Macon, Ga. She is also prominent in social and club life, and is a member of the Music Club, U. D. C., and D. A. R. Mr. Shelverton is a prominent pharmacist, being proprietor of Shelverton's Pharmacy. Issue:
1. Claud Winchester Shelverton; b. Jan. 5, 1892, Macon, Ga.; married April 27, 1921, Hovis Mersenne Ellis. He is an architect and has offices in the Grand Building, Macon, Ga. During the World War he enlisted in the Army and was honorably discharged from second Officers Training Camp at Fort Oglethorpe, Sept. 12, 1917, on account of

being under weight. He was also honorably discharged from Camp Gordon, May 6, 1918, on account of being under weight. Issue:

a. Claude Winchester Shelverton, Jr.

2. William Johnson Shelverton; b. Dec. 10, 1900. P. O. address, 852 First Street, Macon, Ga.

G. Charles Winn Johnson; married Ada Moncrief. P. O. address, Macon, Ga. Issue:

1. Adele Johnson; m a r r i e d Harry P. Flemming. Issue:

a. Winnie Alice Flemming.

2. Winifred Johnson.

III. Elizabeth Anne Johnson; b. 1828; d. 1906; married 1860, John Tomlinson Summers of Statesville, N. C. Issue:

A. Hardin Summers; died age 11 years.

IV. Henry Rogers Johnson, Sr.; b. Oct. 2, 1830, Macon, Ga.; d. Dec. 4, 1904; married first, 1848, Mary Elizabeth Hunt (b. in Pike Co., Ga., Mar. 6, 1832; d. 1863), daughter of Appleton Hunt (b. 1800) and Matilda Guilder (b. 1816; married 1831); he married second, 1864, Matilda Josephine Black (d. Jan., 1922), daughter of William Black and Helen Rawls. His photo is reproduced in this sketch and a sketch of his life, by his granddaughter, Mrs. Minnie Bagley Bradshaw, is given in this chapter. Issue by first marriage to Mary Elizabeth Hunt:

A. Charles Johnson; b. 1849; d. age 9 months.

B. Laura Johnson; b. May, 1858; married Oct. 15, 1878, David Webster Bagley (d. Feb. 14, 1910), son of Daniel S. and Sarah (Mann) Bagley. P. O. address 301 Taylor St., Americus, Ga. Issue:

1. Minnie Elizabeth Bagley; b. Nov. 4, 1879; married July 3, 1906, Charles W. Bradshaw, son of James T. and Nellie (Thomson) Bradshaw. Mrs. Bradshaw has visited the old Taliaferro Estate in Surry County and has been instrumental in securing many records for this sketch. She graduated at Americus High School, June 1898; attended Georgia State Normal College 1898-99; entered Peabody College for Teachers, Nashville, Tenn., Fall of 1899, receiving L. I. Degree, June 1901; did special work in History and Pedagogy, 1901-2. Taught in Burlington, N. C. Graded School, 1902-1904; taught in Americus Graded School, 1904-06. She married July 3, 1906, C. W. Bradshaw of Alamance County, N. C. They lived in Wilmington, N. C. for one year, moving to Greensboro, N. C. in 1907, where they are still residing. Mr. Bradshaw is a very successful cotton merchant. Their only child, Charles William Bradshaw, Jr., was born Aug. 24, 1920. He is unusually bright and gives promise of being a great credit to his family.

2. Henry Johnson Bagley; b. Nov. 24, 1883, Americus, Ga.; married first, June 1908, Mamie Ansley Bailey, daughter of Mr. and Mrs. W. D. Bailey, Americus, Ga.; married second, Aug. 13, 1925, Agnes Metz, daughter of Mr. and Mrs. Otto Metz, Astoria, N. Y. Issue by first marriage:

a. Henry Johnson Bagley; b. March 12, 1911.

b. William Dudley Bagley; b. Sept. 23, 1913.

c. Charles Ansley Bagley; b. April 30, 1922.

3. Daniel Slade Bagley; b. Jan. 9, 1886, Americus, Ga.,; married June 15, 1921, Louise Davis. P. O. address 214 S. Albany Ave., Tampa, Fla. Issue:

a. Daniel Slade Bagley, Jr.; b. March 20, 1922.

b. Salatha Louise Bagley, b. April 18, 1926.

4. Mary Taliaferro Bagley; b. Dec. 20, 1888, Americus, Ga., married Nov. 30, 1910, John A. Wagnon of Milledgeville, Ga., son of Mr. and Mrs. Willard Wagnon. P. O. address, 301 Taylor St., Americus, Ga. Issue:

a. John Alva Wagnon, Jr.; b. Oct. 31, 1911.

b. Lucy Elizabeth Wagnon; b. Nov. 6, 1912.

c. Daniel Webster Bagley Wagnon; b. July 31, 1917.

d. Millard Watson Wagnon;
b. July 13, 1922.

e. Bertram Ennis Wagnon; b.
April 11, 1924.

5. William Webster Bagley; b.
Dec. 30, 1890; married Nov.
24, 1915, Grace Vardeman,
daughter of George Varde-
man, Sparta, Ga. P. O. address Church St., Americus,
Ga. Issue:
   a. William Webster Bagley,
   Jr.; b. Jan. 1919; d. Feb.
   1919.
   b. George Vardeman Bagley;
   b. May 12, 1920.

6. Lilla Josephine Bagley; b.
Nov. 14, 1892; married Dec.
27, 1915. John A. McManus,
son of Mr. and Mrs. Leonard
McManus, Sr., Macon, Ga. He
is a well known admiralty
lawyer of New York City. P.
O. address 549 16th St., Flushing, L. I., N. Y. Issue:
   a. Sarah Mann McManus; b.
   Nov. 11, 1916.
   b. Laura Eunice McManus; b.
   May 27, 1918.
   c. John Alexander McManus,
   Jr.; b. Jan. 10, 1923.

7. Hardin Clay Bagley; b.
April, 1894; d. at the age of
two weeks.

C. Ella Johnson; b. 1860; d. age
7 years.

Henry Rogers Johnson, Sr. had issue
by his second marriage to Matilda
Josephine Black:

D. Minnie Johnson; b. Dec. 21,
1865; d. age 11 years.

E. Walter Allen Johnson; b. Sept.
26, 1867; d. Dec. 16, 1899; unmarried; of Georgetown University;
was too frail to go into business, but he helped to beautify
many spots in Americus. A
majestic avenue of elms is one
of his living monuments.

F. Helen Rawls Johnson; b.
March 11, 1870; d. Nov. 5, 1873.

G. Corrinne Reese Johnson; b.
Sept. 26, 1872; d. Oct. 31, 1873:
Helen and Corrinne died within
one week of each other.

H. Lilla Belle Johnson; b. Aug. 4,
1874, Americus, Ga.; married
Dec. 10, 1902, Norman C. Miller
(b. in Heard County, Ga., Sept.
8, 1871), son of John Isaac Miller (b. Heard Co., Ga., March
17, 1852; d. Nov. 25, 1913) and
Ambrosia Pitman (b. 1855; d.
1872; married 1870). Mrs. Nor-

man C. Miller is very talented
in music and graduated in both
voice and piano from New England Conservatory; then studied
for one year in Florence, Italy.
Mr. Miller was formerly of
Hogansville, Ga. He is a member of the firm, Ginn and Company, Publishers of Text Books,
Atlanta, Ga. and is a man of
very delightful personality, and
has hosts of friends. He is very
much beloved by all members
of his family and his wife's
family. P. O. address, 45
Springdale Road, Atlanta, Ga.
Issue:
   1. Henry Johnson Miller; b.
   Dec. 4, 1906; he is an exceedingly bright boy. He was
   graduated from Emory University this past winter at the
   age of twenty years.

I. Henry Rogers Johnson, Jr., b.
Nov. 24, 1876; d. Oct. 11, 1924
at Americus, Ga.; married
Eugenia Brahan. Issue:
   1. Martha Hayward Johnson;
   b. Dec., 1906.
   2. Eugenia Brahan Johnson; b.
   Feb., 1910.
   3. Anne Johnson; b. 1912.
   4. Katherine Johnson; b. 1914.

J. Joseph Eggleston Johnson; b.
May 1, 1881; married 1899, Alice
Chapman, also a descendant of
Dr. John Taliaferro. P. O. address Box 1483, Lakeland, Fla.
Has degree of M. E. Issue:
   1. Alice Johnson; b. April 27,
   1904; married 1925, James K.
   Stewart, Jan. 4, 1925 at Avon
   Park, Fla. P. O. Address Bartow, Fla.
   2. Anna Margaret Johnson; b.
   Jan. 23, 1906; d. Feb. 6, 1907.
   3. Iris Johnson; b. Nov. 1, 1907.
   4. Joseph Eggleston Johnson; b.
   April, 15, 1910; d. May 27,
   1910.

V. Hardin Taliaferro Johnson; b.
1833; d. 1893; married 1862,
Laura Bragg Mitchell. He was
for many years associated with
the firm Johnson and Harris, in
the Wholesale Grocery business,
Macon, Ga. He was widely
known throughout the State, had
hosts of friends and was loved
and admired by all. Issue:
   A. Albert Sidney Johnson.
   B. Carrie Johnson; b. Griffin,
   Ga., Sept, 8, 1868; married
   Dec. 15, 1885; Julien S.

Rodgers, son of Alpheus Mims and **V i r g i n i a** (Blount) Rodgers. P. O. address, 2346 Riverside Ave., Jacksonville, Fla. Issue:

1. Frank Preston Rodgers; b. Sept. 15, 1886; d. Feb. 16, 1891.
2. Louise Rodger.; b. Dec. 20, 1888; married Dec. 20, 1910, A. C. Schuler. P. O. address, 2224 Lydia St., Jacksonville, Fla. Issue:
   a. Cromer Schuler.
   b. Evelyn Schuler.
3. Julien Sidney Rodgers; b. Nov. 18, 1890; d. Feb. 18, 1891.
4. Ethel Rodgers; b. April 6, 1893; married June 30, 1917, Wilfred T. Coates. P. O. address, 2911 Riverside Ave. Jacksonville, Fla. Issue:
   a. Shirley Coates.
5. Virginia Rodgers; b. Aug. 6, 1895; married Dec. 31, 1919, H. Arthur Irving. P. O. address, 2222 Lydia St., Jacksonville, Fla. Issue:
   a. Jane Irving.
6. Dorothea Rodgers; b. Dec. 18, 1902; married June 30, 1921, Carl F. Emmart. P. O. address, 512 Lyndhurst St., Baltimore, Md.
7. Carolyn Mims Rodgers; b. Feb. 18, 1906. P. O. address 2346 Riverside Ave., Jacksonville, Fla.
8. William Jackson Rodgers; b. Aug. 23, 1913; P. O. address 2346 Riverside Ave., Jacksonville, Fla.

C. Edgar Johnson.
D. Mitchell Johnson.
E. Herbert Johnson.
F. Emmie Cleveland Johnson.

VI. Benjamin Johnson; d. unmarried, 1856; age 21 years.

VII. Mary Beheathland Johnson; b. 1840; d. 1915; married Cornelius Daniels of Connecticut. Issue:
A. Kittie Daniels; died in childhood.
B. Rose Berryman Daniels; unmarried, lives in New York City.
C. Daisy Daniels; died 1913, in Flushing, L. I., N. Y.

War Record of Capt. William Lingo Johnson

In April, 1861, Joseph E. Brown, Gov. of Georgia, ordered twenty companies of infantry to rendezvous at Augusta, Ga., for service in the Army of the Confederate States. "The Sumter Light Guards," Company K., (4th Ga.), commanded by Capt. W. L. Johnson of Sumter County, was mustered in as the Fourth Regiment Georgia Volunteers, commonly known as the "Fourth Georgia." The Regiment left Augusta, May 3rd, arriving at Portsmouth, Va., May 5, 1861. Capt. Johnson retired at the expiration of term of service 1862 and entered the Quartermasters' Dept., under Major George W. Grice, where he remained until the close of the War. He was transferred from Portsmouth, Va., to Americus Commissary. He came to Macon and surrendered to Wilson and was dismissed on parole from the army in April, 1865.

War Record of Lewis Kunze

Lewis Kunze (father of Anne E. (Kunze) Johnson), served six months under Col. William Cumming as a member of the "Volunteer Company of Augusta Independent Blues" in the Expedition to Florida in 1811 and a second campaign under Capt. William Kennedy in Savannah during the War of 1812.

Sketch of the Life of Henry Rogers Johnson, Sr.

Henry Rogers Johnson, Sr. (b. Oct. 2, 1830, Macon, Ga.) was a son of John Clark Johnson, a veteran of the War of 1812, and Beheathland Berryman Lingo. He and his brother, W. L. Johnson, were merchants, dealing in everything from cotton to farm and household supplies. They brought a stock of goods from Macon on the first train that went through to Americus, Ga. Oglethorpe, Ga. was the terminus of the Central of Georgia Railroad for a long while, boasting at one time of a population of 20,000 people, most of whom moved further south when the railroad was extended. They rented a church on reaching Americus, and sold their entire stock of goods before the following Sunday. They opened up cotton business with a mercantile side line and moved their families down.

Henry Rodgers Johnson, Sr. served as private in the early part of the War Between the States; then he became quartermaster; latter part of war he joined Georgia Militia; was cited for an act of bravery at the skirmish of Griswoldville, Ga. After the close of the war, he and Thomas

Harrold opened a cotton warehouse; later Uriah Harrold, the son of Thomas, was his partner. For forty years the firm of Johnson and Harrold was outstanding in Southwest Georgia for honesty, fair dealing and good business. These men helped build Americus; helped to make it a good cotton center.

Henry Rogers Johnson, Sr. attended school only a few years; married at the age of eighteen; but he was constantly improving himself; had a splendid library to which he was continually adding more good books. He was very fond of music, playing the flute himself, while his wife and children played other instruments. He was very ambitious for his children and gave them every advantage. He and his wife traveled quite a bit and always came home with new ideas and new books. In the early eighties he bored a deep well, erected a windmill and installed the first modern water system, with bath tubs, etc., in Americus, Ga. It wasn't long before others were doing likewise. He and his partners had the first phone system in that section of the State, having only four numbers. He befriended many a struggling young man, helped many families both white and black, to buy a home. Their gratitude was very touching; they knew how he valued their love.

He was a man of great determination and would rarely let anything stand in his way. When he was a small boy, he dropped his knife in a mill pond near Macon. After thinking it over, he cut the mill dam, went home and after the water ran out, went back and found his precious knife. No one knew until he was grown that he cut the dam. He died Dec. 4, 1904.

Third Line.
ELIZABETH LINGO

Elizabeth Lingo (called Betsy), daughter of Elijah and Mary Hardin (Taliaferro) Lingo, married first a Rogers; married second, a Baptist minister by the name of Loften. She left several children, living in Alabama; but the writer has been unable to get in touch with her descendants.

Fourth Line
RICHARD TALIAFERRO LINGO—
FIRST MARRIAGE

Richard Taliaferro Lingo (called Dick), son of Elijah and Mary Hardin (Taliaferro) Lingo, was born in Hancock County, Ga., in 1801; d. in Ala.

in 1853; married first, 1825, Mary Frances Slaughter of Baldwin, Co., Ga. (b. 1808; d. 1826); married second, Mrs. Lucinda Humphries Clements. Mary Frances Slaughter's father gave her at marriage a large plantation and several negroes, in Twiggs County, Ga., where she resided until her death. She left one small son. Issue:

I. William Slaughter Lingo; b. in Twiggs Co., Ga. April 20, 1826; d. April 3, 1862; married Aug. 10, 1848, Gabrella Louisa Nash (b. Jan. 6, 1833; d. Aug. 2, 1888). William Slaughter Lingo was a man of executive ability, honor and trust; always discharging his duties without fear and for the betterment of his community and his fellowman. Gabrella Louisa Nash was the daughter of Dr. Reuben Acton Nash of Twiggs Co., Ga. (b. Feb. 4, 1801 in Wilkes Co., Ga.; received Medical Degree at Edinborough, Scotland, 1826; d. in 1869 in Twiggs Co., Ga) and Mary Hart (b. 1810; d. April 27, 1889; married March, 1828). Dr. Reuben Acton Nash was a son of Acton Nash and Margaret Strozier married Aug. 12, 1799 in Wilkes Co., Ga.). Acton Nash was son of Thomas Nash and Mary Acton of Virginia. Margaret Strozier was a daugnter of Peter Strozier (b. in Germany, 1748; d. in Wilkes Co., Ga., 1823; served in Revolution at battle of Kettle Creek, Ga. on Feb. 14, 1779) and Margaret Dozier of Dauge (married in Germany). In 1782 Peter Strozier was given land in Wilkes County, Ga. for Revolutionary services. Mary Hart, wife of Dr. Reuben Acton Nash, was a daughter of Edwin Hart and Avarilla Goodwin Wheeler of Twiggs Co., Ga. Edwin Hart was a son of Watkins Hart of South Carolina; he served as Clerk of old Richland Church, Twiggs Co. from 1815-25. The records of the old church book show that he was well educated and his penmanshi[resembles that of an engraver. In 1825 he attended the banquet at Milledgeville, Ga., given to Washington and Lafayette; his invitation to this ball is now in possession of his descendants. About 1830 he moved to Leon County, Fla., where he died a few years later. William Slaughter

Lingo and Gabrella Louisa (Nash) Lingo had issue:

A. Mary Frances Lingo (b. 1849; d. 1907); married Ira S. King of Wilkinson County, Ga. Issue:
1. Erasmus R. King; married 1902, Mamie Gay. P. O. address Ft. Gaines, Ga. He graduated in law at University of Georgia, where he won the John Temple Graves medal; has for many years been associated with the law firm of King and Castellow of Ft. Gaines; has served for several terms as County Superintendent of Schools of Clay Co., and is now serving his second term in the Georgia State Senate. Issue:
a. Louis Gay King.
b. Hortense King.
c. Carl King; d. 1914.
d. Byron King.
e. Lloyd George King.
f. Hugh King; died in infancy.
2. Elizabeth Lingo King; b. March 20, 1872; married March 16, 1913, William Todd Wall, son of Jasper N. and Caroline (Jackson) Wall. P. O. address Jeffersonville, Ga.
3. William Lingo King; married 1903, Linnie Horton. Issue:
a. Linnie Lingo King.
b. Wade King.
c. Erasmus Ripley King.
4. Sallie King; b. June 24, 1877; married June 19, 1894, Henry B. McCallum. P. O. address 415 W. Howard Ave., Decatur, Ga.
a. Emily Evelyn McCallum; b. Nov. 16, 1899.
b. Mary Katherine McCallum; b. July 11, 1902.
5. Patrick Claiburne King; married Dec. 22, 1910, Bessie Morris. P. O. address Ft. Gaines, Ga. He graduated in law at University of Georgia and has for several years been Solicitor of Superior Court of Clay Co.
a. P. C. King, Jr.
b. Mary Norris King.
c. Willie King.
d. Eleanor King.
e. Nettie King.
f. Elizabeth King.
g. Fred King.

6. Evelyn King; married Dec. 28, 1910, James Beall. P. O. address, Jeffersonville, Ga.
a. Christine Beall; b. June, 1912.
7. Alex S. King; married June 19, 1913, Mattie Camp of Hapeville, Ga. P. O. address Box 119, Atlanta, Ga. Issue:
a. Mary Jane King; b. July 22, 1914.
b. Alex Dawson King; b. Sept. 14, 1916.
c. Sara Eloise King; b. May 27, 1920.
8. Mary Lou King; married Sept. 16, 1913, Wyatt M. Allen. P. O. address, Allentown, Ga. Issue:
a. Willis Ira Allen.
b. Mary Catherine Allen.
9. Carl King; died unmarried, Jan. 1914, age 23 years.
10. Ira King, Jr. P. O. address, Jeffersonville, Ga.

B. Reuben William Lingo; b. 1851; d. 1893; married first, Mollie Bragg, second, Sallie Ballard. No issue by second marriage. Issue by first marriage:
1. William Bragg Lingo; dead.
2. Emmett Lingo.

G. Thadeus Acton Lingo; b. 1855; d. July 1896 at Tennille, Ga.; married 1884, Mrs. Kate Burns McDade (d. April 12, 1913). After he reached the age of maturity, he cared for his widowed mother and sisters. After the removal of the family to Gordon, Ga., he became a member of the order of Railway Conductors, running for several years on the Milledgeville and Eatonton branch of the Central of Georgia; later being transferred to the Wrightsville and Tennille Railroad, which position he held up until the time of his death. He was a consecrated Christian man and enjoyed the admiration of a host of friends. Issue:
1. John Willie Lingo; d. age 6 months.
2. Thad Lee Lingo; married April 3, 1917, Roberta Sparks of Eatonton, Ga. P. O. address Oviedo, Fla. He owns an orange grove and celery farm at Oviedo; was formerly cashier of Bank of Oviedo, but is now in real estate busi-

ness; is Superintendent of Methodist Sunday School and one of the Stewards of the Methodist Church of Oviedo. Issue:

a. Sparks Lee Lingo.

b. Thad Lee Lingo, Jr.

3. Sidney Elijah Lingo; died in infancy.

4. Daisy Aileen Lingo; b. Tennille, Ga., April 12, 1890; married Oct. 6, 1914, Josiah Lee Cuthbertson, son of Thomas Lee and Alice Lauretta (Jones) Cuthbertson, of Union County, N. C., P. O. address 113 Pine street, Chester, S. C. Mrs. Cuthbertson is very talented in vocal and instrumental music and has for several years served as organist of the First Baptist Church of Chester. She is a leader in Church work, being President of the B. W. M. U. of Chester. Issue:

a. Katherine Burns Cuthbertson.

b. Josie Lee Cuthbertson.

5. Harry Meldrim Lingo; d. in infancy.

6. Willie Katherine Lingo; d. in infancy.

D. Elizabeth Lucinda Lingo; b. July 11, 1860; married Nov. 2, 1880, Henry Jones Ivey. P. O. address, 321 Main St., Tennille, Ga. Issue:

1. Mary Lillian Ivey; b. Aug. 9, 1881; d. June 26, 1920; married Dec. 26, 1906, Robert Davis, son of Henry and Jane (Gaddy) Davis. Several years before the death of Mrs. Davis, she began tracing her family history, and had she lived, it was her intention to compile a sketch of the descendants of Dr. John Taliaferro. Since her death numerous records have been added to those she collected and have been incorporated in this sketch. Her photo, taken at the time she received her A. B. Degree, at Brenau College, Gainesville, Ga., age sixteen years, is reproduced in this sketch. No issue.

2. Mattie Stevens Ivey.

3. Henri Louise Ivey; b. Aug. 14, 1888; married April 25, 1911, Wilkinson Mayberry Whitehurst, son of Morgan

and Fannie (Burke) Whitehurst of Twiggs Co., Ga. P. O. address Jeffersonville, Ga. Mrs. Whitehurst received A. B. Degree at Brenau College, Gainesville, Ga., 1907; organizing regent of the Old Marion Chapter, D. A. R., and is now serving her third term as regent of this chapter; recently been appointed to a State Chairmanship of the D. A. R. She has been instrumental in securing many records for this sketch. Mr. Whitehurst is now serving his third term as Mayor of Jeffersonville and is a successful merchant of that place. Issue:

a. Frances Elizabeth Whitehurst; b. Jan. 27, 1912.

b. Henry Ivey Whitehurst; b. Nov. 21, 1913; d. Oct. 8, 1915.

c. Mary Hart Whitehurst; b. Feb. 9, 1918.

4. Willie Catherine Ivey.

5. Adelene Behethland Ivey.

E. Willie Frances Lingo; b. 1862; d. 1884; married William B. Hall. No. issue.

Sketch of Life of Henry Jones Ivey

Henry Jones Ivey, born in Warren County, Ga., Feb. 11, 1847; died in Tennille, Ga., April 3, 1917; was a son of Zacheus Ivey (b. Aug. 21, 1814; d. Dec. 30, 1894) and Elizabeth Grenade (b. Sept. 18, 1817; d. Dec. 13, 1863) married in Warren County, Ga., Dec. 22, 1840. Elizabeth (Grenade) Ivey was the daughter of Joseph Grenade and Catherine Joneston (married in Warren County, Ga., Jan. 27, 1806). Henry Jones Ivey, at the age of sixteen, served in the War Between the States; being confined in a Maryland prison for three months. He was employed for forty-six years by the Central of Georgia Railroad; being Supervisor, later promoted to Superintendent of Bridges and Buildings. He drew plans and superintended construction of the present steel bridge, which spans the Oconee River near Oconee Ga.; also superintended the building of railroads between Savannah and Tybee; Meldrim and Lyons; and the W. & T. extension between Wrightsville and Dublin. In 1891 he became engaged in lumber business at Beech Hill, Ga., operating Keystone Handle Works and shipping handles to all points in the United States and to Hamburg, Germany. He was appointed Postmaster and Ticket Agent at Beech Hill, which position he held until 1912, when, because of ill health, he was forced to give up business and retire to private life. Though quiet and unassuming in his manner, he had the good strong qualities of mind and heart, which gained the confidence of all; was a consecrated Christian man, possessing an even and temperate disposition, but a determined nature. He handled labor successfully on the road and at his mill; was never known to use tobacco, curse or drink, and was loved and respected by all his employees.

RICHARD TALIAFERRO LINGO—
SECOND MARRIAGE

Richard Taliaferro Lingo married second, Nov. 12, 1827, Mrs. Lucinda Humphries Clements (b. in 1803; d. 1883) of Baldwin County, Ga. Shortly after this marriage he moved to Clopton, Ala., where he resided until his death. Issue: (children not named according to age):

II. Sarah Lingo, b. 1828; married first Edmond Riley Brantley, who served two years in Civil War, was captured and died in Lands of Yankey's; married second, Eli Horne, who served in Indian War. Issue by first marriage:

A. William Rufus B r a n t l e y; served seven weeks in Civil War; killed charging breastworks.

B. Eugenia Brantley; b. Mar. 22, 1848; married Aug. 29, 1866, W. J. Blackwell. Issue:
1. ———Blackwell; married A. D. Ryals. P. O. Address Tracy, Ala., Rt. 6.
2. ———Blackwell; married T. J. Radford. P. O. address, Andalusia, Ala., Rt. E.
3. Lora Blackwell; b. June 23, 1879; married Dec. 7, 1902, J. H. Ryals. P. O. address Brundige, Ala. Issue:
   a. Fannie Mae Ryals; b. Sept. 28, 1903.
   b. Wilma Ryals; b. Dec. 10, 1904.
   c. Knox Ryals; b. Oct. 21, 1906.
4. ——— Blackwell; married J. S. Cook. P. O. address Turnerville, Texas.

5. ——— Blackwell; married A. B. Purdue. P. O. address Hartsford, Ala.
6. ——— Blackwell; married W. S. Radford. P. O. address Andalusia, Ala., Rt. A.

D. I. E. Brantley. P. O. address Ozark, Ala., Rt. 6.

E. Elizabeth Frances Brantley (called Bettie); b. July 14, 1856; married Sept. 6, 1874, Spencer Wright, Jr. (b. April 30, 1832; d. Oct. 2, 1903; served four years in Civil War; wounded once; was orderly Sergeant), son of Spencer Wright, Sr. and Nancy Harrell, of South Carolina. P. O. Midland City, Ala., care of W. W. Curry. Issue:

1. Lutie Wright; b. April 28, 1876; d. Aug. 9, 1914; married July 1902, M. C. Burdeshaw. P. O. adress, 6 Hemlock Drive, Columbus, Ga.
2. Minnie Dell Wright; b. June 18, 1877; d. Oct. 12, 1912; married Sept. 3, 1897, J. O. Roberts. P. O. address Abbeville, Ala.
3. Zodie Bell Wright; b. July 27, 1878; married July, 1903, G. W. Tice. P. O. address Enterprise, Ala.
4. Robert Emette Wright; b. Jan. 8, 1880; married Nov. 1911, Annie Hall. P. O. address Dothan, Ala., Rt. 6.
5. Martin Luther Wright; b. Nov. 9, 1881; married Aug. 10, 1902, Lela Johnson. P. O. address, Midland City, Ala.
6. Emma Eula Wright; b. Aug. 7, 1883; married July 8, 1917, W. P. Clark. P. O. address 134 Indiana Ave., Mobile, Ala.
7. Annie McGehee Wright; b. April 22, 1887; married Oct. 6, 1907, A. C. Daniel. P. O. address, 85 West Jeff Davis Ave., Montgomery, Ala.
8. Ottie Virginia Wright; b. April 9, 1889; d. June 3, 1908; married Sept. 1, 1907, E. L. Hardin.
9. Jemmie F. Wright; b. April 29, 1891; married Aug. 1, 1915, W. H. Norton. P. O. address Chickasaw, Ala.
10. Tommie Tuloula Wright; b. Feb. 17, 1893; married April 14, 1912, W. W. Curry. P. O. Address Midland City, Ala.

11. Rubie Lee Wright; b. Nov. 9, 1894; married April 28, 1920, Dr. H. S. Stallings. P. O. address Troy, Ala.

Sarah Lingo had issue by second marriage to Eli Horne:

F. Edward Horne. P. O. address Glenwood, Ala.

G. ——— Horne; married Bill Hilburne. P. O. address, Glenwood, Ala., R. F. D.

III. Richard B. Lingo; married first, Amanda Horne; married second, ———?

Issue by first marriage:

A. William M. Lingo, of Clopton, Ala.; died several years ago.

B. Joseph Franklin Lingo; married Feb. 22, 1888, Ophelia Branan (b. Dec. 12, 1866), daughter of Iverson and Nancy Ann (Balkcom) Branan. P. O. address Milledgeville, Ga. Joseph Franklin Lingo died several years ago. Issue:

1. John William Lingo; b. Aug. 3, 1890. P. O. address Spartanburg, S. C.

2. Lovick Peirce Lingo; b. July 23, 1895; married Katherine Wright of Gray, Ga. P. O. address, Macon, Ga. He volunteered in the World War; was lieutenant in the Aviation Corps, seeing active service in France, where he was cited several times for bravery.

3. Lucile Elizabeth Lingo; b. Nov. 7, 1898; married George W. Allbritten. P. O. address, Albertville, Ala. Issue:

a. Elizabeth Allene Allbritten.

b. Miriam Allbritten.

4. Nannie Claire Lingo; b. July 24, 1901; married Robert W. Russell of Jackson, Tenn. P. O. address Box 275, Amite, La. Issue:

a. Robert W. Russell, Jr.

b. Claire Elizabeth Russell.

c. Carolyn Lingo Russell.

5. Lorene Lingo; b. Sept. 25, 1905; married George S. Davis. P. O. address, Milledgeville, Ga.

Richard B. Lingo had issue by second marriage:

C. Lena Lingo; married ——— West. P. O. address Headland, Ala.

D. Robert M. Lingo. P. O. address Daytona, Fla.

IV. Mary E. Lingo; b. Nov. 26, 1832; d. Jan. 11, 1910; married Rev. William Griffin (b. Jan. 8, 1825; d. Nov. 23, 1884), a Methodist minister. Issue:

A. Laura Griffin; married John Floyd.

B. Josephine Griffin; married Joe Vinson. Both deceased.

C. Henry Llewllyn Griffin; married Fannie Myrick. Both deceased.

D. Robert Slappy Griffin; married Ladonia Vinson.

E. Ella Frances Griffin; married Dock Edmondson. Both deceased.

F. Minnie Griffin; married Newt Hudson.

G. Eli Shorter Griffin; married Lula Vinson.

H. Luther Lawrence Griffin; married Gillie Myrick. He represented Twiggs County at Georgia Legislature.

J. Mattie Griffin; married Ben Reddick.

V. John Taliaferro Lingo; married Bettie Bragg in Wilkinson Co., Ga. No Issue.

VI. Susan Lingo; married James Radford.

VII. Elijah Lingo; married Sallie Hooks; died in Wilkinson Co., Ga. No issue.

VIII. Elizabeth Lingo; b. 1841; d. 1918; married first 1856, Dr. J. J. Cox, (b. 1827; d. 1890); married second, E. O. Prescott. She had issue by first marriage:

A. Mary E. Cox; b. 1859; married 1875, Daniel Claiburne Beville. Issue:

1. Coral Beville; married Remer Y. Jones. P. O. address Valdosta, Ga.

IX. James Taliaferro Lingo; married Gracie Branan; died in Wilkinson Co., Ga. No issue.

X. Selina Lingo; married ——— Hudspeth. P. O. address Headland, Ala.

XI. Fannie Lingo; married ——— Weems. Lived in Alabama.

XII. Nora Lingo; married first, Thomas Mabin; married second, ——— Holland.

Issue by first marriage:

A. Thomas Mabin, Jr.

XIII. Virginia Lingo; married Joe Horne.

Fifth Line.
MARTHA LINGO

Martha Lingo, daughter of Elijah and Mary Hardin (Taliaferro) Lingo, married ——— Gunn. No further information.

Sixth Line.
JOHN RICHARD TALIAFERRO LINGO

John Richard Taliaferro Lingo (called Jack), son of Elijah and Mary Hardin (Taliaferro) Lingo, was born April 23, 1805 in Twiggs County, Ga.; died Jan. 16, 1884 in Marion Co., Ga. He settled in Sumter Co., 1835; later moved to Marion Co., Ga. He married first, Miss Bacon, of Marion Co., Ga.; second a Mrs. Doster of Marion Co., Ga., third, Mrs. Mary (Allen) Bellew. There is no record of issue by second marriage. Issue by first marriage

I. William Lingo; killed in Civil War.

II. Elizabeth Lingo; married ——— Smith. P. O. address, Fordice, Ark. Issue:
A. Joseph N. Smith. P. O. address, Fordice, Ark.

III. Milvinie Lingo; married ——— Warren. P. O. address Troy, Ala. Issue:
A. J. T. Warren. P. O. address, Enterprise, Ala.

Issue by third marriage:

IV. Rebecca Annie Lingo; b. Jan. 16, 1875; died May 27, 1911; married ——— Cunningham.

V. & VI. John Taliaferro Lingo and Hannah Maria Lingo (twins); born April 24, 1878. John Taliaferro Lingo resides at Buena Vista, Ga., R. F. D. 4. Hannah Maria Lingo married Charles W. Webb.

Seventh Line.
MARY HARDIN LINGO

Mary Hardin Lingo, daughter of Elijah and Mary Hardin (Taliaferro) Lingo, was born in Twiggs County, Ga., Nov. 21, 1806; d. June 2, 1885; married July 6, 1826, Joseph John Chappell (b. in Hancock Co., Ga., Aug. 7, 1806; d. May 4, 1878), youngest child of Thomas and Lavina Wheelus (Cox) Chappell. Both lie buried at Bronwood, Terrell County, Ga. Issue:

I. Jasper N. Chappell; b. April 24, 1827; d. Jan. 22, 1828.

II. Lucy Mahala Chappell; b. Nov. 10, 1828; married Jan. 13, 1848, John Chambliss. Issue:

A. Augustus Chambliss; died about 1880.

B. Mary Elizabeth Chambliss; died ———.

C. John Thomas Chambliss; died 1884; married 1879, Leila Merritt. Issue:

I. Dr. John Wade Chambliss; b. Aug. 19, 1881; graduated in Medical School, Emory University, 1907; Chairman Board of Health for City and County for past twelve years; General Practice; served in World War as member of Medical Advisory Board; married Oct. 8, 1908, Annie Pearl Scroggs, (b. Jan. 13, 1881); graduate nurse of Parkview Hospital, Savannah, Ga.; Supt. of City Hospital of Americus, Ga. P. O. address, Doctors Building, Americus, Ga. Issue:
a. J. W. Chambliss, Jr.; b. July 25, 1912.
b. Ross Merritt Chambliss; b. Sept. 5, 1916.

2. Floyd Idus Chambliss; b. Jan. 4, 1884; married July 16, 1909, Lucy Daniel (b. Sept. 15, 1891), daughter of Mr. and Mrs. Ben Jennings Daniel. P. O. address, Columbus, Ga. Issue:
a. Floyd Idus Chambliss, Jr.; b. Jan. 29, 1912.
b. Jacque Merritt Chambliss; b. Aug. 14, 1914.
c. Leon Marshall Chambliss; b. Oct. 5, 1916.
d. Mary Katherine Chambliss; b. Aug. 22, 1919.
e. Leila Nell Chambliss; b. Nov. 17, 1921.
f. Annie Sue Chambliss; b. Nov. 18, 1925.

D. Dr. Joseph Jesse Chambliss; b. 1854; married first, 1886, Laura Ophelia Davis (d. 1888); married second, 1890, Dorcas Ellen Kenner. P. O. 1018 W. Washington St., Phoenix, Ariz.; Issue by first marriage:
1. Davis Royce Chambliss; b. July 4, 1888; married 1911, Clara Pease. Issue:
a. Royce Jesse Chambliss; b. Nov. 28, 1912.
Issue by second marriage:
2. Clyde Kenner Chambliss; b. Jan. 1, 1893; married March 14, 1925, Phebe A. Morrill.

3. Joseph Chappell Chambliss;
b. April 9, 1895; married Nov.
8, 1924, Helen Laing.

4. Mary Chambliss; b. Sept. 4,
1897.

5. John Leo Chambliss; b. Mar.
24, 1902.

6. Catherine Elizabeth Chambliss; b. April 24, 1904.

E. Hardin Ernest Chambliss; b.
May 16, 1857; d. March 11,
1923; married Bessie Chambliss.
P. O. address, Homestead, Fla.
Issue:
1. Mary Chambliss; b. Oct. 20,
1916.
2. Leon Chappell Chambliss; b.
Jan. 4, 1922.
3. Robert Earl Chambliss; b.
July 27, 1923.

F. Mark C. Chambliss; b. 1859;
d. 1871.

G. Benjamin Barton Chambliss; b.
Sept. 10, 1861; married April
24, 1904; Fannie Carrie Merritt
(b. Jan. 6, 1869). P. O. address
1917 Union St., Brunswick, Ga.
Issue:
1. Alton Merritt Chambliss; b.
April 9, 1905; married Nov.
18, 1924, Alice Elizabeth
Evans, daughter of Mr. and
Mrs. D. P. Evans, Brunswick,
Ga. P. O. address, 1123
Reynolds St., Brunswick, Ga.
Mr. Chambliss served in
World War, enlisting in the
Signal Corps, U. S. A. when
only thirteen years old; discharged at Seattle, Washington, in 1921; has served in the
Georgia National Guards
since. Issue
a. William Robert Chambliss;
b. Oct. 12, 1925.
2. Mary Frances Chambliss; b.
April 12, 1907.
3. Susie Elizabeth Chambliss;
b. Jan. 8, 1909.

H. James Rollin Chambliss; b.
April 11, 1863; married May 4,
1893, Henrietta Davidson. P.
O. address Box 284, Homestead,
Fla. Issue:
1. Florrie Belle Chambliss; b.
Aug. 31, 1898; d. Oct. 1, 1912.
2. Lois Vera Chambliss; b.
Sept. 28, 1900; married July
23, 1923, George Flannagan.
3. James Rollin Chambliss, Jr.;
b. July 17, 1902.

4. Mattie Nadine Chambliss; b.
Sept. 13, 1904; married
Thomas L. Graves, Jr., Jan.
19, 1924. Issue:
a. Elaine Graves; b. Dec. 10,
1924.

I. Charles Allen Chambliss; b. Feb.
14, 1866; d. April 23, 1922; married Dec. 15, 1897, Mrs. Juliet
(Bolton) Arrington, widow of
Henry Thomas Arrington. P. O.
address, Jackson St., Americus,
Ga. Issue:
1. Charles Bolton Chambliss; b.
Feb. 18, 1899; married Nov.
26, 1924, Ina Walker of Akron,
Ohio; P. O. address, Toronto,
Ontario, Canada.
2. Mary Sue Chambliss; b. June
27, 1901; married Oct. 27,
1920, Joseph Rufus Lane, son
of Joseph Polk and Georgia
(Russum) Lane. P. O. address, 315 Barlow St., Americus, Ga. Issue:
a. Georgia Lane; b. Oct. 19,
1921.
b. Juliet Lane; b. Sept. 10,
1925.
3. Lauren Morgan Chambliss;
b. July 4, 1902; P. O. address,
Birmingham, Ala.

J. Virgil Homer Chambliss; b.
May 1, 1868; d. Feb. 21, 1906;
married Jan. 8, 1895, Leila
Arrington. P. O. address, Plains,
Ga. Issue:
1. Mark Arrington Chambliss; b.
Jan. 7, 1896; married July 3,
1918, Melba Lunsford. Issue:
a. Valrie Chambliss; b. April
9, 1922.
2. Lucy Chambliss; b. June 13,
1898; married Jan. 9, 1917,
Leon Coogle, (d. Jan. 10,
1919).
3. Eleanor Chambliss; b. Nov.
5, 1901.
4. Virgil Homer Chambliss, Jr.;
b. July 8, 1904.

III. James Thomas Chappell, b. in
Twiggs Co., Sept. 10, 1830; d. Dec.
22, 1899; married Oct. 18, 1885,
Harriet Athalia Stanley (b. in
Laurens Co., Ga., Nov. 17, 1832; d.
Feb. 1, 1918), daughter of Ira and
Janet (Harris) Stanley, and
granddaughter of Thomas McCall.
James Thomas Chappell was by
profession a physician and lived
in Dublin, Ga., up until the time
of his death. He was well educated and far above the average
man intellectually. He was fre-

quently elected a member of the General Assembly of the State of Georgia and of the City Council of the City of 'Dublin, and held other positions of honor and trust. Issue:

A. Judge Ira Stanley Chappell; b. Nov. 28, 1859; married first, Oct. 20, 1885, Missouri Beall Baker, (b. Aug. 7, 1864; d. Dec. 14, 1891), daughter of Rev. William S. and · Maxa (Beall) Baker, and a granddaughter of Thomas N. Beall of Irwinton, Ga. She is buried on the Beall Family lot in the cemetery at Irwinton. A marble monument erected over her grave gives the date of her birth as having been on Aug. 7, 1874, when it should have been 1864, and this is mentioned to correct the mistake, as it cannot be done on the monument without marring the lettering. No issue by this marriage. Judge Chappell married second, June 12, 1900, Cora Elizabeth Mathis, daughter of Robert F. and Martha (Duggan) Mathis. She and her twin sister Dora, who married Robert P. Cooke, of Bolingbroke, Ga., were born July 28, 1879. Judge Chappell is a prominent attorney of Dublin, Ga., and has prepared some of these records of the Lingo-Chappell Family. Judge Chappell had issue by second marriage to Cora Elizabeth Mathis:

1. John Speedwell Chappell, b. Sept. 6, 1901; d. May 27, 1910.

2. Ira Stanley Chappell, Jr., b. Nov. 26, 1903.

3. Katherine Elizabeth Chappell; b. Sept. 28, 1906.

4. Robert Armin Chappell; b. April 27, 1909.

5. Athalia Chappell, b. Aug. 23, 1913.

B. Clifton Thomas Chappell; b. Oct. 30, 1862; d. in Macon, Ga., March 15, 1926; married first, Oct. 17, 1888, Wilena Gertrude Sherwood (b. June 30, 1871; d. June 30, 1894); married second, Jan. 20, 1897, his sixth cousin, Marguerite Claire Doolittle (b. Jan. 10, 1872). Clifton Thomas Chappell was educated in the public schools of Dublin and Macon, and attended the uni-

versity of Georgia at Athens for two terms. He entered business in Macon, as a draftsman in the office of an architect, and then became connected with the Central of Georgia Railway. He left the Central and became paymaster for the Georgia, Southern and Florida Railroad, which position he held for thirty or more years, until that road was taken over by the Southern Railway, and its headquarters removed to Washington City. He was a member of the Christian Church; buried in Rose Hill Cemetery, Macon, Ga. Mr. Chappell manifested great pride in family history and heritage; and in Sept., 1923, began a record of the descendants of Mary Hardin (Lingo) Chappell, which was to have been incorporated in this sketch. His sudden death prevented its completion; and the writer feels keenly, the great loss sustained in his passing. Judge Ira S. Chappell, Dublin, Ga., who was assisting him, has secured the information his deceased brother had collected and it is recorded in this sketch. Both Judge Chappell and his brother have lent invaluable assistance in tracing this branch of the family. Clifton Thomas Chappell had issue by his first marriage to Wilena Gertrude Sherwood:

1. Cecil Cason Chappell; b. June 14, 1891. P. O. address, 155 Second St., Macon, Ga.

2. Sherwood Stanley Chappell, b. June 17, 1894. P. O. address, 155 Second St., Macon, Ga.

Clifton Thomas Chappell had issue by second marriage to Marguerite Claire Doolittle:

3. Clifton Thomas Chappell, Jr.; b. Aug. 19, 1898; d. Sept. 14, 1901 of scarlet fever.

C. Clarence Joseph Chappell; b. Aug. 27, 1864; married Nov. 17, 1897, Lucia Pauline Hardeman (b. Jan. 4, 1876; d. July 26, 1918), daughter of Col. Isaac Hardeman of Macon, Ga., and his wife ——— (Griswold) Hardeman. Issue:

1. Lucia Pauline Chappell; b. Sept. 10, 1898; married June

30, 1921, Alonzo Monk Domingos (b. July 27, 1895). P. O. address, 716 Forsyth St., Macon, Ga. Issue:

a. Pauline Hardeman Domingos; b. Dec. 12, 1923.

b. Lucia Chappell Domingos; b. April 4, 1926.

2. Clarence Joseph Chappell, Jr.; b. Sept. 16, 1900.

3. Isaac Hardeman Chappell; b. Nov. 30, 1903.

4. Logan Stanley Chappell; b. May 25, 1912.

D. Dr. Roy James Chappell; b. Sept. 21, 1866, in Laurens Co., Ga.; married Sept. 18, 1890, Mary Warthen, daughter of Capt. George W. Warthen of Piedmont, Pike County, Ga. P. O. address, Dudley, Ga. Issue:

1. Maroy Chappell, b. Oct. 31, 1894 in Laurens Co., Ga.; married July 3, 1916, Paul J. Jones. P. O. address, Dublin, Ga. Issue:

a. Mary Frances Jones; b. Dec. 4, 1917.

b. Paul J. Jones, Jr., b. July 23, 1919.

2. Warthen T. Chappell, b. July 20, 1897. P. O. address, Dudley, Ga.

3. Joseph J. Chappell; b. March 5, 1907. P. O. address, Dudley, Ga.

E. Vance Lingo Chappell; b. Feb. 5, 1872; married first, Dec. 24, 1897, Annie Clifford Poland (b. Aug. 2, 1874; d. Aug. 14, 1909), daughter of Charles and Mary E. (Knight) Poland; married second, Jan. 18, 1925, Ida Lillian (Jackson) Spence, (b. at Wadley, Ga., Aug. 6, 1879) daughter of William Russell and Margaret Alice (Torrence) Jackson. P. O. address, Dublin, Ga. Issue by first marriage:

1. James Thomas Chappell; b. Feb. 11, 1900; married April 20, 1924, Minerva Lee Franklin. P. O. address, College Park, Ga.

2. Gladys Chappell, b. July 27, 1902. P. O. address, Atlanta, Ga.

3. Elizabeth McCall Chappell; b. March 5, 1904. P. O. address Atlanta, Ga.

4. Maggie Hicks Chappell; b. Nov. 7, 1905. P. O. address, Atlanta, Ga.

5. Karletta Chappell; b. Aug. 24, 1907. P. O. address, Atlanta, Ga.

6. Annie Clifford Chappell; b. Aug. 14, 1909. P. O. address, Atlanta, Ga.

IV. Andrew Lingo Chappell; b. March 17, 1832; d. May 1, 1839.

V. William Harrison Chappell; b. Nov. 28, 1833; d. July 21, 1903 at Shellman, Ga., married Mrs. Nancy P. (Cato) Sanders. Issue:

A. Benjamin Chappell; b. April 30, 1868; d. Jan. 4, 1918; married first, Pauline Bridges, (d. 1894); married second, Nov. 10, 1896, Emma Sword.

B. James E. Chappell; b. Sept. 25, 1872; proprietor of Chappell's Drug Store, Douglas, Ga.; married Dec. 20, 1896, Louella Beasley. Issue:

1. Dr. John Rocher Chappell; b. April 11, 1898; married Aug. 13, 1924, Dorothy Haselton. P. O. address, Box 1137, Orlando, Fla. Issue:

a. Dorothy Haselton Chappel; b. Nov. 10, 1925.

VI. Roxie Ann Saluda Chappell; b. Dec. 9, 1835; d. Feb. 23, 1912; married 1871 Rev. John Harrold Cawood, a Baptist minister. Mrs. Cawood was a teacher at the Monroe Female College (now Bessie Tift College), Forsyth, Ga., shortly before the Civil War. Issue:

A. Julian Chappell Cawood; b. May 24, 1872; married Jan. 29 1899, Hattie Gertrude Weeks. P. O. address, Bainbridge, Ga. Issue:

1. Annie Gertrude Cawood; b. April 8, 1900.

2. James Harrold Cawood; (a son) b. Aug. 31, 1906.

B. James Max Cawood; b. April 1, 1874; at Smithville, Ga.; married June 9, 1917, Myrtle Ross Sanborn (b. Oct. 12, 1890), daughter of Rev. N. R. and Carlista (Greene) Sanborn of Michigan. Rev. Sanborn is a Baptist minister. P. O. address, Americus, Ga. Issue:

1. Roxie Carlista Cawood, b. Sept. 5, 1918; d. Nov. 4, 1920.

2. Myrtle Ross Cawood; b. Jan. 25, 1925.

C. Idus Harrold Cawood; b. Oct. 12, 1876; d. Oct. 29, 1880.

VII. Thomas R. Chappell; b. Sept. 7, 1837; d. Aug. 27, 1841.

VIII. Almeida Chappell; b. Jan. 26, 1840; unmarried; died Oct. 1908, while undergoing a surgical operation at Americus, Ga.

IX. Varilla Behethland Chappell (called Duck); b. March 31, 1843; married 1867, Josiah Webster Jossey. P. O. address, 51 Fairview Road, Atlanta, Ga. Issue:
A. Lorene Jossey; b. Jan. 17, 1868; d. Dec. 17, 1897; married May, 1891, Noah M. McNabb. Issue:
1. Frank Stanton McNabb; b. May 5, 1893; unmarried.
2. William Chappell McNabb; b. Atlanta, Ga., Feb. 17, 1895; married March 19, 1916, Willie Floyd Reeder (b. Atlanta, Ga. July 6, 1892). P. O. address, S. W. 8th St., Miami, Fla. Issue:
a. Alma Lorena McNabb; b. Jan. 24, 1917 in Atlanta, Ga.
B. Leona Jossey, b. April 1, 1870; married Frank L. Stanton in January, 1888. Mr. Stanton is Poet Laureate of Georgia and is also connected with the Atlanta Constitution. P. O. address, Atlanta, Ga. Issue:
1. Valentine Lagree Stanton; b. March 10, 1903.
2. Frank L. Stanton, Jr.; b. May 5, 1905; married Oct. 20, 1925, Dorothy Popham of Atlanta, Ga.
3. Marcelle Stanton; b. Aug. 3, 1907; married Percy Allen Megahee of Thomson, Ga. P. O. address, Atlanta, Ga.

XI. Dr. Thomas Andrew Chappell; b. April 3, 1845; d. July 27, 1917. He was a physician and lived at Bronwood, Terrell Co., Ga., but subsequently moved to Jacksonville, Fla. He married first, Cornelia B. Lawhon, no issue, married second, April 2, 1874, Bettie W. Lawhon (d. Oct. 1, 1885); married third, Adelia Sessions. Issue by second marriage:
A. Dr. Guy Chappell; married Annie Will Carver; he is a prominent physician of Dawson, Ga. Issue:
1. Willie Wilson Chappell.
B. Lucile Chappell; P. O. address, 142 E. First St., Jacksonville, Fla.
C. Mary Floyd Chappell; married first, John Marshall Bolton (d. ———), no issue by this mar-

riage; married second, Smith Parramore Patterson. P. O. address, Jacksonville, Fla. Issue by second marriage:
1. Mary Smith Patterson.
2. Jean Swift Patterson.
D. Bessie Chappell; d. ——— married Henry Archer Ferrell. Issue:
1. Archer Chappell Ferrell; died age five months.
Dr. Thomas Chappell had issue by third marriage to Adelia Sessions:
E. Clifford Cheatham Chappell; married Sarah Eloise Mansfield. P. O. address, Bainbridge, Ga. Issue:
1. James Manfield Chappell.
2. Clifford Cheatham Chappell, Jr.
F. Thomas Andrew Chappell, Jr.; married Gladys Smith. P. O. address, Tampa, Fla. Issue:
1. Thomas Andrew Chappell, III.
2. William Chappell.
3. Mary Lucile Chappell.
G. Louise Chappell. P. O. address, 142 E. First St., Jacksonville, Fla.
H. Helen Chappell. P. O. address, 142 E. First St., Jacksonville, Fla.

XII. Allen Elijah Chappell; b. Nov. 12, 1846; married June 1, 1887, Nora Allen. He is a member of the wholesale grocery firm of Cox and Chappell, Macon, Ga. Issue:
A. Mattie Chappell; b. March 25, 1888; married April 1914, Richard F. Lawton.
B. William Allen Chappell; b. March 9, 1892; prominent merchant of Americus, Ga.

XIII. Joseph John Chappell, Jr.; b. Nov. 28, 1848; d. April 13, 1915, at San Francisco, Calif., where he had lived since 1874; unmarried; was quite wealthy, owning a large section of Imperial Valley land in that state.

War Record of James Thomas Chappell

James Thomas Chappell, son of Joseph John and Mary Hardin (Lingo) Chappell, was Captain of Company "G," in the 49th Georgia Regiment, Confederate States' Army, E. L. Thomas' Brigade, A. P. Hill's Division, Stonewall Jackson's Corps. He was wounded at the battle of Second Manassas while leading a charge on Aug. 29, 1862. After recovering he again entered the service in 1863 and was assigned to the recruiting department as an examining surgeon and stationed at Wilmington, N. C. His Company was known as "Laurens Volunteers," and was formed about March 4, 1862, under a call from Gov. Brown. Sent to Camp Davis at Savannah and formed into the 49th Georgia Regiment on March 22, 1862. Left Camp Davis for Goldsboro, N. C., April 2, 1862; and left Goldsboro, for Richmond, May 24, 1862. According to Folsom's History of the 5th Brigade there were 130 enlisted men. Capt. Chappell participated in the following engagements:

Seven Pines, May 31, 1862.
Mechanicsville, June 26, 1862.
Gaines' Mill, June 27, 1862.
Frazier's Farm, June 28, 1862.
Malvern Hill, July 1, 1862.
Cedar Run, Aug. 9, 1862.
Second Manassas, Aug. 29 and 30th, 1862.

Eighth Line.
PATSY LINGO
Patsy Lingo, daughter of Elijah and Mary Hardin (Taliaferro) Lingo, married ——— Crosby; no further information.

Ninth Line.
ELIJAH LINGO
Elijah Lingo, son of Elijah and Mary Hardin (Taliaferro) Lingo, married his step-sister, Harriet Clements, daughter of Mrs. Lucinda Humphries Clements. He died in Alabama about 1900, leaving several children.

Tenth Line.
TALIAFERRO LINGO
Taliaferro Lingo (called Tol.), son of Elijah and Mary Hardin (Taliaferro) Lingo, married Susan Hale, daughter of James Hale of Twiggs Co., Ga., who married in 1816, Nancy Chappell. Taliaferro Lingo first resided in Crawford County, Ga.; later moving to Sumter County, near Americus, Ga. His mother made her home with him during the declining years of her life. He moved to Arkansas in 1860, where he resided until his death. He left several children, but Georgia and Alabama relatives have lost sight of them.

Eleventh Line.
NANCY LINGO
Nancy Lingo, daughter of Elijah and Mary Hardin (Taliaferro) Lingo, married ——— Simpson; no further information.

Twelfth Line.
LUCY ANN LINGO
Lucy Ann Lingo, daughter of Elijah and Mary Hardin (Taliaferro) Lingo,

married Louis Solomon of Twiggs County, Ga. Issue:

I. Cicero Solomon; married Mrs. Sallie Zachery Finch. Issue:
A. Sallie Zachery Solomon; dead.
B. Lucy Solomon; married John Coombs of Twiggs Co., Ga. P. O. address, Jeffersonville, Ga.
C. Annie Solomon; married Obe Adams. P. O. address, Jeffersonville, Ga.
D. Mamie Lee Solomon; married Marion Burns. P. O. address, Barnesville, Ga. Issue:
I. Cicero Burns.
II. Marcus Solomon. married first Fannie Crocker; second, Jonnie Sauls.
Issue by first marriage:
A. Fannie Solomon.
Issue by second marriage:
B. Louis Edge Solomon.
III. Leonora Solomon; married ———?
IV. Billy Solomon.
V. Clinton Solomon.

Notes: Records from "The Cherokee Land Lottery" containing a numerical list of the names of favorite drawers in said lottery; including soldiers, soldiers of the Indian War, soldiers of the late war (1812), Revolutionary soldiers, soldiers between the years 1784-1797, soldiers by substitute, militia soldiers, widows, orphans, etc., published April 19, 1838 by Harper and Brothers, N. Y., Edited by James F. Smith, Milledgeville, Ga., show the following entries:

23rd Dist. 2nd Sect. Cherokee.
Lot No. 10, Elijah Lingo's Orphans, Wills', Tiwggs Co., Ga.
Lot No. 24 Richard T. Lingo, 319th Baldwin Co., Ga.
6th Dist. 4th Sect. Cherokee.
Lot No. 226 John R. T. Lingo, Wills, Twiggs Co., Ga.

Court Records of Baldwin County, Ga., dated July 23, 1830, show the following entry:

"Ordered that Rhodan A. Greene be and he is hereby appointed Guardian of persons and property of Elijah Lingo, Taliaferro Lingo, Nancy Lingo, and Lucy A. Lingo, minors and orphans of Elijah Lingo, dec., upon giving bond in the sum of $2,000.00 with William Davis and William Gregg, his security. Where upon the said Rhodan A. Greene entered into bond and was duly qualified accordingly."

CHAPTER XI.

ROSE (TALIAFERRO) PORTER

Rose Taliaferro, daughter of Dr. John and Mary (Hardin) Taliaferro, was born in Virginia, and married Joseph Porter, probably, before the removal of her parents from Virginia to North Carolina. This couple resided in Surry County for several years. Joseph Porter, as a "son-in-law," was one of the witnesses of the transfer of lands made by Dr. John Taliaferro to his son, Charles, in 1790-91. The Porters moved to Georgia with Dr. John Taliaferro and settled in Wilkinson County. The old land grants of the Porter Family are still in existence. These grants were no doubt given to Joseph Porter for Revolutionary services, but the writer has no proof of said services, only circumstantial evidence. A creek in Wilkinson County bearing the name "Porter's Creek" was named for Joseph Porter. The will of Joseph Porter was probated in Wilkinson County, Georgia, September term of Oirdinary's Court, 1825. This will names his wife Rose, his daughters, Elizabeth and Behethland, and his sons, Ambrose, Richard Taliaferro, and John. John was the eldest son and his father's executor. The will was witnessed by Sarah Redding.

When Pleasant Plains Church, Wilkinson County, Ga., was founded in 1830, the original church roll named the following Porters:

Ambrose Porter.
Julius Porter.
Richard Taliaferro Porter.
Isaac Porter.
Elizabeth Porter.
Anna Porter.
Mary C. Porter.
Charles Porter.
Rose Porter.

Later the names of Behethland, Lynch, and Julius N. Porter were added. Joseph and Rose (Taliaferro) Porter have numerous descendants, but as the old Porter Family Bible was carried to Irwin County, Ga. when a branch of the family moved there, it has been impossible to connect some of the descendants with this family. Circumstantial evidence indicates that the grandchildren of Joseph Porter have intermarried; thus making it difficult to trace them.

This sketch records only one line of descendants of Joseph and Rose (Taliaferro) Porter; this being that of Richard Taliaferro Porter, which has been carefully compiled by his grandson, Mr. J. E. Hendrix, Mexia, Ala.

—— LINE
RICHARD TALIAFERRO PORTER
Richard Taliaferro Porter, son of Joseph and Rose (Taliaferro) Porter, was born July 25, 1800, near old Red Level Church, Wilkinson County, and was probably his parent's youngest child. He possessed a jovial, good disposition and was always ready for fun. He was of an adventurous nature and wishing to seek a new and better country, he moved with his family, about the year 1853, to the Southern part of Alabama. His cousin, Richard Taliaferro Lingo, moved to Alabama prior to this time. Richard Taliaferro Porter was married to Mary Collins Paul, June 29, 1826. He died Aug. 7, 1882 near Monroeville, Monroe County, Ala. His wife born Oct. 24, 1808, died April 30, 1888 at the same place. Richard Taliaferro Porter and Mary Collins (Paul) Porter had issue:

I. Eliza Ann Elizabeth Porter; b. in Wilkinson Co., March 17, 1828; married Sept. 15, 1842, Alex Stuckey; she died May 4, 1907. Issue:
   A. Daniel Stuckey died ——.
   B. Henry T. Stuckey, died ——.
   C. Wiley H. Stuckey, P. O. address Dexter, Ga.
   D. William A. Stuckey, P. O. address Dublin, Ga.
   E. Erasmus Stuckey, died ——.
   F. Robert Lee Stuckey, died ——.
   G. Edward Lee Stuckey, died ——.
   H. Mary Ann Stuckey, married —— Hall. Address, Danville, Ga.
   I. Missourie Stuckey, married —— Butler. P. O. address, Danville, Ga.
   J. Margaret Stuckey, married —— Denson. Died ——.
   K. Fannie Stuckey, married Hatfield. Died ——.
II. Ann Jane Porter; b. Feb. 19, 1830; d. ab. 1880; married Dec. 29, 1844, —— Pierce. Issue:

A. Thomas F. Pierce; d. ab. 1890; married ———? Issue:
1. Frank Pierce. A d d r e s s Lenox, Ala.
2. Hamp Pierce. A d d r e s s, Lenox, Ala.
3. Andrew Pierce. Address, Lenox, Ala.
4. Sallie Pierce; died ———.

B. Jesse T. Pierce. Address, Lenox, Ala.

C. Elizabeth Pierce; died ab. 1900.

III. Mary Rose Porter; b. Sept. 28, 1831; d. May 18, 1903; never married.

IV. Martha Behethland Porter; b. Jan. 2, 1834; d. April 27, 1857; married Nov. 24, 1853, ——— Phillips, in Barbour County, Ala. Issue:

A. J. Alfred Phillips. Address Elamville, Barbour Co., Ala.

B. Ann Phillips, married ——— Wilkes. Address, Ariton, Dale Co., Ala.

V. Joseph Brice Porter; b. Sept. 26, 1835; killed in Civil War, Nov. 29, 1863; married Nov. 22, 1855, Elefair Barnes, in Barbour Co., Ala. Issue:

A. Susie Porter, married Harper Andrews. Address Ozark, Ala.

VI. Charles Franklin Porter; b. May 12, 1837; d. Aug. 3, 1907; married Sept. 13, 1863, Hettie S. G. Rye. Issue:

A. John Porter. Address, Tallassee, Ala.

B. Frank Porter. Address Samson, Ala.

C. Sallie Porter; died ———.

D. Bennie Porter; died ———.

E. Joe Porter; died ———.

F. Senobia Porter; died ———.

VII. James Henry Porter; b. Sept. 9, 1839, killed in Civil War, May 25, 1863.

VIII. Julius Nicholas Porter; b. Dec. 6, 1841; killed in Civil War, Jan. 14, 1862.

IX. John Ambrose Benjamin Porter; b. Oct. 23, 1843; killed in Civil War, Aug. 12, 1862.

X. Frances Hester Ann Ruth Porter; b. Aug. 13, 1845; d. Jan. 1925; married first ——— Davidson of Monroe County, Ala.; second, Jan. 9, 1862 Robert W. Ryals. Issue by first marriage.

A. "Babe" Davidson, married Benjamin Ryals, a brother of Robt. W. Ryals.
Issue by second marriage:

B. Joseph B. Ryals. Address, Century, Fla.

C. James H. Ryals. Address, Lenox, Ala.

D. Lloyd Ryals. Address, Mobile, Ala.

E. Kimsy Ryals. Address Hurricane, Ala.

F. Kittie Ryals. Address, Flomaton, Ala.

G. Carrie Ryals. Address Flomaton, Ala.

XI. Missourie Ellafair Porter; b. July 25, 1848; d. Nov. 30, 1913; married Nov. 9, 1864, Lemuel Austin Hendrix. Issue:

A. William James Hendrix; b. July 26, 1866; married Dec. 1885, Sarah T. Gepson. Issue:

1. Richard Taliaferro Hendrix; b. Sept. 30, 1886; married Mary Alice Crutchfield; b. March 20, 1890. Issue:
a. Payton Taliaferro Hendrix; b. July 23, 1911.
b. Carroll Austin Hendrix; b. Feb. 23, 1913; d. Feb. 9, 1925.
c. Jacqueline Barboreta Hendrix; b. Oct. 11, 1924.

2. Minnie Lee Hendrix; b. Jan. 1, 1888; married Richard Elbert Dees. Issue:
a. Howard William Dees; b. March 21, 1909.
b. Harwell Joseph Dees; b. Oct. 11, 1911.
c. Lois Laverne Dees; b. Nov. 24, 1913.

3. Lemuel Austin Hendrix; b. Oct. 20, 1889; d. July 18, 1891.

4. William Cleveland Hendrix; b. Jan. 7, 1892; married Fannie Weatherford; b. 1901. Issue:
a. William Cleveland Hendrix, Jr.; b. Aug. 23, 1922.

5. James Edward Hendrix; b. Sept. 8, 1894; killed in action with machine gun Co. 167 Reg., Battle of Chateau Theiry, France, July 26, 1918.

6. Henry Herbert Hendrix; b. July 28, 1896; married Zelma Cornelia English; b. April 16 1905. Issue:
a. Jackson Edward Hendrix; b. Dec. 26, 1924.

7. Lillian Mabel Hendrix; b. Oct. 31, 1897.

8. Albert Leroy Hendrix; b. Oct. 7, 1899; married Mona Jane Nelson; b. Oct. 30, 1904. Issue:
a. James Austin Hendrix; b. Aug. 7, 1922.

B. Henry Alfred Hendrix; b. Dec. 4, 1867, not married; living at Wichita Falls, Texas.

C. Susan E. Hendrix; b. 1869; died at six months of age.

D. Joseph Edward Hendrix; b. Dec. 19, 1871; married Dec. 22, 1897 Leila Coxwell; b. June 17, 1878; d. Nov. 17, 1924, daughter of Hillary Jackson Coxwell and Missourie Lowrey Coxwell. P. O. address Mexia, Ala. Mr. Hendrix is a prominent merchant. He has manifested much interest in his family history and has furnished the writer with these records of the descendants of his grandfather, Richard Taliaferro Porter. Issue:

1. William Alpheus Hendrix; b. Oct. 8, 1899; married Margaret Shields, of Natchez, Miss., Dec., 1920. P. O. address, Brewton, Ala. Issue:
a. Julia Devreaux Hendrix; b. Nov. 2, 1921.

2. Vernon Annette Hendrix; b. Dec. 21, 1901. P. O. address Mexia, Ala.

3. Clifton Hester Hendrix; b. Dec. 3, 1904. P. O. address, Chicago, Ill.

4. Emily Margaret Hendrix; b. Nov. 12, 1906. P. O. address, Mexia, Ala.

5. Myrtle Doris Hendrix; b. Jan. 8, 1908. P. O. address, Mexia. Ala.

6. Edward Byron Hendrix; b. June 5, 1911. P. O. address, Mexia, Ala.

E. Martha Adeline Hendrix; b. May 5, 1873; married Oct. 15, 1890, James Monroe Simpson. Issue:

I. Lillie Mae Simpson; b. Aug. 17, 1891; d. Jan. 22, 1919; married Oct. 20, 1912, Leonard E. Wiggins.

2. Lynda Verdelia Simpson; b. Jan. 28, 1893; d. May 26, 1920; married Dec. 23, 1918, Edward McMillan.

3. Walter Hampton Simpson; b. Jan. 6, 1895; married Oct. 15, 1916, Mattie Stacey. Issue:
a. Woodrow Leroy Simpson; b. Oct. 19, 1918.
b. Mattie Olivia Simpson; b. July 19, 1919.
c. Verdelia Simpson; b. July 19, 1922.
d. Clara Lee Simpson; b. April, 1925.

4. Bessie Lee Simpson; b. May 22, 1898; d. Sept. 28, 1898.

5. Marshall Lee Simpson; b. Jan. 26, 1900; married April 15, 1923, Lottie Brown.

6. James Dennis Simpson; b. Feb. 6, 1902; d. June 8, 1903.

7. Laura Lucile Simpson; b. Nov. 17, 1906.

8. Minnie Irene Simpson; b. Jan. 21, 1908.

9. Herman Clyde Simpson; b. June 24, 1910.

10. Ralph Julian Simpson; b. Oct. 30, 1912.

F. Robert Dennis Hendrix; b. Sept. 6, 1877; married Jesse Amelia Bedgood; b. June 7, 1882. Issue:

1. James Robert Hendrix; b. Nov. 25, 1903.

2. Ralph Collins Hendrix; b. Nov. 15, 1907.

3. Fred Gamble Hendrix; b. Sept. 15, 1910.

4. Leroy Thomas Hendrix; b. Dec. 11, 1913.

G. Richard Jonathan Hendrix; b. Nov. 21, 1878; married Dec. 31, 1907, Clara Coxwell; b. Aug. 16, 1886. No issue.

H. Lemuel Leroy Hendrix; b. Feb. 17, 1880; married Alma Lucile Nettles, b. May 7, 1890. Issue:

1. Barbara Lucile Hendrix; b. Aug. 26, 1917.

2. William Lee Hendrix; b. Oct. 12, 1922.

I. Benjamin Lafayette Hendrix; b. Oct. 18, 1881; married Lillie Rae Ansly, Dec. 1, 1915. She was born Jan. 20, 1896. Issue:

1. Alma Rae Hendrix; b. Nov. 22, 1918.

2. John Austin Hendrix; b June 6, 1920.

3. Benjamin Lafayette Hendrix Jr.; b. Nov. 1, 1923.

4. Charles Rayford Hendrix; b. Nov. 21, 1925.

J. Laura Alice Hendrix; b. June 10, 1885; married Jan. 4, 1911, Alonzo L. Brown; d. May 20, 1922. Issue:
1. Carl Willard Brown; b. May 11, 1914.

K. Jesse Walton Hendrix; b. Oct. 20, 1887; married Carrie Wiggins; b. Sept. 20, 1891. Issue:
1. George Walton Hendrix; b. Dec. 16, 1911.
2. Ida Mae Hendrix; b. Nov. 18, 1914.

XII. Alfred Paul Porter; b. June 8, 1850; d. Sept. 29, 1855.

NOTES

According to information furnished by Mrs. Julia Porter Kitchens, Danville, Ga., Mrs. Kitchens' great-grandmother was Behethland Porter, who married her first cousin, Julius Porter. Julius and Behethland (Porter) Porter had sons:

I. Thomas Porter, married ———? Issue:
A. John Porter, married ———. Issue:
1. Julia Porter, married C. G. Kitchens, Danville, Ga.

B. C. C. Porter.
C. Napoleon Porter.
D. Andrew Porter.
II. Richard Porter, married Sallie Hogan. Issue:
A. Richard Porter.
B. Raz Porter; moved to Irwin County, Ga.
C. Hamp Porter.
D. Griff Porter.

Mrs. Kitchens states that Raz Porter, after the death of his father, moved to Irwin County, Georgia; going with him were his mother, Sallie Hogan Porter, and his grandmother, Behethland (Porter). Mrs. Kitchens cannot identify her great-grandfather, Julius Porter; although, Mr. J. E. Hendrix states that his mother spoke of him as "Uncle Julius." The writer thinks that said Julius Porter was probably a nephew of Joseph Porter, who married Rose Taliaferro, and that Behethland (Porter) wife of Julius, was a daughter of Joseph and Rose (Taliaferro) Porter, and the same Behethland who is mentioned in the will of her father in 1825. This branch of the Porter Family has numerous descendants living in Georgia and Arkansas.

CHAPTER XII.

ELIZABETH (TALIAFERRO) PRUITT

Elizabeth Taliaferro, daughter of Dr. John and Mary (Hardin) Taliaferro; married Oct. 22, 1778 Levi Pruitt, son of Gen. Byrd Pruitt, of Pittsylvania Co., Va. This couple removed to Surry County N. C.; later moved to Warren County, Georgia. Levi Pruitt's will was probated in Warren Co., Ga. on March 11, 1805. Executors were Elizabeth Pruitt and Byrd Pruitt with Matthew McCrary as one of the appraisers. Levi and Elizabeth (Taliaferro) Pruitt had issue:

I. Byrd Pruitt; married a Miss Turner of Warren County, Ga., about 1804.
II. Austin Pruitt; married Nancy Yarbrough in Warren Co., 1800 Issue:

A. Moses Yarbrough Pruitt; b. 1804; married ———? Issue:
1. Samuel Yarbrough Pruitt; married Mary Johnson, daughter of William Andrew Johnson and granddaughter of William and Mary Cummings Johnson of Tennessee. P. O. address, Thomaston, Ga. Issue:
a. Webb Pruitt; m a r r i e d ———.
b. Marion Pruitt married Paul Nelson Johnson.
c. Frank Pruitt.
d. Caroline Pruitt.
e. Samuel Y. Pruitt, Jr.
B. Byrd Pruitt.
C. Elizabeth Pruitt.
D. Turner Pruitt.

CHAPTER XIII.

ANNA (TALIAFERRO) McCRARY

Anna Taliaferro (b. ab. 1768; d. 1864), daughter of Dr. John and Mary (Hardin) Taliaferro, married Jonathan McCrary, son of a Scotch emigrant, in Virginia. This couple moved with their family to Baldwin Co., Ga.; about 1790, settling near the home of Bartley McCrary, brother of Jonathan McCrary. Anna (Taliaferro) McCrary died in Baldwin County at the age of 96 years, death caused by smallpox contracted from her grandson, Andrew McCrary, who had come home on a furlough during the War Between The States; Her will probated in Baldwin Co., Ga. Jonathan and Anna (Taliaferro) McCrary had issue: Two sons and two daughters. Anna Taliaferro has numerous descendants living in Georgia and other southern states; but as they have failed to send in their line of descent, the writer can record only the descendants of her fourth and youngest child, Jane Bartley McCrary, and son Isaac McCrary.

Fourth Line.

JANE BARTLEY McCRARY

Jane Bartley McCrary married her first cousin, James McCrary, son of Bartley McCrary, known as Bartley, Sr. Her will probated in Baldwin Co., Oct. 2, 1882. Jane Bartley (McCrary) left her real estate to her four grandsons, Charles Augustus McCrary, Francis Marion McCrary, Andrew Jackson McCrary, and George Case McCrary; these evidently being children of one or both of her sons. Her daughter, Missouri Holliman McCrary, was the second wife of John Chapman, a very wealthy planter of Twiggs Co., Ga.; he being a son of William Chapman of Wilkes Co., Ga. After Missouri Holliman (McCrary) Chapman's death, her body was carried to Baldwin Co., Ga. and buried in the old McCrary family burial ground. Jane Bartley (McCrary) McCrary took the two children left orphans by her daughter's death and cared for them until after their fathers next marriage. James and Jane Bartley (McCrary) McCrary had issue:

I. Newton McCrary.

II. ——— (a son).

Issue from one or both of these sons:

A. Charles Augustus McCrary.
B. Francis Marion McCrary.
C. Andrew Jackson McCrary.
D. George Case McCrary.

III. Missouri Holliman McCrary; d. June 6, 1853; married, Oct. 10, 1849, John Chapman; b. Jan. 6, 1820; d. Oct. 8, 1892. John and Missouri Holliman (McCrary) Chapman had issue:

A. William T. Chapman; b. July 20, 1850; d. Sept. 18, 1902; married Dec. 12, 1871, Louisa Kate Sinquefield; b. Oct. 23, 1852; d. Oct. 7, 1890. He married a second wife, but no issue by this marriage. Issue by first marriage:

1. Oscar Thomas Chapman; married Dec. 26, 1907, Elizabeth Gilbert Carswell. No issue. P. O. address Jeffersonville, Ga.

2. Eula May Chapman; married Nov. 24, 1892, William Horace Reynolds. P. O. address, 317 Vineville Ave., Macon, Ga. Issue:

   a. Katherine Chapman Reynolds, married Dec. 20, 1922, D. Oscar McCook. P. O. address, 403 First Ave., Macon, Ga.

   b. Bertha Chapman married, March 1, 1924, Edwin Ansley Scoville. P. O. address 317 Vineville Ave., Macon, Ga. Issue: One child, Rose Chapman Scoville.

3. Iverson Parker Chapman married Ruby Powell. P. O. address Whigham, Ga. Issue:
   a. William Chapman.
   b. Iverson Chapman, Jr.
   c. Elizabeth Chapman.
   d. Katherine Chapman.
   e. Ruby Chapman.
   f. Harry Chapman.
   g. Oscar Thomas Chapman.

4. William Green Chapman married Mabel Lamb. P. O. address, Newberry, Fla. Issue:
   a. William Chapman, Jr.
   b. John Sinquefield Chapman.
   c. Kirkland Chapman.

5. Charlie Vincent Chapman married Bertha Logue, (died Dec. 1924). No issue.

B. Martha Jane Chapman; b. Sept. 21, 1852; d. Jan. 6, 1918; married, Jan. 8, 1880, Homer Walter McCrary; b. March 28, 1858; d. March 22, 1915. She was reared in Baldwin County by her grandmother, Jane Bartley McCrary. Issue:

1. Walter H. McCrary married 1st, Mary Yancey Griffin. No issue. Married 2nd Feb. 11, 1915, Nell Griffin. P. O. address Jeffersonville, Ga. Issue:
   a. Walter H. McCrary, Jr.
   b. Martha Nell McCrary.
2. Martha McCrary married Dec. 21, 1911, F. F. Scarborough. P. O. address Macon, Ga. Issue:
   a. Homer McCrary Scarborough.
   b. Walter Richardson Scarborough.
   c. Marcille Scarborough.
3. Lucile McCrary married 1st, Mar. 10, 1914, Robert Henry Edwards; 2nd, James Jackson Thornton, Nov. 8, 1924. P. O. address Tallapoosa, Ga. No issue by either marriage.

Fifth Line.
ISAAC McCRARY

Isaac McCrary, son of Anna Taliaferro McCrary, born Feb. 9, 1806, was married to Melissa Lucretia Nunn, Dec. 28, 1829. He died in Americus, Ga., April 29, 1850. She was born Aug. 3, 1808 and died Oct. 11, 1874. Their children.

I. Laura Henrietta; b. Nov. 21, 1830.
II. Lenora Jean.
III. Lamira Terissa.
IV. Lamanda Melissa.
V. Edmund Blount.
VI. Anna Taliaferro; d. May 10, 1926.

VII. Paul died when two years old, date of birth not known.

Laura H. McCrary was married to Seth Rogers March 15, 1849, by Rev. Joshua Hames.

Leonora J. McCrary was married to John B. Lindsay, Jan. 13, 1853, by Rev. James McCarta.

Lamanda M. McCrary was married to Wills C. Goodwin, Feb. 10, 1856, by Rev. J. W. Hinton.

Lamira T. McCrary was married to John Durkin, Dec. 14, 1865 by Rev. Oneal.

Anna T. McCrary was married to John Perry Chapman, Nov. 27, 1866, by Rev. Geo. H. Coit in Americus, Ga.

Edmund Blount McCrary was married to Victoria Dozier in Georgetown, Ga., Dec. 17, 1872, by Rev. J. B. McGee.

Children of Anna T. and John P. Chapman:

A. Charles Klink Chapman, born Nov. 17, 1867.
B. Lollie Perry Chapman.
C. Anna Lucretia Chapman.
D. John Edmund Chapman.
E. Emma Chapman.
F. Maggie Lamandra Chapman.
G. Albert Henry Chapman.
H. Alice Chapman.
I. Susie Chapman.
J. Elsie Louise Chapman.

Charles K. Chapman and John E. Chapman have the degree of D. D. S.

Charles K. Chapman, married Dollie Johnson.

Lollie P. Chapman, married William H. Chase.

Anna Lucretia Chapman, died when young.

Maggie L. Chapman married Perry Coney Clegg.

Alice Chapman, married Joseph E. Johnson.

Susie Chapman, married Joseph Richard Cooper.

Elsie Louise Chapman, married Frank Roland Coman.

CHAPTER XIV.

CHARLES TALIAFERRO

Charles Taliaferro, son of Dr. John and Mary (Hardin) Taliaferro, was born in Virginia, removed to Surry County, N. C. with his parents. He was a man of prominence in old Surry and represented this county in the House of Commons of North Carolina, 1811-15. After the removal of his father to Georgia, he came into possession of the old Taliaferro estate, located eighteen miles from Mount Airy, which has descended in an unbroken line to his posterity; and is now in possession of his great-grandson, Walter Wylie Lovill, and his great-great-grandson, William Shadrack Lovill, the latter residing at the present time on this historic site. Charles Taliaferro married first, Sallie Burroughs; second Dicie Tucker of Surry County. There was no issue by his second marriage. He died in Surry Co. in 1838. According to the best obtainable records, the children of Charles and Sallie (Burroughs) Taliaferro, named according to age were as follows

First, John Taliaferro.

Second, Elizabeth or "Bettie" Taliaferro.

Third, Charles Taliaferro.

Fourth, Richard Taliaferro.

Fifth, Dickerson Taliaferro.

Sixth, Mark Hardin Taliaferro.

Seventh, Benjamin Taliaferro.

Eighth, Sallie Taliaferro.

Ninth, Mary Taliaferro.

First Line.

JOHN TALIAFERRO

John Taliaferro, son of Charles and Sallie (Burroughs) Taliaferro, was born in Surry County, N. C.; removed to Tennessee, where he was a large land owner and prominent farmer of that state. He married Martha Wright, probably before he moved to Tennessee. Their children were:

I. Charles Taliaferro; m a r r i e d ——? Died in Arkansas. Issue:
A. Will Taliaferro; lived in San Antonio, Texas.
B. George Taliaferro; lived in San Antonio, Texas.

II. Wright Taliaferro; m a r r i e d Betsy Smith. Issue: One son and two daughters.

III. William Taliaferro; married 1st, Miranda Wood; 2nd 1869 his cousin, Martha Franklin (called Pattie), b. July 12, 1831. Mrs. Pattie (Franklin) Taliaferro has the distinction of being the oldest living descendant of Dr. John Taliaferro. She makes her home with her sister, Mrs. Lucinda F. Calloway, and her niece, Mrs. Mayme (Calloway) Jones at Concord, Tenn. She has furnished some valuable information for this sketch and although, advanced in years, manifests a great interest in family history and heritage. She has a double line of descent from Dr. John Taliaferro and her son, Dr. Charles Franklin Taliaferro, has three lines of descent. William Taliaferro had issue by 1st marriage to Miranda Wood:
A. Wood Taliaferro.
B. Maggie Taliaferro; died ——.
William Taliaferro had issue by 2nd marriage to Pattie Franklin:
C. Dr. Charles Franklin Taliaferro; b. Jan. 15, 1870 in Concord, Tenn.; he is a prominent physician of Berwyn, Oklahoma. He married Ida Virginia Bolejack, daughter of Nathaniel Bolejack and Victoria (Bunker) Bolejack of Mount Airy, N. C., and granddaughter of Chang Bunker, one of the Siamese twins. No issue.

IV. Wilson Taliaferro; m a r r i e d ——? Issue:
A. Miranda Taliaferro; married Will Griffey, Georgetown, Tenn.
B. Martha Taliaferro; married ——?
C. Lizzie Taliaferro; married H o w e l l Short, Georgetown, Tenn.

V. Dickerson Taliaferro; married Matt Dobson. Issue:
A. Arch Taliaferro.

VI. Dardis Taliaferro; died unmarried.

VII. George Taliaferro; married 1st ——? 2nd, Liza Goodner. Issue by first marriage:
A. Lorna Taliaferro.
Issue by second marriage:
B. John Taliaferro; drowned.

C. Mattie Taliaferro; married George Cardin, of Chattanooga, Tenn.

D. Annie Taliaferro; married ——— Taylor of East Chattanooga, Tenn.

VIII. Sarah Taliaferro; married Jim Holland. Issue: Several children who moved out West.

IX. Mary Taliaferro; married Shell Boweman. Issue:

A. ——— Boweman; married Shaler James, of Anchorage, Alaska.

B. Mattie Boweman; died ———.

X. Margaret Taliaferro; married Tom Queener. Issue:

A. John Queener, of Lenoir City, Tenn.

B. Charles Queener, of Lenoir City, Tenn.

C. Mattie Queener; married——— Howard, Lenoir City, Tenn.

D. ——— Queener; married Bobbie Davis, Lenoir City, Tenn.

E. Kate Queener; married ——— Davis, Concord, Tenn.

F. Mollie Queener; married——— Baker, in Texas.

Mrs. Ida Virginia (Bolejack) Taliaferro has the unusual distinction of being the oldest granddaughter of Chang Bunker, one of the world renowned Siamese twins. According to the best obtainable records, these twins, Chang and Eng, although born in far away Bangesau, Siam on April, 15, 1811, were for the most part of Chinese descent, their father being of Chinese extraction, went to Siam where he married a woman whose father was Chinese. Their fame might have been denied them, had not their discovery been made by a British merchant at Bangkok, Robert Hunter who aroused the interest of Captain Coffin, the adventurous commander of a "tramp" merchant vessel, and aided the captain in persuading their parents and King Chowpahyi to allow him to carry them away on his boat, small children though they were. After once leaving their native land, they imbibed from the captain his nomadic nature and continued their travels. At the age of eighteen, these boys visited Harvard University, and the records show that Chang, the left twin, was 5 ft. 1½ inches tall, while his brother Eng, the right twin, was 5 ft. 2 inches. After touring the world and having accumulated what was then a considerable fortune, they grew tired of continuous travel and

decided to establish a permanent home for themselves. The nation they chose was our own "land of the free, and home of the brave," so at the age of forty-four they settled in Surry County, N. C., at Mount Airy, then a secluded little village nestling under the shadows of the Blue Ridge Mountains, where they were considered fabulously wealthy. They made good citizens and became very popular, being known everywhere by their American surname of Bunker. In a short while they were struck by one of Cupid's darts, and not being able to resist, they were soon married to two sisters, ages twenty-six and twenty-eight, making new homes for their wives not far distant, and to each union were born several children. Some of the older residents of the community who remember them full well, say that they differed not only in size, but in disposition too— Chang being of a nervous temperament and "high strung," while Eng was usually quiet and retiring, yet they always got along well together, only differing about such minor questions about where to go or what to do. On the night of Jan. 17, 1874, when nearly sixty-three, Chang died at his home of sudden paralytic stroke while Eng was asleep. Awakening in a sudden fit of horror, and realizing that he was linked to his brother's corpse by a band stronger than any steel, Eng expired within a few hours, before medical attention could be given him. Thus passed in this way two of the world's best known and most interesting characters, who had made friends and aroused interest over the entire globe.

Second Line.
ELIZABETH TALIAFERRO

Elizabeth Taliaferro, daughter of Charles and Sallie (Burroughs) Taliaferro, was born in Surry County, N. C. She married Hardin (Hardy) Jones in Surry County. They moved to Tennessee; later removing to Oklahoma. Issue:

I. Calvin Jones:

II. John Jones; married ——— Eldridge.

III. Daniel Jones; married ———? Died ———. Issue:

A. ——— Jones; married Epps Foret or Fout?

B. Dan Jones; married ———? Died ———. Issue:

1. Gladys Jones, Lenoir City Tenn.

C. Charles Jones; married Lulu
Duff. Issue:
1. —— Jones; married Fred
Smith, Concord, Tenn.
D. Sallie Jones; married ——
Eolin, Lenoir City, Tenn.
IV. Daniel Jones. Died ——.
V. Rufus Jones; married Elizabeth
Montgomery. Issue:
A. Joe Jones, Natchez, Miss.
B. Mattie Jones, married ——
Boring, Ferriday, La.
VI. Nancy Jones.
VII. Sarah Jones.
VIII.—— Jones (a daughter);
married —— Cline.

Third Line.
REV. CHARLES TALIAFERRO

Rev. Charles Taliaferro, son of
Charles and Sallie (Burroughs) Taliaferro, is the same Charles Taliaferro
whose life and consecrated, Christian
character is described by his brother,
Rev. Mark Hardin Taliaferro, in
"Fisher's River Scenes and Characters." In character and religion he was
a true Taliaferro; he was highly educated and was a prominent Baptist
minister in old Surry. He was loved
and admired by all for his many good
deeds and for the wonderful Christian
influence which he had over the people
in this community. The oldest members of the Lingo family describe him
as "handsome, wealthy, and a charm-
ing gentleman." A photograph of him
made at the age of fifty-four years, is
reproduced in this sketch. On the
same page are shown photos of his
son Mark Hardin Taliaferro, made at
the age of forty-two years, his grandson C. P. Taliaferro, made at the age
of fifty-three years, and his great-
granddaughter Miss Elizabeth Jane
Taliaferro, made at the age of twenty-
one years. This group shows four
generations of Taliaferros.

Rev. Charles Taliaferro married
first, Jane Whitlock, in Surry County,
N. C. Later he moved his family to
Loudon, Tenn. For several years after
his removal to Tennessee, it was his
custom to make an annual trip to
Macon, Georgia for the purpose of
marketing hides and tallow; Macon
being the best market for his produce
at that time. On these trips he was
a guest in the home of his relatives,
the family of John Clark Johnson. On
Oct. 22, 1839, he married a second
wife, Elizabeth Eldridge, sister of Albert Eldridge. His Family Bible, over
one hundred years old, is now in pos-

session of his grandson, C. P. Taliaferro, Loudon, Tenn., who has
furnished the writer with the following records for this sketch. Rev.
Charles Taliaferro had issue by his
first marriage to Jane Whitlock:

I. John Whitlock Taliaferro; b. in
North Carolina, Feb. 2, 1823; married Jane Ballard. Issue:
A. Samantha C. Taliaferro; b.
Jan. 8, 1847; d. June 6, 1914;
married Jan. 1867, Andrew
Jackson Lillard. Issue:
1. Nannie Lillard; d. July 3,
1904; married Prof. W. T.
Russell. Issue:
a. Robert L. Russell, P. O. Address, Welch, W. Va.
b. Mary Josephine Russell,
married James H. Barnett,
Jr., P. O. R i c h m o n d,
Virginia.
2. John W. Lillard; b. Aug. 15,
1872, in Sweetwater, Tenn.,
married in June 1905, Estella
E. Seybold, daughter of Edward E. and Fannie Seybold.
P. O. address, Sweetwater,
Tenn. Issue:
a. Ruth M. Lillard; b. April,
1906.
b. E. Jack Lillard; b. Nov.
1908.
c. James D. Lillard; b. Feb.,
1911.
d. E. Etoile Lillard; b. Sept.,
1913.
e. Annabell Lillard; b. May,
1916.
f. C. Murrel Lillard; b. Nov.,
1923.
3. Mary Carolyn ("Mollie") Lillard, married Sept. 22, 1892,
Clarence Eugene Harris. Mr.
Harris died Oct., 1925 in
Dandridge, Tenn. Since the
death of her husband, Mrs.
Harris makes her home with
her daughter at 1809 Du Bois
Ave., Tampa, Fla. Issue:
a. Margaret Boyd Harris; b.
at Dandridge, Tenn., July
15, 1893; married Jan. 30,
1918, William Paul Vance.
P. O. Tampa, Fla.
b. Mary Eugenia Harris; b. at
Dandridge, Tenn., Jan. 3,
1901; married Aug. 12, 1923,
Charles Ray Griffetts. P.
O. Rockwood, Tenn.
4. Murrell Lillard, P. O. address,
Atlanta, Ga. Care of Ernest
L. Rhodes & Co.

FOUR GENERATIONS OF TALIAFERROS

Rev. Charles Taliaferro   Mark Hardin Taliaferro

C. P. Taliaferro   Miss Elizabeth Jane Taliaferro

5. Etoile Lillard, married A. L.
Burem. P. O. address Morristown, Tenn. Issue:
  a. Jack Burem.
  b. Helen Burem.
B. Mary Taliaferro.
C. Charles Taliaferro, married
and had several children; moved
away.
D. Sallie Taliaferro; married Allison Everitt; moved to Oklahoma. She has been dead several years. She had at least one
child.
  1. Leonard Everitt. P. O. address, Leon, Okla.
E. Bathilda Taliaferro, married
Alonzo R. Robinson. P. O. address, Morristown, Tenn.
F. Richard Taliaferro, died unmarried.

II. Mark Hardin Taliaferro; b. Dec.
9, 1824, married Feb. 12, 1865,
Louisa Rebecca Beasley. She now
lives at Lenoir City, Tenn., and
is eighty-five years old. Issue:
A. Fannie D. Taliaferro; b. Oct.
15, 1865; married 1899, W. H.
Harrison. P. O. address, Loudon, Tenn. R. F. D. Issue:
  1. Mark Hardin Harrison. b.
  1901. P. O. address, Loudon,
  Tenn. R. F. D.
B. Charles Pleasant Taliaferro; b.
at Loudon, Tenn., Oct. 1, 1871;
married Oct. 11, 1893, Laura
Lowe. Mr. Taliaferro is President of the First National
Bank, Loudon, Tenn., capitalized
at $50,000, which he organized
in 1921. Mr. Taliaferro is also
serving a fourth term as Justice
of Peace for the First District
of Loudon County. He has
furnished these records of his
grandfather's family and is one
of the four generations of Taliaferros pictured in this sketch.
Issue:
  1. Elizabeth Jane Taliaferro; b.
  Sept. 27, 1898. P. O. address
  Loudon, Tenn.
C. Emmieline Eliza Taliaferro; b.
Nov. 20, 1875; married W. H.
Stanfiel, P. O. address Lenoir
City, Tenn. Her mother, Mrs.
Lula Taliaferro, lives with her.
Issue: Two daughters.

III. Sallie Catherine Taliaferro; b.
April 15, 1827; married John D.
Blair. No issue.

IV. Charles Polk Taliaferro; b. Mar.
12, 1829; married Ann Ballard. He

moved to Veal Station, Texas, and
died in 1910. Issue:
A. John Taliaferro; d. at age of
55; near Optima, Okla.
B. Charles Taliaferro.
C. Jennie Taliaferro.
D. Sallie Taliaferro.
E. James Taliaferro.
F. Annie Taliaferro; m a r r i e d
Luther M. Easley, residing at
Ft. Worth, Texas, 2304 Gould
St.

V. Bathilda Ann Taliaferro; b. Oct.
29, 1831; married Albert Eldridge.
Issue:
A. Jesse Eldridge.
B. Charles Eldridge.
C. Kate Eldridge.
D. John Eldridge.
E. Simeon Eldridge.
F. Hardin Eldridge.
G. Dickerson Eldridge.
H. Albert Eldridge.
I. James Eldridge.

Rev. Charles Taliaferro married a
second wife, Elizabeth Eldridge, sister of Albert Eldridge, on Oct. 22,
1839. Issue:

VI. Richard Dickerson Taliaferro;
b. in Kingston, Tenn., May 28,
1841; d. July 25, 1925 at Leon,
Okla.; married July 19, 1885,
Louvenia Neel, (b. in Henderson
Co., Ky., April 27, 1866), daughter
of James F. and Margaret Neel.
He is referred to in Chapter 2 of
this sketch. He saw four years
active service in the War Between
The States, enlisting from the
State of Tennessee; was present at General Lee's surrender.
After the war he moved to Texas,
later to Oklahoma. He was highly
educated and taught the first
school in Oklahoma under an old
oak tree, and hewed out logs for
benches. Issue:
A. Charles Franklin Taliaferro;
b. Jan. 12, 1886; married July
12, 1908 Eula Campbell. Issue:
  1. Miller Taliaferro.
B. James McHenry Taliaferro; b.
Feb. 20, 1888.
C. Samuel Ernest Taliaferro; b.
Sept. 4, 1889; married Sept.,
1908, Blanche E. Everitt. P. O.
address Leon, Okla. Issue:
  1. Ernest Taliaferro.
  2. Opal Taliaferro.
  3. Louvenia Taliaferro.
D. Mollie Jessie Taliaferro; b.
Sept. 25, 1892; married Jan. 25,

1909, Robert S. Woolridge. P. O. address, Leon, Okla. Issue:
1. John Richard Woolridge.
2. Robert S. Woolridge, Jr.
3. Harrell Woolridge.

E. Richard Dickerson Taliaferro, Jr.; b. Nov. 22, 1895. P. O. Leon, Okla.

F. Atlis Louvenia Taliaferro; b. March 29, 1898; d. ———.

G. Dallas Elvis Taliaferro; b. Jan. 31, 1904; married Mar. 22, 1924, Elsie Hastien. Issue:
1. Simon Richard Taliaferro; b. July 2, 1925.

H. Katie Ruth Taliaferro; b. Oct. 27, 1907; d. ———.

VII. William Judson Taliaferro; b. Aug. 6, 1843. He settled in Arkansas, married and left several children.

VIII. Samuel Love Taliaferro; b. April 6, 1845; married first, Miss Waller; second, ———? He left several children and his son, James R. Taliaferro, Lone Grove, Oklahoma, can furnish further information about this family.

IX. Emma Taliaferro; b. 1847; married Washington Rose. P. O. address, Kingston, Tenn. Issue:
A. Charles M. Rose, President of Kingston Bank and Trust Co., Kingston, Tenn.
B. John Dickerson Rose, P. O. address Kingston, Tenn.

X. Jesse Taliaferro; died in young manhood. Never married.

XI. James B. Taliaferro, P. O. address, Wilson, Oklahoma.

The following sketch of the life of the late Richard Dickerson Taliaferro was written by one of his old friends, J. A. Fowler, Duncan, Okla.

"Richard Dickerson Taliaferro came, in the year 1879, to the Dibrell Farm, Chickasaw Nation, Indian Territory. His Post Office at that time was Mayesville, Texas. This farm was located in what is now Love Co., Okla. The Post Office is now Leon, Okla. He had formerly lived at Austin, Texas when he came to the Indian Territory; he made his home with his brother, Samuel L. Taliaferro, and took up farming and stock raising. About six years after his coming here he was married to Louvenia Neel, on July 19, 1885. He lived in this community about 12 years, during which time he also engaged in the Gin and Merchantile business—yet handling cattle and doing some farming. From here he moved to Duncan, Indian

Territory, where he resided for four years; from Duncan, he moved to Simon, Indian Territory, in what is now Love County, Okla.; from there he moved to Cannon's Chapel, where he lived only one year; from there he moved back to the community where he had first settled, (known now as Leon) residing in this place twenty-six years, during which time he farmed and handled merchandise.

He had been converted at the age of twelve years, and being an earnest consistent Christian, he took a live interest in the religious conditions of his community. During the first year, after his coming to the Dibrell Farm, he spent considerable time riding about among the scattered settlements enlisting the interest of those who would go into the organization of a church. He was successful in finding ten other persons, who went into the organization of the Mud Creek Baptist Church on the 18th day of August, 1880. Rev. O. J. R. Colthrop came over from Montague County, Texas, to assist in the organization of this church and it was at this service that Rev. Colthrop recognized his three Civil War comrades, R. D. Taliaferro, Samuel Taliaferro, and James B. Taliaferro. This recognition was occasioned by their singing, as he had heard them sing when serving together in the War Between the States. Mr. Taliaferro was made clerk of the church and served as clerk most all the time until he grew feeble and unable to do the work.

Mr. Taliaferro was a lover of the Hunt; spending much time hunting deer, turkey, and other wilds of the woods, the same being plentiful at that time.

In the year 1884, he was made a Master Mason at the old Jim-town Lodge No. 16, and he rendered faithful service to Masonry in the early days of the settlement in the Chickasaw Nation.

His neighbors knew him as a real friend, and no man doubted his word. He was fearless in the discharge of his duty and was always found on the side of right. His love for home and his family was most ardent and those who visited in his home found it a real home for all who came into it.

He lived a useful life of over more than four score years, enjoying the esteem of all who knew him. His departure was mourned by many and his influence for good lives on in the lives

Mr. Richard Dickson Taliaferro and
Wife, Mrs. Luvenia (Neel) Taliaferro

of his friends and relatives. He helped to carve out a new state from a wilderness and lived to see this new state make a most wonderful progress. He passed out of this life on July 25, 1925. His age at the time of his death was eighty-four years, one month and twenty-five days."

Richard Dickerson Taliaferro is said to have composed the following song, which he sang at every Confederate Reunion that he attended. After he became too feeble to march with the boys in grey, he still sang the song at his home, weeping because he could no longer join his comrades at the Reunion.

(1.)
"Get me my old knapsack, Mary,
And my uniform of grey,
Get my broken helmet, Mary,
For I'll need 'em all to-day.
Get my canteen and my leggins,
Reach me down my rusty gun,
For I'm going out parading
With the boys of '61.

(Chorus:)
"Now I'm ready, darling, kiss me,
Kiss your old sweetheart, good-bye.
Brush aside those wayward teardrops,
Dear, I did not think you'd cry.

(2.)
"Never mind those blood-stains, Mary,
Never mind that ragged hole,
They were left there by a bullet,
That was seeking for my soul.
Just brush off those cobwebs, Mary,
Get my bonnie flag of blue,
For I'm going out parading
With the boys of '62.

(3.)
"These old clothes don't fit me, Mary,
Like they did when I was young.
Don't you recollect how neatly
To my manly form they clung?
Never mind that sleeve that's empty,
Let it dangle loose and free,
For I'm going out parading
With the boys of '63.

(4.)
"Pull my proud belt tighter, Mary,
Fix that strap beneath my chin,
I've grown old and wayworn, Mary,
Like my uniform and thin;
But I reckon I'll pass muster,
As I did in days of yore
For I'm going out parading
With the boys of '64.

(5.)
"Now I'm ready, darling, kiss me,
Kiss your old sweetheart, good-bye,
Brush aside those wayward teardrops,
Dear, I did not think you'd cry.
I am going forth to battle
Cheer up, Mary, sakes alive,
For I'm going out parading
With the boys of '65."

Fourth Line.
REV. RICHARD TALIAFERRO
Rev. Richard Taliaferro, son of Charles and Sallie (Burroughs) Taliaferro, married Elizabeth Ballard. He moved to Tennessee and was a prominent Baptist minister of that state. He had five children, two of whom were:
I. Richard Taliaferro; married 1st, ——?; 2nd, Sophrina Peters, daughter of Sallie (Taliaferro) Peters.
II. Lettie Taliaferro; married ——?

Fifth Line.
DICKERSON TALIAFERRO
Dickerson Taliaferro, son of Charles Taliaferro and Sallie (Burroughs) Taliaierro, married Mary Harris in Surry County, N. C. He represented Surry several times in the legislature. All of his children were born in this county. He later moved to Georgia, settling in Whitfield County, and also represented this county several times in the Georgia State Legislature. Issue:
I. John Taliaferro; b. Mar. 7, 1828; d. 1893; married 1st, Oct. 1, 1859, Frances King, daughter of Sam and Emaline (Lynch) King of Gordon Co., Ga. She died in 1889. John was eighteen years old when his father moved to Georgia. The family settled in Whitfield County. He served in Col Wright's Regiment in the War Between The States. His health failed and in 1862 he moved from Whitfield Co. to Gordon Co.; later removed to Rome, Floyd Co. In 1880 he moved back to Gordon County, where he accumulated large property. He married second, Sarah E. Velvin, daughter of M. J. and Precilla Velvin of Carroll, Co., Ga. Issue by first marriage:
A. Mary Ellen Taliaferro.
B. Samuel Taliaferro.
C. Dickerson Taliaferro.
D. Charles Hardin Taliaferro.
E. George William Taliaferro.
F. John Henry Taliaferro.

II. Charles Taliaferro; married
————Allford.
III. Hardin Taliaferro; married
——— Montgomery.
IV. Dickerson Taliaferro; Sheriff;
killed in making an arrest; un-
married.
V. Wylie Franklin Taliaferro. Mar-
ried ———?
VI. Eliza Taliaferro. M a r r i e d
——— Williamson.
VII. Lucy Taliaferro.
VIII. Sarah Taliaferro.

Sixth Line.

REV. MARK HARDIN TALIAFERRO

Rev. Mark Hardin Taliaferro, son of
Charles and Sallie (Burroughs) Taliaferro, married Elizabeth Henderson
in Surry County. He became a noted
Baptist minister and was one of the
foremost orators of the South. He
moved from Surry County to Tennessee, and later moved to Alabama,
where he edited the Southwestern
Baptist at Talladega. He also resided
for several years at Tuskegee, Ala. He
was the author of several poems,
w h i c h attracted much attention
throughout the South. In 1857 he
visited his old home in Surry County,
N. C., after an absence of twenty
years, and while there the remi-
niscences of his early years naturally
revived, from the influence of that
strange but necessary law in man's
mental structure, association of ideas,
and on his return he concluded to
write out some of the scenes and
stories of that age and section, which
resulted in "Fisher's River Scenes and
Characters." These humorous tales
he published in 1859, and disguising
himself, he used his boyhood nickname, "Skitt," as the author. Judge
L. W. Rigsby, Cairo, Ga., who recently had the privilege of reading a
copy of this book, says, "The reading
of this book has been a real delight
to me. not only because of the matters
it contains and because of the personal interest I feel because of the
relationship of the author and some
of the characters in the book, but
also by reason of the many quaint
and peculiar expressions in the book.
My mother had an older sister, who
used a great many of the expressions in this book, and it was like living over the days of my childhood to
read it. Not only this but a great
many of the stories and anecdotes in
the book had come to me by way of
tradition in the family, evidently hav-

ing come down from Surry County,
North Carolina." Mark Hardin Taliaferro moved from Alabama back to
Tennessee, and was for several years
pastor of the First Baptist Church of
Knoxville. He died at London, Tenn.,
in 1876. After his death, his wife and
children moved back to Alabama.
Issue:
I. Ada Taliaferro; died unmarried.
II. Nancy Taliaferro; married ———
Ham. She had three children,
two sons, who moved away from
Loudon, Tenn., and their relatives
have lost sight of them; a daughter, married and moved to Charlotte, N. C. No further information. It is with much regret that
the writer cannot complete this
line of descendants of this noted
author and minister.

Seventh Line.

BENJAMIN TALIAFERRO.

Benjamin Taliaferro, son of Charles
and Sallie (Burroughs) Taliaferro,
married first, in Surry County, Lucy
Harris; second, Mary Whitlock. According to information obtained from
his eldest surviving relatives, he was
four times married, but the names of
his last two wives are unknown.
Issue by first marriage
I. Hardin Taliaferro.
II. Charles Taliaferro; served in
the War Between The States and
spent ten days at the home of his
uncle, Wylie Franklin, in Surry
County, while off on a furlough.
If living, he resides near Chattanooga, Tenn.
III. Mary Taliaferro.
IV. Harriette Taliaferro.
V. Sarah Taliaferro.

Eighth Line.

SALLIE TALIAFERRO

Sallie Taliaferro, daughter of Charles
and Sallie (Burroughs) Taliaferro
married first, Bill Howard; moved to
Alabama; married second, ———
Peters.
Issue by second marriage·
I. Flora Peters; married ———.
II. Sophrina Peters; married her
first cousin, Richard Taliaferro,
son of Rev. Richard and Elizabeth
(Ballard) Taliaferro. No further
information.

Ninth Line.

MARY TALIAFERRO

Mary Taliaferro, daughter of Charles
and Sallie (Burroughs) Taliaferro,
was born in Surry County, N. C.
April 25, 1800; married Dec. 29, 1827,

her first cousin, Wylie Franklin (b. Dec. 25, 1801; d. June 16, 1891), son of Shadrack Franklin and Judith (Taliaferro) Franklin. This couple resided in Surry County, on the old Dr. John Taliaferro estate. They reared their children in a home that was built by Charles Taliaferro, son of Dr. John, after the latter had moved to Georgia. This historic old home nestled on the top of a beautiful mountain; was roomy, well screened and comfortable. It was occupied by some of the children of Wylie and Mary (Taliaferro) Franklin up until the time it was destroyed by fire in September, 1924. Among the losses which could never be replaced were the old Family Bible, and the photos of Shadrack Franklin, Sr., Wylie Franklin and wife, Mary (Taliaferro) Franklin, and the following Taliaferros, Richard, Dickerson, Charles, Mark Hardin, Sallie, and Elizabeth, these being children of Charles and Sallie (Burroughs) Taliaferro. There are about fifty springs on this old estate. Wylie and Mary (Taliaferro) Franklin had issue:

I. Virginia Franklin; (dead); married West Freeman. Issue:
A. Bettie Freeman; married——— Beamer.
B. Janie Freeman; P. O. Mount Airy, N. C.

II. Martha Franklin; (called Pattie); b. July 12, 1831; married 1869, William Taliaferro. P. O. Concord, Tenn. Issue:
A. Dr. Charles Franklin Taliaferro; b. Jan. 15, 1870; P. O. Berwyn, Okla.

III. Elizabeth Franklin (called Bettie); b. June 1832; d. Feb. 15, 1868; married Dec. 16, 1852, James Lovill. Issue:

A. Walter Wylie Lovill; b. 1853; married Martha Elizabeth Jones, daughter of Francis and Mary (Copeland) Jones, of the State of Virginia. P. O. Mount Airy, N. C. The descendants of Dr. John Taliaferro are indebted to Mr. Lovill for much of the information contained in this sketch. He takes great pride in discussing his family history and has furnished the writer with some interesting incidents of the life of Dr. John Taliaferro, and with records of the Surry County branch of this family. Issue:

1. Wylie Franklin Lovill. P. O. Mount Airy, N. C.
2. James Walter Lovill; married Gladys Virginia Warren. P. O. Mount Airy, N. C. Issue:
a. James Walter Lovill.
b. Martha Tucker Lovill.
3. William Shadrack Lovill; married Ada Beamer. P. O. Mount Airy, N. C. Issue:
a. William Joseph Lovill.
4. Joseph Poindexter Lovill was a civil engineer; died in State of Washington in December, 1912, at the age of twenty-nine.
5. Grover Cleveland Lovill. P. O. Mount Airy, N. C.
6. Dr. Robert J. Lovill (M. D.), married Lucile Kirkman. P. O. Mount Airy, N. C. Issue:
a. Robert J. Lovill, Jr.
7. Elizabeth Lovill. P. O. Mount Airy, N. C.
8. Sallie Matilda Lovill; married June, 1917, Dr. Henry Boyden Rowe (d. May, 1924). P. O. Mount Airy, N. C. Issue:
a. Henry Boyden Rowe, Jr.

IV. Sallie Franklin; died unmarried.
V. Benjamin Franklin; died unmarried.
VI. Judith Franklin; b. Feb. 9, 1838; lives with her nephew, Mr. Walter Wylie Lovill, Mount Airy, N. C. She has assisted the writer in securing much of the information contained in this chapter.
VII. Matilda Franklin; b. June, 1840; d. May 7, 1922. Never married.
VIII. Lucinda Franklin; b. Dec. 14, 1842; married Nov. 1, 1881, James Callaway (b. at Ball Camp, Tenn., Nov. 20, 1838; d. at Concord, Tenn. May 12, 1923). P. O., Concord, Tenn. Issue:
A. Mayme Callaway; b. Aug. 8, 1882; married March 22, 1906, Benjamin Luther Jones, b. July 10, 1881. P. O. Concord, Tenn. Mrs. Jones has contributed much information about the Tennessee branch of the family for this book. Issue:
1. Mary Lynn Jones; b. Dec. 12, 1906.
2. Ruth Franklin Jones; b. Jan. 17, 1909.
3. James M. Callaway Jones; b. Jan. 15, 1911.

4. Shadrack Alan Jones; b. Aug. 14, 1917.

5. Virginia Dom Jones; b. Aug. 21, 1920.

IX. Shadrack C. Franklin; b. July 23. 1845; married first, Feb. 18, 1880, Martha Whitlock (b. Sept. 23, 1851; d. Sept. 22, 1884); married second, Sept. 10, 1885, Bettie Kapp (b. Jan. 22, 1859; d. June 4, 1923). Mr. Franklin formerly lived at Mount Airy, but since the death of his last wife, he now makes his home with one of his sons at Cumberland, Va. Some fifteen years ago Mr. Franklin's Georgia relatives aroused in him an interest in family history and heritage, and he furnished some valuable information to Mrs. Lillian Ivey Davis, Tennille, Ga. (now deceased), and Mrs. Sidney J.

Jones, formerly of Albany, Ga., now of Denton, Texas. Since that time many other records have been added to those originally obtained from Mr. Franklin and have culminated in this sketch. Issue by first marriage:

A. J. W. Franklin; b. May 28, 1881.

B. Charles Franklin; b. June 3, 1883.

Issue by second marriage:

C. Adolphus Franklin; b. Dec. 4, 1886; d. Jan. 30, 1904.

D. Lee F. Franklin; b. Nov. 30, 1888.

E. Bernard S. Franklin; b. July 9, 1894.

Mr. Franklin's children by his second marriage have three lines of descent from Dr. John Taliaferro.

CHAPTER XV.

JUDITH (TALIAFERRO) FRANKLIN

Bernard Franklin was a close friend of Dr. John Taliaferro in Virginia, and moved with his family to Surry Co., N. C., at the same time that Dr. John settled in Surry. He married Mary Cleveland. Three of their sons were Shadrack, Meshech and Jesse. Shadrack Franklin was born, probably, in Orange Co., April 20, 1769, and died in Surry Co., N. C., probably, in Stewart Creek Township, in August, 1860, at the age of 91 years. He was highly educated; possessed a marked degree of wit and humor; was an upright Christian man and a leading citizen in his community. He married Judith Taliaferro, daughter of Dr. John and Mary (Hardin) Taliaferro. She was born 1763 and died 1848. Judith Taliaferro was a patriotic woman and went down to Guilford Court House, only fifty miles from her home, and helped her father nurse the sick and wounded soldiers in Gen. Greene's Army. Shadrack and Judith (Taliaferro) Franklin lie buried in the old Taliaferro-Franklin burial ground in Surry County, N. C.

Jesse Franklin was a private at the Battle of Guilford Court House; was later promoted to captain. After the Revolution he served as Governor and United States Senator of the State of North Carolina.

Meshech Franklin was considered the best educated man in Surry County. His counsel and advice was sought continuously and he was called upon to conduct all the political elections held in Surry and his word was considered law.

Shadrack and Judith (Taliaferro) Franklin had issue:

First, Sallie T. Franklin.

Second, Lucy Franklin.

Third, Mary Franklin.

Fourth, Bernard Franklin.

Fifth, Benjamin Franklin.

Sixth, Betsy Franklin.

Seventh, Martha Franklin (called Patty).

Eighth, Wylie Franklin.

Ninth, John Taliaferro Franklin.

First Line.

SALLIE T. FRANKLIN

Thomas P. Scott, son of Daniel and Ann Radford (Poindexter) Scott, was born in Surry Co., N. C., 1785-1790, and married there in 1810 Sallie T. Franklin, daughter of Shadrack and Judith (Taliaferro) Franklin. The marriage bond is on file in Dobson, the county seat of Surry County, and is dated August 16, 1810, of Thomas P. Scott and Sally T. Franklin. Soon after the marriage they went to Kentucky, where the mother died in giving birth to twins, one of the latter also dying soon. The other child was named Benjamin Franklin Scott, and his grandfather, Shadrack Franklin, went with a daughter to Kentucky and brought back the child when only a few months old, and he was brought up in Surry Co. Thomas Scott married a second wife, but no further trace of him has been found.

I. Benjamin Franklin Scott, son of Thomas P. and Sallie T. (Franklin) Scott, was born in Kentucky, Dec. 21, 1811, and died in Surry County, N. C., May 24, 1873. He married Elizabeth Norman, who was born Dec. 24, 1812, and died May 2, 1901, daughter of William and Delilah (Barker) Norman. Benjamin F. Scott made his will May 23, 1873 and it was proved Sept. 1, 1873, and in it he mentions his wife Elizabeth, son Thomas M. Scott, and daughter Elizabeth E. Scott; making his friend, J. H. Nations executor. Children of Benjamin Franklin and Elizabeth (Norman) Scott taken from his Family Bible:

A. Shadrack F. Scott, b. April 7, 1832.
B. Sally F. Scott, b. Dec. 26, 1833; d. July 15, 1837.
C. Lucinda Scott, b. Sept. 28, 18— (torn).
D. Martha T. Scott, b. Oct. 6, 18 (torn), married James M. Stewart, son of Joel and Milly (Roten) Stewart. He was born in Carroll County, Va., Aug. 2, 1833, and died in Washington, Washington County, Kansas, Nov. 9, 1882. He married in Surry County, North Carolina, March 28, 1851, Martha Taliaferro Scott, who was born in Surry Co., Oct. 6, 1836, and died in Washington, Kansas, July 16, 1912. Issue:
1. Winnie Stewart, born in Washington, Kansas, Nov. 25, 1882, married in Denver, Colorado, May 27, 1918, Carroll Cary Kent, born in Kentland, Indiana, June 23, 1864, son of Alexander James and Rosamond Josephine (Chesebrough) Kent. P. O. address Kentland, Indiana.
E. Mary Scott, b. Jan. 5, 1842.
F. Susan L. Scott, b. Oct. 26, 1844.
G. Berthilda Ann Scott, b. Mar. 26, 1847.

H. Winfield Scott, b. Oct. 16, 1849; d. Nov. 13, 1852.
I. Thomas M. Scott, b. Feb. 3, 1855.
J. Henry Scott, b. Jan. (torn) 1857; d. Nov. 16, 1857.
K. Elizabeth E. Scott, b. June 17, 1860.

Second Line.
LUCY FRANKLIN

Lucy Franklin, daughter of Shadrack and Judith (Taliaferro) Franklin, was born about 1791, and died 1883, aged 92; married Ambrose Johnson, of Wilkes County, N. C. Issue:
I. Franklin Johnson married a Miss Woodrough.
II. Sallie Johnson, married Ambrose Roberts.
III. Pollie Johnson married Jackson McMichel.
IV. Rachel Johnson, married a Mr. Philips.
V. Bettie Johnson, unmarried, living at Jonesville, N. C. in 1884.
VI. Pattie Johnson, married Ervin Parker.

Third Line.
MARY FRANKLIN

Mary Franklin (called Polly), daughter of Shadrack and Judith (Taliaferro) Franklin, died unmarried, age 80 years.

Fourth Line.
BERNARD FRANKLIN

Bernard Franklin, son of Shadrack and Judith (Taliaferro) Franklin, died in Roane County, Tennessee about 1835. He married in Rockford, Surry, Co., N. C., Ann Moore Dobson (called Nancy), who died in Sweetwater, Roane Co., Tenn., March 1884. She was a daughter of William Polk and Mary (Hughes) Dobson. Bernard and Nancy (Dobson) Franklin had issue:
I. William Dobson Franklin; b. Apr. 4, 1822, married Marshall Co., Tenn., Aug. 22, 1848, Mary Ann Hughes, b. Dec. 31, 1829; d. March 1, 1883, daughter of William and Martha (Dobson) Hughes, and they had five children:
A. William Bernard Franklin; b. Oct. 15, 1849.
B. Mary Ann Franklin; b. Oct. 28, 1851; married William Augustus Roberts.
C. Benjamin Franklin; b. April 13, 1856.
D. Henry Dobson Franklin; b. Sept. 7, 1858.

E. Albert Lee Franklin; b. Dec. 1, 1869.

II. Sarah Loutitia Franklin; b. May 1824, married James Alexander Kline. Issue:
A. Mary Ann Kline.
B. William Lowrey Kline.
C. Mary Franklin Kline.

III. Benjamin Franklin; b. May 1830, married Roane Co., Tenn., 1854, Margaret Jane Blair. He was a noted physician. He removed to Osborn, Mo. Issue:
A. William Franklin.
B. Ann Franklin.
C. John Franklin.
D. James Franklin.
E. Benjamin Hill Franklin.

Fifth Line.
BENJAMIN FRANKLIN

Benjamin Franklin, son of Shradrack and Judith (Taliaferro) Franklin, died unmarried. He was killed by falling timber in a storm in Tennessee.

Sixth Line.
BETSY FRANKLIN

Betsy Franklin, daughter of Shadrack and Judith (Taliaferro) Franklin, married Richard Cunningham. No further information.

Seventh Line.
MARTHA FRANKLIN

Martha Franklin (called Patty), daughter of Shadrack and Judith (Taliaferro) Franklin, married Elijah Thompson. He served in the War of 1812. They had issue:

I. Columbus Thompson; married Ada Crockerham. Their children who are now living are:
A. Kimber Thompson. P. O. Jonesville, Yadkin County, N. C.
B. Ben Thompson, P. O. Kapps Mill, N. C.
C. Addie Thompson lives in Va.; married Columbus McMickle (called "Bud").

II. Dr. Kimber Thompson married Lucy McMickle. He was a physician and Baptist clergyman. Issue:
A. Martha Thompson (called Matt), married Aaron Speas; lives at Boonville, Yadkin County, N. C.
B. Mamie Thompson married ——— Woodhouse.
C. Annie Thompson married Paul Edgar Hubbell. P. O. Ypsilanti, Mich. Mrs. Hubbell is very talented and formerly belonged

to the celebrated Ben Greet Players, who reproduce Shakespeare's plays at all the leading colleges in the United States. Mr. Hubbell was North Carolina's Rhodes Scholar to Oxford, England in 1914 and is at present one of the Professors of History at the Michigan State Normal College. They have one child.

III. Ben Thompson, died aged 35 years, unmarried.

IV. Shadrack Thompson married a Miss Beasley. He was a Baptist minister. They had several children.

V. Lucy Thompson died unmarried.

VI. Betty Thompson married Dr. Dudley, a Baptist minister. No issue.

VII. Mary Thompson married Adolphus Kapp. Issue:
A. John Kapp, married Alice Crockerham. P. O. Kapps Mill, N. C. Issue:
1. DeEtte Kapp; b. March 17, 1883; married Frank W. Hanes, Dec. 30, 1909. He was a son of Alfred M. Hanes and Lucy Jane Hanes. Issue:
a. John Alfred Hanes; b. April 26, 1915.
b. Mary Grace Hanes; b. Dec. 2, 1918.
Mrs. Frank W. Haines' P. O. address is Yadkinsville, Yadkin County, N. C.
B. Betty Kapp. She was the second wife of her cousin, Shadrack C. Franklin. The children of Mr. Franklin by his second marriage have the unusual distinction of three lines of descent from Dr. John Taliaferro, Mr. Franklin has a double line of descent; thus giving his children two lines from Judith (Taliaferro) Franklin and one line from Charles Taliaferro and Sallie Burroughs. (See chapter 14 for record of their children.)
C. Nettie Kapp married Jess Allred.

Eighth Line.
WYLIE FRANKLIN

Wylie Franklin, son of Shadrack and Judith (Taliaferro) Franklin married his first cousin, Mary Taliaferro, daughter of Charles and Sallie (Burroughs) Taliaferro. For record of their descendants see chapter 14.

Ninth Line.

JOHN TALIAFERRO FRANKLIN

John Taliaferro Franklin, son of Shadrack and Judith (Taliaferro) Franklin, married Nancy Easley in Surry Co., later moved to Missouri. After the death of his wife, he moved with his son-in-law to California, while some of the family remained in Missouri. They have been lost sight of by relatives in North Carolina. The Easley Family was very prominent in Surry County. They owned the old negro slave called "Ginger Cake Josh," who made and sold ginger cakes on Muster Day in Surry. Muster Day was celebrated as a reunion of old Revolutionery Soldiers. Hamp Hudson, who sold apple brandy, and "Ginger Cake Josh" with his delicious ginger cakes, were very popular among the soldiers and they usually disposed of their brandy and ginger cakes long before the noon hour.

John Taliaferro and Nancy (Easley) Franklin had issue:

I. Shadrack Franklin.

II. William E. Franklin. He was a physician in LaGrange, Tenn.; was killed in the Civil War at Battle of New Orleans.

III. Jesse Warren Franklin, killed at Battle of New Orleans.

IV. James Franklin, married a Miss Martin.

V. Sallie Franklin married ―――― Yankey.

VI. Judith Franklin married Pleasant Hoge. No issue. They moved from Missouri to California.

VII. Mary Franklin.

VIII. Bettie Franklin.

IX. Henry Franklin.

CHAPTER XVI.

FISHER'S RIVER SCENES AND CHARACTERS

(Abstract)

"Fisher's River Scenes and Characters" by Mark Hardin Taliaferro.

These tales are true and are laid in Surry County, N. C., between the years 1820 and 1829. They give a vivid description of old Surry and its people at that time. The following sketch is from this book.

JOHNSON SNOW

Of all the men in that romantic picturesque country, I must yield the palm, in many respects, to JOHNSON SNOW.

He was one of the oldest settlers of Stewart's Creek, near its head, and within a few miles of the "Flour Gap" of the Blue Ridge. "Johnson," for so he was always familiarly called, had not the advantages of even a Dilworth's Spelling Book education. He had learned the common vernacular of the country, with a few additional eccentricities of his own, but he "axed nobody no boot, and could weed his own row, and keep it clean too—that's sartin."

Look at him, and you will believe every word of it, and more too. He is about five feet six inches high, well set, muscularly and powerfully made; but he is good-humored, wears a generous face, and has a warm heart. Well for the "Stewart's Creek Suckers" that he was a good-natured man. He is also fond of good eating, and shows his keeping.

There was a long line of kings in Egypt that went by the common name of "Ptolemy," and to distinguish one Ptolemy from another the people and historians appended an adjunct expressive of the character or habits of each monarch. One of them was called "Ptolemy Physcon," or "Tunbelly." And to distinguish Johnson Snow from the numerous Snows that lived in that region, and to give the reader some idea of the effects of a good appetite, he might with great propriety be called Tunbelly Johnson Snow.

Two things he was particularly fond of, and upon which he flourished whenever he could get them—turnip greens and "hog's gullicks," the "Adam's apple" of a hog's haslet, or the "google," as it is commonly called. Johnson had departed from all technicalities, and called it "gullick." I will add that he would help all his neighbors kill hogs for the "gullicks."

There was an arch, provoking smile ever playing upon his full face, which would attract attention in any crowd, and mark him out as a "rare bird" in any community. He had, moreover, a fund of sharp, provoking wit, running into satire when necessary, which Johnson maintained "were worth more than all yer' college lingo, a plaguy sight." His waggish wit was a terror to the whole country. Woe to the man who happened to fall into some ludicrous mishap! He never heard the last of it from Johnson. He had "a rig" on nearly every man. Johnson Snow was a necessary appendage at every public gathering. "Licker" was at them all, and he loved it as a thirsty ox does pond-water. The fact is that it sharpened his wit, and he would indulge freely for that additional reason.

Johnson Snow possessed, in addition to his waggish wit, a good deal of "hard common sense like a hoss." He was rich in resources and expedients, and seldom failed of a triumph in times of emergency. In all the "tight fits" and "tarnatious snarls" he got into, he would outflight, outquarrel, or outwit; out he would come with "flying colors."

He triumphed over one of the sternest men in the community, as the following incident will show.

There lived in the neighborhood a rigid Baptist and great "Scriptorian," one of the few men in that social region that would not take some of the "good critter," but hated it most cordially. His aversion went so far that he would not let a drunken man tarry with him for the night. He was highly respected by all who knew him, even by the worst drunkards, and bore two titles which were quite honorable then and there. (This was before Americans began to manufacture and apply titles indiscriminately.) He was always addressed very respectfully as "'Squire Charles Taliaferro" and "Cap'en Taliaferro."

Johnson knew him well, and was fully aware of his hatred to his friend "Cap-en Knock-'em-stiff"; but what of that? Ha! Ha! I'm ready for the old 'coon, cocked and primed, and triggers sprung. I'll show him he don't know uvry thing about Scripter afore I'm done with him. This boy has dipped into Scripter as well as stillhouses, sure as gun's iron."

These sentences were uttered by Johnson at a "still-house," not long after he had quit Parson Bellow's church. He had just made a bet with some "jewkers" of a gallon of apple brandy that he could stay all night with "old Taliaferro, and could beat him all holler, too, talkin' on Scripter."

Chuckling as above, he leaves a "still-house" one cold evening, "high up in the picters," and arrived at Taliaferro's gate just at sunset, altered his voice, and hallooed. Taliaferro opened the door, and our hero commenced.

"Hellow, old Scripter; I'm come to stay all night with you. I want to talk all night with you on Scripter. I've hearn you was a reg'lar built screamer in that way, and I want to try my hand with you, sartin. 'Squire, I'll talk all round you. I'll ring-fire you with Scripter. Ha! ha! see here Cap'en, ef you lick me out, you can beat the old Scripter-maker, sartin. I give you far warnin'. No shirkin,' now, sartin."

"You cannot stay, Johnson," replied Taliaferro. "Come when you are sober, and you can stay a week, if you wish; but a drunken man shall not stay all night at my house."

"Don't be too fast, old 'coon," said Johnson; "I'll show you a trick ur two afore I'm done, sartin. You Humph! you Humph!" (calling a negro man named Humphrey); "come here, you bandy-shanked rascal, and take my hoss. Put him up, and in the mornin,' ef he ain't up to his eyes in corn and fodder, I'll larrup you well. Ha! ha! you b'longed to me once, you cathammed puke, but I gulluped you down my gullick in whiskey, and sold you to this rich man, Taliaferro, who's got too big fur his britches, and won't let me stay all night with him. But I'll show him I'm a huckle-berry over his 'simmon, sartin."

Orders were obeyed; the horse was taken, and our Stewart's Creek hero walked to the door and halted. He placed one foot on the doorstep, his elbow upon his knee, his chin in his hand, with a face as long as the president of a club of Pharisees, and commenced his telling s p e e c h on "Scripter."

"Ha! ha! Taliaferro, I read uv you in Scripter. You think I know nuthin' about Scripter, but I'll show you afore I'm done. I know and read of you in that Holy Book. You're that rich man in the parrabul, which you may find by sarching the 16th chapter of Luke, that fared sumptoriously urvy day, and I'm poor Lezzerus. That rich man wouldn't let poor reflicted Lezzerus come into his house, nur will you let me come into yourn nuther. Don't you see the 'nalogy? But that rich man died, and how was it with him, Taliaferro? Be alarmed, sir! Poor reflicted Lezzerus died, too, and how was it with him? Look into Abram's bosom; see him restin' thar, safe as a bar in a hollow tree in the dead o' winter. Ah! you'll see how it will go with you and me in 'that day,' as Parson Beller calls it. When I'm shinin' away in Abram's bosom, like a piece uv new money, where will you be, Taliaferro? Don't Paul, in Hebrews, tell you to be 'careful to entertain strangers—thereby have some entertained angels? What good does all yer Scriptr readin' do you, ef you don't 'ply it better? You'd better be studin' Gale's Almynac, for the good it does you. Ha! ha! you won't let me come into yer house, and even eat the crumbs what falls from your table, now groanin' and screechin' under rich dainties—maybe some hog's gullicks on it too. I'll go out here" (leaving the door, and affecting to weep), "and lie down in yer fence corner, and let yer dogs come and lick my sores. You'll see how it will go with us in that day, Sartin."

"Come back, Johnson," said Taliaferro, "and stay all night. I acknowledge myself beaten for once in 'Scripter.' You certainly got your lesson well while you were in Bellow's church."

Historic Georgia Families
1928 Brochure.

❖

FOREWORD

This concluding Brochure consists of biographies, documents correspondence, genealogies, and opinions ancillary and cumulative to brouchures published 1925, 1926 and 1926-27. In addition to these it contains many miscellaneous genealogies, together with some criticism of Georgia histories and a discussion of the religion of nature.

A list of subjects discussed contains the following: "William Coram, Patriot and wife Ann (Hodo) Coram," "Archibald Swann, Patriot and wife Mary", "Daniel Brunson, Patriot and wife Francis (Stanton) Brunson," "Nicholas Rigby, Georgia Immigrant and wife Sarah," "Errata and Addenda to Hardin Hints and Genealogies with a chapter on the "Welsh Witch Woman", "Errata and Addenda to Georgia Branch of the Virginia Clays," "Johnson Blair, Irish Immigrant and Patriot, with Genealogies of Jonathan Lindley and Documents of other Blairs in Georgia", "Miscellaneous Genealogies", "Georgia History Criticised", "The Religion of Nature."

L. W. RIGSBY.

William Coram, Patriot and Wife Ann Hodo Coram.

Acknowledgement is made to Mrs. W. S. Dozier, Dawson, Ga., and to Mrs. J. L. Davidson, Quitman, Ga,. for information supplied for this sketch:

ERRATA

Date and place of birth given in first page second column of brochure of Thomas Coram is erroneous. Pension record 1850 for Randolph county, Ga., page 854, dwelling 150, family 150 shows Thomas Coram, aged 62, male, farmer, born Georgia. Deborah Coram, female, born South Carolina. This fixes the year of the birth of Thomas Coram, 1788.

WILLIAM AND ANN CORAM

The old Bible of William B. Mitchiner carries the following entry which has been copied and sent me by Mr. George J. Coram of Benevolence, Ga.:

"William Coram born Oct. 2, 1756. Ann Coram born June 12, 1755, married in the year 1783."

Notes of Mrs. J. L. Davidson, Quitman, Ga., contains an abstract of the will of Peter Hodo, Warren county Georgia and in this will he names his daughter, Ann Coram. Peter Hodo was one of the early sheriffs of Warren county, Ga., and his will is of record in that county.

William Coram was living in Wilkes county, Ga., 1793 and that year returned for taxes 420 acres of land adjoining the land of Blandford. Warren county was created this year and the above lands were cut off into Warren. 278 acres of this land was returned for taxes in Warren county in 1794. The land was on B Creek and adjoining lands of Blandford (Clark Blandford). The above land was probably bounty land given for Revolutionary service but have been unable to find record of grant. He probably sold a part of the land between return of taxes 1793 and 1794. Later he must have sold the remainder of the tract because in 1805 which is the first year following of which a tax digest exists for this county I find that Jesse Rickeston returned 637 acres of land for taxes of which Coram and Hall are mentioned as grantors and the land is mentioned as being on Bryer Creek and adjoining land of Blandford. Robert Willis also returned 142 acres in which Corum is mentioned as grantor, the land being on Bryer Creek and adjoining lands of Blandford. I find nothing returned for taxes in this county by Coram this year. The next year of which we find a tax digest is 1818. This year I find that William Coram returned for taxes 132 acres of land on Maddux Creek and bought from Stubbs and adjoining land of Johnson. William Coram returned a poll tax for Thomas Coram this year.

Military Record of William Coram.

War Department, The adjutant General's Office, Washington, Oct. 15, 1925. Respectfully returned to Mrs. W. S. Dozier, Dawson, Ga.

The records of this office show that one William Coram served in the Revolutionary War as a private in the Commander-in-Chief's Guard, Continental Troops, commanded by Captain Caleb Gibbs. He enlisted in March, 1777, to serve during the war, was promoted to sergeant between May 12th and June 4th, 1783, without further information relative to his service. This soldier was from Virginia * * * *

ROBERT C. DAVIS,
Major General.
The Adjutant General by J. M.

Georgia, Warren County.

In the name of God Amen:

I Ann Coram being low of body but of sound mind and disposing memory do make constitute and ordain this my last will and testament.

1. I will that all my just debts be paid.

2. I will and bequeath unto Thomas Coram all that tract or parcel of land situate in the 10th Dist., in the first section in the county of Lee, containing two hundred two and a half acres which is known and distinguished in the plan of said Dist. by the number 206 being a tract of land that I drew.

In witness whereof I do here set my hand and this the 11th of April, 1829.

His   Her
Jason X Hays Ann X Coram L. S.
Mark   Mark
Wm. M. Coram.
Thomas Young.

Georgia, Warren Co., March 1st, 1830.

Jason Hayes and Wm. M. Coram you swear that you saw Ann Coram the Testatrix within name, sign, seal, publish and declare this Instrument of writing to be her last will and testament that in your opinion she was of sound mind and disposing memory that in her presence and at her request and in the presence of each other you became witnesses thereunto and that you Thomas Young the other witness subscribed his name also. So help you God.

His
Jason X Hays
Attest: L. Franklin, Clk. Mark
Wm. M. Coram.

Recorded 9th of March, 1830.
L. Franklin, Clerk.

State of Georgia, Warren County.
Ordinary's Office—ss.

I, C. M. Smith, Ordinary and ex-officio Clerk of the Court of Ordinary of said County, do hereby certify that I have compared the foregoing copy of Ann Coram's will with the original record thereof, now remaining in this office, and the same is a correct transcript therefrom, and of the whole of such original record.

In testimony whereof, I have hereunto set my hand and affixed the seal of the Court of Ordinary, this the 18th day of August, 1925.

(SEAL)   C. M. SMITH,
Ordinary and ex-officio C. C. O.

Archibald Swann, Patriot, and Wife, Mary Swann.

Jordan Rowland married Sally Swann in Greene county between 1787 and 1801. Historical Collections of the Joseph Habersham Chapter D. A. R., Vol III, p82.

Residents of Green county drawing lands in Lotteries taken from phamplet list in office of Secretary of State.

Archibald Swann 141st Dist., Lot 86, 22 Dist., Early county.

John Swann, lot No. 201, Early co.
Joseph Swann, 142, 387, 7, Irwin Co.
Mary Swann, 141, 82, 5 Rabun.
Mary Swan (Illegible) 331, 17, W.
* * *

Archibald Swann of the County of Monroe conveys to John Rawls of the County of Pulaski, lot No. 86 in the 22nd Dist., Decatur county, Georgia. Date Nov. 13, 1824, witness Delamar

2

Clayton and D. Cornwall, J. P. Recorded in Deed Book A, page 177 of the deed records of Decatur county on June 23, 1826. Consideration $500.00.

* * *

Deed records Monroe county, book D, page 180 shows conveyance from Archibald Swann, wife Mary to Davis Smith to the north half of lot of land No. 40 in the 6th District. Date, January, 1826. Test., Green Hill and Wm. P. Henry and Wm. B. Clark, J. I. C.

Residents of Monroe county drawing lands in lotteries as shown by lotteries and index.

21 Dist., 3 Section, 268, Jas Swann, Allens, Monroe.

5 Dist., 4th Section, Cherokee, No. 317, Richard H. M. Swan, Butts, Monroe,, (Walker).

13 Dist., 3 Section, Cherokee No. 122, Stephen Swann, Allen Monroe. (Murray).

16 Dist., 2 Sec., No. 295 Thos. Swanns Orphs, Allens, Monroe.

STATE OF GEORGIA.

By His Excellency Wilson Lumpkin, Governor and Commander in Chief of the Army and Navy of this State, and of the Militia thereof.

To All To Whom These Presents Shall Come, Greeting:

KNOW YE, That in pursuance of the several acts of the General Assembly of this State, passed the 9th of June, and 24th December, 1825, and the 14th and 27th of December, 1826, to make distribution of the land acquired of the Creek Nation of Indians, by a Treaty concluded at the Indian Springs, on the 12th day of February, 1825, and forming the Counties of Lee, Muscogee, Troup, Coweta and Carroll, in this State, I HAVE GIVEN AND GRANTED, and by these presents, DO GIVE AND GRANT unto Mary Swan w. r. s. of Turner's District, Monroe county, her heirs and assigns forever, all that tract of lot of land containing two hundred two and one-half acres, situate, lying and being in the 1st Dist., of the 4th Sec., in the County of Coweta in said state, which said tract or lot of land is known and distinguished in plan of said District by the number Two Hundred and Fourteen, hav-

ing such shape, form and marks as appear by a plat of the same hereunto annexed: To have and to hold the said tract or lot of land, together with all and singular the rights, members and appurtenances thereof whatsoever, unto the said Mary Swan, her heirs and assigns, to her and their proper use, benefit and behoof forever in fee simple.

Given under my hand and the Great Seal of the said State this Fifth day of November, in the year one thousand eight hundred and thirty-two and of the Independence of the United States of America the fifty-seventh.

Signed by his Excellency the Governor, 5th day of November, 1832.

WILSON LUMPKIN,
Wm. W. WELLBORN, S. E. D.

Registered the 5th day of November, 1832.

Archibald Swann died before the above land grant was made but no record of administration of estate is shown and he had probably converted his property into personal property and was residing with one of his children. The land granted to Mary Swann was conveyed by William Cates, attorney for Mary Swann on May 30, 1833 to Arthur D. Meek for a consideration of $150.00.

No administration appears of estate of Mary Swann.

Many records are lost and destroyed in Georgia. This Archibald Swann wife Mary who was probably a Hill were unquestionably the parents of Richard Hill McRae Swann. The family may have originated from a Georgia immigrant as tradition says but Census Record 1850 of family of Richard Swann page 220, Dwelling 974, Family 995, shows:

Richard Swan, aged 51 (or 57), Male, Farmer, b., North Carolina.

Sarah Swan, age 53, Female, b., North Carolina.

John Swan, age 19, Male, b., Ga.

Mary Swan, age 17, Female, b., Ga.

Joseph Swan, age 14, Male, b., Ga.

Mary Swan is not mentioned in Brochure, William, James, Ross, Jane and Emily are not mentioned in Census Records from which it is reasonable to conclude that they were married before this time.

Nicholas Rigby, Immigrant, and Wife, Sarah Rigby.

ERRATA.

Brochure states that W. T. Rigsby was born in North Carolina. Census records disprove this.

6th District, Randolph County, Georgia, 1850—, Dwelling 5, Family 5, page 744.

Wiley Rigsby, aged 40, male, Farmer, born Georgia.

Jane Rigsby, aged 38, female, born South Carolina.

M. A. Rigsby, aged 17, female, born Georgia.

L. J. Rigsby, aged 15, male, born Georgia.

J. R. Rigsby, aged 14, male, born Georgia.

Allen J. Rigsby, aged 13, male, born Georgia.

Eliza Rigsby, aged 11, female, born Georgia.

Ave Rigsby, aged 9, male, born Georgia.

S. D. Rigsby, aged 7, male, born Georgia.

T. W. Rigsby, aged 5, male, born Georgia.

J. A. Rigsby, aged 3, male, born Georgia.

Explanation: Census of 1860 shows Allen J. Rigsby to have been the same as Andrew. Jefferson Rigsby was ten years old at that census and Amos Vatin listed as Ave above had died.

Randolph County, Georgia, 1850, 6th District, page 751, Dwelling 56, Family 56.

Allen Rigsby, aged 80, male, born North Carolina.

Margaret Rigsby, 79, Female, born North Carolina.

Dwelling 80, Family 80.

Samuel Day, 45, male, born Georgia.

Charity Day, 43, Female, born Georgia. (Daughter of Allen Rigsby.)

Robert Day, 21, Jno. W. Day, 18, A. R. Day, 16, M. A. Day, 15, S. E. Day, 14, M. J. Day 12. This shows Allen Rigsby to have been in Georgia as early as 1807.

Allen Rigsby, his son John Rigsby and son Samuel Rigsby served in the war of 1812 and Samuel served also in the Civil War. It is so unusual to find military service extending over so long a period that I am giving the decuments in full which gave me proofs of traditions in the family and information furnished by companions in arms.

"War Department, The Adjutant General's Office, Washington, D. C., March 20, 1924.

Respectfully returned to Mr. L. W. Rigsby, Cairo, Ga.

No one of the names Alan Rigsby, John Rigsby and Sam or Samuel Rigsby has been found on the rolls on file in this office of any organization of North Carolina troops in the service of the United States in the War of 1812.

However, the records show services as follows:

Allen Rigsby, U. S. Rifles (Cap. Thomas A. Smith) enlisted June 12, 1809 by Lt. Thomas Spencer for 5 years. On Oct. 31, 1813, was a sergeant of Capt. Abraham A. Massias' Co., at Camp Point Peter. No further record found.

John Rigsby U. S. Rifles, date of enlistment not shown; was discharged August 7, 1814, at Point Peter by reason of expiration of service, as of Capt. Abraham A. Massias' Co.

Samuel Rigsby, musician, U. S. Rifles (Capt. Ridgeway) enlisted Aug. 7, 1809, by Capt. T. A. Smith, and was discharged August 7, 1814, at Point Peter, by reason of expiration of service, as of Capt. Abraham A. Massias' Co.

ROBERT C. DAVIS,
The Adjutant General.
By J. D. B.

Georgia Soldier Roster Commission, 303 State Capitol, Atlanta, Ga., Aug. 8, 1927.

Hon. L. W. Rigsby, House Representatives, Atlanta, Ga.

My Dear Mr. Rigsby:

We have received the following information relative to Samuel Rigsby:

Samuel Rigsby, Co. F, ("Cuthbert Rifles") 5th Regt. Georgia Volunteer Infantry, enlisted as a musician May 10, 1861. Discharged, disability, Corinth, Miss, May 10, 1862.

I know you will be interested in the following record:

Lewis Johnson Rigsby enlisted as 5th Sergeant, Co. H, 1st Regt., 1st Brigade, 1st Division, Georgia State Troops, Sept. 26, 1861. Mustered out May 5, 1862. Enlisted as a private, Co. G, 55th Regiment Georgia Volunteer Infantry ("Jackson Avengers"),

May 5, 1862. Appointed 5th Sergeant, July 24, 1862. Captured, Cumberland Gap, Tenn., Sept. 9, 1863. Released, Camp Douglas, Ill., prison, June 15, 1865.

Very truly yours,
LILLIAN HENDERSON,
Acting Superintendent.

Before submission of the following documents attention is called to statement in Brochure, page 14, "Allen Rigsby was born in North Carolina about 1770. Nothing positive is known of his parentage." When this was written I had made a dilligent search in North Carolina, presuming from all information at hand that I should have found proofs there. Having failed in this and being without proofs I thought to let the matter rest. Since then, however, I have found documents which appear to bear out tradition, as handed down to me by my grandfather Wiley Taylor Rigsby. The sum of the tradition is that the mother of Allen Rigsby married a man by the name of Wiley Taylor but that their children all took the name Rigsby as preferable to the name Taylor for same cause and that Allen Rigsby named his youngest son Wiley Taylor in honor of his father. I have no recollection that my grandfather assigned any reason for the children taking the name Rigsby. Perhaps the following documents suggest the reason, that is, that as there were no male heirs or legatees to Nicholas Rigsby's estate and as the name would be lost, and as the family had some privileges by reason of a petty title that it was mutually decided that the issue of this marriage should be known as Rigsby, be that as it may, here are the documents of file in the Department of Archives and History, Atlanta, Ga., is the following will:

"This is the last will and testament of me, Nicholas Rigby, of Savannah, in the Province of Georgia, Gentlemen, being of sound disposing memory and understanding. First I will that all my just debts shall be paid as soon after my decease as conveniently may be. Then I give and bequeath unto Sarah, my loving wife, the house wherein I now live in Savannah and the garden lot thereto belonging with the appurtenances for and during the term of her life and as concerning all

the rest of my estate of what kind or nature soever, or to which I am or may be entitled in Possession, Reversion, Remainder or otherwise in England or any other part of his Majestay's dominions as also all legacies, Gifts, Bequests or devises to me made by any person or persons whomsoever or wheresoever My true will meaning and intent in that the same (if real estate) shall be held and enjoyed by my two daughters and co-heirs, Elizabeth and Sarah and their heirs forever as Tenants in Common and as joint tenants they paying out thereof unto their mother, my loving wife, such a sum of money as shall amount to a third part of the value of the said estate and in case of its being personal Estate of what kind soever, I hereby give the same unto my said loving wife and two daughters, share and share alike, and lastly I constitute my said wife and Newdigate Stephens, Gentlemen, Executrix and Executor of this my will. In Witness whereof I have hereunto set my hand and seal the nineteenth day of August in the year of our Lord, 1754.

NICK RIGYBE, L. S.

Signed, sealed, published and declared by testator as his last will and Testament in the presence of us and attested by us in his presence. David Montaigne, Peter Laffittee, Chas. Watson, Georgia."

Ailen Rigsby deeds to Samuel G. Mosley part of lot No. 26 in third District of Walton Co., Ga. 140 acres Consideration $500.00. Book F, page 344.

Allen Rigsby deeds to John Moate 60 acres in lot 11 in the 4th District, Walton Co., Ga., Book H, page 9.

T. W. Rigsby, grandson of Allen Rigsby says that his full name was Allen John Rigsby.

Page 2 Minutes of the Inferior Court of Walton County, Ga., appears the following:

On application of Bryant Lain Adm. of the estate of Sarah Lain, deceased, showing that it will be for the interest of the legatees and heirs of said estate to have the land Estate belonging to said estate divided and opportioned to said heirs and distributed. It is therefore ordered that after due public notice application fit and proper persons be appointed to make said distribution if no objection made to the same, 7th March, 1831.

Walton County Marriages.

Samuel Rigsby and Rebecca Adams, August 2, 1821 by Thomas Watts, J. I. C.; Absolam Hopson and Polly Rigsby, Sept. 28, 1826 by John Jean J. P. "GEORGIA, Walton County.

This indenture made this the fifth day of November, Eighteen hundred and thirty-three, between Allen J. Rigsby of the one part and John McCarty of the other part,, both of the County and State. Witnesseth: that the said Allen J. Rigsby for and in consideration of the sum of One hundred and fifty ($150.00) Dollars, to him in hand paid at and before the sealing and delivery of these presents by the said John McCarty, the receipt whereof is hereby acknowledged, hath granted, bargained and sold and by these presents do grant, bargain, and sell unto the said John McCarty, his heirs, executors and assigns, all that lot or parcel of land situate, lying and being in the third district of said county being that part of lot known in said District by the Number Seven which was assigned to the said Allen J. Rigsby as Legatee of Sarah Lanrs, (Lain), Estate, Known in said division by lot number Three containing thirty-seven and one-half acres.

Together with all and singular the rights and privileges there-unto belonging or in anywise appertaining to his the said John and his H. forever in fee simple. And the said Allen for himself, his heirs, assigns, the

said bargained land and premises unto the said John, his heirs and assigns will warrant and defend against the claims of all and every person whatsoever by virtue of these presents.

In witness whereof the said Allen J. hath set his hand and seal the day above.

ALLEN J. RIGSBY

Signed, sealed and delivered in the presence of Lorenzo H. Cole.

(Seal)   Egbert B. Beale, J. S. C.

Recorded 8th November, 1833. Book K, Page 221.

1820 Census of Walton county, Georgia shows Allen Rigsby head of family. 1 male under 10, 2 between 10 and 16, 1 between 16 and 18, 2 between 16 and 26 and 1 upwards of 45. Heads of Families coming into Pendleton Dist. S. C., between 1800 and 1810 and leaving before 1820 were John, Wright, Daniel and Susannah Rigsby. These were probably of the same family as Allen Rigsby considering their association with other families which were afterwards associated with Allen Rigsby in Georgia.

All this may or may not indicate decent from Nicholas Rigby, of Savannah. Each person can make his or her own deductions. I am inclined to believe that it does. If this is true there can be no Revolutionary Record and the family were probably Tory sympathizers through the influence of Sir Richard Rigby, a member of the British Paliament and advocate of the measures which precipitated the Revolution.

Daniel Brunson, Patriot, and Wife, Frances Stanton Brunson.

From History of Williamsburg, (S. C.), by Bodie, page 84. "Isaac Brunson's will was proved September 7, 1770. He mentions his wife, Mary; his son Daniel; and his other children —his sons, David, Isaac, Josiah, Matthew, Moses and Joshua; and his daughters, Mary Mellett and Susannah."

Stub entries to indents for Revolutionary Claims, O. Q, page 46 (S. C.). "No 234, Lib. O. Issued the 9th April, 1785 to Mr. Daniel Brunson for two pounds seven shillings and one penny half penny sterling for 33 days

militia duty in 1782 and account audited."

Executive Minutes, 1799-1800 p 491. (MSS Volumns in department of Archives and History, Atlanta, Ga.

"On a recommendation of Robt. Fulwood Esquire J. P. of Jefferson, Ordered.

That passports be prepared for Hugh Garity and Daniel Brunson to go through the Indian Nation unto the Western country. Which were prepared and signed."

In a pamphlet index alphabetically arranged of the residents of Houston county drawing land in the Cherokee Lottery in the office of the Secretary of State, Atlanta, Ga., appears the following entry: "Frances Brunson, Widow of Revolutionary Soldier, of Sinclairs District, Houston county, 60-8-3."

Page 215, Cherokee Land Lottery, published by James F. Smith, 1838, appears the following entry: "60 Frances Bruson, w. r. s., Sinclair's, Houston." This was in 8th District, 3rd Section and shows clearly that the letter "n" was inadvertently left out of the name in printing the Cherokee Lottery.

DANIEL BRUNSON'S WILL

GEORGIA, Houston County.

In the name of God, Amen.

I Daniel Bronson of the county and state aforesaid being in perfectly sound mind and memory I make and ordain this my last will and testament in manner and form as follows (to-wit):

First, it is my desire that all my just debts be paid.

Second, I give and bequeath to the heirs of my daughter Sarah Conyers dec'd One Hundred and fifty dollars to remain in the hands of my executor until they become of age.

Thirdly, I give and bequeath unto my granddaughter, Rachel Rebecca Brunson, One thousand and fifty dollars, also one feather bed and furniture.

Fourthly, I give unto my son, William Brunson a horse supposed to be worth fifty or sixty dollars, also one feather bed; also I give unto my daughter, Elizabeth Brunson, one horse supposed to be worth fifty or sixty dollars, together with one feather bed, and unto my daughter, Mary Brunson I give and bequeath a horse supposed to be worth fifty or sixty dollars and also one feather bed.

Fifthly, the remainder of my property both real and personal to be equally divided between David Brunson, Charlotte Bateman, William S. Brunson, Elizabeth S. Brunson and Mary Brunson, but no division to be made of my property during the life time of my wife, Frances Brunson unless there should be property likely to

be wasted, then and in that case it is my wish and I desire that the same be sold or equally divided as aforesaid as my executors may think best. It is my wish that all of my property be under the immediate care and charge of my executors.

Sixthly, I do hereby nominate and appoint my sons, Daniel Brunson and William S. Brunson together with Simon Bateman, my sole executor of this my last will and testament, and I hereby revoke all wills previously made by me.

In witness whereof I have hereunto set my hand and affixed my seal, this 31st January, 1831.

DANIEL BRUNSON. (Seal)

Signed in the presence of:

ALEX SMITH

David Watson

FREDRICK WATSON, Jr.

GEORGIA, Houston County.

Sept. Term 1831, Ordinary's Court.

In open court appears Alexander Smith and after being duly sworn sayeth on oath that the said Daniel Brunson sign and seal the within as his last will and testament and that he was of sound and disposing mind and that he, said David Watson and Frederick Watson, Jr., assign the same as witnesses with himself.

ALEX SMITH.

Sworn to in open Court, Sept. 5th, 1831.

Charles H. Rice., Clk. C. O. T. & C.

Recorded in Will Book A, pages 69 and 70. Sept. 8th, 1831.

I, Simon Bateman and I, William S. Brunson do somenly swear that this writing contains the true last will of the within named Daniel Brunson, dec'd so far as I know or believe and that I will well and truly execute the same by paying first the debts and then the legacies contained in said will as far as his goods and chattels will thereunto extend and the law charges me, and that I will make a tue and perfect inventory of all such goods and chattels. So help me God.

SIMON BATEMAN

WILLIAM S. BRANSON.

Sworn to in open Court, Sept. 3rd, 1831. Charles H. Rice, Clk., C.O.H.C.

Errata and Addenda To Hardin Hints and Genealogies.

Page 86 names as children of Mark Hardin, Wilils Hardin and George Hardin. There appear to have been no such children. Upon a careful examination of records procured since the above was written, Polly Hardin married a George, and Judith Hardin married a Willis. Parties seduring information thought these family names were names of extra children.

Page 86 . Statement is made that children of Henry Hardin were by his second wife, Matilda Jones. Mr. J. M. Carter, a descendant, of Waco, Texas, 86 years of age writes that children were all by first wife. The statement also comes from others.

Page 87. Lineage of Mrs. Ellen Hardin Walworth is given incorrectly. D. A. R. Lineage Book, Volumn 1, Page 2.

"Mrs. Ellen Hardin Walworth, born in Illinois, daughter of John J. Hardin and Sarah Ellen Smith." This error occurred by reason of an abridgment of MSS.

HARDIN.

Abstract of will of Mark Hardin.

Manasses, County Seat of Prince William Co., Va.

In Book C, page 36 is will of Mark Hardin. To his oldest son John Hardin he leaves 250 acres of land in Pr. Wm. Co. To his son Martin Hardin 200 acres in Pr. Wm. Co. To son Mark Hardin 200 acres in Pr. Wm. Co. "To my son Henry Hardin I give 200 acres of land, it being a part of 300 acres I bought of James McDemile on South side of Kittle Run." If these sons should die without heirs, John, Martin, Mark and Henry, the property goes to the daughters, Ann, Elizabeth and Alis. "It is my will that all my sons and daughter Martha shall have two shillings." "To my dear and beloved wife Mary Hardin, I leave one-third of my property. After her death it is to be equally divided among my five daughters, Abigail, Mary, Ann, Alis and Elizabeth, or their heirs. Sons, John, Martin and wife Mary, Executors.

MARK HARDIN.
Sixteenth day of March, 1734."

VIRGINIA STATE LIBRARY
Department of Archives and History.
Richmond, Va.
Certified Copy of Military Record.

This certifies that in a manuscript volume in the Virginia State Library, which is referred to as "War 4" and which contains the names of the soldiers of the Virginia State line on Continental establishment who received certificates for the balance of their full pay in accordance with an Act of the General Assembly of Virginia, passed at the November, 1781, session, and on page 216 thereof appears che name of Henry Hardin. The entry shows that Henry Hardin was a private of infantry and that on the 18th of June, 1784, William Jennings received for him a certificate for L. O. O. It is not stated from what part of the State Henry Hardin came

H. R. McILWAINE,
State Librarian.

WILL OF HENRY HARDIN

(Son of Mark Hardin, French Emigrant and father of Mary (Hardin) Taliaferro.)

"I, Henry Hardin, of Pittsylvania County, Va., being sick and weak but of perfect mind and memory, do constitute and ordain this to be my last will and testament."

"First, I give my land and plantation whereon I now live, containing 232 acres to my grandson Jimmie Hardin (son of Avarillah Wright) to him and his heirs forever."

"Item—I lend to my wife Judith Hardin the one-half of all my movable estate, be it of whatever nature, kind or quality, during her life and at her death I give the same to my grand son Jimmie Hardin (son of Avarillah Wright), and as to my children, towit: Mary Talifero, Mark Hardin, William Hardin, Elizabeth Wilson, Judith Burgess, Martin Hardin, Henry Hardin, Avarillah Wright and Sarah Burkhalter, I give to each of them two shillings and six pence, to them and their heirs forever.

"Item—I give to my grandson Henry Hardin (son of William Hardin) my patent land, lying on the waters of New River, to him and his heirs forever and lastly I do appoint my sons Martin Hardin and Jimmie Hardin executors to this my last will and testament, hoping they will see the same duly performed as my trust is in them reposed as witness my hand and seal, the 25th May, 1796.

(Signed) HENRY HARDIN.

Teste: (SEAL)
CHARLES CARTER,
JOHN WRIGHT,
WILLIAM BURGESS.

(Evidently son of Henry Hardin above.)

Record taken from old Bible of Henry Hardin who married Catherine Cox.

Sarah, born Sept. 8, 1787.
William, born Feb. 22, 1789.
Mary, born 1790.
Cynthia, born 1792.
Jane, born Dec. 22, 1793.
John, born March 31, 1797.
Mark, born March 31, 1797.
Elizabeth, born May 21, 1799.
Nancy, born May 21, 1800.
James Willborn, born May 21, 1802.
Anna, born January 6, 1804.
Martin, born August 14, 1805.
Catherine, born August 6, 1807 .
Susanna, born April 1, 1809.
Richard T., born Dec. 22, 1812.

GEORGIA, Warren County.

In the name of God, Amen.

I Mark Harden of the state of Georgia and County of Warren, though weak and infirm in body, yet of sound mind and memory, do make, ordain and constitute this to be my last Will and Testament.

1. It is my will and desire that my just debts shall be paid, as early as arrangement can conveniently be made for that purpose.

2. I give and bequeath unto my son Henry Harden, the sum of two dollars, to be paid him by my Executor, within twelve months of or after my decease.

3. I give and bequeath unto my son, Mark Harden the sum of two dollars, to be paid him by my Executors, within twelve months of or after my decease.

4. I give and bequeath unto my son Martin Harden, the sum of two dollars, to be paid him by my Executors, within twelve months after my de-

cease.

5. I give and bequeath unto my son James Harden, the sum of two dollars, to be paid him by my Executors, twelve months of or after my decease.

6. I give and bequeath unto my son John Harden, the sum of two dollars, to be paid him by my Executors, within twelve months of or after my decease.

7. I give and bequeath unto my daughters Polly, George, Judith, Willis, and Sally Harden, the sum of two dollars each, to be paid them by my Executors, within twelve months of or after my decease.

8. All the rest of my property both real and personal, then remaining, I leave unto my beloved wife, Frances Harden, and my two daughters, Patsy Harden and Nancy Harden, and my son William Harden, to be used by them in common, as necessity or convenience may require, until the death or undermarriage of my said wife, Frances. Then it is my will and desire that the whole of Estate then remaining to be equally divided among my three last named children, viz. Patsy Harden, Nancy Harden, and William Harden, to them, their heirs and assigns forever.

9. And lastly, I do constitute and appoint my friends Isiah Tucker, Richard Fletcher, Executors, and my wife, Frances Hardin, Executrix in this my last Will and Testament. Hereby revoking disannulling and setting aside all other Wills, Testament and bequests, ratifying and confirming this as my last Will and Testament.

In witness whereof, I have hereunto set my hand and affixed my seal this thirteenth day of April, 1813, and in the thirty eighth year of the Independence of the United States of America.

MARK HARDEN. (Seal)

Signed, acknowledged and sealed in presence of Winder Hillman, John Sell, Robert Walton.

Georgia, Warren county, Court of Ordinary, November Term 1817.

Personally appeared in open Court, Winder Hillman and Robert Walton and being duly sworn deposeth and saith, that they saw the within named Mark Harden sign, seal, publish and declare the within instrument of writing to be his last Will and

Testament, and at the time of his so doing he was in their opinion of sound and disposing mind and memory, and that they also saw John Sell subscribe the same as a witness together with themselves, and being in his presence, they at his request, in the presence of each other, all became witnesses thereunto.

Sworn and subscribed in open court, the date above written.

Test. M. TORENCE, Clk.

ROBERT WALTON.
WINDER HILLMAN.

Georgia, Warren County.

I, C. M. Smith, Ordinary of said County, do hereby certify that the foregoing is a true copy of Mark Mark Harden Will, as the same appears from the Records in this office.

Given under my hand and seal of said Office, This May 25th, 1927.

C. M. SMITH,
Ordinary, Warren Co. Ga.

Notes from Letters of Miss Willie Reynolds of Barnesville, Ga. Relating to Hardin Genealogy.

She writes:

June 2, 1925

Through my maternal grandmother, Mrs. Matilda Harden Holmes I am descended from Adam Harden, Sr. For some while I have been enthusiastc in my Harden ancestry and I have acquired quite a bit of information in regard to Adam Harden, Sr., which I am willing to exchange. These are some of the things I know to be authentic. Adam Sr, was the first Harden to have a land grant in Georgia. I have a certified copy of his will, the names of all his children, and with two exceptions I have learned who each married, though I have not all the marriage records. Family tradition tells of one brother and a sister Eve, or Erin and among my notes I am almost positive I have her marriage record. Adam Jr., was married twice and I have each of the marriage records. He died in Alabama. Family tradition has always been that Adam's (Sr) father was of the Revolution, if not also Adam himself, and many stirring incidents are family history in this connection. It is also family history that in those exciting days, Adam Sr's wife was as courageous as himself."

June 14, 1925

"I am keenly interested in your last letter and my enthusiasm has new impetus from the data relating to Eve Harden Clay and to her brother Adam Harden, Sr. His Guardianship for one of his sister's children, is new data, but it does not help to solve the one special question as to who were their parents and where was their former

residence. I have never found Adam's marriage record, and as was stated in my former letter, I am now uncertain whether his wife was a Sandlin or Tabor, though our family tradition has been that she was a Tabor. In the pension record of Eve Harden Clay, that at the time of enlistment for Revolutionary service, her husband lived in Duplin Co., N. C. but she was marred in Warren County Georgia. Sometime last year I had correspondence with a Mr. Sandlin, Jasper, Fla., and who wrote that his family came from Duplin County, N. C. I have thought Adam may have married there but have found no record. Now that Eve's husband came from there, this idea becomes stronger. I hope in this search you may come upon this marriage record. I have always thought that Adam's father left a will, which, if could be found would solve and positively settle the question of parentage, but thus far it remains hidden. Valentine Harden was closely related to Adam Sr. but it has never positively determined whether he was a brother or first cousin. It s assumed that when Wm. Henry left home he became a ward or a member of Adam Sr's. household as he and Atkinson Tabor Harden were intimately associated through life; as young men they worked together, married sisters and where Wm. Henry went A Tabor followed and they pioneered, estblished homes and died in the same locality. Willianm Henry's son prominent in Georgia Legislature, was Mark Adam, the Adam for Adam Sr., but for whom the Mark has not been determined. I have had considerable correspondence with a descendant of Valentine, who thinks we have a common ancestor. Valentine Harden was wealthy, I do not know whether in his own right right, or whether from property of his wife. My grandmother said Wm. Henry was her first cousinsin, but a descendant of Valentine, thinks perhaps they were second, any how the kinship was close, and Wm. Henry's children were taught to call Tabor uncle and vice versa, but then they married sisters. **** You say that Eve Harden was born about 1772 and assume that Adam was probably born about 1770. I have always assumed that Adam was born about 1760, so judging from the age given to John Harden, Troup Co. father of my maternal grandmother. He died in 1866 and judging from Adam's will the son, William, was the oldest child, and would have been born about 1781, and while they married young in those days. Then John Harden, Troup Co., commonly called Capt. Jack, which title was acquired from his having served in the war of 1812 at which time he was married and lived in Putnam County, Ga., Adam Jr. was married the first time in 1818."

June 23, 1925

"1 have a decided idea or impression that my grandmother said Adam's father was named John, but I have never found the right John. There was a John Nicholas Harden, Revolutionary soldier of N. C., but this is about all I have learned of him. The descendants of Nicholas Harden (supposed brother of Adam) claim that the father of Nicholas was named William and had a land grant for Revolutionary service. The grant however was to Williiam Hardee,, instead of Harden, and was made in 1816. You have doubtless discovered in your research that there were two Col. Wm. Hardens in S. C. during the revolution; one was with General Marion and is the ancestor of Mr. Wm. Harden, Savannah, and the other died in Franklin County and of whose will I have an abstract, but no Adam or Eve appears in the list of his children. I have the names of children of a Henry Harden (1765) N. C. who married Catherine Cox and the names of his children are almost the same as those of Wm. Harden who died in Franklin County. ****** You say a

Nicholas Harden lived in Shenandoah Co. Va., 1785 with 8 members in family. Would it not be worthwhile to learn the names of these members?"

July 6, 1925

"I am inclined to think Adam came to Georgia without his father, and as his sister Eve was with him and married in Georgiia, his mother may have been a widow and may have come with him. I think I have previously written you that my grandmother said Adam Sr's father was named John. She had a wonderful memory, but as she married young, she could easily have been mistaken.***** He (Adam) was not long in Wilkes County, for in 1790, he had a second grant in Washington County. This grant was on Rocky Comfort Creek, perhaps located in Warren County. Recorded in office of Secretary of State Book SSS page 566. ****** I have had a genealogist, reputed the best in Georgia working for me for about three years, and she also has Nicholas in connection with Adam, but as yet she has been unable to give Adam a father, so sometimes I think he must have been like the first old Adam a full grown man, when he was first known and gave me this vexing research or like Topsy he just growed" ******** Extract from letter of Mrs. Ida S. Lambert, Washington, D. C. a descendant of Valentine Harden and his son William Henry Harden, who was prominent in the early history of Georgia, especially in the treaties with the Indians, many being signed at his home in Bartow County, (then Cass and which William Henry named). The Governor wished to name this county Harden in compliment for the service of Wm. Henry, but being modest, he put the honor aside and called it for Cass, who was a Michigan man, so after the war when Gen. Bartow was killed the name was changed from Cass to Bartow. (She refers to letter from Mrs. Millie Harris to Mrs. Lambert.) In your Clay research have you acquired any information of this Mrs. Millie Harris or her descendants? Mrs. Lambert has been working on her Harden line for many years. **** (She says Miss Willie Ivey sends this item) 'While looking over some old records that my sister had I find on a sheet of paper several names that she must have copied from some Georgia reference book and near the bottom of the list she has this item. "Names omitted from Washington County, Adam Harden. She did not write down the name of the reference book from where she got the names, and I have no idea where she found them, but they were evidently names of Revolutionary soldiers. This is the only hint I have of Adam Hardin living in Washington County. ***** Miss Ivey wrote that her sister died some years ago.

July 12, 1925

"In looking over some old records I find this note: "The Hardins came from Scotland about 1700" which will perhaps strengthen your idea that Adam and Eve were of Welsh descent. I imagine that this note was given by some descendant of Adam Harden Jr., as I had corresponded with a party who was making research for his descendants."

Aug. 4, 1925

"The Adam Harden who lived in Sumter County and went from there to Florida was a son of Nicholas and not of Adam Harden Sr., John and Adam Jr., sons of Adam Sr., left Putnam County and went to Monroe County Georgia where they lived several years, and then both went to the young county of Troup, then just established. Both are mentioned in White's statistics as among the early settlers there. John or Capt. Jack as he was commonly called remained, established a home, and was one of the wealthiest and most prominent men of that section of the state. Adam, Jr., on account of the bad health of his wife went to Alabama where his wife died and he married a second time in Lee county, Ala., and there he lived and died about 1872. I have heard that this Adam who went to Florida (son of Nicholas) became quite wealthy."

Aug. 13, 1925.

"Henry Hardin who married Judith Lynch was brother of Martin who married Lydia Waters, and I believe there was also a brother Mark who went to the Carolinas and who it is said was lost sight of.****** "There was a John Nicholas Hardin who was a Revolutionary soldier in N. C. His name was given me by the Secretary of the North Carolina Historical Commission and I tried to get his military record from Washington, D. C., failed and not feeling that a search in N. C. would aid in establishing Adam's parentage I did not make a thorough search of this John Nicholas Hardin's Revolutionary record."

Aug. 26, 1925

"Adam had his grant of land in Wilkes County in 1789, two years after the death of Col. William in 1787, and it is evident his sister Eve was with his family. As I have previously written, I am of the opinion the old records, if any, in Wlkes County wolud furnish more information concerning Adam Harden than those in Washington county, as the first grant was in Wilkes. In May, I had a letter from a Mrs. Davidson, Quitman, who wrote: "If Adam Harden did not actually live in Georgia prior to 1786, he had a grant of land. I have proof of this, but no record of the grant. Maybe some day it will come to light. It was probably a Revolutionary grant too, but that will have to be proven."

Sept 24, 1925

In this letter she doubts that David Clay lost an eye in connection with the defense of the Hardin family during the revolution as she had never heard this tradition from Adam's descendants.

April 4, 1926

Miss Reynolds advises that she has been sick, but is enclosing a sketch of the family of Adam Hardin; same information as in Hardin Hints and Genealogies.

May 2, 1926.

In this letter Miss Reynolds advises that Henry Harden died in Walton County and not in Warrenton as given by me and as taken from sketch of Martin B. Harden as published in Georgia Baptist. She says further that children were by first wife Sarah Cook. This statement is also substantiated in a letter from J. M. Carter, of Waco, Texas. I presume they are correct but it appears strange that a son by first wife should have been named Edward Jones Hardin.

May 23, 1926

"According to notes which I have from Nicholas Harden's descendants the John Harden who went to Tennessee, was a brother of Nicholas. I am told this John went to Tennessee and there married, and then went further West, amassing considerable property. I would not be surprised, however, if John weren't a son, instead of a brother of Nicholas. My informant said this John Harden went from Washington County, Ga., to Tennessee. Nicholas had a son Adam who went to Quincy, Florida, according to the same correspondent."

Jan. 31, 1926.

"My grandmother and her sisters were considered beautiful women, and John Harden, son of Adam Harden, Sr., is said to have been a strikingly handsome man, and they were thrifty folks and exceedingly neat."

April 19, 1926.

"In the copy I have of Adam Hardin, Sr's will,, the name is spelled throughout Hardin. My grandmother always, however spelled it Harden and until you asked about the will, I had never particularly noticed about the spelling. The descendants of Nicholas Harden with whom I have been associated, spell the name Hardin and so are the court records in Monroe County."

May 10, 1926

"Our family tradition is that Adam Harden's father was a John Harden and lived in Virginia, but tradition is not fact."

Statement prelminary to next letter: In the latter part of May 1926, I was in Columbus Georgia in attendance upon the Grand Lodge of Odd Fellows: From correspondence which I had had I was able to locate a great-grand daughter of Adam Hardin, Sr., by his son Adam. I had a long conversation with this lady relating to her grandfather's family, that is Adam Harden, Jr's., and from her learned that she had an uncle John Wesley Harden and from what she told me I thought it quite probable that this was the John Wesley Harden, so celebrated in the Western desperado lore. So I wrote to Miss Reynolds suggesting that she had very probably been handicapped in her search by this fact. The next letter is her reply.

May 31, 1926.

"Yours of the 28th just received and I am keenly interested to know who is John Wesley Harden, of whom I have never previously heard. Adam Harden, Sr., mentions a son John in

his will, but not John Wesley. This son was my grandmother's father, one of the pioneer citizens of Troup Co., Ga. He was commonly called Captain Jack Harden, having acquired this title from having been a soldier in the war of 1812 at which time he was living in Putnam County, Georgia, from which he went to the new county of Troup, where he lived and died an honorable and upright citizen. I have never heard anything dishonorable connected with him or with his family. He had one son John Harden, who lived also in Troup County, but I have never heard of any "Wesley" attached to his name or anything disreputable connected with his life, so I am quite at sea and fail to understand why you say "I have been handicapped in my investigations by reason of John Wesley Harden." Please to explain who he was and how he was connected with my ancestor, John Harden. In all my search and correspondence, this is the first hint I have ever had concerning John Wesley Harden, and naturally my curiosity is excited and stimulated to learn further. You say there is a published history of his life. Have you this history, and how and where is one obtainable. I am keenly interested to read it. Please to tell me ail you know of this John Wesley Harden, and the history of his life. Who is his sister and where is she living. If she is a grand daughter of Adam Harden, Sr., she surely is a very old woman, so I am strongly inclined to think in this particular you are mistaken. As a rule a family cannot keep concealed disreputable facts concerning any one member, for some one is ever only too ready to tell of the Black sheep in any family. The good men do is often interred with their bones, but the evil they do, surely lives after them. Again, if there is a published history of the life of John Wesley Harden, I do not see why his sister should try to repress any facts, if these have already been published and put before the public I should not think there wouuld be any thing to suppress, or any thing to cover up or repress any thing for there is some one to remember and colorfully relate unpleasant or undesired facts. This is human nature, and a characteristic never entirely quenched and trampled underfoot. ***** Surmises do not so much interest me, for I want facts, something solid and positive to build upon, and generally surmises do not amount to much. I do not think because Eve Harden married in Warren county, Georgia proves she was a near relative of Mark Harden, and I hardly think there is a close relationship between these two families. There was a time, however when I wondered if Adam, Sr. may not have been a younger brother of Mark of Warren County. I never found anything to substantiate this idea so I put it aside as hardly probable. My grandmother used to say Adam Harden, Sr. had a brother Mark, but as no Mark ever appeared in our line, and I could find nothing to prove her statement, I have concluded she was probably mistaken, though she had a wonderful memory.

I wish you success, wherever your search may lead, and I am keenly eager to learn all I may of this notorious John Wesley Harden."

The remainder of these letters contain no new information not given elsewhere by documents and as Miss Reynolds health was rapidly failing she ceased to manifest any interest after December, 1926, although I continued sending her the results of my search. In order to give all information in my hands relating to John Wesley Harden, I submit information obtained from his sister and on file in my office.

Correspondence With Mrs. E. I. Howard, Granddaughter of Adam Hardin, Senior.

About the first of May 1926 Mrs. Howard sent me the following information on questionnaires sent to her with request for information. Adam Hardin, born in Putnam County, Ga. (nearest she knows) May 15th, 1800. Died in Lee County, Alabama, 1887 and is buried in cemetery at Auburn, Ala., married first Priscilla Adams, second Ann Elizabeth Fleming. Priscilla Adams Hardin buried at Auburn, Ann Elizabeth Flemming Harden buried at Tuskegee, Ala. She says her mother preferred being buried there where she (Mrs. Howard had cared for her twenty years). Her father, Adam Hardin was twice married, his first wife a Miss Adams.

To them were born eleven children, all dead—James Hardin, H. H. Hardin, Miles Hardin, Thomas Huston Hardin, Adam Hardin, Elizabeth Hardin, June Hardin, Fletcher Hardin and two daughters who died in young womanhood and also a small son. All were buried in Auburn cemetery. Says she has hoped to go there and get names and dates from tombs. His 2nd wife (mother of writer) was Ann Elizabeth Fleming, of Talbotton, Ga. They had six children (names are not very legible but appear to be) Efin Iola Hardin, Adam Sandlin Hardin, Tabor Fleming Hardin, J. Wesley Hardin, Maytie Floy Hardin, and infant. Adam Hardin's wife lives in Miami, Fla. He is dead. They had several children. Tabor F. Hardin a Methodist minister died early, was very promising, having graduated from college in Auburn, with highest honors. Wesley died in Texas. Maytie F. Hardin married Prof. P. D. Arilson (?). They have one child, Mary Flemming Arilson. Address is Ruston, La.

Upon receipt of this information and after conversation with her daughter, I immediately wrote her in regard to John Wesley Hardin and received the following reply:

Tuskegee, Ala., June 4, 1926.
My dear Mr. Rigsby:

Have been slow in answering your letter which I surely appreciate. At the time of its reception, was in the country with a son and his family—several little children—and impossible to concentrate on a reply. First I will tackle the information regarding John Wesley Hardin. The notorious John Wesley was not my brother, whether related, I do not know. My father may have, but died about the time of his famous career. My brother was born in Dallas, Texas about 1867, Sept. 6th. We had moved to that state the year following the close of the Civil war, living nearly a year in Smith county, Johnstown, then moved to Dallas county. Dallas where we lived about four years. My brother was named for the founder of Methodism. My father a staunch Methodist, so all his children were and are. My brother was about 4 years old when we returned to Alabama, Auburn, there he was raised to young manhood. He had an unsettled roving nature which my mother attributed to pre-natal influence. He was never a bad man, though unsuccessful, always in need or being constantly helped by members of his family. He died in the southern part of the state near San Antonio about thirteen years ago, of tuberculosis. How different children of the same family can be. History is always repeating itself. There will always be Cain and Abel, Jacob and Esau:

You may grind them each in the self same mill,
You may bind them heart and brow,
The first will follow the rainbow still,
The other will follow the pow."

There is a good deal more to this letter which must be omitted for lack of space. The letter gives the highest evidence of culture and breeding as well as integrity and convinces me that her brother John Wesley Hardin is not the same person as the notorious John Wesley Harden and this letter is given to correct any misunderstanding that may arise in later years.

Note From Letters from Mrs. Rosamonde Hardin Bogle.

February 24, 1926.

"Nicholas has been the cause of trouble in clearing up my line also, but I will give you the meager information I possess:

"My father, Thomas J. Hardin was the son of William Reeves Hardin. William Reeves, the son of James M. Hardin; James M., the son of Nicholas. No dates known other than James Monroe Hardin, born 1797, died August 6, 1862. Nicholas had a brother, William and a sister, Evie, according to an aunt, who is now dead."

She proceeds to give other information which is included in Hardin Hints and Genealogies and for this reason not repeated here.

April 21, 1926.

"The only information I can get of John Hardin is contained in a letter from my father's cousin, Joe Daniel, of Tennille, Ga., (now dead) in which he says one of the Hardin brothers (the brother of James Monroe) was named John. He was Clerk of Ohoopee Church several years before he moved to Alabama and I feel sure that he lived on the land granted to his father in Washington county as a Revolutionary soldier. His mother was also member of Ohoopee Church. We remember her as Grandma Albritton. You remember she lived with Grandma Smith until she died. This must have been that the widow of Nicholas Hardin married an Albritton as my Grandmother Smith was Sara Hardin."

In this connection I have found that an Albritton returned the land of the children of Nicholas Hardin for taxes in Washington county, Georgia about 1830. Record in the department of Archives, Atlanta, Ga.

Bremerton, Washington, Puget Sound, Navy Yard, Feb. 7th, 1917.

These are the salient facts of a number of letters I have received. I collected these items as they were given me by parties who were posted. The expense of carrying so much paper decided me to condense all in this book. Data of my forebears.

(These are Mrs. Ida Spullock Lambert's Notes:)

Valentine Hardin married Margaret Castleberry about 1790. They lived in Washington Co., Ga. Valentine had the first shingled roof house in the county. Valentine and Margarette children: Rhoda, born in March 12th, 1796, died 1868, married Carter Crew. They lived near Dallas, Georgia. Sallie married James Dowdy. Polly married John Barton, Jackson county, Ga., Jan. 14, 1808. William Henry Hardin, born Jan. 29th, 1798 in Washington County, Ga. nine miles from Sandersville, Ga., married Nancy Cloud, Sept. 21st, 1820 in Putnam county, Ga. She was born in 1800, died 1864, buried in Clay county. William H. Hardin died in 1854 in Bartow county, Ga., buried in the Spullock plot in Rome, Ga. Valentine died in 1800, buried near his home in Washington county, Ga. After his death his widow married Wm. Warren. She died near Carrolton, Carroll county, Ga., in 1850. William Hardin in war 1812.

This data from Miss or Mrs. Camilla H. Davis dated April 6th,, 1900, address 111 Ewing Ark., Oak Cliff, Texas. Her great-grandfather, William Hardin was born in Virginia 1741. He also lived in North Carolina and probably Georgia. Had married Sarah Bledsoe, either Va. or N. C.

Their children, Bledsoe, Henry, Mark, Swan, Richard and Martin. Martin lived and died on ~~Dark~~ River, Tenn. She thinks that William Hardin died about 1810 in Franklin county, Ga. while living with his youngest son, Richard. His wife lived to be 107 years old, buried at College Hill, Miss. His sons, Henry and Bledsoe, died in N. C. Martin lived and died on Duck River, Tenn., each leaving chidlren. Two of the descendants of this family, William and Calloway, were with Gen. Jackson in his Indian wars. Her great grandfather, Col. William Hardin was in the war of 1776, serving with General Francis Marrion. Her grandfather was Swan Hardin, who moved to Texas, 1837, died soon after he moved. He left five sons. Mrs. Davis is the daughter of his second son, Franklin. She asked me if Col. Mark Hardin, my kinsman. Hardins settled in Georgia. Adam in Wilkes Co., 1789, moved to Washington county, 1797. John ,Franklin county, 1797. Martin, Warren county, 1801. Mark, Franklin county, 1806. William, Warren county, 1802. Edward, Screven county, 1805. Martin, Tatnal county, 1810. Henry Warren 1814. William Franklin, 1815. Isaac B. Burk, 1802. * * * * * * * Letter dated Feb. 11th, 1899 from Mrs. Millie Harris, Sandersville, Ga. Mrs. Harris was 75 years old. Her grandfather was Nick Hardin, who is buried at the Hardin burrying ground. She said she had two uncles buried there, one Nick Hardin and one Wm. Hardin. Her grandfather, Nick had one sister named Evie. Mrs. Harris' mother was Mary Hardin and married Wm. Clay. U. S. Senator Clay was from this family. * * * Letter dated April 6th, 1903. This information is from John or Jack Hardin's dather, Adam Hardin's son. She is now 80 years old. Letter written by her granddaughter, Barnesville, Ga. She says her grandfather Adam Hardin came direct from Virginia to Georgia with his family to Putnam county. Eatonton, their market. Adam married a Miss Taber. She was a young lady during the wear of 1776, spun and wove her wedding dress which was of flax." * * * * "Grandma says she well remembers her grandfather Adam Hardin coming to see them in Troupe. She said he was

very handsome and her father, John or Jack. She thinks her father and William Hardin were first cousins. She says she remembers once his bringing to their house a sick daughter with which he was traveling hoping to restore her health. He also had his son, Mark. From her home in Troupe he went to Columbus, Ga., where he had two married daughters, one a Mrs. Spullock. Again she remembers this Mrs. Spullock and her sister making a short visit to their home and she thinks that Mrs. Spullock lives at Rome, Ga. Says her grandfather had a brother, Nick, who lived in Va. * * * Letter from Harperville, Miss., Feb. 26th, 1904. From B. R. Haralson. His mother's name was Jane Hudson Hardin, named for her Uncle Hudson Hardin, son of Adam Hardin, his grandfather, John Hardin died 1867 or 8, 83 years old so he was born 1783 or 84. His mother was born in Putnam, county, Ga., March 1st, 1814. His ancestors were from Virginia. He says they took part in the war of 76 and had property destroyed by the Tories of that date. Aunt said and wrote me Grandfather Wm. Hardin was Clerk of Court of Henry county, McDonough, Ga. Was Indian agent. Help to remove the Cherokee Indians from north Georgia to their reservation west of the Mississippi. In his latter days was a successful planter. (Here follows a letter from Mark A. Hardin contradictory) * * * Letter from J. W. George, Yazoo City, Miss., dated Dec. 16, 1890. He is the son of U. S. Senator George. He is descended from Mary Hunter Hardin.

Rome Tribune-Herald of March 29, 1912 carried notice of the death of Judge J. H. Spullock. Quoting: "Judge Spullock is survived by one daughter, Mrs. R. J. Bell, of Chattanooga, who arrived in Rome last night; and four sisters, Mrs. Ida S. Lambert and Miss Fannie Spullock, of Rome; Mrs. J. E. Murphey, of Portland, Ore., and Mrs. J. K. Butler, of Nova Scotia.

"His father was James M. Spullock, one of the early settlers of this city, and afterwards mayor of Rome. His grandfather was William Hardin and bore the name James Hardin Spullock."

The Morning Tribune, Knoxville, Tenn., Sunday, November 21, 1897 carried an article entitled Original Aristocracy, etc., in which appears the following: As early as June 23, 1833, Tomlinson Fort who then resided at Milledgeville, Ga., B. B. Hargrove, William Soloman, Thomas W. Harris and John Martin, who then resided at Cartersville, Ga. and the same parties with William Harden bought and sold lands in north Georgia.

The Henry County Weekly in its issue of May 13, 1921, carried an article by Scip Speer from which I quote: "The first house built in the town of McDonough was occupied by William Hardin, situated on the north-west corner of the public square. As far back as 1825 the residences were rudely furnished with home-made furniture. For a long time William Hardin owned the only furniture of any consequence in the town. This set was purchased at Charleston, S. C., for $1,000 and hauled by wagon from there to this place. From a clipping which I am unable to identify I take the following. Speaking of Judge James M. Spullock, "He shortly after wooed and wed the daughter of Col. Wm. Hardin who, with Col. Hargrove, were the leading men of the Cherokee country, then just settling up with a white population.

LAST WILL AND TESTAMENT OF
JOHN HARDIN, DECEASED.
GEORGIA, Oglethorpe County.

IN THE NAME OF GOD AMEN: I, John Hardin, of the county of Oglethorpe and said state of Georgia, of sound mind and memeory, blessed be God the extending mercy, knowing that it is appointed for all men to die, and has pleased God to bless me with some of this world's treasures, shall dispose of it in the following manner, viz:

Item—I leave my crop of cotton that is now on hand to pay all my just debts and the use of my family.

Item—I give to my dear beloved wife, Sally Hardin, one negro man, Peter, one hundred dollars, a horse and saddle, bed and furniture.

I lend to my wife, Sally Hardin, the tract of land, I said Hardin, now live, while she ever remains my widow, for the use of herself and the legatees that live with her.

Item—I lend to my beloved wife, until July and Franklin becomes of

age, in case she remains the said Hardin's widow, I lend one negro man, Andrew, one negro man Ben Curtis, and one negro man, Ben Moss, one boy, Joseph, one negro woman, Charity, one negro woman Massy, for the use and support and schooling the children and raising the family.

Item—I leave the tract of land near Lexington to be sold, when convenient, and the money equally divided betwixt my wife, Sally Hardin, and all the legatees.

Item—I give to my beloved daughter, Elizabeth Hardin, one negro girl, Louisa, one negro boy, Louis, one bed and furniture, one horse, saddle and bridle, one cow and calf and two sheep

Item—I give to my beloved daughter, Polly Powell, one negro girl, Jenny, one negro boy, Adam, one bed and furniture, one horse and bridle and saddle, one cow and calf and two sheep.

Item—I give Martha Hardin one negro boy, Benager, one negro girl, Fanny, one bed and furniture, one cow and calf and two sheep, one horse, bridle and saddle.

Item—I leave Lucinda Hardin, my beloved daughter, one negro girl, Cisser, one boy, Washington (in case his eye sight fails him), I leave her George, one bed and furniture, one cow and calf, two sheep, one horse, bridle and saddle.

Item—I leave Permelia Hardin, my beloved daughter, one negro girl, Emily, one negro boy, Terrell, one bed and furniture, one cow and calf, two sheep, one horse, bridle and saddle.

Item—I give my son Benjamin Hardin, one negro girl, Easter, one negro boy Judge, one bed and furniture, one cow and calf, two sheep, one horse, bridle and saddle.

I give to my son, Jno. B. Hardin, one negro boy, Clark, and one negro girl from the estate, one bed and furniture, one cow and calf, two sheep, one horse, bridle and saddle.

Item—I leave to my daughter Caroline, July and Franklin, one negro boy, Van, and she will have a girl from my estate, one cow and calf, two sheep, one horse bridle and saddle.

Item—I leave the plantation and kitchen furniture and the stock and house furniture to my wife and the legatees as it is necessary to keep.

Item—I do further say that, my

182

wife, in case she remains my widow, take out three negroes, such as she may think most proper, and the remainder part of the negroes be equally divided when July and Franklin is twelve years of age.

Item—I lend my wife, Sally Hardin, one negro woman, Aley, until a division takes place.

Item—I give to Frank, a yellow boy, his freedom so long as he lives from the twenty-fifth day of December, 1815.

Item—I give to Linsey, a yellow boy, his freedom so long as he lives from the twenty-fifth day of December, 1815.

Item—I give to Minnie, a yellow girl, her freedom as long as she lives from the twenty-fifth day of December, 1815.

Item—This being my last will and testament made in the year of our Lord, January 29th, 1815. I appoint Joseph Walker and Whittaker Powell my Executors.

JOHN HARDIN (Seal)
Henry Blake
Robert Holmes,
John Holmes, witnesses.

LAST WILL AND TESTAMENT OF SALLY HARDIN, DECEASED
GEORGIA, Oglethorpe County.

I, Sally Hardin, of the County and State aforesaid, do make and ordain this my last will and testament in the following manner—(viz)

Item 1st. I give and bequeath to my daughter, Elizabeth Hardin, a negro girl named Minny to her forever, and one bay mare.

Item 2nd. I give to my son, Benjamin Hardin, one negro man named Frank, and a young sorrell mare to him and his heirs forever.

Item 3rd. I give to my son Jno. R. Hardin, a negro man named Lindsey, and a sorrell horse colt to him and his heirs forever.

Item 4th. I give to my daughter, Caroline Quilian Franklin Hardin, a bed and furniture which was left me by the will of John Hardin, deceased.

Item 5th. The balance of my estate, both real and personal, consisting of a negro man named Peter, a tract of land drawn by me in the late land lottery, my household and kitchen furniture equally divided between Elizabeth Hardin, Benjamin Hardin, and John B. Hardin.

And lastly I leave my son-in-law, Abraham J. Hill, my executor to this my last will and testament. In testimony whereof I have hereunto set my hand and seal, this third day of February, 1823.

SALLY HARDIN. (Seal)
Attest:
Elisha Trammell.
David Robison,
Christopher Bowen, J. I. C.

Col. William Harden's Branch

From a bible now belonging to the descendants of Henry Harden, of Bryan County, Ga.

On the first fly-leaf are the autographs of James Habersham and Charles Harden. To the signature of the latter are added these words:
"Presented to him by his mother, Mary Harden, March 1st in the year 1793."
On the second fly-leaf: "1822. Charles and Henry Harden's Bible."

Family Record.

William Harden (My great-great-grandfather. W. H.) son of William Harden and his wife Agnes (My great great-great-grandfather and great-great-greatgrandmother. I do not know the surname of Agnes, nor can I go farther back than his record in any particular. W. H.) was born November 23rd, in the year of our Lord 1720, and deceased Sept. 12, 1760, aged 39 years, 9 months and 19 days.

Mary Eberson, daughter of Thos. E. and Mary, his wife, born Dec. 13th, 1724. Wm. Harden and Mary Eberson were married July 15th, 1742.

William Harden (The Colonel, my great-grandfather. W. H.) son of Wm. and Mary, his wife born Nov. 8, 1743, and deceased Nov. 28th, 1785 aged 42 years and 20 days.

Thos. Harden, son of Wm. and Mary his wife, born Sept. 8th, 1745, and deceased Sept. 14th, 1747, aged two years and six days.

Rebekah Harden, daughter of Wm. Harden and Mary, his wife, born Dec. 17th, 1747, departed this life June 10, 1806, aged 59 years, 5 months, 23 days. (She married Thomas White. W. H.)

Susannah Harden, daughter of Wm. Harden and Mary, his wife, born April 6th, 1749, and deceased Sept. 12, 1761, aged 12 years, five months and six days.

—

Elizabeth Harden, daughter of Wm. Harden and Mary, his wife, born March 30, 1754, deceased July 24, 1789, aged 35 years, 3 months and 24 days.

Elizabeth Harden, daughter of Wm and Mary his wife, born March the 30, 1754, and deceased July, 24th, 1789, aged 35 years, 3 months and 24 days.

Edward Harden, son of Wm. and Mary his wife, born Aug. 17th, 1757, departed this life July 11th, 1804, aged 46 years, 10 months and 24 days.

Henry Harden, son of Charles and Elizabeth his wife, was born May the 12th, 1783 and died April 30th, 1817, in the 35th year of his age.

Charles Harden and Elizabeth Miles (formerly Hunt) married July 30, 1782.

Charles Harden, son of Chas and Elizabeth, born Aug. 9, 1788, died March 15, 1815.

It is not necessary to bring this record down to a more recent date. Col. Wm. Harden had a son William, by this first wife Sarah..............., and it is possible that he had others; but it seems that only William was living at the time of his father's death. His first wife died some time between the year 1775 and the year 1777. He married the second time the widow of John Perkins who was born Sarah Cussings and married, first, John Perkins, and after his death Col. Wm. Harden.

By his second marriage Col. Wm. Harden had a daughter who died young, and three sons; Charles Murray Harden, Edmund Bellinger Harden, and Thomas Hutson Harden who was born after the death of his father, and was my grandfather.

WM. HARDEN.

The estate of Martin Harden, deceased in account with

Cash Paid To	Voucher No.	Amt.
Clk Court of Ordinary	1	$ 8.31
E. W. Doubleday	2	7.12
Craig & Daffin	3	23.44
B. M. Shaw Tax Collector	4	32.08
Hunt & Thomas	5	115.70
D. M. Whaley	6	13.00

George King for latter for use of plantation	7	5.10
For gathering stock	8	219.00
E. H. Kemp	9	5.00
Paid J. Donalson & Co., for negro clothing	10	179.95
Columbus Engineer office	11	5.50
N. Harley	12	138.86
Expenses of hands when gathering stock		15.00

Commissions on 768.06 paid out $19.20
Commissions on $2243.20 Received $56.07 — $75.27

John Harden, Adminstrator from the 13 July, 1838 until 31 Oct. inclusive.

By cash on hand at the death of the intestate as mentioned in the appraisement	$1448.25
By Cash collected of	
B. Crawford on note	97.20
B. Crawford on interest	9.00
W. T. Crawford on note	103.53
H. G. Crawford on note	108.66
W. H. Owens note and int.	1050.00
I. W. Keith	200.00
Perishable property	226.56

Sworn to and subscribed in open court.

JOHN HARDEN.

ATTEST: A. D. Smart, C. C. O.

The estate of Martin Harden, deceased in account with

To Cash Paid	Voucher No.	Amt.
M. L. and L. L. Harden	1	$2985.00
Richard Fletcher, Attorney for Sarah Harden	2	3162.00
Mark Harden, Attorney for Mark Harden	3	3338.85
F. Gorden, Attorney for Henry Harden	4	3162.00
William Young	5	3162.00
William G. Harden, Attorney for Martha and Jacob Garrard	6	3162.00
William G. Harden	7	3162.00
O. M. Whaley	8	64.25
William G. Harden	9	3292.00
W. H. Harden, Attorney for Clark Blandford	10	3162.00
Joseph Irwin	11	51.00
Isaac Brunson	12	300.00
Harden and Taylor	13	162.23
Inlow Evans	14	26.00
Hill and Danson	15	16.75
Lott Warren	16	50.00
C. B. Strong	17	50.00
J. Donalson & Co.	18	87.79
B. Crawford	19	54.33

N. Hanley	20	253.54
I. I. Williams	21	1.50
W. W. Hair	22	305.50
Moses Shaw	23	10.00
H. Manley	24	2.50
C. B. Strong	25	51.00
B. M. Shaw	26	20.50
A. D. Smart	27	11.75
Steam Boat Ellin	28	10.75

John Harden, Admr. from the 1st Jan. 1839 to 31st October, inclusive.

By balance on hand from	$1399.87
By cash received from sale of negroes, cotton, etc.	32169.94
By cash on notes and accounts	4132.37
By cash from Joseph Irwin on book account	33.08

Sworn to and subscribed in open court.

JOHN HARDEN, Admr.

ATTEST: A. D. Smart, C .C. O.

The estate of Martin Harden, deceased in account with John Harden his Administrator from 1st January, 1840 to 31st. December, inclusive

To Cash paid	Vou. No	Amt
William Young	1	$1326.32
Sarah Harden	2	1000.00
W. W. Garrard	3	1000.00
M. D. Harden for the hands of James Harden	4	400.00
John Harden	5	1000.00
Thomas A. Brown	6	1000.00
C. B. Strong, Attorney for estate	7	50.00
L. T. Bailey, Attorney for estate	8	50.00
Clark Blandford	9	500.00
Clark Blandford	10	500.00
May George	11	1000.00
Joseph Irwin	12	6.37
A. D. Smart	13	1.25
Thomas Bush	15	1.00
N. Manley	16	98.03
R. A. I. Rolley	17	500.00
A. D. Smart	18 ·	2.00
William Chapman	19	5.00
Taxes	20	20.07
C. B. Strong, Atty	21	100.00
S. T. Bailey	22	100.00
Henry Harden	25	1000.00
R. C. Sommege	26	1.00
M. A. Pattot	27	12.00
Recorders office	28	25.00

Sworn to and subscribed in open court May Term, 1840. JOHN HARDEN
A. D. SMART, C. C. O.
The estate of Martin Harden deceased in account current with John Harden, from 1st. January, 1843 to 31st December, inclusive.

1842   To Amount Paid

Date	Vou. No.	Amt.
Mch. 8. C. Blandford	1	$200.00

1843   To Amount Paid

Date	Vou. No.	Amt.
Dec. 14. C. C. Young	2	39.50
Dec. 18. Robert Myers	3	15.37
Feb. 25. Martin N. Garrard	4	140.00
Nov. 25. Martin N. Garrard	5	50.00
Dec. 9. Conway Smith	6	50.00

Apr. 4. To amount paid John P. Gaulden commissions for collecting which receipts should have been returned but has been overlooked·as per voucher number   7 90.10

Sworn to and subscribed before me, this 19th day of February, 1844.

HOHN HARDEN, Admr.

ATTEST: John P. Dickenson, C. C. O.
1844. The estate of Martin Harden deceased in account with John Harden, his Administrator, from January 1st, 1841 to December 31st, inclusive.

Date.	Vou. No.	Amt.
Oct. 9. Samuel Gaines, com. for collecting	1	$34.19
Apr. 23. Hayes & Crosland com. for collecting	2	40.00
Feb. 26. S. T. Bailey com. for collecting	3	100.00
Apr. 27. C. C. Strong com. for collecting	4	100.00
Hayes &Crosland com for collecting	5	22.50
Tax for year 1841	6	2.53
Oct. 6. Isaac R. Harris	7	6.05
Feb. 22. John M. Caine	8	7.50
Aug. 29. Warren & Wardman	9	8.00
James & Coon	10	6.75
Oct. 16. I Faryerson, Jr. collecting fee	11	10.00
Oct. 9. Warren & Wardman	12	32.00
To Thos M. Bush Clk Jackson Co.		
Sept. 29.	13	3.00
Nov. 13	14	3.43
Nov. 13.	15	3.43
Nov. 13.	16	5.50
Nov. 13.	17	13.61
Nov. 13.	18	3.43
Nov. 13.	19	3.43
Aug. 31. C. W. Dupont	20	254.23
D. Harrell	21	667.60
Wann & Scarborough amt. of cost in the case of Pipi Mobley for the account of John Harden	22	1767.00

Sworn to and subscribed before me this 2nd day of May 1842.

JOHN HARDEN

A. D. Leonard, C. C. O.

The estate of Martin Harden, deceased, in account current with John Harden, Administrator from Jan. 1st, 1844 to July 1st 1845.

To Cash paid	Vou. No	Amt
Thos Baltzell, Atty.	1	$2992.14
Martha N. Garrard	2	522.00
A. G. Semuns, Atty.	3	631.00
A. G. Semuns, Atty.	4	100.00
R. Myers (Marshall)	5	65.00
R. Myers (Marshall)	6	22.75
R. Myers (Marshall)	7	32.71
R. Myers (Marshall)	8	19.91
Wm. P. Duval, Atty (in Florida money)	9	200.00
George T. Ward	10	60.00
Wm. L. Durham	11	50.00
C. C. Young, Atty.	12	150.75
A. W. Sneed	13	25.00
Ben G. Alderman	14	10.43
Tax for 1844	16	7.83
A. D. Smart	17	4.50
F. R. Pittman	18	3.25
R. C. Lunency, Clk. Tatnell County	19	5.00
St. Joseph Sims	20	8.00
F. R. Pittman	21	2.00
Rich K. Long	22	3.00
F. R. Pittman	23	2.00
A. A. Allen, Atty.	24	3.45
A. A. Allen, Atty.	25	32.00
Robt. Myers, Marshall	26	43.00
A. A. Allen, Atty.	27	20.00
A. A. Allen, Atty.	28	20.00
A. A. Allen, Atty.	29	20.00
Mary George	30	3162.00
Clerk C. L.	31	5.00
A. A. Allen	32	17.75
I. P. Gaulden, Atty.	33	1152.84
A. A. Allen	34	9.50
Jno R. Hayes	35	407.52
John Harden (distributed) as per voucher	36	6454.00
Heirs of Jas. Harden	37	615.23
W. G. Macon, exr. of M. L. Harden	38	153.80
Guardian for minor heirs of Blanford	39	200.00
Judith Young (by atty)	40	200.00
Sarah Harden " "	41	200.00

Sworn to and subscribed in open court July Term, 1845.

JOHN HARDEN

ATTEST: John P. Dickenson, C. C. O.

The estate of Martin Harden, deceased in account current with John Harden, his Administrator, from Jan. 1st, 1842 to December 1842.

Cr. This amount paid on the judgment obtained by Jesse Scott or Martin

Harden as per voucher no	1	$5676.58
Dec. 20 paid J. Long	2	385.00
Jan. 1 paid C. Blanford	3	300.00
Nov. 16 Martha Garrard	4	330.00
Jan. 5 C. Blanford	5	300.00
Aug 12 Mary George	7	1301.00
Aug. 2 Henry Harden	6	400.00
Mch. 8 L. L. Harden	8	300.00
Mch. 5 Jacob Garrard and Martha Ann Guardian by Attorney	9	1250.00
Mch. 3 Elias H. Kemp	10	50.59
July 6. F. Dickenson	11	1.37
Mch. 3. E. W. Kemp, shf.	12	39.22
Mch. 6 Paid D. Wamle	13	3.75

DR. By Amount Collected $10737.49

Sworn to and subscribed before me this 23rd day of January, 1843.

JOHN HARDEN, Admr.

ATTEST: A. D. Smart, C. C. O.

Est of Martin Harden deceased in account with John Harden, Admr.

To Cash Paid	Vou. No.	Amt.
Mary George	1	$992.00
Judith Young	2	300.00
R. R. and S. B. Hines and S. T. Bailey	3	390.00
A. A. Allen	4	92.00
A. A. Allen and M. W. Sneed	5	50.00
I. P. Dickenson, Clerk Court of Ordinary	6	7.25
I. P. Dickenson, Clerk Court of Ordinary	7	1.12
Marshall for land tax	8	7.83
Marshall for land tax for 1843	9	8.06

Sworn to and subscribed before me this 3rd day of August, 1846.

JOHN HARDEN, Admr.

J. P. Dickenson, C. C. O.

THE STATE OF GEORGIA

Dept. of Archives and History

I, Ruth Blair, State Historian and Director of the Department of Archives and History of the State of Georgia, do hereby certify, That the pamphlet, LAND GRANTS, 1784-1787 showing a list of the warrants issued by the Land Court for the County of Washington from its establishment to the sixth day of August, 1787, inclusive, shows on page 25 that Nicholas Hardin received 200 acres on headright; that Adam Hardin received 200 acres on headright (page 27); and that Isaac Hardin received 600 acres, distinction not shown (page 30). Said pamphlet, signed by Joseph Miller, O. W. C., Nov. 16, 1797, is on file in this Department.

In testimony Whereof, I have hereunto set my hand and affixed the seal of my office, at the Capitol, ,in the city of Atlanta, this 6th day of August in the year of our Lord One Thousand Nine Hundred and Twenty Seven and of the Independence of the United States of America the One Hundred and ....
RUTH BLAIR, State Historian.
(SEAL)

THE WELSH WITCH WOMAN.

There was living in Wilkinson Co. Georgia, 83rd Subdivision, 1850, in the family of her daughter, Sarah Hatcher, an old woman who was listed in the Census of that year as follows: "Eve Clay, aged 80, female, born in Georgia". There was living at the time of collecting the material for this sketch, in Wilkinson, County, Ga., Mrs. Susié Gilbert, in Washington County, Ga., Mrs. Mary Trawick, and in Florida Mrs. William Connell, each of whom remembered Eve Clay as mentioned above and from them I obtained the salient points of this sketch together with traditions from my mother who remembered her quite well and who left notes relating to her.

Eve Clay, above is the same person as often referred to as Eve Harden. She had a sister and brothers as shown in Hardin Hints and Genealogies. In addition to these it now appears that Valentine Hardin was also a brother, a careful study of the foregoing correspondence and documents together with family characteristics makes this conclusion inevitable.

In my opinion she was of the same family as the Hardens of Savannah and the Hardens of Athens. Other members of this family resided in Pennsylvania and also in North Carolina. The family also was related to that family of Lewises known as Irish John Lewis and through this family of Lewises were related to Mitchell Clay. I give this merely as my opinion and it is also my opinion that John Hardin, father of Adam et al was a son of William Hardin, originally of Wales.

Eve Hardin was born in Georgia in 1770 of Welsh descent . During the early days of the revolution the family refugeed from state of Georgia to the Southwestern part of Virginia where John Hardin, her father participated in Dunmore's war. Later the family refugeed from this frontier settlement into Pennsylvania her father serving in the Pennslyvania Militia, from Pennslyvania the family refugeed into either North Carolina or Virginia in the vicinity of Orange County, if not within the borders of that county. At the close of the revolution the family came into Washington County, Ga., that is the children came and it is presumed that the father was dead, having died in either Pensylvania or in North Carolina or Virginia, presumably in Orange County, North Carolina. The three earliest Hardins coming to Georgia were Isaac, Adam and Nicholas. Isaac appears to have gone back to Virginia and presumably he was an uncle of Adam, Eve, and others.

Reader is referred to "Clay Errata and Addenda" in connection with the above.

Sept. 26, 1792 Eve Hardin was married to David Clay in Warren County, Georgia. Presumably she was living at that time either with her brother Adam or her Uncle Isaac. Very little is known of her married life except that which is included in The Georgia Branch of the Virginia Clays and Their Celebrated Cousins" but what we do know is rather unfavorable. She had a violent temper, was selfwilled and could not be reasoned with when her temper was aroused. David Clay was a man of considerable property and owned a plantation in Washington County and one in Wilkinson County. When she was overcome with one of these rages he quietly removed himself to his 'Washington County Plantation until the storm blew over when all was quiet until the next time.

Her husband died before 1820 and the more minute part of this sketch begins with her widowhood.

After her husband's death she remarried, but the marriage was not happy. Her second husband sent her to my grandfather's on the pretext that he was sick. He was living at that time in what is now Terrell Co. and Eve was living in Wilkinson. She went horse back carrying a negro woman with her. When she returned home she found that her husband, negroes and mules had disappeared. She was left with lands, a horse and one negro. She immediately set out in pursuit of her husband and slaves and followed them to some place either on the Gulf near Port St. Joe or Savannah. The family are not exactly agreed as to the place, but wherever it was her husband and negroes had taken ship and that was the last she ever knew of either. Whether this deranged her mind or whether she had been of the same disposition all along I do not know but now began a peculiar kind of life.

Going back a little. After the death of David Clay and before the children began to leave home, Eve Clay had fried ham for breakfast one morning. The older children knew, or thought they knew, that there was no ham in the smokehouse. They immediately began to inquire of their mother as to where she got the ham. She would not tell them or give any explanation. The older children refused to eat breakfast unless she would tell and she refused to tell, so they went to work breakfastless and no member of the family, to this day knows any more about the ham than when the discussion first started.

In personal appearance she was of medium size with gray eyes and at the time of which I write her hair was white. It was probably auburn in earlier life. She was restless, filled with boundless energy, without shame and of a most determined disposition and violent temper.

She had a great store of Welsh superstitions and of Scotch Closeness. She united these and practiced the profession of Palmistry and "fortune-telling". In this she traveled considerable distances, usually going horseback and carrying her serving woman with her. The practice of her profession proved profitable and she was accustomed to have in her possession considerable amounts of silver. She went as far as Savannah, and even to the Gulf Ports and wherever she went her art was in demand. Her temper, and her rather uncanny skill in foretelling or rather guessing the coming future events, built for her quite a reputation. This with her age and appearance and peculiar conduct soon attracted to her the appelation of "The Witch Woman."

Her children disapproved of this kind of existenec and every effort was made by them to get her to abandon her fortune telling and these excursions but without avail. The struggle between Eve and her children over this, was long and persistent with Eve continuing to do as she pleased. The children finally scattered out and Peyton Clay built Eve a house near his home. Here she lived for a number of years all alone and it was here that Mrs. Susie Gilbert knew her. Her serving woman appears on the scene no more and from now on we find Eve travelling on foot. Peyton Clay was wealthy and it is presumed that there was a deliberate attempt made to prevent these excursions, but to no avail. She was too independant to ask for a horse or to be carried and on more than one occasion traveled from Wilkinson County to Sumpter and Terrell counties on foot. Her children would send her back when her time was out.

She lived to an extreme old age and got to where she could not walk a foot log. This did not prevent her, however, from going when and where she pleased. There were no bridges and she would wade the creeks at the fords and one on occasion gave some of her grand children a severe scolding because they had seen her come to a creek and wade it and did not offer to take her up and carry her across on the horses which they were riding home from the field. They had wanted to see her wade the creek and did not let her know they were there until after she had crossed the creek. I think that she was justified in her indignation at her grand children at this time.

Her grand children were divided as to her supernatural powers, some believed in her possessing such powers and others did not. My mother had no faith in her possessing such powers but her sister Francis who married Hiram Wadsworth did. Mrs. Luvinia Connell still relates this circumstance as proof of Eve's powers. "Judith Lucindy, my sister died quite young. Before her death I was very sick and my mother was expecting me to die. Grandma (Eve) was at our house. At that time Judith was well and playing about. Mother asked Eve to tell her if I was going to die. Grandma told my mother that I was not going to die but that Judith was. I got well but Judith was soon taken sick and died."

Mrs. Trawick remembers Eve coming over in Washington County to visit relatives. She says that at that time she was very old and always came on foot. She says that all of the children were afraid of her, and that people called her a Witch. Mrs. Gilbert of Wilkinson County gives the same account of her.

She lived to be very old and is given by White as an instance of longevity in Wilkinson County. When enfeebled by age her daughter Sarah Hatcher appears to have taken her in her home and to have given her the necessary care and attention. Age had finally done what man had been unable to do, that is subdue and tame her proud and imperious spirit.

These characteristics of Eve has appeared in other members of the family to a much lesser extent. In collaterals it has rarely ever gone beyond eccentricity, but in my opinion John Wesley Hardin of Texas was of this family and this characteristic explains hs life and conduct, Henry Clay of Wilkinson County must have inherited a share and I have seen it in others to a less extent. As a matter of fact I have felt the surge at times in myself. This characteristic was so marked that a common expression among all descendants when one lost his or her temper was "Watch old Eve." That was all that was necessary to cool the temper and restore tranquility.

Now in concluding this sketch, I know of nothing better for all descendants to do than to adopt this as a permanent motto "Watch old Eve". Whenever we become indignant, when we are tempted to fly off the handle, when we have the urge to do some foolish or eccentric thing lets remember our motto "Watch old Eve." Time and the diffusion of her blood among the blood of many others has nearly destroyed the potency of this characteristc, but is likely to be renewed at any time by a series of marriages among her descendants or with some other family of similar blood lines and with similar characteristics. She had many good and noble qualities but it is by this characteristic that she is remembered and it is from this char-

acteristic that we descendants can most profit, that is in a negatve way by guarding against the development of this characteristic within our hearts. "Watch old Eve" and while others glory in the deeds of some illustrious ancestor let us profit by correcting those defects which may have been transmitted to us and in perfectng the virtues inherited and in the acquisition of virtues not inherent, thus honoring our sires and excusing their delinquencies.

HARDIN NOTES.

Oct. 17, 1803

William Hardin of Frankln County, Georgia mentions in will which is abstracted in Historical Collections of Daughters of Revolution, Page 252. Beloved wife, sons, Martin, Mark, Swan, Henry, Richard; daughters, Cynthia, Sarah and Sucka or (Sookey). This William Hardin appears to have been a son of Henry Hardin and Judith Lynch. See test of Swan and Jerusha Harden, page 232, Georgia D. A. R.

Land Grants.

16 District 2, Section No. 93, b Levisa Harden (w) Yorks Stewart. Fields Harden Sen. Wilkinson Co. (Note).

Nov. 12, 1801, Martin Hardin, Warren County 350 A. (Note).

1st District, 4 section, 933c Adam Hardin 374 Putnam.

12 District, 1st Section, 980 c Adam Harden, Lesters, Monroe.

15 District, 2 section 650 b Ann Harden, W. Gorves, Bibb.

25 District, 2 section (Cherokee) 123 Asa C. Hardin 404 Gwinett.

20 District, 3 Section 107c B. B. Hardin, Doziers, Columbia.

5 District, 1 Section, 723 c Benjamon Hardin, Doziers, Columbia.

16 District, 1 Section, Cherokee 106 (fr) Benjamin B. Hardin, Doziers, Columbia (Union Co.)

14 District, 1st Section 1188 b Chas. A Harden 20 Bryan.

26 District, 3 Section Cherokee 85 Charles A Harden 20th Bryan (Walker County.)

14 District, 2 Section Cherokee, 129 Charles A. Harden, 20th Bryan.

5 District, 1 Section 796, c Edward Harden, Athens, Clark.

20 District, 2 section, 734 c Edward J Harden, Valleans, Chatham.

6 District, 4 Section, Cherokee 252 Edward R. Harden, Athens Clark (Walker Co.)

17 District, 3 Section 577 c Elias Harden, Butts Monroe Co.

5 District, 3 Section, Cherokee, 153 George Hardin Collings, Oglethorp (Cass Co.)

28 District, 3 Section, Cherokee, 25 Henry Harden, Hearns Butts, (Walker Co.)

11 District, 3 Section, Cherokee 283 Henry Harden, Hearns Butts, (Murray Co.)

11 District, 1 Section, 967 c Henry Hardin, 419 Walton.

12 District, 2 Sec., Cherokee 111, Henry Hardin, Albersons Walton.

12 District, 4 Section, Cherokee 84, Henry F. Harden, Silmans Pike (Walker Co.)

5 District, 4 Section, 157 Henry F. Harden, Silmans Pike, (Floyd Co.)

14 District, 2 Section, Cherokee 200 Kezekiah Hardin, Hills, Stewart.

3 District, 1 Section, 34 c Hudson Harden, Moores Randolph.

15 District, 4 Section, Cherokee, 123 Hugh M. Harden, Sanderlins Chatham, (Floyd Co.)

16 District, 4 Section, 475 b James Harden, Lesters Monroe.

3 District, 4 Section, 98 c Jas. M. Harden, McGinnis, Jackson.

15 District, 2 Section, 1160 b James P. Hardin 404, Gwinnett.

21 District, 3 Section, 161 c Jas. Hardin, Silmans Pike.

4 Dstrict, 1 Section, 648 c James Harden Lesters Monroe.

17 District, 1 Section Cherokee, 232 Jane S. Harden or Newsons, Thomas.

21 District, 3 Section, 565 c Jesse Hardin, Jackson.

2 District, 1 Section, 139 c J. G. and B. A. Hardin Orphans, Merriwether.

24 District, 2 Section, Cherokee 317, J. G. & B. A. Hardin, Crows Merriwethers.

Irwin County, District 11, No. 13, John Hardin, Twiggs, Hodges, Dec. 15, 1824.

20 District, 3 Section, 1155 c John Hardin, Talleys, Troup.

16 District, 2 Section 1160 c Joseph Hardin, Lovens, Henry.

16 District, 2 Section, 177 c Josiah Harding, Williams Walton.

15 District, 2 Section, 749 b, Josiah Harden, Cliftons Tatnall.

14 District, 3 Section, Cherokee 46

Mary Harden, h a Bowers, Elbert. (Murray.)

25 District, 3 Section Cherokee 142 Nicholas Harden, Robinsons, Fayette, (Walker.)

3 District, 4 Section, 1209 b Martin Harden 53 Emanuel.

Irwin County, District No. 12, No. 134, Marten Harden, Tatnal, Tharps, Dec. 13, 1826.

8 District, 1 Section, Cherokee, 114 Matilda A. Harden W. S. L. W. 20th Bryan (Union.)

27 District, 2 Section, Cherokee, 296 Nancy Harden, W Carpenters Tatnal.

11 District, 4 Section, Cherokee, 174 Robert M. Harden, Cliftons Tatnal (Walker)

11 District, 2 Section, Cherokee, 52 Robert R. Hardin S. L. W., Ballards, Morgan, (Gilmer.)

13 District, 2 Section, Cherokee, 12 Rhoda Hardin mi f a Bowers, Elbert, Cherokee.

15 District, 2 Section, 351 b Richard T. Harden, Roysters, Franklin.

5 District, 1 Section, 1156 c Stephen L. Harden, Doziers, Columbia.

2 District, 4 Section 134 c Thomas Harden, Clelands, Chatham.

4 District, 2 Section, Cherokee, 261 Thomas H. Harden (Cherokee).

Irwin County Dotun No. 9 128 Thomas Hardin Columbia County Pullens District, Nov. 10, 1829.

2 District, 1 Section, 1275 c Thomas Harden Pecks, Columbia Co.

14 District, 1 Section 260 b Thomas Hardin Pecks, Columbia Co.

Irwin County District 12, 396, William Harden, Oglethorp, Davenports, Nov. 25 1827.

21 District, 2 Section, 834 c Wm. Harding Albersons, Walton.

19 District, 3 Section 900 c Wm. S. Hardin, Talley's Troup.

18 District, 3 Section, 460 c Wm. W. Hardens orps Bells Columbia.

CLAY ERRATA AND ADDENDA.

Page 64 add to children of W. A. and Minnie Clay Webb, 7" Bobbie Bird Webb born January 27, 1904; 8" Judge Webb b Dec. 28, 1906; 9" Jewell Clay Webb b Aug. 22 1911.

Page 71 Mary Elizabeth Clay m Drewery Morgan Davis April 26, 1877.

Page 57 Rebecca Collier Etheridge was married only once and to James M. Kilpatrick. Their daughter Nancy Kilpatrick was twice married, first to Merrell Kenedy Bishop, these were the parents of Agnes Rebecca Bishop Clay. After the death of Bishop Nancy (Kilpatrick) Bishop married Joseph H. Pierce.

36, 6'. Iverson Greene Gayden.

Mrs. R. L. Tullis, box 188, Baton Rouge, La., who was formerly Miss Octavia Tulls and whose husband is Dean of the Law School of the Louisiana State University furnishes me with the following information:

Iverson Greene Gayden born Amite county, Mississippi, January 19, 1825, died Nov. 17, 1896. Married first, Mrs. (widow) Ellen Scott Keller, born Scott, daughter of Judge and Mrs. Thomas Scott, of East Feliciana Parish, Louisiana; she died in 1862. Married next, Martha Jane Thompson, daughter of Obediah Morton Thompson and his wife, Mary Jane Williams Thompson. Issue:

By 1st marriage:

A' Agrippa Gayden, married 1st, Octavia Perkins; next, Katie Perkins. Their children are Octavia, maried to Dr. James J. Robert, of Baton Rouge; and Lewis Perkins Gayden, married to Peachey Woodson.

B' Minerva Gayden, married Eli Norwood Perkins, address, Myrtlewood, Ala., issue, a'—Mary Eleanor Perkins, b'—Agrippa Gayden Perkins and Ellie Perkins.

C'—Ellen Gayden married Isaac Duncan Norwood, address, Norwood, La. Issue: a'—Minerva Norwood, b' —Thomas Street Noorwood, c'—Nellie Norwood, d'—Frank Lewis Norwood.

D'—Mary Gayden married Harry S. Perkins, address Baton Rouge, La. Issue: a'—Lewis Gayden Perkins, b' —Mac Bridges Perkins, c'—Georgie May Perkins, d'—Iva Gayden Perkins.

By second marriage:

E'—Julia Lea Gayden married 1st, Dr. Samuel J. Perkins, married second E. L. Woodside. No issue by either marriage. Address, Baton Rouge, La.

F'—George Lea Gayden married Irene Keller, five children, address, Gurley, La.

G'—Iva May Gayden, died June 7, 1896.

H'—William Percy Gayden, married Gertrude Brownlee of Clinton, La. No issue. He died March 11, 1911.

I'—Joseph Redhead Gayden, died Feb. 19, 1913.

J'—Octavia Perkin Gayden married Robert Lee Tullis, of Baton Rouge, La. No issue.

K'—Iverson Greene Gayden, Jr., married first, Mamie Hands, of New Orleans; second, Georgia Hands, of New Orleans. No issue by either marriage.

L'—Margaret Kirby Gayden married Donald Derickson, of Meadville, Penn. Issue, Gayden Derickson, 1311 Henry Clay Ave., New Orleans, La.

N. B.—In Goodspeed's Memoirs of Louisiana, published about 1890, appears a sketch of the Gayden family, the material for which was supplied by Iverson Greene Gayden, the subject of this paper. In the same book appear sketches of the Norwood, Perkins and Keller families among whom were marriages of the Gayden sons and daughters. Iverson Greene Gayden was a soldier in the Mexican War, in the company of Jefferson Davis. He won a medal for distinguished service. He was enlisted in the Civil War in an East Feliciana Parish, La. company, but did not engage in active service.

William Clay

William Clay, son of Henry Clay and Mary Mitchell Clay, has proven rather elusive to genealogists as well as have his children. He must have absented himself and family from Virginia for a period of time otherwise the Virginia records would show more relating to him. He may have resided in Pennsylvania but I have a suspicion that he resided in Georgia for a time and that Joseph Clay the first of Savannah was of this line. Genealogies and historical mention controvert this but are too indefinite and vague to furnish positive proof to the contrary and such descendants of Joseph Clay as I have discussed the matter with all claim relationship with Henry Clay, the Great Commoner. If their claims are well founded then their descent must have been thru this William Clay. His wife was, in my opinion, Anne Lewis, possibly the daughter of Irish John Lewis, if not, then, there must have existed a relationship, and David Lewis, of Surrey County, North Carolina must have been related. William Clay and wife, Ann, made deed to parts of lands taken by will from William Clay's father, but on June 26, 1765, William Clay deeded lands to son, Obed, without wife's signature. We have evidence since publication of Brochure showing that Pearce Clay of Washington Co., was not a son of this William but a grandson as stated by my mother in her notes. This limits the known children to Mitchell, William and Obed Clay. Soon after the death of his wife, William Clay went to the Southwestern part of Virginia together with other members of his family. On May 2nd, 1771 he deeded land in Bedford County to Eleazer Clay, and regardless of his age joined the forces in defense of the white settlements from the Indians in Dunmore's War and was the first white person killed in the battle although I have found no authorities giving more than his family name.

Mitchell Clay

Documents relating to Mitchell Clay are rather meagre. He must have married in Henrico County Virginia, and much earlier than that stated by Johnston as will appear later. Having received his grant of land for service in the French and Indian War it is quite probable that he moved with his family which at that time consisted of his father into what was then Augusta County Virginia, about 1765 or 6. This section was largely settled by Scotch and Irish and some Welsh. Among the families occupying the new country were the Lewises and Hardins, Hardins of both Huguenot and Welsh extraction, and several with the given name of John. Mitchell Clay soon settled a farm and established his residence on the extreme frontier as we have seen in the "Georgia Branch of th Virginia Clays" but it was not long before these frontier settlements were threatened by Dunmores' War. This was the beginning of a very exciting existence for the settlers and especially for the Clay and Hardin families. Times were perilous and every person able to bear arms joined in the general defense. William Clay, the old grandfather, Mitchell, the son, and David and Ezekial Clay, the grandsons as well as three John Hardins. One of these was John Hardin, son of Mark Hardin of Prince William County. He was wounded in McDonald's expedition and later died. One was the father of Adam, Eve, etc., the other I am unable to identify. (see Thwait, Reuben G. Documentary History of Dunmore's war, pages 155 and 421.)

David Clay.

David Clay served in Dunmore's war 51 days with his father Mitchell and Brother Ezekiel. They found their own provisions. Thwaits p 200, 397. After the close of Dunmore's war the Clay family and several others remained until the beginning of the Revolution. Their exposed position made their residence exceedingly precarious and they were advised to move, but the Clay family refused to move, and remained during the entire war, however about 1777 or 8 the more cautious decided to seek a safer place and several families refugeed into Pennsylvania where several of them had orignally come from. David Clay was one of the guards and guides for these families on their pilgrimage and remained to serve in Pennsylvania Militia. John Harden with his family was one of the families to take refuge in Pennsylvania and he also served in the Pennsylvania Militia.

John Harden, 7th Class, 4th Battalion, Cumberland Co., Militia, Penn. Archives, 5th series, Vol. 6, page 285.

David Clay, 7th Class, 7th Battalion of Cumberland County, Militia, Penn. Archives, 5th Series, Vol. 6, Pages 252, 488,489. Entered service March, 1778. David Clay may have gone back into Virginia for brief periods during the Revolution but I have found no records to prove it beyond question.

Both John Harden and David Clay must have remained in Pennsylvania for some time but I find no record as to when they left Pennsylvania. From Pennsylvania they both went to North Carolina where both the Clays and Hardens had relatives. David Clay enlisted in the 10th North Carolina Regiment from Duplin County, N. C. and served with Lewis Harden, but I am unable to say whether he was a brother of John or a son but I think he was a brother. John Harden may have come to North Carolina and have died there or he may have died in Pennsylvania. Nicholas Hardin was in Orange County, North Carolina for a short time, from which I infer that if the family did not come to this county they came to the vicinity.

Aside from this record I am inclined to believe that the family resided in Orange County North Carolina from the following circumstances. David Clay was one eyed having lost this eye in an encounter with the Tories. The Tories were raiding a settlement in which the Hardens lived. David Clay resisted the Tories but was overpowered and captured. The Tories mistreated him in some way from which he received an injury that resulted in the loss of an eye. According to my recollection of my mother's account he was not in regular service at the time and he escaped from these Tories. This is all rather vague but I have been so positive that I would find the Hardins with the Clays durin the Revolutionary period that the search has been confined to territory adjacent to David Clay's family or himself at all times. Now if we examine the history of Orange County, N. C., immediately following the close of the Revolution the conviction grows that it was in Orange County North Carolina that David Clay lost his eye and that it was immediately after the close of the war, that this occurred. Rioting and confusion lasted for some time between the Patriots and Tories, even after peace had been made between the Colonies and Great Brittain.

David Clay must have gone back to Virginia after this perhaps about 1784. He was evidently away at the time of the attack on Mitchell Clay's family by the Indians because no mention is made of him in this connection.

Both David Clay and his nephew Pierce came to Georgia soon after the raid of the Indians on the home of Mitchell Clay. It is quite probable that the widow of Ezekial came to Georgia also. Both settled in Washington County Georgia. After the county of Wilkinson was created David Clay removed to that county but he retained his Washington County plantation until his death.

Records fail to disclose any grant of land to David Clay in Georgia for his Revolutionary services. There is no doubt in my mind, however but that he received such a grant in Washington County, Georgia. A great many grants to soldiers of the Revolution are not shown by index. Pierce Clay evidently married Martha Rose in Washington County Georgia soon after David Clay married Eve Harden

and must have acquired the real estate of David Clay after his death because he owned about 3,000 acres of land in 1830 as shown by tax digest of Washington County Georgia.

WILLIAM JAMES CLAY—AND ERRORS CORRECTED.

When I wrote the chapter of The Georgia Branch of the Virginia Clays dealing with the family of Pierce Clay of Washington County Georgia, I relied upon Johnston and Memoirs of Georgia as authority. I suspected some errors in each but did not imagine these errors to be so serious and glaring as they have proven to be. I failed to make as thorough an investigation of records and documents as I should have before accepting these authorities. My excuse for this is that descendants failed to manifest the interest in the work which I thought they should and from the further fact that it was stated in Memoirs of Georgia that the Grandmother of Senator A. S. Clay was Margaret Rose. I presumed that this information was supplied by Senator Clay himself and it was such a disappointment to me to find a man occupying the exalted position held by Senator Clay not knowing who his father's mother was that I regretted ever having undertaken the writing of a sketch of this branch of the family. However a more thorough investigation and a better opportunity for research has placed a different light upon the matter and in justice to the memory of Senator Clay and other descendants of Pierce Clay I am giving this brief treatment of the family's lineage.

William James Clay was the father of Senator A. S. Clay, a son of William Monroe Clay and a grandson of Pierce Clay of Washington County, Georgia. He was born in Washington County but moved to Cobb County quite early and lived there until his death which occurred in 1911. He raised his family near Austell and from his old neighbors I have learned considerable of him.

From them I learn that he was a plain, honest unpretentious, hardworking farmer in moderate financial circumstances and not given to extravagence. He gave his children such educational opportunities as the locality afforded but did not send them to college. When his son Alexander Stephens Clay entered college it was a friend of the family, Columbus Blair, who advanced the funds for his entry into school. Later A. S. Clay and D. W. Blair were law partners at Marietta, one the son of William J. Clay and the other the son of Columbus Blair, one to occupy a seat in the U. S. Senate and the other on the Bench of that Judicial Circuit.

Notwithstanding the honesty, industry, piety and sterling character of William James Clay, he failed to achieve any degree of distinction. His intelligence and true nobility of character failed to receive that recognition which they no doubt would have, had it not been that he never amassed a fortune and that he had an impediment in his speech which constantly embarassed him and caused him to be of a retiring disposition. This impediment of speech is a characteristic occasionally met with among descendants of those Clays intermarrying with the Welsh Hardens and is perhaps the result of some nervous condition that sometimes manifests itself in bursts of temper. David Lewis of Surry County North Carolina appears to have had the same trouble and I suspect that the characteristic came from the Lewis family.

The closest ties of affection existed between Senator Clay and his father during their entire life, and regardless of what others might withhold of recognition the Senator knew his father for what he really was and rendered to him that love and honor which he deserved and which is so becoming in this relationship.

The father rarely ever missed an opportunity of hearing his son speak if within a reasonable distance and the son always invited his father to a seat of honor on the rostrum. Those who failed to understand accused the Senator of playing politics, when clearly no such intention existed.

The foregoing explains to my mind the errors in Memoirs of Georgia. It is evident that when the publishers were seeking data for the publication of the sketch of the life of Senator Clay that the Senator refered them to his father for the information relating to the family history. The re-write man must have gotten confused with the information from these two sources. Whoever took notes must have misunderstood Martha and thought the old gentleman said Margaret Rose. Martha Rose evidently married Pierce Clay in Washington County about 1794.

It is most assured that part of information mentioned in connection with William Monroe Clay was intended for Pierce, and the whole is inaccurate, confusing, misleading and not authoritative. I will now give an exact quotation from the sketch refered to.

Memoirs of Georgia, Vol. 1, Page 503 contains the following statements relating to Clay ancestry of Senator A. S. Clay, "Alexander S. Clay, lawyer, Marietta, Cobb Co., Ga. son of W. J. and Ann (Peck) Clay, was born in Cobb county, in 1853. On his father's side he is of Scotch descent, his great-grandfather having emigrated from Scotland to this country about the middle of the last century, and settled in Virginia, where he lived and died. His paternal grandparents were W. M. and Margaret (Rose) Clay. He was born in Virginia in 1764, migrated to Georgia and settled in Washington County toward the close of the last century. He accumulated quite a large estate-owning 3,000 acres of land in one body—became one of the largest planters, and was one of the wealthiest citizens of the county at the time of his death, which occurred in 1853, in the ninetieth year of his life. Mr. Clay's father was born in Washington county in 1828, was reared on the plantation and has continued farming as his life occupation. He served three years during the war between the states, and is a member of the Methodist Church, of which he is a stewart."

In 1820 there were only two families of Clays enumerated in Washington County in Census of that year. One was Pierce Clay with 1 male between 10 and 16, 1 male over 45, 1 female under 10 and 1 female over 45. The other was William Clay. His family consisted of 1 male under 10, 1 male between 26 and 45, 1 female under ten and two females between 16 and 26. (These last two were probably Mary Hardin Clay and her sister as we know that her father died quite early).

In 1830 there were three Clay families and only three enumerated in the census of Washington County Georgia. These were. Pierce Clay whose family consisted of 1 male over 45 and no other members. John Clay whose family consisted of 1 male between 20 and 30, 1 male under 5 and 1 female between 15 and 20. William Clay whose family consisted of 2 males under 5, 1 male between 5 and 10, 1 male between 20 and 30 and 1 male between 30 and 40, 2 females between 5 and 10, 1 female between 10 and 15 and 1 female between 30 and 40.

This I believe disproves the above extract from Memoirs of Georgia. Johnston has 'been shown to have been in error as to dates and ages and I am positive that Pierce Clay was a son of a brother of David Clay as stated by my mother. Then which brother?

There is just one brother to which he may be assigned, Ezekiel Clay. The other brothers have been accounted for and eliminated. Ezekiel Clay was old enough to participate in Dunmores war in 1774 and must have soon married and Pierce Clay was born soon afterward before 1780.

Considering the locality, the unsettled state of affairs, and the condition of the early records of this section I doubt that the marriage record will ever be found. His wife was evidently Millie Pierce and married after the death of Ezekiel Clay and came with her second husband to Wilkes County Georgia. I do not know who her second husband was and have no positive evidence as to her first marriage but Millie Clay Hester's statement together with several other circumstances satisfies me that Ezekiel Clay married Millie Pierce and that these were the ancestors of the Clays of Washington County.

TALLIAFERRO ERRATA.

Page 136. Date of marriage of J. T. Chappell and Harriet Athalia Stanley should be Oct. 18, 1855.

Page 135. Mary Hardin Lingo Chappel and Joseph John Chappell had a son, Benjamin T. Chappell who gave his life for his country during the Civil War. Name inadvertently omitted from brochure.

Johnson Blair, Immigrant and Patriot

Tradition among the descendants of Jane R. Blair Rigsby and descendants of her collateral relatives is that Johnson Blair was an Irish Immigrant. Thomas Wiley Rigsby, the only surviving child of Jane R. Blair Rigsby says that Johnson Blair was her father, his mother his authority. He says further that his mother told him of a brother John, a brother William who was blind from the result of a lick received on the back of his head with a bottle, and a brother, Andrew. He does not remember to have ever seen any of his Blair relatives and does not remember having heard of any other members of the family except Rob Vatin. He is living at this time and I have consulted him frequently. He says that to the best of his recollection his mother told him that her mother was a Roberson, that she married a Vatin and that Jane R. Blair Rigsby had a half brother, Rob Vatin. I have accepted this as being correct for some time although not exactly in accord with my recollection of statements made by my father and grandfather. My father had a brother named Amos Vatin Rigsby. I once enquired as to the reason for this peculiar name and I was informed by them that he was named for an old man connected with the family in some way and I am now of opinion that this was a man named Vaughten who came to America with Johnson Blair, perhaps a half brother, and that Robert Vatin mentioned by T. W. Rigsby was Robert Blair, probably Robert Vatin Blair as there appears to also have been a Robert Keating Blair in Georgia about this time.

Another matter remembered by me but not recalled by T. W. Rigsby relates to the Lindley family. He fails to remember any thing of this family while I remember hearing them discussed in the following connection: Margaret Johnson, relict of John (?) Johnson, Irish immigrant and supposed to have been a relative of Johnson

Blair and a fellow passenger to America, lived to be one hundred eighteen years of age. She was the grandmother of Wiley Taylor Rigsby whom Jane R. Blair married and it was related to me that after her death her body was propped up in bed and her pipe placed in her mouth. It was related to me that the Lindleys were connected with this in some way and I have thought that Jonathan Lindley was probably furnishing her a home at the time and that it was at his home that her death occurred.

James Lindley, son of Jonathan Lindley and Nancy Blair Lindley had a queer sence of humor. A few circumstances will serve to illustrate this and helps to identify Nancy Blair as a daughter of Johnson Blair.

During slavery James Lindley was away from home until late at night. Returning he found a wagon loaded with corn standing on the river (Alcovy?) bridge. This incensed him and he proceeded to push the wagon and corn into the river. Reaching home he found that the wagon was one of his that one of his slaves had left on the bridge as a result of an accident.

At another time he was out at night at a neighborhood distillery and got "tight." Considering it a good time to get even for numerous practical jokes which he had played upon them, others of the party proceeded to black his face and hands. As soon as he had sobered sufficiently he returned home. His wife failed to recognize him and screamed. Mose, a house servant, ran to the rescue of his mistress and also failing to recognize Lindley began to give him rather a severe beating. Lindley would halloo "It's me Mose", Mose not recognizing the master's voice would reply "I know it's you" and keep up the beating until at last Lindley's wife recognized his voice and stopped it.

No one enjoyed telling of these circumstances better than did James Lindley himself.

It was related to me at Powder Springs by one of the older members of the family, that he, when very old and knowing that he was shortly to die, decided to see how his old friends would take his death and rigged out a dummy figure, spread a sheet over it and sent for his friends with the message that Jim Lindley was dead.

Concealing himself he awaited their coming and listened to their conversation until one of them decided to look at the body, when Jim came out of concealment and they all enjoyed the joke together.

Notwithstanding this strange freak of practical joking he was much loved and respected and a leader in every community in which he lived. I remember that some member of the Lindley family was credited with putting the pipe in "Granny" Johnson's mouth and I suspect Jim.

Blair Immigrants to Georgia.

Tradition in the family and its various branches agree in the main as to details of the voyage to America. According to this tradition the voyage was long and tedius because of storms encountered and calms. One tradition is that the ship either had to put back, or into some port in order to secure extra supplies. The immigrants consisted principally of families and Nancy Blair is said to have been a child, some place her age at 6 months and others at 6 years. That she was a child is authenticated by the fact that a child's bonnet was long preserved among her descendants, and said to have been worn by her on the voyage from Ireland. Every fact and circumstance of this voyage points circumstantially to the ship described by Jones in his History of Georgia, Volume 2, page 120, as follows: "In March, 1768, the General Assembly passed an act 'encouraging settlers to come into the province.' That substantial aid might be rendered to those who sought to avail themselves of its provisions, the sum of £1,815 sterling was appropriated to be disbursed in certificates by commissioners named for that purpose. Contrary to the expectation of the colonists this act was returned disapproved by the king. Meanwhile, resting upon the inducements extended in that bill, and encouraged by Messrs. Galphin and Rae, one hundred and seven Irish Protestants came to Georgia in December of that year. It was necessary that they should be cared for. The public faith of the colony, as expressed in the intentions of the legislature, stood pledged for their accommodation and assistance. During the recess of the legislature the governor and council, without hesitation, provided homes for them in the fork of Lambert Creek and the Great Ogeechee River, looking to the next General Assembly to reimburse them for all expenditures in this behalf, and in feeding these newcomers until they could clear farms and plant and gather their crops. The town which they there builded was called Queensbury, and DeBrahm describes it as inhabited by about 70, and its environs by above 200 families, mostly Irish, from which it is generally called the Irish settlement."

I have been unable to secure further direct evidence relating to this settlement.

Not being able to secure more definite information necessitates giving evidence in great minutiae, relating to these Blair immigrants:

Will of Rachel Blair of file in Jefferson County, Georgia:

Date—day of October, 1801. Rechel Blair, State of Georgia, county of Jefferson, gives to mother, Elizabeth White bond against estate of John McNeely, dated 1773, signed John McNeely, Wit. Samuel Blair "If my mother should never come from Europe" then property goes to brothers and sister, John Blair, Margaret Blair and David White. Wm. McNeely named as executor, test Hugh McNeely and Rachel Crosley."

Georgia D. A. R., p 324.

Thomas Hayney, of Pendleton Dist., S. C., Jan. 31, 1821—Sept. 3, 1821 (?).

Wife Elizabeth land in Franklin Co., Ga. Slaves to be freed at her death. Land in S. C. sold, and half to go to brother Hugh Haney, and to Elizabeth Blair and her heirs: Both of whom if living are now in County Antrim, Ireland, near Clough Mills. If not called for in 7 years to be used for the poor of the district. Slaves not to be hired out or removed from Georgia, or S. C. Exrs: James McDill, Hugh Wilson, William Turner. Wit: Robert McKenney, Margaret and Elizabeth McDill."

James Blair of St. George's Parrish drew 100 acres 1770 p 92, of land. Index, office of the Secretary of State. Jefferson County Authorities are agreed that James Blair was an Irish Immigrant.

The above documents show John

Blair, Margaret Blair, Rachel Blair, James Blair, and Samuel Blair to have been immigrants to Georgia. Now in connection with this and traditions as to Johnson Blair lets consider the Act of August 20th, 1781, Roster of the Revolution, p 194 "That any person or persons who shall produce a certificate from the commanding officer of the district to which he belongs, to the legislature (on the total expulsion of the enemy from it)" etc. This was to provide for refugees who were leaving the state at that time as well as those who had already left because of British activities. The Blairs had, many of them, already left the state and had rendered service at the Cowpens immediately preceeding the passabe of the act and were possibly by their example, an inspiration to its passage. Tradition says that they were under Morgan and that they served at Kings Mountain. At any event upon the declaration of peace and the opening of the land Court at Augusta we find on deposit in the Department of Archives and History, Atlanta, Ga., the following documents:

Certificate of John Twiggs to service of Samuel Blair. Prays for bounty in Franklin county but only find a 50 acre tract drawn, in Richmond county index of land grant book. Roster of the Revolution, p 32. Petition of Sibbiah Blair petitions for land in Washington county, p32. This petition has the name William Blair endorsed across the back of the petition but there is no accompanying certificate. The executive minutes however show a grant to William Blair's orphans and in Clark county, part of which was originally in Washington county, I find the following conveyance. It is poorly written and errors in recording appear to have been made. The writing being poor I may have made others in copying. It is my opinion that this was the grant authorized to have been made to the orphans of William Blair on the application of Sibbiah Blair:

"State of Georgia, Clark County.

Know all men by these presents, that we Bartlet Wooten, Johnson Riggnold (Renfrow?), John Blair, Spencer Reynold (Renfrow?) William Nobles, Henry Huff, John Armstrong (Sen.), John Springer, Philip Tigner, John Henderson, William Johnston,

Swan (Susan) Thompson, Anderson Fambrough and John Kilgore, of State and county aforesaid, have sold unto William Milton of the county of Greene and State aforesaid all our right and title, claim, estate and in-trust from us our heirs and assigns belonging to us or claiming by us of our certain unascertained one thous-and acres of land each survey made the 7th and 8th day of August, last for our head rights now passed through the county surveyors office of said county for seven (?) thousand acres of land on the waters of the Oconie and we do hereby authorize the said William Melton to take through the general surveyors office said works as above mentioned and obtained.

Granted over our own names after-wards to be applied to her own use and benefit as she may think proper and necessary to be done in and about the premises. In witness whereof we have hereunto set our hands and seals, this 8th of December, 1804.

Interlined before assigned of gree-ing.

Bartlet (X) (his mark) Wooten, Johnson Renfrow, John Blair, Spen-cer Renfrow, William Nobles, Henry Huff, John Armstrong, Job Springer, Philip Tigner, John Henderson, Wil-liam Jameston, John (X) (his mark) Kilgore, Anderson Fambrough, Susan Thompson. (Seal after each name.) This—day December, 1804.

Attest: Alex Hall, J. P., John Smith, John W. Addle.

Clark County Book of deeds A, p371.

There is no positive proof, and there is a considerable delay in time but I am of the opinion nevertheless that these were the orphans and the rep-resentatives of orphans mentioned in executives minutes as orphans of William Blair and that William Blair was the husband of Sibbiah and they were both dead at the time of the execution of the above deed. This William I think was the brother of Johnson Blair. In support of this be-lief I present an abstract of deed taken from Clark county deed records, Nov. 7th, 1835: John Blair, of New-ton county, Ga., deeds to Needham McLeroy of Clarke Co. Ga. 75 acres in Clarke Co. and watered by Dove Creek. Test. Jonathan Lindley and Wilburt Hunt. Acknowledged before

Virgil W. Akridge, J. P. In Walton Co. Ga. James Blair with James Lindley witness will of Andrew Blair, James Blair took conveyances from Cordy Barnes and James Lindley and executed conveyances to John Sum-merson, George Willingham land in Newton county at present 1824. Re-corded in record book 1827-1834, Wal-ton county. James Lindley vs James Blair. Blair confessed judgment for $300.00. This James Blair 1820 was between 26 and 45 years of age, wife between same ages, and there were two girls between 10 and 16.

In a photostat copy of MSS sent me appear the following: "Blair, Johnson, (Private), John Twiggs B. G." See appended letters.

The following records were copied by L. W. Rigsby from old Bible in possession of William B. Blair of Cobb County, Ga. This is the old Bible records of Joseph Blair, son of George Blair, Irish immigrant:

Joseph Blair was born 6th day of March, 1801.

Elizabeth Blair was born the 27th day of January, 1808.

Sarah Blair was born the 19th day of April, 1826.

Allen Blair was born the 1st day of August, 1824.

Margaret Blair was born the 17th day of May, 1831.

Loid Blair was born, January 10th, 1834.

Columbus Blair was born 29th day of November, 1836.

James Blair was born 8th day of March, 1839.

Albert Blair was born 4th day of June, 1842.

Washington Blair was born the 9th day of April, 1845.

W .B. Blair was born the 30th day of October, 1848.

Joseph Alby Blair was born Nov-ember 26th, 1852.

Joseph Blair and Elizabeth Stock-ton was married the 28th day of December, 1827.

Martin McElreath and Sarah Blair was married October the 26th, 1844.

Charles James and Margaret Blair was married September 19, 1847.

Allen Blair and Marindy Newburn was married April 11th, 1850.

Columbus Blair and Sarah M. Kedd was married January 1st, 1857.

Loyd Blair and Piety S. James was married November the 7th, 1858.

Loyd Blair and L. M. Kedd was married August 15th, 1861.

W. B. Blair and Sarah E. Danforth was married June 3rd, 1866.

Joseph A. Blair died June 7th, 1854, aged 1 year,, 6 months and 11 days.

Piety S. Blair departed this life September 17th, 1859.

Albert Blair died May 6th, 1862, aged 20 years and 4 months and 2 days.

Loyd Blair died the 1st day of December, 1862, age 29 years and 10 months and 21 days.

Joseph Blair departed this life April 2nd, 1871; age 70 years, 1 month and 15 days.

Elizabeth Blair, the wife of Joseph Blair, died July 13, age 79 years 5 months and 16 days.

At the time of copying these records W. B. Blair stated as follows: George Blair, Irish Immigrant, married Elizabeth Yarbrough. Joseph Blair was the eldest child. Other children were Jane Blair who married James Clay. They moved to Carrol county and from there to Texas. Mittie Blair married Amon Yarbrough. Charles Blair never married. Died in Mexican war. George Washington Blair moved to Texas after Civil War. John Blair moved to Calhoun county, Ala., where he died. He left a son named William Blair. Joseph Blair had a cousin named Nancy Bowen but does not know her maiden name. Other traditions are that George Blair had a brother, William, and a brother, "Wash." This indicates another Blair immigrant to Georgia.

DEPARTMENT OF STATE
Atlanta, Ga.,
November 18, 1927.

Judge L. W. Rigsby,
Cairo, Georgia.

Dear Judge Rigsby:

I have your lettter of the 14th instant relative to the record of Revolutionary service of Johnson Blair.

I have just examined the manuscript copy of the list of Georgia Revolutionary Soldiers, which was later published by Dr. Lucien Lamar Knight, at the time he was State Historian, and I find opposite the name of Johnson Blair, a notation to the effect that a certificate of service was issued by General Twiggs.

I don't know whether you are aware of just what has taken place in the past decade relating to these certificates of service and I am going to recite as nearly as I can, the facts. The certificates of service of the Revolutionary Soldiers were on file in this office when I came here 17 years ago, and at the time Dr. Knight decided to publish the Roster of Revolutionary Soldiers, we gave him access to all the records in the office and turned over to him ,to be copied, all the certificates of service, which you will note are published in the said roster. After the copy had been completed, the certificates were returned to this office and were deposited here until the General Assemb.y passed a law requiring all State Departments to deliver to the Department of Archives, all records and books not in general use and at the time the State Historian called delivered to him a large quantity of documents and records which had been on storage and file in this office for an age or more and among such records were the certificates of service of Revolutionary Soldiers.

The work of indexing and the proper filing of such old records required quite a lot of work and extended over quite a period of time, but they are now properly indexed and filed so that they are readily accessible in the office of the Department of Archives and History. Miss Blair and I have made a careful examination of such files and the certificate of service of Johnson Blair as a Revolutionary Soldier is not on file in the Department of Archives, although there is no doubt in my mind that this document, once was among such files, but as to its whereabouts now, I regret I am unable to say.

Johnson Blair did not take advantage of his privilege of making out the necessary papers for the purpose of procuring a bounty land grant of 287½ acres of land and I believe when you were here in the summer made investigation as to this feature.

If you can suggest in any way in which I can assist you further in this matter, I shall be glad to have you write me.

With kindest regards, I am
Yours very truly,
A. T. HARRIS,
Chief Clerk.

DEPARTMENT OF STATE
Atlanta, Ga.,
December 19, 1927.
Hon. L. W. Rigsby,
Cairo, Georgia.
Dear Mr. Rigsby:

I have your letter of the 17th relative to the grant of land to Nancy Blair in Lee County, will say that this property is now in Terrell Co., Georgia, it being a part of the territory taken to form said county in 1856.

I am sending you photographic copy of a portion of the list of the manuscript copy of the Revolutionary Soldiers as was compiled by Captain B. F. Johnson, who was at one time connected with this office. You will note that immediately to the right of the name of Johnson Blair that the name of John Twiggs appears, which indicates that John Twiggs had been given a certificate as to the Revolutionary Service of said John Blair.

Yours very truly,
A. T. HARRIS

With this, so far as I am able to learn, the name of Johnson Blair disappears from the records. I have searched the early records as published of all the original States and also the census records. I do not find any record of Johnson Blair by that name but do find a John Blair in both North and South Carolina who I can identify with considerable certainty as Johnson Blair. I do not find a John Blair in Georgia, however, whom I can identify. In Greene County, Ga. I find the following in a pamphlet index to deeds:

"Blair to Tisdale B 677"
"Blair to Keating B 405"
"Blair to Moore, Book 4 page 3"

The first two conveyances have been removed from book, the third is as follows:

STATE OF GEORGIA:

THIS INDENTURE made this sixteenth day of January in the year of our Lord one thousand eight hundred and four and in the twenty eight year of the Independence of the United States of America between John Blare and Jane, his wife, of the County of Greene and State aforesaid of the one part and Joshua Moore of the County and State aforesaid of the other part WITNESSETH that the said John Blare and Jane his wife for and in consideration of the sum of five hundred dollars to them in hand well and truly paid by the said Joshua Moore at or before the sealing and delivery of these presents the receipt whereof is hereby acknowledged have granted bargained sold released and confirmed and by these presents do grant bargain sell release and confirm unto the said Joshua Moore his heirs, assigns a certain tract or parcel of land lying and being in Greene County and aforesaid state containing one hundred acres more or less beginning at a Black Oak on the north side of the branch running north 16 w 36 chains to a sweet gum corner, thence south 85 E 47 chains to a pine corner, thence S 86 E 3 chains to a post Oak corner, thence down the said branch to the beginning together with all and singular the rights members appertenances thereof whatsoever to the said tract of land being belonging or in anywise appertaining and the remainders, reversions, rents, issues and profits thereof and every part thereof to HAVE AND TO HOLD the said tract of land and all and singular the premises and appurtenances thereunto belonging as aforesaid and every part thereof unto the said Joshua Moore, his heirs and assigns to the only proper use benefit and behoof of the said Joshua Moore, his heirs and assigns forever and the said John Blare and Jane his wife and his heirs and assigns and every other person and persons whatsoever shall and will warrant and forever defend by these presents. IN WITNESS whereof the said John Blare and Jean his wife have hereunto set their hands and seals the day and year above written.

JOHN BLAIR, (Seal)
JEAN BLAIR, (Seal)
Signed, sealed and deliv-

ered in the presence of:
Solomon Burford,
Mitchel Burford,
Jonathan Shockley.
March the 5th 1804, the above deed
proven agreeable to Law.
JOHN ARMOR, J. P.
Registered this 5th of March 1804.
J. L. FANNIN, (Illegible)
Tho Carlton Clk.
GEORGIA, GREENE COUNTY.
I, E. J. Stanley, clerk of the Super-
ior Court of said County, do hereby
certify that I have compared the
foregoing copy of deed from John
Blair and Jean Blair to Joshua
Moore, of said County and State
with the original record thereof, now
remaining in this office, and the same
is a correct transcript therefrom,
and of the whole of such original
record, and that said court is a court
of record.

In testimony whereof, I have hereunto set my hand and affixed the
seal of the said court, this the 21st
day of May, 1928.
E. J. STANLEY, C. S. C.
Greene County.
(SEAL)

The fact that this deed was signed
by the wife of John Blair is some
evidence that they came into Georgia from some other state. This, I
think was the same John Blair, who
later, upon the death of his wife,
Jean Blair, went back to Mecklinburg
County, North Carolina and married
Nancy Eakes. That he was a soldier in the Revolution is proven by
land grant to wife Nancy Blair, resident of Washington County. Land
in Lee, now Terrell County, No. 222,
11th District, 1st section.

We have no further interest in
this John Blair than to establish the
fact that he has no direct bearing
upon Johnson Blair. He may have
been the son of William Blair. This
family of Blairs appear to have settled at a later date in Washington
County, Georgia,, ' Capt. Worthins
District. This was in the northern
part of the County. Another family
of Blairs appear to have settled in
the lower part of the County, near
Cedar Creek. This family appears
to have been that of George Blair,
said to have been an immigrant.
These Blairs were evidenely of the
same family as the Blairs of Vir-

ginia and in my opinion were related
to the McCalls of whom Hugh Mc-
Call was a member.

Having exhausted information relating to Johnson Blair we will now
proceed with his children.

Proof as to relationship of William Blair, of Walton County, Georgia, to Jane R. Blair is positive and
conclusive. Tradition from T. W.
Rigsby as to William Blair's blind-
ness is corroborated by all of the
older descendants of William Blair as
well as details and circumstances.
Mrs. J. C. McKown in a personal in-
terview went into all of the details
in the presence of T. N. Lindley and
Dr. Lindley, of Powder Springs and
before learning of the tradition from
T. W. Rigsby. T. N. Lindley and
Dr. Lindley had already been informed of the tradition as related by T.
W. Rigsby. All were agreed that
Jane R. Blair Rigsby and William
Blair were either brother and sister
or half brother and sister.

In addition to traditions and circumstances related before, all descendants are agreed that Nancy Blair
who married Jonathon Lindley was a
sister of this William Blair and for
this reason we give considerable genealogies and facts relating to Jonathan Lindley as an aid in clearing
up the mystery surrounding Johnson
Blair.

From old books which I have read
and statements which I have heard
made there must have been a family
of Blairs in Ireland, County, Antrim,
designated locally as the Johnson-
Blairs, presumably from a frequent
intermarriage with the Johnson family. In my opinion Johnson Blair
was of this family of Blairs. It may
have been that there was confusion
because of this, or that his name was
contracted into John. Be that as it
may, the evidence to my mind is clear
that he appears on the records in
both North Carolina and South Carolina simply as John Blair. I am
inclined to believe that the name was
Johnson and that Twiggs gave it
correctly but it may have been John
given as Johnson because of the circumstances as given above.

That Johnson Blair was a resident
of Orange County, North Carolina,
quite early as a refugee from Georgia is shown by the following facts;

Jonathon Lindley was a resident of this county at the time of his marriage to Nancy Blair, Census records of 1790 were destroyed but on a tax return prior to 1800 John Blair returns poll but no real estate, and State records of North Carolina, Vol. 22, p 416 "A pay roll of Capt. Nathaniel Hart's company of the Orange Regiment of Militia that were in the late expedition against the Insurgents of this Province. John Blair 68 days @ 2s, L 6-16-0. No other Blair is mentioned on Tax Roll and Census of 1800, Orange County North Carolina shows no John Blair and the only Blair shown is James Blair who then was between 26 and 45 years of age, had one boy, under ten, three girls, under ten, and his wife was between 26 and 45 years of age. A tradition given by Mrs. J. C. McKown is that her Sorrels and Blairs, ancestors served together in the Revolution and were at the battle of the Cowpen's and Kings Mountain. I find that Thos Sorrell, Ben Sorrell, and Lewis Sorrell mentioned as Revolutionary soldiers in North Carolina.

That he left North Carolina at an early date is shown by the Census records of Jane R. Blair, Rigsby, (See Rigsby Sketch) and also Census record of James Lindley and wife Mary Blair Lindley. All three of these were born in South Carolina, over a period of time from 1797 to 1812. During this period I find no Johnson Blair in South Carolina and Secretary of State, South Carolina, informs me that no Johnson Blair ever received a grant of land from the State of South Carolina. I do find however in Abbeville County, S. C., 1810, John Blair head of family, over 45 years of age, 1 son under 10, 1 between 10 and 16 and 1 between 16 and 20. The only other Blair resident in the district at that time was Hugh Blair. Now in 1820 there were residents in Abbeville County, South Carolina William Blair, over 45 with males 2 under ten, 1 between 10 and 16, 1 between 16 and 18, 1 between 16 and 26, 2 females under ten, 1 between 10 and 16 and 1 over 45. Also Catherine Blair with 3 males under 10, 2 between 10 and 16, 1 female between 10 and 16, 1 be-

tween 16 and 26 and one between 26 and 45. (Query?) Was this the widow of John Blair? I do not think so. A careful examination of Census returns show that children do not correspond. Administration on the estate of William Blair (See docments) indicate most strongly that he was a resident of Abbeville County South Carolina, 1820. William Blair's records of children,, date of death of wife, age given of children and number of children in Census of 1820 indicates that there were children in the family not belonging to him. He is credited with 5 males before 1820 when Bible record mentions only one born prior to 1820 and one born in December of this year. He is credited with 2 girls under 10 and 1 under 16. The descendants are not at all clear as to several Blair names mentioned in Bible as will be seen by reference to appended correspondence relating to the family of William Blair. Tradition is that there was a second marriage but no proofs and all the Blair children credited to William Blair could not have been his. Circumstances indicate that he married Andrew Blair's widow, and that some of the children in record were Andrews. It is possible that William Blair may have taken the minor children of Johnson Blair after the death of Johnson Blair, or that Andrew Blair took them or that they were divided between the two. It is all confusing and nothing can be stated positively as to that. It is certain in my mind, however, that the John Blair in Abbeville in 1880 was the same as Johnson Blair.

Comparing census record of William Blair, of Walton County, 1830, with Bible records we find that there was a female living with him in 1820 that was not with him in 1830. This female was over 45 years of age in 1820, his first wife was dead at that time and this must have been his step-mother. There is no evidence of Johnson Blair or John Blair, father of William, et al., or his widow, ever coming to Georgia. Wiley Taylor Rigsby and Jane R. Blair certainly were married in Georgia, probably Gwinnett County, no Blairs were in that county in 1820, 1830 or 1840, neither were there Vatins. Rigsbys moved into the county before 1830

and out before 1840, while there was
a land grant to one Robert Blair to
land in Gwinnett County, there is no
record of him as a resident of the
county. True the records of the
county have been burned but it hardly seems probable that a member of
the family could have resided in the
County long without some trace having been left either in the Census
Bureau, among the land grants or
elsewhere. There are many other
circumstances too numerous to enumerate and without details, such as the
facts that Jane R. Blair Rigsby mentioned the details of the loss of the
eyesight of William Blair with fre-
quency and detail enough to fix the
fact on the memory of T. W. Rigsby, the fact that her name is written in the records, Jane R., indicates
that there was another Jane in the
family and William had a daughter,
Jane, that there was no other probable home in Georgia save in the
home of William Blair or Andrew,
etc., etc., etc. Records of Abbeville,
S. C. have been destroyed by fire for
period covered I am informed by the
authorities in S. C.

ANDREW BLAIR.

T. W. Rigsby remembers hearing
his mother mention her brother, Andrew but can give no details. Census records from Walton County, Ga.,
1820 show Andrew Blair head of a
family with 2 males under ten, two
between 10 and 16, 1 between 26 and
45; 1 female under 10, 1 between 16
and 26 and 1 between 26 and 45. He
owned one negro March 1, 1821 in
Walton county. Andrew Blair makes
will bequeathing all property to wife,
Martha for life to be disposed of at
her discretion. No children named.
Signed Andrew Blair by mark. Witness James Lindley and James Blair.
Books of Wills and returns 1819 to
1827, page 22.

JOHN BLAIR AND OTHER
CHILDREN.

John Blair certainly never came to
Georgia. I doubt that any of his
children ever came. I have found
none of his descendants. It is my
opinion that this is the same John
Blair that resided for a time in Washington County, North Carolina, later

Washington County, Tennessee. I
think that his family came to South
Carolina about 1819 and soon after
his death. He certainly was not the
ancestor of the Blairs of Loudon Co.,
Tennessee.

I am positive that there were other
children, not named by W. T. Rigsby,
but do not care to enter into specula-
tion in regard to them and so leave
the question for others to complete
the list.

Following Records Copied by L. W.
Rigsby from Cemetery at
Powder Springs, Ga.

James Lindley, born Dec. 9, 1797,
died Dec. 29, 1886 aged 89 years and
20 days.

Mary Lindley born Feb. 20, 1797,
died June 27, 1864.

From old Bible in possession of Mrs.
Jno. C. McKown; Powder Springs,
Ga., and known as the Blair Bible,
copied and notes made by L. W. Rigsby.

William Blair and Rosey McCal-
ister was (born) Married, February,
14th, A. D., 1793. (N. B.—This record
was evidently taken from an older
Bible.)

James Lindley and Mary Blair was
married October 3rd 1815.

William W. Lindley was born Nov.
1st, 1816.

Rosannah Lindley was born Jan.
25th, 1819.

John Benson Lindley was born Feb.
29, 1825.

James Marshal Lindley was born
July 8th, 1827.

Margaret Jane Lindley was born
June 27th, 1831.

Louisa E. Sorrells was born Nov.
30th, 1836.

Charles N. Sorrells was born Mch.
19th 1838.

Mary J. Sorrells was born July
9th, 1842.

Martha F. Sorrells was born July
3rd, 1845.

James T. Sorrells was born Jan.
29th, 1848.

Robert A. Sorrells was born April
26th, 1850.

John M. Sorrells was born July 6th
1855.

Rosannah McCalestar was born the
5th day of December, 1773.

Sarah Blair was born March the
23rd, A. D., 1794.

Mary Blair was born February the 20th, A. D. 1796.

Margaret Blair was born September the 4th, A. D. 1798.

Elizabeth Blair was born December the 6th, A. D. 1800.

Anne Blair was born March the 29th, A. D. 1804.

John Wilson Blair was born July 22nd, A. D. 1807.

Caroline Blair was born the 22 day of March, 1811.

Jinny Blair was born the 31st day of August, 1812.

Martha Caroline Blair was born March 16, 1819.

William Smith Blair was born Dec. 6, 1820.

Andrew Blair was born December the 14th, A. D. 1822.

Marinday Blair was born A. D., Jan. 28, 1825.

Charlotte Harrison was born the 3rd day of May, 1809.

Louisa Blair was born September the 30th 1827.

James Blair was born Sept. the 5th A. D., 1825.

Emily Blair was born Jan. 1st, A. D. 1832.

James Lindley was born December the 9th, 1797.

John M. Sorrells Died Feb. the 20 1917.

Jonathon Lindley was born Feb. 23, 1814.

John W. Blair was born (illegible. Appears to have been a very old record.)

Jonathan Linly.

John Osborn was born Oct. 15th, 1803.

Kinon Kotton Mote was born April 12th, 1848. (N. B. Said to have been no relation.)

Elizabeth Smith died Sept. 4th, 1886.

Martha Baggett died Feb. 12, 1912.

Rosanah Blair, Deceased, the 10th day of September, 1816, aged 43.

Lendie M. Sorrells was born Dec. the 12th, 1874. (N. B. This name is written over a name beginning John Remainder illeligible.)

Letter J. (remainder is illegible.)

Jane Blair was born August 31st, 1812. (The letter J as above does not appear to be apart of name Jane Blair but is at beginning of name.

Margaret Carpenter departed this life February 29th, 1836.

Robert H. Lesley was born Febru-

ary the 25th, 1828.

William B. Sorrells was born Dec. 7th, 1854.

Lonard (Leonard) B. H. Sorrells was born 19th March, 1858.

Eliza Sorrells was born July the 23rd, 1873.

H. D. Sorrells was born January the 5th 1876. (N. B. Attempts has been made to scratch this out.)

Robert A. Sorrells died August 13, 1927.

Mary J. Ward died October the 3rd, 1917.

Charles N. Sorrells departed this life August 30th, 1862, being killed at Manassas Va.

Mary M. Lindley departed this life June the 27th, 1864, she being sixty-eight years, four months and ven days of age.

Robert A. Sorrells and Julia E. Phillips, his wife, were married Oct. 31, 1872.

H. D. Sorrells was born January 25th, 1876.

Elva Ada Sorrells was born Sept. 5th, 1878.

Marriages From Walton County Court of Ordinary. By L. W. Rigsby.

Thomas Lesly and Caroline Blair Feb. 28, 1826.

Jonathan Lindley and Milley Henry Nov. 15, 1827.

Jacob Carpenter and Margaret Blair, March 11,1830. Marriage performed by James Lindley, J. P.

Jesse H. Atchinson and Miss Jane Blair, August 4, 1831.

Russel B. Sorrells and Miss Rosannah C. Lindley, Nov. 7th, 1833.

Wills and Administrations.

March 1, 1821, Andrew Blair makes will of all property to wife, Martha for lift to be disposed of at her discretion No children named. Signed, Andrew Blair, by mark. Witness, James Lindley and James Blair. Book of Wills and Returns, 1819 to 1827, page 22.

Jesse H. Atchinson granted letters of Administration on estate of William Blair, Sept. 4, 1837.

In one of the returns of the above administrator appears the following item (Page 117 book of returns for 1839) "To going to South Carolina and back, in all 7 days and finding myself and horse at two dollars per

day, $14.00."
James Lindley vs. James Blair,
Deft. Blair confessed Judgment for
$300.00. Record book 1827-1834
Conveyances.
James Blair to George Willingham,
Feb. 14th, 1824, Book F, Page 35,
both of Walton County, Ga. Land in
Walton County when surveyed now
Newton County, Lot 313 in 4th Dis-
trict
Cordy Barnes to James Blair, book
E, page 81, Dec. 18, 1823.
James Lindley to Wm. Blair, book
F, Page 106, both of Walton County,
lot No. 81 in 3rd district, June 23,
1825.
James Blair to John Summerson,
Lot No. 26, in 3rd District. Date,
Feb. 6th, 1827.
James Lindley to James Blair, 50
acres land in lower half of lot No.
26 in 3rd District on Beaverdam
Creek.

CORRESPONDENCE.
Atlanta, Ga., 9-2-1927.
Mr. Rigsby; Sir:
Yours to hand. Contents noted.
I am a son of John Wilson Blair and
Minerva Poole. There is only three
of us living. Myself; Olie Cunning-
ham, Baird, Texas; Henry Blair, Tye,
Texas. I have four children living;
Bessie Huckeba, Atlanta, Ga., Rt. 9;
Evie Rakestraw, Dallas, Ga.; Lillie
Einl, Atlanta, Ga., Mason Ave; and
Hershel Blair, Rt. 9 Atlanta, Ga. My
father's father lived in South Caro-
lina, was blind for many years, is as
full a description as I can give of my
family.
I know but very little of my father's people. I never saw any of them.
J. M. BLAIR, Atlanta, Ga.
Route 9. c|o W. C. Huckeba.
"Baird, Tex., 9-9-1927.
L. W. Rigsby, Cairo, Ga.
Your letter of Sept. 3rd to hand.
I will answer the best I can.
First, my father, John Wilson Blair
and mother Minerva Pool Blair had
ten children—two of which are living,
myself and one brother, Henry Blair,
who lives at Tye, Texas. He has four
children; one niece in California, her
parents are dead, don't know her address; six nieces and nephews living,
five in Texas and two in Georgia. I
am a widow. My husband is dead. I
had one child, died when 3 years old.

My mother's father's name was
John L. Pool and my Mother's Moth-
er's name was Minerva Jane Pool.
My father had two brothers and three
sisters—Uncle Mack Blair and Uncle
Jim Blair. Both died in Fannin Co.,
Texas and left one child living. All
I know.
OLLIE CUNNINGHAM"

"Baird, 9-20-1927.
L. W. Rigsby, Cairo, Ga., Dear Sir:
Have just received yours of the 14th
and will give you all the information
I can of my father's people. My
grandfather, Blair, was married
twice. My father was by his first
wife. I don't know how many chil-
dren he had by his first wife. I had
an aunt by the name of Betsey but I
forgot who she married. She died in
Georgia when I was a small child.
His second wife came to Texas with
her children, Uncle Jim, Uncle Mac
and one girl, Aunt Emley, which all
died after I came to Texas. Aunt
Emley married a man by the name of
Ligh Farris and they both died in
Gracon Co., Texas and Mac and Jim
Blair and their mother died in Hunt
Co. I never saw them but I assisted
Aunt Emiley and she said that Jim
Blair never had any children but
Uncle Mac Blair had one boy and his
name was Mac but I don't know where
he is. Uncle Mac and Jim came to
Georgia with the Texas Rangers and
that was the last time my father ever
saw them. Now my father had 10
children. My two brothers and two
sisters came to Texas and the rest
all died in Georgia except my eldest
brother, Jim, who is living there now.
He married John Mohorns' daughter
and he had 5 children, but I think
there is only 3 living but I don't know
about them as I left there when I was
18 years old. My oldest sister Seaby
Blair married a man by the name of
Jim Priest and came to Texas when
I was a child. She only lived 14
months after she came and she has no
children. My next sister, Lula Blair,
married a man named Bull Chapman.
She had 5 children. She also came to
Texas and her and all her children are
dead but one and she married a Mr.
Thompson and is in California. My
two next brothers, Joe and Henry,

came to Texas and brother Joe died
leaving no children and Henry is still
living. He married a Miss Crutchfield and has five children, 3 married
and one single and has 2 grand children. He lives at Tye, Texas, 30
miles west of here. So there is only
three of us children living. I married
Jim Cunningham and had one child
and she died when she was three
years old. I don't know of any Clays
that married a Blair. So this is all
I remember about my father's people.
I am planning to come to Atlanta,
Ga., some time the first of next year
and may buy me a home there. So
if I do would be very glad to meet you
as I would like to meet some of my
father's people and if there is any
thing else I can do to help you in this
would be glad to do so I have some
friends in Hunt Co., and I will see if
I can find out any more about the
Blairs there and let you know if I do
so. Hoping I have made this plain to
you I am very respectfully yours,

OLLIE CUNNINGHAM."

Above letters are from descendants
of William Blair by his son John Wilson Blair. The following letters are
from descendants by his daughter
Elizabeth who married Henry Mitchell. His daughter Mary, married her
cousin, James Lindley, and information regarding her is included in the
Lindley Genealogies.

"Douglasville, Ga., Oct. 5, 1927.
Mr. L. W. Rigsby, Cairo, Ga.,
Dear Sir:
In reply to your letter of August
30th. I have failed to find the old
family Bible. Elizabeth Blair Mitchell was my grandmother. She died
Nov. 15th, 1883. I remember very
well, she was 83 years old. My grandfather died May 3, 1859, was 56 years
old when he died. My grandmother
had two sisters, one married a Milford, the other a Lindley. She also
had one brother, John Blair. These
are all I know of. She had 8 children,
5 boys and 3 girls. All are dead.
None of their children live in Georgia
now but my father's family and one
sister's family. My father raised 11
children, 4 boys and 7 girls, 6 living
now . If not providentially hindered I
will be at Macon during the Masonic
Grand Lodge. If you happen to be
there or have a friend there would be

glad to see you. Perhaps could give
you some information that I have not
written. Would be glad to hear from
you again.
Respectfully,
W. H. MITCHELL."
"Ladonia, Tex., Feb. 7, 1928.
The Pioneer Institute, Cairo, Ga.
Gentlemen: My grandmother (my
father's mother) was Miss Elizabeth
Blair (married to Henry McDonald
Mitchel.). Was a sister-in-law to
Mrs. Francis Blair, now living at
1339 13th Place Tulsa, Oka. Grand-
mother was also a descendant of Ire-
land; having crossed over here at the
age of six years.
I have an adopted brother living in
Georgia, Henry M. Mitchell. I fail
to have his address but it can be ob-
tained from Frank M. Mitchell, Mc-
Cauley, Texas.
Bill Mitchell, brother of Henry M.
Mitchell has children, one namely, J.
H. Mitchell, Ida, La., R. 3. Valuable
information might be obtained
through him.
Yours respectfully,
MRS. N. C. MILFORD."
Douglasville, Ga., Oct., 20, 1927
Dear Sir:
I received your letter today and
will give you all the information I
can. Aunt Rosie Mitchell's husband's
name was Lewis Hopgood. She had
three children. Two of them are dead,
one is living but I do not know the
address of the one that is living. I
don't remember anything about Francis Marion Mitchell. My grandmother's name was Betsy Blair. She married Henry Mitchell. I will give you
the children's names. William Mitchell married a Stewart and they are a.l
in Texas but I don't know their address. Uncle Frank Mitchell married
a Stewart and they had nine children.
Five are still living but I don't know
the address of but one of the boys and
that is Henry Mitchell, Douglasville,
Ga. Aunt Polly Mitchell married Lyse
Crow, they went to Texas. I don't
know anything about any of their
children but one, her address is Fannie Lee, Bloomberg, Texas. I am sure
she can give you some information if
she will. Write her. Uncle Jack
Mitchell married and they had one
child but he is dead. Uncle Jack was
killed in the civil war. Jane Mitchell was my mother. She married Lew-

is Jones and he was killed in the Civil War and he left three girls. One of them got burned to death when she was small, my sister and I are still living. My sister married Jim Prickett. Their address is Douglasville, Ga. All of the old set of Mitchell's are dead. I can remember seeing my old Uncle Johnnie Blair, my grandmother's brother when I was a small child. I will answer all the questions I can as far as I know.

MRS. C. W. MOSS,
Douglasville, Ga.

Queen City, Texas
October 31st, 1927.

L. W. Rigsby, Cairo, Ga.

Sir:

Mrs. W. C. Moss sent me your letter she received from you dated Oct. 17, she is my cousin. Our mother's were sisters. Aunt Rosa Hobgood was their sister too. Her husband's name was Lewis Hobgood. They had three children, William, Frank and Mary, but I do not know the address of either of them. If they are living you can find them by writing to Henry Mitchell at Douglasville, Ga. Francis Marion Mitchell was my Uncle. He married Tinie Stewart. You write to Mrs. W. W. Rickerson, Russellville, Ala., at 148 Washington Street. She can tell you the whereabouts of all of Uncle Frank's children and their names. She is the oldest one of the children. Pollie Mitchell was my mother and she married Elias L. Crow. There is four of us children; Mrs. Fannie Lee, of Queen City, Texas, Route 2; John A. Crow, Texarkana, Ark, Lincoln, Ave; Mrs. Lou Wall,, Galveston, Texas, 1610 Ave N½; Mrs. Geneva Westmoreland, Bloomberg, ,Texas. Jonathan Mitchell never was married. He died when he was a young man. Jack Mitchell married Susan Jones. He died in the Civil war service, their only child's name was Jefferson. He is dead. Henry M. Mitchell married Sarah Stewart. You write to Mrs. N. C. Millford, Ladonia, Texas. Jane Mitchell married Louis Jones, she has three girls. Mrs. W. C. Moss and Minnie Griggs, both of Douglasville, Ga., and Senie Prickett, of Milledgeville, Ga. My mother, Mrs. Pollie Crow and all of her brothers and sisters are all dead. If what I have written you will be of any information I will be glad and if not, commit these lines to the waste basket.

Yours truly,
Mrs. Fannie Lee, Queen City, Tex.

Jonathan Lindley and Nancy Blair Lindley.

Nancy Blair is identified as being a sister of William Blair by all of the best informed descendants and there are none who dispute the fact. We have found no dates relating to Jonathan Lindley other than those shown by Census records and appended documents. We do not have the date of his birth, marriage or death or the birth of Nancy Blair. She died May 27, 1840 according to information furnished by Mrs. J. L. Beeson. It had been presumed that she was married about 1796. I am sure that this is entirely too late and that the presumption arose because of the date of the birth of James Lindley which is known and that it was presumed that the marriage occurred within two or three years before this date. This is evidently an error as will be shown from the following documents which will also convince us that there were several more children than those we have succeeded in locating: Jonathan Lindley was living in Walton County, Georgia in 1820. His family consisted of 3 males under 10, 1 under 16, 1 between 16 and 26 and 1 between 26 and 45 which last was clearly an error, it should have been over 45. The females were 1 under ten, 1 between 16 and 26 and one over 45. The family are agreed that he came to Georgia from Pendleton Dist., S. C. The census there for 1810 shows Jonathan Lindlay head of family of 3 males under 10, 1 between 10 and 16, 1 between 26 and 45, 3 beyond 45; females 1 between 10 and 16, 1 between 26 and 45 and 3 beyond 45. Now if we compare these two returns for the same family we are forced to the conclusion that both Jonathan Lindley and his wife were more than 45 at that time, 1810. Keeping this in mind in 1800 we find Jonathan Lindley in Orange County, N. Carolina and at that time there were as follows: One male under 10, 1 between 10 and 16, 1 between 16 and 26 and 1 between 26 and 45; 4 females under 10, 1 between 10 and 16, 1 between 26 and 45. This makes a total of 9 children in 1800, and I have proof that 4 were born after this but of these thirteen known chi.dren, and I think there were seven more, we have only found eight which persuades me to believe that Nancy Lindley was born before 1860 perhaps considerably before this. N. C. state records, Vol. 18, p413, shows Jonathan Lindley named as a Justice of the Peace, page 375 shows that he was a member of the House of Representatives and that he was a member of the Constitutional Convention 1788 which persuades me that he was born some time before 1760 that is between 1755 and 1760. Marriage must have occurred during the Revolution, therefore, we can approximate the date of marriage as being between 1770 and 1775. Now there was among the descendants at Powder Springs Georgia until destroyed by moth's a baby's bonnett said to have been worn to America from Ireland. More will be said of this bonnett as we proceed. This fact proves that Johnson Blair's first marriage was in Ireland and that the fami.y came to America before 1770. Tradition is that Jonathan Lindley sympathized with the Crown during the Revolution, which tradition I accept as correct. However, he must have been a man of unusual personality and have enjoyed a high share of the confidence and esteem of his fellow citizens in order to receive the votes of confidence and commendation so soon after the close of the war. His wife was the daughter of a Patriot, whose brother was perhaps in the Patriot army and Jonathan Lindley appears to have furnished a refuge for the aged and indigent after the Revolution. He owned considerable property in Orange county, North Carolina, on some of which Lind.ey's Mill, the scene of a battle in the Revolution was probably located, and there are some indications that he rendered service to the Patriot cause but not definite. We will now proceed to give children, so far as we have been able to find them and their descendants.

A. James Lindley b Dec. 9, 1797. B. Ruth Lindley b before 1800. C. Lethie Lindley b Sept. 18, 1803. D. Jennie Lindley b Dec. 16, 1804. E. William Lindley b about 1806. F. Jonathan Lindley, Jr., b Feb. 22, 1808. G. Thos. Lindley b Jan. 16, 1810. H. Elisha H. Lindley b Jan. 25, 1816.

Comparing this with the census re-

cord of Walton County 1820 we find 2 boys and 1 girl, all under ten not named in above list while from the Census of 1800 in Orange County we find that that Census included 2 boys not named and three girls not named. If these were all children of Jonathan Lindley then they had sixteen children of whom I have record of but eight.

James Lindley

1A

James Lindley b Dec. 9, 1797, S.C., d, Dec. 29, 1886 at Powder Springs, Ga. Married his first Cousin, Mary Blair, dau. of William Blair (b Feb. 20, 1797 d June 27 1864) Oct. 3, 1815. James Lindley served as Justice of the Peace, was Sheriff of Walton County and a teacher. Issue: a- William W. Lindley. b- Rosannah Lindley, c- John Benson Lindley, d- James Marshall Lindley, e- Margaret Jane Lindley.

1Ab

Rosannah Lindley b Jan. 25, 1819, m Russell B. Sorrells Nov. 7, 1833. Issue: 1'- Louisa, 2'- Charles N. Killed at second battle of Manassas, 3'- Mary J., 4'- Martha F., 5'- JamesT, 6'- Robert A., 7'- John M., 8'- Eliza Sorre.ls m John C. McKown and is in possession of the old Blair Bible, 9'- Leonard, 10'- W. B. Sorrells.

N. B. Mrs. McKown was asked the following questions by me "Please give all information possible about the Sorrels fami.y. What was the name of the Ancestor who was in the Revolution? Give all the facts as you have heard them." To this she made the following answer: "My great grandfather, whose name I can't recall served in the Revolution under the command of General Dan Morgan and was wounded in the Battle of the Cowpens" This question was propounded because of the tradition among the older members of the family that her Sorrells and Blair ancestors were companions in service during the Revolution.

Mr. J. W. Moon, 956 Stewart Ave., S. W., Atlanta, Ga. says that Russell B. Sorrells was a son of Charles Sorrells and that he thinks that Charles Sorrells was a son of Benjamin Sorrels.

Charles Sorrells was a representative in the General Assembly of Geor-

gia 1813 and 1814 and Mildred Sor-
rells as the widow of a Revolutionary
Soldier residing in Madison County,
1827, Caldwells Dist, drew lot of land
No. 71, 20th District, 1st section, Gold
Lottery. See page 21 Gold Lottery.

1B

Ruth Lindley married Job Smith.
Issue: a- Jonathan Smith, b- Lettie
Smith died at two years of age, c-
James Smith, d- Melissa Smith, e-
Mary Smith, f- Wm. Smith, g- Milk
Smith, h- Nancy Smith, i- Thomas
Smith, j- Ruth Smith, k- Mattie
Smith, l- Elisha Smith.

1C

Lethie Lindley (1803-1872) married
Thomas Camp (1800-1877) Issue:
a Nancy Camp, b Ruth Camp, c Joseph L. Camp, d Delilah Camp (m
Job Smith), e Jefferson Camp (m Annie Westmoreland), f Benjamin F.
Camp, g Jane Camp (m Thomas
Lovelace), h Parmelia Camp, i Elisha
Camp, j Wilson Camp, k Jot Camp (m
1st Lears 2nd............), l Letita Camp,
m Marth Camp, n Ellen Camp.

1Ca

Nancy Camp b Nov. 15, 1821, d
1879, m William Covington Selman,
1836. Issue:
1' Delilah Selman, 2' Letitia Selman, 3' Elizabeth Selman, 4' James
Wilson Selman born April 17, 1843,
5' Jefferson Selman.

1Ca4'

James Wilson Selman born April
17, 1843, died June 20, 1908, married
Lucinda Catharine Riley who was
born Feb. 21, 1850, died Nov. 21, 1908
and to them were born:
A' Leola Selman, B' James Selman,
C' Linton Stephens Selman, D' William Arthur Selman, E' Neva Riley
Selman, F' Jean V. Selman.

1Ca4A'

Leola Selman married Jasper Luther Beeson, President of the Georgia
State College for Women at Milledgeville, Ga. He was born Aug. 30, 1867
in Keener, Etowah County, Ala., and
a biographical sketch of his life is
contained page 223, Ga. Official and
Statistical Register, 1927, and a more
extended sketch page 586 Vol. III
History of Georgia by Clark Howell.
Dr. Beeson is the author of the Beeson Genealogy, a valuable contribution to the history of this family
which emigrated from England in
1682.

Mrs. Beeson has been of wonderful
help in this work and furnishes this
bit of interesting information: "Thos.
Camp who married Lethie Lindley
and who are the common ancestors of
this line was a son of Elizabeth Camp
who married Joseph Camp; Elizabeth
Camp was a daughter of Thomas
Camp and Susannah Waggoner, Thos.
Camp was the son of John Camp, b
1743 married 1768 Mary Tarpley, b
Oct. 30, 1740. Mary Tarpley was the
daughter of James Tarpley, a well to
do merchant of Williamsburg, Va.
He was a partner with Hon. Hugh
Blair, Dr. George Gilmer and William
Prentiss. In the steeple of old Bru-
ton Parish church still hangs the old
bell which is engraved "The gift of
James Tarpley, 1761" Issue:
a' Catherine Selman A. B. State
College for Women and A. M. Peabody College for teachers,, 1925, married Samuel Brown Wright, June 26,
1926.
1Ca4'B' James Selman married
John Alexander.
1Ca4'C' Linton Stephens Selman
married James Plaxico. Issue: a, Linton Stephens Selman, Jr., b' Martha
Riley Selman, c' James Selman.
1Ca4'D' William Arthur Selman
married Elizabeth Crouch. Issue a'
Dorothy Selman, b' Margaret Selman.
1Ca4'F' Jean V. Selman married
Carrie Pritchard. Issue: a' Caroline
Selman, b' Norma Belle Selman.
1Cb Ruth Camp married John Baggett. Issue:
1' Jane Baggett, 2' Tom Baggett,
3' Nancy Baggett, 4' John Baggett,
5' Ellen Baggett, 6' Susie Baggett, 7'
Bud Baggett, 8' Beulah Baggett, 9'
Lou Baggett.
1Cc Joe L. Camp born Douglas
county, Feb. 2nd, 1824, married 1st,
Martha Anderson, 2nd, widow Eliza
Lindley. Issue: 1st marriage.
1' M. R. Camp, 2' Hattie E. Camp,
3' D. C. Camp, 4' R. W. Camp.
1Cc Benj. F. Camp born Douglas
County married first Lula Smith, 2nd,
Sarah J. Scott. Issue first marriage:
1' Lula Camp, Second marriage 2'
T. N. Camp, 3' C. A. Camp, 4' B. F.
Camp, Jr.
1Ch—Parmelia Camp m Sandy
Morris Issue: 1' Billie Morris; 2' Ed
Morris; 3' Joe Morris; 5' Johnnia
Morris.
1Ci Elisha Camp married first a

Burke and second a Selman. Issue by first marriage:

1' Joe Camp. 2' Cora Camp, 3' Burke Camp, 4' Bettie Camp, 5' Ellen Camp, 6' Jot Camp. By second marriage: 7' Mary Lou Camp.

1Cj Wilkes or Wilson Camp married Mary Smith. Issue:

1' Forest Camp, 2' Lucia Camp, 3' Luke Camp, 4' Moses Camp, 5' Peggy Camp.

1Ck. Jot T. Camp twice married and had children, of these I have learned of only two, Thomas and Lethie. Lethie married F. Humphries and lives at Dade City, Florida.

1Cl Letitia Camp married William Walden, Issue:

1' Viola Walden, 2' Victoria Walden, 3' Tom Walden.

1Cm Martha (Mat) Camp married Thomas Abercrombie. Issue:

1' Lindley Abecrombie, 2' Lila Abercrombie, 3' Sanford Abercrombie, 4' Lottie Abercrombie.

1Cn Ellen Camp was twice married first to a Mr. Duke and second to a Mr. Lewis: Issue By first marriage; 1' Tom Duke. By second marriage, 2' Benjamin Lewis, 3' Nannie Lewis, 4' Holmes Lewis.

1D Jane (Jennie) Lindley b Dec. 16, 1804 died July 30, 1873, married Hope Hull Camp (b Oct. 30, 1803, d July 16, 1864). Issue:

a Hope Hull Camp b Dec. 9, 1843, killed during Civil War at Chancellorsville, Va., May 31, 1863. b Henry Clay Camp b Dec. 4, 1841, died of Typhoid Fever at Richmond, Va., May 21, 1862. c Elizabeth Camp, d Thomas G. Camp, e Benjamin Camp, f Joseph Ray Camp, g Asbury Camp, h Geo. W. Camp,, i Jonathan Camp, j James Camp, k Martha Camp.

WILLIAM LINDLEY

1E William Lindley born about 1806, married Eliza (?). Issue: a- Nancy, b- Elizabeth, c- Elmira. William died early in Walton county and family moved to Texas.

JONATHAN LINDLEY, JR.

6F Jonathan Lindley born Feb. 23, 1808, married Mildred Henry, Walton County, Ga., Nov. 15, 1827. (She was a daughter of Dr. Charles Hendry and wife, Nancy McGhee. Used same spelling as in records). Issue: a- Ann Charlotte Lindley, b- Sophia, c- James, d- Augustus Highsmith, e- Josephine, f- Charles.

6Fa Ann Charlotte Lindley married Dr. Artistides Reynolds. Issue: 1'- Adalaide Reynolds, 2'- Portia, 3'- Ella, 4'- Jessie, 5'- Homer V., 6'- Dr. Artistides, Jr., 7'- Frank, 8'- Walter, 9'- Willie, 10'- Cenci.

6Fb Sophia Lindley married Milton J. Magbee. No further information.

6Fc Augustus Highsmith Lindley married Anna Muse Bowen. Issue: No information from descendants.

THOMAS LINDLEY

1G Thomas Lindley, born Jan. 17, 1810, died July 8, 1882, married Elizabeth Rossie Scott. Issue: a- Harriet Lindley, b- Jonathan P. Lindley, c- William Lindley, killed at the battle of Knoxville, Tenn., during the Civil War, d- Nancy Lindley, e- Elizabeth Lindley married a Butner, f- Thomas Park Lind.ey, g- Julia Lindley, h- Elisha H. Lindley, i- Georgia Lindley, j- James M. Lindley, k- Ida Pauline Lindley, 1- Samuel Pierce Lindley.

1Ga Harriett Lindley married first Daniel C. Campbel., Jan 10, 1852, after his death she married William Knox, March 5 1867. Issue 1' Mary Campbell married A. J. Stewart. No issue.

1Gb Jonathan P. Lindley born Oct. 4, 1832 died Nov. 30, 1864 married Asenth Newell, Nov. 2, 1853. Died in Civil War. Issue: 1'- Hattie E Lindley married Henry Arno.d, 2'- Mary S. Lindley, 3'- Thomas N. Lindley of Powder Springs, Ga., 4'- Fannie I Lindley.

1Gc William Lindley was killed at the battle of Knoxville, Tenn. and left no descendants.

1Gd Nancy Lindley born Feb. 3, 1837 married W. H. Scott, Sept. 4, 1860, died July 19, 1891. Issue: 1'- Charles Scott, 2'- Edward Scott, 3'- Lon Scott, unmarried, 4'- Willie Scott, 5'- May Scott born 1870 died 1888.

1Ge Elizabeth Eliza Lindley born Oct. 12, 1844 married J. C. Butner, on Sept. 14, 1865. Issue: 1'- William Edgar Butner born Feb. 7th, 1868, died June 25, 1927. 2'- John Lindley Butner, born May 30, 1870, 3'- Ida Butner, born June 19th, 1875, married Walker Florence, no issue.

1Gf Thomas Park Lindley, born Jan. 25, 1849 married Georgia Turner Aug. 6, 1868 died June 28, 1916. Issue: 1'- Mitchell Lindley, 2'- Esca Lindley, 3'- Agnes Lindley.

1Gg Julia Lind:ey, born April 3' 1847 married J. J. Calloway, May 12,

1870 died Feb. 20, 1897. Issue: 1'-Lillian Calloway, 2'- Jim Calloway, 3'- Ross Calloway, 4'- Lindley Calloway, 5'- Howard Calloway, 6'- Annie Calloway.

1Gh Elisha H. Lindley b Nov. 4, 1851 married Sannie E. Turner, May 6, 1875,died April 21, 1910. Issue: 1'-Ida Lindley, 2'- Mamie Lindley, 3'-Bernice Lindley, 4'- William Lindley.

1Gi Georgia Lindley born Dec. 5, 1853 died June 27, 1926, married Dr. Robert R. Murray Nov. 10, 1886. (Dr. Murray was twice married). Issue by this marriage: 1'- Robetta R. Murray, 2'- Wilhelmina Murray.

1Gj James M. Lindley born March 20, 1856 married Louella B. Turner, Dec. 10, 1879 and died June 26, 1923. Issue: 1'- Myrtle Lindley, 2'- Nina Lindley, 3'- Chester Lindley, drowned at Wilmington N. C., 4'- Mittie Lindley, 5'- Harry Lindley, 6'- Gladys Lindley.

1Gk—Ida Pauline Lindley, b Powder Springs, Dec. 13, 1861, d Dec. 12, 1894, m Walker Scott, Dec. 20, 1882. Issue: 1'—Clara Scott, 2'—Kate Scott, 3'—Neva Scott, 4'—Hattie Scott, 5'—Agnes Scott

1Gl—Samuel Pierce Lindley, b March 16, 1859, m 1st, Mollie B. Howell, Jan. 4, 1883, 2nd Callie Corhran. S. P. Lindley died Aug. 1, 1902. Issue: 1'—Estelle Lindley, 2'—Posey Lindley, 3'—Ross Lindley, 4'—Sam P. Lindley, 6'—Sarah Lindley.

ELISHA H. LINDLEY

1H Elisha H. Lindley born Jan. 25, 1816 married first Sallie Smith, second Jane Scott. He was a member of the Secession convention, organized Company D of the 7th Georgia Regiment in which he served as Lieutenant, remained in the County until the surender at Appomattox. Represented Cobb County in the General Assembly 1875-76 and was killed in a wreck on W. A. Railroad, Oct. 12, 1876. Issue by first wife: a- Jonathan F. Lindley born Sept. 2nd, 1837. A member of his father's company in the Civil War and died without issue, by second wife, b- Martha Jane Lindley, c- Elizabeth C. Lindley, d- Wi.liam D. Lindley b Dec. 5, 1845, e- Nancy A. M. Lindley, f- John Thomas Lindley born Sept 2nd 1852, g- James Franklin Pierce Lindley.

1Hb Martha Jane Lindley b July 6th, 1843 married Dr. J. F. Cotton,

Oct. 25, 1860. He was a graduate of Johns Hopkins and a friend of Dr. Crawford W. Long. Issue all dead.

1Hc Elizabeth Lindley born July 4th, 1843, at Powder Springs Ga. married William J. Manning (born April 12th 1843, Chester S. C.) Feb. 28, 1867 at Powder Springs, Ga. Elizabeth Manning died May 16th 1918, William Manning died Nov. 19th 1915. Issue: 1'- Jessie Lane Manning born Nov. 6, 1867 died Sept 5, 1872, 2'- Julius Franklin Manning born March 16, 1871, 3'-Lula Jane Manning born Feb. 7th 1874, 4'- Sarah Elizabeth Manning born Feb. 25th, 1879.

"Marietta, Ga., Jan. 23, 1928.

Mr. L. W. Rigsby, Cairo, Ga.

Dear Mr. Rigsby:

Your letter received asking for information of the descendants of Johnson B.air. I am sorry I haven't had time to reply before this. My sister Lula and I can not buy a book but I hope the information I am sending will be a help and you will be successful in getting the family history to complete the sketch.

Your request for information of William D. Lindley (Bud). When very young joined the army, was a member of First Confederate Ga. Regiment, and was killed in the battle of Peachtree Creek, July 20th, 1864. Body left on battle field.

My grandfather, Elisha H. Lindley had a splendid record. His mother was a Blair but I don't remember her name. I heard my mother Elizabeth Lindley Manning tell of the bonnett she wore over from Ireland. Also of a chest she had. These are in possession of some of the Lindley family at Powder Springs. Some one has my great Grandfather Lindley's Bible.

I copied all the records in my grandfather Elisha H. Lindley's Bible.****

Wishing you success with your Historical Sketch, I am,

Yours truly,

SARAH MANNING"

N. B. I have been unable to find the bonnett, the chest or the Bible. All are agreed that they existed at one time but a.l I can learn is that moths ate the bonnett up.

1He Nancy A. M. Lindley b Oct. 27, 1848 at Powder Springs, Ga., married Saxon Alexander Anderson. Issue: 1'- Katherine Jane, 2'- William Patrick.

1Hf John Thomas Lindley born Sept. 2, 1852 at Powder Springs, Ga., married Margaret Anderson (b Mar- 28, 1859) Newton County, Georgia Is- sue: 1'- Charles Hamilton, 2' Ludie, 3'- Blanche.

1Hg James Franklin Pierce Lind- ley born March 13, 1856 at Powder Springs, Ga., died Sept. 30, 1920, mar- ried Annie Catherine Lackey Decem- ber 23, 1880 at Powder Springs, Ga. She was a daughter of Charles Lackey and Catherine Anderson Lackey. Is- sue: 1'- Guy H., 2'- Lucille, 3'- Pierce Baxter, 4'- Robert H., 5'- Ethel K.,6'- Fred Saxon, 7'- Joe R.

NOTES RELEVANT TO GEORGIA BLAIRS.

Blair, Joseph.

Joseph Blair, wife named Rebecca, Maiden name unknown, moved from Connecticut to Taylor County, ,Geor- gia. Died about three miles from Rey- nolds. Was probably born about 1800 perhaps earlier. He was of either Scotch or Irish descent and his wife was not born in America. Issue:

Hiram Blair, married and died in Taylor County, Ga., Mack Blair went to Leon County, Fla., Appie Blair (son) moved to Texas, Benjamin Blair, killed in Civil War, James Blair moved to Thomas County, Ga. Barbara Blair married Cage Amerson, Matilda died in Taylor county unmar- ried, Milbreath moved to Texas, un- married when left Georgia and went with brother Appie, Linnie Blair mar- ried James West and died in Albany, Ga., Joseph Blair married Mary Math- is.

Above information supplied by Mrs Mary (Mathis) Blair now 87 years old and resident in Leon County Fla.

The following land grants to Blairs were taken from various sources, principally the Cherokee Lotteries as published, the Gold Lotteries, the Ir- win County Lotteries, and from the General Index in the office of the Sec- retary of State. There may be inac- curacies, but on the whole will give, I think a fairly exhaustive list of the early Blair settlers in Georgia.

Georgia Land Grants to Blairs.

To Adam Blair of Philips District, Monroe County, number 730, Fourth District, Third section, Gold Lottery

page 231.

To Adam Blair of Phillips District, Monroe County, number 279, 23 Dis- trict, third section, Cherokee, p 289 (Floyd Co.)

To Arthur K. Blair of Garners Dis- trict, Washington County, number 6, third District, second section, Gold Lottery p 122.

To Elizabeth Blair, orphan, of Gar- ners District, Washington County, No. 178, 26 District, third section p 308 Cherokee (Walker County.)

To Elizabeth Blair, orphan, of Gar- ners District, Washington County, No. 461, 4th District, third section page 229, Gold Lottery.

To George Blair of Garners District Washington County, number 995, 3rd district, 2 section, Gold Lottery p 130.

To George Blair, number 451 in Jackson County in 1827, p 683, index.

To George Blair, Ellis District, Ra- bun County, number 23, 2nd district, 1st Section, Gold Lottery, p 59.

To George Blair, Harris, number 165, 7, Appling County, Laurens Co., Index.

To George Blair, Kendails 7---5--- Dooly, Hancock County, Index.

To Geeorge Blair of Ellis District, Rabun County, number 446, 21 Dis- trict, third section, p 284, Gold Lot- tery.

To George W. Blair, number 270, 24th District, 2nd section, Gold Lot- tery—170, (Murray and Gilmer Co's.)

To George W. Blair, Ellis, 270, 24-2, Rabun County Index.

To Henry B.air, of Folsom's Dis- trict Lowndes County, number 962, 17 District, third section, Lottery (Cher- okee) page 244.

To Hugh Blair, Columbia County, number 122,18,578 Index.

To Hugh Blair Sr., 11th 70-26 ....

.... County not given. Index.

To James Blair, Habersham, 333,- 1835-145 also 140-1838-582 (Index.)

To James Blair, Franklin County, 200-1813-313 also 800-1813-315 Index.

To James Blair, 530-1810-236, Franklin County Index.

To James Blair, St. George's Par- rish, 100-1770-92 Index.

To James Blair, Kendalls, 13-17 Henry County, Hancock County, In- dex.

To James Blair, Crows, Pike Coun- ty, numbe 826, third district, 4 sec- tion.

To James Blair, R. S. Whitehead, 27-6-1 also 97-20-2 Habersham County Index.

To James Blair R. S. of Whitehead District, Habersham County, number 27, 6 district, 1st section, Cherokee p 9 (Union and Lumpkin Counties).

To James Blair R. S. Whitehead District, Habersham, number 97, 20 District, 2 section Cherokee, p 145 (Cobb).

To James Blair, Sr. Powells 41-9-Irwin (Franklin Co.) Index.

To James B. Blair, Clarke Pentecost 147-8- Appling, (Clarke County Index).

To James B. Blair, number 415 Walton County, number 943, 3 District 4 section Gold Lottery p 317.

To James B. Blair, of Garners District, Washington County, number 220 16th District, 4th section Gold Lottery p 322.

To Jemima Blair W. of Walkers, Columbia, number 235, 10 District, 1 section (Cherokee p 41).

To Janet S. Blair orphan of Richmond County, number 332 in 6th District of Appling County.

To Janette S. Blair, orphan, number 398-321-third District, Early county (Richmond County Index.)

To Jemimah Blair (widow) Gartrellis District, Columbia County, number 299-15-Early.

To Jemima Blair widow of Walkers District Columbia, number 247-20 District, third section Gold Lottery-271.

To John C. Blair Ellis Rabun County 116-7-4 (Index) See also Cherokee p 349 (Land in Walker County.)

To John D. Blair, of Garners District Washington County, number 201, 15th District, third section Cherokee p 268 Land in Cass County.

To John D. Blair, of Garners District, Washington County, number 214, 8th District, third section, Cherokee p 218 in Murray County.

To Joseph Blair of Mitchells, Marion County, number 836, 19th District, 2nd section Gold Lottery, p 181.

To Levi C. Blair, of Edward District, Franklin County, number 838, 19th District, 2nd section Gold Lottery, Land not described in note.

To Mary Blair Burke County 200-1789-348-555.

To Middleton Blair, of Bowers District Elbert County, number 474, 1st. District, 1st. section G. L. p 9.

To Powell Blair of Powells District, Franklin County, May 21, 1832 (Irwin County, District 9).

To Robert Blair, Marshalls District 256-7-Gwinnett (Baldwin County Index.)

To Samuel Blair of Richmond County 50-1785-316 (Index)

To Thomas Blair, Talbot County. No description in note.

To Thomas Blair Tramels 83-19-B (Clarke 1806 Index.)

To Thomas Blair, Book, 269-6-Early (Washington County Index, 1806.)

To Thomas Blair, Pool 134-9 Rabun (Washington County Index, 1806.)

To Thomas Blair, Phillips District, Monroe County, number 704, 16th District, 2nd section Gold Lottery p 150.

To Thomas H. Blair Telfair, Cooks 104-11-3 (Note) Cherokee p 237.

To Thomas Blair, of Phillips, Talbot, number 500, 2nd District, 1st section (Gold Lottery p 13.)

To Thomas R. Blair, of Garners District, Washington County, number 103, 12th District, 3rd section (Murray county.)

Wade and Mims Blair, Screven 200-1802-647-Note.

To William Blair-Liberty County 300-1806-298 (Note).

To William Blair 119 District Richmond County, number 128,17th. District, 4th section, Gold Lottery p 325.

To William Blair Jr. Phillips (Monroe) ? 5-5-3 (Note)

To William Blair McCranies District, Montgomery County 235-6-Henry County (Note).

To William Blair, Jr. Phillips District Monroe County, number 5, 5th District, 3rd section Gold Lottery p 193.

To William Blair, Sr., of Phillips District, Monroe, number 70, 12th District, 4th section Cherokee p 384 Land in Walker County.

Johnson Blair's widow said to have married a Vatin (Vaughten) only recod found of family of this man is as follows: Whorton Vaughten drew land in Burke County as follows 200 acres, 1791 page 121.

From the old tax digests in 1825 I find the following Blairs returned property for taxes in Washington County, Georgia.

George Blair returned property for land lying in Washington County, Ga. and 202½ acres lying in Dooly County, Georgia.

John Blair returned property for taxes in Washington County, Georgia. Nancy Blair returned 150 acres of land for taxes in Washington County, Georgia. All of the parties returned taxes in Captain Worthins District.

In 1830 there was returned by the Blairs residing in Washington Coun-ty, Georgia in Captain Motts Company land as follows: George Blair 200 acres of land in Washington County. John D. Blair 202½ acres in Lee County.

Robert K. Blair 138 acres of land in Washington County, Georgia, and 202 and one-half acres in Lee county, Ga., and the orphans of James Blair 202½ acres in Lee County, Georgia, and also James Blair 202½ acres in Lee County, Georgia.

Miscellaneous Genealogies, Blewett

The History of the Georgia Baptist, page 36, Biographical Section has the following Sketch of Willliam J. Blewett. This was Wiley J. Blewett and with this correction I quote.

"He was born in Anson county, N. C., March 12th, 1812. He with his parents emigrated to Decatur county, Georgia in 1833. In April, 1834, he united with the Richland Creek church and was baptized by Elder A. Belcher. In 1835 he was licensed by that church to preach the Gospel. Sometime after this, at the solicitation of the Cotton Hill church, in Randolph county, he was ordained to the full work of the ministry, Elders O. and A. J. Cumbie officiating."

"In Florida he identified himself with the cause of missions, and, perhaps, had an important agency in the introduction of the present articles of faith of the Florida Association. He preached along the Florida and Georgia line, beloved by the people as an earnest, faithful servant of the Lord Jesus, and was instrumental in doing great good."

Rev. J. R. Bluett, Climax, Georgia, pastor of the Long Branch Church successor to Richland Church, is a son of above

WATSON.

Mrs. J. R. Patterson, granddaughter of Frederick Watson who married Martha Frederick, wrote me from Norman Park, Ga., July 7th 1927, in response to request for information relative to Daniel Watson as follows: "I don't know anything about the family. He (Daniel) was my father's grandfather and Daniel Brunson was my grandfather but he died many years before I was born. So I don't know anything about his brothers and sisters, but J. G. B. Watson my father had two brothers, Elbert David and James. James died young. His sisters, Mary, Delilah and Sarah. Mary married Lewis Pollock, Delilah married her cousin Jess Watson, Sarah married Joseph Hancock. They lived in Houston and Pulaski County. Mary had four boys. J. G. B., Frederick, Pinkney, E. D. and one one girl Martha. Delilah had several children also. I don't remember their names. They all have been dead many years. I do not know the names of Daniel Brunson's brothers and sisters nor who they married. My mother was the youngest child. I can't give any information about Martha Frederick nor Frederick Watson's father and mo'her. I don't know anything about John and William C. Watson. They might have been related to my father. I do not know anything about Daniel Watson who lived in Wilkinson County, either. My Uncle E. D. Watson married Sarah McDonald. Their children Martha, Catherine, Mary Jane, Flora Crawford, Georgia and Angeline; 2 boys James Frederick, John Greenberry. One boy was a lawyer the other a doctor. All the family are dead".

In a post-scrip she says, "My uncle Elbert David Watson was ordinary in Lee County, Georgia 15 or 20 years. He died in Smithville, Ga. Has been dead several years."

BURKHALTER.

(By Mrs. John F. Little,
Washington, D. C.)

Sarah Hardin, the 9th child of Henry Hardin and Judith Lynch was born 1763. She was twice married, first to James Loyles in Pittsylvania County, Va., and second to John Burkhalter. By her first husband 3 children were born, James, Lucy and one other. James Loyless died about 1787 in Wilkes County, Ga. She married her second husband, John Burkhalter, May 29, 1792 at the home of her brother, Mark Hardin in Warrenton, Warren County, Ga. By this union there were six children: 1 Harriet, born August 19, 1793, m Moses McKinney, Sept. 21, 1811. 2 Redan born Dec. 15, 1795. 3 Samuel born April 27, 1797, married Thomas Pate, June 27, 1815. 4 Martin Hardin, born Dec. 27, 1799. 5 Averella born Oct. 21, 1801, married Kitchen McKinney, Dec. 21, 1815. 6 David Newsom, born Sept. 17, 1803, married Ann Eliza Short, April 26, 1826.

Children of David Newsom Burkhalter and Ann Eliza Short were: 1 John Thomas Burkhalter married Fannie Weaver and they had one daughter, Carrie, who married Edward Elder of Barnesville, Ga. They had several children: 1 Cliff Elder, a promising attorney of New York City. 2 Ann Eliza married Thomas Colquitt, whose children are Ex Governor O. B. Colquitt, of Texas, Will, John and one daughter Eula. 3 Sarah Martha married Steven Woodruff. 4 Harriett, m John Wesley Brown. They had one daughter, Mollie, who was married twice, first to Mr. Brown, second to Col. W. B. Short, of Buena Vista, Ga. They had three children: Lieut. Will Brown; Esther married Mr. Stevens and Ruth married Mr. Freeman C. McClure. 5 Fletcher married James Wiggins and had one daughter Claud, who married Mr. Edward Reeves and lives in Augusta, Ga. 6 David Newsom married first Miss Berta Brown, second Lula Hooks. 7 Dorothy Chamberlayne Burkhalter married Judge Thomas Lumpkin, children were: Lucy, Joe, Burke. Lucy married John Hall and lives at Douglas, Ga. Her children are Lucy, Julia, John Lawton and Carrie. 8 Virginia Burkhalter married a distant cousin, John Lawson Burkhalter and they live in Warrenton, Georgia. Their children are Mary Thomas Burkhalter, married John Franklin Little, Evelyn, Eugenia married Henry Latimer Hall, Fletcher, James Seaborn, Robert Icalia married Evelyn Jetter and Anna Frances married Robert Bell. Children of

Mary Thomas Burkhalter and John Franklin Little are May Katherine Little married Jasper Marion Beall and Lieut. John Franklin Little, Jr., married Mary Peele.

Sarah Hardin's husband, John Burkhalter and his father, Michael Burkhalter who married Martha Newsom, were both soldiers of the Revolution. Mrs. W. B. Short, Mrs. J. F. Little, Mrs. Lillie Hall Walker and about ten more have gone into the D. A. R. on their records. I have the old Hardoin or Hardin coat-of-arms, gotten for me in France by Mrs. Dolores B. Colquitt. Mamie Burkhalter Little is a member of the League of American Pen Women, American Colonists and Daughters of American Revolution.

John Burkhalter who married Sarah Hardin ran away from home and joined the Revolutionary Forces when his father was brought home wounded. Martha turned her home over to the sick and wounded and nursed and administered to the sick and wounded. This she could well afford to do as Michael was a man of some means. This information was handed down through Mrs. Dollie Woodall, a granddaughter. She was quite old and she could give some splendid information on the Burkhalter line. Martha Burkhalter received a land grant in Warren County in 1752.

GRIFFIN

Lewis Griffin married Martha Boyett. Presumably in Washington Co. The family came into Southwest Georgia from Washington County and lived in the southern part of the county. Children were: Burrell, Major, John, Frank, Shadrack, Dempsey, Dennis, Sallie who married John Clay first, second Edward Crutchfield, and Harriett, who married Benjamin Ward. John Griffin moved to Texas, Benjamin Ward moved west, descendants of others are some in Georgia, some in Florida and others in other States.

Lewis Griffin is supposed to have come into Georgia from the Carolinas, either North or South Carolina. soon after the Revolution. When I was a very small child Burrell Griffin son of Lewis Griffin above, then a very old man, used to give a very spirited account of the Battle of Bunker Hill. It was my understanding that some of his family, presumably father or a grandfather was in this Battle. It was a rare treat to hear this rendition of this historic battle. It may have been described by others with more accuracy, but never by any that could impart to it more fire of patriotism or dramatic effect.

HARRISON.

Benjamin Harrison, came to Southwest Georgia from Pulaski County, Georgia soon after the organization of Early county. He, perhaps, has the most numerous list of descendants of any other of our early Settlers, at least resident in Grady County. He was a soldier in the war of 1812, a member of the Baptist church, a man of financial importance in the early settlement and has stamped the characteristic of thrift and industry upon his progeny. He was twice married, in each instance to women of prominent and respectable families of Southwest Georgia. First marriage was to ....Bush, second marriage to .... Dykes Issue:

Thomas Harrison married Nancy Grice, James Harrison married Elizabeth Reynolds and these were the parents of B. R. T., A. J., T., Mary, who married Andrey Graham, and others, Matthew Harrison married Jane Matthis, William Harrison married Martha Ann Sanders, Jack Harrison married Patsy Jones and these were the parents of William S. Harrison,, financier, Benjamin Harrison who married Elizabeth Clay, and John Harrison, assassinated, Nancy Harrison, married Jonathan C. Hawthorne, Celia Harrison, never married, Polly Harrison married Silas Jones.

HAWTHORNE

The first highway opened in Grady County according to the best information was the Hawthorn Trail running North and South between Cairo and Whigham. This road is said to have been surveyed by Elder William Hawthorn one of the first settlers in this section and who settled just South of Tired Creek from the present city of Cairo. The family was originally from North Carolina but were in Georgia several years before coming to this section. He appears to have been a member of the old Hepzibah Association as early as 1813 because we find him named with one Pearce as among the ministers and preachers agreeing to continue to preach in the usual

mode, which appears to have been a kind of voluntary missionary service. History of Georgia Baptist, p 87. He was residing in Pulaski County, Ga., in 1818 at the time of the survey of Early and returned for taxes, 1 poll, 1 slave, 1923 3-4 acres of land in the 19th district.

It was soon after this that he came to this vicinity. He continued his ministerial labors and was instrumental in establishing both Tired Creek and Richland Creek Churches, forming a member of the presbytery in the constitution of each. He took occasional long trips back to his old neighborhood and even into the Carolinas. On some of these trips he imbibed rather freely and would make his acknowledgements at next conference, his congregation freely forgiving for these lapses. William Hawthorne took an active part not only in the organization of the churches but also in the organization of Decatur county. He was one of the commissioners to select the county site for Decatur Co., (Bainbridge) and represented Decatur County in the State Senate 1827 being the second senator from the county, the Hon. James Brown having preceeded him. This legislative experience was nothing new for he had represented Pulaski county in the General Assembly in 1817. In 1833 Jonathan Cliborn Hawthorn, son of E.der William was a member of the lower house together with George R. McElvey from Decatur. A considerable portion of the old homestead is still owned by descendants, Elder William is buried at Tired Creek but the Hawthorne Cemetery contains the remains of many of the descendants.

His grave is marked by a monument, the headstone of which is cracked and crumbling but there can still be deciphered the following inscription, "Sacred to the Memory of Elder William Hawthorn. Died May 15th, 1840, aged 84 years."

His old Bible is now in the possession of Elias O. Hawthorn and it is from this family Bible and these old monuments that the ensuing records are taken. He served in the war of the Revolution and for this service he drew land in lottery of 1827. Roster the Revolution 365.

Elias Owen Hawthorne, a grandson now living says that the father of El-

der William Hawthorne was a soldier
in the revolution together with sons
Nathaniel and William; that Nathaniel was killed about the close of the
Revolution and that another son was
born after the Revolution and named
Nathaniel for his brother. Mr. Hawthorn's information and documents
given later is our authority for the
following genealogies.

John Hawthorne, soldier in Revolu-
tion, of Roberson County, North Car-
olina. Sons were, 1 Nathaniel ,first,
2 William and 3 Nathaniel, second.
William Hawthorn married Meleachy
Cliburn. Issue: A- Jonathan Cliburn
Hawthorn married Nancy Harrison.
Children all dead.

B- Elias Owen Hawthorne married
Thena Lee. No issue.

C- Timothy Hawthorne married
Martha Kelly. Family went to Texas.
(probably Joshua Timothy.)

D- William Bryant Hawthorne married Elizabeth Jones.

E- Millie Hawthorne married a Kelley.

F- Patsie Hawthorne married Robert Jones.

William Bryant Hawthorne.

William Bryant Hawthorne married
Elizabeth Jones. They lived near the
Hawthorne Cemetery in a house still
standing and were important members of the community during their
time. Issue

a- John C. Hawthorne married the
widow Mrs. C. L. Norton who was a
Heisler before her marriage. She was
the mother of E. A., Sam, George and
Z. Norton but there was no issue by
Hawthorne.

b- Mary Hawthorne married John
Godwin who was a son of Steve God-
win who came to this section with the
Hawthornes and his brother Aleck
Godwin who went to Mitchell county.

c- William B. Hawthorne, married
first Louisa Massey and second Mildred Stallings.

d- Elizabeth Hawthorne married
James I Connell. No issue.

e- Meleachy Hawthorne married
John Jones who died in the Civil War.

f- Mellie Hawthorne married Abe
Massey.

g- Patsie Hawthorne married Geo.
Ray.

h- Nancy Hawthorne married Ganes
S. Key.

i- Elias Owen Hawthorne married

Francis Melvina Hughes.

j- Martha Louisa Hawthorne married John R. Taylor.

BIBLE RECORDS.
Births.

Elizabeth Melecha Hawthorne was
born May 19th, 1866.

Lougemia Hawthorne was born Oct.
26, 1867.

Marietta Hawthorne was born Aug.
11th, 1869.

E. H. Ray was born Dec. 22, 1866.

John Cliburn Hawthorne was born
Jan. 12th, 1744.

Nancy Hawthorne was born July
29th, 1854.

Elias Owen Hawthorne was born
July 9th, 1857.

Martha Louisa Hawthorn was born
April 11th, 1860.

Elizabeth Jones was born April 16,
1821.

John Cliburn Hawthorne was born
Nov. 20th, 1837.

Mary Cliburn Hawthorne was born
Aug. 16th, 1839.

Melecha Hawthorne was born July
14th, 1841.

William Bryant Hawthorn was born
July 14th, 1843.

Elizabeth Hawthorne was born Dec.
27th, 1845.

Milbra Hawthorne was born Dec.
30, 1847.

Patsey Hawthorne was born Sept.
16th, 1850.

Patsy Hawthorne was born Feb.
28th, 1875.

DEATHS.

Mollie Massey died Nov. 24th, 1870
Melecha Jones died May 14th, 1864.
W. B. Hawthorne died April 27th,
1887.

John Cliborn died April 27th, 1826.
Mary Cliborn died April 27, 1832.
Martha Concel died Sept. 22, 1824.
Elias O. Hawthorne died Feb. 19
1846.

William Hawthorne died May 15th,
1846.

John C. Hawthorne died Sept. 22,
1848.

Meleachy Hawthorne died March
26, 1866. Aged 99 years, 3 months and
21 days.

Marriages.

William Bryant Hawthorne and
Elizabeth Jones were merried on the
29th day of January, 1837.

William Bryant Hawthorne, Jr., and
Louisa Elizabeth Massey were mar-

ried May 11th 1865.

John Godwin and Mary C. Hawthorn were married May 11th, 1853.

John H. Jones and Melecha Hawthorne were married Aug. 14, 1856.

Able M. Massey and Mollie Hawthorne were married March 16, 1865.

John E. Hall and Bedde Dora Hawthorne were married Sept. 14th 1890.

The following inscription copied from Tombstone at the old burying place. "In memory of Maleachy Hawthorne. Died March 26th, 1866. Age 99 years, 3 months and 21 days.

The above information taken from copies furnished by John B. Hawthorn great-grand son of Elder William Hawthorne. The following is taken from original document kindly loaned by Mr. Hawthorne.

"North Carolina, Roberson county" Know all men whom it may concern that I Nathaniel Hawthorne, of the above State and County do by these presents convey and make over and deliver unto the possession of William Hawthorne of the State of Georgia, and County of Pulaski for the use of my father, John Hawthorne, all and singular the properties, Real and personal and perishable which was conveyed to me by deed of gift by my said father, John Hawthorne in presence of William Bodiford and Leonard C. Thomas who were subscribing witnesses to said conveyance, which conveyance, or deed of gift was made to me for the purpose of supporting my father through this life and whereas my aged father possesses a disposition to move to the State of Georgia and desires that my elder brother William Hawthorne should supervise his business and take care of his person. I therefore by these presents relinquish all claim, right, title and interest in or to the property designated and for the purpose of confirming the same for the above purpose as above mentioned 1 hereby bond myself, my heirs, executors, administrators and assigns forever by these presents. Signed, Sealed and acknowledged in the presence of William Bodiford and Benjamin Freeman, Jr.

(Seal)   Sept. 18, 1820.

NATHANIEL HAWTHORNE.

Nathaniel Hawthorne Relinquishment to William Hawthorne. Roberson County. May Term, 1821. This deed was proven in open court by the

Oath of William Bodiford and ordered to be registered. R. C. Binding,C. Registered in the Registers office of Roberson County, Book T, page 43. Neeiv Bins, Register.

HICKS

As we catch the name Hicks as it flashes here and there across the pages of history in connection with our Indian affairs our interest is intrigued and we fain would conjure more facts and circumstances from the silent past. Larger libraries than those to which we have had access may show more, there may be private records which will illustrate and illumine the family's history more but at present we must surmise that this family was connected with those mentioned in the following instances, but in what way we are unable to say.

Writing of Walker County, Knight says in Georgia's Landmarks, Memorials and Legends, Vol 1 page 100. "Dogwood was an Indian town situated on the headwaters of Chickamauga Creek. The principal chief was Charles Hicks, a man of vigorous mind, who embraced the Moravian faith. Elijah Hicks was his son. It is said of him that he would not disgrace any circle ,either in appearance, manner or conversation."

About 1833 an old news paper carried the following notice. "At a meeting of the National Council of the Cherokees, the following resolution was adopted; 'Resolved by the National Committee and Council that an agent shall be appointed to solicit donations from individuals, or societies, in the United States for the purpose of establishing a National Academy for the Cherokees." Signed John Ross, president; Major Ridge, speaker; Pathkiller, principal chief; Charles R. Hicks, Head Chief and Treasurer; Alexander McCoy and Elias Boudinot, Clerk's, Georgia's Landmarks, Memorials and Legends.

Evans in his History of Georgia, p 203 shows that Elijah Hicks and Major Ridge went to Washington as Representatives and addressed a letter to the President. Hicks opposed the sale of the lands of the Indians and his conduct was approved by the Indians. He appears to have succeeded his father as Chief or to have been connected with a different part of the tribe. Page 228 of Evans History records as follows: That in 1834 a band of Indians broke open and robbed a smokehouse. Eli Hicks, a friendly Indian chief who was in favor of the removal of the Indians followed these Indians with only two companions. Overtaking the Indians and remonstrating with them was shot and died from the wounds in two days.

Georgia's Landmarks, Memorials and Legends, page 627, writing of Gordon County, Mr Knight describes the murder of a prominent Indian named Hicks at a Green Corn Dance by two outlaws, presumably white, and who lived for a long time in a cave near the mouth of Oothcaloga Creek.

Mr. E. F. Dollar, a prominent farmer living on the Hawthorn Trail a short distance South of Mizpah Church, and who is a great-grandson of Raford Hicks gives me the following account of the Hicks family who settled in this section.

Raford Hicks, who was the ancestor of the Hicks of this section of the State came here direct from the Indian Nation and was himself of Indian descent with a high degree of Indian blood. He does not remember the name of his wife or anything about her. He had two sons, Nat Hicks who did not remain long in this section, but he does not know what became of him and William Hicks who was Mr. Dollar's grandfather. He remembers his grandfather who died about the age of 65 years and about 58 years ago. He married Annie Norris but the Norris family did not remain long. His mother used to keep as a souvenir of this Norris family the claw of a panther, about which the following was related. One night soon after the Norris family had come into this section and before their cabin was finished, curtains being the only doors and windows, the old lady Norris awoke and could not go back to sleep Several log heaps were burning in front of the house. The old lady got up and went out to set around one of these fires and smoke her pipe of tobacco. She had a small dog that went with her. The dog soon raised a disturbance and became very much frightened at something in the dark. The old lady could see nothing but became alarmed at the actions of the dog and went into the house. Next

morning she told of the circumstances and the family went to look for tracks. A panther's tracks were discovered near where the old lady had been setting. A hunt was organized and the panther soon found and treed. He was shot out and the claw preserved in the family as a memento.

William Hicks and his wife Anne Norris Hicks had children as follows:
John Hicks went west.
Newton Hicks went to Florida.
Putnam Hicks married and left issue. One son Andrew and a girl Annie Eliza.
Thursby never maried.
Demarious (Babe) married Thomas Jefferson Dollar and were the parents of Mr. E. F. Dollar, supplying this information. Mr. Do.lar served the County of Grady as Sheriff during the early days but soon retired from politics and spends his time looking after his farming interests and his interest at a resort on the Gulf.

POWELL.

William Powell was evidently living along the route of the Bainbridge and Thomasville Road before it was opened. It passed his old homestead and the grave of self and wife is about a quarter of a mile South of the road and North of the Curry Cemetery over in Decatur County. As his posterity has played so important a part in the development of this section it is fitting that I give some attention to this family. He was one of the first settlers in this section, possessed considerable property, was named as trusteee of the Decatur Academy created by the Legislature of 1829, was one of the Judges of the Inferior Court and was a man of liberal views and charitably disposed towards his fellow man. He was born Nov. 11, 1783 and died Dec. 15, 1836, his first wife who was before her marriage Sarah Bigham was born on June 17, 1792, and died April 16, 1852. This information was taken from the monument over the grave by me. If we could accept Memoirs of Georgia as authority we would say that this was his second wife because it is stated in that work Vol. 1 page 591 that his wife was Sarah Turner. This work is so filled with error and other errors are apparent in this Sketch that I will only say that Wi.liam Powell had issue as follows: 1- Kedar,

2- Jane married Sutton H. Trulock, 3- Sarah married Albert Cunningham, 4- Margaret married James McElven, 5- Benjamin F., 6- William, 7- Louisa, married Dr. Bruce.

Kedar Powell, (1)

Kedar Powell was executor of his father's will which is of probate in Decatur County. He was one of the early Sheriff's of Decatur and represented the county in the Legislature in 1834 and again in 1861-2-3. (born July 19, 1810 and died Sept. 4, 1879.) He resided for a time in Florida, later about eight miles south of Cairo on the Hawthorne Trail, but his death and interment was in Cairo. He was twice married, first to Martha Ann Lasseter and second to Melvina Bell. Issue by first marriage A- William Powell, by second marriage B- John, C- Margaret married Geo. A. Wight. D- Benjamin Franklin, E- Sarah married.............. F- Hugh P, G- Elizabeth married Wiley C. Pittman of Thomasville, H- Amanda married Rev. J. W. Arnold.

Benjamin F. Powell, (5)

Benjamin F. Powell represented Decatur county in the legislature 1851-2, 1853-4, 1855-6, 1857-8, 1865-6, 1869-70. I know of no descendants and presume that he died without issue.

William Powell, (6)

William Powell (born Jan. 1, 1830, died May 29, 1892) married first a Donaldson and second Mrs. Emma Knighton. Issue by first marriage A- William E., B- G. D., C- Eugene, D- Frederick M., by second marriage E- Wight, F- Luellen, G- Jeff Davis, H- Ruth.

POULK (PAULK)

The Poulk family of this section is the same as the Paulk family of the central section of the State. They are all descended from Micajah Poulk or Paulk, Scotch immigrant who came to Georgia before the Revolution and who was one of those Georgians who refugeed from the State when it was overrun by the British. At the close of the Revolution he returned to the State and James McNeil certified to his service in the Revolution and Paulk requested his bounty land in Washington County, Georgia, and an executive order was granted for the land as prayed for. The name of his wife is unknown to the writer and the

names of all the children have not been learned. Of sons there were Jacob who married a Henderson, Thos. Paulk, Micajah Paulk, Henry Paulk, James Paulk and George Paulk. Of the girls Rebecca Paulk married a Vickers, Mary Paulk, married a Tucker and Margaret Paulk married a Smith. A son William Paulk married Catherine Waters. She was also known as Kate Waters. William did not live long before he died leaving two boys and perhaps several girls. The boys were Micajah and William. The widow married Phillip Ragon and his wife lived to an advanced age. They were the parents of J. J. Ragan, long a justice of the Peace, Jourdan Ragan, Alfred L. Ragan, and General Ragan. There was also a girl. Micajah Poulk was the progenitor of the Poulks of Cairo, William Poulk had a son, John, who went west with a son, William, and died.

Richland Creek Church.

This was not the first Baptist Church constituted in this vicinity but it is given here by reason of the fact that it is the first church constituted in the vicinity along the Hawthorne Trail. It was situated just North of Richland Creek near the old McElvey Mill, neither sign of church or cemetery remains except a headstone at some distance marking the grave of an aged negro. It was constituted Aug. 16, 1828 under authority of an arm from Tired Creek. Presbytery consisted of William Hawthorn, Lewis St. John and Theo Hardie. Among the members participating in the organization were Francis Smallwood, Wiley Pearce, Augustus C. Barlow, Wiley Horn, John Blewett, Tom, (a colored man), Mary Smallwood, Mary Trulock, Huldah St. John, and Kesiah Bell. A partial roll of members were F. Smallwood, W. Pearce, A. C. Barlow, W. Horn, J. Blewett, Wiley J. Blewett, Tom (colored man) Mary Smallwood, Mary Trulock, Mary Mills, Huldah St. Johns, Kesiah Bell, John Adams, Margaret Adams, W. C. Lester, S. Castelow, Nancy (colored woman), N. Rackley, Harmon Neal, Sabra Neal, E. A. Arline, Ann M. Lester, Zilpha Pharer, Reuben Dubose, Ann Burkitt, Nancy Horne, Martha Horn, Mahala Windham, Kesia colored woman). The mission question arose in the church in an unguarded moment and the church fell a martyr to the cause of Missions and was finally dissolved on the 2nd Sunday in April, 1858. This furnishes us with a partial list of the early settlers in this particular section and the information is taken from the old minutes of the Church. Mizpeh further up the trail is the legitimate successor of old Richland Church, of the Primitive persuasion and Long Branch of the Missionary division.

N. B. At the old Hawthorne Cemetery at the foot of the monument which marks the last resting place of Meleachy Cliburn Hawthorne there is a small grave which has been pointed out to me as the place where a little boy by the name of Horne was buried. He, as related to me, was the son of one of the first settlers and the story regarding his death may be of interest in future years as illustrating some of the difficulties encountered by the early settlers.

He and a smaller brother were crossing Tired Creek Swamp when a large wild cat or panther sprang from a tree upon the back of the larger boy. He called to the younger brother for help to secure his knife but the younger boy ran in fright and left his elder brother to battle alone with his bare hands, he not being able to secure his knife without assistance. As soon as the younger child reached home with the news a party ran to the scene but the viscious animal had already accomplished its hellish design and the boy was dead, litterally ripped to shreds by the large cat.

Another tradition which persists in regard to this Horne family is that the elder Horne brought into this section the first cotton gin which was a small affair operated by hand.

The old McElvey mill was erected near old Richland Church. It was known later as the Sapp mill, now abandoned, perhaps forever. The church had been abandoned and all signs obliterated before my first recollection, but many of our neighbors had loved ones buried in the old cemetery. In securing dirt to build the dam for the mill it was said that many of these graves were dug up and the people became indignant but talk was all it ever amounted to .

WHIGHAM.

Thomas Whigham, for whom the town of Whigham received its name was a son of John Whigham,, Irish immigrant and Revolutionary soldier. He with a brother, William Whigham came into this section from Jefferson County, Ga., before 1830. It is presumed that this family were of the Queensboro settlers before the Revolution. The family were related to a family of Pattersons but whether or not Thomas Whigham's wife was a Patterson is unknown to this writer. His children were, Robert E. Whigham, married Elizabeth Lodge, Mary Whigham married a Hickey and lived near Recovery, Ellen Whigham died unmarried, John Whigham married but name of wife is unknown to writer. He went to Civil War and never returned, Thomas Whigham, William Whigham, Nancy Whigham married David Cooper. They were the parents of L. D. S. Cooper who married John A. Rigsby. Joseph Mossman Whigham married Margaret Oates, daughter of James Oates whose wife was a Little, supposed to have been the daughter of William Little, Irish Immigrant and Revolutionary Soldier. This family of Littles is supposed to have been of the Queensboro Colony also and related to James Little who married Mary Ann Margaret (Polly) Rigsby, James Whigham married first Phronia McNair and second Ellen McNair, Abbie Whigham married Milton Thomas.

Church membership was with the Associate Reformed Presbyterian Church at Hack, Ga.

TRULOCK.

The financial interest of the section surrounding Whigham and Climax has been largely controlled by the Trulock and Powell families so long that the memory of man runneth not to the contrary. The Trulock family is said to be of English origin, to have first settled in Maryland emigrating from Maryland to Darlington District South Carolina where Sutton Hines Trulock was born Oct. 23, 1800. He came with a brother J. H. Trulock to Decatur county about 1826, settling near Climax. He maried Jane Powell daughter of William Powell, wife Sarah, Sept. 22, 1829. She was born June 7, 1812. Issue: 1- Delia married Dr. Peacock, 2- Missouri B. married John T. Harrell, 3- Gordon B. 4- Zimmerman, 5- Mary L. married J.

W. Maxwell, 6- Sallie D., 7- Andrew
J. Trulock.

So finish our labors in repose to a
mother's request.

A Southwest Georgian's Criticism of Georgia History.

Cairo is the Capital of Grady county, Georgia and is situated on the Atlantic Coast Line Railway between Savannah Georgia and Montgomery Alabama and on the Lone Star Trail leading from Los Angeles California to Saint Augustine Florida. Through Cairo this is known as State Route Number 38. Whigham seven miles West is on the same railroad and the same highway. The Bainbridge and Thomasville Road formerly traversed much of the same territory as is now traversed by State Route 38 from Thomasville to Bainbridge, but as Cairo and Whigham have been settled since that road was first opened it does not touch either of these cities.

One of the oldest, if not the oldest road, in this section was that leading from Albany Georgia by way of Tallahasse Florida to the Gulf and known as the Hawthorn Trail. It passed through the present city of Camilla, Georgia and between Cairo and Whigham, crossing the Slough in Mitchell County, Richland, Tired, Turkey, Sofkee, Buck, and Horse Creeks in the present county of Grady and the Ochlochnee River in Florida, passing between lakes Jackson and Iamonia in Florida to Tallahassee. This road was probably a part of, or near, an Indian Trail leading from the Great Lakes to the Gulf, and partially travelled by Desoto on his exploration of this section. Another trail supplemental to this appears to have followed the general route of the Dixie Highway from Tallahassee northward to the road branching off below Iamonia Stores and crossing the river at Hadley Ferry bridge. The trail first mentioned must have crossed Ochlochnee River near Fairbanks Ferry, the supplemental trail must have crossed near the shallow ford south of Walden's bridge.

Grady County is bounded on the North by Mitchell County on the East by Thomas County, Georgia, on the South by Leon and Gadsen Counties, Florida and on the West by Decatur County, Georgia. Cairo is approximately 14 miles West of Thomasville,

25 miles East of Bainbridge, 38 miles North of Tallahassee, Fla. and 25 miles south of Camilla.

The county is more or less hilly with soil varying from a stiff clay to a light sandy loam. Average elevation is about 375 feet. Except in the Nort-western part of the county, springs and running streams are the rule, with well drained hills and plains between. The most of these streams ultimately reach the Ochlochnee River, those which do not flow into crevices or sinks to join an underground or subterranean stream flowing under the north western part of the county, except in high water when the under ground outlet becomes insufficient to carry off the water, then the sinks fill up and the water over-flows into the slough and runs into Flint river.

Among the streams flowing into Ochlochnee river from the West may be mentioned: Barnetts, Brumbley, Tired, Buck and Horse Creeks, from the East, Lees, Walden, Wolf and Hadley Mill Creek. In the Northwestern part of the county there may be mentioned the following disappearing underground: Bay Pole Creek flows into Bay Pole Sink, over flows into Big Fish Ponds and the Slough, Oakey Woods Branch flows into sink at Jordan Mill, Barrow Branch flows into Barrow Sinks at Barrow Old Mill, Water Fall branch flows into Waterfall Sink on Waterfall plantation, Spring Hill branch flows into Lime Sink at Jackson Old mill, Man Bone Creek flows into Sink of the Level.

The slough mentioned above, first touches Grady County a few miles to the South-west of Pelham and extends in a south-westerly direction and then crosses the western boundary of the county a few miles north-west of Whigham. The characteristics of the country to the north of this slough is in marked contrast to the country south of the slough. North there are no running streams or springs except a few large springs along the Flint river. This country extends through the western part of Mitchell county and the eastern part of Dougherty counties and is traversed by the Dixie Highway leading from Albany, Georgia to Tallahassee, Florida.

When the country was first settled the native growth abounding in this section was in the lower part of the section and south of the slough and along the swamps, oak, hickory, ash, sweet gum, black gum, tupular gum, poplar, bay magnolia, etc., while along some of the larger streams some cypress might be found. The up-lands were covered with a very magnificent growth of yellow pine. These pine groves should not be confused with "pine barrens" as has been frequently done. To the North of the slough the growth was principally pine, cypress, haw, wild plum and wild apple.

Webster's New International Dictionary gives as a noun "Barren-A tract of barren land;" level more or less wooded tracts of land, commonly characterized by a light, sandy soil and a distinctive biota; as pine barrens, oak barrens, etc. U. S."

The yellow pine with its ever-green foliage, its long straight trunks, its cluster of limbs at or near the top, its tendency to sway in the breeze and sough its solemn dirge, is one of the most magnificent trees that grow. A forrest of trees, such as these, all soughing their requiem in unison is awe inspiring and makes an impression never to be forgotten. They are found on high lands and clay plateaus most often and seldom or never on low lands. In sandy soils they send their tap roots down to an unbelievable depth, but on up lands and clay plateaus their tap roots do not penetrate the soil so deeply and consequently they are more easily uprooted in storms. These peculiarities of the pine has given rise to certain local expressions among which are the following:

Clay Root-That part of a pine tree which has been turned up exposing the clay when up-rooted by a storm or otherwise.

Harrican-A section of country where the pine timber has been blown down by a hurricane or storm.

Old Harrican-A section of country where the pine timber was destroyed by a storm a considerable time in the past. The fallen timber has usually been destroyed by fires and a young growth of timber is beginning reforestation.

Horsen Log-A log blown down but not up-rooted and the trunk of the tree still clinging to the stump and elevated some distance in the air.

Deadening-A tract of land where the timber has been circled preparatory to clearing after the timber has died. Term is not used after land has been put under cultivation.

These lands were carpeted with wiregrass, wild oats, wild ginger and other grasses. There was a native growth of huckleberries, Goose-berries, black berries, wild grapes, Bullaces, etc.

This country was not such a country as a pine barren is defined by Webster. The first use I have found of the word was by Fidalgo of Elvas 1540 where it occurs as follows, "Apr. 20, 1740. Lost in a pine barren. Six days consumed in fording two rivers and in an effort to find a way of escape." I suspect that he used the word, meaning the same thing as Harrican is now used locally or was used earlier in this section.

The territory was originally included in Early County created in 1818, and originally extending some miles into the present state of Florida. Decatur was organized in 1823 and then Thomas in 1825. Grady county was created from territory taken from Decatur and Thomas 1905 and organized Jan. 1, 1906. Seminole County was organized under Act of July 8, 1920. These three counties, Seminole, Decatur and Grady constitute the major portion of original Early county lying along the Florida line. A small portion of Thomas county on the west side was originally in Early county the remainder was in Irwin county. Dougherty County was organized under Act of Dec. 15, 1853 and Mitchell County under Act of Dec. 21, 1857. These three, Grady, Mitchell and Dougherty counties contain the territory traversed by Desoto, through which the Hawthorn Trail furnished a Highway for settlers to migrate to this section, through which an ancient Indian trail must have anciently furnished a way of travel for the red man, and the territory which we have for study.

Let us digress here for a brief mention of one of the natural curiosities.

About three-fourths of a mile east of the Hawthorn Trail and one and one half miles southeast of Mizpeh Church is a sink known throughout this section as Blowing Cave. At the bottom of the sink and extending at an angle under the ground is a small opening fifty or sixty feet from the top. At times there issues from this cavern a gentle breeze or a strong wind while at other times there is a suction. At other times it is quiet, no breeze or wind stirring. Various explanations have been given of this phenomena, some think that there is a connection by an under ground passage with the Gulf of Mexico and that the breeze is caused by the ebb and flow of the tides, others think that it is caused by running water underneath the ground, others that it is caused by the variations of the temperature of the atmosphere in an underground cavern and the outside atmosphere. I had the opportunity of studying this for several days about twenty-five years ago. Since then I have lost my notes made at the time but the conclusion I reached was that the wind motion was caused by the direction and velocity of the wind in the vicinity. The wind I think blows into this cavern when blowing in one direction and out when blowing in a different direction. I hear of another one of these caves to the south-west and it is my opinion that when one blows the other sucks and vice versa.

Cairo was first incorporated in 1870 but the first English settlements in the vicinity began soon after 1818. It is probabl· that there were Spanish settlements before Oglethorpe settled Savannah. The fertility of the soil, undulating topography of the country, the salubrious climate, the friendliness of the natives, the nearness of the Gulf, New Port and St. Marks, Fla., with the accessibility of sea foods and salt, the game in the forrest, the fish in the streams, the water-power easily available for grinding grain and the Old Trail leading down on the East side of Flint river induced a rapid settlement of the country by the best families from the older settled sections of the state. Some of these were descendants of the first settlers along the coast, some from Burke, or Richmond and some from those settlers which came into the State im-

mediately after the Revolution from the older States. A later wave of immigrants came directly from the older States, one settlement being known as the North Carolina settlement because so many of the settlers had come from that State. This settlement or settlements was a few miles south of Whigham. Many of the first settlers were in the war of 1812 and some few in the Revolution.

In the perceeding genealogies may be found some evidenc of the character of settlers who pioneered their way into this section. Full credit has been given to the character of the settlers from other states, but the earliest settlers, descended from original Georgians are constantly humiliated by being accused of being descended from "poor debtors, unfortunates and criminals." I would be derelict in my duty should I fail to set forth the facts as I find them as they relate to these charges which I believe to be unsupported by facts and to be the outgrowth of a strategical dissemination of propoganda immediately preceeding the settlement of the coast section of Georgia, of which more later.

Among our earliest settlers were immigrants from Ireland and descendants of such. Some of these were evidently passengers on that ship which reached Savannah in December 1768 or closely related to them and descended from the Royal Irish Stem which traces its lineage back through Milesius to the Pharoes and to the Bible genealogies. (See O'Harts Irish Pedigrees.) In support of this contention further I present first a list of the settlers drawing land in the neighborhood of old Queensboro and who were probably among the first generation of descendants the original heads of families and also a list of the early settlers of this section for comparison. The first list is taken from Georgia's Land Marks and Memorials, the other from History of Thomas county, Georgia by W. I. McIntyre.

QUEENSBORO LIST.

Albritton, Z.,
Allen, John,
Alexander, David and Hugh,
Atkinson, Thomas,
Barr, Matthew.
Barren, Samuel,

Bartholemew, John,
Beatty, Mitchell and Thomas,
Blair, James,
Boggs, James and John,
Breckenridge, James,
Brown, John and William,
Bryant, John,
Busby, John,
Campbell, John,
Cary, John,
Chambers, John,
Chestnut, Alexander,
Colman, Isaac,
Cook, George,
Cooper, Robert,
Crozier, John,
Dickson, John,
Dorton, M.,
Dubose, Isaach,
Douglas, David.
Duncan, Robert,
Evans, John,
Finley John,
Fleming, James R. and Samuel
Fleeting, Richard,
Gamble, John,
Gervin, Robert,
Gilmore, John,
Gray, R.,
Green, John,
Greer, David,
Haden, James,
Hampton, Joseph,
Hancock, D.
Hanna, Robert and William,
Harding, William,
Hardwick, Garland, C. W., W. P.
Harris, James,
Hogg, James,
Hartley, Sherrill,
Harvey, James,
Hogg, James,
Hurd, Henry,
Ingram, John,
Irvin, David and Isabella,
Johnson, Joseph,
Kennedy, John,
Laremore, Isaac,
Lewis, Henry,
Little, Samuel,
Lyle, Matthew,
McAllister, Samuel,
McClinigan, John and Elizabeth
McConkey, William,
McCreery, William,
McCroan, James and Thomas,
McCulloch, Patrick,
McCutlers, B.,
McGee, Patrick,
McIlrow, Adam,
McEelvey, James and John,

McMichan, Moses and James,
McNeil, Daniel,
Mack, John,
Mackay, Patrick and William,
Martin, John,
Maynard, John,
Meriwether, James,
Miller, Robert,
Mineely, John,
Moore, Andrew and Matthew,
Morrison, Adam and John,
Murdock, John,
O'Neal, Arthur,
Paulett, Jesse,
Peel, John, Richard,
Prior, Robert,
Purvis, Jesse,
Reese, John,
Robson, Clotworthy,
Rodgers, James, Robert, Edward,
Russell, David,
Sampson, Robert and William,
Sanford, Love,
Saunders, Joseph,
Scott, John,
Shellman, M.,
Simpson, James,
Slatter, Jesse,
Skelly, William,
Stevens, Walker,
Thompson, Edward, Geo., James,
Todd, John,
Toland, John,
Tonkin, James,
Tucker, Henry,
Tweedy, Esehte,
Warnock, John and Robert,
Warren, Benjamin,
Wilson, John,
Witherup, Seb.,
Wolfington, Thomas.
Early settelers in Territory now
embraced in Grady, Decatur and Sem-
inole Counties, Georgia (1830—40).
D After name shows residence in
Decatur county—1830.
  T After name shows residence in
Thomas county—1840.
Abbott, Wm. W., T
Adams, Dennis, T
Adams, Nancy, T
Adams, Thomas, T
Adkins, Samuel, T
Alligood, Wright, D
Arline, Henry, D
Asley, Jesse, D
Atkinson, Daniel, T
Atkinson, Henry, T
Atkinson, Hiram, D
Atkinson, James, T
Baggett, Peter, T

Baley, Isham, D
Bailon, Lewis, T
Ballard, Edward, T
Barber, Asa, D
Barker, Joseph, T
Barnes, James, D
Barnes, James, T
Batchalder, Bennett, D
Barr, John G., D
Barr, Thomas G., D
Belcher, Abner, D
Belcher, Daniel, D
Bell, Duncan, D
Bell, Jeremiah, D
Bell, Margaret, D
Bell, Walter, D
Belton, Solomon, D
Bennit, Elisha, D ,
Bird, James, D
Bishop, Abner, D
Bishop, George, D
Bishop, Samuel, D
Black, William A., T
Blackshear, James J., T
Blackshear, Thomas T., T
Blanset, James, D
Blewed, John, D
Bodiford, Vincent, D
Bole, Levi, T
Bole, John, T
Bolen, Willam, D
Boon, Joshua, D
Bostwick, Levi, D
Bostwick, Littlebury, D
Botsford, Theophillis, D
Boyce, George, D
Boyd, Phillip, D
Boyet, Isaac, D
Brain, Newton, D
Braswell, James J, T
Braswell, Kindred, T
Braswell, Marada, T
Braswell, Samuel, Jr., T
Braswell, Samuel, Sr., T
Braswell, Simeon A., T
Brescoat, James, D
Brewton, John, D
Brock, Daniel, D
Brock, Isaac, D
Brock, Martha, D
Brown, George, T
Brown, James, D
Brown, James, Sr., D
Brown, William, D
Brown, William, D
Browning, Daniel, T
Browning, John C., T
Browning, Simpson, T
Browning, William, T
Bryan, Alfred, T
Bryan, Daniel, D

Bryan, Elender Jane, D
Bryan, Nathaniel, T
Bryan, Stephen, T
Bryan, William, D
Bryan, Wm., T
Bryan, Wm. J., T
Bucklow, John, D
Buie, John, D
Buie, Margaret, D
Bullock, Robert, T
Burkit, Alexander, D
Buts, James, D
Butler, Elisha, T
Butler, Elisha, D
Burvis, Mary, D
Canniday, John, D
Carter, Michael, D
Castelow, Stephen, D
Castler, William H., D
Carlton, John, T
Cartledge, James, D
Chamblin, Asa, D
Chandler, William, D
Chapman, James, T
Chason, John, D
Chason, Reuben, D
Chastain, John, T
Chester, Abner, D
Chester, Abel, D
Chisam, Robert I., D
Churry, Samuel, D
Clary, James, D
Clewis, John, D
Cloud, John, D
Cloud, Lilpha, D
Cloud, Reuben, D
Corbet, George B., T
Cooper, John J., T
Cooper, Lewis J. , T
Collier, John J., D
Collins, William, T
Collins, Jesse, D
Collins, Ezekiel, D
Collins, William, D
Colman, Manning, T
Colwell, William L, D
Conner, Willis, D
Cook, Joel, D
Cook, John D
Cook, Johnson, D
Cook, Willis, D
Cravy, Joshua, D
Crawford, Ann, T
Crawford, Bennet, D
Crawford, Hardy, D
Crawford, Milton, D
Croff, Dawson, D
Crosby, Edward, T
Crutchfield, Edward, T
Cumby, Azariah, T
Cumby, Elizabeth, T

Cumby, James C.	T
Curry, Duncan,	D
Cursey, Bud,	D
Darsey, Joel,	D
Davis, Jesse,	D
Davis, Jesse H.,	D
Davis, Joseph,	D
Deborce, Reuben,	D
Debrough, Samuel,	D
Degraffenreid, John,	D
Dickey, Shadrick E.,	T
Dickenson, Francis,	D
Donaldson, Anna,	D
Donaldson, James,	D
Donaldson, Jonathan,	D
Donaldson, John,	D
Donaldson, Nancy,	D
Donaldson, William, Jr.,	D
Donaldson, William, Sr.,	D
Duglas, Alexander,	D
Duglas, Daniel B.,	D
Dubose, Peter P.,	T
Dykes, Isaiah,	D
Elkins, John,	D
Elkins, William,	D
Elkins, Wm.,	T
Elkins, Young,	D
Ellice, Willis,	D
Elwell, Benjamin	T
Emanuel, Caswell,	D
Emanuel, David,	D
Emanuel, John,	D
Evans, James,	D
Everett, Josiah,	D
Fain, Thomas P.,	D
Fain, Thomas, Sr.,	D
Fairchilds, Mary,	D
Faircloth, Abraham,	T
Faircloth, Eldred,	T
Faircloth, Jacob,	T
Faircloth, John,	D
Faircloth, Joshua,	T
Farior, Frederick,	D
Fenn, Elija,	D
Ferrel, Ansel,	T
Ferrel, Hutchins,	T
Finkley, George W.,	D
Forde, James,	D
Forbes, James,	D
Forbes, Richard,	B
Forson, Wm. I.,	T
Frazzer, Stark,	T
Freeman, James,	D
Freeman, John,	D
Freeman, Thomas H.,	D
Gamble, Hugh,	T
Gains, Geo. G.,	D
George, Daniel,	D
George, Eli,	D
George, Isaih,	D
Gibson, Jeptha,	D

Gibson, Jobe,	D
Gibson, Sylvanus,	D
Gideons, Isaac,	D
Gideons, Jesse,	D
Gilbord, Henry,	D
Gilbert, Jeptha,	D
Glover, Drewery,	D
Glover, Jesse,	D
Godden, Alexandria,	D
Godden, Stephen,	D
Godding, Stephen,	T
Gowen, Chas. G.,	D
Grace, Major C.,	T
Grady, Dennis,	T
Graham, Andrew,	D
Granard, Solloman,	T
Gray, David,	D
Gray, Mincha A.,	D
Grider, Jacob,	T
Griffin, Benjamin,	D
Griffin, Burrell,	T
Griffin, Dempsey,	T
Griffin, James,	D
Griffin, John,	T
Griffin, Lenn,	D
Griffin, Lewis,	T
Griffin, Major,	T
Griffin, Micajah,	D
Griffin, Shadrack,	T
Griffin, William,	D
Guyton, Joseph,	D
Hadley, Lewis L.,	T
Hagan, Stephen,	D
Hagans, James,	D
Hair, Elijah,	D
Hair, Edmond,	D
Hair, Thomas C.,	D
Hair, William,	D
Handley, James M.,	D
Harden, Marten,	D
Hargreaves, John,	D
Harnedge, George,	D
Harriel, Dempsey,	D
Harriel, Elijah,	D
Harrell, Isaac,	D
Harriel, Jacob,	D
Harriel, John,	D
Harrell, John,	D
Harrell, Moses,	D
Harrell, Wm. D.,	D
Harren, Edmond,	D
Harren, Howell,	D
Harris, John,	D
Harrison, Benjamin,	D
Harrison, Thomas,	D
Hart, Levi,	T
Harvin, Mary,	T
Harvin, William N.,	T
Hasard, John,	D
Hawthorne, Elias O.,	D
Hawthorne, Jonathan,	D

Hawthorne, Nathaniel, D	Kent, William, D
Hawthorne, William, D	Killin, William, D
Hays, Davis, D	King, Thomas, D
Hayes, William E., T	Knettles, Samuel, D
Henderson, John, T	Lamb, Islam, D
Hesters, John, D	Lambert, James, D
Hesters, Thomas, D	Lambert, Noah, D
Hesters, Thomas, T	Lanam, Squier, D
Hicks, John, D	Lassiter, Mary, D
Hicks, Nathaniel, D	Lawrence, George, D
Hicks, Ralph, D	Lee, Ebenezer, D
Hill, Hannah, D	Lee, John, D
Hilyard, Silas, D	Lester, Isaac, D
Hines, Starling, D	Lester, William C., D
Hines, Thomas, D	Lewis, Prior, T
Hodge, Elisha, D	Lewis, Thomas B., D
Hoge, Jacob, .D	Lewis, Wiley, D
Holten, Gideon, D	Lewis, William, D
Hopson, Hardy C., T	Long, George W. D
Hopson, Warren A., T	Lunn, John, D
Horne, Henry E., D	McCauly, Malcom, T
Horne, Wiley, D	McCrelys, John, D
Howell, Arthur, D	McCrone, Thomas, T
Hutchens, Anthony, D	McDaniel, Buckner, D
Hutchens, Asa, D	McDaniel, Daniel, D
Hutchenson, John, D	McDaniel, John, D
Ingraham, Hugh, D	McDaniey, William, T
Ingraham, John, D	McElvey, William, D
Ingram, William, D	McGowen, Alexandria, D
Israel, John, D	McGowen, Anthony, D
Jackson, Williams P., D	McGowan, Jacob, D
Jernigan, Laney, T	McGowen, Joseph, D
Johnson, Absalom, D	McKenzy, Daniel, D
Johnson, Daniel B.,	McKinis, John, D
Johnson, Hiram, D	McNair, Daniel, D
Johnson, Jesse P., D	McLendon, Eliza, T
Johnson, Jacob, D	McSwain, Floria, D
Johnson, John, D	Magany, Reddick, D
Johnson, Levi, T	Malone, Robert, D
Johnson, Samuel, D	Maloy, John, D
Johnson, Timothy, D	Man, John W., D
Johnson, William,	Mansfield, Frederick,
Joice, Michael, D	Mansfield, William, D
Jones, Alvis, D	Maples, Thomas, D
Jones, Elizabeth, T	Martin, Frances A.,
Jones, John, T	Martin, William, D
Jones, John,	Mathis, James, D
Jones, Josiah, D	May, David, D
Jones, Matthew, D	Meek, Reuben, D
Jones, Robert, D	Megainey, McClendon, D
Jones, Sarah, D	Melone, John, D
Justice, David, D	Malone, William, D
Kallahand, James, D	Merritt, Wiley, T
Keith, John W., D	Miller, Ebenezer G.,
Kelly, Jones, D	Miller, Jacob, D
Kelly, Malakier, D	Miller, James I., D
Kelly, William, D	Miller, James I., D
Kelly, William W., D	Miller, John, D
Kemp, Elias, D	Miller, Jonathan, D
Kemp, George W., D	Mills, John B., D
Kemp, John, D	Mills, Littlebury, D

Miller, William, D
Mobley, Daniel, D
Montgomery, D
Moore, Levi W., D
Moore, Thomas, D
Moore, Matthew R., D
Morgan, Duncan, D
Morgan, John,
Morgan, Reuben, Jr., D
Morgan, Reuben S., D
Murfey, Hiram, D
Neels, James T., D
Nell, Herman, T
Newberry,, Isaac, T
Newbury, John, D
Newbury, Sarah, D
Newsome, Elender, D
Nicholson, Duncan, D
Nobles, William, D
Obrien, Arch T., D
Obrian, David, D
Obrian, Lewis, D
Oliver, Thomas, D
Oneel, Daniel, D
Owens, Levi, D
Owens, Lott, D
Owens, Whitman, D
Owens, William, D
Owens, William M., D
Parham, Ransom,
Parice, Matthews, D
Parice, Wyatt, D
Parmer, Charles, D
Pate, Charley, D
Pate, Zacheus, T
Peacock, Alexander, T
Peacock, James, T
Phillips, Isaac, D
Plant, Jason, D
Pierce, Wiley,
Pike, Wm. H.,
Pitts, Stephen, D
Pollock, John, D
Portervint, Jno. G., D
Posey, Shadrack, T
Pope, Nathaniel, D
Pound, George C., D
Porter, Mark A., T
Powell, James,
Powell, William, D
Powers, John, D
Prevatt, Presley, T
Price, Joseph R., D
Proctor, Synthia, T
Rackley, Nathan, D
Ragan, Philip, D
Rankins, David, D
Rankins, John, D
Rawls, Benjamin, D
Rawls, John, D
Rawls, Joseph, D

Rawls, William H., T
Reeves, Isham, D
Regans, Chas., D
Regans, Daniel, D
Regan, Roberson, D
Rials, Jane,
Ricks, Harris, D
Ricks, John, D
Rich, George W., D
Rich, John, D
Rich, Sarah,
Rich, Stephen, D
Ridley, David, T
Rigdon, Ephraigh, D
Roberson, John, D
Roberson, Noah,· D
Robertson, Josiah, D
Runnels, William, D
Sadler, James, D
Saper, William, T
Sanders, John, D
Sanders, Logan, D
Sanders, William, D
Sanders, Wm. C., T
Sanders, Wright, D
Sansbury, Mordica, D
Sapp, James, D
Sapp, John G., D
Sapp, Margaret, D
Sapp, William, D
Scarborough, Stiring, D
Scott, Jacob, D
Scott, William, D
Sellers, Samuel, D
Sellers, Simeon, T
Sellers, William, T
Sellers, Wright, T
Sewel, Chas., D
Shaw, Daniel K., D
Shaw, Jeremiah, D
Shepherd, Lyman, D
Shepard, Wm., T
Shores, Isaac, D
Simmons, John, D
Simmons, John,
Singletary, Brayton, T
Singletary, David, T
Singletary, Henry, T
Singletary, James B., T
Singletary, Joseph, T
Singletary Nelson, T
Singletary, Richard W., T
Singletary, Wm. I., T
Slade, Jeremiah, D
Slade, Jno., T
Sloan, Allan, D
Smallwood, Francis, D
Smart, Edmond, D
Smith, Henry, D
Smith, Michael, D

Smith, Philemon,
Smith, Seth D.,   T
Smith, Shadrack,   T
Spann, John,   D
Spears, Allen,   T
Spears, William,   T
Spell, William,   D
Spence, Isaac,   T
Sphers, John L. W.,   D
Spooner, Adam,   D
St. John, James,   D
St. John, Lewis,   D
Strickland, Neel,   D
Strickland, Reuben,   D
Stoubt, John,   D
Sutton, Elizabeth,   D
Swicord, David,   D
Taylor, Bartholomew,   D
Taylor, Burrell,   T
Taylor, Dempsey D.,   T
Taylor, Jeremiah H.,   D
Taylor, Joseph,   T
Taylor, William,   D
Tate, Sarah,   D
Thomas, Bud C.,   D
Thomas, Lewis,   D
Thomas Hezekiah,   T
Thomas, Rachael,   T
Thompson, James,   T
Thompson, Nelson,   T
Tinsley, Green,   D
Tipton, Benjamin,   D
Tilson, Eson,   D
Tootle, Richard,   D
Touchstone, Stephen,   D
Travis, Asa,   D
Tredway, Thomas,   D
Trulock, James,   D
Trulock, Sutton H.,   D
Tucker, Barna,   D
Umhrey, John,   D
Van Landingham, Benjamin,   D
Van Landingham, Peter, Sr.,   D
Van Landingham, Peter, Jr.,   D
Vickery, Eli,   T
Vickery, Tesse,   T
Walden, Marten,   D
Walls, Birch,   D
Walsingham, Wm. H.,   T
Ward, Benjamin,   T
Waters, David,   T
Waters, George,   D
Waters, John,   T
Welch, Richard,   T
Wenzer, William,   D
West, Williams,   D
Wester, Elias,   D
White, Henry,   D
White, John,   D
Whiddon, Eli,   D
Whiddon, John,

Whiddon, Matthew,   D
Whiddon, William,   D
Whigham, Thomas,   D
Whigham, William,   D
Williams, Isaac,   D
Williams, Nathan,   D
Williams, Samuel,   D
Williams, William,   D
Williford, William,   D
Windham, Mahaley,   D
Wilson, Jeremiah,   T
Womack, Benjamin,   T
Woodruff, William,   D
Yarbrough, Joseph,   D
Yearby, George,   T
Yearby, William,   T
Young, Elijah R.,   D
Young, William,   D
Yawn, Isaac,   D
Yawn, John,   D
Yawn, Martin R.,   D
Yawn, Patrick,   D
Zeigler, Israel,   D

A comparison of the names in the two preceeding lists taken in connection with Miscellaneous Genealogies furnishes strong circumstantial evidence that many of the early settlers of the Eastern part of Early County as first organized were of the same racial stock as the settlers of Queensboro.

No other ship ever reached America with immigrants whose descendants have more reason for pride of ancestry than that ship, the name of which I have been unable to find and the list of immigrants of which appears to be lost, which arrived at Savannah in December, 1768, and whose passengers settled Queensboro. They paid their own passage money, received no bounty, and it appears that they received their land in common by right of sufferance. It was their children I think that received individual grants. They had not been settled long before the Revolution began. They sought peace, but when the action of the British became onerous, they fled the colony and threw the weight of their influence with the colonies and when the fortunes of the colonies were in the balance and their liberties at its darkest ebb, remembering their native land and the age old series of oppressions which had been imposed upon them there, they joined the Continental forces and at the Cowpens and Kings Mountain and many another bloody battlefield, by the added weight of their arms assured the triumph of the cause of liberty.

There are few if any of the older settlers of this section who do not have one or more lines of descent from these settlers.

The names of the Heroes of the war of 1812 were commemorated in the names of Thomas County, named for General Jett Thomas, a soldier of the war of 1812, Decatur County named for Commodore Stephen Decatur and Bainbridge named for William Bainbridge who took prominent parts in the perilous times just preceeding this war. Many of the first settlers had served in the war under Jackson, Blackshear or Hardin.

Many of the early settlers are also descended from the first settlers of the State through one or more lines. Because of frequent reference to the poor debtors and the suspicion cast upon the first English immigrants to Georgia in the histories (?) of Georgia but little effort has been made to preserve any record of this descent. Because of the condition of the state's colonial records the lineage of many of our families are difficult to connect with these early settlers. However, it does exist and existing deserves some mention here. Savannah is supposed to have been founded for poor debtors and the unfortunate class of Europe and the first settlers reputed to have been taken from the prisons. I believe this to be false. I do not question the recitals in documents or what historians have to say about the purpose of the settlement in so far as the literature of the time shows or the purpose is stated, but I do question that this was the real reason for the settlement or that the settlement was actually made by the class as described. My incredulity arises from the following circumstances. I have never found a single instance in literature of any kind relating the circumstance of the release of any individual from imprisonment to come to Georgia or the name of a single individual who was released from prison. I have compiled and carefully examined a large list of representative first settlers which I here give.

A partial list of early settlers of the Province of Georgia, compiled

from Jones, Knight and Historical Collections of Joseph Habersham, Chapter Daughters of the American Revolution, Vol III. (w, shows name taken from will; d, from deed and K, from Georgia Land Marks and Memorials.)

A.

Robert Adams, of St. Andrews Parrish, (1775), w.

William Aglionby, of Savannah, (1738), w. John Wesley refused to receive him as a God-father because he was not a communicant.

William Alexander, of Province of Georgia, (1760), w.

Amelia Alther, of St. Galena, Savannah, (1770), w.

William Anderson, of St. Johns Parish, (1772), w.

Benjamin Andrew (Midway), K.

James Andrews, of St. Johns Parrish, (1770), w. (Midway), K.

Thomas Atwell, of Savannah, d.

Francis Arvin, of Savannah, (1769), w.

B.

Hannah Betz, of Province of Georgia, (1770), w.

Josiah Bryan, of Christ Church Parish, (1774), w.

Timothy Bowling, wife, Elizabeth and daughter, Mary, d.

Lewis Bowen, d.

William Brown, John, d.

Peter Bailou, d.

Joseph Butler, of Privince of Georgia, (1760), w.

John Bowles, of Savannah (1776), w.

John Bowles, of Savannah, (1776), w.

James Baillow, of Savannah (1777), (1747), w.

James Thomas Brooks, of Savannah, (1770), w.

Raphaeal Bornal and wife, Jews. K.

Thomas Baillie, of Savannah, (1773), w.

Elizabeth Brownson, of Newport, (1775), w.

Hannah Bradwell, of St. Johns Parish, (1775), w.

Michael Beuer, of Christ Church Parish, (1775), w.

John Peter Bretton, of Savannah, (1770), w.

Urban Buntz,, of Province of Georgia, (1774), w.

Richard Baker, of St. Johns Parish, (1774), w.

Edward Barnard, of St. Pauls Parish, (1775), w.

Hainery Ludwig Buntz, of St. Matthews Parish, (1774), w.

Barbara Buntz, of St. Matthews Parish, (1775), w.

Benjamin Baker, (Midway) K.

Samuel Bacon, (Midway) K.

Richard Baker, (Midway) K of St. Johns Parish, (1774), w.

Samuel Burnley, (Midway(, K.

Jonathan Bacon, (Midway), K.

Kenneth Baillie, of St. Johns Parish, (1766), w.

John Martin Boltzais, of Ebenezer, (1763), w.

William Butler, of Ogeechee, (1759) w.

Solomon Boyking, (1770), w.

Isaac Barksdale, of Augusta, (1757) w.

Samuel Burnley, of St. Johns Parish, (1767), w.

Rebecca Baker, of St. Johns Parish, (1767), w.

Hugh Burn, of Christ Church Parish, (1767), w.

William Baker, (1764), w.

Sigmon Betz, (1764), w.

Joseph Bacon, of St. Johns Parish, (1764), w.

Adam Bosomworth, of Colony of Georgia, (1757), w.

Thomas Bosomworth (Jones). Married Mary Matthews widow who was a widow Musgrove, having been married to a Musgrove at the time of the settlement of the Colony. She and her Musgrove husband were living at the present site of Savannah before settlement by the whites, a half breed before her marriage, she was claimed by the Indians to be a sister of Malatcha. She and the colonist had considerable trouble and difference over title to some of the lands in Georgia. Bosomworth had been a Chaplain of one of Oglethorpe's Regiments and historians have dealt severely with his wife's claim but quoting from Lippincott's History of Georgia, "In 1751, the restless intriguer (referring to Bosomworth) revived his claim. It was litigated in the English courts for many years, and at length partially decided in his favor; but one Levy claiming a moiety of the lands by previous purchase of Bosomworth, a new suit was instituted, which from Levy dying not long after, has never been legally settled." (page

97). Are historians justified in their treatment of this subject?

Mary Bateman, of St. Johns Parish, (1772), w.

Michael Bohrman, of St. Matthews Parish, (1771), w.

Michael Burkholder, (1762), w.

Henry Lewis Bourguin, of Savannah, (1774), w.

Richard Buntley, of St. Johns Parish, (1771, w.

Joseph Butler, Jr., of Great Ogechee, (1760), w.

Isaac Brabant, of Province of Georgia, (1763), w.

Ann Bullock, of Province of Georgia, (1762), w.

Mary Bryan, of Savannah, (1766), w.

C.

Richard Cannon, d

James Carwall, d.

William Cox, and wife Frances, d.

Wi.liam Cox, Jr., d.

Thomas Christie, d, (1754), w, of Savannah. Thomas Christie together with William Calvert and Joseph Hughes named by trustees to take and convey title to settlers. He also appears as recorder in a warrant issued on the 8th day of August, 1737 for the arrest of John Wesley, Clerk, upon the complaint of William Williamson, and his wife Sophia Williamson, ne Hopkins.

Paul Cheeswright, d.

Thomas Chenter, d.

Joseph Cooper, d.

Henry Close, wife Hannah and daughter, Ann, d.

Robert and John Clark, d.

Joseph Coles, d.

Thomas Causton, d. He was senior bailiff, a position corresponding to that of our Superior Court Judge and also had charge of the distribution of the supplies for the colonies. His wife was the Aunt of Sophia Hopkins who had been the sweet-heart of John Wesley, and who later married William Wi.liamson. He was in charge of the grandjury which returned the indictment against Mr. Wesley on the 8th day of August 1737. Mr. Wesley departed the colony on Dec. 2nd, 1737 without having been tried. On June 2nd, 1738 the Trustees began to make investigations of the accounts of Causton. (See Jones Vol. 1 p 267 also Howell, Vol. 1 page 208). He was ordered to London denied any wrong doing and upon arrival in London and being required to produce vouchers which were in America, started back to Georgia for these vouchers and died and was buried at sea without ever having come to trial. (See Jones Vol. 1 page 271). These are the facts gathered from the authorities examined. Causton has been painted in the blackest character possible. Is the evidence sufficient?

David Cohen del Monte, d. Jew, K., Wife and daughters, Grace, Abigail and Hannah.

Jacob Costa, Jew K. (Jacob Lopez de Crasto d).

Thomas Carter, of St. Johns Parish, (1774), w.

Thomas Chewter, of Savannah, (1734), w.

Nathaniel Clark, of St. Johns Parish, (1761), w.

Robert Campbell, of Savannah, (1766), w.

George Cubdage, of Colony of Georgia, (1758), w.

Daniel Clark, of Augusta, (1757), w.

Mark Cave, of St. Patrick's Parish, (1767), w.

George Cothbert, of Christ Church Parish, (1768), w.

James Corneck, of Christ Church Parish, (1773), w.

Christopher Chappel, of Christ Church Parish, (1774), w.

Hugh Clark, of Colony of Georgia, (1771), w.

Clement Crooke, wife Harriet, (1770), w.

John Cable, of Province of Georgia, (1762), w.

Christopher Campher, of Christ Church Parish, (1774), w.

Joseph Camuse, of Savannah, (1764), w.

Giles Church, of Christ Church Parish, (1771) w.

Teleman Cuyler, of Savannah, (1772), w.

Patrick Clark, of Augusta, (1756), w.

John Coffee, of Savannah, (1759), w.

Thomas Cross, of Savannah, (1768), w.

Elias Crispin, Vice-Dean of Island of Guernsey, (1763), w.

James Cuthbert, of Christ Church Parish, (1770), w.

Lawrence Clark, Savannah, (1770), w.

John Clubb, of St. Simons Island, (1770), w.

D.

John Dearn, d.

Aaron Depevia, K.

Abraham DeLyon, K.

John Desborough, d.

Isaac de Val, d.

David de Pas, d.

Jacob Lopez d' Olivera, d.

James dormer, of Province of Georgia, (1747), w.

Lydia Dean, of Savannah, (1761), w.

John Davis, of Christ Church Parish, (1761), w.

Daniel Deviroux, of Province of Georgia, (1766), w.

John Doors, of Savannah, (1777), w.

John Davis, of St. Philips Parish, (1773), w.

Raymond Demere, of St. Simons Island, (1766), w.

Daniel Demere, Savannah, (1758), w.

Thomas DeValle, Indian Trader, of Georgia, (1758), w.

John DeVeaux, of Little Ogeechee, (1759), w.

Richard Dobbyn, Savannah, (1759), w.

Andrew Darlin, Sunberry, (1760), w.

Robert Davis, of Province of Georgia, (1771),w .

John Baptist Dolony, of Savannah, (1770), w

John Devine, of Savannah, (1737), w.

Robert Donaldson, of St. Andrew's Parish, (1768), w.

David Douglas, of Augusta, (1759), w.

W. M. Dunham, of St. Johns Parish, (1769), w.

Paynter Dickinson, of Christ Church Parish, (1767), w.

David Drummond, Savannah, (1761), w.

Daniel Demetrie and wife Ann, w.

Daniel Dunnom, (Midway), K.

E.

Thomas Egerton, d.

Thomas Ellis, d.

Andrew Elton, of Savannah, (1776) w.

William Ely, of Savannah, (1775), w.

William Erwin, of Savannah, (1776)
w.

John Eppinger, of Savannah, (1777)
w.

Thomas Eaton, of Savannah, (1767),
w.

John Elliott, of Midway in Georgia,
(1765), w.

John Emanuel, of St. Georges Parish, (1768) w.

David Emanuel, of St. Georges Parish, (1768), w.

Andrew Elliot, of Savannah, (1771)
w.

F.

Walter Fox, d.

Joseph Fitzwalter, d, of Savannah,
(1742), w.

Hugh Frazier, d.

Magdalene Fountain, of Savannah,
(1754), w.

John Fox, of Ft. Argyle, (1746),
w.

Samuel Fulton, of St. Andrews Parish, (1775), w.

Joshua Ferguson, of State of Georgia, (1777), w.

John Forbes, of Province of Georgia, (1775), w.

Geo. Frazier, of Savannah, (1775),
w.

John Flerl, of St. Matthews Parish,
(1776), w.

Benjamin Farley, of Province of
Georgia, (1765), w.

A.exander Fyfee, (1756), w.

David Fox, of Christ Church Parish, (1766), w.

Charles Flerl, of St. Matthews Parish, (1764), w.

Mary Flerl, of St. Matthews Parish, (1764), w.

George Faul, of St. Matthews Parish, (1767), w.

Penelope Fitzwaller, of Savannah,
(1765), w.

James Fox, of Christ Church Parish, (1773), w.

Benj. Fox, of Christ Church Parish, (1773), w.

Richard Fox, of Christ Church Parish, (1771), w.

Martin Fenton, of White Bluff, Ga.,
(1768), w.

David Fox, Little Ogeechee, (1760)
w.

Thomas Fraser, of Christ Church
Parish, (1772), w.

Benjamin Francis, of Province of
Georgia, (1774), w.

Wm. Francis, of Grantham, Christ

Church Parish, (1772), w.

George Frazer, of Abecorn, (1751)
w.

John Fitch, of Christ Church Parish,
(1762), w.

John Farley, of Savannah, (1763),
w.

Nicholas Fisher, Savannah, (1769)
w.

James Fitzimonia, of Savannah,
(1759), w.

G.

John Grady, d.

John Graham, d.

Thomas Gapen, d.

John Goddard, d.

William Gough, d.

Beasley Gough, d. Knight quoting
from Dr. James W. Lee in his account
of John Wesley's leaving Georgia says
Vol 2 page 635 of Landmarks and Memorials. "Wesley refused to enter
into the necessary recognizances, and
a warrant for his arrest was accordingly issued. To avoid further trouble
he determined to fly, like Paul from
Damascus. He left the place secretly
by night, in the company of a bankrupt constable, a ne'er-do-well wifebeater, named Gough, and a defaulting barber." It must have been Beasley Gough or William and Wesley had
made up for one of the counts in the
indictment returned against Wesley
charged. "By repelling Wm. Gough
from the Holy Communion" (Holwell
Vol. 1, page 207.)

Peter Gordon, d.

Robert Gilbert, d.

William Gibbons, of Christ Church
Parish, (1769), w.

John Goldwire, of St. Matthews
Parish, (1774), w.

Benjamin Goldwire, of Christ
Church Parish, (1766), w.

Wm. Gilbert, of Island of Wilmington, (1775), w.

James Garvey, of Christ Church
Parish, (1772), w.

Gaspar Garbut, of Savannah, (1772)
w.

Thomas Goldsmith, of St. Philips
Parish, (1772), w.

James Goodall, of St. Georges Parish, (1768), w.

John Grover Fellow, of Kings College Cambridge, (1772), w.

Rosanna Gregory, of Christ Church
Parish, (1774), w.

Antony Gotere, of Savannah, (1772)
w.

Patrick Graham, of Josephs Town, Georgia, (1755), w.

John Gibbons, of Christ Church Parish, (1770), w.

John Giovaorili, (1770), w.

George Gray, of Province of Georgia, (1766), w.

Mungo Graham, Savannah, (1766) w.

Michael Germain, of Savannah, (1753), w.

John Gallache, of Christ Church Parish, (1769), w.

Richard Gamble, of Province of Georgia, (1770), w.

John Gorton, (Midway), K.

Isaac Girardeau, (Midway), K.

William Graves, (Midway), K.

John Graves, (Midway), K.

Richard Girardeau, (Midway). K.

William H. Horn, d.

Robert Hanks, d.

Joseph Hughes, d.

Robert Hows, Wife Anne, d.

.ichard Hodges wife Mary, daughters, Mary, Elizabeth and Sarah, d.

Isaac Nunis Henriques, wife and son, Shem, K and d.

Nicholas Horton, Savannah, (1774) w.

Wm. Harvey, of Williamsburg, on Ogeechee, (1744), w.

Presylla Houston, of Savannah, (1772), w.

Samuel Holmes, Planter, (1772), w.

John Hobson, of St. Pauls Parish, (1767), w.

Wm. Hickson, of Province of Georgia, (1770), w.

Frederick Holzendorf, of Savannah, (1767), w.

Francis Harris, of Savannah, (1771) w.

David Hughs, of St. Georges Parish, (1770), w.

George Heyd, St. Matthews Parish (1770), w.

John Harwell, of Augusta, (1755), w.

James Herron, of Christ Church Parish, (1771), w.

James Huston, of Christ Church Parish, (1774), w.

John Howell, of St. Georges Parish, (1771), w.

James Habersham, the Elder, of Province of Georgia, (1775), w.

Benjamin Horn, of Province of Georgia, (1775), w.

Henry Hamilton, of Savannah, (1760), w.

Sir Patrick Houston, of Christ Church Parish, (1761), w.

Robert Johnson, d.

Edward Johnson, d.

Noble Jones, d. He was a Captain of Marines and lived on the Isle of Hope at his plantation known as Wormsloe, (Jones Vol. 7, p 148). He rendered distinguished service at the battle of Bloody March in the war of Jenkins Ear, led a charge against Spanish troops under Sebastian Santio and Magaleeto on the 7th of July, headed a troop of horse to receive Mary Bosomworth and Indians when trouble threatened and by his firmness and promptness in disarming the Indians prevented serious trouble between the whites and Indians. April 8th, 1751 he was commissioned register of the Province of Georgia. June 13th, paraded the militia which had been organized into four companies at Savannah, he having been appointed a Colonel. Was an assistant to Patrick Graham, president of the Colony, and later a member of council. He remained loyal to the crown but died during the troublesome times, having rendered distinguished service to the colony of Georgia and established a family that has rendered distinguished service to the state to this day and is now perpetuating the History of the State in the Wormslow Library at or near Savannah, Georgia.

Noble Wimberly Jones, d. son of Noble Jones, signed a call for the earliest meeting of the patriots in Savannah, elected speaker of the Georgia House of Assembly, deposed by Governor Wright, styled one of the morning stars of liberty and declined to leave his father's sick bed for a seat in the Continental Congress in Philadelphia. One of the line married a widow Nutall, of Jefferson County, Florida, and a few years ago I visited the old home while the old Library was still there and was much interested in an examination of the old books and MSS. which I learn have since been removed to New York.

Edward Jenkins, Sr., d.

Edward Jenkins, Jr., d.

William Jones, of Province of Georgia, (1768), w.

John Jagger, of Province of Georgia, (1760), w.

David John, of St. Georges Parish, (1764), w.

235

Margaret Jeankins, of Colony of Georgia, (1772), w.

Francis Jones, of Province of Georgia, (1774), w.

Samuel Jeans, (Midway), K.

K.

John Kelley, d.

John Kitt, of Province of Georgia, (1761), w.

Darby Kennedy, of St. Georges Parish, (1777), w.

Henry Kennan, of St. Josephs Town, of Georgia, (1767), w.

Bryan Kelly, of Province of Georgia, (1766), w.

Theobold Keiffer, of Province of Georgia, (1766), w.

Savannah Kennan, of Christ Church Parish, (1742), w.

Wm. Kennedy, of Savannah, (1769) w.

Charles Keys, of Savannah, (1754), w.

L.

William Little, wife Elizabeth, d.

John Lawrence, d.

Moses Le Deama, d.

John Lupton (Midway), K.

Capt. Thomas Lee, of Savannah, (1778), w.

Moses Linus, of St. Georges Parish, (1767), w.

Isaac Lines, of Province of Georgia, (1766), w.

Evan Lewis of St. Georges Parish, (1766), w.

John Lewis, of Province of Georgia, (1763), w.

Thomas Lloyd, of Savannah, (1765) w.

Roger Lacy, of Thunderbolt, (1736) w.

James Love, of Savannah, (1768) w.

Thomas Lloyd, of St. Pauls Parish, (1771), w.

John Long, of Whit-march Island, (1773), w.

J. W. Levonroy, of Province of Georgia, (1733), w.

Abraham Lewis, of St. Johns Parish, (1774), w.

Jacob Lewis, of St. Andrews Parish, (1774), w.

John Lester, of Exeter, Eng., now Savannah, (1761), w.

M.

Robert Moore, d.

Francis Muggridge, d.

James Muir, d.

Thomas Millidge, wife Elizabeth,

and male heirs, d.

William Mackay, d. (Gentlemen).

Samuel Marcer, d.

William Mears, d.

John Musgrove, d. (1734), w.

Abraham Minis, d. (1754), w. Wife and daughters Leah and Esther, K.

Sarah Mitchell, (Midway), K.

Mr. Mlena, K.

John Mitchell, (Midway), K.

Joseph Massey, (Midway), K.

Jacob Matthews, of Savannah, (1741), w.

Capt. Martin Moreland, of London, England, (1751), w.

Peter Morel, of Savannah, (1752), w.

Dan Mackentosh, of Darien, (1748), w.

Henry Manly, of Frederica, (1746) w.

Alexander Moon, of Province of Georgia, (1747), w.

John McGilvery, of Province of Georgia, (1748), w. Was this the father of Alexander?

Peter Miller, of Savannah, (1742), w.

Edward McGuire, of Savannah, (1761), w.

Andrew Moorman, of Province of Georgia, (1762), w.

William McPherson, of St. Johns Parish, (1761), w.

Thomas Morgan, of Savannah, (1778), w.

Roderick McLoud, of Province of Georgia, (1775), w.

Joseph Money, of St. Pauls Parish, (1774), w.

Clement Martin, of Province of Georgia, (1775), w.

Patrick Mackay, of Sunberry, (1768), w.

George Mauer, of St. Matthews Parish, (1775), w.

J. Boul Miller, of St. Matthews Parish, (1773), w.

John Morell, of Christ Church Parish, (1775), w.

Audley Maxwell, of St. Johns Parish, (1769) w.

Robert McClatchie, of Province of Georgia, (1766), w.

Laughlin McBean, of Augusta, (1756), w.

John McFarland, or Savannah, (1766), w.

Lewis Michel, of Province of Georgia, (1767), w.

William Moore, of St. Matthews

Parish, (1762), w.

Mary McGuire, of St. Johns Parish, (1773), w.

John Martin of St. Johns Parish, (1772), w.

Charles Maran, of St. Johns Parish, (1772), w.

John Boul Miller, of St. Matthews Parish, (1772), w.

John Mackay, of Province of Georgia, (1733), w.

John Maxwell, of St. Phillips Parish (1777), w.

James McHenry, of Savannah, (1767), w.

Donald Mackay, of St. James Parish, (1768), w.

Mrs. Mary Maxwell, of St. Philips Parish, (1770), w.

John McLean, of Little Ogeechee, (1773), w.

Robert Miller, of St. Johns Parish, (1773), w.

John Ledwig Meyer, Practitioner of Physic, (1764), w.

Ann Munford, of Province of Georgia, (1762), w.

Elias Miller, of St. Georges Parish, (1769), w.

John Murphree, of St. Georges Parish, (1770), w.

George Maures, of St. Matthews Parish, (1775), w.

Mathew Maure, of Province of Georgia, (1770), w.

Clement Martin, the Elder, of Province of Georgia, (1771), w.

Thomas Matthew, of Province of Georgia, (1769), w.

Richard Milledge, of Province of Georgia, (1768), w.

Polsen Miller, of Savannah, (1771), w.

David Murry, of Christ Church Parish, (1770), w.

Peter Miller, of Savannah, (1771), w.

Hugh Mackey, of Island of Jamaica, (?), w.

N.

Dr. Nunis and Mother, Mrs, Nunis, K.

Daniel Nunis, K.

Moses Nunis, K.

Shem Noah, K. The latter was a servant. The former were Portugese and Dr. Nunis an able physician.

William Norman, (Midway), K.

Malcolm Nelson, of Savannah, (1778), w.

Barack Norman, of St. Johns Parish, (1765), w.

William Norman, of St. Johns Parish, (1773), w.

Robert Nichols, of St. Johns Parish, (1768), w.

O.

Joshua Overend and wife, Mary, d.

David Olivera, K.

Jacob Olivera, wife and sons, Isaac and David, and daughter, Leah.

Rev. John Osgood, (Midway), K., (1773), w.

Josiah Osgood, (Midway) K. (1770) w.

Christopher Orten, Minister, Savannah, (1742), w.

John Owens, of Savannah, (1775), w.

Charles Odensell, of Christ Church Parish, (1773), w.

P.

John Penrose, d.

Thomas Pratt, d.

Robert Potter, d.

Jeremiah Potter, d.

James Papot, d.

Samuel Parker, wife Jane and son, Thomas, d.

Samuel Parker, Jr.

Henry Parker, d. (1773), w.

Thomas Peacock, (Midway), K.

Mary Powell, of Savannah, (1776), w.

Mary Palmer, of Savannah, (1761), w.

Thomas Parker, of Province of Georgia, (1759), w.

John Paddero, of Province of Georgia, (1763), w.

George Palmer, (1777), w.

Margaret Papot, (1776) w.

John Patten, of Savannah, (?), w.

John Perkinson, Commander of Ft. George, (1766) w.

Seth Place, of Tybee, (1757), w.

Elizabeth Pryce, of Province of Georgia, (1759), w.

de Daniel Phitner, of Province of Georgia, (1737), w.

Margaret Page, of Savannah (1778) w.

John Pye, of Savannah, (1755), w.

Amie Prunier, of Savannah, (1755) w.

John Randolph Pury, of Savannah, (1756), w.

John Pettigrew, of Augusta, (1766) w.

Nathaniel Polhill, of Burkley county S. C., (1756), w.

Joseph Premer, of Savannah, (1768) w.

Edmond Pierce, of Savannah, (1767) w.

Joseph Parker, of Savannah (1766) w.

Thomas Peacock, of St. Johns Parish, (1769), w.

John Platter, of Province of Georgia, (1767), w.

Solomon Prather, of St. Matthews Parish, (1755), w.

John Pettigrew, of Sunberry, (1775) w.

Q.
John Quarterman, (Midway), K. (1767), w.

John Quarterman, of Province of Georgia, (1763), w.

R.
Charles Philip Rogers, d.

Samuel Nunez Ribero, d.

Daniel Ribero, d.

Moses Nunez Ribero, d.

Nicholas Rigby, of Savannah, wife Sarah, daughters, Sarah and Elizabeth, (G), w.

Hugh Rose, of St. Peters Parish, S. C., (1761), w.

Badazier Reifer, of Ebenezer, (1775), w.

Michael Reiser, of St. Matthews Parish, (1775), W.

John Frances Reinier, of Province of Georgia, (1773), w.

Hugh Ross, of Province of Georgia, (1762), w.

Conrad Rahn, of Ebenezer, (1773), w.

Mary Reinier, of St. Matthews Parish, (1776), w.

Thomas Ross, of Province of Georgia, (1759), w.

Capt. John Robinson, of Savannah, (1758), w.

Alexander Rose, of St. Johns Parish (1767), w.

John Rovere, of Savannah, (1767), w.

Israel Roberson, of Wrightsboro, Town, (1773), w.

Daniel Ross, of Augusta, (1759), w.

John Ross, of Augusta, (1759), w.

Charles John Frederick Reitler, of Province of Georgia, (1766), w.

William Russell, of Savannah, (1768), w.

Simon Roviere, of Christ Church Parish, (1766), w.

Thomas Red, of St. Georges Parish, (1768), w.

John Mathias Reinstetler, of Vernonburg, (1776), w.

S.
Monte Sauls, d.

Benjamin Shaftell, d. (1765), w. Wife Perla.

Richard Spencer, (Midway) K.

John Stephens, (Midway), K. (1759), w.

John Stewart, Sr., (Midway), K.

John Stewart,, Jr., (Midway), K.

Mrs. Lydia Saunders, (Midway), K.

Joseph Smith, of City of New York, (1764), w.

William Simpson, Chief Justice of Georgia, (1766), w.

Thomas Salter and wife Anna of Province of Georgia, (1753), w.

William Sluder, of Province of Georgia, (1751), w.

Thomas Salter of Savannah, (?), w.

William Spencer, of Christ Church Parish, (1776), w.

John Stewart, of St. Johns Parish, (1776), w.

Ebenezer Smith, of St. Pauls, Parish, (1774), w.

Robert Smallwood, of St. Johns Parish, (1774), w.

Michael Stutz, of Christ Church Parish, (1770), w.

Joseph Stanley, of Savannah, (1770) w.

Thomas Shruder, of Christ Church Parish, (1775), w.

Agnesia Seckenger, of Ebenezer, (1776), w.

George Seaprit, of Savannah, (1775), w.

Mary Smith of Savannah, (1763) w.

Charles Story, of Savannah, (1763), w.

William Sludder, of Augusta, (1756), w.

Morgan Sabb, of Province of South Carolina, (1760), w.

Richard Spencer, of St. Johns Parish, (1767), w.

Joseph Summer, of Little Ogeechee, (1759),w . .

John Stewart, of St. Johns Parish, (1769), w.

Peter Stedeler, of St. Georges Parish, (1769), w.

John Summerville, of Savannah, (1773), w.

Matthew Smallwood, of St. Johns Parish, (1772), w.

David Smith, of Sunberry, (1773), w.

Thomas Schweighofer, of Ebenezer, (1772), w.

George Schweghofer, of Ebenezer, (1772), w.

Mary Spry, of St. Johns Parish, (1771), w.

William Simpson, of St. Johns Parish, (1772), w.

Edward Sommerville, of Savannah, (1762), w.

John Smith, of Savannah, (1770), w.

Edward Splatt, St. Johns Parish, (1773), w.

Andrew Seckinger, of St. Matthews Parish, (1772), w.

Solomon Shed, of Province of Georgia, (1768), w.

Heinrich Sturman, of Savannah, (1769), w.

Hannah Stewart, of St. Johns Parish, (1770), w.

John Street, of Savannah, (1768), w.

George Strobhar, of Christ Church Parish, (1772).

T.

James Turner, d.

Daniel Tibbeau, wife Mary Magdalene, and male heirs, d.

Thomas Tebbit, d.

Peter Tondee, d., (1775), w. He was a famous tavern keeper during revolutionary days of which much has been written.

John Todd, of Province of Georgia, (1756), w.

Edward Tennatt, of Province of Georgia, (1761), w.

Michael Tattershell, of Province of Georgia, (1775), w.

John Tinley, of Augusta, (1760) w.

Stephen Tasian, of Province of Georgia, (1762), w.

Jacob Telfair, of Savannah, (1769), w.

George Thomas, of Savannah (1766) w.

Richard Thompson, of St. Matthews Parish, (1767), w.

David Tsuan, of Christ Church Parish, (1775) w.

U.

David Unseld, of St. Matthews Parish, (1770), w.

V.

John Vanderplank, M. Veneral, K.

Mary Vanderplank, of Savannah, (1758), w.

Thomas Vincent, of Savannah, (1766), w.

W.

John Warren, wife Elizabeth, son William, d.

James Willoughby, d.

John West, d.

James Willson, d.

William Waterland, d.

John Wright, d.

Ludwig Weidman, of Ebenezer, (1769), w.

Joseph Watson, of Colony of Georgia, (1757) w.

Nevil Wainwright, of Savannah, (1754)), w.

Benjamin Williamson, of St. Georges Parish, (1774), w.

Samuel Wagner, of Province of Georgia, (1775), w.

Sarah Watson, of Savannah, (1771), w.

John Francis Williams, of St. Pauls Parish, 1774), w.

Charles Whitehead, of St. Georges Parish, (1770), w.

John Martin Wright, of Colony of Georgia, (1749), w.

Wm. Wright, late of New York, now of Savannah, (1756), w.

Christopher Wisenbackner, of Savannah, (1767), w.

Joseph Wright, of Christ Church Parish, (1771), w.

George Williams, of Christ Church Parish, (1773), w.

Wentworth Webb, of St. Philips Parish (1771), w.

Thomas Westberry, of St. Johns Parish, (1773), w.

Robert Wright, of Savannah, (1773) w.

Jasper S. Whiteheart, of Savannah, (1757), w.

Charles West, of St. Johns Parish, (1766), w.

Thomas Whitehead, of St Georges Parish, (1765), w.

Richard Williamson, of Christ Church Parish, (1773), w.

Thomas White, of Province of Georgia, (1770), w.

Stephen Williams, of Province of Georgia, (1770), w.

Samuel Way, of Midway, (1757), w.

Edward Way, of St. Johns Parish, (1762), w.

Joseph Way, of St. Johns Parish, (1766), w.

Absalom Wells, of Province of

Georgia, (1768), w.

George Whitfield, of Savannah, (1770), w.

Charles Watson, of Savannah, (1770), w.

Parmenas Way, (Midway), K.

Mo3es Way, (Midway), K.

Edward Way, (Midway), K.

Nathaniel Way, (Midway), K.

John Winn, (Midway), K.

Y.

Thomas Young, d.

Isaac Young, of Christ Church Parish, (1766), w.

William Young, of Savannah, (1776), w.

Jacob Yowel, d.

Z.

Bartholemew Zouberbuh:er, Rector Christ Church Parish, (?), w.

Mathias Zeitler, Savannah, (1776), w.

The foregoing list of early settlers, while not complete, is representative. The character of the families represented and the limited knowledge of them which we are able to secure at present precludes the assertion that they were either of the poor debtor or criminal class. Other facts inconsistent with these statements in our early histories that the settlement of Georgia was an act of philanthropy are that Thomas Coram, the only member of the board of trustees with a reputation for philanthropy (except in connection with the Colony Georgia) retired as trustee after his first year's service; provisions were made for importation of servants by the first settlers and these were personal servants, not slaves; immediately upon arrival of the colonies fortifications were begun and many other details of conduct indicative of the purpose to hold the colony against possible attempts to secure it by other powers.

The question must occur here as to why should such representations have been made at the time if the colony was not intended as a refuge for the unfortunate class. The answer lies, in my opinion, in the condition of the times. England was Protestant, and Spain and France Catholic. Georgia belonged to Spain under the authority of the Pope and this claim had color of title from treaties existing between England and Spain. England was aware that Spain would consider the settlement of Georgia an act of aggression and to forestall Spain the project was proposed for poor debtors of Europe and delegated to Trustees. The first ship brought settlers native of Portugal, Spain and Bavaria, as well as from England. The trustees were English, they had the right of selection and rejection and were thus enabled to furnish such military forces as might be needed to maintain the colony for England. Historians have given but little if any consideration to this question. Oglethorpe, Wesley and Whitfield were great men and immensely admired in their day; yet each had been under attack in Georgia; Oglethorpe had been court-martialled and acquitted, of charges made in Georgia; Wesley had been indicted and left Georgia at night, and Whitfield had made a failure of his orphan home. Our historians have been more interested in protecting the reputations of these great men than in giving the facts regarding the average citizens. The result of this has been that Georgia is suffering from misrepresentation abroad and our people do not have that pride of ancestry, spirit of patriotism, and inclination for service to their State which no doubt would prevail if they knew the facts of the early settlers of the colony. At this late day the task of rescuing these facts from the pages of oblivion must be that of the genealogist until such a time as a sufficient array of facts has been marshalled to supply the historian with data for correcting the errors in the history of our state.

Now stepping back nearly two hundred years before Oglethorpe settled Savannah, Ga., and the English colonization of Georgia began, the history of Georgia by the white race began in that section which we have been discussing.

Tallahassee, F.orida before the advent of the white man was in the midst of an Indian's winter paradise. The hills and forests to the North of the Indian town, which was about two miles south of the present city of Tallahassee, protected them from the cold north winds, the pines provided fuel, the gulf, sea food, the surrounding fresh waters, fish, and the forests, game.

From the evidence of Indian Trails

and from a study of the character of the resources of the various localities and the necessities of the aborigines, Tallahassee must not only have been a winter pleasure resort but also a trade center, at which during the winter months there was an exchange of stone implements and pottery for various commodities from the South. The character of this early town, Tallahassee, is indicated by its name which according to the Rev. Milton A. Clark as related in A Lost Acadia, (page 4) means Broken Down Town, referring, no doubt, to the fact that it was inhabited principally during the winter months.

During the winter of 1539 and 1540 a party of white men headed by De Soto appeared upon the scene and spent the remainder of the winter among the Indians, no doubt studying their language and learning all that they could about the surrounding country. Nothing is known with certainty as to these winter months. Perhaps supply ships were anchored off St. Marks; certainly some of the Spaniards would be diligent in acquiring a knowledge of the Indian language and securing as definite information of the country which they were to explore as shortly as possible.

We learn from Jones (Vol 1, p 38) that two hundred thirteen horses were put on shore in Florida, (p 38), there were also burden bearing mules, fleet grey hounds, savage blood hounds and grunting swine, and artillery. The order of the King of Spain provided for 500 men and among them were twelve priests, eight clergymen, four monks. (p 45). We learn that the thirteen sows had multiplied until there were three hundred swine in camp from which it is certain that De Soto had no little herd of hogs at Tallahassee which he drove through the country on the march.

As March drew near the Indians began making preparations to disperse to their summer locations and De Soto and his band likewise for their march of discovery and exploration. March the third, 1540, O. S., which corresponds to February 23rd, under our present system of recording time, De Soto began his celebrated march from Anhayca, which is reputed to be two miles south of the present city of Tallahassee, Fla. The

line of march must have consisted of mounted men, several pack animals, several foot men, a drove of hogs which were driven along the main line of march, some artillery and camp equipment. The mounted men must have furnished an advance guard and headed various expeditions of exploration to spy out the country, both to the right and left of the main line of march. The rate at which the herd of hogs could travel would determine the rate of speed of the march as they were the slowest of the animals. It is estimated that this rate of travel of the main line of march could not have been more than ten or fifteen miles per day and more likely ten than more. On the seventh day, O. S., of March, they crossed the Ochlocknee river, traveling north. This must have been near what is now known as Walden's bridge and tradition says that when the section was first settled an Indian trail crossed the river about one half mile from what was formerly known as the Shal.ow Ford. This must have been the line of march. This trail led through the present city of Cairo and De Soto must have camped near Cairo on the night of March the 7th, 1540.

After breaking camp on the morning of the 8th, De Soto continued his march to the north. Every circumstance indicates that he reached the main Indian trail leading from the Gulf to the Great Lakes on this day and some where near what is known as the Pearce Court ground. It must have been on the 9th that De Soto had the encounter with the Indians described by Jones as follows:

"Within the next forty-eight hours the Indian village of Capachiqui was reached. At the approach of the Spaniards the natives fled; but when five of the Christians visited some Indian cabins, surrounded by a thicket, in rear of the encampment, they were set upon by Indians, lurking near, by whom one was killed and three others badly wounded. Pursued by a detachment from the camp, the natives fled into a sheet of water filled with forest trees whither the cavalry could not follow them."

When this country was first settled and for some time following there was an Indian village in the general vicinity of Camp Flats and another near the Waterfall plantation. One of these must have been the village of Capachiqui. Man Bone Creek flows between these sites of ancient villages, tradition is that this creek was named for a man's bones and from the best information obtainable it appears that the name was given by the surveyors surveying and mapping out the country and was the English equivalent of the Indian name. I suspect that this creek received its name from the first white man whose bones were to rest in Georgia soil.

DeSoto must have remained two days in the vicinity of the slough and this Indian village, perhaps burrying the dead and treating the wounded. He departed on the 11th, where Jones says, "Departing from Capachiqui on the 11th, and traversing a desert, the expedition had on the 21st, penetrated as far as Toalli." Here Jones draws conclusions from the use of the word desert. Had he been familiar with the country through which the line of march was traveling his conclusion would no doubt have been different. De Soto's line of march from Anhayca had, so far been through a country abounding with hills and running streams, with springs and a varied growth: At Capachiqui he was on the slough. A large stream flowed under the ground of which his expedition could know nothing. They found numerous streams flowing to the north or the northwest whose waters disappeared under the ground. Crossing the slough and traveling north a marked change in the appearance of the country demanded instant attention. No longer were there running streams, or springs. The country was nearly level. They were likely in an "old harrican," the Indians had probably burned the grass and nothing was more natural than to mistake the country for a desert, but he who travels over the Dixie Highway today, traversing much of the same territory from Albany to Camilla, would not fall into this error, but viewing the magnificient homes, the wonderful vistas of pecan groves, the beautiful hedges or the fields of cotton, corn, mellons, or peanuts would never think of this as having once been described as a desert, but rather as a wonderful land of promise. I wonder if these

Spanish explorers had been more intent upon the agricultural possibilities of this section or if they had been able to visualize the country as it now is, if the history of this section would have been the same or if a Spanish colony would not have been planted here rather than the scattering and half-hearted Spanish missions which came later.

We can not definitely determine the Indian village of Toalli but as it was within a ten days journey by the expedition from Capachiqui and within a two days journey from the Ocmulgee river we must conclude that it was somewhere in the vicinity of the present County of Wilcox.

Not only is this section of Georgia the oldest explored part of the state but in all probability it is the oldest from point of continuous occupation by a Christian people. In Herbert E. Bolton's recent book, "Spain's Title to Georgia," page 24: "The center of a new movement was Apalache, with San Luis (now Tallahassee) as its focus. Towards this important region in the back country French and English pirates on the Gulf, empty flour barrels at San Augustin, and the demand of the royal fleets for wild turkeys pointed the finger of prophecy. The Apalache Indians had long been asking for missionaries, but for lack of funds and workers the petition could not be answered until 1633. Then the guardian of the head monastry at San Augustin trudged westward and answered the call. Twenty years later there were nine flourishing missions at San Luis. Some of them drew neophites from the region that is now southwestern Georgia."

The Indians living within the present boundaries of Grady county were certainly friendly to the whites and while the settlers in other sections were having their troubles those in this section lived in perfect friendliness and accord. These two following incidents will illustrate the spirit of friendliness that existed between the two races.

Elder William Hawthorn first settled along the waters of Tired Creek. At the time of making this settlement a small Indian village was located near the forks of the roads beyond the creek on the lower Whigham road. These Indians remained friendly and afforded Elder Hawthorn every aid and assistance in establishing himself. One of the orphaned Indians was provided for by Hawthorn and remained as a member of his household for seven years. When the trouble broke out between the whites and Indians from neighboring settlements neither the whites nor Indians here were involved to any considerable extent, if at all. Other Indians were dissatisfied with this condition and sought to create trouble. In furtherance of this desire a scheme was devised to assassinate Hawthorne in such a manner as to leave evidence to cause the white settlers to suspect the friendly Indians of being guilty of his assassination, thinking in this manner to cause a breach which would involve the friendly Indians in the, then prevailing, Indian war.

Soon after day one morning Elder Hawthorne heard a turkey yelping in the nearby woods. He secured his rifle and went to look for the turkey, but instead of going straight from the house he took a circuitous route so as to approach the sound of the turkey call from the growth of timber. He located the call as coming from among the branches of a large oak. Creeping forward noiselessly and keeping another large tree between him and the tree in which he supposed the turkey to be, he approached quite close to the supposed turkey. Looking around the tree for the turkey he was startled by an arrow which struck the tree just a few inches from his head and glanced off. He recognized at once that the supposed turkey was an Indian seeking to entice him within reach to kill him. He knew his danger. While he had his gun he did not know the exact location of the Indian. He could neither retreat or move without taking the risk of receiving an arrow. After considering for some time and remaining entirely motionless he determined upon what appeared to him the only safe course of action. Having reached his decision he examined the priming of his gun and seeing that everything was in readiness, exposed himself just long enough to tempt another arrow from the Indian, which missed. Taking advantage of the time necessary for the Indian to secure another ar-

row and fit it to the string Hawthorne stepped from concealment and shot the Indian from the tree.

He failed to recognize the Indian and left him lying where he fell. Returning to the house he dispatched the Indian lad who was living with him to the village of the friendly Indians with the news of what had happened. The Indians came and looked over the ground after which they dispatched a runner to the village in what is now Thomas county where the Indian belonged and these Indians came and took the body away. In this way their scheme was foiled and the whites and Indians still remained friendly..

As the troubles grew more serious between the Indians in other sections runners were sent out calling the whites and their families into the fort near Bainbridge. The settlers did not want to go. They discussed the matter with their Indian neighbors and the Indians advised them to go to the fort and promised to care for the property of the whites, and thus it was arranged. The white settlers all resorted to the forts for protection from the Indians and the Indians cared for their property. After the trouble was over and the white people returned to their homes they found their cows and calves, their hens and biddies and all their property cared for just as well as if they had remained to look after it themselves.

These traditions have been given to me by children and grandchildren of the first settlers. I remember only one of the first settlers, Millie (Ward) Hester, and remember only one circumstance as related by her, nevertheless these circumstances have come from so many sources that I believe they are correct in all important particulars.

There are now residents in this section, descendants of first settlers who trace their descent from one line of Indian ancestry, and there is but little doubt that there was an infusion of Spanish blood among the Indians here long before the advent of the English race.

W. I. MacIntyre, of Thomasville has compiled a complete list of heads of families for this section covering the period 1830 and 1840. Let those who have a remaining doubt as to the character of our people procure this list and study the lineage of them as they please. The result can be only to show that the early settlers of Southwest Georgia belong to the best families of America and that they have by their accomplishments demonstra'ed this.

I acknowledge descent from among the first settlers in Georgia. Instead of being a poor debtor or an unfortunate he appears to have been a Gentleman and to have owned property in Georgia, England and Ireland. I have learned enough about a few hundred other first settlers, whom I would be be just as proud to acknowledge as a foreparent as the one I do acknowledge. I believe Georgia settlers to have been of the best blood. To teach Georgia History in such a way as to discredit our early settlers is an imposition upon our school children. To describe the pine lands of Southwest Georgia as pine barrens is deceptive. Let those who live in sections, if there be such, where their pine lands may be properly described as pine barrens so describe them, but do not so describe the pine lands of Southwest Georgia. Let those who are descended from "poor debtors" or the unfortunate class of Europe so describe their ancestors, but name them and show their circumstances, and do not so class the ancestors of the settlers of Southwest Georgia.

Southwest Georgia, not only was settled by the first families and their descendants, but it has produced numbers of notable men. Few of these are thought of in connection with Southwest Georgia, the State and nation at large claiming them.

Georgia boasts of "Uncle Remus" and Sidney Lanier, justly so, but the sweetest singer and the Greatest writer of Georgia dialect was a native South-Georgian, Montgomery M. Folsom. When will his recognition come?

Many of Georgia's public officials have been the sons of other states. The conduct of many of these has been such as to cause Georgia to blush with shame and their parent States to befoul Georgia with their criticism for the conduct of their progeny. Governors guilty of making illegal grants of the lands of Georgia as enumerated by the late S. G. McLendon, Secretary of State, History of the Public Domain of Georgia, page 65, were Walton Telfair, Matthews and Irwin. Of these George Walton was born in Prince Edward County, Virginia in 1749. Edward Telfair was born in Scotland in 1735, having lived in both Virginia and North Carolina before coming to Georgia. George Matthews was born in Augusta County, Virginia. Jared Irwin was born in Mecklenburg County, North Carolina.

Matthews, above, was the Governor of the State at the time of the passage of the celebrated Yazoo Act, and regardless of what others may say of us, when our failings are itemized and the responsibility brought home to the guilty parties, Georgia is exonerated.

James L. Seward, Peter E. Love, Nelson Tift, Archibald T. MacIntyre, William E. Smith, Philip Cook, John C. Nicholls, Henry G. Turner, Charles F. Crisp, Benjamin E. Russell, Charles R. Crisp, James M. Griggs, Elijah B. Lewis, Seaborn A. Roddenbery and Frank Park are a few of those who have held positions of honor and trust from Southwest Georgia in the past. At present E. E. Cox, Walter F. George, Judge R. C. Bell, and Judge Roscoe Luke are representative citizens of Southwest Georgia. We commend these names and these men to the consideration of the nation. No suspicion of graft, or corruption, or moral turpitide has ever attached itself to any or either of these. So far as I am able to learn every single citizen of Southwest Georgia who has been honored by the State has proven worthy of the trust reposed in him. What more can be said of the people of a section?

The Religion of Nature.

The religion of nature is recognized throughout the Scriptures. "The Heavens declare the glory of God; and the firmament showeth his handiwork." Reason teaches that if the Scriptures are the revealed word of God that nature will teach the same lessons for He is one, and the author of both.

Nature functions thru laws. These laws are ordained and established by the great Law Giver. Man's comfort and existence is dependent upon a knowledge of these laws. Learning these laws he learns something of the One who prescribed the laws and from this there is a beginning of the Religion of Nature.

The first problems confronting man are, food supply, protection from enemies and the elements, and the establishment and perpetuation of the social relations. He first learns to utilize and take advantage of those things which nature has provided for his welfare, next how to adapt nature to his requirements, then how to pit the forces of nature against each other.

Each step in his development necessitates another step, and the next still another. The making of the first spear was a forecast of a shield, the beginning of agriculture required storage facilities for the products grown, and when men began to domesticate cattle and keep herds the necessity for a preservative for meats arose and it was only a question of time before man would understand somewhat of the chemistry of salt. Likewise the acquisition of goods was the mother of barter and exchange and the grandmother of transportation.

As these develop so does religious thought. From these gropings there emerges a religion whose first propounders receive the grateful acclaim from those who understand and recognize the truths contained in the creed. There usually spring up imitators, charlatans and hypocrites who with innovations and minute technical and fanciful interpretations pervert the truth to the gratification of their desires or the advancement of themselves.

If we examine the religions of the peoples who have reached a degree of development worthy of observation, after having eliminated formality and practices prescribed by priests or medicine men, we find the essential features of the religion of nature which are as follows: A belief in

The existence of a Great Spirit with a Spiritual Kingdom.

The existence of an evil force operating to man's injury.

That the will of the Great Spirit is that man should attain to the highest physical, intellectual, moral and emotional development to which it is pos-

sible for him to attain.

This appears to have been the stage of the religious belief of the American Indian in Georgia, when it was settled. (See Howell's History of Georgia, Vol1, page 21, et seq.) This is in accord with the fundamental teachings of the Christian religion.

The primary purpose of the religion of nature being the development of man to the highest physical, intellectual, moral and emotional state to which he may attain, makes it necessary for those seeking the accomplishment of this purpose to know the laws prescribed by the great lawgiver by which this purpose may be approached if not attained.

Nature teaches that most imperfections are transmitted by the laws of heredity. Every grower of seed and breeder of stock recognizes this law and selects his seed or breeding stock in accordance with this law. That the same laws govern the human family can not be questioned by one who has given any attention to the question, and has had opportunity for observation. Half-breeds, mulattoes, and similarity of the characteristics and the personal appearance of the members of families illustrate the fact that this law does operate among humans but the extent to which it extends and the amount of the worries and troubles of life that are directly traceable to this law is beyond the comprehension of the best informed of the most interested people.

The truth of this law is recognized in the scriptures and could hardly be made clearer or more forceful than in the commandments where God says "I the Lord thy God am a jealous God, visiting the iniquity of the fathers upon the children unto the third and fourth generation of them that hate me; and shewing mercy unto thousands of them that love me, and keep my commandments." The flood was sent upon man because the sons of God had intermarried with the daughters of men and man's age was shortened from eight and nine hundred to one hundred and twenty years. Noah was selected to be saved from the flood for two reasons, he was a just man and perfect in his generations. (See 6th chapter of Genesis.)

I suspect that the doctrines of election, predestination and foreordination are nothing more than a recognition of this law of inheritance as applied to human beings. Faith in the scriptures inclines to a belief in the law of heredity and a careful study of nature supplies positive proof of the law as applied to humans.

Then if heredity plays an important part, as it does, in the development of man to the highest state of physical, intellectual, moral and emotional perfection to which he may attain how may this law or these laws be utilized to attain this primary purpose of religion and the will of the Great Spirit. Nature's methods are harsh and Christian people are repelled by their severity, yet, unless some steps are taken among Christians to conform to this law, Christian nations will eventually perish from the face of the earth.

Legislative enactment is impractical and will never receive the sanction of a Christian people. In my opinion sane, rational education of boys and girls in these fundamental truths so that they will enter matrimony with a knowledge of the danger surrounding an improper or unsuitable match, and with an opportunity to know something about the antecedents of those with whom they associate will promote the cause. Unless the Christian youth receives practical instruction in the laws of heredity in the human family before the age of mate selection youth will, in ignorance, resent all helpful advice. Parents and adults all too often volunteer advice predicated upon financial or social or other reasons entirely foreign to the laws of heredity than otherwise, and youth, sensing a false premise, rebels against parental authority and friendly advice. I have failed to find an intelligent youth who refused to give attentive consideration to reasons presented, based upon correct grounds looking to the probable effect upon issue of marriage. In this instance youth is wiser than age, and recognizing that a life time must be spent in the society of such companion as is taken and the issue of such union, is more concerned with a congenial companion and a happy fireside than with wealth or social position, which is a correct view. When youth sees that there can never be a pleasant family life because that the issue of

the union will probably be weaklings, feeble minded, degenerate or otherwise abnormal then youth will exercise a caution which adults fail to recognize. However they must be shown that it is a fact and they are justified in this , because all too frequently would be advisers are not actuated by the best interest of the individuals or their posterity but are simply trying to gratify preconceived prejudice or further some pet scheme of their own.

Facts must be presented from a source in which the youth has implicit confidence. Unfortunately I know of no such source in America. Now, when tempted to bewail divorce courts, deplore degenerates and criticise youth, first stop and consider.—Youth receives no training or instruction fitting it for the proper selection of a life companion and if by chance such instruction is received there is no reliable source from which it can obtain information as to even its own antecedents much less that of associates from which a companion must be selected. In failing to provide such instruction for American youth and to supply a source of information for youth from which it may acquire the facts essential for mate selection, we are supplying the gist for divorce mills, inmates of insane asylums, and criminals for courts to fuss over, and taxing ourselves to exhaustion to take care of an unnecessarily abnormal and dependent product of this neglect. If the primary purpose of religion is development of man to the highest physical, intellectual, moral and emotional state possible, we must in the final hearing plead guilty to a neglect of the first essential of its accomplishment.

This is only one of the lessons that nature teaches. The cotton seed we plant influences the crop but it is influenced more by the preparation of the soil, the fertilizer used, the cultivation given, the character of the soil, the climatic conditions, etc. To make the best crop every factor affecting the plant must be given attention, and the plant must be guarded against its enemies, or else the boll weevil or something else will destroy the best of our efforts. Likewise, the blood of the pig, the calf, the colt, the chick, etc., is important, but of more importance is pasturage, feed and attention. All this in natural course, yet the time comes when if neglect to breeding is persisted in the strain "runs out" and new blood must be resorted to or extinction follows.

The human family is influenced by forces or factors without itself in a similar manner, but being an intelligent creature soon acquires the power to adapt its environment, somewhat to its needs. This power of adaption and the ability to wisely make selections is dependent somewhat upon instruction and environment of the earlier years and here the responsibility rests upon those who have the charge of the instruction, the training and the disciplining of these years. I fear that many have acquired the idea from modern high pressure evangelism that the Christian religion is such a miracle worker that it will make a man anew over-night. I would not detract from the Christian religion one iota, but if the Christian religion has this power I have not seen it so operate but to the contrary I have observed that the humble Christian is engaged in a constant warfare progressing slowly towards the goal, never attained, of perfection. They are working out their Salvation with fear and trembling. I do not deny the power of Jesus to save. Nature teaches the ability of selection even among plant life, the sugar cane selects the elements of sugar, the potato starch, the tobacco nicotine and other plants other properties from the same soil, the same fertilizer, the same water and the same air. I do not understand what this power is but know that it exists. Cows have been bred to select the food elements and convert it into milk and others to convert it into beef, hens to make eggs or flesh, and dogs to chase fox, set birds, tend the sheep, etc. These properties are either inherent in the plants or animals or have been developed by breeding and selection. Man, however, being an intelligent creature, arrives at an age and experience when he may acquire control of the power of selection as it relates to himself and when he has reached this age we say that he has arrived at the age of accountability. Man now becomes a free agent and adopts some philosophy of life. His future depends upon what this

philosophy of life is; whatever it is, it will in future determine the nature of his selections. Jesus taught a philosophy of life like unto many others in many respects and in harmony with the Religion of Nature, but clear of errors and imperfections of other religions. Happy is he who can learn of Jesus and understand his philosophy of life, rid of misinterpretation, perversions and superstitions for all such will he save, in, that man accepting this philosophy, will begin the selection of those elements from his daily life that enters into and builds character, and helps to bring men to a state of the highest physical, intellectual, moral and emotional development possible.

Georgia had two of the greatest men of modern times who were intimately connected with her early history whose lives illustrate this, John Wesley and Benjamin Franklin. Each approached the same purpose from a different point of beginning but each reached the same practical result. Then Georgia had tribes of red men where the same religious purpose was manifested and the same philosophy of life was held as was held by Wesley and Franklin,—that is, the bringing of man to the highest state of perfection possible. The red man's philosophy went little if any beyond the physical development, but in this it was strict to the point of cruelty. It must have accomplished this single-fold purpose however if we are to credit such information and traditoin as are left for us. I have seen evidences of this in the remnants of the Indians of this section now remaining in Florida, in their near perfect physique, their immobility and perfect control of and co-ordination of their limbs and muscles.

John Wesley was the son of Christian parents, received a pious training and Christian education and imbibed a correct philosophy of life with his mother's milk, but it was not until after his ordination and after his ministry in Georgia that his conversion occurred.

Benjamin Franklin was deprived of much of his early training in the home, received little education in the schools of the time, but on reaching years of accountability gradually began to build a philosophy of life based upon nature, cold intelligence and fact, refusing to accept the scriptures and skeptical on all points but accepting the primary purpose of religion as has been stated. Having adopted this religion of nature as his philosophy of life and after having brought one of the most powerful intellects of all time to bear on the question from every possible angle arrived at the same conclusion as did Wesley. Wesley's religion was a religion of faith, Franklins of knowledge; Wesley believed because thus sayeth the law, Franklin believed because having mastered many of the secrets of nature and having carefully compared the scriptures with known truths found that the prohibitions of the scripture were prohibited because wrong and in violation of nature.

Wesley so ordered his life and reduced his affairs to discipline as to give rise to name "Methodist". John Wesley was John Wesley's own boss and when John Wesley played truant it was John Wesley who took him to task. Benjamin Franklin was Benjamin Franklin's boss. He was not always on the job but on the whole did a pretty good job of the bossing business. Neither of these men were willing to leave the entire responsibility of their development in the hands of God but displayed their zeal in behalf of the desired purpose, and in my opinion, their greatness and success is surpassed by no man.

Georgia Historians have seen fit to make of Oglethorpe and Wesley demigods, presumably to induce the young to accept them as ideals after which to model their lives. I doubt that this tendency has done more than to fill the minds of the young with disgust. Certainly the treatment of the first settlers has had this effect upon our young. The iniquitious result of this treatment of our history has been incalculable. When we lament too much politics, when we bemoan our like of statesmen, when we deplore the tendency of public officials to engraft into our body of laws, boards, commissions and regulations entirely foreign to our history and traditions we are simply voicing our condemnation to so much of written history

of our state that results in this condition.

History has its place in the religious development of a people, but any religious development to be permanent and of beneficial effect upon the people must be founded upon truth. When historians are willing to suppress truth, history become worthless if not dangerous. So likewise biography and genealogy.

Hugh Blair is to English composition what Gray is to Anatomy or Blackstone is to law. He shows, page 394 and 395 in his lecture on Rhetoric and Belles Letters in the edition of 1858 that the proper object of the historian is to record truth for the instruction of mankind, that as the primary end of history is to record the truth,—impartiality, fidelity, and accuracy are the fundamental qualities of the historian; that such facts should be recorded as enable us to apply the transactions of former ages for our own instruction; that wisdom is the great end of history; that it is designed to supply the want of experience; that its object is to enlarge our views of the human character and to give full exercise to our judgment on human affairs."

Now, the object of religion as is taught by the laws of nature, being the development of mankind to the highest physical, intellectual, moral and emotional condition to which he may attain, and the lives of Wesley and Franklin, have, if properly presented, the most wholesome and inspiring effect upon the young. Each of these was the architect of his own fortune. Each labored successfully in the building of his own character, in the overcoming of defects, and in shaping his life to a pholisophy of life founded on truth, in other words, theirs was a natural religion.

Genealogy, history and religion are one an inseparable. These three constitute the Scriptures. Each plays its part in the drama of life and the development of the race. For mankind to reach that state of physical, intellectual, moral and emotional development for which he is destined, each must be recognized, and our lives made to conform to their lessons.

INDEX.

INDEX.

INDEX.

INDEX.

INDEX.

www.ingramcontent.com/pod-product-compliance
Lightning Source LLC
Chambersburg PA
CBHW061005280326
41935CB00009B/846